THE BEST

PLACES TO KISS™

IN THE NORTHWEST

(AND THE CANADIAN SOUTHWEST)

A Romantic Travel Guide

COMPLETELY REVISED 7th EDITION AND UPDATED

by

Laura Kraemer & Linnea Lundgren

BEGINNING PRESS

Other Books in the

BEST PLACES TO KISS™
Series:

The Best Places to Kiss in Northern California, 4th Edition $13.95

The Best Places to Kiss in Southern California, 4th Edition $13.95

The Best Places to Kiss in Hawaii, 3rd Edition $14.95

Any of these books can be ordered directly from the publisher.

Please send a check or money order for the total amount of the books, plus $5 for shipping and handling per book ordered, to:

**Beginning Press
13075 Gateway Drive, Suite 300
Tukwila, WA 98168**

All prices are listed in U.S. funds.
For information about ordering from Canada or
to place a credit card order, call (206) 444-1616.

Art Direction and Production: Studio Pacific, Deb McCarroll
Cover Design: Studio Pacific, Deb McCarroll
Managing Editor: Laura Kraemer
Editors: Miriam Bulmer, Kris Fulsaas, and Sheryl Nelson
Printing: Publishers Press
Contributors: Audra Ang, Paula Begoun, Stephanie Bell, María Christine
Brown, Miriam Bulmer, Allison Carter, Kristin Folsom, Elizabeth Janda,
and Kerry Tessaro.

Copyright 1986, 1988, 1990, 1992, 1994, 1997, 1998 by Paula Begoun

First Edition: June 1986
Second Edition: June 1988
Third Edition: June 1990
Fourth Edition: December 1992
Fifth Edition: December 1994
Sixth Edition: January 1997
Seventh Edition: December 1998
1 2 3 4 5 6 7 8 9 10

BEST PLACES TO KISS™

is a registered trademark of Beginning Press
ISBN 1-877988-24-3

This book is distributed to the U.S. book trade by:
Publisher's Group West
1700 Fourth Street
Berkeley, CA 94710
(800) 788-3123

This book is distributed to the Canadian book trade by:
Raincoast Books
8680 Cambie Street
Vancouver, B.C. V6P 6M9
(800) 663-5714

"As usual with most lovers

in the city, they were

troubled by the lack

of that essential need

of love—a meeting place."

Thomas Wolfe

Publisher's Note

Travel books have many different criteria for the places they include. We would like the reader to know that this book is not an advertising vehicle. As is true for all *The Best Places to Kiss* books, the businesses included were not charged fees, nor did they pay us for their review. This book is a sincere, unbiased effort to highlight those special parts of the region that are filled with romance and splendor. Sometimes those places, such as restaurants, inns, lodges, hotels, and bed and breakfasts, were created by people. Sometimes those places are untouched by people and simply created by God for us to enjoy. Wherever you go, be gentle with each other and with the earth.

The publisher made the final decision on the recommendations in this collection, but we would love to hear what you think of our suggestions. We strive to create a reliable guide for your amorous outings, and in this quest for blissful sojourns, your romantic feedback assists greatly in increasing our accuracy and our resources for information. If you have any comments, criticisms, or cherished memories of your own from a place we directed you to or a place you discovered on your own, feel free to write us at:

Beginning Press
13075 Gateway Drive, Suite 300
Tukwila, WA 98168

We would love to hear from you!

"What of soul was left,

I wonder, when the

kissing had to stop?"

Robert Browning

Contents

The Fine Art of Kissing 1

   Why It's Still Best to Kiss in the Northwest 1

   You Call This Research? 1

   Rating Romance 2

   Kiss Ratings 2

   Cost Ratings 3

   Wedding Bells 4

   The Most Romantic Time to Travel 4

British Columbia 7

   Vancouver and Environs 9

   Vancouver Island 55

   Gulf Islands 131

   Sunshine Coast 153

   Whistler and Environs 169

Washington 191

   Seattle and Environs 193

   Puget Sound Area 237

   San Juan Islands 293

   Olympic Peninsula 329

   Southern Washington Coast 359

   Washington Cascades 373

   Yakima Valley 409

Oregon 421

   Portland 423

   Willamette Valley 441

   Eugene and Environs 451

   Oregon Coast 459

   Oregon Cascades 507

   Southern Oregon 527

Index 557

The Fine Art of Kissing

Why It's Still Best to Kiss in the Northwest

This is the seventh edition of *The Best Places to Kiss in the Northwest,* and we are proud to still be a regional best-seller and one of the most popular travel books in the area. Our readers are constantly reminding us that our reputation as one of the few travel books that candidly and critically review romantic properties is well earned and a breath of amorous fresh air.

We admit a strong bias in our feelings about the Northwest. Without question, this area provides the best kissing territory anywhere in the continental United States and Canada. As is true for every edition, our research is enthusiastic and our criteria increasingly more restrictive. If we recommend a place for romance, we want to be sure your lips and emotions will be satisfied. Disappointment can be a near disaster where the heart is concerned.

Beginning Press also publishes *The Best Places to Kiss in Northern California, The Best Places to Kiss in Southern California,* and *The Best Places to Kiss in Hawaii.* After all this lip-chapping research, we find it even easier to rave about the Northwest.

We are confident that you will relish this glorious part of the world as much as we do. More than any other area in the United States, the Northwest has a splendor and peacefulness that is apparent throughout. And along with the beauty of nature's handiwork, the people here have a style and attitude that are quietly conducive to intimacy and affection. Northwesterners know a secret: The more intimately acquainted you are with the earth, the more intimate you can be with each other. In short, we can't think of a better region for romance.

You Call This Research?

This book was undertaken primarily as a journalistic effort and is the product of ongoing interviews, travel, thorough investigation, and critical observation. Although it would have been nice, even preferable, kissing was not the major research method used to select the locations listed in this book. If smooching had been the determining factor, several inescapable problems would have developed. First, we would still be researching, and this book would be just a good idea, some breathless moments, random notes, and nothing more. Second, depending on the mood of the moment, many kisses might have occurred in places that do not meet the requirements of this travel guide. Therefore, for both practical and physical reasons, more objective criteria had to be established.

You may be wondering how, if we did not kiss at every location during our research, we could be certain that a particular place was good for such an activity? The answer is that we employed our reporters' instincts to evaluate the heartfelt, magnetic pull of each place we visited. If, upon examining a place, we felt a longing to share what we had discovered with our special someone, we considered this to be as reliable as a kissing analysis. In the final evaluation, we can guarantee that when you visit any of the places listed, you will be assured of some degree of privacy, a beautiful setting, heart-stirring ambience, and romantic accommodations. What you do when you get there is up to you and your partner.

Rating Romance

The three major factors that determine whether or not we include a place are:

- **Privacy**
- **Location/view/setting**
- **Ambience**

Of these determining factors, "privacy" and "location" are fairly self-explanatory, but "ambience" can probably use some clarification. Wonderful, loving environments are not just four-poster beds covered with down quilts and lace pillows, or tables decorated with white tablecloths and nicely folded linen napkins. Instead, there must be other engaging features that encourage intimacy and allow for uninterrupted affectionate discourse. For the most part, ambience was rated according to degree of comfort and number of gracious appointments, as opposed to image and frills.

If a place has all three factors going for it, inclusion is automatic. But if one or two of the criteria are weak or nonexistent, the other feature(s) have to be superior before the location will be included. For example, if a breathtakingly beautiful panoramic vista is in a spot that's inundated with tourists and children on field trips, the place is not included. If a fabulous bed and breakfast is set in a less-than-desirable location, it is included if, and only if, its interior is so wonderfully inviting and cozy that the outside world no longer matters. Extras like complimentary champagne, handmade truffles, or extraordinary service earn brownie points and frequently determine the difference between three-and-a-half and four-lip ratings.

Kiss Ratings

The lip rating preceding each entry is our way of indicating just how romantic we think a place is and how contented we were during our visit.

The following is a brief explanation of the lip ratings awarded each location.

No lips = Reputed to be a romantic destination, but we strongly disagree

❤ = Romantic possibilities with potential drawbacks

❤❤ = Can provide a satisfying experience

❤❤❤ = Very desirable

❤❤❤❤ = Simply sublime

Unrated = Not open at the time this edition went to print, but looks promising

Romantic Note: If you're planning to celebrate a special occasion, such as an anniversary or birthday, we highly recommend telling the proprietors about it when making your reservation. Many bed and breakfasts and hotels offer "special-occasion packages," which may include a complimentary bottle of wine, breakfast in bed, fresh flowers, and special touches during turndown service, such as dimmed lights and your beloved's favorite CD playing in the background to set the right romantic mood. Restaurants are also sometimes willing to accommodate special occasions by offering free desserts or helping to coordinate a surprise proposal.

Cost Ratings

We have included additional ratings to help you determine whether your lips can afford to kiss in a particular restaurant, hotel, or bed and breakfast. (Almost all of the outdoor places are free; some charge a small fee.) The price for overnight accommodations is always based on double occupancy; otherwise there wouldn't be anyone to kiss. Unless otherwise indicated, eating establishment prices are based on a full dinner for two (which includes an appetizer, entrée, and dessert for each person), excluding the cost of liquor. Because prices and business hours change, it is always advisable to call each place you plan to visit, so your lips will not end up disappointed.

Romantic Note: The exchange rate for Canadian funds at the time this book went to press was about $1.42 Canadian to $1 U.S. The cost ratings for Canadian establishments included in our book are based on Canadian currency.

Lodgings

Inexpensive	**Less than $100**
Moderate	**$100 to $130**
Expensive	**$130 to $175**
Very Expensive	**$175 to $250**
Unbelievably Expensive	**More than $250**

Restaurants

Inexpensive	**Less than $30**
Moderate	**$30 to $50**
Expensive	**$50 to $80**
Very Expensive	**$80 to $110**
Unbelievably Expensive	**More than $110**

Wedding Bells

One of the most auspicious times to kiss is the moment after you've exchanged wedding vows. The setting for that magical moment can vary, from your own cozy living room to a lush garden perched at the ocean's edge to a grand ballroom at an elegant downtown hotel. As an added service to those of you in the midst of prenuptial arrangements, we have indicated which properties have impressive wedding facilities. For more specific information about the facilities and services offered, please call the establishments directly. They should be able to provide you with menus, prices, and all the details needed to make your wedding day as spectacular as you have ever imagined.

Romantic Note: If wedding bells aren't in your near future and you are going to an establishment that specializes in weddings and private parties, call ahead to ensure that a function isn't scheduled during your stay. Unless you hope that seeing a wedding will magically inspire your partner to "pop the question," you might feel like uninvited guests.

The Most Romantic Time to Travel

The Northwest is so spectacular, it's hard to imagine any time of the year that would not be romantic. Each season and hour has its own special joy: winter skiing, cuddling by the fireplace on a chilly day (that can be any time of year here), summer sunshine, mesmerizing fall sunsets, the exuberant rebirth of nature in the melting wet spring. Even in overcast conditions (again, any time of the year), if you prepare properly there is no reason to postpone investigating the splendor that hovers around every turn in the Northwest.

So don't be one of those couples who wait until summer to travel and then decide not to go because it might be too crowded. Oh, and about the rain—it does. Enough said.

"To be thy lips

is a sweet thing and small."

e. e. cummings

BRITISH COLUMBIA

Vancouver and Environs

Vancouver is a phenomenal example of a big city done right. Towering skyscrapers, flashing lights, steel-girded bridges, and heavily trafficked one-way streets sprawl for miles, but this vintage urban landscape is softened by surrounding snowcapped mountains, forested parks, and the island-flecked Strait of Georgia. International cruise ships ferry passengers from around the globe to this popular Canadian port of call, renowned for its impressive scenery and world-class cultural activities.

In the Vancouver area, there is something for everybody. Visitors can take in views of downtown's sophisticated architecture from the forested acreage of Stanley Park or from the peak of Grouse Mountain (accessible via an aerial tram). Outdoor enthusiasts will be impressed by the area's provincial parks and woodland, nearby ski slopes, and abundant wildlife. If you prefer tamer encounters with nature, seek out the flawlessly manicured gardens scattered in fragrant pockets throughout the city. Those who arrive in Vancouver with shopping in mind (and many do) can wander for hours in the multitude of stores, boutiques, and art galleries crowded around colorful Robson Street, artist-oriented Granville Island, and historic Gastown, where a steam clock regularly pipes out the time. The **VANCOUVER ART GALLERY** (750 Hornby Street; 604-662-4719) has a stellar permanent art collection and more than a dozen additional temporary exhibitions every year. The **VANCOUVER SYMPHONY ORCHESTRA** (601 Smithe Street; 604-684-9100) and the **VANCOUVER OPERA** (845 Cambie Street; 604-683-0222), along with local theater groups, offer outstanding productions year-round. Your options in this lively city are endless. Once you've sampled what Vancouver has to offer, your notions of urban life will never be the same. Before you know it, you're likely to find yourselves making plans to return.

Like most cities, Vancouver has serious traffic, particularly on the bridges at rush hour. Getting around on foot or via public buses is recommended whenever possible. Another option is the **AQUABUS** (604-689-5858), which offers commuter ferry service in False Creek from five terminals. Though it is arguably touristy, the Aquabus is a convenient and interesting way to see the city's sights without having to contend with traffic (a definite romantic plus). Two other public transportation options include the **SKY TRAIN,** a monorail system that links downtown Vancouver with some of its suburbs, and the **SEA BUS,** a passenger ferry that crosses to North Vancouver.

Cost ratings for British Columbia listings are in Canadian funds. American travelers should check the exchange rate or ask an innkeeper to figure out the cost in U.S. dollars.

If you plan to explore this vast area, we highly recommend that you purchase a detailed map. For more personal travel guidance while in British Columbia, consult the Visitor Information Centres scattered generously along most major roads and in most towns. The people here are lovely; you should stop in just to say hello and get your first taste of Canadian hospitality. For Vancouver information, contact the **VANCOUVER TOURIST INFORMATION CENTRE** (Plaza Level, 200 Burrard Street, Vancouver, B.C. V6C 3L6; 604-683-2000; www.tourism-vancouver.org).

Romantic Warning: Be aware that timing border crossings to and from Canada at Blaine, Washington, can be exceptionally tricky due to the long lines of cars encountered at different times of the day and year. Peak travel times during the summer and weekends are the worst, but traffic can be very fickle and there is no telling when you may have to endure a serious wait.

Vancouver

Hotel/Bed and Breakfast Kissing

❧❧ **ARBUTUS HOUSE, Vancouver** Set on a quiet street near biking and jogging trails, this 1920s home is a calming retreat at the edge of Vancouver's prestigious Shaughnessy district. A lilac-colored tiled fireplace warms the formal living room, and the adjoining dining room's rose-colored walls, cozy window seat, and beautiful antique clock contribute to a serene setting. Guests looking for more casual relaxation can enjoy the lounge at the back of the house, which offers comfortable couches, a television, plenty of books, and a view of the garden.

Upstairs, the contemporary but sparsely decorated Magnolia Room is enhanced by a private deck, accessible through French doors, as well as a washed-oak queen-size bed. While the Dahlia Room is small, it feels cozy and feminine thanks to its queen-size white iron bed, leaf green walls, and garden view. If you're staying in either of these rooms, be aware that the bathrooms (complete with large step-up tubs) are down the hall. For the most privacy, choose the top floor's Sunset Suite, an airy 550-square-foot perch. Here you'll find mountain and water views, a comfy sitting area with a gas fireplace and TV/VCR, a sleigh bed, and high, sloped ceilings.

A four-course breakfast awaits guests each morning, either in the dining room or on the large garden deck. **4470 Maple Crescent; (604) 738-6432; inexpensive to moderate; minimum-stay requirement; closed December-mid-January.**

❧❧❧ **BRIGHTON HOUSE, Vancouver** Hidden in a residential area that marks Vancouver's original townsite (a location many visitors never stumble upon), Brighton House is a charming surprise. Its location on the high side of the street affords clear views of the mountains and a stretch of working water-front—but just wait till you see the sights inside.

Tucked into matching alcoves on the second floor are two pretty rooms, one decorated in French country style with a four-poster bed and the other done up in a folk-art motif. The mirror-image rooms both have small sitting areas with tables for two, large semicircular windows, handsome fabrics and furnishings, sloped ceilings, and cozy decks where you can nibble on breakfast and lounge on wicker chairs while watching tugs chug by in the distance. Both have similar en suite bathrooms, although the one belonging to the French country room is more elegant, with its skylight, glass-block wall, and marble-surrounded air-jet tub.

Downstairs, guests can enjoy a comfortable living room with striped couches and a fireplace, as well as a small wisteria-draped back deck (alas, with no view) that catches the afternoon sun. Breakfast is a bountiful affair of muffins, fruit, egg dishes, and pancakes, proudly presented by the extremely helpful innkeeper. **2826 Trinity Street; (604) 253-7175; inexpensive to moderate; minimum-stay requirement seasonally.**

COLUMBIA COTTAGE GUEST HOUSE, Vancouver Located on a corner in a quiet residential neighborhood, this modestly adorned Tudor-style home is chock-full of antiques. Though a bit on the cramped side, the home's interior is reminiscent of an English country cottage. Lace curtains, Oriental carpets, and blond wood floors adorn the lovely common areas, where guests can enjoy a glass of sherry in front of the fireplace. The five guest rooms, four of which are located on the first and second floors of the main house, offer cushy feather beds covered with luxurious linens and down comforters. Bright, contemporary fabrics and color schemes combine modern flair with old-world charm. The fifth room, situated in the converted basement, is called the Garden Suite. It offers the most space and privacy, with a private entrance, kitchen area, and separate living room and bedroom. The wrought-iron sleigh bed is a decisive romantic touch, but we prefer the authentic charm of the upstairs rooms.

In the morning, the professional chef/host prepares a full gourmet breakfast that may include freshly baked bread, muffins, and croissants, various frittatas, fresh fruit and juice, and, of course, coffee and a selection of teas. Before setting out on your day, take a stroll through the lovely back garden or, if you are up for a healthy walk, visit nearby QUEEN ELIZABETH PARK (see Outdoor Kissing). **205 West 14th Avenue; (604) 874-5327; www.novamart.com/columbia; moderate to very expensive.**

ENGLISH BAY INN, Vancouver Located in Vancouver's West End, this unassuming English Tudor–style home is a treasure just waiting to be discovered. You'll feel soothed just stepping inside the peach-hued sitting room, where fresh flowers, a fire in the hearth, and port and sherry on the antique sideboard welcome guests. Upstairs is a jaw-dropping dining room, complete with massive Gothic-style mahogany antique table and chairs, an imposing fireplace, and gilded accents. Guests gather here to partake of breakfasts that may include such delights as chicken and peppers in phyllo dough, chocolate chip scones, and an array of fresh fruits and juices.

Four of the five guest rooms are rather small, but make up for this shortcoming with a generous helping of style, including antique armoires, Louis Philippe four-poster beds, and windows or French doors that open to the back garden. The romance quotient goes way up, however, if you decide to stay in the inn's one suite. This two-story hideaway includes a charming, antique-filled sitting room below and, up a short flight of stairs, a boudoir complete with its own wood-burning fireplace, sleigh bed, and a sloping ceiling accented with skylights. In the bathroom, antique stained glass windows set off the spa tub. Although English Bay Inn is just a stone's throw from the sea wall and **STANLEY PARK** (see Outdoor Kissing), if rain is tapping on the roof and you are snuggling in the light of the many candles, you'll find it hard to imagine leaving this hideaway at all. **1968 Comox Street; (604) 683-8002; moderate to very expensive; minimum-stay requirement on weekends.**

❀❀❀ **FOUR SEASONS HOTEL, Vancouver** Although Vancouver's Four Seasons is filled with old-world style and run with the exacting attention to detail that is the hallmark of this luxury chain, it lacks some of the personality and charm that many associate with a romantic getaway. The main entrance is an unfortunate introduction to the hotel: It's located adjacent to the Pacific Centre shopping mall entry and guests must ride an escalator to reach the lobby on the second level. Here, leather couches and elegant shops elevate the ambience. The 385 guest rooms are ample and tasteful, with refined furnishings —although some of the decor could use updating. Upper-level rooms are recommended for their city views; some rooms on the west side of the building have water views. Once you're happily ensconced in your private chamber, you'll enjoy the kind of attentive yet unobtrusive service that has long made the Four Seasons famous. **791 West Georgia Street; (604) 689-9333, (800) 268-6282 (in Canada), (800) 332-3442 (in the U.S.); expensive to unbelievably expensive; recommended wedding site.**

Romantic Suggestion: For an elegant fine-dining experience, we recommend **CHARTWELL** (see Restaurant Kissing) on the hotel's first floor. For a lighter, less formal repast, try the **GARDEN TERRACE**, with its hanging greenery, orchids, and rattan furnishings in an atrium-like setting.

❀❀ **GEORGIAN COURT HOTEL, Vancouver** The Georgian Court, a classic high-rise hotel, offers traditional lodgings in the city, excellent service, and upscale dining—without an intimidating price tag. None of the 180 spacious guest rooms has a view to speak of (aside from views of office buildings), but rooms on the third floor offer private balconies. Lacquered wood furnishings, queen-size beds, and upscale, modern fabrics and color schemes create a pleasant, comfortable ambience in all of the rooms. Prices are surprisingly reasonable, and even the two luxurious Penthouse Suites with jetted tubs are less expensive than some of the standard hotel rooms found elsewhere in the city. Guests can make use of the hotel's small workout room and whirlpool, then dine at the famous **WILLIAM TELL RESTAURANT** (see Restaurant Kissing), or sit at an outdoor bistro table for pub fare. In addition, neighboring Yaletown is a lively destination for window-shopping or a night on the town, so take an evening stroll to enjoy the surroundings before retiring to your room. **773 Beatty Street; (604) 682-5555, (800) 663-1155; inexpensive to very expensive.**

❀❀❀ **HERITAGE HARBOUR BED AND BREAKFAST, Vancouver** Just across the Burrard Bridge from downtown Vancouver and just across the street from English Bay, this Kitsilano-area bed and breakfast has an ideal location on a tree-lined street. Guests can stroll or bike around the promontory of Kitsilano Point and Vanier Park, hop on the "foot ferry," wander to colorful Granville Island, or simply cozy up on the beach and gaze at the city skyline before returning to their pleasant accommodations a few steps away.

A new home built in Victorian style, Heritage Harbour offers an airy interior with high ceilings, hardwood floors, and a spectacular stained glass window. The guest parlor downstairs and the appealing library lounge upstairs both offer large windows that bring in spectacular views and fireplaces that warm the interiors on rainy days. The two guest rooms are well spaced for privacy, and each has its own detached bathroom. The Garden Room has no view, but boasts high ceilings, a romantic four-poster bed, and a large private balcony overlooking the garden—making it an ideal choice for longer stays. The Harbour Room is more snug but still well appointed, with rosy walls and French doors that overlook the park, bay, city skyline, and mountains. Gourmet breakfasts are served at an antique dining room table; guests often relax with coffee in the front garden before starting the day's adventures. **1838 Ogden Avenue; (604) 736-0809; www.vancouver-bc.com/HeritageHarbour; moderate to expensive; minimum-stay requirement seasonally.**

❀❀❀ **HOTEL VANCOUVER, Vancouver** This 1887 heritage building with the distinctive peaked copper roof is a venerable city landmark and a welcome change from typical downtown high-rise hotels. Gracious, old-world elegance is apparent everywhere, from the gargoyles peering down from the stone facade to the well-heeled travelers gliding in and out past imposing doors. Inside the lavish lobby are upscale shops, ornate chandeliers, and a popular raised piano bar that's an ideal place to cozy up with a coffee drink and indulge in some free-style people watching.

Recent renovations have updated the 550 rooms with style. Yesteryear's slightly dated furnishings have been replaced with gleaming mahogany pieces, floral draperies, down duvets, and lighter color schemes. The mauve marble bathrooms are lovely, although some are quite small. Guests can make use of the hotel's glass-enclosed pool, or, for a nominal charge, visit the full health club.

For the epitome of personalized service, stay on the Entrée Gold ninth floor. Among other enticements, guests here have complimentary health club access and a private concierge, plus leisurely breakfasts and afternoon hors d'oeuvres served in the sumptuous new lounge, with brocade chairs, English china, and windows that reveal a slice of water and mountains between skyscrapers. **900 West Georgia Street; (604) 684-3131, (800) 441-1414; expensive to unbelievably expensive.**

Romantic Suggestion: You won't have to leave the property in search of an impressive meal, because the Hotel Vancouver is brimming with options. **GRIFFINS RESTAURANT** (moderate to expensive), adjacent to the lobby, is a little too bustling to be particularly romantic, but the dining room's tall ceilings, cheery yellow walls, hardwood floors, and remarkable, reasonably priced meals distinguish it from most hotel restaurants. Griffins is especially popular for lunch, due to an outstanding buffet featuring gourmet delights. For a truly romantic repast, we recommend the hotel's newly opened restaurant and wine bar, **900 WEST** (604-669-9378; expensive to very expensive; reservations required; lunch Monday–Friday, dinner daily). Decorated to resemble a luxury ocean liner, this cavernous restaurant offers impeccable service, Canadian regional cuisine, and live music in the adjoining wine bar.

❦❦❦ THE JOHNSON HERITAGE HOUSE BED AND BREAKFAST, Vancouver

Tucked away on a quiet, upscale residential street, this 1920s Craftsman-style home is filled with charm and a good dose of whimsy. The Great Room is a wonderful entrée into the experience to come: crimson couches, Oriental rugs, and a huge brick fireplace lie just steps from antique carousel horses and gramophones, which the hosts collect. Just beyond, a stone-floored kitchen opens onto a dining room with hardwood floors, windows to the garden, and a vintage cash register.

The daylight basement holds one guest room, which has been renovated and improved with larger windows, a stone fireplace, and a brass bed. Upstairs, options include one room with a white iron bed and mountain views—the bath is down the hall, but private, with a claw-foot tub—and another with an antique Indonesian bed and a new en suite bathroom filled with barbershop antiques. In the latter, a new two-person balcony bedecked with grapevines overlooks the garden.

For special occasions, though, the Carousel Suite is the Johnson House's pièce de résistance. Here, highlights include a luxurious canopy bed, hardwood floors, inviting sitting area, Persian rugs, a pitched pine ceiling, and a new gas fireplace edged in slate. Lovely views of Grouse Mountain are a bonus. But quirkiness has not been left behind: A row of gramophones and a giant antique gas pump occupy one corner. A startlingly spacious bathroom rounds out the floor plan; its skylights, tile shower, separate soaking tub (with room for only one), and a collection of sensual mermaid sculptures promise to make bathtime a delight. **2278 West 34th Avenue; (604) 266-4175; www.johnsons-inn-vancouver.com/index.html; inexpensive to expensive; no credit cards; minimum-stay requirement; closed November–March.**

☙☙ **A LITTLE GREEN HOUSE ON THE PARK, Vancouver** If you're in a Bohemian mood, check out the Grandview neighborhood—a Berkeley-esque collection of shops, ethnic restaurants, and stores featuring organic goods that invites adventuresome exploration—and spend the night just a stone's throw from the action in this turquoise-green townhouse across the street from a local park. In the backyard, a roomy hot tub is ensconced beneath a trellis and surrounded by beautiful gardens. The newly renovated back porch has a covered roof with skylights, an overhead heat lamp, and open sides to allow guests to curl up in their robes after a soak in any kind of weather. Inside, the owners have decorated their home with sleek style, including blond hardwood floors, modern black couches, contemporary art, and a cozy window seat covered with comfy pillows.

Upstairs, the two guest rooms have private baths and a contemporary look. Flower boxes line the small private balcony in small but engaging Parkview, which faces (not surprisingly) the park across the street. A striped comforter drapes a pretty wrought-iron bed, and French country antiques add a romantic accent. A TV/VCR is discreetly tucked away, and the bathroom has a jetted single tub. Aptly named Gardenview, the room across the hall, faces the gardens in the backyard. A little plain but still very comfortable, this room is furnished with eclectic antiques, contemporary linens, and a double steambath/shower equipped with complimentary aromatherapy products.

An elaborate homemade breakfast served in the stylish modern kitchen, the raised dining area off the living room, or the countrified backyard is the ideal prelude for a day spent exploring the city. **1850 Grant Street; (604) 255-3655 (June–October), (604) 255-0815 (off-season hot line); inexpensive to expensive; closed mid-December–February.**

☙☙❧ **THE METROPOLITAN HOTEL, Vancouver** Set in the heart of downtown, this contemporary boutique hotel retains a bit of Asian flair from its previous incarnation as a Mandarin Hotel. A small, elegant lobby is marble floored and enhanced by Oriental rugs, unusual flower arrangements, and intriguing artifacts, including an ornate gilded wall screen that separates the sitting area from the reception desk. With 197 guest rooms, the Metropolitan can feel more intimate than a larger business hotel; however, the rooms tend to feel a bit conservative despite a recent renovation that has freshened the decor. Those with small terraces offer views of the surrounding cityscape. Suites are decidedly better appointed, with Asian art pieces and spacious white marble bathrooms with soaking tubs and glass-enclosed showers. Guests have free access to the small but well-maintained health club, which includes an indoor lap pool under an enclosed atrium, as well as squash and racquetball courts, a weight room, whirlpool, sauna, and an on-call masseuse.

For amorous encounters, the Metropolitan's "Romance Packages" are worth checking into. For a slight extra charge, your stay can include a bottle of sparkling wine, chocolate-dipped strawberries, and assorted fruit upon arrival. Breakfast in bed or at the hotel's restaurant, parking, taxes, and service charges are also included for your convenience. **645 Howe Street; (604) 687-1122, (800) 667-2300; www.metropolitan.com; moderate to very expensive; recommended wedding site.**

Romantic Suggestion: DIVA AT THE MET (see Restaurant Kissing) is the Metropolitan's jewel, a sleek and sexy eatery for intimate dining any time of day.

❦❦❦ **"O CANADA" HOUSE, Vancouver** Canada's national anthem was written in this beautifully restored 1897 Victorian, just a few blocks from the bustle of Robson Street in downtown Vancouver. Today, as you walk through the lovely landscaped garden, you'll feel like you're at your favorite great-aunt's home—you know, the one with exquisite taste. The owners, who are antique restorers and collectors, have made certain that every detail is a testament to loving care.

Rich wall-to-wall carpeting, a cheery fireplace, stunning museum-quality light fixtures, and historic family photos grace the living room, where sherry is served to guests in the afternoon; an adjoining back parlor has its own adorable miniature fireplace and more antique furnishings. A lavish dining room table is set for a full gourmet breakfast beneath a breathtaking antique chandelier. Tucked away is a guest pantry perpetually stocked with hot and cold drinks and homemade baked goods, which guests can feel free to take on trays to their rooms. Other thoughtful amenities are restaurant menus and maps to assist guests in selecting the perfect romantic dinner or stroll each evening.

The six tasteful rooms all include generous en suite baths, TV/VCRs (complimentary movies are available for checkout), plush bathrobes, and details such as original light fixtures, faux fireplaces, and period armoires. The North Suite is a roomy, appealing choice for romance, featuring a fluffy feather duvet atop the king-size bed, plus lovely architectural detailing and a spacious bathroom with an enticing claw-foot tub. A top-floor double suite has skylights and two sleigh beds under sloped ceilings, plus a separate sitting area/breakfast nook. For complete privacy, the former carriage house in the back garden has recently been transformed into a charming one-room cottage, complete with a gas fireplace and private brick patio surrounded by lilacs. **1114 Barclay Street; (604) 688-0555; www.vancouver-bc.com/OCanadaHouse/index.html; moderate to very expensive; minimum-stay requirement on weekends.**

❦ **OGDEN POINT BED AND BREAKFAST, Vancouver** Just across the street from English Bay on Kitsilano Point, this restored 1915 home boasts a spectacular vista. Unfortunately, while one view room is worthy of your romantic attention, much of the decor and ambience here feels old rather than antique.

For a romantic encounter, the only room to reserve is the English Bay Room, which has a large enclosed porch that faces the water and is bathed in the morning sun. Here, you and your sweetheart can enjoy a private breakfast in front of the huge picture window and its magnificent panorama. Alas, the en suite bathroom and separate shower are incredibly tiny (to retain the architectural integrity of the home), and the carpet and bedding are fine but unremarkable. However, a few original pieces of furniture are tasteful touches. Other options upstairs include a double room and a twin room that share one full bath and one half-bath. A communal coffee room for guests is rather bare, with only a plain table and chairs plus a few historic photos for atmosphere.

Breakfasts are "upscale continental" rather than full, and are served on the front porch or in the wood-paneled dining room at an antique table. A rich wood-paneled foyer with an antique grandfather clock leads to the parlor, which has a view of the water but is filled with worn furniture; the TV in the corner of the parlor seems out of place among the antiques. **1982 Ogden Avenue; (604) 736-4336; moderate to very expensive; minimum-stay requirement.**

❤❣ **PACIFIC PALISADES HOTEL, Vancouver** Although the lobby here screams large chain hotel, the centrally located Pacific Palisades has a genuinely romantic disposition—beginning with floor-to-ceiling windows that bring in the water views. In addition, each floor holds only a handful of rooms, which makes the hotel feel small and personal. (You'd never guess there are 233 units.) Better yet, most of the rooms are exceedingly roomy—even the studios. TVs are discreetly hidden in wood cabinets, and plump down duvets give the beds an inviting appearance. Though the decor is fairly hotel standard, contemporary artwork and water or mountain views make most of the rooms feel stylish and upscale. Fresh orchids spice up the standard but attractive bathrooms.

Guests have complimentary use of the hotel's health club, which features a 55-foot indoor pool, whirlpool, sauna, weight room, suntan and massage service, and even bicycle rentals (which will save you a lot of frustration with battling Vancouver's ever-increasing traffic). **1277 Robson Street; (604) 688-0461, (800) 663-1815; www.shangri-la.com/shangri-la/hotels/1/1home.html; expensive to unbelievably expensive.**

❤❤❤ **THE PAN PACIFIC HOTEL, Vancouver** This mega-hotel doesn't seem to be a romance destination at first glance: Entering the huge structure, which is always filled with streaming crowds, feels a bit like being in Grand Central Station. The hotel is part of an expansive waterfront complex that includes a shopping mall, restaurants, a cruise ship dock, and a convention center (where something is almost always going on). So be prepared to push your way through exhibitors, cruise passengers, tourists, and somewhat sterile, cold decor before you even get to the reception area, much less your room.

On the upside, this is an exciting place with a cosmopolitan feel that comes from being the hub of many happenings in the city. Even better, it sits at the water's edge, just steps from Gastown and downtown Vancouver. Many of the 506 rooms showcase spectacular views of water, mountains, and sky; soft color schemes, down duvets atop king-size beds, and chic marble bathrooms add to the experience. A mere four of the deluxe rooms have luxurious sunken jetted tubs, and they are almost always booked, so call ahead. All guests have access to an ultra-modern health club, which includes an outdoor pool and sundeck, sauna, Jacuzzi tub, weight room, and even a paddle tennis court for some healthy fun with your loved one. **300-999 Canada Place; (604) 662-8111, (800) 663-1515 (in Canada), (800) 937-1515 (in the U.S.); www. panpac. com; expensive to unbelievably expensive; recommended wedding site.**

Romantic Suggestion: The Pan Pacific Hotel has several excellent restaurants, the most notable of which is **FIVE SAILS** (moderate to expensive), which serves Pacific Rim cuisine. Its dining area is small but elegant, with floor-to-ceiling windows that frame views of the waterfront and snow-dusted foothills. If you want sweeping views without a full meal, visit the airy **CASCADES LOUNGE,** where cozy chairs and a live pianist add to the romantic mood.

❧❧ **PENNY FARTHING INN, Vancouver** Comfortable and casual in style, this bed and breakfast is ideal for couples who want to put their feet up in the antithesis of stuffy, formal accommodations. The bright turquoise 1912 heritage home is ensconced on a funky residential street amid an assortment of eclectic older homes, near the trendy Kitsilano district. Inside the front parlor, timeworn antiques are enlivened by the rose and pale green decor and a new green-tiled gas fireplace. Upstairs, Bettina's Boudoir features sea green walls, a pine four-poster bed, and a private deck overlooking the garden; a new rose-colored tiled fireplace enhances the small sitting area. Across the hall, recent renovations have blessed Sophie's Room and Lucinda's Room with private baths.

The top floor is devoted to Abigail's Attic, a hideaway that's almost like a small apartment. Furnishings are modest and appear a bit worn, but the sloped ceiling and skylights add charm—plus there's an appealing tiled bathroom and plenty of space for a private breakfast, which can be brought upstairs upon request. All rooms have TV/VCRs, CD players, phones, and fridges.

A full breakfast is served in the back garden when weather permits. If the day is gray, enjoy your morning meal beside a stained glass window and fireplace in the warm, homey dining room, which is stacked with board games and frequented by the owners' cats. **2855 West Sixth Avenue; (604) 739-9002; www.pennyfarthinginn.com; inexpensive to moderate; no credit cards; minimum-stay requirement on weekends seasonally.**

❀❀❀❀ **SUTTON PLACE HOTEL, Vancouver** Sutton Place enjoys a reputation for top-of-the-line accommodations, dining, and service in the heart of the city. Although the exterior looks more like a pink-hued medical complex than a luxury hotel, inside is an oasis. A cream and dusty rose palette, with pale Oriental rugs and sweeps of beige marble, provide a tasteful backdrop for European artwork and antiques. Many top businesspeople and chic travelers choose this property for personalized attention, so you and your loved one can expect outstanding service from the moment you arrive.

Rooms are attractive and bright, with luxurious maroon and gold upholstered furniture, marble-tiled bathrooms, and all of the expected amenities. Guests have access to Le Spa, the hotel's health, fitness, and beauty center, which includes a year-round pool with a spacious sundeck, set beneath a glass roof. **845 Burrard Street; (604) 682-5511, (800) 961-7555 (in Canada); expensive to unbelievably expensive; recommended wedding site.**

Romantic Suggestion: Start your leisurely Sunday with a truly decadent brunch at **FLEURI** (see Restaurant Kissing), Sutton Place's signature restaurant. A cozy spot for a cocktail is the **GERARD LOUNGE** (moderate), which offers a limited menu that is more inspired than typical bar fare. The ambience here is a contrast to the very feminine decor of the rest of the hotel: the comfy leather armchairs, banquette couches, a crescent-shaped mahogany bar, low lighting, and fireplace will make you feel like you're in a richly appointed Parisian men's club. (Alas, some men's club smoke might increase the resemblance.)

❀❀❀❀ **TREEHOUSE BED AND BREAKFAST, Vancouver** Don't take the name too literally—the Treehouse Bed and Breakfast is not a woodsy, rustic retreat, although it is indeed sheltered from busy 49th Street by towering trees. There's a unique, Zen-like feel to this ultra-modern beige stucco and glass-block home; its ivory-and-cream color schemes, clusters of candles, and contemporary artwork and sculptures are designed to soothe overstimulated senses. Lengths of honey-colored fabric drape low white couches in the stylish common living room; a beige marble dining table, glowing fireplace, and large windows draped in flowing gauze are affectionate extras. On warm days, a large guest deck is the spot for unwinding with a cup of tea.

All three suites have private baths, TV/VCRs, mini-fridges, and views of the slightly overgrown but wonderful backyard, which holds an abundance of trees and a serene Japanese garden. Guests are welcomed with touches that show the owners' attention to detail: luxurious slippers and robes, and homemade bath salts, gels, and shampoos.

Cost ratings for British Columbia listings are in Canadian funds. American travelers should check the exchange rate or ask an innkeeper to figure out the cost in U.S. dollars.

On the main floor, the Pacific West Suite has Western-style details such as plaid linens and wood carvings; it also features a small private bathroom with a one-person Jacuzzi tub. The minimalist Far East Room is a little too snug for an extended romantic encounter, but has a nice, cool Japanese flair thanks to a black lacquered bed and sliding doors that open to the shady Japanese garden. The place to go for romance is the Treetop Suite, which occupies the entire third floor and features a jetted Jacuzzi tub for two in the skylit bathroom. In the bedroom, gauzy fabric drapes a beautiful wrought-iron four-poster bed, and a private, spacious outdoor deck and small but well-appointed sitting area overlook the pretty backyard.

A lavish four-course breakfast, which often includes edible flowers and Japanese garnishes, can be delivered to your room (a definite romantic plus) or enjoyed with other guests at the chic dining table. Breakfast is served on black dishes and sparkling crystal. **2490 West 49th Avenue; (604) 266-2962; www.treehousebb.com; inexpensive to expensive; no credit cards; minimum-stay requirement on weekends seasonally.**

❀❀❀❀ **WATERFRONT CENTRE HOTEL, Vancouver** Just across the street from **THE PAN PACIFIC HOTEL** (see above), the polished Waterfront Centre Hotel surveys views of Burrard Inlet, where seaplanes and cruise ships come and go against a backdrop of tree-covered mountains. Come here for the best in big-city accommodations. Gold-hued marble floors and columns plus floor-to-ceiling windows impart an air of luxury to the elegant yet welcoming lobby. The 489 spacious guest rooms are soothingly decorated in tones of salmon, beige, and cream, and all have pretty marble bathrooms. Artistic lamps, lovely watercolors, and original artwork add dashes of color and a feminine air, and picture windows frame extraordinary water views in most of the rooms. Corner rooms are especially inviting, with an abundance of windows and bathrooms that are a bit more spacious.

None of the units feature Jacuzzi tubs, but guests can pamper themselves in the health club's heated outdoor pool, large hot tub, and sauna. An on-call masseuse is available to knead away the stress you're attempting to leave behind, and consistently excellent service makes this hotel getaway even more relaxing than most.

For an extra charge, you can reserve one of the 48 rooms on the Entrée Gold floor. These rooms feature fluffy down duvets instead of bedspreads, 24-hour concierge service, a complimentary breakfast, and afternoon hors d'oeuvres in the view lounge (with large outdoor deck), among other personal touches. "Romance Packages" are also available for an extra charge and include complimentary breakfast, champagne, roses, and free valet parking (isn't your beloved worth it?). Overall, this is one of the most pleasant places to pamper yourselves in Vancouver. **900 Canada Place Way; (604) 691-1820, (800) 441-1414; www.cphotels.com/cp.htm; expensive to unbelievably expensive; recommended wedding site.**

❦❦❦ **WEDGEWOOD HOTEL, Vancouver** In a city filled with towering high-rises, the intimate and manageable Wedgewood Hotel combines small-hotel charm with the efficiency and attention to detail of a larger property. A recent facelift has given the facade, awnings, and lobby a rich elegance that's apparent from the moment you arrive. Step inside to view the impressive chandelier, welcoming fireplace, and original artwork that grace the foyer.

Of the 89 rooms, most are either "executive level," with small bar areas for entertaining guests, or one-bedroom suites, with French doors and spacious balconies. Almost all rooms have foliage-draped decks overlooking the bustle of Robson Square below. The decor is warm and comfortable, with paisley bedspreads and pale wood accents. Alas, the recent remodel has not cured the dim lighting and cramped feel of the hallways, so be prepared when you make your way to your lovely room. **845 Hornby Street; (604) 689-7777, (800) 663-0666; expensive to unbelievably expensive; recommended wedding site.**

Romantic Suggestion: Don't miss having a cocktail, tea, or dinner at the hotel's revitalized BACCHUS (see Restaurant Kissing), which is now a swanky, sexy night spot.

❦❦❦ **WEST END GUEST HOUSE, Vancouver** Only six blocks from STANLEY PARK (see Outdoor Kissing) and within walking distance of Robson Street's shops, the West End Guest House is a real find. This electric pink turn-of-the-century home is dwarfed by two large, modern apartment buildings on either side in a neighborhood that is almost exclusively high-rises. Inside, the decor is a bit loud for some tastes, but there are plenty of lovely touches: framed black-and-white photographs, a gas fireplace, crystal chandeliers, floral and paisley wallpaper, and bay windows festooned with lace curtains. Afternoon sherry is served in the refined living room; in nice weather you can enjoy iced tea on the front porch. A new pantry is stocked with baked goods, tea, and coffee for guests. After a big day in the city, retreat to a sundeck with a retractable awning or a small backyard patio; both are open to guests, and they are perfect spots for quiet relaxation with your sweetheart.

All eight guest rooms boast quaint private baths, and soft down quilts covered with handmade bedspreads; some also have beautiful brass beds and either a skylight or a ceiling fan. Two junior suites have the added romance of French doors and fireplaces. The basement has been remodeled to combine two rooms into a single large suite. While the new furniture, wallpaper, gas fireplace, and sauna shower are all very nice, this suite still feels too much like a converted basement to win high romance ratings. Instead, go for the Grand Queen Suite on the attic level, with a canopied brass bed, parlor area with fireplace, and the roomiest bathroom, with a claw-foot tub. In the morning, breakfast is served in the main dining room or may be delivered to your room. **1362 Haro Street; (604) 681-2889; moderate to very expensive; minimum-stay requirement on weekends.**

Restaurant Kissing

❤❤❤❤ **BACCHUS, Vancouver** The recently remodeled restaurant in the WEDGEWOOD HOTEL (see Hotel/Bed and Breakfast Kissing) is now even more romantic than it used to be. In the lounge area, burgundy and gold club chairs, a sleek mahogany bar, and velvet banquette couches fronting a massive stone fireplace make this a popular gathering spot for tea, brunch, or evening cocktails. Though the room is most aglow at night, come after the chattering post-work crowd thins for better atmosphere and a chance at quiet conversation (not to mention a good table). A couple of steps beyond is the intimate restaurant, with high velvet seats, stunning light fixtures, gorgeous gilded sconces, and semi-separated dining areas for privacy.

The northern Italian fare includes pastas and risottos as well as wonderful local mussels in a zesty roasted garlic broth; entrées include a rich osso buco with tomato-fennel white wine sauce and a melt-in-your-mouth beef tenderloin with roasted pepper relish, potato and ricotta flan, and mushroom balsamic essence.

Tea or brunch by the sunny windows can be a marvelously cozy affair, highlighted by delightful, nonintrusive service, decadent baked goods, and inspired light dishes. Clink your cappuccinos over crab cakes and polenta, eggs Benedict, or the fabulous cranberry biscotti. **845 Hornby Street, at the Wedgewood Hotel; (604) 689-7777, (800) 663-0666; moderate to expensive; breakfast, lunch, high tea, and dinner daily, brunch Saturday–Sunday.**

❤❤❤ **BISHOP'S, Vancouver** Popular with visiting celebrities and well-heeled locals alike, Bishop's is one of the city's favorite restaurants. Modern artwork and extravagant flower arrangements add a dash of color to the minimalist interior of this two-level bistro, where a handful of tables are cloaked in white. On the lower level, large picture windows let in ample daylight but look out to the busy street. For a more romantic ambience, we recommend the upper level, where the lack of windows enables you to focus your full attention on each other.

The menu features nouvelle cuisine with an emphasis on fresh regional ingredients, and the wine list is extensive. To start, try the warm walnut-crusted goat cheese or house-cured wild sockeye gravlax; you might move on to the pan-seared scallops with lemon grass or the roasted duck breast with sun-dried Okanagan fruit and candied ginger glaze. Seasonal fish, such as the legendary ginger-steamed halibut or smoked black cod, is always a memorable choice. The skilled chef, together with the professional and polished wait staff, will make this an evening to remember. **2183 West Fourth Avenue; (604) 738-2025; www.settingsun.com/bishops; expensive to very expensive; dinner daily.**

❤❤ **BREAD GARDEN, Vancouver** If your sweet tooth is begging to be indulged, you've come to the right city: Vancouver is awash in bakeries and pastry shops. Set in a cozy storefront among clusters of other charming shops, the Bread Garden—Vancouver's original bakery/café—is one of our favorites. Opt for a decadent dessert after a night at the theater or a buttery croissant to begin a lazy morning. You can enjoy your treats at one of the handful of tables in the bakery's casual interior or get a "to go" bag and dine at one of Vancouver's scenic outdoor spots (see Outdoor Kissing). **1880 West First Avenue; (604) 738-6684; inexpensive to moderate; breakfast, lunch, and dinner daily.**

Romantic Suggestions: The Bread Garden is by no means the only good bakery in town. We also recommend **TERRA BREADS** (2380 West Fourth; 604-736-1838), **ECCO IL PANE** (238 West Fifth; 604-873-6888), **CARMELO'S PASTRY SHOP** (1399 Commercial Drive; (604-254-7024), and **VITO'S PASTRY SHOP** (1748 Commercial Drive; 604-251-6650). The latter two shops are located in **LITTLE ITALY,** a neighborhood in the east part of town near Commercial and 12th Streets, which is worth exploring for a diverting hour or two.

✿✿✿ **CAFÉ IL NIDO, Vancouver** Tucked in an alley and set back from the bustle of Robson Street, Café Il Nido provides delectable Mediterranean cuisine in an intimate atmosphere. Rich saffron-colored walls, black accents, green carpet, and a handful of polished mahogany tables covered with white tablecloths and topped with fresh flowers distinguish this small Italian hideaway. Dried flowers and contemporary artwork decorate the walls, and sconces provide soft lighting in the evening. Feast on intimate conversation and oven-roasted chicken stuffed with Camembert, scallops, and dried apricots in a romaine sauce, or perhaps a pan-seared fillet of salmon accompanied by a trio of melon sauces and garnished with pink-shelled scallops and tiger prawns. Outdoor seating is available on warm summer afternoons. Due to this restaurant's lunchtime popularity with the business crowd, however, you may want to skip lunch and come back for dinner instead, when you can enjoy your privacy to the fullest. **780 Thurlow Street; (604) 685-6436; moderate to expensive; lunch Monday–Friday, dinner Monday–Saturday.**

✿✿✿ **CAFFE DE MEDICI, Vancouver** Robson Street is stuffed to the brim with specialty shops, bakeries, cafés, bistros, superb restaurants, and designer boutiques, cutting a half-mile course through downtown. Caffe de Medici holds court in one of the swankier clusters of shops, somewhat away from the bustle. This elegant Italian restaurant is artistically decorated with high arched ceilings, chandeliers, and terra-cotta-tiled floors warmed by Oriental rugs. Plush drapery frames its many large windows, ornate Italian oil paintings grace the walls, and each table is topped with crisp white linens, fresh flowers, and a candle to add a soft glow to your evening.

The restaurant has grown over the years, and the furnishings seem a bit timeworn, but the unmistakably romantic interior remains lovely. Antipasto and pasta dishes are standouts, and desserts are exquisite. Crowds impart a bit of a power-lunch feel in the daytime; come in the evening for a more affectionate flavor. **1025 Robson Street; (604) 669-9322; www.settingsun.com/italy001.html; moderate to expensive; lunch Monday–Friday, dinner daily.**

❦❦❦ **CHARTWELL, Vancouver** Stepping inside this elegant restaurant at the FOUR SEASONS HOTEL (see Hotel/Bed and Breakfast Kissing) is like entering a private club: Dark wood paneling, detailed murals, and a stately fireplace make this an ideal choice for a blustery Northwest winter evening. And once you're happily ensconced in the glowing dining room, you'll be treated like royalty. Like most hotel-based restaurants, Chartwell offers dishes to suit every taste, but everything is done with good taste. Seafood is a specialty, with choices ranging from scallion-studded swordfish to miso-glazed mahimahi; carnivores will relish the herb-marinated pheasant breast, rack of lamb, veal chop, or venison. Vegetarian options are also offered. After a long, lovely evening spent here, you may find it difficult to leave—even if it's just to wander upstairs to your room. **791 West Georgia Street, at the Four Seasons Hotel; (604) 689-9333, (800) 268-6282 (in Canada), (800) 332-3442 (in the U.S.); expensive; breakfast, lunch, and dinner daily.**

❦❦❦ **CINCIN, Vancouver** This crowded, popular Mediterranean restaurant overlooking Robson Street owes its name to a popular Italian toast, and rightly so: The celebratory, good-time feeling here will inspire you to raise your own glasses. At the top of a tiled staircase, the inviting dining room is distinguished by high ceilings, arched windows, warm sponge-painted walls, and colorful murals. The immense wood-fired oven and grill are highlights of the open kitchen, where gourmet pizzas and focaccia are prepared. Other menu items include paella, veal tenderloin carpaccio, a velvety roasted squash soup with grilled endive and marjoram, plus a signature porcini-crusted sea bass on crab and leek mashed potatoes. The bar offers single-malt scotches and grappas for post-meal toasts. **1154 Robson Street; (604) 688-7338; www.cin-cin.com; moderate to very expensive; lunch Monday–Saturday, dinner daily.**

Romantic Suggestion: Due to the lively clientele, the dining room isn't particularly quiet; an outdoor balcony enclosed with greenery offers a quieter alternative when weather permits. Also, a newly renovated wine cellar seats up to 25 people among over 3,000 bottles if you're planning an occasion.

❦❦❦ **DELILAH'S, Vancouver** This restaurant and bar at the base of the Coast Plaza Hotel (no affiliation) in Vancouver's West End has emerged as an elegant hot spot, with a swanky, eclectic lounge look. Many people come to Delilah's just for the bar and its famous two-page martini menu. Trendy young swingers elbow in to see and be seen while sipping a cran-tini or other high-octane concoction. Perfect mood lighting sets off the small dining room, which offers a frescoed ceiling with cavorting cupids plus snazzy red velvet booths along the room's perimeter; brocade chairs hug candlelit tables in the center.

The menu has many appealing offerings, including a lovely salad of shrimp, grapefruit, pistachios, and baby greens with pink peppercorn vinaigrette, and entrées such as New Zealand scallops with herb gnocchi and Chilean sea bass with an orange-ginger-soy glaze. However, we find the method of ordering a bit disconcerting. Diners are handed a fill-in-the-blank, prix fixe menu that they hand back to their server rather than giving their order verbally; it comes across as strange instead of novel. Still, this place is a peach. **1789 Comox Street; (604) 687-3424; moderate; dinner daily.**

Romantic Suggestion: Tables here are placed very close together and the place is often full. For real intimacy, request a booth or—better yet—one of the two separate booth alcoves with velvet drapes that can be closed partway to cut down on distractions.

❀❀❀ **DIVA AT THE MET, Vancouver** Already acclaimed as one of the best *hotel* restaurants in the city, Diva at the Met is now thought of as one of the best restaurants in the city, period. This contemporary restaurant is separated from the Metropolitan Hotel's lobby by a wall of beautifully etched glass. A colorful picture of (what else?) a diva hangs above the open bar in the front entrance, lending a touch of whimsy to the ultra-modern, multilevel dining room. Beige and white linens drape the well-spaced tables, which are topped with candles and copper salt and pepper shakers. Depending on your mood, you can reserve a table in front of the exhibition kitchen and watch the adept chef prepare your meal, or cozy up in a secluded banquette in the upper dining room (an appropriate spot for a few discreet kisses).

Evening is undoubtedly the most romantic time to dine here, and the food is consistently superb. The rare-seared tandoori ahi tuna is done to perfection, as is the grilled veal chop with artichoke and potato frittata. No matter how full you feel, do not pass up the decadent desserts here. Instead, request the dessert sampler, which offers small tastes of everything. **645 Howe Street, at the Metropolitan Hotel; (604) 602-7788; www.metropolitan.com/diva/index.html; moderate to very expensive; breakfast, lunch, and dinner daily.**

Romantic Note: Diva offers a table d'hôte pretheater, three-course menu that is very reasonably priced and includes complimentary parking (a definite plus in this busy city).

❀❀❀ **FLEURI RESTAURANT, Vancouver** Newly renamed and now the only full-service restaurant at the elegant **SUTTON PLACE HOTEL** (see Hotel/Bed and Breakfast Kissing), Fleuri has the refined ambience of a European manor—complete with floor-length floral tablecloths, damask wall coverings, and original artwork. A gourmet menu and polished service add to the special-occasion flavor. However, because it is so close to the airy main lobby, the arrangement seems a bit too open for a truly intimate romantic encounter; request a table in the rear of the restaurant—ideally, the "alcove table" (No. 50)—for a more private tête-à-tête with your loved one.

Brunch here is a decadent treat, with an array of international specialties, French pâtés, fresh omelets, and delicious desserts. Live jazz adds to the atmosphere. At dinner, opt for the chef's Fresh Sheet selections, highlighting the bounty of the region. Saturday evenings, the "Taste of Atlantis" seafood buffet is offered; for some unforgettable sweets with your sweetie, don't miss the Chocoholic Bar, served Thursday, Friday, and Saturday evenings. **845 Burrard Street, at the Sutton Place Hotel; (604) 682-5511, (800) 961-7555 (in Canada); expensive; lunch and dinner daily, brunch Sunday.**

❀❀❀ **GIANNI RESTAURANT, Vancouver** It may not be the quietest place for a romantic meal, but if you're in a lively mood this restaurant is a consistent pleaser. Traffic speeds by at a frantic rate on Granville Street, so it isn't at all surprising that the pace at Gianni is equally brisk. Though it can be difficult to get a table and sometimes even more difficult to hear yourselves over the clanking of dishes in the open kitchen, there are several good reasons why this restaurant continues to draw crowds. The lovely narrow dining room boasts cathedral ceilings, and the terra-cotta-colored walls are appointed with hand-woven tapestries and Italianesque sculptures. White linens and fresh flowers adorn the well-spaced tables, where you are catered to by the friendly, helpful wait staff. From the antipasto to the interesting gourmet pastas to the consistently fresh seafood, the Italian fare here is some of Vancouver's best. So don't expect the crowds to diminish anytime soon—we have a feeling they're here to stay. **2881 Granville Street; (604) 738-7922; moderate to expensive; lunch Monday–Friday, dinner Monday–Saturday.**

❀❀❀ **HERMITAGE, Vancouver** Situated on vibrant and always crowded Robson Street, the Hermitage is a surprisingly quiet refuge and a definite romantic find. Brick walls warm the dining room's French country–style interior, appointed with antiques and country knickknacks. A fire roars in the corner hearth, which is accented with copper kettles and other vintage cookware, and candle lanterns flicker at fairly well-spaced tables covered with elegant white fabric. Whether you opt for the lobster terrine and goat cheese salad or rack of lamb with Dijon mustard crust, you'll be treated to true regional French country cooking. And then there are the fresh home-baked desserts; forgoing them would be a sin. **115-1025 Robson Street; (604) 689-3237; moderate to expensive; lunch Monday–Friday, dinner daily.**

❀❀❀ **IL GIARDINO, Vancouver** Like an Italian villa, Il Giardino is a welcoming place to linger, sip some wine, enjoy the sounds of laughter and clinking dishes, and smile at your sweetheart. The high ceilings, terra-cotta tile floors, and lively rooms inside this beautifully restored Victorian home make meals feel like an extended private party. Eating outside is just as heavenly if you prefer to unwind on a welcoming vine-draped brick terrace with wood-fired oven and fireplace. The menu emphasizes pasta and game, including fresh veal and pheasant with rich, delectable sauces. One warning: This popular restaurant is packed during lunchtime on weekdays and also on Friday and Saturday nights. When most of the tables are filled, the romantic ambience suffers. Try for a table somewhere other than adjacent to the open kitchen. **1382 Hornby Street; (604) 669-2422; expensive; lunch Monday–Friday, dinner Monday–Saturday.**

❀❀❀❀ **LE CROCODILE, Vancouver** Forget every negative French restaurant stereotype you've ever heard: Le Crocodile will change your mind. The gracious staff, the beautifully presented meals, and everything else will win your hearts. Casual refinement describes the small dining room, with its goldenrod-colored walls, polished mahogany chairs, starched white linens, and sprigs of fresh flowers on each table. Dimly glowing candle lamps and wall sconces, plus saffron half-curtains shielding the room from the busy street outside, are ideal touches for intimacy. The inviting restaurant is always busy (reservations are a must), but even with a full house, the noise level remains low, service is attentive, and you and yours will be well taken care of.

Authentic French dishes fill the menu, and there is usually an extensive list of daily specials. Escargots in edible pastry shells, fresh sautéed duck liver with grilled quail in port wine sauce, and boneless rabbit with wild mushroom and spinach stuffing are just a few of the delectable offerings available. **100-909 Burrard Street; (604) 669-4298; moderate to expensive; reservations required; lunch Monday–Friday, dinner Monday–Saturday.**

❀❀❀❀ **LE GAVROCHE, Vancouver** Le Gavroche, offering a menu that combines traditional French with a Northwest twist, is a standout for romantic dining in the Vancouver area. Situated downtown in a renovated Victorian home, this restaurant offers views of the distant bay from tables scattered throughout the home's original dining and living rooms. Hardwood floors, floral wallpaper, impressive antiques, and a glowing fireplace make the restaurant feel intimate yet polished. Fresh flowers and candle lanterns sparkle atop white linens at every table, and when weather permits, guests can dine in the sunshine on the outdoor deck.

Though ultra-formal dining doesn't always translate into romance, Le Gavroche's staff strives to make everyone feel comfortable and welcome in this setting. Not surprisingly, the food is a gastronomic triumph. Indulge in the sea bass cassoulet, lobster in Thai curry, or delicate marinated mahimahi; for dessert, we recommend the signature lili cake, an almond and hazelnut meringue confection. If you're celebrating (which you probably are at this restaurant), don't forget to splurge on a special bottle from one of the top wine cellars in the city. **1616 Alberni Street; (604) 685-3924; expensive to very expensive; lunch Monday–Friday, dinner daily.**

❀❀❀ **LUMIERE, Vancouver** When it's time to splurge, Vancouver's chic set comes to this somewhat minimalist space, and no wonder. The small yet dramatic dining room features black ceilings, pale wood floors, and arty black-and-white prints on the white walls. While the room might feel a bit cold for some tastes, it is a study in understated elegance. Besides, the exquisitely balanced food and impeccable service will soon warm you up to the place. Dishes are delicate yet full of flavor; the cuisine is best described as contemporary French. Appetizers might include escargots with local wild mushrooms in a roasted garlic froth; warm smoked black cod salad with Yukon gold potatoes, leeks, arugula, and horseradish; or seared Sonoma Valley foie gras with citrus fruits. Entrées range from roasted Peking duck with Israeli couscous to herb-crusted rack of Australian lamb with truffle jus. The Chef's Tasting Menu or the Vegetarian Tasting Menu can provide an ideal introduction to the delights, with eight manageable courses including cheeses and desserts. A complementary flight of wines from the fine wine list is available for both of these well-chosen menus. **2551 West Broadway; (604) 739-8185; very expensive; dinner Tuesday–Sunday.**

❦❦❧ **MANGIAMO!, Vancouver** Located in the burgeoning Yaletown district, across from the busy Yaletown Brewery, this elegant eatery attracts lively crowds. Though the restaurant works hard to keep things intimate, it can be a challenge when the place fills with Vancouver trendies on a Saturday night. So while the small tables in front and the bar seating at the open kitchen can be fun, try to score a table in the warm and well-appointed back dining room for a more intimate evening. Here you'll find floral draperies, dark hardwood floors, and beautiful light fixtures illuminating wine bottles stored in a dramatic wall unit. The best bet for romantic dining in nice weather is the lilac-draped back patio, sheltered by striped awnings and warmed by heat lamps as Italian opera music filters through hidden speakers.

The menu is best described as spirited Italian, with entrées including Quebec duck breast with pinot noir reduction and wild mushroom polenta, lamb osso buco with saffron risotto cake, and grilled mahimahi with calamari orzo and fire-roasted yellow peppers. A selection of gourmet pizzas and pastas, plus an extensive list of antipasti, rounds out the menu. Once you do make up your mind about what to order from the many delectable selections, do what the restaurant's name suggests: *Eat!* **1116 Mainland Street; (604) 687-1116; expensive; lunch Monday–Friday, dinner Monday–Saturday.**

❦❦❦❧ **PICCOLO MONDO RESTAURANT, Vancouver** One block south of lively Robson Street, Piccolo Mondo provides a calm refuge from the city.

Cost ratings for British Columbia listings are in Canadian funds. American travelers should check the exchange rate or ask an innkeeper to figure out the cost in U.S. dollars.

White columns and cherry-stained wood floors graced with Oriental carpets lend stylish elegance to the small, two-level dining room. Layers of beige fabric give the windows a fashionable look, lovely artwork depicting Italian scenes hang on a turquoise wall, and the well-spaced tables are topped with white linens, candles, silver, and fine china.

Although the setting may seem formal, the gracious staff will make you feel at home. You'll want to linger for hours, savoring the ambience. Authentic northern Italian cuisine is the specialty here, and the pasta dishes combine the freshest herbs and cheeses with rich, silky sauces. Squid-ink risotto with scallops, veal tortellini in creamy mustard sauce, and salmon with sea urchin and lemon sauce are standouts. Ask the owners to select the right wine to accompany your meal from their list of award-winning Italian wines. **850 Thurlow Street; (604) 688-1633; www.piccolomondoristorante.com; moderate to expensive; lunch Monday–Friday, dinner Monday–Saturday.**

❤❤❤ **THE PROW, Vancouver** Once you make your way through the mammoth Canada Place complex to this restaurant poised on the water's edge, you'll be glad you did. The view is simply spectacular. Three distinct dining rooms overlook Burrard Inlet, set off by mountains, glittering city lights, and imperious ships forging their way through the water. Dressed in pale peaches and greens, each dining area is pretty and the tables have room to spare. Perhaps the most attractive room is the one that resembles a greenhouse, with tiled floors, expansive windows, and abundant foliage. Outdoor seating in a geranium-trimmed patio is also available and a great choice for a lunch spent watching seaplanes take off.

While some of the preparations are not the most inventive, the seafood is consistently fine, almost allowing the restaurant to transcend its touristy location. We say "almost" because the dining room is consistently packed, a situation that interferes with intimacy. Still, the desserts are generous—and, well, there's that view. **999 Canada Place, Suite 100; (604) 684-1339; moderate to expensive; lunch and dinner daily, brunch Saturday–Sunday.**

Romantic Note: If the Prow is crowded, you can relax awhile next door in the CASCADES LOUNGE of THE PAN PACIFIC HOTEL (see Hotel/Bed and Breakfast Kissing). This immense, airy, echoing bar boasts the same astonishing view as the restaurant, through arresting floor-to-ceiling windows. When the weather is warm, we recommend walking hand in hand along the outdoor walkway that leads to the Prow, or visiting the observation deck above it. You'll find lots of kiss-inspiring lookout perches.

❤❤❤ **RAINCITY GRILL, Vancouver** On the west side of the city, Denman Street is a lower-key version of Robson Street, but its abundant coffee bars and specialty shops attract more locals than tourists. Raincity Grill is another Denman denizen, and locals rave about this lovely little restaurant located just a few yards from the seawall and English Bay. The intimate space is warmed by amber-hued lighting and tea candles on the tables; windows face out to active Denman Street in front and the bay on one side. Unfortunately, the tables are placed close together, and the acoustics in this small room aren't the best for romance; don't be surprised if you have to lean in to converse with your loved one on busy nights. Luckily, in the summer months, a deck facing the water eases some of the space constraints.

The menu emphasizes Pacific West Coast fare; signature items include a grilled Caesar salad with preserved lemon; local sea bass with horseradish, fennel, gnocchi, and caper oil; and a tender veal chop with warm potato–green bean pancetta salad and a dried fruit glaze. To complement your meal, choose a bottle from the extensive selection of exclusively Northwest wines (from British Columbia, Washington, Oregon, and northern California). For dessert, try digging two forks into the unbelievably decadent cranberry-toffee pie with crème fraîche—now that spells romance! Service is knowledgeable and prompt, and the helpful sommelier offers wine recommendations for each menu item. **1193 Denman Street; (604) 685-7337; expensive; lunch and dinner daily, brunch Saturday–Sunday.**

🌸🌸🌸🌸 **SEASONS IN THE PARK RESTAURANT, Vancouver** Sister to Stanley Park's **TEAHOUSE RESTAURANT** (see below), this stunning establishment is slightly less crowded (but still touristed), which gives it a distinct kissing advantage. Roosting high on a hilltop in emerald green **QUEEN ELIZABETH PARK** (see Outdoor Kissing), Seasons enjoys a sensational view of the park, Vancouver's skyline, clouds hovering above the North Shore Mountains—and the sunset, if you time things right. Both dining rooms have an enormous live tree as their centerpiece, atrium-style glass ceilings, and walls of windows that showcase the breathtaking scenery. Though the restaurant is open and airy, the atmosphere is intimate and casually elegant, with white linens, low lighting, and tapered candle lanterns at each of the well-spaced tables.

Fresh seafood specials, including grilled B.C. salmon and roasted sea bass, supplement the straightforward Continental menu. Your meal will be good, but a sunset from this vantage point is something to cherish forever. **Cambie and 33rd Avenue, in Queen Elizabeth Park; (604) 874-8008, (800) 632-9422; moderate to expensive; lunch Monday–Friday, dinner daily, brunch Saturday–Sunday.**

🌸🌸 **THE TEAHOUSE RESTAURANT, Vancouver** Set in an old-growth forest in Stanley Park, the Teahouse Restaurant has the dubious dual distinction of being both a major tourist attraction and also one of the more beautiful places to dine in British Columbia. In spite of the crowds it draws, the Teahouse remains a truly extraordinary kissing place. Much of this property's charisma comes from the location: It rests in the middle of a verdant lawn overlooking English Bay and Vancouver Island. The building itself is dazzling—half of it is an evergreen-colored country home, the other half a glass-enclosed atrium.

Here you can watch the sun gently tuck itself into the ocean for a peaceful night's rest—as long as you have reservations, that is. Everyone knows about the Teahouse Restaurant, including busloads of tourists, so reservations are a definite must.

Although the kitchen serves fairly standard Pacific Northwest cuisine that is a tad too basic and generally oversauced, if you order carefully you'll find that the seafood and pasta dishes can be tasty when prepared simply. Besides, the view is so ravishing you'll hardly feel disappointed. **Stanley Park at Ferguson Point; (604) 669-3281, (800) 280-9893; moderate to expensive; reservations recommended; lunch and dinner daily, brunch Saturday–Sunday.**

❦❦❦❦ **VILLA DEL LUPO, Vancouver** In a neighborhood that's almost exclusively high-rises, this two-story Victorian home turned restaurant looks unassuming but is full of delightful and romantic surprises. Sage-colored walls, bold artwork, and hardwood floors dress up the three cozy dining rooms; each is slightly different, but all are warm, welcoming, and freshly decorated. There are only about six tables in each area, so intimacy is assured. (A wood-burning fireplace makes one of the rooms especially snug.) This is a place for special occasions without pretension—a place lively enough to avoid any hint of stuffiness, but with an intimate, upscale ambience. Service is gracious but can be on the slow side—don't come here for a pre-event meal—but a meal here is an event in itself, so come prepared to spend the whole evening lingering over a great feast.

Start off with freshly baked sun-dried tomato bread or focaccia, then move on to appetizers such as calamari tubes stuffed with mushrooms and herbs or buffalo milk mozzarella with grilled eggplant and organic tomato salad. Entrées are not standard Italian fare, not by a long shot—local ostrich scaloppine, tuna loin with ricotta and spinach gnocchi, and veal steak accompanied by morels stuffed with foie gras are among the memorable offerings. Desserts are equally unforgettable, including a dramatically presented lemon tartlet with homemade gelato and the vanilla bean and cane sugar crème brûlée, not to mention top-notch cappuccinos and a selection of grappas or eaux-de-vie to cap your meal. *Bene. Molto bene!* **869 Hamilton Street; (604) 688-7436; moderate to expensive; dinner daily.**

Romantic Note: A wine cellar can be reserved for special occasions. The privacy factor is nice, but the room feels rather claustrophobic to us—particularly since the main rooms are so lovely.

❦❦❦ **WILLIAM TELL RESTAURANT, Vancouver** Renowned for its intimate setting, the William Tell caters almost exclusively to romance-minded couples. And its location near the Queen Elizabeth and Ford Theatres makes it a natural choice for a big night on the town. Although part of the restaurant has been recently converted into an airy, contemporary bistro with an outdoor terrace, French doors still open into the William Tell's heart of hearts: the main dining room. Here, a crystal chandelier softly illuminates rich green walls and a handful of tables covered with crisp white linens. European artwork is spotlighted by glowing wall sconces in this exceedingly formal and radiant setting.

Fortunately, the food is as impressive as the ambience. A newly revised menu includes traditional beef dishes, Swiss-inspired fare, and local seafood. Desserts are to die for, but don't expire until after you've tried, say, the white and dark Belgian chocolate terrine set on berry coulis and praline sauce, or delicate crêpes prepared tableside. **765 Beatty Street, at the Georgian Court Hotel; (604) 688-3504; expensive to very expensive; breakfast, lunch, and dinner daily.**

Outdoor Kissing

❦❦❦ **BOTANICAL GARDENS, Vancouver** The Vancouver area boasts many acclaimed, exquisite, and lush gardens, but the most beautiful are the **VANDUSEN BOTANICAL GARDENS** (5251 Oak Street; 604-878-9274; $5.50 per adult), the **UNIVERSITY OF BRITISH COLUMBIA BOTANI-CAL GARDEN** (6804 Southwest Marine Drive; 604-822-4208; $4.50 per adult), the **BLOEDEL FLORAL CONSERVATORY** (3030 Cambie Street; 604-257-8584; $3.30 per adult), and the **DR. SUN YAT-SEN CLASSICAL CHINESE GARDEN** (578 Carrall, in Chinatown; 604-689-7133; $6.50 per adult). Each one has its own captivating beauty. Coaxed from the earth by skilled artisans, the verdant presentations are creative and dramatic. Sculpted shrubbery, specially pruned trees, tranquil ponds, and exotic arrangements are all here for your pleasure. Of course, there are the occasional tour buses to look past, but depending on the season you could be the only ones walking through these elysian paradises. Come in the early morning or late afternoon to avoid the majority of tourists. **Recommended wedding sites.**

❦❦❦ **HYAK WILDERNESS ADVENTURES LTD., Vancouver** Located one hour from Vancouver, the Chilliwack River is churning with white water and (if you'll pardon the phrase) a thrill a minute. River rafting through rugged canyons, unanticipated gorges, and momentary still water along riverbanks crowned with cedars and pines makes for a trip that is nothing short of sensational. Depending on the season, the impact of your excursion can vary from awesome to electrifying. Packages are available for one-, two-, or six-day adventures. It is all an immense amount of fun, even if you've never been in a wet suit before or are afraid of how you'll look in one. Let go and jump in; the surging water is terrific. **Chilliwack and Thompson Rivers; (604) 734-8622, (206) 382-1311, (800) 663-RAFT; $98 to $249 per person; call for information and reservations; closed October–April.**

❦❦❦ **QUEEN ELIZABETH PARK, Vancouver** Queen Elizabeth Park, home of the **BLOEDEL FLORAL CONSERVATORY** (see the Botanical Gardens review above), is located at Vancouver's geographic center. Take the short, winding, tree-lined drive up to a lookout peak where you can enjoy panoramic views of the city and its surroundings. Although this park is popular, it isn't nearly as crowded as **STANLEY PARK** (reviewed below), so affectionate hand holding or an intimate picnic is possible while you enjoy the natural beauty Vancouver has to offer. **Free admission; recommended wedding site.** *At 33rd Avenue and Cambie Street.*

Romantic Suggestion: You will see plenty of signs for **SEASONS IN THE PARK RESTAURANT** (see Restaurant Kissing), where you can eat up the view while you dine.

❀❀❀ **ROCKWOOD ADVENTURES, Vancouver** If you're eager to spend a "green day" in Vancouver, call Rockwood Adventures. Although guided tours preclude truly romantic moments, Rockwood Adventures' friendly guides can only be considered a romantic asset, as they lead you to some of Vancouver's most awe-inspiring (and kiss-inspiring) destinations. You can learn more about the life cycle of the Pacific salmon at the Capilano Fish Hatchery along the spectacularly lush Rain Forest Walk in the Capilano River Canyon, drink in spellbinding views of a virgin coastal rain forest in Lighthouse Park in Burrard Inlet, seek out spectacular hidden corners of **STANLEY PARK** (see below), or take a scenic journey to nearby Bowen Island. Couples who are looking for a physical challenge will enjoy the steep climb up **GROUSE MOUNTAIN** (better known as the Grouse Grind; reviewed on page 40). Or ask about an ultimate outing on a floatplane—if you can afford the $1,000 price tag. Rockwood Adventures guarantees a scenic perspective of Vancouver you won't find anywhere else. **1330 Fulton Avenue; (604) 926-7705, (888) 236-6606; www.cool.mb.ca/rockwood; $45 to $190 per person.**

❀❀❀❀ **STANLEY PARK, Vancouver** Stanley Park is Vancouver's version of Central Park: a verdant oasis in the heart of a bustling city. Within its boundaries you can explore thick forest, green hilly lawns, jewel-like lakes, and paved trails weaving through 1,000 acres of cloistered parkland. Almost an island, the park projects into the water, with English Bay on one side and Burrard Inlet on the other. From the **SEAWALL PROMENADE**, which wraps around the park, to the engaging aquarium, abundant picnic areas, lengthy shoreline at Sunset Beach, picturesque restaurants, and vista after scenic vista, Stanley Park provides a much-needed respite from the cityscape. And it's just moments away! Of course, this means it draws thousands of locals and visitors at all times of the year, which doesn't leave much room for privacy. But the surroundings are so welcoming that you'll easily forgive the busloads of camera-clicking tourists and find yourselves a corner to call your own—at least for a while. **Free admission; recommended wedding site.** *In the West End, just off Georgia Street.*

Romantic Suggestion: If you work up an appetite while exploring the park (and if you remembered your wallet), THE TEAHOUSE RESTAURANT (see Restaurant Kissing) is an ideal spot for lunch in the park.

West Vancouver and North Vancouver

If you time it right and manage to avoid rush-hour traffic on Lion's Gate Bridge or Highway 1 West, you can trade Vancouver's urban sprawl for more residential and forested North Vancouver or West Vancouver in a matter of minutes. (If you do happen to get stuck in traffic, rest assured the wait is worth your while.) Nestled in the foothills of the North Shore Mountains, adjacent to several provincial parks, this region features tranquil scenery and settings that are undeniably conducive to our favorite activity: kissing, of course! Better yet, we found a handful of properties designed for couples with just that in mind.

Hotel/Bed and Breakfast Kissing

❦❦ **BEACHSIDE BED AND BREAKFAST, West Vancouver** Nestled in an upscale residential community, this semi-contemporary home is perched at the water's edge. Waves lap at the driftwood logs that have settled on the beach fronting the property. Views of Vancouver span the horizon in the distance and can be enjoyed from the vantage point of a large deck or a steamy hot tub set right on the beach. While the Beachside's setting is, without exaggeration, picture perfect, the five guest rooms could use some major updating. Brown carpeting and mismatched furnishings and linens lend a dated feeling to many of the rooms, several of which lack water views due to their location at the back of the house.

Having said that, the oceanfront Honeymoon Suite is still worth your romantic consideration and is the only real reason to book a reservation here. The suite needs some new furnishings and carpet, but offers panoramic views of the water, ample privacy, a private entrance to the beach, and exclusive use of an en suite Jacuzzi tub the size of a small swimming pool. (However, we found that the chlorine smell and locker room–type shower almost counteract the romantic novelty.) Runner-up is the adjacent Seaside Room, with a fireplace, new step-up jetted tub in the small bathroom, and sliding doors to a private patio and the communal hot tub beyond.

Guests are encouraged to make themselves at home in the comfortable fireside living room or dining room enclosed by floor-to-ceiling windows that face the water. In the morning, a full breakfast is enriched by the sound of waves lapping against the shore. **4208 Evergreen Avenue; (604) 922-7773, (800) 563-3311; inexpensive to expensive; minimum-stay requirement seasonally.**

❦❦❦ **LABURNUM COTTAGE, North Vancouver** Haloed by towering evergreens, this picturesque Victorian country home looks slightly neglected on the outside, but the real appeal lies beyond the initial impression. The remarkably pretty setting is what makes this place a gem: Miniature bridges traverse a trickling mountain stream and winding footpaths meander through the colorful, manicured English gardens that embrace this one-and-a-half-acre retreat. You'll think you've stepped into a Jane Austen novel.

Five of the six options for guest accommodations here face the tranquil garden, ensuring calm privacy. However, we found some dated touches, an odd assortment of artwork, and furnishings that weren't the freshest.

The guest rooms in the main house, three upstairs and one down, are quite snug, but still cheery and bright with country accents and down comforters; all overlook the garden. The self-contained Summer House, right in the middle of the garden, offers the most seclusion, but the narrow, rectangular floor plan makes it seem even smaller than it is. Although it lacks a garden view, a second private cottage called the Carriage House has been renovated to include a fireplace, kitchenette, and comfortable sitting area, plus a new soaker tub in the small bathroom.

High tea and sherry are served in the formal English-style living room of the main house, where windows allow views of the colorful flowers outside. A full breakfast is presented in the atrium-like dining area, which brims with sunlight. **1388 Terrace Avenue; (604) 988-4877; moderate to very expensive; minimum-stay requirement in cottages; closed January–February; recommended wedding site.**

❀❀❀ THE PALMS GUEST HOUSE, West Vancouver Located in an impressively upscale residential neighborhood, this contemporary home just steps from the water has magnificent views. Guests are encouraged to make themselves at home in the owner's elegant upstairs living quarters, fashioned with high ceilings and skylights, classical columns, and beautifully finished hardwood floors. Watch the boats on English Bay from the expansive outdoor deck or lounge on the lawn in the large backyard, surrounded by tall trees.

The four guest rooms here all have beautiful views of the water and surrounding stands of evergreens. Although some of the color schemes are a little too jarring for our tastes, the en suite bathrooms, embroidered sheets, and private water-view balconies are a rare find. If you've got serious romancing in mind, the regal Ambassador Suite—the only room larger than standard bedroom size—is the main reason to stay here. A two-sided fireplace warms the bathroom and bedroom at the same time. Deep green satin bedding drapes an immense four-poster bed and contrasts with the spotless white carpet. Nearly the size of a bedroom itself, the glamorous white-and-green-tiled private bathroom has a glass-enclosed shower and a double Jacuzzi tub beneath a picture window that reveals an exceptional water view. You can even watch the sunset from the privacy of your own big balcony. Other amenities in this sumptuous suite include a TV, telephone, and stereo.

Tea is offered to guests in the afternoon, and a generous gourmet breakfast is served in the elegant dining room, which shares the same lovely water views. A butler's pantry adjacent to the common rooms provides coffee and snacks throughout the day. Since the formal, feminine feel of the common areas and the rooms won't appeal to everyone, the best bet would be to come in the summer, when the appeal of the view is universal. **3042 Marine Drive; (604) 926-1159, (800) 691-4455; www.vancouver-bc.com/palmsguesthouse; moderate to very expensive; minimum-stay requirement seasonally.**

❤❤❤❣ **THISTLE DOWN HOUSE, West Vancouver** In this newly renovated, 1920s-era country inn, discriminating guests will find true style, comfortable sophistication, and an air of refined tranquillity among antiques and art from around the world. Tucked behind towering pines across the Lion's Gate Bridge from Vancouver and near the Capilano Suspension Bridge and **GROUSE MOUNTAIN** (see Outdoor Kissing), Thistle Down House is the perfect showplace for the proprietors' backgrounds in hotel management and interior design.

Each room has its own flavor, but all include framed art prints, antiques, custom soaps from London in the en suite baths, goose-down duvets, and other tasteful touches. (TVs are available upon request only—a policy we appreciate.) The Snuggery is somewhat snug but not too much so, with its own fireplace, stained glass windows in the bathroom, and Persian carpets. Upstairs, Mulberry Peek has elegantly draped bay windows on all sides, a private rooftop balcony, and a bird's-eye view of the half-acre of lush lawn below. Sweet Tibby's boasts a sleigh bed and an adjoining reading alcove with a sloped roof that gives it a "hidden attic" ambience, plus a lovely all-white bath with the original stained glass windows. Memories lacks a garden view, but is a large room with stunning antiques, plus a tiny dressing area with a marble-topped antique vanity.

All of the rooms are lovely, but for the ultimate in romance we recommend Under the Apple Tree, a suite-like downstairs hideaway where you'll find a sunken sitting area with a gas fireplace and comfy couch for snuggling. Wraparound bay windows face the spectacular tree that gives the room its name, glass doors open directly to the garden, and an antique wardrobe and headboard add charm. The elegant white Swiss linens that grace all the rooms also drape the king-size bed in the suite. The large and sumptuous bathroom is appointed with an air-jet tub for two with marble surround, heated floor, and a marble vanity.

Gourmet silver-service breakfast might include portobello mushroom crêpes with Ayrshire bacon, smoked salmon and herbed cream vol-au-vent, or chicken and mushrooms in cream sauce with four-cheese polenta. The meal is served in a honey-hued, Craftsman-style dining room, adjacent to a guest parlor with leather couches, an antique piano, and a large brick fireplace. **3910 Capilano Road; (604) 986-7173; moderate to very expensive.**

Restaurant Kissing

❧❧❧ BEACH HOUSE AT DUNDARAVE PIER, West Vancouver

Nestled right on the beach at West Vancouver's scenic Dundarave Pier is this forest green 1912 building where, a plaque explains, until the late 1930s the Stevenson sisters hosted many illustrious visitors in their tearoom. Today it's still a scenic and special gathering place—particularly on sunny days, when there's no better place to be than on the large patio facing the water, sheltered by a glass windbreak and yellow-and-white-striped umbrellas. Inside, the large dining room is pleasant but fairly standard in decor; either sit by the window or save this restaurant for a nice day and an outside table.

The menu is filled with West Coast specialties. For dinner, follow a sunset stroll on the promenade with lobster and potato gnocchi, Australian lamb loin, or braised duck confit with fried sweetbreads. Instead of a buffet, the limited but inspired brunch menu features such eye-openers as cornmeal-crusted Fanny Bay oysters, grilled raisin bread pudding, and spiced air-dried chorizo hash and eggs. **150 25th Street; (604) 922-1414; moderate to expensive; lunch and dinner daily, brunch Saturday–Sunday.**

Romantic Suggestion: The seawall walk that begins just outside the restaurant is perfect for a romantic stroll with water and city views. The wide promenade is well maintained and includes benches, flower boxes, and telescopes along the way. In-line skates, bikes, skateboards, and dogs are prohibited, keeping the route calm and civilized.

❧❧ BEACH SIDE CAFE, West Vancouver

Tucked into a cheery storefront on bustling Marine Drive, the Beach Side Cafe is one of the more "happening" places to dine in West Vancouver. The pace can feel a little frantic at the peak of the evening, but the lovely setting and fabulous fresh food ensure a pleasant repast after strolling hand in hand by the shops along the way.

Tiles in the entrance give the restaurant a Mediterranean flair, accented with blond wood, round columns, and jazzy fabrics. White linens drape the well-spaced tables, several of which are cozied into window alcoves that overlook the street beyond. When the weather cooperates (and sometimes even when it doesn't), you can dine on the heated terrace at an umbrella-shaded table with a view of **STANLEY PARK** (reviewed on page 33) and Kitsilano across the water. Sunsets here are remarkable and worth celebrating.

The kitchen strives to be creative and rarely disappoints. Unique preparations of seafood, such as pan-seared scallops with an Oriental noodle pancake, are highlights, and the lemon meringue pie is heavenly. **1362 Marine Drive; (604) 925-1945; expensive; lunch and dinner daily, brunch Saturday–Sunday.**

❧❧ CAPERS CAFE, West Vancouver

You may be surprised (as we were) to find a little gem of a cafe at the back of a health-food-oriented grocery store;

even more surprising is the discovery that it provides a desirable setting for a special meal at almost any time of day. Well, seeing and eating (with a kiss or two thrown in for good measure) is believing. Still, early morning (before the grocery opens) and dinnertime (after the grocery has closed for the evening) are definitely the most suitable times for intimate dining here. The deck is the perfect spot for an informal breakfast.

The casual wood-paneled interior is appointed with white tablecloths, forest green accents, and a large deck with a view of English Bay. Soft classical music adds to the ambience. Not surprisingly, the menu is almost entirely vegetarian (except for several seafood items), and the whole-wheat, organic, al dente pasta is a dream come true. Everything we sampled was excellent, and the service was professional and friendly. We realize this is an unusual setting for a romantic encounter, but we still think it is worth considering if you admire wholesome cooking served with elegant flair in a casual setting. **2496 Marine Drive; (604) 925-3374; inexpensive to moderate; breakfast, lunch, and dinner daily.**

❦❦ CHESA RESTAURANT, West Vancouver

Chesa's garden-like interior is a welcome oasis along well-traveled Marine Drive. Oriental carpets cover hardwood floors in the sunny dining room, which is filled with bouquets of exotic flowers. White latticework separates clusters of tables covered with white and red linens and topped with fresh flowers. Primarily meat-based, the menu features Continental cuisine with West Coast influences. Entrées like duck parfait with port wine and Amaretto; veal diced with white wine, mushrooms, and shallots; and the fresh seafood of the night are usually good, but sometimes miss the mark. Desserts, however, are always tantalizing and entirely too good to exclude (try the signature meringue swan floating in a pool of Belgian chocolate). If you didn't save room, we recommend kissing until you have some! **1734 Marine Drive; (604) 922-2411; moderate to expensive; lunch Tuesday–Sunday, brunch Saturday–Sunday.**

❦❦❦ LA TOQUE BLANCHE, West Vancouver

Don't let your first glimpse of this French restaurant dissuade you from dining here. Located behind a gas station and convenience store, La Toque Blanche has much more to offer than is first apparent. Step inside the softly lit dining room and you'll see exactly what we mean. Tall windows in the dining room face away from the gas station (thank goodness) and offer views of two towering evergreens in the parking lot instead. A recently renovated interior now provides a Renaissance Italian flavor, with pale yellow walls and a gleaming mahogany bar.

Cost ratings for British Columbia listings are in Canadian funds. American travelers should check the exchange rate or ask an innkeeper to figure out the cost in U.S. dollars.

The updated French Continental menu is remarkable, with an emphasis on seafood and game. Starters include smoked duck carpaccio and grilled rare tuna with avocado and prawns; exquisite entrées include grilled tenderloin of beef with port wine reduction, smoked black cod with lobster mashed potatoes, and grilled veal chop with roasted red peppers.

The name of this restaurant, La Toque Blanche, refers to the white "hat" awarded to chefs depending on their talent. We can't give hats of approval, but we can award lips of approval. Both are deserved. **4368 Marine Drive; (604) 926-1006; moderate to expensive; dinner Tuesday–Sunday.**

❦❦❦ **SALMON HOUSE ON THE HILL, West Vancouver** Sometimes a spectacular view is enough to establish a place's romantic dining credentials, and the Salmon House is a case in point. Poised high on a hillside, the restaurant surveys superlative views of Vancouver and its busy waterways. Much to our delight, the Salmon House also offers an innovative seafood-oriented menu that equals (and sometimes almost surpasses) its impressive setting—particularly their "fresh sheet" specials and their always stellar signature dish: B.C. salmon cooked over green alderwood.

Designed to look like an authentic Northwest lodge, the expansive terraced dining room is decorated with Native Canadian artwork, hand-carved canoes that hang from a sloped knotty pine ceiling, and a glowing brick fireplace. Wooden tables and green booths fill the interior, and all afford glimpses of the water through the wall of windows fronting the restaurant. Reserve a table near the window, order the savory salmon or the Cajun-dusted fried green tomatoes, then sit back and let the evening drift by your ringside view of the world. **2229 Folkestone Way; (604) 926-3212; www.salmonhouse.com; moderate to expensive; lunch and dinner daily, brunch Sunday.**

❦❦ **SALUTE!, West Vancouver** You won't even notice the heavy traffic on Marine Drive as you enjoy the consistently delicious fare served up by this vintage Italian eatery. Reproductions of Michelangelo's Sistine Chapel paintings embellish the walls, and terra-cotta tiles accent the floor of the small but charming dining room. White linens lend elegance to tables aglow with candlelight and surrounded by shiny black-lacquered chairs. Everything on the menu is fresh and worth trying, from the grilled oysters and antipasto appetizers to the penne pasta sautéed with fresh tomatoes and vodka (unusual but wonderful!). Desserts are equally tempting and impossible to resist. **1747 Marine Drive; (604) 922-6282; moderate to expensive; lunch Monday–Friday, dinner Monday–Saturday.**

❦❦❦ **THE SAVOURY RESTAURANT, North Vancouver** Harbored at scenic Deep Cove, in the quiet reaches of North Vancouver, this casually authentic French restaurant is situated at the end of a row of storefronts overlooking a peaceful waterfront park. A wall of windows in the airy dining room showcases views of boats bobbing in the marina and majestic mountains ascending above the cove. The relaxed but pretty dining room is colorfully decorated with deep maroon walls, green columns, and a sparkling black-tiled floor. White linens give each table elegant flair, and nearly every seat in the house has a glimpse of the water. In the spring and summer, you can dine on the outdoor terrace, which shares the same views. Savoury's cuisine displays southern French and Basque influences used to enhance the fresh, local ingredients. You won't find fresher seafood anywhere, and the mussels are among the best we've ever sampled. **107C-4390 Gallant Avenue, at Deep Cove; (604) 929-2373; moderate to expensive; dinner Tuesday–Sunday.**

Romantic Suggestion: After you've lingered over the views and eaten your fill, take a walk through the adjacent waterfront park or nearby **CATES PARK** (several minutes via car from the restaurant on Dallarton Highway), both of which offer numerous spots to stop and smooch at the water's edge.

Outdoor Kissing

❀❀❀❀ **CYPRESS PROVINCIAL PARK, West Vancouver; GROUSE MOUNTAIN, West Vancouver; MOUNT SEYMOUR PROVINCIAL PARK, North Vancouver** One extraordinary aspect of Vancouver is that in its very own backyard are three separate mountains high enough above sea level to be active ski areas, and they are only about 30 minutes from the city (45 minutes if you take your time or get lost). It is quite feasible to spend an invigorating day on any of these mountains hiking, swimming in lakes (depending on the season), gazing out over the stupendous views, or skiing, and still have more than enough time to get back to the city and dress up for an elegant dinner downtown.

On a moonlit winter's eve, adventurous couples may consider doing the above scenario in reverse. After an early dinner in the city, gather your cross-country ski equipment, toss it in the car, and drive up to Cypress Provincial Park. There you can make tracks over the sparkling white snow until the park lights shut off at 11 P.M. *These three mountain areas are accessible from Highway 1 and Highway 1A/99. To get to Mount Seymour Provincial Park, follow the signs from Highway 1 heading east from the Lion's Gate Bridge. Cypress Bowl Road in West Vancouver takes you to Cypress Provincial Park. Capilano Road in West Vancouver leads to Grouse Mountain.*

Romantic Warning: These park areas are well known. Grouse Mountain tends to be the most touristy of the group, but it also offers dining on top of the world overlooking the city lights. Call ahead for general information about Grouse Mountain or for dinner reservations (604-984-0661). Needless to say, the crowds are worst during the summer and on sunny weekends.

❀❀❀❀ **LIGHTHOUSE PARK, West Vancouver** At the southwestern tip of West Vancouver is a peninsula called Lighthouse Park, a small fragment of granite hanging on to the mainland. From the parking area, the shores of the

Strait of Georgia and the cliff tops of the parkland are both only a brisk 15-minute walk over trails through rocky forest. As you stroll along the trails, you can inhale fresh sea air mingled with the scent of sturdy fir and spruce trees. At trail's end, you'll get a far-reaching view on a clear day. On a cloudy day, Lighthouse Park obligingly resembles the kind of dense forest that exists deep in the distant Canadian Rockies, enabling you to feel far away from city life. The two of you will scarcely remember how close civilization really is. *From Highway 1/99 in West Vancouver, take the 21st Street exit to Marine Drive. Follow the signs on Marine Drive to Lighthouse Park.*

❦❦❦ LYNN CANYON SUSPENSION BRIDGE, North Vancouver While

everyone and their aunt are lining up at the extremely popular Capilano Suspension Bridge, you can discover the bridge less traveled. There are free admissions and no tourist shops, and when school is in session you may even have a certain amount of privacy. The suspension bridge across Lynn Canyon hovers and sways (as suspension bridges are inclined to do) over a rocky, forested gorge where a waterfall and river etch their way through the canyon floor below. On the other side of the bridge are trails that lead to a boulder-strewn brook with freshwater soaking pools. You can cross over the rocks and find a refreshing niche all to yourselves. **Free admission.** *Take Highway 1 east from the Lion's Gate Bridge and follow the signs to Lynn Canyon Park.*

Romantic Warning: Trails here are periodically washed out, and the crystal-clear pools, which look inviting, can be dangerous due to unexpectedly swift water. Be cautious, stay on the trails, wade in the shallows, and the solitude will be invigorating.

❦❦ MARINE DRIVE, West Vancouver Marine Drive borders, at water's

edge, a stellar residential and commercial neighborhood in the Vancouver area. Summertime graces this road with perfect views of the city and Vancouver Island. During the fall, overcast rainy days make this sinuous road more reclusive, emphasizing its dark, rocky cliffs and the thick, moist foliage that veils the houses along the way. Stores and restaurants here have a quaint, congenial style. Major banks and gas stations are scattered throughout, but for the most part this area is a quieter alternative for a stroll or drive than Vancouver.

Besides being scenic, Marine Drive has an added attraction: Several satellite roads lead northward and connect with two alternate routes to Whistler—Cypress Access Road through **CYPRESS PROVINCIAL PARK,** and Capilano Road over **GROUSE MOUNTAIN** (see Outdoor Kissing). Let the beauty of the drive lead you wherever your hearts desire. *Heading north over the Lion's Gate Bridge, turn west onto Marine Drive, which follows the southern shoreline of West Vancouver.*

Romantic Alternative: Adjacent to Marine Drive, just west of the Lion's Gate Bridge, look for a waterfront park called **AMBLESIDE.** The long, winding sidewalk that outlines the park is bordered on one side by a stone seawall with marvelous views of the water and city, and on the other by grass and playgrounds. This is a much smaller, less crowded version of the seawall in **STANLEY PARK** (reviewed on page 33), and the better romantic option if crowds are something you like to avoid.

Ladner

Set on the Fraser River Delta, Ladner is a quiet farming and fishing community. Located only about 30 minutes south of downtown Vancouver, it's a pleasant alternative to staying in the city, but not so far away that you can't take advantage of all the fine dining and entertaining options Vancouver has to offer.

Hotel/Bed and Breakfast Kissing

❤❤❤**THE DUCK INN, Ladner** If you dig ducks, waddle up to this hideaway for mallard mania and more. You'll get your own little waterfront cottage, a garden shaded by a weeping willow, and plenty of waterfowl to keep you company. If excessive duck decor doesn't ruffle your feathers too much, this is the perfect place to nest.

The three-room suite—above the innkeeper's cluttered workshop and salmon smokery—grants unobstructed views of the Fraser River from the king-size bed, living room, and kitchen. Behind the duck-motif shower curtain is a jetted tub, and the refrigerator holds an already prepared Northwest breakfast. Savor the innkeeper's smoked salmon, along with bagels, cream cheese, cereals, and a jar of milk with cream on top. For indoor entertainment (besides kissing), there's a wood-burning fireplace, CD player, and TV/VCR. When the sun shines, take the canoe out for a spin or bike to the dikes five miles away. Sit on your private patio and watch fantastic sunsets, inspect the fishing vessel moored below you, or feed your new web-footed friends. If you're lucky, you may get a speedboat ride compliments of the multitalented and friendly innkeeper. **4349 River Road West; (604) 946-7521; expensive.**

❤❤❤❤ **RIVER RUN COTTAGES, Ladner** Don't delay checking into the River Run. You'll want to spend as much time as possible savoring the surroundings. Located along the Fraser River in a houseboat community, this four-suite bed and breakfast will charm you with its uniqueness. Special touches abound throughout, from the chocolate-chip cookies and bountiful snack bowl to fresh flowers at every turn.

Make some waves of your own in the Waterlily, an adorable floating home that gently rocks when big boats go by. Inside you'll find such amenities as a queen-size loft bed, small kitchenette, woodstove, pillowed window seats, fish tank, CD player, and highly polished wood. (If you are tall, you may have trouble negotiating the tiny claw-foot tub/shower and sleeping loft.)

Three onshore cottages, built on pilings, are just as alluring. Each is equipped with a fireplace, CD player, private entrance, and small refrigerator. The Netloft is a snug, two-level retreat featuring a Mexican tile floor, a woodstove, skylights, hardwood floors, and a built-in queen-size captain's bed on the upper level that showcases views of the river. By the light of the moon, simmer and smooch in the deep Japanese-style soaking tub on the deck. The other two adjoining cottages are equally cozy and charming, with French doors that open onto flower-laden private decks that jut out over the river. The Keepers Quarters is slightly more spacious, with a two-person Jacuzzi tub in the lovely bathroom and a massive log bed draped with a down comforter in the separate bedroom. We especially liked the other cottage, known as the Northwest Room, which features local and Native American artwork, an enticing queen-size bed fashioned from pine logs, and, most intriguing of all, a two-person waterfall shower surrounded by river rock and cascading plants.

To make you feel thoroughly pampered (as if just staying here isn't enough), a full gourmet breakfast can be delivered *literally* to your bed at a prearranged time. After a leisurely morning, borrow a two-person kayak and paddle to No Name Island for a picnic. **4551 River Road West; (604) 946-7778; www.cimarron.net/canada/bc/riverrun.html; expensive to very expensive.**

Romantic Suggestion: River Run's romance package isn't your run-of-the-mill regular. In addition to a three-course dinner at a local restaurant and a bottle of bubbly, the deal includes—surprise!—chocolate body paint. The paintbrush is optional.

Tsawwassen

Best known as a terminal for ferries headed to and from Vancouver Island, the nondescript town of Tsawwassen has several glorious sand-swept beaches. Because its beaches are not well known, you're almost guaranteed to find a private spot on the sand to sit and watch eagles soaring and blue herons fishing until the sun goes down.

Hotel/Bed and Breakfast Kissing

☙☙☙ **SOUTHLANDS HOUSE BY THE SEA, Tsawwassen** A wildlife preserve in the backyard, a golf course bordering the front, and plenty of peace inside await at this multifaceted bed and breakfast. While it may sound odd, the curved, taupe structure resembles a cross between a Tuscan villa, a West Coast contemporary home, and a lighthouse. It all works to form a unique building that blends into the grasslands of adjoining Boundary Bay Regional Park.

The best (and most private) room, the Tower Suite, resides in the abstractly designed lighthouse section. Unfortunately, its two bedrooms, hallway bath, and cozy upstairs reading nook are geared for groups of four. Too bad. However, once you see the four suites in the Carriage House—each with private, standard bath, simple decor, warm colors, wooden blinds, and fireplaces—all is forgiven. The small Elephant Tusk Room is our favorite; we liked the subtle African safari theme, black bedspread accented with zebra-striped pillows, and elephant-motif art. However, if you're here for a honeymoon and not a safari, you may prefer the larger, floral-decorated High Country Suite, with French doors opening onto a patio, a double-seated shower, and huge king-size bed.

Journey downstairs into the main home or out on the patio for a breakfast that brings plenty of fruit to the table: healthy smoothies, fruit kabobs, and/or fruit salads. Top that with baked goods and, perhaps, smoked-salmon scrambled eggs or apple pancake with orange-ginger syrup, and you'll be ready to explore the park's pathways. Afterward, lounge in the open backyard or soak sore muscles in the hot tub while listening to the birds and savoring expansive views of the delta. **1160 Boundary Bay Road; (604) 943-1846; moderate to expensive.**

Point Roberts, Washington

Due to a geographic quirk, the tiny rural town of Point Roberts is actually located in the state of Washington, but because it is so close to the Canadian towns of Ladner, Tsawwassen and Vancouver, it belongs in this section of the book. Even if you don't book a reservation at the lip-worthy bed and breakfast we recommend, this quiet farming community set at the edge of Boundary Bay is well worth an afternoon visit.

Hotel/Bed and Breakfast Kissing

❤❤ **MAPLE MEADOW, Point Roberts** Get back to nature at this picturesque farmhouse, enclosed by a white farm fence and surrounded by horse pastures, farm relics, and a whimsical garden. An exuberant Doberman welcomes guests at the front gate (don't worry, he's very friendly) and ushers them into the authentic country home. Inside, Northwest meets the Old West with an assortment of antique saws, cowboy hats, knickknacks, a stuffed raccoon, and dozens of period antiques. Guests are welcome to make themselves at home here or take a soak in the outdoor Jacuzzi tub that overlooks an immense 200-year-old maple tree and a grassy pasture. Appointed with comfortable patio furniture, the outdoor deck and veranda are wonderful places to sit and fill your lungs with fresh country air. And if you're in the mood for a walk, the beaches of Boundary Bay are just minutes away.

Although two of the three guest rooms here (Knotty and Cedar) share baths, the self-contained Old Pumphouse cottage offers more than enough privacy for romance-minded couples. Homey and snug, the cottage's countrified interior is outfitted with a claw-foot tub, an elevated king-size bed, and embroidered white linens. Your only neighbors are the three resident horses, and the only sounds are that of the creek nearby (and maybe the occasional car). In the morning, flip on the porch light and—voila!—coffee is delivered to your door. Later, enjoy a fresh country breakfast served in the main house, featuring such local specialties as crab omelets, salmon quiche, or lemon-ricotta pancakes. Guests who are interested can rise early with the innkeepers and accompany them as they attend to their farm chores (including gardening). Your vision of the country will never be the same! **101 Goodman Road; (360) 945-5536; inexpensive to expensive.**

White Rock

Located 30 minutes south of Vancouver, the town of White Rock sits just north of the U.S. border. Though White Rock isn't touted as a romantic destination, its miles of sandy beaches and a beach promenade lined with specialty shops and restaurants are wonderfully pleasant. We also discovered a bed and breakfast that is worth a stop if you've got romance in mind.

Hotel/Bed and Breakfast Kissing

❧❧❧ **DORRINGTON BED AND BREAKFAST, White Rock** In spite of its location in a not-so-romantic upscale suburban housing development, everything about the Dorrington is impressive. Immaculately manicured grounds envelop the contemporary wood-and-brick mansion, which in turn holds cathedral ceilings and impressive artwork. All four guest rooms are located upstairs, and all have private bathrooms.

Northwest atmosphere is captured in the Mountie Post, a new room that resembles a log cabin. Get cozy in the pine bed accented with corkscrew willows or pad around in the provided bear-claw slippers. The door to the bathroom even resembles an outhouse, but luckily things are much nicer inside. The traditionally elegant Victorian Room contains an antique four-poster bed covered with beautiful pink-and-white-striped linens. Well worth the extra price you're asked to pay, the Windsor is the most romantic room in the house (and the reason this property was awarded three lips). A canopied queen-size brass bed takes up a large part of the spacious suite, which is additionally appointed with Oriental carpets, lovely antiques, and European sculptures. A fireplace warms a cozy sitting area in the bedroom, and the oversize marble bathroom features a large Jacuzzi tub, separate glass-enclosed shower, twin basins, a bidet, and even a heated towel rack and floor. A bottle of chilled champagne is a complimentary bonus.

There's also an upstairs library, complete with a "stuffed" Mountie to keep you company. Downstairs, enjoy a game of pool or pinball in the game room. But if you want to play pinball, you'll have to battle it out with Pepper, a pint-size, canine pinball wizard.

Breakfast is served in the formal dining room or in the beautifully appointed lounge, adorned with a floor-to-ceiling river rock fireplace, hunter green walls, and surrounding windows. (Request the custard-like French toast Raphael, a house specialty, accompanied by a vanilla latte.) On sunny mornings, breakfast can also be served outside on the shady deck. This vantage point overlooks the lush backyard, tennis courts, and a small bridge that crosses over a fishpond to a roomy hot tub set beneath the open sky. **13851 19A Avenue; (604) 535-4408; www.bbcanada.com/508.html; moderate to very expensive; minimum-stay requirement for the suite.**

Restaurant Kissing

❤❤ **GIRAFFE RESTAURANT, White Rock** White Rock's waterfront is certainly breathtaking in its beauty, as well as its restaurant selection. The main street is lined with eateries, ranging from busy ice-cream parlors to see-and-be-seen spots. At the top of the street, Giraffe adds some refinement to the bustling beach scene. Fusion is the word that best describes both the decor and the food. While the woven leather chairs look medieval rather than modern, and the big, bright artwork clashes with the Asian-motif wallpaper, the setting is pleasant and elegant, with linen-covered tables, fresh flowers, and soft, sultry jazz playing in the background. The only drawback: Summertime brings a cast of thousands to the beach. Parking is difficult, and the restaurant can get crowded. Reservations are a must.

The Northwest Coast fusion cuisine combines a variety of disparate elements in new and pleasing ways; we were smitten with the intriguing salads (the grilled peach, prawn, and asparagus salad with smoked Gouda vinaigrette is outstanding) and the equally engaging entrées that blend textures, flavors, and fruits together quite wonderfully. Sea bass with black cherry and balsamic glaze and lamb with an apricot-mint chutney are prime examples of culinary fusion done right. Desserts are simply divine, especially the espresso crème brûlée and pear-pecan-chocolate tart. **15053 Marine Drive; (604) 538-6878; expensive; reservations recommended; lunch and dinner daily, brunch Sunday.**

Langley

The town of Langley is best described as a quiet farming community that grew up fast. Located at the doorstep of Vancouver, this area weaves together country settings with urban amenities (and traffic congestion). We stopped here on our way up north and had the fortune of finding a remarkable bed and breakfast. Even if you're just passing through, you should stop by to tour the gardens or have tea (see Hotel/Bed and Breakfast Kissing).

Hotel/Bed and Breakfast Kissing

❤❤❤ **TUSCAN FARM GARDENS, Langley** The moon has been known to spark romance, especially in a garden dedicated to the night orb. Step into the lovely moon garden, filled with flowers that radiantly reflect the moonbeams, and you'll see what we mean. This 80-acre working flower farm, bordered by forest and farmland, blooms with romance opportunities. During the day, stroll down Lavender Lane or Rhodeo Drive, a walkway lined with hundreds of rhododendrons. Hang out in the Secret Garden's hammock, or drive your own golf cart to the secluded beaver pond. At night, sit in the moon garden and see what happens.

In the Italian-style farmhouse's lobby, dried lavender hangs from rafters and a small, country-style store pleases the senses with herbed soaps and oils, homemade jams, lavender dream pillows, and potpourri. Upstairs, three bedrooms decorated in an uncomplicated yet elegant fashion offer queen-size beds bedecked with fluffy down comforters and pillows, kitchenettes, fir floors, and standard baths. A bubbling rock fountain provides the only background noise, since TVs, radios, and telephones are absent. Of the three suites, spacious and sunny Magnolia is our favorite thanks to its fireplace and covered private balcony. Breakfast fixings are already in your room, so, come morning, enjoy your meal in the beautiful garden. **24453 60th Avenue; (604) 530-1997; www.tuscanfarmgardens.com; moderate to expensive; call about seasonal garden tours and tea; call for seasonal closures.**

Romantic Suggestion: Garden tours are available seasonally; call for times. And don't miss the afternoon tea, featuring lots of lavender-infused treats.

Fort Langley

This historic town situated on the banks of the Fraser River was once a Hudson's Bay Company trading post and still retains much of its authentic character. Stroll down tree-lined streets past restored buildings, browse through the boutiques and art galleries, or have lunch at one of the many cafés and restaurants—many of which reside in the older buildings. We found one kiss-worthy bed and breakfast about five minutes outside Fort Langley. However, once you arrive you might not want to leave, so we recommend visiting the town first.

Hotel/Bed and Breakfast Kissing

❧❧❧ **EAGLE'S REACH, Fort Langley** Want to add a little fun to your romance? This is the place to stay and play. Perched on a cliff overlooking the Fraser River, this huge contemporary home (modeled after a "Street of Dreams" home in Seattle) has plenty to keep you and your sweetheart entertained. Practice your short game on the three-hole mini-golf course, hold hands while hiking through the woods, play pool or pinball in the game room, smooch while watching a flick on the big-screen TV, or, most romantic of all, swim by candlelight in the indoor saltwater pool, which can be reserved for you alone.

No expense was spared in providing entertainment, nor in decorating the spacious house: Cherry-wood walls and trim adorn most rooms, large windows provide breathtaking views, the library is stocked floor to ceiling with books, and the kitchen area is a cook's dream. In addition to two guest bedrooms upstairs, one room is dedicated to the innkeeper's doll collection. Tons of teddy bears line the huge hallway desk, which also harbors a computer for guests to use. While big is the byword downstairs, both wonderfully decorated guest rooms tend toward the small side, although they do offer en suite standard baths, TVs, coffeemakers, and complimentary golf balls. We liked the Silhouette Room, thanks to its river views, creamy color scheme, and big, bright bathroom. The Artist's Retreat overlooks the manicured front lawn and is more masculine in design, with burgundy shades, a plaid duvet, black-and-white photographs, and Mission-style furniture. For the utmost in privacy and space, venture next door to the two-level Coach House above the garage. English country decor, a private deck, full kitchen, living room with fireplace, and a queen-size sleigh bed make this a pleasant place to stay. Plus, guests here also have use of the garage.

Choose between two options at breakfast time. Coffee, juices, and baked goods are available all morning for early birds and slugabeds alike. A full breakfast, featuring such treats as apple-juice spritzers, tropical fruit soup, baked oranges drizzled with chocolate sauce, and fluffy Belgian waffles, awaits those who come down at 8:30 A.M. Load up: You'll need lots of energy to play the game of love . . . as well as other activities. **24658 87th Avenue; (604) 888-4470; moderate.**

Harrison Mills

Hotel/Bed and Breakfast Kissing

❧❧ **HARRISON MILLS COUNTRY HOUSE, Harrison Mills** We'll break the bad news first: It rains a lot up here. Now the good news: If the day is gray and wet, you can stay here. There's a lot you can do in this bed and breakfast without ever venturing outside. Amenities include a darling three-tiered, old-fashioned movie theater (popcorn included); an indoor hot tub and sauna in the cedar-planked sunroom; a (rather dark) game room complete with pool table, fireplace, and TV/VCR; and a well-stocked, cozy library on the second floor. You may hope the rain stays all day.

Perhaps the gray days are what inspired the owners to paint this large Victorian farmhouse Day-glo yellow. However, the odd color somewhat complements the green surroundings: The home sits smack-dab in the middle of a Christmas tree farm. Inside, the palette is more mellow. The eclectic decor is sprinkled with interesting antiques, plenty of paintings (the innkeeper once owned an art gallery), classic Victorian wood accents, and too many animal-

---

Cost ratings for British Columbia listings are in Canadian funds. American travelers should check the exchange rate or ask an innkeeper to figure out the cost in U.S. dollars.

skin rugs. Guest have the run of the house and can even use the kitchen (except the heavy-duty stove).

Three small rooms with en suite baths on the second floor are small and ordinary, but have decent views. Hidden on the third floor, the light and spacious Winston Churchill Room offers kissing couples plenty of mix-and-match seats to smooch on, two beds (queen-size and double), wonderful views of the farm and mountains, a chess table, and a standard, small bath. Privacy is the biggest plus up here.

When we visited, the innkeeper was reluctant to disclose any breakfast recipes (we don't know why), but hinted that specialty crêpes and other sweet offerings are presented with homemade blackberry jam. One thing is certain: Breakfast, served in the formal dining room, is a fine-dining affair with candles and good china. **828 Kennedy Road; (604) 796-0385, (800) 551-2511; expensive.**

Romantic Suggestion: If the sun does shine, walk a mile down a country road to the **KILBY STORE AND FARM** (Kilby Road; 604-796-9576; open daily). Thankfully, this farm/museum/general store is charming and authentic rather than country cute. Spend an hour exploring what farm life was like in the 1920s, followed by tea or lunch in the Harrison River Tea Room.

❀❀❀❀ **ROWENA'S INN ON THE RIVER, Harrison Mills** Almost too picturesque for words, every inch of this stunningly renovated bed and breakfast, situated on the banks of the Fraser River, will generate romantic aspirations in even the most jaded of city-tired spirits. Quite a saga lies behind this property, which comprises 160 immaculate acres of smooth lawn, towering evergreens, and undulating hillside poised along the river. Several scrapbooks and photo albums help illustrate the story. For our purposes what counts most are the five exceedingly affectionate rooms in the main home and, more notably, the two cedar cabins tucked into the trees.

Rowena's is modeled after a quaint English manor. Attention to detail and fastidious elegance are evident throughout, from the glass-walled solarium (where breakfast is served) to the sunken living room adorned with crystal chandeliers, silk-covered sofas, two pianos, an expansive marble fireplace, and a sweep of bay windows that bring the enchanting outdoors inside. Upstairs, the handsomely decorated rooms, with their thick down comforters, attractive seating arrangements, and specialty soaps and shampoos, are perfect in every way. Still, as wonderful as these rooms are, they pale in comparison to the cabins, which border a pond and the property's golf course. River-rock fireplaces, heated slate floors, striking furnishings, exquisitely cozy beds, and impressive bathrooms complete with air-jet tubs and glass showers distinguish these ultra-romantic retreats. We liked the secluded On the Pond Cabin, with its deck extending over the water. The By the River Cabin resides too close to the 11th-hole's fairway for our comfort. Speaking of which, the gorgeous 18-hole golf course that winds its way around the home is available to guests. (Book a tee time with your reservation.) If chasing after a ball isn't your thing, swim laps in the 70-foot blue-tiled pool or play footsie in the soothingly steamy outdoor hot tub.

Rowena's serves dinner nightly in the heritage dining room. Guests are seated first, but reservations are also available to the public (make them well in advance). The decor and scenery are sumptuous, and the food equals its surroundings. The kitchen's creativity transforms remarkably fresh ingredients into divine meals. If culinary adventure intrigues you, order the chef's "throwaway" menu. For $60 per person, you'll be treated to whatever the chef decides to whip up that night. Just don't make any other evening plans: Our four-course meal took four hours!

While Rowena's sounds like paradise, two things did disappoint us. First, there is a severe lack of rainy-day activities. Sure, you can kiss, but you may be kissing for a long, long, long time. The downstairs common area is too formal to cuddle up in, and at dinnertime it's not private. The upstairs lounge is nicer, but there are no magazines, games, or other visual entertainment. (Other bed and breakfasts in the area are much better suited for indoor play, with game rooms, theaters, and libraries.) Second, service can be standoffish and not very informative. No one greeted us upon arrival, and when we were shown to our room, little details were neglected (such as telling us how to turn off the piped-in music and, more important, that the outdoor gates are locked at 11 P.M.). If you can put such things aside (and bring a good book for rainy days), the two of you will certainly enjoy the splendid surroundings. **14282 Morris Valley Road; (604) 796-0234, (800) 661-5108; expensive to very expensive.**

Harrison Hot Springs

For more decades than anyone can remember, Harrison Hot Springs has attracted throngs of tourists and locals alike who want a quick and easy escape from the city. Located one and a half hours northeast of Vancouver, it is a mixed bag of treats. From any viewpoint, the town is located in an idyllic setting. Low-rise buildings (mostly newly constructed condos) hug the shore of Harrison Lake, backdropped by evergreen-clad mountains and foothills. If you can see around the RVs and campers, it is truly a site (and sight) to behold, especially in the off-season (which means anytime but summer).

Where are the hot springs the town is named for? The actual springs burble out of the ground into a holding reservoir, five minutes from the front lobby of the **HARRISON HOT SPRINGS HOTEL** (see Hotel/Bed and Breakfast Kissing). Unfortunately, the temperature of these springs is far too hot for swimming. But don't let your sore muscles be dismayed at this news; a large, public pool in town recycles the hot sulfur-laden spring water into freshwater and cools it down to an agreeable 102 degrees Fahrenheit. Unfortunately, the pool resembles a high-school gymnasium, so don't expect a romantic atmosphere. You may want to stay at the Harrison Hot Springs Hotel, which offers three hot pools for hotel guests only.

Hotel/Bed and Breakfast Kissing

❦ **HARRISON HOT SPRINGS HOTEL, Harrison Hot Springs** Historic Harrison Hot Springs Hotel has long been a local landmark, and for decades it was the lone getaway in this region. Originally built in 1885, then destroyed by fire and rebuilt in 1926, it has undergone several face-lifts and additions since. Unfortunately, perhaps due to the lack of competition, this sprawling hotel is in desperate need of serious attention. It lacks any warmth or style, being little more than a random cluster of nondescript buildings filled with motel-standard rooms and a jumble of restaurants and meeting rooms. Its popularity has not waned over the years, but that speaks more for the surrounding beauty of Harrison Lake and rolling hills than the accommodations themselves.

Without question, the best reason to stay at Harrison Hot Springs Hotel is the hot spring water, filtered and cooled to a variety of temperatures to accommodate a range of tolerance levels, then piped into one indoor and two outdoor pools reserved exclusively for guests. Tennis courts, massage facilities, an exercise room, a nine-hole golf course, and lakeshore hiking trails provide additional ways to keep busy, and during high season you can dance nightly to the rhythms of a local four-piece band that plays rock and roll and country ballads. (The ballroom has a flavor all its own, hovering somewhere between nostalgia and kitsch.)

When it comes to food, we encourage you to eat elsewhere in town. The hotel's two restaurants can be described as mediocre at best, with very steep prices, and the ambience is reminiscent of a 1950s catering hall. **100 Esplanade; (604) 796-2244, (800) 663-2266; moderate to very expensive; minimum-stay requirement on holidays.**

❦❦❦ **LITTLE HOUSE ON THE LAKE BED AND BREAKFAST, Harrison Hot Springs** If you venture out to Harrison Hot Springs, this endearing bed and breakfast may be the best place to call home for the duration of your stay. On the shores of Harrison Lake, far enough from town to feel remote and private, this impressive log cabin home is anything but little. The several thousand square feet of living space, with a generous portion dedicated to the bed and breakfast, are filled with simple comforts. Unfortunately, the best views of the lake (from inside) are from the owner's private quarters. Nonetheless, the four rooms are delightful, warm, and romantic. All have en suite bathrooms (with heated floors), fireplaces, semiprivate balconies, CD players, TV/VCRs, and phones. The simple Scandinavian decor is highlighted by plush beds, fresh flowers, and stained-glass and hand-stenciled accents. The individual color schemes are most evident in the bathrooms. Which room to choose? For an authentic log-cabin look, book Algonquin, with its log-beamed ceilings, skylights, and high four-poster queen-size bed. For comfort and romance, try Cookham, which offers a two-person soaking tub in one corner, as well as a lovely canopy bed. Its counterpart, Grafton, also has a two-person tub with a window view. Done up in mauves and pinks with sloping ceilings, this room is perhaps the coziest. However, tall people should watch their head! Last, but not least, Metchosin is dedicated to folk art and antique decor. Although the room is tiny, the cedar-planked bathroom is not. Bubble away in the air-jet tub for two or venture onto the deck and watch Cyril the squirrel.

Guest are encouraged to relax in a large common room outfitted with a games table, billiards table, VCR (with lots of romantic videos), piano, and a number of chairs and couches in front of the large granite fireplace. Don't miss the CD collection, which includes dozens of lovey-dovey selections from *Lullabies for Lovers* to *Bach at Bedtime*. Afternoon tea is included in your stay, as well as turndown service complete with Hershey's kisses placed on your pillow. The innkeepers have certainly made many efforts to keep you happy, comfortable, and entertained.

At 8:30 A.M., an eye-opener "mug 'n' muffin" basket is delivered to your door. When the breakfast bell rings at 9:30, get set for a feast. The brunch-style breakfast may include broiled tomatoes with Parmesan cheese, crêpes, a selection of fruits, and specialty pies such as country salmon pie or a feta cheese/asparagus pie.

If you can move after such a meal, a hot tub awaits on the backyard deck. The only drawback is that it borders the innkeeper's quarters, which diminishes the privacy. For some ideal kissing spots, head up to the rooftop patio or take a walk along the beach (if the water level is low enough), although expect company from Tasha, the easygoing German shepherd. Better yet, take the canoe out on the lake and cuddle. Just don't rock the boat too much. **6305 Rockwell Drive; (604) 796-2186, (800) 939-1116; www.littlehouse onthelake.com; expensive to very expensive; minimum-stay requirement seasonally.**

Restaurant Kissing

❀❀❀ **LA CÔTE D'AZUR, Harrison Hot Springs** Once a hot spot on Vancouver's Robson Street, this restaurant packed up its pots and now delights dinners in Harrison Hot Springs with its magical French cooking. For the most part, you are in for a treat, with classic presentations, flavorful seasonings, and incredibly fresh ingredients. Utilizing a vast selection of local produce, meat, and fish, the chef creates robust, country-French creations such as marinated portobello mushrooms, a simple goat-cheese salad, sea bass poached in a delicate saffron bouillabaisse, and roast duck in a Pernod sauce with zesty juniper berries. If you're lucky, dessert will be as delicious as it is entertaining. As the chef whipped up sabayon beside our table, all heads turned to watch the show. The interior has a delightful rustic charm and warmth lacking in the other restaurants in town. What's more, the owner/chef visits each table to make sure all is well. This splendid culinary outpost should be at the top of your dining list when visiting the area. **310 Hot Springs Road; (604) 796-8422; www.lacotedazur.com; moderate to expensive; dinner daily; closed January.**

"You may conquer with the sword,

but you are conquered by a kiss."

Daniel Heinsius

Vancouver Island

Vancouver Island is ferry accessible for car and foot traffic from the following ports: Seattle, Anacortes (one and a half hours north of Seattle), Port Angeles (on the Olympic Peninsula), Tsawwassen (30 minutes south of Vancouver), Horseshoe Bay (in West Vancouver), and Westview (on the Sunshine Coast, north of Vancouver). The Victoria Clipper, a foot-traffic-only ferry, docks in the heart of downtown Victoria after a two-and-a-half-hour passage from Seattle. Another passenger-only ferry travels between downtown Vancouver and Victoria. For information on fares and schedules, contact the British Columbia Ferries (250-386-3431, 888-223-3779 in Canada; www.bcferries.bc.ca), Washington State Ferries (206-464-6400), Port Angeles Black Ball Transport (360-457-4491), or Victoria Clipper (206-448-5000). Be aware that during peak travel times you can spend a long time in line if you take your car. Trial by ferryboat is one of the hazards of summer or weekend travel.

Traveling to Vancouver Island is an unconditional romantic must, simply because it has everything that two people in love could want to share. Covered by deep forests and miles upon miles of wilderness, this enormous island is also known for its rugged beaches, bustling fishing communities, rustic lodges, quaint bed and breakfasts, magnificent hotels, and a mountain range that spans its nearly 300-mile length.

The mostly uninhabited north-central section is noted for untouched mountain terrain, abundant wildlife, and pristine scenery. The comparatively overdeveloped eastern coastal areas are still marbled with long, lazy beaches. Except for the congenial fishing villages of Tofino and Ucluelet, the central west coast is entirely wilderness. Along the southwestern coast, near the towns of Sooke and Metchosin, more unspoiled wilderness is accentuated with rocky beaches and extensive forestland.

Victoria, on the southern tip of the island, presents a stark contrast to the rest of the island. Distinguished by lavish gardens, charming tearooms, and old-world architecture, the capital of British Columbia also has a multitude of tourist traps and scores of international visitors. (Actually, much of Victoria's English style is self-consciously marketed to attract visitors.)

Cost ratings for British Columbia listings are in Canadian funds. American travelers should check the exchange rate or ask an innkeeper to figure out the cost in U.S. dollars.

Romantic Warning: Signs on this island are not always clearly marked. (In fact, sometimes signs aren't even visible.) Be sure to bring along plenty of maps and an extra dose of patience. The Island Highway runs north and south along the length of the entire island and can be agony to travel. As the only main thoroughfare on the island, it gets dreadfully crowded and, unfortunately, not everyone wants to go as fast as you might.

Romantic Note: Canada charges a 7 percent goods and services tax (GST) in addition to a hotel tax. Most places will warn you about these extra charges, and you'll notice that it can be a hefty addition to your bill. The GST portion of your accommodation bill and some purchases are refundable directly from the government if you are not a resident of Canada. Most places provide the required forms and information explaining how you can submit your receipts for reimbursement. If you have further questions, call the **SUMMERSIDE TEXT CENTRE** (800-668-4748 in Canada; 613-991-3346).

Romantic Reminder: The exchange rate for Canadian funds at the time this book went to press was about $1.42 to the U.S. dollar. The cost ratings in this section are listed in Canadian funds and correspond with the chart at the front of the book. For example, an establishment that charges $140 Canadian per night is listed in the expensive range. American travelers should keep in mind that this price translates into about $100 U.S. per night, so it is actually considered moderate in U.S. dollars. The rates are listed in Canadian funds due to the fluctuating exchange rate, and for the ease of use by our Canadian readers. Innkeepers are accustomed to translating funds for travelers from the States if you need assistance figuring out the U.S. dollar value.

Victoria

As much as possible, this book excludes big tourist draws, and without question Victoria is a sprawling center of tourist activity. But Victoria's charisma is hard to ignore, even in summer when the crowds swell beyond romantic tolerance. The famous Empress Hotel, stately Parliament Building, Butchart Gardens, the parks, museums, cobblestone streets, cozy restaurants, and Edwardian-style shops, combined with a thriving harbor and marina framed in the distance by the Olympic Mountains, make the city an Anglophile's nirvana. And it can be particularly wonderful during the off-season. It may even make you feel lustfully regal.

Romantic Suggestion: Victoria is a wonderful walking city, and you would do well to leave your car at home. (When you see the summer crowds and read about the hassle and cost involved in bringing your car, you will see what we mean.) If you are staying anywhere within a ten-block radius of Government Street, most of what you'll want to see and do is easily accessible. Victoria's bus system, **B.C. TRANSIT,** can take you anywhere in the city; call for information about bus routes (250-382-6161).

The following information and directions may sound complicated, but once you choose your route, it is just a matter of hopping on a ferry and crossing the water. No matter how you get there, Victoria is definitely worth the trip.

From Seattle: The **VICTORIA CLIPPER** (206-448-5000 in Seattle, 250-382-8100 in Victoria, 800-888-2535), operates a passenger-only ferry service year-round. This trip is hardly inexpensive (about $94 U.S. per person round-trip), but the high-speed, water-jet-propelled catamarans will get you there relatively comfortably and somewhat quickly (in about two and a half hours during off-seasons). However, from spring until the end of summer, the crowds and a first-come, first-served boarding system can produce a headache. Arrive early if you want to avoid an aspirin.

From Seattle you can be in Victoria in just 35 minutes by zooming off on **HELIJET AIRWAYS** (250-382-6222 in Victoria, 800-665-4354; www.helijet.com). Besides beating the clock, you'll also beat the crowds since there's a 12-passenger limit per helicopter. These cushy copters fly low enough for you to see some spectacular scenery too. Landings are surreal. Prices can be a bit unreal too, depending on availability. Once you arrive in Victoria, you're only a 20-minute walk from downtown, or you can hop on the complimentary shuttle that drops you off at the Empress Hotel. Helijet also serves Vancouver.

Another airborne option is taking a floatplane that lands in Victoria's Inner Harbour. **KENMORE AIR** (425-486-1257 in Kenmore, 800-543-9595; www.kenmoreair.com) offers several daily flights between Seattle and Victoria. Round-trip flights cost around $150 U.S. per person.

PRINCESS MARGUERITE (800-668-1167) offers the only car-and-passenger ferry departing from Seattle. It makes just one round-trip sailing per day, from mid-May through mid-September, so if you are traveling at any other time of the year and need your car with you, skip ahead to another option. It costs to take your car with you (around $156 U.S. round-trip for the car, driver, and one passenger), but the ship is comfortable, with a bar, two restaurants, and a game room. The trip takes about four and a half hours each way. If the length of the trip doesn't bother you and you are not taking your car, you can be a walk-on passenger for about half the price charged by the Victoria Clipper. Reservations are recommended if you are driving on.

From Port Angeles: **BLACK BALL FERRY TRANSPORT** (360-457-4491 in Port Angeles, 250-386-2202 in Victoria) runs a car-and-passenger ferry between Port Angeles and Victoria. Call for information about fares and sailing schedules. If you do plan to take your car, this route can be a traveler's worst nightmare thanks to the first-come, first-served boarding system. During peak season you have to get your car in line at least 12 hours in advance. That's right, 12 hours! And no matter how slowly you shop, there simply aren't 12 hours worth of places to browse in downtown Port Angeles. A time-saving option is to leave your car in a convenient and inexpensive nearby parking lot and walk onto the ferry fairly cheaply.

The passenger-only **VICTORIA EXPRESS** (360-452-8088 in Port Angeles, 250-361-9144 in Victoria) is an additional option between Port Angeles and Victoria. Call for information about fares and sailing schedules.

From Vancouver via Tsawwassen: Perhaps the easiest and most frequent runs to Vancouver Island are from the Tsawwassen, B.C., ferry terminal, just 30 minutes south of Vancouver. (This ferry docks in Sidney, about 20 minutes north of Victoria.) The huge, fastidiously maintained ferryboats leave every hour. Summer weekends can be intense, but you only have to wait a sailing or two even at the busiest times. You can also make reservations on some runs. **BRITISH COLUMBIA FERRIES** (604-943-9331 in Canada, 250-386-3431 in the United States, 604-444-2890 for reservations). A second nearby option is the Anacortes-Sidney ferry run by **WASHINGTON STATE FERRIES** (206-464-6400). Unfortunately, the wait on both the U.S. side (Anacortes) and the Canadian side (Sidney) can be long, particularly on weekends and holidays.

Hotel/Bed and Breakfast Kissing

❀❀❀❀ **ABIGAIL'S HOTEL, Victoria** The breakfasts alone are enough to make you want to stay at Abigail's forever. The aromas of lemon-pepper bacon, fresh herb scones, and other savories drift up the stairway in the early A.M. And even though the rooms are delicious and divine, you'll be down at the breakfast table in no time. Prepared by a professional chef, the multicourse meal offers exceptional choices, including lemon-pecan muffins, fruit crêpes, and poached eggs with smoked trout in tortillas. But breakfasts are just part of the story. Every nuance of comfort and class has been attended to at this European-style inn. (Expect a good climb, though; there's no elevator to take you and your luggage to the second or third floors.)

Surrounded by lovely English gardens, the classic 1930 Tudor mansion and new matching Coach House are located several blocks from downtown on a relatively quiet cul-de-sac. The original mansion has 16 rooms, all designed with two things in mind: romance and pampering. Features include private spa tubs framed in elegant Italian marble, wood-burning fireplaces, plush carpeting, pedestal sinks, and thick goose-down comforters. Even the smaller rooms are sunny and nicely decorated, although they don't have all the amenities. Of course, the most expensive "Celebration Rooms" are the crème de la crème, and they're worth it. Six such rooms are found in the Coach House, located alongside the main building. Unlike many add-ons, this new edition blends beautifully with the historic mansion. The large rooms feature all the luxuries you would expect and then some. A few have balconies and all have two-person Jacuzzi tubs. Arts and Crafts–style furnishings, set off by William Morris wallpapers and fabrics, foster a classic, yet comfortable ambience. The only problem with the Coach House is those tempting aromas from the kitchen don't reach this far unless you order breakfast in bed, which arrives in a large wicker basket for an additional fee.

In the main building, a wood-burning granite fireplace warms the library on the main floor, where sherry and hors d'oeuvres are served each afternoon. If you have a special occasion to celebrate, or can invent one, Abigail's is an ideal place to come. Attractive celebration packages, which don't skimp on the goodies, are also available. **906 McClure Street; (250) 388-5363, (800) 561-6565; www.abigailshotel.com; expensive to very expensive.**

❀❀❀ **ANDERSEN HOUSE, Victoria** Bed and breakfasts in historic homes typically feature furnishings from the corresponding period, but this 1891 Queen Anne Victorian is boldly decorated in a fresh, artistic style. From the moment you enter the bright and open parlor with its high ceiling, hardwood floor, African masks, and Picasso- and cubist-influenced artwork, you know that the Andersen House is run by an artist.

The five guest rooms display different personalities, but each one has a private entrance, CD player, and telephone. On the top floor, the sunny Casablanca Room is decorated with Persian rugs on the hardwood floors, a four-poster queen-size bed, and a lovely boxed window seat. A small, south-facing private deck shows off the distant Olympic Mountains, and a curved staircase leads down to the lush backyard garden. Also on the top floor is the Captain's Apartment, a spacious two-bedroom unit with a small kitchenette, a slipper-shaped claw-foot tub framed by a stained glass window, and a two-person shower with an old-fashioned spigot that sends down a spray similar to a warm, gentle rain. At the time of our visit, plans were in the works to add jetted tubs and fireplaces to these rooms. (We'll miss the small slipper tub, but the new additions will enhance the romance factor and lip rating.) Perhaps the most romantic and private room is the ground-level Garden Studio, which has a two-person Jacuzzi tub surrounded by gray marble salvaged from the old Empress Hotel. Outside its private door is the property's English-style perennial garden; if there's a chill in the air, light a fire in the old Franklin fireplace and bask in the warmth on the Cape Cod–style garden furniture. During the day, dappled sunlight streams through the branches of 100-year-old weeping willow, pear, and apple trees onto a curvaceous brick patio and numerous garden statues. (We think the backyard is worth four kisses.) **301 Kingston Street; (250) 388-4565; www.islandnet.com/~andersen; expensive to very expensive; minimum-stay requirement on weekends.**

❀❀❀ **ARUNDEL MANOR, Victoria** A ten-minute drive north of town center, this lovely 1912 Craftsman home sits on a grassy knoll overlooking Portage Inlet. Arundel Manor is a truly classic Victorian-style bed and breakfast, complete with all the appropriate, engaging details: handsome antiques and family heirlooms, stained glass windows, a stone fireplace, silver service, English china, and a charming innkeeper who makes gourmet breakfasts. Morning repasts such as salmon-stuffed crêpes with béarnaise sauce are served to guests at individual tables. Ask if the lemon preserves are available; if they are, spread some over freshly baked goodies or fresh fruit crêpes for a tasty treat.

The four guest rooms upstairs, each done in a comfortable Victorian manner, are spacious and exceedingly comfortable; all have private baths, although one is detached. The Rose Room and the Plum Room, with private balconies overlooking the water and the Sooke Hills, are the best. A collection of artwork embellishes the walls; dried flower arrangements add a touch of nature. The fluffy multicolored carpeting found throughout the home may be warm on the tootsies, but it detracts from the historic feel. Plans are in the works to tear it out and refurbish the beautiful hardwood underneath.

The verdant grounds are punctuated by wild gardens, large Douglas firs, Garry oaks, and several benches. Down near the water is a secluded bench underneath a growing tunnel of honeysuckle where you can sit in sweet solitude as the sun dips below the horizon. **980 Arundel Drive; (250) 385-5442; www.victoriabc.com/arundelmanor; moderate to expensive; closed November–January.**

Romantic Suggestion: Private guided kayak tours of Portage Inlet (a bird sanctuary) depart from the water below Arundel Manor ($30 Canadian per person for a two-hour tour, $45 Canadian per person for a four-hour tour). Bird-watching, peaceful paddling conditions, and spectacular sunsets are typically included, but ultimately depend on Mother Nature's plans.

❤❤❤ **BEACH COTTAGE, Victoria** If you want to disconnect from the world for a while, get out your Gold Card and check into this waterfront accommodation, which is sure to inspire some love connections. The petite Beach Cottage, set right on Cadboro Bay, has been remodeled specifically with couples in mind, and you will have the place to yourselves. The single bedroom, which is extremely spacious, holds an antique pine king-size sleigh bed and a two-person Jacuzzi tub. Pale hardwood floors in the living room set off the country-style decor, and a wood-burning fireplace with a massive river-rock hearth adds ambient warmth. There is another fireplace in the entertainment room, but you will probably prefer to stay in the living room, where you can gaze through the expansive windows that cover one wall and provide outstanding views of the bay and nearby marina. The sunny little kitchen is equipped with everything you need to whip up a meal, or you can walk to a small village nearby that offers the essentials: a coffee shop, restaurant, and grocery store.

If moonlight puts you in the mood, relax in the outdoor Jacuzzi tub beside the house. Another romantic option is to wander along the small stretch of beach right outside your door and across a small lawn. At night you can watch the moonlight dance on the water and listen to the waves stroke the pebbled beach.

While busy Victoria is thoroughly charming, this cottage will transport you to a slower, magically serene place in time. Best of all, you're only 15 minutes from downtown, so really you get the best of both worlds. **Reservations through Beaconsfield Inn, (250) 384-4044; www.islandnet.com/beaconsfield; unbelievably expensive; minimum-stay requirement.**

❀❀❀❀ **BEACONSFIELD INN, Victoria** Many inns promise old-world elegance, romance, and class, but few live up to their claims. This beautifully restored Edwardian manor delivers on all three, while also providing a turn-of-the-century haven for rejuvenating city-tired spirits. The friendly staff are professional, unobtrusive, and readily available to make you feel at home.

Lavish, fragrant flower gardens brighten the inn's classic hunter green and cream exterior. The garden seems to accompany you indoors as you pass through a plant-filled sunroom with a bubbling fountain. Beyond, rich mahogany walls and a roaring fireplace warm the main entrance. Leather love seats, walls of bookcases, and a gas-log fireplace make the library a perfect retreat for afternoon tea or evening sherry.

Seven guest rooms are located on the first and second floors, and two suites occupy the lower garden level. A half split of champagne, fancy chocolates, and fresh flowers from the garden await in each room. Truly, the most difficult decision to make here is which room to stay in. All have gorgeous antiques, leaded stained glass windows, Ralph Lauren linens, down comforters, and attractive color schemes. On the main floor, the pretty peach-toned Parlor Room has three walls of original leaded stained glass windows, making it the brightest room of all. Upstairs, the especially handsome Emily Carr Suite sports dark houndstooth and paisley Ralph Lauren linens, navy blue print wallpaper, and a massive polished bedstead in the bedroom area. The spacious sitting area features a wood-burning fireplace and a two-person Jacuzzi tub, hunter green walls, a high ceiling, and hardwood floors. A crystal chandelier sparkles above the two-person shower in the bathroom. The Veranda Room next door is considerably smaller and has no fireplace, but you'll hardly notice once you discover the jetted tub for two surrounded on two sides by picture windows. On the lower level, the Gatekeeper's Suite has a separate sitting area with a gas-log fireplace and corner whirlpool tub for two. Floral linens and a half canopy adorn the queen-size bed, and a little patio is connected to the gardens in front. The ground-level location of this room keeps it nice and cool in the summer, but we must note that you may hear noise from above and next door, even though the owners have made efforts to correct it. Rising above it all is the Attic Suite, the perfect place for privacy. Once you're up here, you won't be down anytime soon. Sink into love seats in front of the wood-burning fireplace or take a soak in the jetted tub.

A gourmet three-course breakfast is served in the inn's original dining room or in the bright sunroom. Tables for two help keep breakfast a semiprivate affair if you so desire. If savoring fancy breakfasts and lounging around this Edwardian oasis make you feel like a wet noodle, a brisk walk to town may be in order. Since you are only four and a half blocks from the downtown core, it won't be much of a strain, and you can hurry back to your room in no time. **998 Humboldt Street; (250) 384-4044; www.islandnet.com/ beaconsfield; very expensive to unbelievably expensive; minimum-stay requirement on weekends seasonally.**

❦❦ **THE BEDFORD REGENCY HOTEL, Victoria** First impressions can fool you. The downtown Bedford Regency Hotel looks grand on the outside, but the cavernous lobby is a disappointment: the outdated wicker furniture, pale colors, huge mirrors, and an out-of-place green whale-watching information desk turned us off. The dirty, wood-paneled elevator didn't leave a favorable impression either. Luckily, the hallways and rooms are more inviting. The 40 modern rooms have been done up in shades of peach and burgundy or yellow and green. (Some odd colors sneak in, such as the wet bar with a bright gold sink, royal blue faucet, and brownish orange granite countertop. Also, the rooms look good at first glance, but upon closer inspection you might find stains on the chairs and an abundance of wall marks and scratches.) Queen-size beds are graced with white goose-down comforters, and the bathrooms were clearly built for a couple in love to enjoy together. Some rooms feature huge tiled shower stalls with two jets, while others have spa tubs; some have wood-burning fireplaces (with the kindling prepared for you), and a few have everything, including separate sitting rooms and views of the Inner Harbour.

The hotel's downtown location provides ideal proximity to Victoria's best dining and shopping. And you can't beat the Bedford Regency if you want readily available information on whale-watching tours. Whatever your plans, begin your day with a complimentary buffet-style breakfast served downstairs in the **RED CURRANT CAFE** (moderate). **1140 Government Street; (250) 384-6835, (800) 665-6500; www.victoriabc.com/accom/bedford.html; moderate to very expensive.**

Romantic Warning: The courtyard rooms have flower boxes but no views, and because they look directly across to other units it is necessary to keep the shades down if you expect to have any privacy at all. This is not the best situation on a hot summer day, when you'll want to open a window.

❦❦❦ **CARBERRY GARDENS, Victoria** Tucked away in a residential area, Carberry Gardens is a comfortably appointed bed and breakfast that's rich with charm and clean as a whistle. The second floor of this 1907 home holds three guest rooms, two of which are especially suited for romantic travelers. Both offer plush down comforters, hardwood floors, Oriental rugs, and private baths. The Master's Room has lovely floral linens on the four-poster bed, a wood-burning fireplace, and a claw-foot tub. Catch morning rays on the comfortable window seat overlooking an ancient oak tree in the front yard. The Balcony Room, also equipped with a claw-foot tub, is especially nice on summer nights, when you can sit and stargaze from the large balcony. Due to its private bath across the hallway, the King Room, named after the large king-size bed, is less amorous than the other two rooms but still worth considering. Although most hallway bathrooms put the chill on romance, this one is equipped with an attached balcony overlooking the backyard garden, which makes up for the inconvenience.

The rooms are free of TVs and phones, but the comfortable guest parlor on the main floor is equipped with those modern conveniences. Three-course gourmet breakfasts are served family-style in the main-floor dining room, which is adorned with some interesting antiques, including an old rocking chair and a treadle sewing machine. Enjoy classical music as you feast on brandied currant scones, fruit topped with honey-lemon yogurt, and hot dishes such as roasted vegetable omelets, homemade chorizo sausage, and corn-and-spinach flan. **1008 Carberry Gardens; (250) 595-8906; www.carberry gardens.com; expensive.**

No lips DASHWOOD MANOR, Victoria We dashed in and out of here as quickly as possible. This well-known and well-publicized historic inn has flunked the test of time. While the waterfront location is beautiful and the home's exterior is certainly regal, the dark Victorian interior might put a damper on the flames of romance. **One Cook Street; (250) 385-5517, (800) 667-5517; moderate to unbelievably expensive.**

❧❧❧❧ THE EMPRESS HOTEL, Victoria Palatial and elegant, the Empress Hotel is to Victoria what Big Ben is to London, what the Eiffel Tower is to Paris, and so on. The $45 million renovation of the 1908 building is old news now, but the results still look new and unequivocally spectacular.

Among the Empress's dominions are the opulent **PALM COURT**, with its $50,000 stained glass ceiling that must be seen to be appreciated; the formal, architecturally grand **EMPRESS DINING ROOM** (see Restaurant Kissing); the charming café called **KIPLING'S**; and the unique **BENGAL LOUNGE AND PATIO**, casual only in comparison with the other dining spots here, but with a wonderful British Colonial feel. All are stupendous. Alas, these public areas can feel like a museum, complete with gawking tourists. Still, you would be remiss if you didn't visit the Empress and linger a while over tea and crumpets or sherry and dessert in the handsome, eminently comfortable **EMPRESS TEA LOBBY** (see High Tea Kissing). Outside, in the perfectly manicured rose garden, potential kissing spots await discovery among the magnolia trees and flower-covered trellises.

If you can afford the steep tariffs, an overnight stay here is definitely worthwhile. (Luckily, off-season package rates are more reasonable.) There are more than 100 room configurations, but all 460 rooms have private baths, polished furnishings, ceiling fans, and duvets.

For romance, we have two suggestions. Journey to the seventh floor, originally the staff quarters, to where eight cozy (read: small) Attic Suites await. All are individually decorated, and all are equipped with either a four-poster, canopy, or round bed romantically stationed within a turret. Because these suites are accessible only via a private staircase, you'll feel quite removed from the hustle and bustle below. If you can afford to foot the bill, request one of the 25 Entrée Gold Suites, where everything is private—from the concierge to the handsome lounge. (You'll love passing the lines of tourists at the main check-in desk as you head to your own private check-in on the second floor.) These spacious rooms—occupying both the second and third floors—offer incredible views of the Inner Harbour. King-size beds and large, sunny bathrooms with built-in TV speakers are additional enticing amenities. The dedicated staff go out of their way to attend to your every need, while a complimentary breakfast and afternoon hors d'oeuvres and cocktails can be enjoyed in the exclusive Entrée Gold lounge. "First-class" doesn't begin to describe the experience. **721 Government Street; (250) 384-8111, (800) 441-1414; www. cphotels.com; expensive to unbelievably expensive; recommended wedding site.**

❦❦❦❦ A HATERLEIGH HERITAGE INN, Victoria This Victorian bed and breakfast has been beautifully restored to preserve its turn-of-the-century charm while providing modern-day comforts few romantics can do without. Located near the south side of the Inner Harbour, this 1901 home still has its original hardwood floors, leaded windows, and intricate stained glass.

Six lovely rooms occupy the first and second floors, and each is blessed with high arched ceilings, tall windows, separate seating areas, and hand-painted tiles in the bathrooms. All are exceedingly clean and comfortable, but the best of the bunch are Day Dreams (the Honeymoon Suite) and, our personal favorite, the Secret Garden. Located on the first floor, Day Dreams is indeed the perfect place to dream the day away, with its rose and plum color scheme, enormous front windows, queen-size bed, and hardwood floors. In addition, this is the only room with a double Jacuzzi tub (three other rooms have one-person Jacuzzi tubs). The Secret Garden, a sunny room on the second floor, is the ideal hideaway, with a queen-size bed covered by a gorgeous tapestry bedspread, a step-up Jacuzzi tub, lovely antiques, and a small porch affording views of the Olympic Mountains and neighborhood rooftops.

A full gourmet breakfast is served family-style in the formal dining room at 8:30 A.M. sharp. You won't want to be late for the exotic fruit plate, chocolate-zucchini bread, and the house specialty—scones filled with smoked-salmon scrambled eggs and drizzled with hollandaise sauce. The amiable innkeepers also serve up interesting stories about the home's history, give a weather report, and relay news on what's happening in Victoria that day. **243 Kingston Street; (250) 384-9995; www.haterleigh.com; expensive to very expensive; minimum-stay requirement seasonally.**

❦❦❦ THE HOLLAND HOUSE INN, Victoria Filled with plenty of color and natural light, along with a dash of Mediterranean flair, the Holland House does much to brighten up Northwest days (and nights). The sun-kissed Georgian-style home—reminiscent of an Italian villa—will warm you up to romance in no time.

Ten rooms in the main house are tastefully done up in either solid colors or florals. Shades of egg yolk yellow, poppy orange, and deep plum brighten and soothe, while the prints add elegance and softness. Whatever the color or pattern, all rooms are elegantly appointed with antiques, hardwood floors covered with Oriental rugs, goose-down duvets, and private balconies. Private, standard bathrooms are the norm, and every room has a telephone and TV. Some also feature gas-log fireplaces, canopied or four-poster beds, and intimate sitting nooks. Since each is decorated differently, it's hard to specify which ones have the most romantic potential. We particularly like one fireplace room, elegantly decorated in black and white with red accents. Toile de Jouy wallpaper and a matching bedspread add a French country touch. The staff are extremely service oriented and will gladly help you find a room that suits your taste.

At the time we visited, Holland House was just completing four deluxe rooms in the new Carriage House adjoining the main building. Complete with fireplaces, window seats, and double soaking tubs (one has a jetted tub), these additions are bright and spacious, and should keep cuddling couples happy.

Morning brings a gourmet breakfast served at one large table in the cheery solarium. If you want to burn off calories from your morning meal of stuffed French toast or huevos rancheros, take a short walk along tree-lined residential streets to Beacon Hill Park, the waterfront, or downtown. **595 Michigan Street; (250) 384-6644, (800) 335-3466; www.hollandhouse.victoria.bc.ca; moderate to very expensive.**

❧❧❧❧ **HUMBOLDT HOUSE, Victoria** Privacy is a necessary element for romance, and this bed and breakfast specializes in providing it. The tall and skinny "shotgun"-style Victorian home is located on a quiet street lined with historic buildings. The nearby grounds of St. Anne's Academy provide a park-like feel with large lawns, plenty of trees, and few, if any, people. It may seem strange that downtown Victoria awaits only a few blocks away.

Inside, additional romantic elements come into play. A grandfather clock marks the entrance of the small, cozy parlor, where you can help yourselves to sherry as you relax in front of a blazing fireplace. All five guest rooms have inviting linens, wood-burning fireplaces, CD players, and Jacuzzi tubs tucked away in elevated corners framed by windows. (The tubs in the three upstairs rooms are spacious enough for two people.) Pop open the waiting bottle of champagne, nibble on homemade chocolate truffles, and revel in the solitude.

In the colorful Mikado and Oriental Rooms, sexy black Jacuzzi tubs are set apart from the bedrooms by Japanese-style screens. Edward's Room has a subtle Middle Eastern theme; the Gazebo Room resembles a garden with its

Cost ratings for British Columbia listings are in Canadian funds. American travelers should check the exchange rate or ask an innkeeper to figure out the cost in U.S. dollars.

terra-cotta-tiled Jacuzzi area and hand-painted vines and flowers winding along the vaulted ceiling. The Celebration Room is by far the grandest of all. Lovely white linens grace the immaculate queen-size bed, which is crowned by a sophisticated lace canopy and a lighted archway. Pretty floral prints adorn the elegant drapes and matching sofa. Classical art, angelic sculptures, and potted plants abound, and a glittering chandelier hangs overhead. While every room is well done, we recommend booking on the top floor so you won't hear the pitter-patter of other couples' feet and the reverberations of adjacent Jacuzzi tubs.

Champagne reappears at breakfast time. Be sure to raise a toast to what we consider the Humboldt House's best privacy feature: the ingenious two-way butler's pantry found in each room. At a specified hour, the proprietors deliver a picnic basket filled with breakfast goodies, champagne, and orange juice to the pantry. There's no contact with the outside, and the two of you can enjoy seafood crêpes, eggs Benedict, or French toast in your own romantic world. **867 Humboldt Street; (250) 383-0152, (888) 383-0327; www. humboldthouse.com; very expensive; minimum-stay requirement on weekends seasonally.**

❀❀❀ JOAN BROWN'S BED AND BREAKFAST, Victoria

There's plenty going on here, in fact, possibly too much. The dynamic Joan Brown begins by welcoming guests into her home as only she can. She is right at home in this grandiose Georgian Italianate mansion stuffed to overflowing with bric-a-brac.

Set in a refined neighborhood near Craigdarroch Castle, this stately property has high beamed ceilings, several fireplaces, gorgeous stained glass windows, formal English gardens, polished wood floors, and the original wood staircase. Rooms come in a variety of sizes, but all are furnished with pieces that are ostentatiously ornate and rather out-of-date. Plentiful sunlight brightens this already colorful home. Some rooms have private baths; the others share facilities. The larger rooms, particularly the one with high ceilings on the ground floor, are the grandest but also the gaudiest. Only one small room, off the dining area, could be called pleasingly simple; it features a four-poster queen-size bed, separate entrance, and deep soaking tub. Uninviting little "DO NOT TOUCH" notes are sprinkled throughout the house, along with reminders about breakfast time. Speaking of which, a generous, full breakfast is served in the ornate dining room, which is adorned with Spode china, fresh flowers, and a massive chandelier. **729 Pemberton Road; (250) 592-5929; inexpensive to moderate; no credit cards.**

❀❀❀ LAUREL POINT INN, Victoria

Laurel Point Inn may look like just another massive condominium complex lining Victoria's Inner Harbour, but this 200-room hotel contains some extremely stylish suites with phenomenal views. The trick is knowing specifically which rooms to choose. Start by tossing out the brochure; it is entirely misleading, with pictures of only the most exclusive suites. Next, rule out the entire north wing. These boring hotel rooms are more than just rough around the edges. That leaves the south wing. Narrow the choices here by requesting an Outer Harbour view. (The city-view rooms located closer to the water are also acceptable, but depending on their location, you run the risk of looking directly at the neighboring high-rise.)

What's left on the south wing are studio-style junior suites, one-bedroom suites with separate sitting areas, and panoramic penthouse suites with unobstructed views and wonderful amenities. Prices start at $250 Canadian in these categories, but when you see your room you'll be glad you were choosy. An atmosphere of Pacific Rim–style simplicity and elegance prevails in these suites, with their taupe and sand decor, punctuated by black accents, blond wood furnishings, shoji-style sliding doors, granite tables, Asian art pieces, and L-shaped couches. Deep soaking tubs and glass walk-in showers highlight large bathrooms lined with Italian marble. Floor-to-ceiling windows open to glass-enclosed balconies overlooking glorious views of the Outer Harbour and the majestic Olympic Mountains. While we seldom mention hallways for romantic ambience, the south wing's halls are worth visiting for their exquisite Asian art pieces displayed in museum-like glass cases. Also, the comfortable lobbies next to the elevator feature some lovely views.

Outside, be sure to visit the large reflecting pond and the tiny Japanese garden framed by a waterfall cascading over granite boulders. This hideaway gets an extra kiss from us. Romance packages here include the usual goodies, but for some bathtime excitement, request a Bath Bomb. Once in the tub, this ball explodes with bright colors and soothing aromas.

The hotel's dining rooms, **COOK'S LANDING LOUNGE** and **CAFE LAUREL**, are dated, have mediocre food, and don't hold a candle to the glass-enclosed **TERRACE ROOM**. However, summer rays are the only ones you'll be able to bask in here; it's open from June to mid-September only. **680 Montreal Street; (250) 386-8721, (800) 663-7667; www.victoriabc.com/ accom/laurelpoint; very expensive to unbelievably expensive; recommended wedding site.**

💋💋 **THE MAMITA, Victoria** The Empress Hotel isn't the only classic place in town to spend the night. There's also *The Mamita*, a 1927 motor yacht that back in the olden days was the flagship for the Royal Yacht Club. Now in leisurely retirement, the 50-foot boat docks at Laurel Point Bay in Victoria's Inner Harbour with other fashionable, albeit newer, yachts.

Step aboard and you'll discover a solid teak interior filled with art deco designs, Persian rugs, bright red cushioned couches, and a tiny, cluttered galley (kitchen). Moonlight shines through the all-window wheelhouse onto a comfortable but small double bed. (You can close the blinds if you wish.) On sunny days, perch on the foredeck and watch seaplanes go by and seals at play. On rainy days, grab a blanket and cuddle underneath the boat's covered aft deck. While it's a little rustic and a tad weathered, this is the perfect place for privacy and 360-degree views of the energetic Inner Harbour. **Reservations through Andersen House, (250) 388-4565; www.islandnet.com/ ~andersen; expensive; minimum-stay requirement.**

Romantic Warning: A luxury liner this is not. Be prepared for tight spaces below, small showers, tiny toilets, and precarious steps and narrow pathways. You'll also have to walk a block (through a nice neighborhood) to the Andersen House for breakfast. And, last but not least, if you're perched on the foredeck during the day, onlookers will ask boatloads of questions. However, the fun part is you can tell them *The Mamita* is all yours . . . at least for a few days.

❀❀❀❀ **MULBERRY MANOR, Victoria** Luxury and history will embrace you in this renovated Tudor mansion set in a gorgeous neighborhood. Famous Victoria architect Samuel Maclure constructed the beautiful, stately home in 1926, reportedly rolling out the red carpet for the lady of the house—i.e., the boss. Red carpets continue to roll, so to speak, when guests arrive today.

As you enter, the main floor whispers of grandeur with its plush, chintz-covered sofas and chairs, hardwood floors, and embroidered carpets. A bay window in the parlor allows views of the perfectly maintained grounds, which extend almost an acre. The elegant dining room, where a full gourmet breakfast is served come morning, is appointed with rich red walls and china displayed in an antique cabinet. Anywhere else, all this opulence might come across as gaudy, but here everything is tastefully and beautifully executed.

The three individually decorated guest rooms are embellished in understated, classic English style with thick down comforters and fluffy feather beds. Decorated in yellow and blue, the Jasmine Suite is the largest room, with a huge old-fashioned bathroom, brass bed, wood-burning fireplace, and expansive balcony. The Rosewood Room, with a detached bath, is outfitted with pink floral linens and has a four-poster bed with a half canopy. The romantic Angel Room, done up in a black-and-white cherub motif, features a private balcony. The grounds are as lovely as the home, with a backyard duck pond that's as popular with courting waterfowl as it is with courting couples.

In the morning, soft classical music fills the air as you enter the grand dining room and behold the lavish breakfast spread: yogurt, muesli, fruit compote, scones with lemon curd, and a delicious hot entrée such as poached eggs with smoked salmon on a toasted English muffin. Only the best will do here, and everything is served on fine Spode china. Lingering over breakfast has never been so enjoyable or elegant. **611 Foul Bay Road; (250) 370-1918; www. mulberrymanor.com; moderate to expensive; minimum-stay requirement.**

No lips OAK BAY BEACH HOTEL, Victoria Long-standing reputations, no matter how undeserved, sometimes refuse to die. The Oak Bay Beach Hotel is known as Victoria's only seaside hotel (that much is true), which explains why it is so popular and often fully booked. The gorgeous setting, overlooking the open waters of the Strait of Juan de Fuca and the often-snowcapped Olympic Mountains, is impressive, and the half-timbered Tudor mansion is striking. Yet inside, the 51 rooms are amazingly second-rate and in serious need of refurbishing. Beds in most rooms have been appointed with down comforters or duvets, but unfortunately they don't make up for dreary colors, unattractive artwork, and a musty odor that seems to permeate the entire building. The third-floor rooms, which flaunt the highest price tags and best views, are the ones that require the most restoration. Even the handful of recently renovated rooms were done poorly and still look tacky.

The parlor is the most attractive part of the hotel (which isn't saying much). Antique sofas, large windows facing the ocean, a blazing fireplace, and a square-beamed ceiling contribute to a distinctive old-world ambience. BENTLEY'S ON THE BAY (expensive) is the hotel's restaurant. Each table is topped with flowers and green and ivory tablecloths, while a brick hearth glows at one end of the dining room. Despite the wonderful views of Oak Bay, its afternoon tea service is shoddy and the presentation just okay. **1175 Beach Drive; (250) 598-4556, (800) 668-7758; very expensive to unbelievably expensive.**

🐚💧 OCEAN POINTE RESORT HOTEL AND SPA, Victoria Notice how the word "resort" comes before "hotel"? If you find that love blossoms on the tennis court or after a refreshing mud wrap, this is your place. Go elsewhere for amorous hotel ambience. Encompassing almost the entire north shore of the Inner Harbour, the massive, contemporary building faces the Empress. Take some time to enjoy the grand, modern lobby, with ceiling-high windows overlooking the harbor.

Unfortunately, only a handful of the 250 guest rooms appeal to romantics, and even some of these resemble your average green and pink hotel room. Two loft suites add some dimension, height, and larger windows, but the view is of the working (industrial) side of the harbor. There's one honeymoon suite and only one Jacuzzi room. If you don't mind a standard room, push for an Inner Harbour view—that's one romantic aspect of this hotel. As for the spa, it's reputed to be the best in town, with everything from therapeutic massage to squash courts to sessions with a personal trainer. Book ahead for the beauty services: Locals come here too, and things can get busy. **45 Songhees Road; (250) 360-2999, (800) 667-4677; www.oprhotel.com; very expensive to unbelievably expensive.**

Romantic Note: One of the best dining views in town can be found in the resort's VICTORIAN RESTAURANT (see Restaurant Kissing).

No lips OLDE ENGLAND INN, Victoria This place is a classic example of Olde English decor gone old. The inn—a historic re-creation of an English village that has turned into a tourist trap—has been around forever, and much of its popularity stems from its proximity to Anne Hathaway's Thatched Cottage—a replica of a 16th-century home. Even though the inn bills itself as charming and romantic, we recommend you steer clear. The lobby is as dark and dreary as a dungeon, rooms are overly frilly with oddly shaped bathrooms (note the head-hitting ceilings), and everything else looks as if it needs a dusting with Old English Furniture Polish. While this place advertises itself as "A Taste of Olde England," it's a stale one. **429 Lampson Street; (250) 388-4353; expensive.**

♥♥♥⁌ **PRIOR HOUSE, Victoria** When the Edwardian style of architecture hit Victoria's housing scene, architects went wild adding footage. Prior House, an 8,500-square-foot Edwardian Revival mansion built in 1912, is a perfect example, with over two dozen rooms. Luckily for lovebirds, several of these stately rooms cater to romance.

Seven guest rooms are spread throughout the home's two top levels and at the garden level. Most spacious and romantic are the 1,000-square-foot Windsor Suite and the equally grand Lieutenant Governor's Suite. Hidden away on the top floor, the Windsor Suite is popular with honeymooners. While not decorated as lavishly as the other rooms, it's comfortable, and the Jacuzzi tub beneath the skylight lets moonlight bathe you as well. French doors open to a small private patio facing the Strait of Juan de Fuca, and a gas fireplace (with an annoying ticking timer) will keep you cozy at night. The Lieutenant Governor's Suite on the second floor is appointed with Austrian hand-printed draperies and a wood-burning fireplace. An unusual headboard created from an antique sofa crowns the bed. The most striking feature, however, is the enormous bathroom, lavishly decorated with crystal chandeliers, gold swan fixtures, mirrored walls, a TV, and a huge Jacuzzi air-jet massage tub in green marble. Even the towels are oversize! Some people have had picnics in this lavish spot. (Did we mention there's a fridge hidden behind mirrored walls?) Such modern appointments seem a bit out of place in this historic manor, but who's complaining?

Less extravagant (and less expensive) rooms are also available. No matter which room you choose, all have fireplaces, TV/VCRs, and old-fashioned European decor, with richly colored walls and antique furnishings. If that's not enough, all of the upstairs rooms have views (some better than others).

Common areas are inviting and warm, thanks to the many fireplaces throughout. The owners have put much thought into restoring the mansion, adding such details as hand-loomed English Axminster carpets, period lighting, and a sprinkling of family antiques. A carved stone terrace with plush green lawn chairs looks onto meticulously groomed lawns, perennial gardens, and a magnificent copper beech taller than the four-story inn. The terrace is the setting for a delicious afternoon tea, featuring such home-baked treats as salmon-and-chive scones and scrumptious Welsh griddle cakes. (The feast moves inside to the library if the weather is bad.) In the morning, enjoy an elaborate breakfast of Scottish oat pancakes or smoked-salmon mousseline presented in the formal chandeliered dining room, or arrange to have it delivered to your room. If you can tear yourselves away from all this eating and lounging around, the beautiful grounds of Government House and popular Antique Row on Fort Street are only a short stroll away. **620 St. Charles Street; (250) 592-8847; www.priorhouse.com; expensive to unbelievably expensive.**

♥♥ **SCHOLEFIELD HOUSE, Victoria** Third in a row of matching Italianate homes, Scholefield House does much to keep in line with history. Built in

1892 by one of British Columbia's earliest historians, the home is authentically Victorian through and through and still retains many original features, such as those practical picture rails. Good thing, too, since there are plenty of ornately framed pieces throughout. In the Queen Victoria Room, portraits of Her Majesty adorn the room, which is decorated in burgundy and hunter green, her favorite colors. The room's queen-size bed, walnut antiques, and antique claw-foot tub are augmented with books and manuscripts about the queen's life.

If being surrounded by representations of Queen Victoria's face isn't your cup of tea, get regal in the King Suite. Outfitted in blue and gold, this masculine alternative has a wood-burning fireplace, claw-foot tub, tall ceilings, and a bed fit for a king, with the royal lion standing guard above. A small table framed by a beautiful bay window makes a perfect and private breakfast spot. Green thumbs might enjoy the Secret Garden Room, which overlooks the backyard and has a queen-size bed and shower. Upon arrival, guests can imbibe a glass of Scholefield's own wine and relax in the small, simple upstairs library. Downtown Victoria is just a hop, skip, and jump away for those wanting to hit the town.

Edible flowers and fragrant herbs from the garden find their way into five-course champagne breakfasts. Lavender scones, carrot-pineapple muffins, and eggs Florentine are some of the dishes you can savor while seated in the sunny dining room teeming with antiques and overlooking tree-lined Vancouver Street. Presiding in front of the fireplace is Mr. Galileo, a friendly white feline. All guests leave with a packet of dried herbs from the garden. If you have cats at home, the innkeeper will include something for them too. **731 Vancouver Street; (250) 385-2025; www.scholefieldhouse.com; moderate to expensive.**

SWANS, Victoria If you like being in the heart of the action in every sense of the phrase, you will appreciate Swans' location. Set in downtown Victoria, on the corner of Wharf Street and Pandora Avenue, this 1913 warehouse-turned-hotel retains a number of historic architectural touches, such as the original rafters and exposed brick walls. Guest rooms feature full kitchens, separate dining areas, living rooms, oversize windows, cathedral ceilings, small balconies, TVs, and phones. The 29 units come in three configurations: studios and one- and two-bedroom units. The studios and one-bedroom lofts are the coziest. Modern and Northwest artwork along with fresh flowers brighten every room, but the nondescript contemporary decor and slightly-off color schemes remind you this is just a hotel. Nevertheless, these are spacious rooms in which to set up temporary housekeeping while touring Victoria, and the location is incredibly convenient. **506 Pandora Avenue; (250) 361-3310, (800) 668-7926; www.islandnet.com/~swans; moderate to expensive.**

Romantic Warning: Rooms above the main-floor pub can be noisy. Unless you plan to stay out most of the night yourselves, you won't appreciate the clamor from downstairs.

Romantic Note: Also in the building is the **FOWL & FISH CAFE** (moderate to expensive), featuring fresh oysters, tapas, and West Coast cuisine. The colorful decor is warmed by gorgeous flower displays, exposed brick walls, and wood rafters hung with dried herbs and copper pots.

Restaurant Kissing

❀❀❁ **CAFE BRIO, Victoria** Looking more like it belongs in Tuscany than on Fort Street (a.k.a. Antique Row), this restaurant adds a touch of warmth to the neighborhood. A charming patio, edged by swirly wrought-iron gates, frames this sun-kissed villa that serves Pacific Northwest food with Tuscan flair.

Earth tones heat up the interior, which is decorated in neo-Renaissance style with Italian wall statues, gilt-framed mirrors, lighting fixtures salvaged from an old mansion, and modern paintings hung every which way. The narrow dining room, which is plagued by outside noise, can have a decidedly unromantic decibel level. While the noise can't be helped, avoid the unprotected tables and hide in one of the pine booths, just right for two.

Simplicity defines the cooking style, with an emphasis on light, delicate flavors set off by robust accents. The beet risotto proved an excellent accompaniment to pan-fried halibut cheeks. The delicate sea bass, served atop flavorful cider-braised cabbage, leeks, and pancetta, is superb. Desserts, however, can't be defined as simple: pear tarte Tatin, banana and caramel pudding, and grilled pear with citrus mascarpone are outstanding. We only wish the lunch menu had more than four dessert choices. Overall, you'll leave Cafe Brio feeling satisfied by the flavors, but not stuffed by heavy sauces. And that's all the better for romance later on, isn't it? **944 Fort Street; (250) 383-0009; moderate to expensive; lunch Monday–Friday, dinner daily.**

❀❀❀❀ **CAMILLE'S, Victoria** Camille's has been voted "Victoria's Most Seductive Restaurant" in our personally conducted, highly scientific, two-person poll. From the moment you enter this irresistible lower-level restaurant, you'll see why. Right away you feel significantly removed from the turmoil of the city, and that helps set the mood for quiet conversation and hand holding. Two dining rooms are tucked in here, but for romantic purposes you should request a seat in the second one, hidden away in the back. Hundred-year-old brick walls adorned with contemporary art blend well with linen tablecloths, stained glass lamps, and a rustic assortment of decorative books and wine bottles. A few individual tables are separated from the rest of the room by wooden partitions that create extremely private booths. The affable staff works together to make your experience as warm and wonderful as you can imagine. Be sure to read the wine list, which is not only witty and entertaining, but also offers suggestions for special-occasion wines.

A delightful lineup emphasizing fresh fish, locally grown produce and meats, and various Mediterranean dishes is prepared in a health-conscious manner. Enjoy freshly baked bread as you decide between appetizers like phyllo triangles stuffed with goat cheese and caramelized shallots, or the five-pepper-corn-crusted ahi tuna carpaccio. For dinner we recommend pan-seared duck breast with fig, orange, and sherry compote; the rack of lamb; and, if in season, the baked halibut with cabernet and black bean jus, which is divine. Desserts are just as interesting and just as luscious. For a pick-me-up, indulge in the tiramisu spiced with a citrus liqueur or share the maple-orange crème caramel. Mmmmm—it's almost as sweet as kisses. Almost. **45 Bastion Square; (250) 381-3433; www.camillesrestaurant.com; expensive; dinner daily; call for seasonal closures.**

CASSIS BISTRO, Victoria Far from the madding tourist crowds is this little neighborhood bistro. Actually, it's not that far away, but most tourists don't bother walking 15 minutes to Cook Street to find this eclectic restaurant that's popular with locals. A mix of abstract, thickly painted art hung on butter yellow walls gives the room a hip but elegant feel. However, the antique lamps and mismatched chairs, although funky, don't complement the art. Nevertheless, the place is tiny, cozy, and warm, with natural light by day and candlelight at night. There are plenty of two-person tables throughout, but unfortunately not by the wonderful large front window.

The small menu covers a lot of ground, with flavors and influences as common as French and as exotic as Moroccan. Mix and match with the tapas selection or split menu items, which can be ordered in small or large portions. The generally flavorful dishes are accompanied by interesting touches, including a salad bedecked with grilled mango and halibut served with harissa sauce. Some dishes are only okay; we were not enamored with the bland crab cakes. Global influences continue into the desserts. The Mexican-chocolate brownie accompanied by a scoop of roasted-banana ice cream tastes just like paradise. **253 Cook Street; (250) 384-1932; moderate to expensive; dinner Tuesday–Sunday, brunch Sunday.**

CHEZ DANIEL, Victoria This quaint little restaurant almost blends into the row of shops lining Estevan Avenue, but once you step inside you're in for a romantic treat. Copper pots adorn the walls and wine bottles abound throughout the two tiny dining rooms. The burgundy and forest green color scheme, crisp linens, soft harp music, and flickering candlelight add class, but the amateurish artwork (with prices scribbled on Post-It notes) detracts a bit.

Chez Daniel offers some elegantly prepared dishes. Don't miss the choice appetizers, including admirable escargot in garlic butter. Entrées such as filet mignon, veal Madeira, and roasted duck with chestnuts are superior. While tender enough to cut with a fork, the Châteaubriand tableside presentation was as bland as unsalted butter. The table d'hôte menu is reasonably priced for a French restaurant and offers an impressive assortment of the kitchen's best efforts. While the food is wonderful, service is at best informative and at worst indifferent. Most of all, it's as slow as escargot. But have patience: This meal is worth waiting for. **2524 Estevan Avenue; (250) 592-7424; expensive; dinner Tuesday–Saturday.**

❦ **DA TANDOOR, Victoria** Savory aromas singing of exotic spices will make your mouth water in anticipation when you enter Da Tandoor. However, the decor is less appealing to the senses. There are too many tables to call the dining room intimate, and too many silk plants and fake pink flowers to call it elegant. However, hanging brass lanterns, Persian rugs, Indian silk paintings, and intricately carved sandalwood screens lend some authenticity. Tandoori dishes (baked in a clay oven) are the house specialty, but the Indian- and Pakistani-style curries are also notable. *Taza sagg*, fresh spinach cooked with green onions, herbs, and spices, is a pleasing complement to the chicken curry in spicy tomato and onion sauce. This is one of the most frequently recommended restaurants in Victoria. Dinner, and not the decor, will explain why. **1010 Fort Street; (250) 384-6333, (800) 384-6333; moderate; dinner daily.**

❦❦❦ **THE EMPRESS DINING ROOM, Victoria** Dinner at the Empress is a regal treat. The two formal dining areas, each appointed with chandeliers, upholstered high-backed chairs, and beautiful tapestried walls, are equally elegant. Both are highlighted by candles, fine china, pressed white linen tablecloths accented with a single lily, and exceptional service. The only difference is one offers an outstanding harbor view while the other offers a harpist, whose soft music adds extra enchantment. For romance, we especially recommend the tables for two set by the large harbor-view windows.

Like everything else at the Empress, the food, which draws on local delicacies, sets a high standard. Specialties include rack of lamb, roasted baby chicken infused with wild B.C. mushrooms, smoked duck breast, black cod chowder, and a unique yellow squash and flower petal soup. When the dessert cart is wheeled your way, let go your willpower and submit to the sweets. **721 Government Street; (250) 384-8111; www.cphotels.ca; expensive to very expensive; dinner daily.**

❦❦❦ **HERALD STREET CAFFE, Victoria** Typically when so many locals love one place, you can't go wrong eating there. That's the case with the Herald Street Caffe, where a line of locals often waits outside. (Hint: Make reservations.) Since day one—more than 18 years ago—the kitchen has consistently dished out fresh, innovative Northwest-Asian cuisine that keeps everyone happy

---

Cost ratings for British Columbia listings are in Canadian funds. American travelers should check the exchange rate or ask an innkeeper to figure out the cost in U.S. dollars.

and full. What do we recommend? Everything. Start with a spinach salad that has a refreshing honey-ginger dressing good enough to eat alone (and who says that about salad dressings?). A local favorite is the pan-roasted chicken sautéed in creamed Dijon and served with apple-currant relish. Creamed whole-seed mustard infused with mint accents the rack of lamb, which is outstanding. Or try the generous bouillabaisse, with a fennel-chardonnay broth and toasted-almond pesto. Desserts are a must! The banana–coconut cream pie is a dream, while the lemon pie, made with whole lemons, will have you puckering up in no time—good practice for later on.

Bold artwork, dark plum wainscoting, chocolate butter-cream walls, and huge floral arrangements lend a stylish edge to the casual dining room. Ask for a window seat when you make your reservation. The view is just the sidewalk and street, but the active atmosphere seems a little calmer around the edges. **546 Herald Street; (250) 381-1441; expensive; reservations required; lunch Wednesday–Sunday, dinner daily, brunch Sunday.**

❤❤ **IL TERRAZZO RISTORANTE, Victoria** Although the tables are a bit too close together and the room is busy with activity, this restaurant's charm will quickly win you over. Exposed brick walls and archways are adorned with colorful artwork, while wrought-iron candelabras hang overhead. Hardwood floors, handkerchief-like floral tablecloths, and candlelit tables promote an intimate and casual ambience. Large windows face a quaint brick courtyard, which is the real romantic spot here. Hanging flower baskets, black marble tables, and wrought-iron chairs embellish the patio, while seven brick hearths and several space heaters help things heat up on cool evenings. Tiny white lights sparkle in the potted trees and surrounding greenery.

Excellent northern Italian cuisine is served by the knowledgeable wait staff. We recommend the spinach risotto; spaghetti with clams, tomatoes, roasted garlic, and black pepper, prepared in a white wine sauce; or the roast duck served on penne pasta with shiitake mushrooms and ginger. You won't be disappointed by anything this kitchen puts together. **555 Johnson Street, off Waddington Alley; (250) 361-0028; moderate to expensive; lunch Monday–Saturday, dinner daily.**

❤❤ **THE MARINA RESTAURANT, Victoria** This massive waterfront restaurant dishes out mediocre cuisine while diners concentrate on the magnificent views. The contemporary interior also pales in comparison to the outside scenery, which encompasses Haro Strait and the forest of masts rising from Oak Bay Marina below. Dozens of four-seat tables blanket the lower level, so you'll be bumping elbows with your neighbor. Your only chance for privacy awaits in the booths encircling the restaurant's bar.

An extensive menu features seafood from the Pacific Northwest and beyond, including Vancouver Island clams, Dungeness crab, Prince Edward Island mussels, Alaskan halibut, and other catches of the deep. A tastefully decorated sushi bar is tucked behind the restaurant's entryway. The food is reputed to be better here, so fill up on nigiri sushi, traditional rolls, or a variety of dinner combinations.

As for the Marina's food, the local clams in a spicy tomato broth proved to be delicious, but the crab cakes looked and tasted like mass-produced salmon burgers, and a thick, overcooked Parmesan cheese crust plopped right off our oven-baked sea bass. Desserts, luckily, offered some excitement. Chocoholics should try the chocolate fetish—five tiny chocolate creations, including a chile-laced crème brûlée certain to spice up the night. **1327 Beach Drive; (250) 598-8555; expensive; lunch and dinner daily, brunch Sunday.**

Romantic Alternative: Downstairs from the restaurant is the more casual **CAFE DELI** (250-598-3890; inexpensive), with an espresso bar and glass-enclosed pastry cases sporting the usual assortment of goodies.

Romantic Journey: If you are coming from downtown Victoria, drive via the winding, scenic waterfront route. However, take along a cup of time and a pint of patience, as this route is not always well marked. If you do get lost, you can wander through some of Victoria's nicest neighborhoods until you're back on track.

❦❦ **ROGERS' CHOCOLATES, Victoria** If you're trying to woo your beloved while in Victoria, we recommend an age-old tactic: chocolate. Most experts agree that the way to another's heart is through the stomach, or, in this case, the sweet tooth. Simply follow Government Street a few blocks north of the Inner Harbour and there, in the midst of a plethora of shops and cafés, you'll find Rogers' Chocolates. Once you step foot inside, we guarantee you won't leave empty-handed.

This old-fashioned chocolate shop is a chocoholic's dream come true, with dark wood paneling, tiled floors, and enough sweets to last a lifetime. Chocolates are handmade fresh every day in the back of the shop, according to the original recipes Charles W. "Candy" Rogers perfected in the late 1800s. The creams, almond brittle, caramels, truffles, and other creations are wrapped in colorful packages and placed seductively in glass display cases. What could be sweeter than a chocolate kiss? **913 Government Street; (250) 384-7021; open daily.**

❦❦ **THE VICTORIAN RESTAURANT, Victoria** Despite its name, The Victorian Restaurant lacks the frills, lace, and burgundy and green color schemes prominently displayed elsewhere in the city. This fine dining restaurant, located in **OCEAN POINTE RESORT HOTEL AND SPA** (see Hotel/Bed and Breakfast Kissing), is instead elegantly decorated in shades of taupe, brown, and black, and ornamented by a magnificent five-foot-high floral centerpiece. Most tables are designed for four people, which is a thumbs down on coziness, but thumbs up on privacy—i.e., you aren't sitting in your neighbor's lap. Walls of windows look across the Inner Harbour at the historic Parliament Building and the Empress Hotel, outlined after dark by thousands of sparkling lights.

The four-course dinner proves a better deal than the pricey à la carte menu, but can be a roller-coaster ride in terms of taste. (We must note that regardless of culinary appeal, all presentations are beautiful.) Our appetizer of smoked salmon and sea bass was flavorful, but the lamb sirloin in a caramelized pecan crust was chewy and bland, and we wondered where those pecans were. What was supposedly Kahlúa crème brûlée was, alas, just plain old vanilla. Service is strictly formal, not friendly. Go here to see the city lights dancing on the water; just don't expect the food or the service to illuminate the night. **45 Songhees Road, at Ocean Pointe Resort Hotel and Spa; (250) 360-2999, (800) 667-4677; expensive to very expensive; dinner daily.**

High Tea Kissing

Sharing high tea is a thoroughly English, utterly civilized way to spend a late afternoon together. And no other town in North America offers this delightful ritual with as much style, dedication, and abundance as Victoria. Presentations differ widely, as do the prices. Some places employ the traditional white gloves and silver service, while others provide a more eclectic display on floral-patterned china. Prices range from $9 to $25 per person, depending on your surroundings, but the customary basics are always the same: fresh fruit, dainty finger sandwiches (with crusts cut off), delectable pastries, rich Devonshire cream, and tea properly steeped in a china teapot and kept warm by a tea cozy.

The ritual of afternoon tea began in China, where tea making was considered an art form. Later, tea was used for meditative purposes by Japanese Buddhist monks. High tea as we know it was initiated in the 19th century, when the Duchess of Bedford noticed a "sinking feeling" each afternoon and decided to ask some of her genteel girlfriends to join her for afternoon refreshments.

Since no trip to Victoria would be complete without a taste of tea, we have reviewed the most well-known places for savoring high tea in the city. Although many of these restaurants serve other meals as well, our romance ratings largely reflect their tea presentations.

No lips BLETHERING PLACE, Victoria Frumpy, a bit dumpy, and certainly cluttered, this popular-with-the-tourists tea place is located in the affluent Oak Bay neighborhood. Housed in a traditional Tudor building, the casual English country-style dining room is appointed with oak chairs, pastel floral tablecloths, and lace curtains. The walls are covered with a hodgepodge of English-theme items, and up front there's a shop with all sorts of tea souvenirs. While having tea here won't break your budget, it may ruin your appetite. Our scone was basically a big blob of white bread with currants, and the wait staff were about as lively as the long, dowdy country dresses they wore. Save your appetite, and chitchat over tea elsewhere. **2250 Oak Bay Avenue; (250) 598-1413; inexpensive to moderate; breakfast, lunch, high tea, and dinner daily.**

❧❧❧ **BUTCHART GARDENS DINING ROOM, Victoria** Sometimes location is everything. Views of the Butchart Garden's famous flowers from every window make this a refined and regal place for high tea. The building, originally Mr. and Mrs. Butchart's home, offers two seating areas. For more privacy, journey to what used to be the breakfast nook, which features floral wallpaper and large windows overlooking the Italian gardens. A bit more open is the solarium, a lovely sun-filled spot cooled by mint green walls, white linen tablecloths, and fresh flowers. Greek statues and Chinese vases displaying leafy tropical plants bring the garden indoors. Although tea is a tad pricey, the setting is spectacular and the serving of tea sandwiches, homemade sweets, and scones is generous. Of particular interest is the edible-flower sandwich made from organically grown purple pansies. Take a bite so you can truly say you experienced the beautiful sights, smells, and tastes of THE BUTCHART GARDENS (see Outdoor Kissing). **800 Benvenuto Avenue; (250) 652-8222; moderate to expensive; call for seasonal lunch hours, high tea and dinner daily.**

❧❧❧ **THE EMPRESS TEA LOBBY, Victoria** Visitors from far and wide come to the Empress for high tea each afternoon. This is undoubtedly the most formal white-glove tea in Victoria, and the setting is posh beyond words. Locals are bemused by the exorbitant price visitors are expected to pay for high tea. Most agree that it's not the food itself you're paying for, but the experience of taking tea at Victoria's most beloved landmark.

Once the grand entrance to the hotel, the lobby has been transformed into the main tearoom. During the summer, tea is served under the stained glass dome of the nearby **PALM COURT;** however, the Tea Lobby is the most sought-after locale. Two enormous marble fireplaces stand at either end of the room, crowned with portraits of Queen Mary and King George V. Intricately carved columns rise upward to an elaborately detailed rose and pink ceiling. From the crystal chandeliers to the hardwood floors, you'll be awed by such stately splendor. As you nestle in one of the overstuffed chairs or floral upholstered couches clustered around the tables, you can savor finger sandwiches of smoked salmon, deviled egg, cucumber, and watercress; sip the Empress's own blend of tea; and converse contentedly while a pianist or a string quartet plays softly in the background. A packet of Empress tea is presented when you leave so you can enjoy their tea again at home. **721 Government Street; (250) 384-8111, (800) 441-1414; www.cphotels.ca; expensive; reservations required; high tea daily.**

Romantic Note: Reservations are a must for high tea, especially during the busy summer months. Also, visitors are asked to observe a semiformal dress code while taking tea at the Empress; shorts and T-shirts are not suitable attire for teatime.

Vancouver Island

❧ **JAMES BAY TEA ROOM AND RESTAURANT, Victoria** Given the state of disrepair at the James Bay Tea Room, you may wonder if we are serious about recommending this little spot. Well, despite the weathered exterior and old interior, this charming Tudor-style home feels entirely authentic. British knick-knacks clutter the small dining room, and portraits of English monarchs, past and present, cover the walls. The scones are edible, the tea is drinkable, but avoid the mediocre sandwiches if you know what's good for you.

Perhaps what feels so genuine about tea here is that there is no big production around the event, and the lack of pretension may be a welcome change of pace for some. On the other hand, someone who has never experienced a high tea may want a grand presentation, complete with white gloves. In that case, somewhere like the Empress Hotel would probably be (pardon the pun) your cup of tea. **332 Menzies Street; (250) 382-8282; inexpensive to moderate; breakfast, lunch, high tea, and dinner daily.**

❧❧❧ **POINT ELLICE HOUSE, Victoria** Some of the best tea in town can be found, well, out of town. A five-minute ferry ride from the Inner Harbour transports you back in time to the peaceful oasis known as Point Ellice. This Italianate villa, built by the prominent O'Reilly family, appears to have remained virtually unchanged since the 1860s, and currently displays a large collection of Victorian antiques and heirlooms. Each room in the house has been re-created to depict the daily life of the O'Reilly family at the turn of the century. You can rent a cassette player at the entrance and take an audio tour of the charming house. Tours last roughly a half hour and can be added to your high tea for an additional small fee.

Afternoon tea is served on the croquet lawn, where views of the water and gardens inspire a feeling of serenity. White wicker chairs are clustered together on the grass, with a few set beneath a shady canopy. High tea here consists of fresh fruit, finger sandwiches, and scones with cream and homemade jam, followed by a light dessert of fruit tart, shortbread, and lemon-poppyseed cake. You can choose between coffee, lavender lemonade, or the house tea, a unique blend of Ceylon and China black. Tea servers wear the traditional dresses of servants in the late Victorian era.

Later, stroll around the grounds and enjoy fragrant gardens filled with poppies, honeysuckle, jasmine, lavender, hollyhocks, and lilacs. There's also a small gift shop, a heart-shaped rose garden, and a trail called the Woodland Walk leading to the beach through overgrown ivy. Trees and shrubbery enclose the property and serve as natural insulation from the noisy industrial area nearby. Overall, the excellent food, lovely setting, and reasonable rates make Point Ellice a wonderful afternoon escape. **2616 Pleasant Street; (250) 380-6506; inexpensive; high tea daily; closed early September–early May, with special openings during holidays; recommended wedding site.**

Romantic Suggestion: The best route to Point Ellice is via the VICTORIA HARBOUR FERRY COMPANY (250-480-0971; $4 per person one-way).

(Your only alternative is a short but rough-and-tumble drive through Victoria's unattractive industrial district.) Simply hop aboard one of the little green-and-white mini-ferries zipping around the harbor. Yes, it is a touristy thing to do, but tourists are everywhere in Victoria, so if you can't beat 'em, why not join 'em?

Outdoor Kissing

❧❧❧❧ **THE BUTCHART GARDENS, Victoria** You really can't kiss here—it's just too crowded. But if you want a preview of what heaven looks like, tour these elysian, astonishing gardens. Each flower seems to have been hand-stroked to full bloom, the hedges could have been trimmed with a scalpel, and the sinuous pathways must have been carved from the earth by artisans who knew how to create a model Eden. All 50 acres are sublime. Especially wonderful are the rose, Japanese, and Italian gardens. Before descending into the sunken garden, once the site of a limestone quarry, stop a moment to take in the incredible panorama of dazzling flowers and sculpted bushes below. Most summer evenings you can enjoy colorful illuminations of the gardens and Ross Fountain. And Christmastime at the gardens will make you believe in Santa Claus again. So ignore the crowds, concentrate on the flowers, breathe in the perfume of fresh blossoms all around, and hold hands tightly. **800 Benvenuto Avenue; (250) 652-4422; $15.50 per adult; call for seasonal hours.** *Heading north on West Saanich Road (Highway 17A), turn west onto Benvenuto Avenue and follow the signs to the gardens.*

Romantic Note: If you happen to visit around teatime, the **BUTCHART GARDENS DINING ROOM** (see High Tea Kissing) is worth a stop. You can also grab a quick bite at **THE BLUE POPPY RESTAURANT** (inexpensive), also located at the gardens. It may not be fancy, but it is the prettiest cafeteria we've ever seen, with cream-colored walls, a jungle full of plants, and skylights that allow sunshine to stream in.

❧❧❧❧ **MOUNT DOUGLAS PARK, Victoria** Although only minutes away from downtown Victoria, Mount Douglas Park is light-years away from tourists and city sounds. This 500-acre rain forest on the ocean's edge is surprisingly quiet and serene. A walk down one of the many beach trails brings you out to a winding stretch of shoreline. From here you can look out across island-dotted Haro Strait. Don't forget to bring a blanket and picnic provisions so you can spend a leisurely afternoon here without interruption. **Free admission.** *From Highway 17, eight kilometers (five miles) north of downtown Victoria, exit east onto Cordova Bay Road. Follow this road south to the park.*

❧❧❧ **VICTORIAN GARDEN TOURS, Victoria** Sure, Butchart Gardens is spectacular, but if you want to see, smell, and savor some of Victoria's hidden gems without swarms of people, this is your tour. From herb farms to English gardens, Victorian Garden Tours caters to the preferences of its guests. The proprietor, a garden aficionado, knows Victoria's garden community like the back of her hand and, with advanced notice, can design trips to private and public gardens. On our trip, we visited a wonderful 100-year-old rhododendron garden at a private residence. The outing was more exploratory than educational and, best of all, only the birds and flowers kept us company. We finished with a lovely English tea followed by flowery talk. Groups are small, transportation is provided, and the schedule's relaxed, so sit back and smell the flowers together. **(250) 380-2797; tours start at $29 per person; reservations required.**

❦❦ **WHALE WATCHING, Victoria** Catching a glimpse of an orca in its natural habitat is truly an unforgettable experience. With Seacoast Expeditions, you can cruise around Victoria's coastal waters in search of marine wildlife and beautiful scenery. Whale-watching trips depart daily from **OCEAN POINTE RESORT HOTEL AND SPA** (see Hotel/Bed and Breakfast Kissing) on the Inner Harbour and explore 30 to 50 miles of orca territory. Trips last about three hours and accommodate up to 12 passengers, plus a driver and a university-trained naturalist. In addition, each 23-foot Zodiac boat comes equipped with a hydrophone for listening to whale vocalizations. Life suits are provided for your safety (and for warmth), but be prepared to get wet anyway.

June and July are the most likely times to spot orcas, but other wildlife can be seen anytime. Look for porpoises, minke whales, sea lions, harbor seals, bald eagles, and other marine birds. If you have your heart set on seeing an orca, an additional $10 (per person) will reserve a pager that will alert you when a whale sighting can be guaranteed. **Seacoast Expeditions, 45 Songhees Road, on the boardwalk level of Ocean Pointe Resort Hotel and Spa; (250) 383-2254, (800) 386-1525; $79 for a three-hour trip; reservations recommended; tours daily April–October.**

Sidney

Restaurant Kissing

❦❦❦ **DEEP COVE CHALET, Sidney** This secluded restaurant overlooking Saanich Inlet is quintessentially French and enticingly romantic. A good 30-minute drive north from Victoria, the enchanting building is set on manicured lawns dotted with trees and enclosed by low brick walls. Inside, tables draped in white linens stand in stark contrast to dark wood columns, and large picture windows afford stunning views of the inlet. Everything is gracious and elegant, with a congenial, homey feeling.

Prices are high, but every dish is beautifully presented and prepared with the greatest skill. Choice entrées include flavorful lobster bisque, savory crêpes with mushrooms in a smooth beurre blanc sauce, an airy yet rich cheese soufflé, and perhaps the best escargot in puffed pastry to be found anywhere. Meats and fish are always perfectly prepared, and the sauces are light but distinctive. **11190**

Chalet Road; (250) 656-3541; expensive to very expensive; lunch and dinner Tuesday–Sunday.

Romantic Warning: Lunchtime at the Deep Cove Chalet is often plagued by swarms of tourists, who seem to arrive by the busload. Dinner may be your best option when planning a romantic interlude.

❀❀ **DUNSMUIR LODGE AND RESTAURANT, Sidney** Perched on a mountainside with 180-degree views of Sidney, the Gulf Islands, and Vancouver's mountain ranges, this restaurant certainly deserves a Best Scenery award. The bad news is that Dunsmuir Lodge is first and foremost a conference center, and it looks like one. Built to accommodate hundreds, the large dining room is decorated with Japanese-style lamps, a selection of art, and a massive fieldstone fireplace, all set against light pink walls. Views require some neck stretching, but are still spectacular. They're even better in the upstairs lounge, which serves casual dinners in summertime.

As for food, the restaurant attracts top talents from Victoria's major hotels and offers reasonably priced à la carte and prix fixe dinners. With a concentration on Northwest cuisine, the kitchen delivers such specialties as shiitake-crusted sturgeon, seared venison, and Pacific salmon fillet with baked Swiss cheese polenta. **1515 McTavish Road; (250) 656-3166, (800) 255-4055; web.uvic.ca/~dunsmuir; moderate to expensive; lunch and dinner daily.**

Romantic Warning: We recommend coming here for dinner; the lunchtime buffet often brings in busloads of tourists.

Romantic Note: The 45 plain-looking rooms here are geared to conventioneers. However, the lodge is trying to attract guests during the off-season (mainly summer) and offers some impressive and reasonably priced romance packages. Amenities are few, but the food is good and the hiking, in 100 acres of forest park, is excellent.

❀❀❀ **THE LATCH COUNTRY INN, Sidney** Tucked away in a residential area, this imposing timber lodge was originally built in the 1920s as a summer residence for one of British Columbia's lieutenant governors. Today it's a lovely, flower-trimmed country inn where Euro-Pacific-style cuisine is served in two handsomely appointed dining rooms. Soft lighting and candles on each table enhance the burgundy accents and light up the polished native woods embellishing the walls. Shelves of antique books in one dining room and a gas fireplace in the other add to the warm ambience. During summer, casual patio seating overlooking the neighboring marina is set up to accommodate guests who prefer the outdoors. Good service and fine meals make the Latch a welcome addition to Sidney's dining scene. **2328 Harbour Road; (250) 656-6622; www.leaphere.com/latch/thelatchcountryinn; moderate to expensive; dinner Wednesday–Monday; closed January.**

Romantic Option: Five handsome guest rooms are available on the second floor of the inn (inexpensive to very expensive). The dark wood paneling continues upstairs, and each room features rich color schemes; private baths, down comforters, telephones, and TVs are additional amenities. Ask about the inn's "Romantic Gourmet" packages, which include a three-course dinner and continental breakfast with an overnight stay.

Brentwood Bay

Hotel/Bed and Breakfast Kissing

❤❤ **THE BOATHOUSE BED AND BREAKFAST, Brentwood Bay** Want to add a rustic touch to your romance? This secluded beach cottage poised on the waters of Brentwood Bay will do the trick. Just pack lightly, because a long flight of stairs is before you. Once you reach the rust-red hideaway, lounge the day away on the covered porch, sunbathe on the private dock, or take the dinghy out for a row. Even on a gray day the light blue and white interior livens things up, along with a sailboat quilt, fresh flowers, and lots of windows. A small kitchen and tiny library room add to the charm. Cuddling up at night comes naturally here, since the cottage lacks a fireplace.

Although the Boathouse is cute, don't expect four-star facilities. You'll have to sleep on a sofa hide-a-bed, and then there's the issue of the bathroom: 17 steps are between you and the loo. Thankfully, this is not your average outhouse. Resembling a sauna with wood panels, the cozy quarters come equipped with a glass-enclosed shower, toilet, and old-fashioned water basin with pitcher (notice we didn't say sink and faucet).

Respecting guests' desire to be alone, the proprietors deliver a breakfast basket in the early evening and then leave you be. If you can endure the uphill trot to the toilet and sofa bed sleeping, this cottage can't be beat for charm, coziness, and cleanliness. **746 Sea Drive; (250) 652-9370; www.pacificcoast.net/~boathouse; expensive; call for seasonal closures.**

Romantic Suggestion: Turn that dinghy into your own little love boat. Pack a picnic and row to a nearby beach where your only company may be a curious seal, otter, or bald eagle. Or row to Butchart Gardens and enjoy the day there (only a ten-minute row).

Metchosin

Metchosin is located roughly midway between the bustling city of Victoria and the rural town of Sooke. Travelers passing through experience the merging of these two distinct worlds, as residential neighborhoods begin to thin out along Metchosin's scenic coastline.

Hotel/Bed and Breakfast Kissing

❤❤❤ **SEASIDE BED AND BREAKFAST, Metchosin** A potential deterrent to staying at this contemporary seaside estate is that you might not want to leave:

The setting is simply spectacular. A rocky shore with lapping waves frames the front of the Mediterranean-style stucco home; in the distance the snowcapped Olympic Mountains are visible across the sparkling blue waters of the strait. And it's all waiting just 20 minutes from downtown Victoria.

The three suites here feature private entrances, eclectic artwork, and terry-cloth robes. Two three-room suites are situated in the main house. One features a living room surrounded by windows, a sliding glass door that opens to a private tiled patio, and skylights that frame the heavens. The other has a bedroom overlooking the beach and ocean. If it's privacy you seek, wind your way up the outdoor wooden stairs to the one-bedroom penthouse apartment in a separate building. This suite, which overlooks the entire gorgeous property, has its own deck, a kitchen equipped for light cooking, rattan furniture, and a color TV. Whichever suite you choose, rest assured that all three offer a prime atmosphere for relaxation. The furnishings are comfortable though simple (some pieces are outdated), but all the proper amenities are seen to with great care.

The two highlights of this property are the 50-foot-long seaside swimming pool (heated to 85 degrees) edged by natural rock and carved cement, and the oceanside hot tub. Each morning the amiable innkeeper serves a full breakfast in the dining room of the main house or out on the patio when weather permits. **3807 Duke Road; (250) 478-1446; expensive; minimum-stay requirement.**

Outdoor Kissing

❦❦❦ THE ITALIAN GARDENS AT ROYAL ROADS UNIVERSITY, Metchosin Who would have thought that a university campus would be a good place to kiss? Royal Roads University not only has a prime kissing spot, but it has a castle to go along with it. Hatley Castle, otherwise known as the administration building, is the centerpiece of the campus, with its ivy-covered stone facade. (Tours of the castle are conducted daily for $2 per person.) Directly beside the castle are the incredible Italian Gardens, which hearken back to an era when gardens were essential elements for romance.

A surrounding stone wall, which keeps the gardens partially hidden, is open near the west end of the castle to allow entry for visitors. Inside, a brick pathway traces the perimeter of the upper level. Columned trellises with flowers and gnarled branches creeping through the latticework create a shady shelter overhead. Continue along the path into the sunshine and into the brilliant colors of spring. Crumbling statues seem completely at home in this wonderland of lilacs, foxgloves, poppies, and rhododendrons. Descend the steps to the second level, which has larger vegetation and more open lawn space than the previous level. Here, a few benches strategically placed beneath the trees provide excellent sites for embraces. The gardens are fairly secluded, especially during summer, but don't be surprised if you happen upon one of the friendly peacocks that roam the campus. **2005 Sooke Road (Highway 14);**

(250) 391-2511; free admission; parking fee. *Enter the campus at Royal Roads University through the main gate on Sooke Road. Keep left on the main road and you will see Hatley Castle near the center of campus. The Italian Gardens are located directly beside the castle.*

Sooke

The undeveloped and reasonably undiscovered town of Sooke lies about 30 kilometers (20 miles) west of Victoria. Starting here and continuing for another 65 kilometers (40 miles) north to the town of Port Renfrew, this area has not yet been claimed by civilization, which translates into plenty of wide-open spaces for you and yours. Miles of rugged forested terrain, outstanding views of the Olympics across the Strait of Juan de Fuca, rocky isolated beaches, and notable accommodations present many options for enamored travelers seeking solitude and Canadian Southwest beauty. After you've wrapped up all the obligatory tourist requirements in Victoria, be sure to include extra time for this remarkable stretch of coastline and countryside.

Hotel/Bed and Breakfast Kissing

☙☙❧ **COOPER'S COVE GUESTHOUSE, Sooke** Kissin' and cookin' are two essential ingredients for romance. Such a combo comes together at this waterfront bed and breakfast where one of the innkeepers is a professional chef. You'll not only get first-class food served in a comfortable home, but perhaps some cooking lessons as well. (The kissin' part is left up to you two.)

While food is at the forefront here, the romance factor could use a bit more zest. It seems the proprietors realize this and, at press time, plans were being finalized for a new room with a fireplace and a Jacuzzi tub à deux on the private deck. We find this prospect quite promising considering the improvements already made throughout the house and garden. For the time being, this contemporary West Coast–style home provides three comfortable, simply decorated, sun-filled rooms with waterfront views. The Fireside Room, complete with a queen-size sleigh bed, en suite bath, fireplace, and private balcony, is our romantic favorite. Below the house, a lovely, glass-enclosed deck adorned with potted palms holds—but doesn't hide—the hot tub. Colorful flower, herb, and vegetable gardens spill over the terraced gardens to the harbor below.

Homemade truffles and sherry greet guests upon arrival, and in the morning a buffet breakfast is prepared by the proprietor/chef. Enjoy smoked salmon and Swiss chard omelets, strawberry crêpes touched with peach liqueur, or waffles topped with an orange-walnut sauce at the windowside table for two.

Cost ratings for British Columbia listings are in Canadian funds. American travelers should check the exchange rate or ask an innkeeper to figure out the cost in U.S. dollars.

5301 Sooke Road; (250) 642-5727; www.sookenet.com/coopers; moderate to expensive; minimum-stay requirement on weekends.

Romantic Note: The proprietor/chef is expanding the kitchen in order to offer cooking classes for guests. Following an introductory walk through the herb and vegetable gardens, you'll learn how to make delectable delights in the kitchen. Perhaps afterward you'll be inspired to whip up your own recipe for romance.

💋 **FOSSIL BAY RESORT, Sooke** Six identical cottages, perched side by side on a rocky cliff bordering the Strait of Juan de Fuca, make up Fossil Bay Resort. Each unit offers a king-size bed, wood-burning brick fireplace, terra-cotta-tiled floors, a full kitchen, TV/VCR (along with satellite TV for an extra charge), an unobstructed view of the glistening water, and a partially covered outdoor patio with a hot tub for two. The rooms are too stark to be considered intimate, but the views and the Jacuzzi tubs help compensate for this shortcoming. **1603 West Coast Road (Highway 14); (250) 646-2073; www.fossilbay.com; very expensive; minimum-stay requirement.**

Romantic Warning: Coffee and tea are the only breakfast fixings provided with your stay, so be sure to stop at the grocery store before coming—the nearest market is about 25 kilometers (16 miles) away.

💋💋 **FRENCH BEACH RETREATS, Sooke** What's your pleasure—the Ocean Treehouse, where you can enjoy a cozy liaison in the woods, or the Retreat, an 1,800-square-foot oceanfront cedar home available for your exclusive use? Both reside on three acres of old-growth woods with trails leading to rocky, secluded bluffs.

The octagonal Treehouse is tiny, with windows all around, hardwood floors, a mishmash of furnishings, and Turkish throw rugs. A queen-size bed covered with a sumptuous down comforter is the room's centerpiece, and bookshelves crammed with knickknacks, an old stereo, TV/VCR, and books line the walls. A bowl of fruit, wine, and other goodies greet you upon arrival, and a continental breakfast awaits in the small refrigerator so you can wake at your leisure and encounter only each other.

The Retreat is a steal when shared by several couples (it can accommodate up to eight guests) but is rather pricey for just one couple. Like a vacation rental with all the comforts of home, this contemporary coastal property features a full kitchen furnished with all the necessary utensils and initial breakfast fixings, two bedrooms, a sleeping loft, queen-size beds with down comforters, double-sided wood-burning fireplace, and two bathrooms (one with a Jacuzzi tub for two). Furnishings are slightly worn and outdated, but the views are timelessly beautiful. **983 Seaside Drive; (250) 646-2154; expensive to unbelievably expensive; minimum-stay requirement.**

Romantic Warning: Children are welcome at the Retreat, which is a potential romantic deterrent if you've booked the Treehouse for peaceful seclusion.

Romantic Note: The ownership at French Beach Retreats has recently changed; this review is based on a visit prior to the changeover.

❧ ❧ ❧ ❧ **HARTMANN HOUSE BED AND BREAKFAST, Sooke** Sooke is full of delightful surprises, including this wonderful bed and breakfast. At first we were skeptical of the location along Highway 14, but once we opened the gate, walked uphill through a glorious front yard filled with flower gardens, and came upon an English country cottage tucked well away from the road, we knew we had found something special.

Handcrafted cedar furnishings abound throughout the cottage and gardens, and attention has been paid to every detail. A massive Colonial-style fireplace warms the guest living room, where, on cooler days (which aren't unusual around here), you can enjoy complimentary afternoon wine and cheese while cuddling on softly padded wicker furniture. In warmer weather, relax in the tranquil garden on more wicker chairs or on the cedar swing built for two. The foliage is lush enough to create semiprivate sitting areas, a romantic bonus.

The highlight here is the Honeymoon Suite, a self-contained cottage that was literally built around a four-poster "barley twist" king-size canopied bed. Handcarved from western red cedar, this work of art inspires superlatives: It is one of the nicest, largest, and most romantic beds we've ever seen. From this comfortable vantage point, you can look through the two-way fireplace to an oversize whirlpool tub encircled by emerald green tile. Chinese wool carpet, black-and-white photographs, chintz fabric, and gorgeous woodwork lend elegance to this open and light-filled suite. When you finally emerge from underneath the feather duvet, you'll find breakfast awaits in the private butler's pantry. Open the outside doors, let the garden greet you, then crawl back into that wonderful bed and enjoy your meal.

While the Honeymoon Suite is sublime, the two plush guest rooms in the house are extremely nice. Both have fluffy feather comforters, lace curtains, hardwood floors, and all the comforts you could want. The Bay Window Room feels light and airy, with white wicker furniture, white and pale blue linens on the king-size bed, a private bath, and French doors leading into the garden. The smaller Garden Room offers a four-poster queen-size pineapple bed with a lace canopy and floral linens. Soft lighting in this room may make reading difficult, but kissing shouldn't be a problem. The only drawback is that the bath is across the hall; thankfully, terry-cloth robes are provided.

Sunrise summons a full gourmet breakfast, served at a table for four adjacent to the open kitchen where your gracious hosts work their magic. Spiced rhubarb parfait topped with mint, shrimp omelet with tomatoes and feta cheese, and waffles with strawberry maple syrup and whipped cream are just a few examples of the delectable entrées that may grace your plates. And what could be more romantic than heart-shaped blueberry bran muffins? **5262 Sooke Road (Highway 14); (250) 642-3761; www.amazinggetaways.com/hhinn; moderate to very expensive; minimum-stay requirement.**

❀❀❀ **LIGHT HOUSE RETREAT, Sooke** Call it garage-sale chic. Call it postmodern. Call it eclectic. Whatever you dub the decor at this retreat, there is one description that fits uniformly: It's unique, and, for the right couple, it can be very romantic. Owned by a former photojournalist, the multilevel, multidimensional concrete home feels like an art gallery, with interesting art set off by tall white walls. Look around and you'll see African masks and rugs, Bedouin veils, a whale bone, Chinese screens, and plenty of bold, colorful, sometimes abstract, works by Northwest artists. Much of the furniture was gathered from garage sales, resulting in a mix-and-match motif with a whimsical, worn-out touch.

Ring the bell before you descend the steep stairway to the home. Privacy is highly respected here. Of the four rooms, our favorite is the Aviary Tower, perched at the top of the home. Use your imagination, and you can envision this glass-enclosed room as the top section of a lighthouse with a huge wraparound deck. Open and light, the room speaks simplicity with a sky blue futon, Danish-style furnishings, bamboo curtains, and Japanese floral print accents. At night, moonlight bathes the room as you bathe in the Jacuzzi tub for two. Another option is the Keeper's Cottage, set below the main home. The eclectic decor, private deck, claw-foot tub, fireplace, kitchen, and upstairs sleeping loft make this another ideal, and perhaps more private, hideaway. As for the two other rooms in the main house, opt for the smaller Beacon's Reach, complete with a queen-size bed, a Jacuzzi tub for two surrounded by mosaics, and a double shower.

Leaning toward a leisurely style of breakfast service, the proprietor sets out baked goods made with organic flours and local fruits. Whenever you're ready, enjoy your breakfast in the high-ceilinged common room or partake on the deck. Afterward, hang around in a hammock, stroll around the yard (which is a work in progress), or journey down the steep pathway to where the waters of Muir Creek meet the Strait of Juan de Fuca. **107 West Coast Road; (250) 646-2345, (888) 805-4448; www.sookenet.com/lighthouse; expensive; minimum-stay requirement seasonally.**

❀❀ **MARGISON GUEST HOUSE, Sooke** One guest room and a small cottage are available for your consideration at this bed and breakfast in the center of Sooke. The cottage, hidden from the main house by a tennis court and a tall laurel hedge, offers the utmost in privacy, but not much space. Don't get stuck in the bedroom, which is literally the size of the queen-size bed. Despite the squeeze, we found the cottage quite adorable (and affordable), although a bit dated in decor. Breakfast awaits in the refrigerator and may include home-made scones or muffins, fresh fruit, bacon, and eggs (compliments of the hens next door in the chicken coop).

The room inside the main home features Victorian decor with a four-poster bed and a mishmash of throw rugs. Legal types will find lots of engaging but unromantic reading material here: An outstanding collection of law books dating from the early 1800s lines the walls. The private bath offers an extra-long soaking tub. This room, located between the front door and the private kitchen area, could be noisy on nights when the Margison House is open for dinner (see the Romantic Note below). **6605 Sooke Road; (250) 642-3620; moderate to expensive; call for seasonal closures.**

Romantic Note: Four-course, West Coast–cuisine dinners are served in Margison Guest House's lovely restaurant Thursdays through Saturdays during the summer (expensive). Guests have a choice between two entrées, one of which is usually seafood. Dining here is worth a try, as well as a few kisses.

❤❤❣ MARKHAM HOUSE BED AND BREAKFAST, Sooke

If you'd like to retreat to the country after a busy day of sightseeing in Victoria, Markham House is the place for you. This pale yellow Tudor home is tucked into the trees on a ten-acre estate on the outskirts of Sooke. From the moment you enter the circular driveway to the time you depart, you'll be surrounded by abundant gardens and woodlands. The sprawling yard has been landscaped with flowers, greenery, a lovely pond, and even a par-three golf hole. Above the home, winding trails await exploration and will reward your effort with views of Sooke Harbor.

Afternoon tea is served upon your arrival. Relax by the fireplace in the parlor amid the innkeepers' eclectic combination of Scottish and Asian antiques, or in warm weather exit through the French doors and repose on the veranda and admire the hanging baskets of flowers. A small pond, where rainbow trout occasionally ripple the water, and a lovely iris garden are in full view. You can revisit this scene in the morning while enjoying a full breakfast on the veranda or in the nearby breakfast room.

Three guest rooms occupy the second floor of the main house. Two are a bit on the small side, but each offers terry-cloth robes, feather beds covered with pretty duvets, and views of the surrounding gardens. The eclectic mix of antique furnishings continues in both rooms, and the private bathrooms are rather ordinary (one is detached); however, chocolates and turndown service are much-appreciated touches. A third room, the newly refurbished Garden Room, is the room for romance (at least in the main house). Overlooking the pond, this large room is done in shades of olive green with floral accents. Chandeliers and matching wall sconces provide much of the light. Cuddle by the gas fireplace, savor breakfast in the sitting area, or soak in the Jacuzzi tub. A sprinkling of antiques, from an 18th-century Chinese chest to a mirrored Scottish armoire, add to the elegance.

From the main house, follow a trail to the Honeysuckle Cottage. Trees excavated from the property now form the bark-covered foundation of this cedar-shingled home. Inside, the secluded cabin is graced with hardwood floors, Oriental throw rugs, a queen-size feather bed, and an ingenious makeshift kitchenette hidden away in a Belgian pine armoire. An old-fashioned woodstove stands in the corner, while the open-beamed ceiling slopes heavenward. The decor is a bit too mismatched for our tastes, but such glorious privacy more than makes up for it. Bathing suits are optional in your own private hot tub, located just steps away on the wooden deck. In the morning, guests at the Honeysuckle Cottage can join the others for breakfast in the main house or opt for a basket of goodies to be delivered to their door. **1853 Connie Road; (250) 642-7542, (888) 256-6888; www.sookenet.com/markham; inexpensive to moderate.**

❀❀ **OCEAN WILDERNESS INN AND SPA RETREAT, Sooke** An interesting blend of homey comforts, spa amenities, and touches of elegance makes Ocean Wilderness an intriguing getaway. Surrounded by old-growth forest and set on an ocean bluff, the log structure has a lovely tree-framed view of the water and mountains. At one edge of the property, a Japanese gazebo holds a seawater-filled hot tub that overlooks the ocean through the trees. Private soaking times can be reserved, but before you get wet, be sure to hike down to the wonderful beachfront, where tidal pools and breathtaking views will greet you. If heavy-duty relaxation is in order, journey to the small spa in the main home, where massages, herbal wraps, seaweed wraps, and mud baths await. (The mud and seaweed are supplied compliments of the local waters.)

The log cabin's dining room and reception area are romantically rustic. The dark-stained log walls create a cozy, somewhat dark atmosphere, yet settings at the long breakfast table are extremely elegant, with fine china, white linens, silver, and crystal. The nine guest rooms, located in a wood-framed wing that was added to the original log cabin, hold an eclectic mix of antiques, plush furnishings, and handmade canopied beds. Some of the frilly touches and embellished fabrics are a bit much, but you can't go wrong with the second-floor rooms, which have two-person soaking tubs, private entrances, and large, private, glass-enclosed sundecks that share in the scenery.

Wake-up coffee is delivered to your room on a silver tray with fresh flowers in the early morning. A full country breakfast can also be delivered to your door if you request it the night before. Otherwise, breakfast is served next to the crackling fire in the log-cabin section of the home. **109 West Coast Road (Highway 14); (250) 646-2116, (800) 323-2116; www.sookenet.com/ocean; inexpensive to very expensive.**

❀❀❀ **POINT-NO-POINT RESORT, Sooke** Set on one mile of waterfront and 40 acres of untamed wilderness, Point-No-Point has been welcoming travelers since the early 1950s. It all started with just a couple of cabins (still standing and in pretty good condition, considering their age), but today there are 22 units available. Furnishings in some cabins are a little too dowdy for romantic-minded travelers, but each cabin does have a fireplace, full kitchen, and private bathroom. Luckily, none have TVs, phones, or radios, so you should have no outside distractions—except for the ocean view.

Most suited for a lovers' getaway are the new Blue Jay and Otter Rooms, two suites that form a duplex. Nonetheless, each has a full kitchen, wood-burning fireplace, living room, 18-foot-high windows with water views, and a queen-size bed tucked into a cozy sleeping loft. Water amenities abound, including a marble soaking tub and two-person shower in the bathroom. However, the real romantic draw is the private hot tub on the deck—now *this* is a place to kiss. (Several other private cabins have hot tubs as well.)

Trails with foliage-covered stone archways lead down to a nearby inlet and a gorgeous sandy beach—another fantastic kissing spot. The pure, rugged beauty of Point-No-Point seems eons away from civilization, and the isolation of this place can spell romance. **1505 West Coast Road (Highway 14); (250) 646-2020; inexpensive to very expensive; minimum-stay requirement on weekends and seasonally.**

Romantic Note: Food is not included with your stay, so bring your own breakfast provisions. Lunches, afternoon tea, and Northwest-cuisine dinners (moderate) are served in the small dining room adjacent to where you check in. The water and mountain views are simply stupendous, and the sunny dining room is charming. Binoculars are placed at every table in case an eagle soars overhead or a whale happens to swim by in the distant surf. On warm days you can enjoy your meal and the great outdoors on the casual deck.

❀❀❀❀ **RICHVIEW HOUSE, Sooke** Steam bath or deep soaking tub? That's the most difficult choice you'll face when selecting a room at this cliffside bed and breakfast. All three rooms offer panoramic views of the Strait of Juan de Fuca and are furnished with simple, handcrafted wood furniture reminiscent of Scandinavian design. All have queen-size beds, cozy fireplaces, and private entrances. It's the bathrooms that differ.

The downstairs bedroom is located just off the living room area. Double doors protect you from any noise in the living room, but unfortunately not from noise emanating from above. Inside the bathroom, a green marbled, two-headed shower doubles as a steam bath. Place a drop of essential oil in the steam spout, sit on the wooden stools, and inhale. It's downright therapeutic. If poaching is more your style, the two upper bedrooms offer deep tubs located on outdoor decks. Both of these rooms feature beach-stone and slate wood-burning fireplaces, skylights punctuating the slanted ceilings, and radiant-heat floors that give the rooms seductive warmth. Outside, the broad, grassy lawns are ideally suited for unobstructed views of the Olympics and the water, but lack any sort of secluded areas for private smooches. Just be prepared to kiss out in the open.

Romantics can arrange to have breakfast served in their room; otherwise, the sun-filled sitting room is a nice alternative. As the morning fog makes way for the sun, enjoy such treats as cantaloupe in a ginger-honey sauce, rhubarb-pecan muffins with peach-mango jam, caramelized sweet rolls, and cheese blintzes smothered with mixed berries.

Once the sun is out, enjoy a walk along **WHIFFIN SPIT**, which is a must for nature lovers, bird lovers, and lovers in general. Later on, you'll be pleased to find that the restaurant at SOOKE HARBOUR HOUSE (see Restaurant Kissing) is only moments away. **7031 Richview Drive; (250) 642-5520; www.islandnet.com/~rvh; expensive.**

❦❦❦❦ **SOOKE HARBOUR HOUSE, Sooke** It is no wonder that Sooke Harbour House has gained nationwide acclaim and earned an excellent reputation for both its inn and restaurant (see Restaurant Kissing). Travelers from all walks of life continue to be surprised and satisfied by the unique experience offered here, at the end of a quiet Sooke road. A fantastic water's-edge setting, subtle elegance, and Northwest charm make Sooke Harbour House an exceptional, but very expensive, getaway.

Recent remodeling added 13 fabulous new rooms to the existing 13. No detail has been overlooked in the regionally inspired suites, and the views of Sooke Bay, the Strait of Juan de Fuca, and the Olympic Mountains are captivating. Regardless of which you choose, you'll find yourselves in the lap of luxury. Each suite features a wood-burning fireplace, a separate sitting area, views of the water, a vaulted ceiling, beautiful furnishings, and a wet bar. Other amenities include local artwork, king- or queen-size beds, plush linens, balconies or patios, and oversize tubs or outdoor Jacuzzi/soaking tubs. Which room to choose? We had a hard time deciding, but the Thunderbird Room, a split-level, top-floor suite with a king-size bed, claw-foot tub, steam shower with a view, and soaker tub on the deck, is outstanding. The ground-level Seal Room also ranks high with the biggest double-headed steambath/shower we've ever seen, a private jetted tub on the terrace, and a gorgeous king-size bed. The Blue Heron Room, one of the original and most popular rooms, has the best view in the house and a large whirlpool tub beside a river-rock fireplace. Fresh cookies, a bowl of fruit, and port are set out in all rooms.

It will not be easy to leave your sumptuous accommodations. Thankfully, you can lounge around all morning—gourmet breakfasts are delivered to your door. Lunch, also included with your stay, is served in the celebrated dining room or, if you plan to spend the day exploring the region, you can request a picnic basket. **1528 Whiffen Spit Road; (250) 642-3421, (800) 889-9688; www.sookenet.com/sooke/shh; very expensive to unbelievably expensive (price includes breakfast and lunch); call for seasonal closures; recommended wedding site.**

❦❦❦◗ **SOOKE RIVER ESTUARY BED AND BREAKFAST, Sooke** The Harbourside Cottage, one of two options at this lovely romantic retreat, was designed around a two-person jetted tub, which sits majestically in the corner. At night, dim the lights, turn on the Vermont Castings stove, sit in the bubbles, and enjoy a glass of Sooke River Estuary wine while looking out onto the water. The cozy cottage sits on two acres of waterfront property, next to the main house but far enough away to guarantee a certain degree of privacy. Large windows and French doors fill the simply adorned room with light, while oak floors, oak window trim, and a floral-print duvet on the queen-size bed add warmth. Other amenities include a double-headed shower in the teal green bathroom, a CD player, small kitchen, washer and dryer, and a private deck with lounge chairs, barbecue, and a hummingbird feeder. A delicious made-to-order breakfast, served on Yorkshire Rose china, is delivered to your room at a prearranged hour. Sit back on the rattan chairs and start the day off with strawberry yogurt, specialty pancakes, and a smooch.

While the cottage is definitely our top pick for romance (and what sparked the high kiss-rating), the one guest room inside the home will do if the cottage is occupied. The Waterfront Suite, the top section of the West Coast contemporary home, is similar in decor to the cottage, except heavier on the pink floral tones and with a four-poster queen-size bed. The spacious but somewhat bland bathroom has every amenity you could want: an extra-long, window-enclosed whirlpool tub, a double-headed shower with window (at eye level, of course), and a dry sauna for two. The bathroom also doubles as the gateway to a semiprivate deck on the lawn. And like the guests in the cottage, you won't need to get up early for breakfast; it's brought to your room on a linen-covered rolling table at whatever time you desire. **2056 Glenidle Road; (250) 642-4655; www.sookenet.com/sookeriver; expensive.**

Romantic Note: With advance notice, the host can make a personalized wine label for any special occasion.

💋💋 WATER'S EDGE COTTAGE AND BED AND BREAKFAST, Sooke Skip

the guest room in the main house and go straight to the beach cottage at this bed and breakfast. While the bedroom is adequate (and slightly exotic, with a magnificent hand-carved ebony bed from Bali), it doesn't compare to the private cottage below. Walk through a small orchard of peach, apple, and kiwi trees to the restored blue and white, one-bedroom retreat 110 yards below. A wraparound deck overlooks the beach, which is easily accessible via your own private pathway. Hardwood floors, a full kitchen, Indonesian rattan furniture, a wood-burning fireplace, CD player, and a sunny sitting area make the interior a bright and comfortable place to kick up your heels and kiss. Enjoy the sounds of the water from the small bedroom, accented with simple Shaker-style furniture and a queen-size bed with down comforter. Elbow room isn't a problem in the bathroom: It's big enough to hold laundry facilities plus everything else.

Another romantic feature is a hot tub, which resides in the middle of the orchard. While it can be reserved and a wood fence provides limited privacy, we wish it were closer to the cottage. Oh well. Soaking among the fruit trees does have one advantage: You can reach up and pluck an apple from the 100-year-old apple tree. Some poached fruit for dessert, perhaps? **5641 Sooke Road; (250) 642-4864, (800) 307-7556; www.victoriabc.com/accom/ watersedge.html; inexpensive to expensive.**

Restaurant Kissing

❤❤ **THE GOOD LIFE BOOKSTORE CAFE, Sooke** The Good Life, a casual eatery and small bookstore in Sooke, has taken on a new life. When we visited, new owners were updating the menu, but not the decor. You'll find the same antique wooden tables in the two dining rooms, which are separated by etched glass windows. However, the dandelion-colored walls, large windows, and light jazz mixed with candlelight dining lend an elegant touch. Kissing couples (or book lovers) may want to compare notes on the latest romance novel in one of two secluded tables bordering the bookshelves. We liked the one with the funky, high-backed velvet chairs the best.

The new and improved menu emphasizes Pacific Rim cuisine with some Latin flavors thrown in by the Brazilian chef. Favorites include phyllo-wrapped stuffed chicken served with a berry-ginger reduction, delicious curried seafood wraps, and baked salmon adorned with a light strawberry velouté sauce. A bounty of berry dishes fills the dessert menu, including a somewhat satisfactory blackberry-rhubarb crumble. **2113 Otter Point Road; (250) 642-6821; moderate; lunch and dinner daily.**

❤❤❤❤ **SOOKE HARBOUR HOUSE, Sooke** Prepare yourselves for a memorable experience—Sooke Harbour House has a stellar reputation. The menu reads like an exotic novel, and every dish comes out looking glamorous, sprinkled with colorful, edible blossoms and leaves. With a menu that changes nightly, it's exciting to see what the chefs will come up with next. The ingredients are undoubtedly the freshest around; an herb garden supplies the seasonings, and an outdoor tank houses the shellfish. Speaking of which, you'll find some seafood not seen on many menus: wild gooseneck barnacles, sea cucumbers, and sea lettuce. If you are up for trying new things, this is the place to start. And, if your love of adventure is strong, have the chef decide the menu for you. That's what we did, and we were treated to a variety of Northwest foods that ranged from good (pan-seared idiot fish with a carrot reduction) to fabulous (halibut in a beet-root coulis accented with an asparagus terrine and eggplant caviar). The evening ended with a rhubarb consommé topped with salmonberry ice cream.

The dining room is located on the main floor of the newly expanded two-story country inn (see Hotel/Bed and Breakfast Kissing), where a lovely fireplace, accented by duck decoys, casts a warm glow over the room. Northwest art covers the walls, including everything from totemic carvings to decorated crab shells. Each table is dressed in white linen and adorned with fresh flowers and a single tapered candle. Try requesting a window seat so you can also partake

---

Cost ratings for British Columbia listings are in Canadian funds. American travelers should check the exchange rate or ask an innkeeper to figure out the cost in U.S. dollars.

---

of wonderful views of the strait and the surrounding gardens. Just be sure to note what type of flowers caress the exterior walls of the dining room. (Answer: passionflowers, of course.) **1528 Whiffen Spit Road; (250) 642-3421; www.sookenet.com/shh; very expensive to unbelievably expensive; dinner daily (breakfast and lunch available for guests only); call for seasonal closures.**

Outdoor Kissing

❀❀❀❀ **CHINA BEACH AND FRENCH BEACH, Sooke** These two beaches are separated by a few miles, but they share similar settings and a rugged character. Ramble through young, replanted forests, visit formidable groves of ancient trees, or explore pebbled beaches pocked by tidal pools. Surefootedness is a prerequisite for the hike to China Beach, because you will occasionally have to make your way over projecting headlands of rocky coast and woods. At either location, you can bask on the shore in solitary glory while being lulled by the water's music. Beautiful views are abundant along this relatively undiscovered coastline, about an hour's drive from bustling Victoria. *Follow Highway 14 past Sooke. Sixteen kilometers (ten miles) down the road is a sign for French Beach. Reach French Beach via a short tree-lined path that leads down to the shore. Farther along Highway 14, about two kilometers (one mile) past the town of River Jordan, look for the China Beach sign. China Beach is accessible via a 15-minute walk through a rain forest.*

Romantic Note: French Beach has a well-maintained 69-unit campground set in old-growth forest. It is one of the most picturesque sites on the entire island for setting up a tent for two. Call ahead to make camping reservations (800-689-9025).

❀❀ **EAST SOOKE REGIONAL PARK, Sooke** Whether you're planning a short morning jaunt or a rugged all-day hike, East Sooke Regional Park provides 3,500 acres of wilderness with phenomenal views. Follow one of the many trails that wind through beautiful beaches and pristine forest. Swimming is also recommended at these beaches if you dare to take the cool plunge. **Free admission.** *From Victoria, take the Old Island Highway (Highway 1A), which turns into Sooke Road (Highway 14). From Sooke Road, turn south onto Happy Valley Road and follow it to Rocky Point Road, which soon becomes East Sooke Road. Follow this road to the park's main entrance.*

❀❀❀❀ **WHALE WATCHING, Sooke** Sighting a whale is an exhilarating experience. The grace and agility of these aquatic giants is amazing. Resident and transient orcas circle the island and are clearly visible from most shores from June through September. Boat excursions are also available to take you out to greet them during known feeding times. No matter how you encounter these creatures, it will be a singular moment in your lives that you will always treasure. **Sooke Coastal Explorations, 6971 West Coast Road (Highway**

14); (250) 642-2343; www.sookenet.com/coast; $60 to $70 for adults; trips daily May–October.

Romantic Suggestion: For an additional charge, you can reserve a beeper that will page you when an orca sighting is reported. After you are notified, simply rush down to the nearby marina, zip up in a flotation suit, hop into the Zodiac, and you are guaranteed to catch a glimpse of the magnificent creatures.

Port Renfrew

Outdoor Kissing

❤❤❤❤ BOTANICAL BEACH, Port Renfrew Tide pools full of sea urchins, crabs, starfish, chitons, coralline sea algae, and other saltwater animals thrive along this rock-clad beach. At low tide the ocean world opens up for your viewing and entertainment. It is an adventure worth sharing, but please tread lightly and leave the creatures alone; this wonderland is an integral part of nature and should stay that way. Be sure to wear sturdy shoes; the beach pathway can be muddy, and walking over the rock formations on the beach can prove tricky. *Sixty-five kilometers (40 miles) north of Sooke, just outside Port Renfrew. Driving along the scenic, winding, and narrow road between these two towns takes about one and a half hours.*

Malahat

Hotel/Bed and Breakfast Kissing

❤❤❤❤ THE AERIE RESORT, Malahat In terms of grandeur and extravagance, nothing in the Pacific Northwest or the Canadian Southwest quite compares to The Aerie. This grandiose, sparkling white Mediterranean-style villa with clinical green accents looks as if it belongs in Beverly Hills or Los Angeles. The only reminders that you are still in the great Northwest are the fresh mountain air and serene setting on a forested hillside. The 25-minute drive from Victoria is beautiful, but some highfalutin guests choose to helicopter in (the resort has a landing pad specifically for this purpose). The Aerie itself offers absolutely stunning views of the distant Olympic Mountains, tree-covered islands, and a peaceful fjord below—and sunsets are unforgettable.

While there's no doubt you'll love the view, reactions to the interior are less predictable. From the moment you arrive at the sprawling, multiterraced resort, you'll either love the decor or hate it. Those in the former category adore the opulent, Austrian-influenced designs. They love getting lost in the overstuffed sofas, admiring themselves in ornately carved mirrors, and falling into plush, four-poster beds. Those in the latter group dismiss the interior as nouveau riche Hollywood fluff with a confusion of styles, patterns, and 1980s pastels.

Whatever your opinion, one thing you can't argue about is choice. The 28 rooms and suites come in six styles, most offering sexy tubs for two, private decks with glorious views, and other sensuous appointments. No expense has been spared in outfitting the beds with ultra-thick down comforters and cotton-silk sheets.

At the top of the line are the eight lavish, multilevel Aerie Suites, each with a large hydro-massage tub framed by columns in the center of the room, a gas fireplace, a king-size four-poster canopied bed, and an extra-large deck. Unfortunately, some of the decks offer little privacy, and many have views of the tennis courts or parking lot in the foreground. (This may seem minor, but at these prices you have a right to be picky.) The new Residence Suites, which we recommend for those seeking a newer look and a lot of privacy, are separate from the main building. Inside these high-ceilinged and high-priced suites indulgences await, from a grand leather sleigh bed across from a large soaking tub to gas fireplaces and steam showers. All overlook a beautiful shallow pool as well as a poor excuse for a castle that was built across from the resort. (It's not affiliated with The Aerie.)

Standard rooms, located one floor below the main building's reception area, are not nearly as grand but still fall in the "very expensive" price category. Some have small balconies with incredible views, but they are right next to the balconies of neighboring rooms. Also, these rooms have red exit signs above the patio door (probably for safety reasons, but they detract from the ambience and state the obvious). Finally, we must mention that the faux marble touches (found in every bathroom and even on some furnishings) look too artificial and compromise the otherwise glamorous fantasy of staying at The Aerie.

A generous full breakfast, included with your stay, is served in the elegant dining room overlooking the inspiring mountain scenery. Dinners here are also a four-lip experience (see Restaurant Kissing). If you love opulent decor, you'll adore this place. If not, concentrate on the scenery and your sweetheart. **600 Ebadora Lane; (250) 743-7115; www.aerie.bc.ca; very expensive to unbelievably expensive; recommended wedding site.**

Romantic Note: A full-service spa is open for all of your pampering needs and offers some wonderful massage packages for two. The Aerie also boasts two hot tubs. We recommend the outdoor one with the view; the indoor one is stuck inside a dark, unappealing room. A beautiful glass-enclosed pool, equipped with water jets, is the perfect place for an evening dip.

Restaurant Kissing

❀❀❀❀ **THE AERIE RESORT, Malahat** Who would have thought that a wooded hillside in the middle of nowhere could harbor an extravagant resort? Well, The Aerie is nothing if not extravagant, and you are sure to enjoy a heart-stirring meal at this "castle in the mountains." Located on a Malahat mountainside, The Aerie's dining room offers a 180-degree view of the Olympic Mountains and the twinkling lights of Port Angeles across the Strait of Juan de Fuca. This awesome vista enhances an opulent, if somewhat dizzying, interior filled with glittering chandeliers, faux marble columns, a medley of artwork, high-backed upholstered chairs, perfectly pressed white table linens, and massive floral arrangements. Above you is a 14-karat gold-foiled ceiling. If you can't kiss here, it's only because you're too overwhelmed to pucker up.

French-inspired cuisine made with fresh West Coast ingredients is the kitchen's forte. Artfully presented dishes such as Caribbean lobster tail in a delectable herb crust and pheasant with juniper-port sauce are exceptional. We recommend the tasting market menu, which brings delightful and surprising dishes to the table such as stinging nettle and mussel soup and pan-seared stuffed pheasant. Try to save room for dessert: The Grand Marnier soufflé and chocolate nougat mousse are satisfying finales. **600 Ebadora Lane; (250) 743-7115; www.aerie.bc.ca; very expensive to unbelievably expensive; dinner daily.**

Romantic Note: There are no dress requirements here, but most guests save up to come to The Aerie for a special occasion. Attire can be relatively formal.

Shawnigan Lake

Hotel/Bed and Breakfast Kissing

❦❦❦ WHISTLESTOP SHAWNIGAN LAKESIDE BED AND BREAKFAST, Shawnigan Lake Book two train tickets to this delightful bed and breakfast that actually has its own train stop. Give the E&N Railway (which runs from Victoria to Courtenay) advance notice and they'll drop the two of you off at the Whistlestop. From there, you can walk up the hill to a large, lodge-like home made of planked cedar with forest green trim where five rooms await, all decorated in railroad themes. The Santa Fe is splashed with quasi-Southwest decor, while the Orient Express Room shimmers in Asian opulence, highlighting Chinese vases and a large gold fan framed over the brass queen-size bed. In the marbled, emerald green bath, a beautifully etched Chinese dragon brings the beveled mirror to life. Hop on the fast track for romance in the three-room TGV Suite (named after the French bullet train), which offers views into the courtyard garden. This suite features Raphael-inspired paintings, a king-size canopy bed swathed in German lace, a gas fireplace, and a double jetted tub, which generates its own kind of heat. Why the entire suite is floored with cold kitchen tile instead of carpet we'll never know. The remaining two rooms here are comfortable but less suitable for romance-minded couples.

In each room, decorative wallpaper and whimsical touches (like conductor's hats) are a feast for the eyes, if sometimes a bit too cute. Private decks and en suite standard baths are also included in your ticket.

The grassy grounds extend from the home, past the train tracks, to beautiful Shawnigan Lake. Play croquet on the lawn or volleyball on the beach, or row boats across the lake to a nearby waterfront restaurant. After a day of play, reserve the hot tub hidden in a private gazebo, which overlooks the lake.

Before breakfast, the proprietor delivers coffee and baked goods to a table outside your door. Once you're rolling, select items from a breakfast menu that even includes dessert and eat in the open kitchen area, which holds enough red counters, red tiles, and red chairs to keep everything rosy for romance. **1838 Baden Powell Road; (250) 743-4896; expensive to very expensive; recommended wedding site.**

Romantic Note: Call the Whistlestop for information on the E&N Railway. You can also arrive by floatplane and, of course, by car.

Restaurant Kissing

❤❤ **SUNFLOWER CAFE, Shawnigan Lake** Don't blink or else you might miss this cafe located in the one-stop-sign town of Shawnigan Lake. The one-room restaurant is hidden below the main road in a tiny yellow house. Inside there's space for only half a dozen tables, which ranks this restaurant high on the privacy scale. Be forewarned, though, that depending on the time of day, you might be surrounded by locals who congregate and chitchat within the purple and green walls of this family-owned favorite.

More funky than charming, the Sunflower could use some cultivation, such as removing the old fluorescent and track lighting. But at night, candlelight contributes to a cozier atmosphere. Service is small-town friendly, while the food is big-city sophisticated. The chef, formerly of the Four Seasons Hotel and The Aerie, whips up West Coast cuisine in the little kitchen below. Creamy tomato-basil soup with vodka, a salad with 17 varieties of greens, and seafood linguine in a Pernod cream sauce have been known to appear on the small, changing menu. **1753 Shawnigan–Mill Bay Road; (250) 743-3663; moderate to expensive; call for seasonal hours; reservations recommended.**

Cowichan Bay

Restaurant Kissing

❤❤ **THE MASTHEAD RESTAURANT, Cowichan Bay** With views of bobbing fishing vessels and the forested hills across the water, the Masthead is a picturesque spot to dine (if you can manage to find parking). Colorful flower boxes accent the weathered dockside building that houses the dining room. Inside, white linens, fresh flowers, and candlelight create a subtle romantic mood. Fresh fish, the kind that almost jumps from the boat onto your plate, is the specialty here. Succulent Fanny Bay oysters, steamed Dungeness crab, and wild British Columbia salmon are served with French flair and are remarkably good. **1705 Cowichan Bay Road; (250) 748-3714; moderate; dinner Tuesday–Sunday.**

Duncan

Duncan is known in these parts as the "City of Totems." Its 66 totem poles pepper the downtown area and stand out of place along the town's strip of industrialized freeway. Besides the handful of romantic accommodations described below, these totem poles are the only feature distinguishing Duncan from the other nondescript towns along the Trans-Canada Highway.

Hotel/Bed and Breakfast Kissing

❀❀❀ **GROVE HALL ESTATE, Duncan** Venerable oak trees usher you to the end of a long driveway, where a magnificent turn-of-the-century Tudor mansion awaits. The entire estate boasts 17 acres of gardens, sweeping lawns, and accessible lakefront. Once you've slipped your feet out of your shoes and into a pair of soft Indonesian silk slippers, you'll feel as if you've been transported to another place and time. Depending on your perspective, you may also feel like you've wandered into a museum. Intriguing antiques collected from Asia and the Middle East are tastefully and elegantly showcased throughout the mansion's luxurious interior, where deep red Oriental carpets grace gleaming pine floors.

Two exotic guest suites upstairs are thoroughly impressive. A huge, handcrafted 400-year-old Chinese wedding bed is the star of the spacious Singapore Room (our favorite), which is accented with stunning antiques and a view of the lake and gardens. If this picture-perfect escape has a flaw, it can only be the detached bathroom facilities. An extra sitting room and a private balcony provide even more space in the lovely Indonesia Suite, which showcases unique art pieces and batiks from that part of the world. Indonesian fabrics and prints in all of the rooms are unusual but add authenticity. For the most privacy, rent the self-contained cottage situated at one end of the property. If you have a penchant for the 1930s, you'll love it; otherwise, the furnishings and linens might feel somewhat dated.

In the evening, gourmet appetizers are served in the mansion's formal dining room, which offers views of the lake. Appropriately regal breakfasts of fresh fruit and juice, eggs, bacon, and pancakes are also served here in the morning. **6159 Lakes Road; (250) 746-6152; moderate to very expensive; no credit cards.**

❀❀◗ **NORTH HAVEN BED AND BREAKFAST, Duncan** The shortage of quality accommodations in the town of Duncan will leave your hearts aching. One exception is this turn-of-the-century heritage home, set on three and a half acres of landscaped countryside. Lovingly renovated, the white home is trimmed in blue and has a stone foundation. From the large wraparound porch, you can survey the property's gorgeous flower gardens, white gazebo, small rock-lined pond, and rose arbor.

The interior is just as impressive as the outside. Stunning drapes and Oriental rugs in the parlor complement the hardwood floors and antique Victorian furniture. In the library, you can cuddle in front of a fire, enjoy a breathtaking view of Mount Prevost, listen to soft music, or watch an old movie together.

All three guest rooms are immaculately kept and smell of freshly cut flowers. With plush carpeting, private bathrooms, and fluffy white robes in each room, comfort is assured. Each room has been tastefully decorated in subtle tones and furnished with polished antiques. A beautiful mahogany headboard crowns the queen-size bed in the Orchard Room. The Prevost Room features an impressive view of Mount Prevost and its private bathroom is appointed with a claw-foot tub; unfortunately, guests must sleep in two twin beds—not ideal for a romantic getaway. We were especially taken with the Garden Room, which has an antique cherry-wood canopy bed and a cozy window seat.

If in the morning you still desire privacy, the two of you can enjoy a breakfast of eggs Benedict, French toast, or blueberry pancakes outside on the front porch. Otherwise, enjoy a candlelit repast in the elegant dining room, under a brass chandelier and surrounded by fresh roses from the garden. **1747 Herd Road; (250) 746-4783, (800) 585-1822; www.seaside.net/northhaven; very expensive; recommended wedding site.**

❧❧ **SAHTLAM LODGE AND CABINS, Duncan** Do yourself (and your partner) a favor by calling for directions before you attempt to drive here. Don't rely on that old standby, "We'll pull over and ask for directions," because there ain't nobody out here to ask, folks! Once you're here, however, the solitude and lush surroundings will seduce you.

Sahtlam Lodge, which resembles a large, weathered log cabin, was originally built as a fishing and hunting retreat in the 1920s. It retains a rustic character, albeit with modern conveniences. *Sahtlam* is Salish for "a leafy place," and the definition fits. Located along the beautiful Cowichan River, the lodge and four accompanying cabins are hidden amid lofty trees and grassy meadows.

The main lodge doesn't have any rooms, but does house the **SAHTLAM LODGE RESTAURANT** (see Restaurant Kissing), itself worthy of a visit. Sleeping quarters are found in the cabins, with the most romantic being the Meadow Cabin, set next to a duck pond and overlooking the river. Its amenities include a wood-burning fireplace, a kitchenette, and a cedar-and-glass bedroom with a vaulted ceiling and river-facing windows. The other alternative is the Gatekeeper's Cottage, which is near the entrance but affords some fenced-in privacy along with an outdoor hot tub. The two other cabins are designed for larger groups (read: families with kids).

On the first morning you'll awake to find a complimentary basket filled with breakfast fixings. Read the enclosed recipe and plan on cooking, since breakfast is made "in-house" by you.

Romantic retreats abound, from the river's intermittently sandy beach to a hiking trail across the river. Once you pull yourselves across the river in a suspended handcart, you can walk for miles without seeing a soul. If things get too hot, inner-tube or swim in the lake-fed river. Come evening, cool down by strolling through the lighted arbor adjacent to the lodge. **5720 Riverbottom Road West; (250) 748-7738; www.islandnet.com/~sahtlam; expensive; minimum-stay requirement on weekends.**

Restaurant Kissing

❀❀❀ **INGLENOOK RESTAURANT, Duncan** Set just off the main highway and surrounded by flower gardens, this two-story Tudor home holds one of the nicer restaurants on Vancouver Island. Reservations are highly recommended; walk-ins are difficult to accommodate due to nonstop crowds. Rustic yet elegant, the three upstairs dining rooms feature knotty pine walls and an eclectic mixture of watercolors, modern artwork, and vintage antiques. The well-spaced tables are accented by white linens and surrounded by beautifully embroidered chairs. Classical music in the background sets the perfect mood for a leisurely evening. Service is gracious and efficient, even when understaffed.

The kitchen specializes in German cuisine, featuring primarily meat and poultry dishes. During our visit here, the most memorable appetizer was the Brie baked in phyllo, perfectly complemented by a dollop of fruity mango sauce. We shared, but we were so taken with this dish, we came very close to ordering two. **7621 Trans-Canada Highway; (250) 746-4031; moderate to expensive; reservations recommended; dinner Tuesday–Sunday.**

❀❀❀ **QUAMICHAN INN, Duncan** Set just off the road on a knoll overlooking the Cowichan Valley, Quamichan Inn's four dimly lit dining rooms occupy the lower level of a handsome Tudor home. Crystal chandeliers, antiques, and glowing fires help to make this one charming location for dinner. Silver candelabras and maroon linens give every table an elegant appearance, although the floral carpeting that runs throughout is extremely dated.

When the weather is clear, the most romantic spot to dine is outside on a rock patio overlooking verdant lawns, gardens, and a footbridge that crosses a little fishpond. The menu features meat and seafood; we recommend the latter, particularly the generous Seafood Taster's Platter, which overflows with mussels, clams, scallops, crab, fish, lobster, and every other imaginable delicacy from the sea. **1478 Maple Bay Road; (250) 746-7028; moderate to expensive; dinner Wednesday–Sunday.**

Romantic Note: The inn also has bed-and-breakfast rooms upstairs, but they are definitely not recommended for romantic interludes. Smells and sounds from the restaurant too easily travel upstairs, and the decor leaves much to be desired.

❀❀ **SAHTLAM LODGE RESTAURANT, Duncan** Even if you're not an over-night guest at **SAHTLAM LODGE AND CABINS** (see Hotel/Bed and Breakfast Kissing), we encourage you to visit this property's restaurant, located in a weathered 1920s fishing and hunting lodge filled with antiques and lodge-related bric-a-brac. Besides its secluded location, this restaurant boasts excellent waterfront views. One wall of the dining room is all windows, which look onto the Cowichan River below and the dense forest beyond. Simple country living is the theme here, and the handful of tables lining this wall are decorated with floral linens, while dried flowers hang from rafters above. Folding screens separate many tables—a nice touch for a small room. If you arrive early for your reservations, you can start the evening by snuggling up in lounge chairs near the immense stone fireplace.

The kitchen offers a simple menu of Pacific Northwest seasonal dishes, including lamb with chèvre, three-mushroom stew, and beef with pistachios and green peppercorns. A roasted chicken, sprinkled with sea salt, herbs, and garlic, is made for two to share. Looking around at the tables, most of which are occupied by couples, it's no surprise that this dish is the house specialty. **5720 Riverbottom Road West; (250) 748-7738; moderate to expensive; reservations required; dinner Thursday–Sunday.**

❀❀❀❀ **VINOTECA, Duncan** There's nothing like driving along a country road and discovering a wonderful little restaurant tucked inside a farmhouse that borders a vineyard. Vigneti Zanatta Winery, a family-owned winery and farm, is such a place. The owners have restored a 1903 farmhouse back to its original simplicity and charm. The small dining room holds several tables covered by floral linens, which is a pity since hidden underneath is beautiful gray marble. In fact, colorful marble touches abound throughout—from fireplace to front porch. Butter-colored walls, accented by colorful modern art and white drapes encircled with decorative grapevines, add contemporary flair. Wavy-paned windows look out onto 27 acres of vineyard and the logged mountains above; try hard to ignore the shabby empty pool in the foreground.

Wines are served by the taste (two ounces), glass, or bottle, and include an almondy auxerrois and light but full-bodied pinot gris. They're expertly matched to the small but interesting menu, which highlights fresh farm products. Risotto takes center stage, along with other Italian-Northwest creations, while catches of the day may include ahi tuna or black sea bass (sorry, the region's otherwise ubiquitous salmon isn't served here). Consider taking advantage of the set menu—a tasty way to go at a reasonable price. **5039 Marshall Road; (250) 748-2338; moderate to expensive; lunch and dinner Tuesday–Sunday, brunch Saturday–Sunday; call for seasonal closures.**

Romantic Option: The tasting room, open noon to 4:30 P.M., Tuesday through Sunday, sells wine and deli fixings. Enjoy a spontaneous picnic on the wraparound porch or journey into the vineyard and dine alongside the grapes.

Chemainus

Many people wonder what exactly the town of Chemainus did to earn its triumphant nickname, "The Little Town That Did." Here's the story. Once an economically depressed logging community, this small, undistinguished burg completely transformed itself with a revitalization project implemented in 1980. World-class artists were solicited from all over British Columbia to paint a series of murals on storefronts throughout town. These impressive illustrations enthrall thousands of tourists a year, and, as a direct result, Chemainus is now thriving.

Although the murals are interesting, you do have to contend with an overwhelming number of visitors, all flocking here to see the same thing. What most people don't know, however, is that there are other kiss-worthy reasons to visit Chemainus.

Romantic Suggestion: Near the south end of town stands a large, peach-colored building that houses the **CHEMAINUS THEATRE** (9737 Chemainus Road; 250-246-9800, 800-565-7738; tickets begin at $22). Popular plays and musicals such as *Little Shop of Horrors* and *A Christmas Carol* generally run in season between mid-February and December. Whether you choose to have dinner at the theater or opt for a more romantic rendezvous before curtain call, watching a show is bound to add dramatic spark to your evening. Call for a complete schedule of plays and times.

Hotel/Bed and Breakfast Kissing

◆◆◆ **BIRD SONG COTTAGE BED AND BREAKFAST, Chemainus** Fronted by flower gardens and a trickling fountain, this white and lavender home looks too precious to be real. It is real, though, from the beautiful Victorian furnishings to the larger-than-life oil paintings and the live birds trilling sweet songs. Fancy antique hats, part of the innkeepers' ongoing collection, are tucked in every nook and cranny, while a crackling fire warms the parlor. On summer evenings, retreat to the wraparound veranda, where an inviting porch swing provides the perfect spot to sip tea and share a kiss or two.

Bird Song Cottage offers three guest rooms: one just off the common area, and two more upstairs. Nightingale, on the main floor, is outfitted with plush green linens and a crisp white coverlet, pale green walls, a cozy window seat, a private bathroom with a claw-foot tub, and a door that opens to a small patio and colorful gardens. Upstairs, Blue Bird and Hummingbird are smaller, with slanted dormer ceilings. Both offer private bathrooms, freshly ironed linens, and lots of country Victorian charm.

In the morning, a full gourmet breakfast is accompanied by live piano music in one of the prettiest rooms in the house: an airy garden room awash in flowing white lace and hanging flowers. Two caged parakeets, appropriately named Romeo and Juliet, flutter in the background as guests enjoy such goodies as strawberry pancakes, quiche, or asparagus crêpes. **9909 Maple Street; (250) 246-9910; inexpensive; closed January.**

❀❀❀ **LITTLE INN ON WILLOW STREET, Chemainus** Affectionately referred to as "the world's smallest luxury hotel," this entire property is available for rent—in a manner of speaking. Enveloped by lovingly manicured flower gardens, this miniature, red-turreted gingerbread-style castle has only one guest room. A complimentary bottle of chilled champagne is the first of several distinct romantic details you will encounter here. At the touch of a finger, a fire burns in the hearth, illuminating a queen-size canopy bed veiled in richly colored fabric. A Jacuzzi tub, built for two, is sheltered in the corner of the bedroom, which is furnished with baronial European antiques and a TV/VCR. With such romantic amenities as these, you may never want to leave your room at all. Unfortunately, you may have to venture outside come morning, because breakfast provisions are not provided with your stay. **9849 Willow Street; (250) 246-4987; expensive.**

❀❀◖ **ONCE UPON A TIME INN, Chemainus** Once upon a time, a massive rose Victorian home sat peacefully just blocks from the water, until one day it was transformed into a beautiful bed and breakfast full of antiques. Now it provides a setting where the two of you can make up your own romantic fairy tales. The four immaculately kept guest rooms located on the first, second, and third floors are lovingly decorated with handsome antiques and sumptuous floral linens; all have full or partial views of the water. The Main Suite, adorned with floral wallpaper, hardwood floors, and lace curtains, features a large bathroom with a claw-foot tub and a glass corner shower. The smaller Angel Room and Rose Room share a detached bathroom (decidedly unromantic) with a claw-foot tub and rose-colored wainscoting. On the third floor, the amazing Skylight Suite is well worth the ascent up the stairs. Filled with contemporary furnishings and boasting a huge sitting and dining area, spacious bathroom, and a heavenly king-size bed, it has the best view in the house.

Located next door to the main house is a game room where rainy days (a Northwest certainty) can be whiled away playing a game of pool or watching videos. In the main house, you can relax in the guest parlor, which is filled with Victorian furnishings and knickknacks, or play a duet at the grand piano in the corner. Just off this main parlor is the breakfast room, where guests can enjoy a full breakfast that includes fresh fruit topped with French vanilla yogurt, freshly baked breads and pastries, and a scrumptious entrée such as blueberry French toast or waffles. **9940 Cedar Street; (250) 246-1059; inexpensive to moderate.**

Cost ratings for British Columbia listings are in Canadian funds. American travelers should check the exchange rate or ask an innkeeper to figure out the cost in U.S. dollars.

❦❦ **PACIFIC SHORES INN, Chemainus** A carved statue of a sea captain with a telescope keeps watch from the rooftop of this light blue gabled inn. Situated on a corner in a residential neighborhood, Pacific Shores Inn is owned by the same company as the **LITTLE INN ON WILLOW STREET** (reviewed above). Although the three suites at Pacific Shores are less luxurious than its sister property, they are still very attractive and the prices are as reasonable as they get. Amenities include full kitchens, TV/VCRs, tasteful country Victorian furnishings, and private entrances to ensure your sense of isolation in each room.

A lovely Edwardian canopy bed is a particularly enchanting feature in the Duchess Room, which is accented with a down comforter, white lace curtains, and beautiful antiques. A cozy breakfast nook surrounded by windows is a delightful place to start your day in the Princess Room. The King Room has the most spacious quarters, with its full kitchen, dining area, living room, bedroom, and bathroom. Whichever room you choose at Pacific Shores, you'll need to come prepared with plenty of breakfast fixings for a leisurely morning together. **9847 Willow Street; (250) 246-4987; inexpensive.**

Restaurant Kissing

❦❦ **HUMMINGBIRD TEA HOUSE, Chemainus** Don't overlook this unassuming little teahouse, tucked away on a residential street in Chemainus. Yellow walls and unfinished floors give the eclectic interior a warm and cozy feeling, while flowers in the windows and single candles on each table add a touch of romance. The restaurant holds only eight tables; we recommend sitting in the back room, where you can escape the hustle and bustle of the kitchen.

The dinner menu changes weekly, but usually offers a choice of pasta, seafood, and meat dishes. Begin your meal with an appetizer the locals rave about and keep coming back for—the warm goat cheese salad on greens with sun-dried cranberries, peppers, and sautéed mushrooms, topped with a walnut vinaigrette. This delectable combination of hot and cold ingredients will make your taste buds sing! For hearty appetites, the grilled New York steak covered with sautéed mushrooms is an excellent choice. If you still have room after your generous entrée, dessert is a must. The chocolate cheesecake will melt in your mouth. By the way, be prepared to be fussed over by the owners—the service here is impeccable. **9893 Maple Street; (250) 246-2290; expensive; lunch and dinner Wednesday–Monday.**

❦❦ **THE WATERFORD RESTAURANT, Chemainus** Located on the sunny main floor of a renovated Victorian home, the Waterford is one of the more popular lunch spots in Chemainus. The restaurant's cheerful café-style ambience is enhanced by teal and white textured walls adorned with watercolors by local artists, although the rest of the decor is unremarkable. Intimate it's not, and the service can be iffy, but the kitchen's specialty crêpes are among the best we've tasted and well worth a visit. Dinner fare is a bit heartier, with entrées such as duck Montmorency, prawns Provençal, and scallops served in a Pernod cream sauce. Outdoor dining in the summer is available on a flower-lined patio facing Maple Street. **9875 Maple Street; (250) 246-1046; moderate to expensive; reservations recommended; lunch and dinner Tuesday–Sunday.**

Ladysmith

Ladysmith offers few accommodations of any kind, so the serenely beautiful forested surroundings are all but unspoiled. Nevertheless, we did find a couple of romantic possibilities that will put you in the heart of this glorious natural landscape.

Hotel/Bed and Breakfast Kissing

❦❦ **ESTUARY ESTATE BED AND BREAKFAST, Ladysmith** This bed and breakfast is for the birds! Indeed, you'll see more bald eagles, hummingbirds, sparrow hawks, kingfishers, and great blue herons than people. When we visited this new home, perched above a waterfront bird refuge, the proprietors had their telescope pinpointed on an aerie. Throughout the day we watched bald eagle parents feeding their hungry chicks. Although there's no guarantee you'll see these majestic raptors, you're bound to see something colorful flying by. There's also Sophie, an adorable Toto look-alike who doesn't fly, but loves to entertain.

Lovebirds—the human variety—will find a special love nest here. A two-room cottage, with full kitchen, queen-size bed, and sitting area, resides above the detached garage. While it's a bit apartment-like, you'll have this roost all to yourselves. Additional accommodations in the main home consist of three large bedrooms—one with private bath—on the top floor. Each room includes a queen-size bed, roomy closet, and outstanding views of the water below. Those sharing the hallway bathrooms can choose between the full or half bath.

While romantic amenities are not abundant, we found the suburban home beautiful, bright, exceptionally clean, and certainly unique. The proprietors built it themselves, with beautiful hardwood floors, large windows, and classical Craftsman-style touches throughout. In the afternoon you can sample their homemade wine while sitting in the elegant living room; in the morning, when the birds start to sing, have breakfast on the deck. **302 Roland Road; (250) 245-0665; inexpensive to moderate; no credit cards.**

Romantic Note: All of the bedrooms face the quiet waterfront, which is good: There's a freeway on the other side of the home. The proprietors have planted plenty of trees along their property in an attempt to reduce noise. While traffic noise exists during the day, in the morning and at twilight all you can hear are the birds.

❦❦ **YELLOW POINT LODGE, Ladysmith** Yellow Point Lodge is well known for many reasons: its remote location, its extensive beach and secluded coves bordered by 180 acres of forest, the attentive staff, the laid-back ambience, and the 200-foot seaside saltwater swimming pool. There is no need to do anything more strenuous than deciding what to wear to the three hearty family-style meals and two teas (included in the price of your stay) served daily in the handsome main lodge.

Upon arrival the first thing you might detect is the noticeable lack of children anywhere in sight. They aren't allowed here, which is an emphatic romantic advantage. Perhaps the second thing you'll notice, particularly in the warm and inviting main lodge, is the fact that everybody seems to know each other. This is not an illusion—they really do know each other. A unique reservation system ensures that guests are guaranteed the same room on the same date one year later (and every consecutive year after that, if they so choose). As a result, many of the people you see have been spending the same week together, year after year, for a long, long time. Most who come here consider it an advantage, but it can feel uncomfortable when you're the only ones who don't know anybody else.

Lodgings here are eclectic. Romantically speaking, we recommend the newer white beach cabins that line the ocean shore, tucked among tall pines. Down comforters, sitting areas, private bathrooms with showers, and incredible water views make these the most desirable options. The sprawling property also holds many other accommodations in assorted price ranges, including rooms in the main lodge that offer some water views and unluxurious furnishings, and cottages that feature private bathrooms, beautiful ocean vistas through lofty pine trees, and very rustic decor. The least desirable choices are the barracks and the cabins with communal bathrooms, unless you're really in the mood to rough it. **3700 Yellow Point Road; (250) 245-7422; moderate to expensive; minimum-stay requirement on weekends and holidays.**

Restaurant Kissing

❤ **THE CROW AND GATE NEIGHBORHOOD PUB, Ladysmith** If you've never visited the English countryside, this authentic British pub overflowing with rustic appeal and old-world charm is the next best thing. Surrounded by rolling meadows and tall pines, the small Tudor-style house and its captivating rose arbor provide refuge to weary, hungry travelers. Guests can dine inside at wooden tables arranged near the stone fireplace or outside (where the cigarette smoke is not as thick) at picnic tables shaded by umbrellas. The mediocre food, mostly traditional British fare, consists of hearty sandwiches and pub-style samplings. **2313 Yellow Point Road; (250) 722-3731; inexpensive; lunch and dinner daily.**

❤❤ **THE PRINTINGDUN BEANERY, Ladysmith** Looking for a friendly spot to linger over dessert and espresso? Simply head over to the Beanery and sit for a bit. This quaint coffeeshop offers a limited selection of soups, salads, sandwiches, and desserts, as well as a variety of coffee choices. The cheery interior is a lovely blend of parquet floors, dark green walls, and burgundy accents. Fancy candles, painted flowerpots, and Victorian-style knickknacks are displayed for sale along a brick wall, while baked goods tempt sweet tooths from the pastry counter near the entrance. A handful of tables, set beneath tall ceilings, provide a delightful place to chat the afternoon away. **341 First Avenue, Unit A; (250) 245-7671; inexpensive; lunch Monday–Saturday; live jazz every other Friday night.**

Nanaimo

Industrialized and overdeveloped Nanaimo, one of the largest cities on Vancouver Island's east coast, doesn't offer much for romantic travelers. But once you step outside the city limits, the kissing can begin.

Hotel/Bed and Breakfast Kissing

❤❤❤ **THE PEPPER MUFFIN COUNTRY INN, Nanaimo** We were beginning to think that Nanaimo had very little to offer in the way of romantic possibilities until we discovered the Pepper Muffin Country Inn. This blue ranch-style home, laid out on seven acres of peaceful countryside, provides city-weary travelers with a welcome respite from Nanaimo's commercialized core. Here, the only distractions are the friendly *baahing* of sheep and the occasional *mooing* of cows in the surrounding pastures. So slow your pace, breathe in the country air, and relax.

The inn offers three small guest rooms and one newly constructed suite. All feature plush carpeting, private en suite bathrooms, TV/VCRs, terry-cloth robes, and comfy duvets draped over cozy beds. Mauve walls add warmth to the two rooms on the main level. The Mountain Room has a lovely brass double bed crowned by a diamond-shaped window; its best feature, however, is the small sitting alcove with several windows showcasing views of Mount Benson. On the opposite side of the dining room is the Meadow Room, which surveys views of the neighboring farmland. More masculine in nature, the River Room is located upstairs near the tastefully decorated common area. It features lovely mahogany and cherry-wood furnishings, blue walls, a plaid duvet on the queen-size bed, and a private deck for taking in the serene surroundings.

A recent addition is the Bridal Suite—also located on the second floor and done up in a New England style. It includes all the amenities of the other rooms, plus a gas fireplace, four-poster cherry-wood bed, separate sitting area, and jetted tub set beneath a window in the bathroom. For special occasions, ask about the Bridal Package, which includes extras like champagne, fresh flowers, chocolates left on your pillows, and in-room breakfast.

If the cozy rooms and peaceful setting don't fully set your hearts aglow, check out the community hot tub waiting for you beneath a gazebo on the patio at the back of the house. Or stroll hand in hand to the back of the property, where you can stake your claim to one of the secluded spots along the river.

In the morning, mouthwatering aromas will tempt you out of bed and lure you to the countrified central dining room. There you'll find a full breakfast of fresh fruit, muffins, and other goodies arranged on the buffet table, plus a hot dish such as French toast, omelets, or breakfast quiche. Large windows let in the morning sunlight, the walls are adorned with hand-painted flowers, and polished hardwood floors add a touch of elegance. **3718 Jingle Pot Road; (250) 756-0473; www.island.net/~pog; inexpensive to expensive.**

❀❀❀ **YESTERYEAR FARM AND GUEST HOUSE, Nanaimo** Talk about a change of pace! Once you've settled down on Yesteryear's 33-acre working farm and made friends with the amiable farm animals, the city will feel light-years away. Explore the orchards, admire the flower and vegetable gardens, or relax by the tranquil pond. Learn more about the well-cared-for chickens, rabbits, horses, oxen, and sheep who call this rural place home. Guests are encouraged (but not expected) to participate in seasonal farm activities, ranging from haymaking and fence building to gardening and berry picking.

Two of the three reasonably priced guest rooms are worth recommending. Both the Gatehouse and the Carriage Room are filled with gorgeous antiques, blond hardwood floors, and private baths with glass-enclosed showers. We were especially partial to the Gatehouse, with its cozy sitting area, queen-size maple sleigh bed, and lush linens. Couples with a sense of adventure are the best candidates for the remaining option: the Hay Loft, situated on the upper floor of the adjacent barn, beside an actual hayloft. The shower for this suite is located in the wash rack with the horses (hard to believe, but true!). Definitely for horse lovers only!

Complete your experience with a delicious, homemade farm breakfast of freshly squeezed juice, piping hot pancakes, and bacon and eggs, served to guests in the cozy main house or on the outside deck when the weather permits. **3055 Quennell Road; (250) 245-4297; inexpensive.**

Restaurant Kissing

❀❀❀ **MAHLE HOUSE RESTAURANT, Nanaimo** If you're ready to escape Nanaimo's overdeveloped core, head out to the rolling countryside for a breath of fresh air at this lovingly restored farmhouse turned restaurant. You'll know it when you see it: Just look for the only bright orange building in sight. Inside, hardwood floors, Oriental rugs, and stained glass windows adorn the home's original living areas, which have been converted into charming dining rooms. French doors open to a bright sunroom that functions as a second, more casual dining room. Here diners enjoy views of an expansive grassy yard and English perennial gardens. At night, wall sconces cast a soft glow on the peach-colored walls, colorful local artwork, and tables draped with floral linens.

Wonderful smells float in the air, whetting your appetite for the menu's variety of seafood, meat, and pasta dishes. Appetizers include tasty choices such as carrot and ginger soup, deep-fried Havarti cheese, and duck breast salad served with an Oriental dressing. We had difficulty deciding between the Dungeness crab cakes and the roasted leg of lamb, so we ordered both and shared. Desserts change daily and are worth saving room for. **On the corner of Cedar and Hemer Roads; (250) 722-3621; www.island.net/~mahle; expensive; reservations recommended; dinner Wednesday–Sunday; call for seasonal closures.**

Romantic Note: If you're dining on the appropriate day of the week, be sure to try the "Adventurous Wednesday": The chef prepares a surprise multicourse meal in which each person at the table gets something different for every course. Sharing is a must for this one!

❤❤❣ **THE WESLEY STREET RESTAURANT, Nanaimo** This upscale, contemporary restaurant is a welcome change of pace in Nanaimo's industrial core. If the two of you want to have an urbane evening of jazz (live on Friday and Saturday evenings, taped the rest of the week), you won't be disappointed here. Cushioned booths and intimate tables, complemented by pink and maroon tablecloths and topped by fresh flowers, fill the dining room. Eclectic artwork adorns the pink and maroon walls, and large windows look out on a quaint shopping area. Noise from the open bar spills over to the small, intimate dining room, which lends a slightly bustling atmosphere on busy nights.

Fresh, artfully presented entrées will exceed expectations. We recommend the halibut with a pineapple curry sauce and the pan-seared duck in a tantalizing Szechuan black bean glaze. Don't leave out dessert; the chocolate caramel cake will satisfy your most passionate sweet cravings. **1-321 Wesley Street; (250) 753-4004; moderate to expensive; lunch and dinner daily.**

Nanoose Bay

Hotel/Bed and Breakfast Kissing

❤❤❤❣ **PACIFIC SHORES NATURE RESORT, Nanoose Bay** Whatever preconceived notions you have of time-share accommodations may be discarded when you see Pacific Shores' stellar interiors and spectacular beachfront location. Everything about Pacific Shores can soothe city-tired temperament—even the prices. The 52 (soon to be 76) impressive units are set on almost 15 acres of awe-inspiring land that is immaculately and lovingly maintained. Though time-shares usually leave nonowners out in the cold, several rental units are available when a space hasn't been reserved.

Most of the units are adorned with richly colored draperies framing beautiful bay windows that look out over the water. Contemporary appointments are comfortable and handsome, though a bit on the commercial-prefab side for some tastes. Still, Jacuzzi tubs, fireplaces, heated bathroom floors, TV/VCRs, pleasing linens, and four-poster beds in the large master bedrooms more than compensate for the store-bought ambience.

Prices are linked to the unit size and view you request: The larger the unit and the better the view, the more you pay. If money isn't a consideration, don't forget to request a view of Craig Bay when booking your reservation.

A garden nursery, movie rental shop, fitness center, outdoor Jacuzzi tub, and indoor swimming pool are all available to guests. Outside, waves lap at sandstone beaches and strategically placed lighting illuminates the seawall nature walk. You'll be so enthralled with this property that you may be too distracted to kiss, at least for the first few moments. **1655 Strougler Road; (250) 468-7121; inexpensive to very expensive.**

Parksville

Sorting through Parksville's overabundance of roadside motels and beachfront accommodations is no easy task, and we wish we had more to show for our extensive research. Parksville's lovely stretch of beach, bordering Craig Bay and overlooking resplendent views of the mountains, has experienced a condominium/rental explosion. Large signs shout at you from the highway. Some properties have mowed every tree in sight and now resemble mainland suburbia. The majority of this area's standard economy motels are not worthy of note, for all the obvious unromantic reasons (outdated decor, traffic noise, and rambunctious children, to name a few.) But if Parksville's beach is calling your name, don't worry. We did find a few affectionate locales that are bound to inspire romance.

Hotel/Bed and Breakfast Kissing

❦❦ **TIGH-NA-MARA RESORT HOTEL, Parksville** Don't be dissuaded by the less-than-attractive sign along the freeway or by the fact that this place is often overrun with families and kids during the summer months. With its tranquil setting, myriad walking trails, beach access, lovely water views, and a reliable restaurant (see Restaurant Kissing), Tigh-Na-Mara is Parksville's best option when it comes to romantic accommodations.

The resort is spread out over 22 acres of Douglas firs and madrona trees, and bordered on one end by a sandy beach. Amid all this scenery, 45 free-standing log cabins and several buildings housing condominiums hold the resort's 142 units. The one- or two-bedroom log cabins offer exposed log walls, wood-burning beachstone fireplaces, full kitchens, comfortable sitting areas, and small private decks with barbecues. While they are undoubtedly more cozy and private than the condos, their rustic interiors could use some sprucing up.

We recommend the individually owned condos that tower over the sparkling shoreline. Each spacious unit features magnificent views, a queen-size bed, stone fireplace, cedar-paneled living room, full kitchen, and sliding glass doors that open to a private deck with a ringside view of the water. Even though these condos are individually owned, Tigh-Na-Mara controls all the decor decisions, so most feature attractive contemporary furnishings. Some units are blessed with large Jacuzzi tubs, and those in Building C have them in the bedroom so you can gaze out at the water as you soak away the evening. Units in Building C also boast king-size beds and new kitchens done up in pretty blue tiles.

If you are traveling on a budget, you can stay in some less expensive units in an adjacent lodge; these units are within close proximity of the resort's recreational facilities, which include steam and exercise rooms, an indoor pool, a community Jacuzzi tub, and outdoor tennis courts. **1095 East Island Highway; (250) 248-2072, (800) 663-7373; www.tigh-na-mara.com; inexpensive to very expensive; minimum-stay requirement on weekends and holidays.**

Restaurant Kissing

❤❤ **MACLURE HOUSE INN RESTAURANT, Parksville** One of the last places you would expect to find a romantic restaurant is in the middle of an ordinary resort complex, especially when it's situated behind the main office and laundry facilities. Nevertheless, here it is, and warmly inviting too. Originally built in 1921, the Tudor-style building has been handsomely renovated to retain all of its original charm. The interior is dimly lit and bathed in the amber glow of a gas fire, with polished dark wood moldings and paneling. Windows draped in lace frame views of the Strait of Georgia in the distance.

Lunch and dinner are both worthwhile. Our appetizer of hot Camembert rolled in almonds and served with a fresh plum sauce was flavorful, and the classic Caesar salad had exactly the right proportions; unfortunately, the French onion soup was unbearably cheesy. The raspberry torte we ordered for dessert was almost too rich, but we "suffered" through it anyway. **1015 East Island Highway; (250) 248-3470; moderate; reservations recommended; breakfast, lunch, and dinner daily.**

❤❤ **TIGH-NA-MARA RESTAURANT, Parksville** Tigh-Na-Mara's restaurant is housed in a large log cabin–style building near the resort's entrance. A crackling fire in the stone hearth warms the polished pine-and-stone interior, where wooden tables and floral curtains create an informal atmosphere. In the summer, choose a table on the glass-enclosed terrace that borders the restaurant on three sides.

The friendly staff serves up consistently good dinner selections seven days a week. Try the saffron scallops with a side of mushroom risotto; the lamb medallions sautéed with rosemary, garlic, and tomato; or the smoked chicken served over a bed of penne pasta and garnished with basil, sun-dried tomatoes, mushrooms, garlic, and cracked pepper. Breakfast and lunch are also served here, but because Tigh-Na-Mara is a hot spot for conferences during the day, the ambience at dinner is much more conducive to romance. **1095 East Island Highway, at the Tigh-Na-Mara Resort Hotel; (250) 248-2072, (800) 663-7373; www.tigh-na-mara.com; moderate to expensive; breakfast, lunch, and dinner daily, brunch Sunday.**

Outdoor Kissing

❧❧❧ **MACMILLAN PROVINCIAL PARK, Parksville** Highway 4 winds its way across Vancouver Island, over mountain passes and alongside quiet creeks, and eventually cuts through MacMillan Provincial Park. This 336-acre (136-hectare) forest is also called Cathedral Grove for its gorgeous display of Douglas firs. Most of the trees here sprouted after a fire swept through the forest about 300 years ago; however, the largest tree standing is more than 800 years old. Nature trails extend throughout the forest on both sides of the highway, through old-growth forest and trees draped in moss. The longest trail follows the Cameron River, another takes you to Cameron Lake, and Cathedral Trail makes a short loop through the forest. Even during the busy summer months, the park provides a refreshingly cool spot in which to stretch car-cramped legs and commune with nature (and each other) before continuing on to your final destination. **(250) 954-4600; free admission; day use only.** *From Parksville, head 32 kilometers (20 miles) west on Highway 4 toward Port Alberni.*

Tofino

Beginning at Parksville, a winding 120-kilometer (75-mile) trip west on Highway 4 takes you across the central mountains of Vancouver Island to the remote side of the island. For the last few miles of this panoramic drive, beautiful scenery surrounds you on your descent to sea level. When you finally reach road's end, the highway splits: One road forks north to Tofino, the other south to Ucluelet. Both towns are essentially fishing villages and whale-watching ports of call. Both pride themselves on being noncommercial places where you can charter boats for fishing and touring. But for heart-stealing pursuits, Tofino is the destination of choice.

Tofino is everything a small town should be: unpretentious and amiable, with streets and neighborhoods set like small constellations along the volatile, rocky oceanfront and the marinas of the calm inner bay. Environmentalists and artists flock here to escape the citified hustle of the island's "other" side. Several waterfront resorts line the shore along the main road into Tofino and have unobstructed views of the beach and ocean. In town you'll find a few basic shops and casual restaurants. Nothing here gets in the way of the scenery. Get close, kick back, and discover a place that remains unmarred by the woes of city life.

Romantic Note: The tourist season in Tofino is brief and intense. During

July and August the best accommodations are so difficult to come by that you should consider timing your visit for a less popular season. In fall or winter, the two of you will practically have the entire area to yourselves.

Hotel/Bed and Breakfast Kissing

❀❀ **BEACHWOOD, Tofino** This self-contained apartment has everything you need for a private, reclusive getaway. Though rather plain and unembellished, it is comfortable and spacious. Situated on the second floor above the owner's garage, it features a complete kitchen (provisions are up to you), dining room, and living room, all drenched with daylight that floods in from overhead skylights. The bathroom is exceedingly small, but the claw-foot tub makes long soaks a treat and helps to compensate for the cramped quarters. Perhaps the best reason to consider this spot is its location across the street from the endless, spectacular shoreline. Meandering along this stretch of beach is a four-lip experience not to be missed. Take advantage of it, any time of day or night, regardless of the weather conditions. **1368 Chesterman Beach Road; (250) 725-4250; moderate; minimum-stay requirement seasonally.**

❀❀❀ **CABLE COVE INN, Tofino** Don't be fooled by the unpretentious exterior of this building, because it does not accurately depict the luxury that awaits inside. Once you're secluded in one of the inn's six wonderful guest suites and you've savored the magnificent ocean views from your private deck, any doubts will dissipate. Poised high on a cliff, the inn looks out to the surf pounding against the rocks below—an utterly breathtaking sight. Just as magnificent are the accommodations. Beautiful, softly colored linens drape the handsome cherry-wood four-poster beds, and sunlight pours in through skylights in the second-floor rooms. Gas-burning fireplaces, marble Jacuzzi tubs, and glass showers for two are distinctly romantic attractions in every room. Corner rooms feature sliding wooden doors that open to wraparound decks where cedar chairs provide ideal seating to take in the scenery. Colorful Native Canadian art accentuates the contemporary flair of the inn.

Although this inn has the privacy and professional attitude of a hotel, the innkeepers live right next door and see to personal touches, making it feel more like a bed and breakfast. Hot beverages are brought directly to the rooms every morning, and a variety of juices and freshly baked goods are available in the common sitting room for all to enjoy.**201 Main Street; (250) 725-4236, (800) 663-6449; www.victoriabc.com/accom/cablecov.htm; moderate to very expensive; minimum-stay requirement seasonally.**

Cost ratings for British Columbia listings are in Canadian funds. American travelers should check the exchange rate or ask an innkeeper to figure out the cost in U.S. dollars.

❤❤❤ FRASER'S VIEW BED AND BREAKFAST, Tofino

This contemporary home is situated right on the water, and almost every room benefits from this illustrious vantage point. Fortunately, the innkeepers do not rely on location alone, and they have spent time and energy on all three of their guest suites. These units have private entrances, down comforters, original handcrafted pine furnishings, wood-burning stoves or fireplaces, and private bathrooms. Our favorite is the Storm Suite, with its wraparound windows, breathtaking views, and a lavish fireplace surrounded by floor-to-ceiling beach stones. The Wolf Suite has an even better view, plus a private balcony, glass-fronted wood-burning stove, a vaulted ceiling, wood wainscoting, and a queen-size bed. In the Whale Suite, a handmade goose-down comforter drapes a rustic pine queen-size bed. This room also features an entire wall of windows that afford a peekaboo view of the ocean through a stand of trees.

A short path at the rear of the house wanders through the trees to the beach, where you can stroll hand in hand along the water, watch for whales, or just lounge on the sand. If you want to wash off after a beachcombing expedition, a semiprivate outdoor shower adds an adventurous romantic touch, if you can brave it.

In the morning, Starbucks coffee, freshly baked breads with homemade jams, fresh fruit salad and juice, and smoked-salmon omelets are brought directly to your door for you to enjoy at your leisure. **1329 Chesterman Beach Road; (250) 725-2489; www.bbcanada.com/1397.html; moderate to expensive.**

Romantic Note: Since the time of our visit, Fraser's View has come under new ownership.

❤❤ GULL COTTAGE, Tofino

Cottage is a misnomer: This massive green and white country Victorian home with a wraparound porch is far from small. The downstairs common areas and four upstairs guest rooms are filled with comfortable contemporary furnishings and local artwork. By far the best choice is the Rainforest Suite, where a beautiful pine sleigh bed has a cushy, thick feather mattress and a deep red comforter. Bay windows showcase the serene forested setting, and a spacious en suite bathroom features a large soaker tub. The Jay and Spruce Rooms are more spartan, but still offer four-poster beds, pretty linens, and views of the forest. We do not recommend the Chickadee Room for romantic interludes because it has two twin beds and shares a detached bathroom with the Spruce Room. After a day of play, relax in the community hot tub located on the deck in the backyard. A full gourmet breakfast is served downstairs at one large, elegant table each morning. **1254 Lynn Road; (250)725-3177; www.bbcanada.com/1401.html; inexpensive to moderate; minimum-stay requirement on weekends.**

❤❤❤ MIDDLE BEACH LODGE, Tofino

Middle Beach Lodge is one of Tofino's more popular romantic destinations, and we can see why. A long, bumpy gravel drive leads you away from the highway and into the forest, where a lovely wood lodge and its newly constructed counterpart are perched above a sandy beach and the roaring Pacific. Myriad decks and lookouts throughout the original lodge make the ocean seem much closer, and a steep staircase zigzags down to the beach. An immense stone fireplace is the focal point of the main lounge, where guests can relax or cuddle up close on overstuffed sofas. Polished hardwood floors and pine furnishings, along with spectacular panoramas of the crashing waves, create a sense of West Coast simplicity that continues throughout both buildings.

The 26 "At the Beach" guest rooms are located in the lodge's original wooden structure. Most of these rooms have lovely ocean views, but even those without this advantage are worth your romantic consideration. Simple and almost plain, the attractive European country decor is enhanced with bouquets of dried flowers, wood accents, and puffy down comforters that you can hardly refrain from diving into. Best of all, this section of the lodge does not allow children, so the quiet setting remains tranquil.

Just down the beach, a new lodge and several cabins have been built along a rocky oceanfront bluff known as the Headlands. Rustic Northwest charm is provided by burlap curtains, dried flowers, hand-carved beds, hardwood floors, and wood accents, and many of the guest rooms feature decks that command panoramic ocean views. Private decks wrap around the adjacent cabins, which boast knotty pine walls, antique trunks, and ladder lofts. Several cabins have Jacuzzi tubs and convenient kitchenettes.

Those looking for more space or traveling with another couple may want to check out the newly constructed duplex or the four free-standing cabins; these accommodations offer two bedrooms and private hot tubs.

A generous continental breakfast is served in the elegant dining room or can be enjoyed in the main lounge beside a raging fire. In the evenings, the kitchen serves up dinners of barbecued salmon, fresh Dungeness crab, or halibut for both guests and nonguests. Even though dinner is not included in your stay, you'll want to stick around for these fresh fish feasts (expensive). **400 McKenzie Beach Road; (250) 725-2900, (800) 954-8588; www.middlebeach.com; moderate to very expensive; minimum-stay requirement seasonally.**

❀❀ **PACIFIC SANDS BEACH RESORT, Tofino** If you value incredible views over plush accommodations, Pacific Sands may be the place for you. If luxury and intimacy are more your style, you'll want to stay elsewhere. This sprawling, condominium-style development hugs a mile-long stretch of coastline along Cox Bay, offering fantastic water views from all 64 units. Manicured lawns separate the three-story buildings (whose weathered exteriors are in desperate need of paint), and the crashing surf is just footsteps away.

Unfortunately, the units here aren't nearly as spectacular as their surroundings. Even though they have all the amenities of an upscale motel, they feel somewhat impersonal and dated. Small mini-apartments in the newer sections are decorated in pastel color schemes and feature wood-burning fireplaces, small kitchens, TVs, comfortable living rooms, separate bedrooms, and sliding glass doors that open to private balconies or patios. The original section offers units with similar furnishings and decor, and the top-floor rooms sport cathedral ceilings and the best panoramic outlooks. The recently constructed Sand Dollar Suite, with its two bedrooms, two bathrooms, kitchen, gas fireplace, and deckside hot tub, is more geared for families or couples traveling together. On the third floor of the newer section, the Cox Bay and Sunset Point Suites feature hot tubs on private decks for soaking beneath the stars, as well as down comforters on the king-size beds; these suites are clearly the best option for romance-minded couples. **1421 Pacific Rim Highway; (250) 725-3322, (800) 565-2322; www. travel. bc.ca/a/pacificsands; moderate to expensive; minimum-stay requirement seasonally.**

Romantic Warning: Steer clear of the ten rustic cabins that sit near the water's edge. These cabins are situated too close to one another to be private, they lack fireplaces, and their furnishings are mediocre at best.

❤️❤️ **SPINDRIFT, Tofino** Homes that reside directly on the rugged ocean shores of Tofino are envied for their treasured location. Spindrift, a blue cedar-sided residence, is sited on just such a corner of forested sand. Inside, the living room, with its hardwood floors, floor-to-ceiling windows, and efficient fireplace, is an ideal spot for guests to watch the daily tidal processions change the shoreline's appearance. For more privacy, seclude yourselves in one of the three attractive guest suites. Though Window-by-the-Sea does not have the luxury of a sweeping view, it does give a peekaboo glimpse. It also has a kitchenette, a private entrance, a cozy dining nook, and plenty of room due to the fact that the bed folds up into the wall. And don't worry about tracking in sand from the beach—this suite has linoleum floors (not elegant, maybe, but very practical). Although smaller than Window-by-the-Sea, the Garden Suite is just as attractive and features the same amenities. You can catch only a small glimpse of the ocean from this room, but with the beach only 50 steps away, you can stroll down to the water for a closer look.

For the ultimate views, book the eclectic Pacific Suite, where vaulted hemlock ceilings soar above an antique double bed, a fireplace with a raised hearth, and a huge soaking tub set next to windows. Though the decor is mismatched, glorious towering windows display spectacular ocean views from every corner of the room. **1373 Chesterman Beach Road; (250) 725-2103, www.pixsell.bc.ca/bb/198.htm; inexpensive to expensive; no credit cards; minimum-stay requirement seasonally.**

❤️❤️❤️❤️ **THE WICKANINNISH INN, Tofino** This exquisite property is set on a rocky cape that juts out from the western tip of Chesterman Beach. Here guests can experience the best of both worlds: Frosty white surf crashes against the jagged rocks that front the inn, while Pacific Rim National Park secludes it in a blanket of tall trees. Elegance and nature are the focus here, a fact that's apparent the moment you open the large wooden doors to the engaging lobby, where floor-to-ceiling picture windows showcase breathtaking views of the ocean, and attractive contemporary furnishings are set off by copper accents and dark slate floors. Throughout the inn's many hallways, stunning black-and-white photographs and prints by local artists are tastefully displayed for guests to enjoy in passing.

Each of the 46 guest rooms is decorated with unique recycled-wood furnishings in rich earth tones, and all offer views of the pounding Pacific from tall windows and private balconies. The rooms have been constructed in such a way that it's very difficult to see or be seen by neighboring balconies; you'll feel very much alone with the crashing surf and your loved one. Other romantic amenities include large soaking tubs, gas fireplaces, refrigerators, microwaves, coffeemakers, fluffy robes, and down duvets draped over king- or queen-size beds. Several room types are available: standard bedroom suites, several-room suites with king-size beds, rooms with two queen-size beds, and rooms with a queen bed and a double sofa sleeper. Every room has a lovely tiled bathroom, and six rooms on the main level feature wonderful Jacuzzi tubs.

Downstairs, you'll find a fitness room with peekaboo views of the ocean. At the time of our visit, a spa facility was in the works, which, when completed, will offer a variety of services such as massages, manicures, pedicures, facials, and body treatments. After a relaxing day of beachcombing or storm watching, you'll be pleased to discover that one of Tofino's most romantic dining options is conveniently located on the main floor of the inn. Don't miss **THE POINTE RESTAURANT** (see Restaurant Kissing) for the perfect finale to a perfect day. **Osprey Lane at Chesterman Beach; (250) 725-3100, (800) 333-4604; www.wickinn.com; unbelievably expensive; minimum-stay requirement seasonally.**

Restaurant Kissing

❤️⛵ **ORCA LODGE RESTAURANT, Tofino** Tofino is a fishing village, so it isn't at all surprising that the local restaurants have exquisite seafood. Orca Lodge Restaurant's fare is delicious, and its dining room has a casual, friendly gettogether state of mind. The bar area sports a pool table, and the small, casual dining room is crowded with burgundy-clothed tables. Affectionate touches include wraparound windows that look out to untamed gardens and a large brick wood-burning fireplace that radiates a warm glow.

Servings here are generous, and the fresh seafood is excellent, particularly the king salmon covered in a light pesto sauce. Herbed focaccia is served along with a saucer of balsamic vinegar and extra-virgin olive oil for Italian-style dipping. **1254 Pacific Rim Highway; (250) 725-2323, (800) 725-2320; moderate to expensive; call for seasonal hours; closed January–mid-February.**

Romantic Note: ORCA LODGE also has eight guest rooms, none of which are of any romantic interest.

❀❀❀❀ **THE POINTE RESTAURANT, Tofino** This is *the* place to dine in Tofino, a place where Northwest elegance, culinary expertise, and the area's natural glories are brought to culmination each evening around sunset. The Pointe's location, on the jagged rocks of Chesterman Beach, is absolutely stunning. Large picture windows afford 240-degree views of the dramatic ocean and untamed natural surroundings; during winter storms, waves actually roll in beneath the restaurant's foundations and splash up against the windows! The dining room's hand-adzed cedar post-and-beam construction is the epitome of Northwest architecture. Twenty-foot ceilings soar above a circular wood-burning fireplace set in the middle of the room, and innovative rock candleholders set each wooden table aglow. Even with the bar near the entrance, the dining area remains quiet throughout the evening. To top it all off, service is attentive without being pretentious.

As the sun goes down and the lights dim, you and your sweetheart will enjoy fresh local seafood items prepared to utter perfection. An impressive selection of Pacific Northwest wines is available to accompany just about anything on the menu. Begin your meal with a sampling of local oysters, followed by a thick New York–cut steak or an entire fresh crab. (Bibs are available, so go for it!) As for desserts, our favorites are the double chocolate mashed pot brioche, and the organic pear and apple pie served with a side of cinnamon ice cream. When an experience like this beckons, why eat anywhere else? **Osprey Lane at Chesterman Beach, at the Wickininnish Inn; (250) 725-3100, (800) 333-4604; www.wickinn.com; expensive; breakfast, lunch, and dinner daily.**

❀❀ **RAIN COAST CAFE, Tofino** If simple is your idea of enchantment, you will adore this intimate little café located only steps from the ocean. Soft jazz flows throughout the small, dimly lit dining room and the large, bare picture windows frame breathtaking views of the water. The interior of the café is best described as minimalist, with its cement floor, natural wood tables and chairs, and simple flower vases and candles. While the decor is spare, the food is anything but ordinary; you can expect quality and freshness in every bite. The chef's Mediterranean fettuccine with artichokes, peppers, and sun-dried tomatoes, tossed with olive oil and white wine, is al dente and flavorful, and the wild rice cakes with roasted garlic, herbs, ginger sauce, and cashews are uniquely memorable. **1-120 Fourth Street; (250) 725-2215; moderate; lunch and dinner daily.**

❀❀ **WEST COAST CRAB BAR, Tofino** Fresh seafood is abundant in the Pacific Northwest, and we've certainly eaten our share, but we'd never tasted crab quite so succulent or delicious as the crab served here. It doesn't get much fresher than this: You can actually watch your future entrée swimming in a tank at the restaurant's front entrance. The casual two-level dining room overflows with nautical paraphernalia, including tables laminated with maps and a boat hanging from the ceiling. Not the most romantic of settings, but the food is so exceptional you won't think twice. Crab-stuffed mushroom caps will warm up your taste buds for the main course: tender, fresh crab served with a cup of drawn butter. Don't hesitate to order a whole crab for each of you, even if you're small eaters. It's a lot of work to crack them, and you'll develop quite an appetite. (You'll also make a big mess, so ask for lots of napkins.) **601 Campbell Street; (250) 725-3733; moderate to expensive; dinner daily; call for seasonal closures.**

Outdoor Kissing

❀❀❀❀ **LONG BEACH, Tofino** Located between Tofino and Ucluelet, Long Beach offers everything that restless surf lovers could want. Several hiking trails run adjacent to the shoreline, which is defined by rocky cliffs, smooth white-sand beaches, old-growth rain forest, and wooded picnic areas. Romantic possibilities here are infinite: You can walk along the extensive beach, hike through the forest bordering the shore, or seek the water for a salty frolic. An amazing number of surfers will be out trying to catch a wave at many spots along the beach; watching them can be quite entertaining. *Just off Highway 4, on the west side of the road, as you head north toward the town of Tofino.*

❀❀❀❀ **WHALE WATCHING, Tofino** Everything about whale watching is romantic. Imagine yourself and your loved one staring out from an open Zodiac at the cliff-lined Pacific Ocean and forested islands haloed in shades of deep, lush green. The cool morning air swirls around you as you clasp each other close for protection against the chill. As you scan the calm blue water, your thoughts are overwhelmed with the vastness before you. Suddenly, in the distance, breaking the stillness of a sun-drenched early spring day, a spout of water explodes from the ocean surface, followed by a giant, arching black profile. After an abrupt tail slap, all is stillness once again. Even if you're not sitting next to someone you care about, you're likely to grab the person nearest you and yell, "Wow, look at that!"

Maybe it's the excitement of knowing that such an immense, powerful creature can glide so effortlessly through the water with playful agility and speed. Or it could be the chance to "connect" with a civilized mammal that knows the secret depths of an aquatic world we can only briefly visit and barely understand. Whatever the reason, a sighting of these miraculous creatures is best shared with someone special. **Chinook Charters: (250) 725-3431, (800) 665-3646. Jamie's Whaling Station: (250) 725-3919, (800) 667-9913 (in western Canada only); www.jamies.com. Remote Passages: (250) 725-3330, (800) 666-9833 (in Canada only); www.island.net/~remote. Moderate.**

Romantic Note: The height of the gray whale migration season is in March and April, though orcas reside here year-round.

Ucluelet

Ucluelet (pronounced "You-clue-let") occupies its own little peninsula on the west side of Vancouver Island. Its name is derived from a First Nations word meaning "safe harbor," but today the town is better known as the whale-watching capital of the world. March through May is the supreme time for catching a glimpse of the 20,000 gray whales that make their annual migration past Ucluelet's shores. In addition, fishing and scuba diving attract many visitors to this area each year, and the breathtaking scenery of Barkley Sound provides a spectacular backdrop for kayaking, sailing, and charter motorboating.

Hotel/Bed and Breakfast Kissing

❀❀❀❀ **A SNUG HARBOUR INN, Ucluelet** The surroundings alone would make A Snug Harbour Inn an enviable place to stay, but the scope of the architecture and the thoughtfulness of the romantic details demonstrate heartwarming considerations as well. Terraced decks, incredible views, plenty of windows, large rooms, and incredibly alluring bathrooms are all part of this luxurious romantic getaway. Nestled on a cliff overlooking the Pacific Ocean, the inn is perched on a remarkably beautiful stretch of land. From the deck off the main sitting room, a dramatic, sweeping view of the waves pounding against the rocks below will take your breath away. For a closer look, a pathway that the owners call a "stairway from the stars" leads to the beach below. A helicopter pad is available for guests who want to arrive by air.

There is no doubt that you will be in the lap of luxury at this idyllic, one-of-kind retreat. The four guest rooms here are exquisite; all are appointed with fireplaces, unique furnishings, private balconies with spectacular ocean views, and lavish private bathrooms with jetted tubs. If you are wondering which one to choose, we suggest the Sawadee or the Atlantis. The Sawadee Room promises an intoxicating evening, with its captivating ocean view, simple yet exotic decor, and imported Thai artwork. Teak appointments include the fireplace mantle, ceiling, and headboard. There is even a tub-side fireplace surrounded by beach stone where two can easily soak together for hours on end. For those with more contemporary preferences, the Atlantis is adorned with vivid yellow walls, black laminate furnishings, and an exceptional view. Even more enticing is the huge Jacuzzi tub with a cascading waterfall in the bathroom.

After a night of bliss, enjoy a breakfast of fresh fruit, pastries, seafood quiche, and Belgian waffles in the Great Room. When you've finished your meal, saunter over to the nautically decorated sunken sitting room and enjoy an awe-inspiring view of the Pacific from the panoramic windows. If you are curious, the friendly innkeeper (who bears an uncanny resemblance to the Skipper from *Gilligan's Island*) and his wife will tell you all about their adventures at sea. **460 Marine Drive; (250) 726-2686, (888) 936-5222; www.ucluelet.com/asnugharbourinn; unbelievably expensive.**

Restaurant Kissing

❧ **THE MATTERSON HOUSE RESTAURANT, Ucluelet** Ucluelet doesn't offer much in the way of romantic dining establishments, so locals have come to rely on the next best thing: the Matterson House. This tiny restaurant is sure to satisfy your stomachs; just remember to bring your own serving of romance to keep your hearts occupied while you eat. Established in 1931, the yellow home is enclosed by a white picket fence and fronted by a small porch. Inside, a handful of tables covered in maroon linens are scattered around the informal, one-room dining area. The casual service matches the casual decor, which toes the line between eclectic and mismatched despite a few endearing touches like hardwood floors and lacy white curtains. Choose from a variety of burgers, soups, and sandwiches on the menu before heading off to more romantic surroundings. **1682 Peninsula Road; (250) 726-2200; inexpensive; breakfast, lunch, and dinner daily.**

❧❦ **WICKANINNISH RESTAURANT, Ucluelet** Wickaninnish is the name of an outstretched beach with hundreds of weathered logs strewn like toothpicks on the shore. A large wooden building with the same name houses an information center, a museum of Native Canadian culture, and a restaurant, all set on the edge of the sandy shore. The information center and museum, together known as the Interpretive Centre, are educational points of interest but hardly romantic. On the other hand, the restaurant is exceptionally romantic, particularly during the off-season, when the tourists are home waiting patiently for summer.

The views are the real reason to come here. Although it is surrounded by windows that showcase the beach and the moody, ever-changing sea, the wood-crafted waterfront dining room is exceedingly casual. Threatening winter storms, dramatic high tides, and still summer days make for a scene that at one moment may be languid and silent, and the next violent and thundering. Regardless of what excitement nature is providing, the Wickanninish Restaurant will serve you tasty fish and chips, salads, and sandwiches while you sit back and watch the show. **1 Wick Road; (250) 726-7706; inexpensive to moderate; dinner daily; call for seasonal closures.**

Romantic Suggestion: After an early dinner, if the weather permits, hike along the beach or through the woods along nature trails that run behind the building. When you're done, return to the restaurant and drink a toast to the day you've shared together.

Fanny Bay

Hotel/Bed and Breakfast Kissing

❤❤❤ **SHIPS POINT BEACH HOUSE, Fanny Bay** Eagles, blue herons, Canadian geese, seals and sea lions, and other wildlife can be observed from the vantage point of this picturesque beach house perched at the tip of Ships Point Peninsula. If you want to get even closer to Mother Nature, you can launch a rental kayak from the property's sandy beach or ask the gracious innkeepers for a boat tour of the area's wildlife. Nature is the focus of this luxurious country inn, encompassed by lush flower gardens and adjacent to a protected forest and bird sanctuary. Panoramic views of the ocean, mountains, and Denman Island are visible from nearly every room in the house.

Hospitality is important to the enthusiastic innkeepers, who welcome you to their home like old friends. Help yourselves to a complimentary drink from the "people fridge," relish the views from the deck, or listen to your favorite CD in the airy living room, distinctively appointed with deep red walls and modern artwork. Home-baked treats await guests in each of the seven small but endearing guest rooms, all with private baths. Native Canadian artwork and gorgeous down comforters lend appeal, even in the rooms with twin beds. For romantic purposes, we recommend Tequila Sunset, with its gorgeous water views, cheery fabrics, and enticing queen-size bed. Although it was being remodeled at the time of our visit, the Raphael Room looks promising. Romance is certainly assured with its fireplace, view of the water from the queen-size bed, and sunken bathroom containing a soaker tub for two.

Also on the property are two rooms in the nearby Long House. The Eagle's Nest Loft upstairs contains a private deck, jetted tub, and a fireplace. At the time this book went to press, the owners were in the process of renovating the second room in the Long House, and from all appearances, it will be a comfortable suite right on the water.

Delectable appetizers and wine are served at sunset every evening, and for an extra charge the innkeepers are delighted to have you as their guests for a three-course gourmet dinner, served family-style at one large table. Delicious breakfast aromas waft through the halls in the early morning, providing extra incentive to get out of your comfy bed. Savor heart-shaped gingerbread scones topped with homemade jams, orange soufflé pancakes, grilled pineapple, and Fanny Bay oyster omelets in the family-style dining room. After breakfast, the main deck is an inviting spot to leisurely sip your latte or espresso while taking in the lovely water views. **7584 Ships Point Road; (250) 335-2200, (800) 925-1595; www.shipspoint.com; moderate to unbelievably expensive; minimum-stay requirement seasonally; recommended wedding site.**

Union Bay

Restaurant Kissing

❧❧ **HARBOUR VIEW BISTRO, Union Bay** This small, unassuming restaurant doesn't look like much from the outside. In fact, you may have trouble finding it unless you know to look for a brown trailer-style building hidden among a row of storefronts. Once you find it, however, you'll see why this restaurant rates high on the coziness scale. Four tables, each topped with pink tableclothes and candles, occupy the tiny dining room, while an old woodstove warms the eclectic interior. When it comes to dining, the restaurant's reputation precedes it. The menu features baked Prince Edward Island mussels in garlic butter, crêpes Florentine, rack of lamb, salmon and steak entrées, and chocolate mousse for dessert. **5575 South Island Highway; (250) 335-3277; moderate to expensive; lunch Wednesday–Saturday, dinner Wednesday–Monday.**

Courtenay

Courtenay sits roughly in the center of the Comox Valley and provides a segue to the area's many recreational activities. Most visitors come here to ski the slopes at **MOUNT WASHINGTON** (see Outdoor Kissing), hike along the alpine meadows and lakes, fish in the Strait of Georgia, or golf at Vancouver Island's premier golf course. While the town itself is hardly a romantic destination, once you stray from its commercialized stretch of highway, the area's natural wonders are yours to explore.

Restaurant Kissing

No lips LA CRÉMAILLÈRE, Courtenay La Crémaillère has a long-standing reputation as the most romantic place to eat in Courtenay. Why this reputation has lasted so long, we can't say. This cream-colored Tudor home certainly has a pleasant enough setting alongside the Courtenay River, which allows for serene water views from the covered Garden Terrace. But that's where any hint of romance begins and ends. The decor, which was once touted as old-world elegance, is now simply old. Dated brown and cream carpeting, coupled with heavy wooden beams, make the dining rooms seem dark and almost dingy. Tired valances line the windows, and posters of paintings by Renoir are tacked haphazardly to the pale yellow walls. It's definitely time for a face-lift.

Cost ratings for British Columbia listings are in Canadian funds. American travelers should check the exchange rate or ask an innkeeper to figure out the cost in U.S. dollars.

Authentic French entrées fill the menu at La Crémaillère. Among the many fish, meat, and pasta choices, we recommend the more traditional entrées such as the rack of lamb or stuffed pheasant. (These are the dishes that keep the regulars coming back year after year.) Steer clear of the Louisiana egg Creole—it's just too mediocre to bother—and the sole amandine isn't anything you couldn't concoct in your own kitchen. With such depressing decor and unimpressive food, we couldn't even bring ourselves to stay long enough to order dessert. Now that's saying a lot! **975 Comox Road; (250) 338-8131; expensive; lunch Wednesday–Friday, dinner Wednesday–Sunday.**

❤❤ **THE OLD HOUSE RESTAURANT, Courtenay** Don't be too distracted by the neighboring log-processing factory, which operates in full swing during the day; you'll hardly notice it once you've been enveloped by the charming country ambience and lovely garden setting of the rustic Old House Restaurant. Willow trees and thick green lawn carpet the backyard, where the Courtenay River flows by umbrella-shaded tables set on a latticed open-air deck.

Built in 1938, the historic riverfront home has four old-fashioned dining rooms, each one dominated by dark wood beams, unfinished walls, and wood-burning fireplaces. Our favorite has an enormous beach-stone fireplace and lots of hanging plants. Antique furnishings, floral fabrics, and leaded glass windows throughout the restaurant reflect the building's historic past, although the vinyl tablecloths are less than formal. While the kitchen does a good job with standard items, unusual fresh ingredients turn up in imaginative combinations. Turkey schnitzel cordon bleu; peppered Fanny Bay oysters; and a warm scallop and wild mushroom salad, served on a bed of fresh spinach with oyster mushrooms and a raspberry vinaigrette, are a few of the rare finds on the interesting menu. **1760 Riverside Lane; (250) 338-5406; inexpensive to expensive; breakfast Saturday–Sunday, lunch and dinner daily.**

Outdoor Kissing

❤❤ **MOUNT WASHINGTON, Courtenay** Be sure to call for directions before you set out for this resort; it took us a lifetime and a half to find it. If you're in an adventurous mood, you'll appreciate the 25-minute drive (it takes much longer if you get lost) along graveled or snow-covered country roads that lead from Courtenay to the ski slopes of Mount Washington. During the off-season (mid-June through mid-October), as you dangle above the golden land on the mile-high ski lift, you can study the scenic Comox Valley, the Strait of Georgia, and the Beaufort Mountain Range. During ski season, numerous runs boast great skiing and amazing scenery. It might not be Whistler, but at least the lines are shorter. **(250) 338-1386; www.vquest.com/alpine; $40 for an all-day lift ticket; call for directions.**

Comox

Hotel/Bed and Breakfast Kissing

❦ **FOSKETT HOUSE BED AND BREAKFAST, Comox** Set on five acres near the Strait of Georgia, Foskett House offers both seclusion and easy accessibility to the water. The small outback-style ranch house is enveloped by pines and Garry oaks and situated far from any signs of big-city life. Here, the two of you can truly hide away from the rest of the world.

Although the two guest rooms are cozy and pleasantly decorated with rustic furnishings, they are more homey than romantic. Done up in a safari theme, the Natal Room has white mosquito netting draped over the queen-size bed, and secondhand antiques. For complete seclusion, ask for the Mbona Room, which is located in a separate cabin adjacent to the main house and has its own private entrance. You will feel at home in the warmth of this private hideaway, which contains a small wood writing desk, rocking chair, cozy bed, and vintage photos of the innkeepers' relatives and forebears.

Outside, you can lounge on the patio and enjoy the beautiful daffodils and rose tree near the pond, or take a walk along the trails that crisscross the rear of the property. Simply cross the street and you'll be at the water's edge. On chilly days, relax by a fire in the snug parlor, which features works by local artists and by the hostess herself. In the morning, a luscious breakfast that may include freshly squeezed juice, heated citrus compote, Swiss muesli, and smoked-salmon omelets is served in the family-style dining room, or outside on the veranda when weather permits. **484 Lazo Road; (250) 339-4272; www.vquest.com/ foskett; inexpensive.**

Campbell River

With a population of more than 20,000, Campbell River is brimming with shopping malls and condominium complexes—definitely not our idea of romantic. Still, it is home to some of the island's best fishing resorts (fisherfolk refer to it as the salmon capital of the world), and it's very close to the pristine wilderness of **STRATHCONA PROVINCIAL PARK** (see Outdoor Kissing).

Hotel/Bed and Breakfast Kissing

❦❦ **PAINTER'S LODGE, Campbell River** It's between 5 A.M. and 9 A.M., and you're sitting in a rocking boat out in the middle of a serene channel of water, waiting for a slight tug on the end of your fishing pole. Snowcapped summits surround the two of you with silent majesty, amplifying your sense of supreme isolation. Even if fishing isn't your idea of romance (and even if it's raining), the scenery alone is bound to inspire some passionate moments. And keep in mind, there are some who kiss best after they've landed a king or two.

Painter's Lodge is an angler's delight and has been for more than 60 years. Canadians and Californians flock here to test their patience and skill. A fire several years back served almost as a blessing in disguise: The lodge has been entirely rebuilt and the result is an elegant, attractive, modern wood complex nestled right on the water's edge. Wood accents, peaked ceilings, and private decks add charm to the 90 otherwise sparse hotel rooms and four additional cabins. French doors open onto private patios in every room; some face spectacular water vistas while others have views of the outdoor pool and landscaped gardens. Corner suites are particularly enticing, with surrounding windows and slanted wood ceilings. At the end of the day, head down to the glass-enclosed fireside lounge, with its huge stone fireplace and comfortable seating; it's a prime place to gaze at the water and revitalize yourselves for another go-around of fighting off the dogfish and weeds. **1625 MacDonald Road; (250) 286-1102, (800) 663-7090; www.obmg.com; expensive to unbelievably expensive; closed November–mid-March.**

Romantic Suggestion: PAINTER'S LODGE RESTAURANT (see Restaurant Kissing) is the nicest place to dine in the vicinity.

❧❧ STRATHCONA PARK LODGE, Campbell River

A long, winding mountain road delves into the rugged wilderness of Strathcona Provincial Park and delivers you to Strathcona Park Lodge. Set at the edge of a crystal-clear mountain lake, the red hewn-log buildings are encircled by an astounding collection of snowcapped peaks. Strathcona is, without question, a visual paradise. There are no other facilities around for miles, and that sort of isolation has an enchantment all its own. But enchantment can be relative, given the eclectic assortment of accommodations. You really need to be the camping type to appreciate this location, as some of the cabins have few or no modern conveniences. Calling Strathcona Lodge rustic is truly an understatement.

Despite the rugged quarters, if you want outdoor adventure, the friendly and professional staff here is dedicated to sharing the mysteries and excitement of the park. They offer guided hikes as well as instruction for any mountain and water activity you could desire: kayaking, rappeling from cliffs, glissading down glaciers, wildlife viewing, hiking, canoeing, fishing, sailing, and camping. The lodge's brochure lists a rare selection of packaged challenges for all ages and skill levels. Even if you are not staying at the lodge, the park is a magnificent area to explore on your own, with exquisite vistas and picturesque countryside.

You may be thinking yes, that all sounds great, but not necessarily romantic unless you're dating Paul Bunyan. But after you have explored the rustically appointed lodge and cabins set around the lake, as well as the new alpine chalet, wandered into the wilderness for a breathtaking hike, and enjoyed three hearty family-style meals served daily, you will be convinced that this is an extraordinary place for nature-loving couples. **Highway 28, 48 kilometers (30 miles) west of Campbell River; (250) 286-3122; www.vquest.com/strathcona; moderate to expensive; minimum-stay requirement seasonally.**

Restaurant Kissing

❀❀ **PAINTER'S LODGE RESTAURANT, Campbell River** Floor-to-ceiling windows command brilliant ocean views in this expansive timbered dining room. Tables are well spaced alongside the windows to ensure that each party has ample privacy and unobstructed views. Fresh flowers, white linens, candles, and fine china give the dining room its formal appearance. During our visit, the service was gracious and very efficient, but the items on the small gourmet menu sounded much better than they tasted. We recommend sticking to the more basic seafood entrées and focusing on the views (and, of course, each other). **1625 MacDonald Road; (250) 286-1102, (800) 663-7090; expensive; breakfast, lunch, and dinner daily; closed November–mid-March.**

Outdoor Kissing

❀❀❀❀ **STRATHCONA PROVINCIAL PARK** Your first sight of Strathcona Provincial Park's 518,000 acres (210,000 hectares) of legendary wilderness will leave you speechless. Sheltered in the heart of Vancouver Island, far, far from the reaches of civilization, snow-shrouded mountains ascend above sunlit glades and shimmering, crystal-clear lakes. Thick, lush moss clings to bare branches and tree trunks, and rushing waterfalls tumble over rocky summits into lazy, slow-moving creeks that meander through the forest and disappear underground. Roosevelt elk and black-tailed deer forage for food on the forested hillsides, while brightly colored birds twitter in the high boughs of the evergreens. And these are just glimpses. We urge you to come and witness the sights and sounds of the park's spectacular isolation and scenery firsthand. Myriad hiking trails and nature walks allow visitors access to this heavenly region. **(250) 954-4600; free admission.** *Campbell River and Courtenay are the primary access points to the park. From Campbell River, follow Highway 28 west; from the Island Highway in Courtenay, follow signs to Forbidden Plateau.*

Port Hardy

Outdoor Kissing

❀❀❀❀ **CAPE SCOTT PROVINCIAL PARK AND SAN JOSEF BAY, Port Hardy** Cape Scott is on the northwestern tip of Vancouver Island and feels like the end of the world. It is accessible via a dusty gravel-and-stone logging road. Though the park is not very far from Port Hardy, because of the road's condition you'll need longer to get here than you'd think from looking at a map. Once you've arrived, however, you'll be ecstatic that you underwent the ordeal; this park is the epitome of magnificent wilderness.

At the beginning of the hiking trail, you make a dream-like transition from the gravel-pit road to a land filled with the elfin spirits of nature. A flat walkway of wood planks is the only sign of civilization you're likely to see all day; you are guaranteed privacy.

From the trailhead, meander for three kilometers (two miles) past trees draped in moss and streamered with sunlight, until the path opens onto an enormous sand-laden horseshoe bay called San Josef, which you can claim exclusively for yourselves. Waves breaking on the beach fill the air with a rhythmic pounding. The U-shaped bay is bordered by forested hills where very few people have gone before. Be sure to mark where you leave the trail when you reach the bay, or it will be tricky to find that spot again. **Free admission; (250) 954-4600, (250) 949-7622.** *Just south of Port Hardy, follow the poorly marked logging road toward the town of Holberg for 45 kilometers (28 miles). At the end of the road, you'll pass a government-run meteorology station as you proceed to the parking area at the head of the trail. A very short climb reveals the path.*

Romantic Warning: Because Cape Scott is so remote, acquire a detailed map and complete information from the visitor center in Port Hardy before you head out there. If you plan on backpacking, the need to be prepared for adverse weather conditions cannot be stressed enough. Weather can be severe and excessively wet, bordering on torrential. Visitors are advised to use caution while camping or hiking here. Cougars and bears are prevalent, and the running water is not drinkable.

Gulf Islands

Salt Spring, Pender, Mayne, Saturna, Galiano, Gabriola, Denman, Hornby, Quadra, and Cortez Islands are accessible via ferryboat from Tsawwassen (just south of Vancouver), from several locations on Vancouver Island, and between the individual islands. Call ahead for ferry information (250-386-3431 in Victoria) or visit British Columbia Ferries' Web site at www.bc ferries.bc.ca. Depending on the season and during most weekends, reservations and advance payment may be necessary to assure your place on the ferry. Departure times are limited, so be sure to make your travel plans with this in mind.

Scattered like a heavenly constellation, the Gulf Islands lie nestled between Vancouver Island and mainland British Columbia. There are more than 300 forested isles, whose populations vary from zero to several thousand, and all of them are places of transcendent splendor and solitude.

A handful of the Gulf Islands are accessible by ferryboat, and all have what's required to give you hassle-free, all-absorbing time away from everything except nature and each other. Whichever island you choose, you will be certain to find bed and breakfasts set on hilltops or hidden in the woods, intimate restaurants where "leisurely" is a way of life, oceanfront parks with sweeping views of the other islands, and miles of meandering paved roads that lead to island privacy. Nothing will be able to distract you from the out-of-this-world scenery and the eyes of the person you love.

Romantic Note: If you are planning to visit more than one island during your trip, we can't stress enough the importance of calling ahead for ferry schedules. Island hopping is not as easy as you would think, with some ferries offering only limited transportation at strange hours. It's possible to get stranded on one of the smaller islands overnight if you don't pay close attention to return sailing times (there aren't any on certain days). We recommend bringing along a healthy sense of adventure and a dose of patience when relying on ferry transportation between the islands.

Salt Spring Island

Salt Spring Island has experienced a bed-and-breakfast explosion. That means a lot of work for a travel writer and a lot of confusion for travelers choosing accommodations. Sometimes having only a few choices is better (or at least easier) than having too many. Still, after exhaustive—and kiss-intensive—research, we discovered the best this wonderful island oasis has to offer.

Romantic Note: Due to Salt Spring Island's size and popularity, we recommend calling the properties you intend to visit well ahead of time for reservations and specific directions.

Hotel/Bed and Breakfast Kissing

❦❧ ANCHORAGE COVE BED AND BREAKFAST, Salt Spring Island

Perched above a quiet cove not far from the town of Ganges, this wood-shingled home rests easily among a stand of madrona trees. A community hot tub and the owners' sailboat are harbored at a long wooden dock extending from the property's white-shell beach. Chocolate Island stands not too far offshore, and on any afternoon one may witness a parade of boats, seaplanes, and kayaks passing by. If you wish to join this waterway procession, hop in one of the complimentary canoes or rowboats for a leisurely tour around the cove.

Three extremely basic guest rooms occupy the bottom part of the house at Anchorage Cove. For romantic purposes, we recommend only the two with full-on water views and corner locations (the third room has very limited views of the water and a half bath). Simple and rustic, the Blue Heron and Kingfisher Rooms feature Quebec antiques, country artwork, wooden headboards, and modern bathrooms. Best of all, neither of the rooms has a TV to distract you from quiet time together. Guests can also unwind in the shared common area, which comes equipped with a billiards table, a large TV hidden away in an armoire, and a tiny kitchenette.

Mornings bring full breakfasts of muffins, banana bread, and fresh fruit, as well as a hot entrée like salmon strata or pancakes. During summers, breakfast can be enjoyed outside on the dock; in less cooperative weather, it is served upstairs in the spacious kitchen area with views of the water through large windows. **449 Long Harbour Road; (250) 537-5337, (888) 537-5360; www. anchoragecove.com; moderate to expensive.**

❦❦❦❧ ANNE'S OCEANFRONT HIDEAWAY, Salt Spring Island

High above the ocean, amid tall trees, this large contemporary home offers romantic wayfarers several cozy common areas, a private exercise room, an outdoor hot tub with views of the water, and two wraparound verandas where guests can unwind while gazing at the peaceful surroundings.

Four luxurious guest rooms are located on the upper level of the home, with a separate entrance to ensure the utmost in quiet. Each has a private bathroom with affectionate amenities such as plush towels and bathrobes, massage tubs, soft lighting, and heated floors. Most have queen-size beds draped with sumptuous down comforters, and all are impeccably decorated with quality furnishings. Although each room is stunning, our favorite is the Garry Oak Room. A queen-size canopy bed with Laura Ashley linens majestically occupies the center of the room, and a whirlpool tub invites long

Cost ratings for British Columbia listings are in Canadian funds. American travelers should check the exchange rate or ask an innkeeper to figure out the cost in U.S. dollars.

soaks beside the gas fireplace. In the octagonal Pacific Yew Room, ten windows facing five different directions allow views of the forest and water from the beautiful pewter canopy wedding bed. This is the only guest room without a balcony, but with all the surrounding windows, you won't miss it at all. French country decor and bleached wood furniture make the Arbutus Room a cozy place to relax, and views of the water can be enjoyed from its side balcony. For a spectacular panoramic view of the ocean, request the Douglas Fir Room, a spacious room tastefully decorated in rich colors. Unfortunately, this room comes with two twin beds, which doesn't afford the best cuddling, but they can be combined to make a short king.

Morning brings a gourmet, four-course breakfast of oven-fresh muffins and cinnamon rolls, succulent Salt Spring lamb, a creative egg dish, and plenty of fresh fruit, served in the family-style dining room. (You can also relish the gorgeous ocean view along with your meal at a cozy table for two set right next to the windows in the sitting room.) After your meal, walk down the winding path to the water and watch as boats and marine life pass by. **168 Simson Road; (250) 537-0851, (888) 474-2663; www.bcyellowpages.com/advert/ a/annes_ocean_hideaway.html; unbelievably expensive.**

❦❦❦ BEACH HOUSE ON SUNSET, Salt Spring Island
Poised on a rocky bluff above a waterfront cove, this enticing bed and breakfast is miles away from the bustling villages of Ganges and Vesuvius. You can actually watch eagles diving for fish right outside your window.

Your most secluded option here is a self-contained cedar cabin that rests on an incline above its own private cove. Wraparound decks and bay windows allow dramatic views of sensationally gorgeous sunsets over the mountains of Vancouver Island. Although the decor here is dated and rustic, the absolute privacy helps to compensate. Snuggle in thoughtfully provided bathrobes as you rest on your deck watching otters and seals frolic in the waves.

Three delightfully plush rooms are located in the main house, with private decks that offer the same water views as the cabin. All three rooms boast eiderdown comforters, feather pillows, lovely floral fabrics, and separate sitting areas. One is furnished in wicker; another has a stunning wrought-iron canopy bed cloaked in white fabric, which contrasts beautifully with the dark green walls. Sophisticated and subtle, with a taupe color scheme and sumptuous linens, the third and newest suite has a claw-foot tub in the bathroom and a fireplace. There's also an outdoor shower at the back of the house for those daring enough to take the plunge!

Breakfast is a culinary event at the Beach House; one of the innkeepers was schooled at the Cordon Bleu in Paris. Delicacies such as blueberry coffee cake, salmon quiche, fresh brioche, soufflés, homemade sausages, and unusual fruit drinks will greet you in the morning. **930 Sunset Drive; (250) 537-2879; www.saltspring.com/beachhouse; expensive to very expensive; minimum-stay requirement seasonally; call for seasonal closures.**

❦❦❦ **BEDDIS HOUSE BED AND BREAKFAST, Salt Spring Island** Fruit trees and perennials border the walkway leading to a turn-of-the-century white farmhouse surrounded by more than an acre of manicured lawns outlined by white fences. This building holds the property's common area, where comfy floral couches sit in front of a wood-burning stove and large windows afford picturesque views of the water through tall trees.

The adjacent carriage house holds the three guest rooms, two on the main floor and one taking up the entire second floor. Each one has a private bathroom with pedestal sink and claw-foot tub as well as attractive linens, country knickknacks, glass-fronted woodstoves, and private decks with views of the lovely surroundings and the tranquil strait. The Gingham Room is done up in pale yellows and blues, with hardwood floors and plenty of country freshness; the Butterflies Room boasts English country decor, a lovely green damask duvet cover, floral wallpaper, and a four-poster pine bed. We especially recommend the Rose Bower Suite; this top-floor suite has been appointed with a king-size four-poster bed, mauve walls, lovingly restored antiques, and a spacious bathroom that holds a six-foot claw-foot tub.

In the morning, wander next door to the main farmhouse for a full country breakfast of fresh fruit, home-baked breads, and an ever-changing hot entrée, all served at one long table with views of the ocean and gardens. Afternoon tea and baked goodies are served in the guest parlor or out on the expansive front porch when weather permits. **131 Miles Avenue; (250) 537-1028; www. saltspring.com/beddishouse; expensive to very expensive; minimum-stay requirement seasonally; call for seasonal closures.**

❦❦ **BOLD BLUFF RETREAT, Salt Spring Island** Bold Bluff Retreat is not your typical Northwest getaway, but that's what makes it so wonderful. Nestled on 100 acres of rocky oceanfront land, this property can be reached only via the owner's motorboat. While this can be an inconvenience, it also guarantees that you won't be bothered by the rest of the world.

Two rental cottages are set at opposite ends of Bold Bluff's sprawling property. Located in a grove of trees behind the owner's private home, the 1940 Garden Cottage is best described as rustic, with its fir floors, weathered cedar walls, and fully equipped kitchen. What this cottage lacks in modern conveniences, it more than makes up for in quiet, antique charm. The tiny old-fashioned bath holds a claw-foot tub, and the living room features a hand-painted writer's desk. A woodstove cranks out heat in the winter.

Farther away, the second, more basic Salty's Cabin is poised literally at the water's edge on a rocky outcropping. Floor-to-ceiling windows capture views of the water and glimpses of herons, eagles, and owls—your only neighbors. Listen to the sound of the waves lapping below you as high tide brings the water right below the deck. This is the cabin for couples who prefer to rough it, with a composting toilet, a small kitchenette with just the basics, and an outdoor shower. (You'll feel like one with nature after your first day here!) You are truly sheltered from the outside world here: There's no road nearby, and no telephone, TV, or electricity (lights are all solar powered). Cozy up next to a woodstove or explore the nearby acres of forest; you might even catch glimpse of an eagle's nest. **1 Bold Bluff; (250) 653-4377; moderate to expensive; no credit cards; minimum-stay requirement; call for seasonal closures.**

Romantic Warning: Meals are not included with your stay, so come prepared with groceries and other personal necessities. Just in case you've forgotten something, the owner will ferry you back and forth to the island's "mainland" for a charge. However, there's no guarantee it will be service with a smile. When we made a special request for an after-dinner pickup, the reception was far from welcoming—i.e., no introductory pleasantries or small talk. Another warning: Don't expect any assistance from the innkeeper getting into and out of the boat. If you are unfamiliar with boats, this one can be very difficult to negotiate, especially if you have luggage and the water is choppy.

❀❀❧ CRANBERRY RIDGE BED AND BREAKFAST, Salt Spring Island

Located on a bluff and surrounded by colorful gardens, Cranberry Ridge Bed and Breakfast has one of the most magnificent panoramas imaginable, with a mesmerizing 180-degree view of the islands, inlets, and the imperial snowcapped mountains of the mainland. Charming and immaculate, the three ample guest rooms are located in the bottom section of the house. Cozy sitting areas appointed with wicker and willow furniture look out at the stunning scenery through floor-to-ceiling sliding glass doors found in every room. The Country Room and the Twig Room have Jacuzzi tubs, and the latter boasts a wood-burning fireplace. All have the added comfort of terry-cloth robes and feather beds draped with handmade patchwork quilts. Each room opens onto an expansive deck where a large hot tub sits, perfect for stargazing during late-night soaks.

In spite of all this praise, we should mention that when the shades are opened to let in the beautiful view, you'll initially feel rather exposed to other guests who are enjoying the deck (especially if you're in the Wicker Room, the one nearest the hot tub). To remedy this situation, the innkeepers have installed frosted, one-way glass; now other guests can't see you, but you can still see them. Still, this slight inconvenience is a small price to pay for the endless views and affectionate ambience. And we haven't even mentioned the gourmet five-course breakfast that might include baked pears with whipped cream, smoked-salmon eggs Benedict, and stuffed French toast: utterly delicious and satisfying. **269 Don Ore Drive; (250) 537-4854, (888) 537-4854; www.cranberryridge.com; moderate to expensive; minimum-stay requirement.**

❀❀❧ GREEN ROSE BED AND BREAKFAST, Salt Spring Island A hidden

pathway alongside a lovely waterfront home leads down to the lower part of the house where you'll find the entrance to your own little beach retreat. There's only one suite here, so the only people you have to contend with are the innkeepers, who live in the upper part of the house, and they respect your privacy as much as you do.

Cream walls and large windows brighten the interior, throw rugs warm up the tiled floors, and every room in the suite faces the water. White linens and a thick down comforter make the queen-size bed perfectly inviting, while a seashell-lined mirror and wooden boats bordering the bathtub add charm. The sitting room has been endowed with a gas fireplace, distressed pine furnishings, and more nautical accents, and a small kitchenette area is hidden away behind louvered doors. Even though your kitchenette comes stocked with plenty of breakfast fixings, freshly baked croissants and muffins magically appear on your doorstep each morning. You might decide to spend the entire day on your private, secluded patio, watching the boats pass by, or you could head down to the cement platform at the water's edge and dangle your feet in the water as you kiss. **388 Scott Point Drive; (250) 537-9927; moderate; minimum-stay requirement.**

❤❤❤ **HASTINGS HOUSE, Salt Spring Island** Hastings House is a sparkling gem of a country inn, poised over Ganges Harbor and set on 25 acres of rolling, wooded hills crisscrossed by inviting trails and bordered by the water. Everything about this elite property will tug at your heartstrings, from the 16th-century Sussex-style Manor House to the five charming buildings that hold ten distinguished rooms, all with private bathrooms and pale color schemes. Unfortunately, Hastings House will also pull at your purse strings, even if you select one of the smaller, more plainly decorated accommodations. And the strings may break altogether if you want a two-story suite with a classic stone fireplace and two bathrooms. On the other hand, this is certainly the most romantic option: The less expensive rooms are nice, but some are small and most have standard baths.

Every morning, before a four-course breakfast is served in the fireplace-warmed Manor House, a basket of fresh pastries and hot coffee is delivered to your door. As the Hastings House brochure aptly states, "Meticulous attention is given to character, courtesy, comfort, calm, and cuisine," and we can personally vouch for that. As your day progresses, enjoy the afternoon tea, stroll in the gardens, watch the sheep in the pasture, or take a trip into town on a bike. **160 Upper Ganges Road; (250) 537-2362, (800) 661-9255; expensive to unbelievably expensive; minimum-stay requirement on weekends; call for seasonal closures.**

Romantic Note: If your wallet can stand one more splurge, make dinner reservations at the **HASTINGS HOUSE RESTAURANT** (see Restaurant Kissing) or at **SNUG** (very expensive), the property's more casual dining room, which offers a four-course prix fixe menu. Both are open to the public, although guests do receive reservation priority.

❀❀ **MALLARD'S MILL BED AND BREAKFAST, Salt Spring Island** Everything about this bed and breakfast is unique and enticing. Sheltered in a forest grove, the recently constructed wood home is an architectural achievement. Part of the building is supported by cement stilts and propped above a small pond, where water spills from a large rotating waterwheel. An outdoor hot tub and a cabana with a shower overlook this tranquil setting, and a nearby greenhouse provides herbs and vegetables for morning meals. Guests can even hop on board a miniature railroad that wraps around the house for full-scale views of the property. Like we said, unique.

Daylight floods through skylights in the home's interior, which is appointed with wicker furnishings and hardwood floors. Coffee, tea, and cookies can be enjoyed in this comfortable setting at all hours. Four sparingly appointed guest rooms feature a turn-of-the-century motif; hand-sewn patchwork quilts cover the beds, and several rooms have gas fireplaces and views of the churning waterwheel through large picture windows. All rooms have private baths.

A newly constructed honeymoon cottage called Otter Tail is by far the most appropriate choice for romancing. Secluded in the trees, it offers a king-size bed, gas fireplace, a dock that stretches out over the pond, and the utmost in privacy. A Jacuzzi tub for two is set beneath a skylight in the bathroom, making this a cozy spot for evening stargazing. In the morning, a three-course gourmet breakfast is delivered by the train to this unit; the rest of the guests are served in the cheery kitchen or at two-person tables on the outdoor patio overlooking the pond. Blueberry pancakes, seafood omelets, homemade breads, and fruit crêpes are just a few of the delicious treats you can expect. **521 Beddis Road; (250) 537-1011; www.saltspring.com/mallardsmill; moderate to expensive; minimum-stay requirement on weekends seasonally; call for seasonal closures.**

❀❀❀ **THE OLD FARMHOUSE BED AND BREAKFAST, Salt Spring Island** Nestled among spreading trees, bountiful orchards, and colorful gardens, this revitalized turn-of-the-century farmhouse has everything you'll need for an outstanding getaway. A private entrance leads to four cheerful guest rooms located in a separate building that is attached to the main house by a terracotta-tiled hallway. Each room features high dormers, down comforters, a private balcony or patio that overlooks the peaceful landscape, and color accents that correspond to the room's name (e.g., the Blue Room). Special romantic touches include hot coffee or tea delivered to your door in the morning and a decanter of sherry and two miniature crystal glasses placed on each room's bedside table. Outside, you can relax in the two-person hammock or sip iced tea in the intimate gazebo tucked away in the fruit orchard.

Breakfast here is the talk of the town. Served at one large table in the elegant dining room, the gourmet country meal is meticulously presented. Selections may include delicious homemade cinnamon buns, croissants, and muffins; blended fruit smoothy drinks; and egg soufflés filled with tangy berries and topped with powdered sugar. Don't worry if you can't finish your bountiful portion; the hosts provide plastic "doggy bags" so guests can snack on unfinished goodies later in the day. **1077 North End Road; (250) 537-4113; expensive; minimum-stay requirement on weekends seasonally; call for seasonal closures.**

Romantic Warning: Although the innkeeper is always hospitable, you may experience occasionally abrupt and somewhat harsh interactions. When we were late arriving, we found ourselves being scolded for the inconvenience we caused.

❦❦ A PERFECT PERCH BED AND BREAKFAST, Salt Spring Island

Formerly called A Pauper's Perch, this accurately renamed contemporary home commands one of the most spectacular views on Salt Spring Island. Ensconced at the top of a steep forested hillside and surrounded by five acres of undeveloped woodland, A Perfect Perch overlooks sloping valleys, lush forests, the Coast Mountains, and the waterways surrounding the island. In this quiet refuge from the island's ever-increasing hustle and bustle, guests can soak up the magnificent views from the vantage point of each room's private deck.

Though it is slightly more expensive than the other choices, the Honeymoon Suite (also called the Parker Room) is the real reason to come here. A wedding dress adorns the wall above the queen-size four-poster bed, and plentiful amounts of sunlight stream through the many windows. A two-sided fireplace sheds warmth into both the bedroom and bathroom. The spectacular bathroom also offers a double-size Roman soaking tub surrounded by windows that offer an awesome view of Mount Baker. A complimentary bottle of champagne accompanies your stay in this suite. The two downstairs suites have been completely redecorated and are bright and cheery, with white wicker furniture and crisp linens draped over queen-size beds.

Savor a five-course breakfast served in the innkeeper's dining room, with views to the side. Exotic dishes such as grilled spiced oranges, smoked salmon frittatas, and bananas flambé may be among the offerings. In the warmer months guests can eat outside on the expansive deck. **225 Armand Way; (250) 653-2030, (888) 663-2030; www.saltspring.com/perfectperch; expensive; minimum-stay requirement on weekends seasonally; closed mid-November–February.**

❦❦❦ SALTY SPRINGS SPA AND SEASIDE RETREAT, Salt Spring Island

Set on a manicured grassy bank across the street from the ocean, these peculiar-looking "Gothic arch" chalets create a strange first impression. Spiny wooden frames enclose the decks on each of the 12 closely arranged private cabins. However, there is nothing strange about most of the heartwarming interiors; all have knotty pine walls, high arched ceilings, abundant skylights, full kitchens, and wood-burning stoves. Each unit also has an airy living room overlooking the water, and a snug bedroom, separated from the living room by shutters, with the same view. Best of all, guests can soak by candlelight in the large, bright red jetted tub placed in each unit's red-tiled bathroom. If you prefer more modern decor, book a cabin that has been recently updated or one of the two newly built chalets that sit at the edge of the forest. These newer chalets feature the same amenities as the others, but with more up-to-date furnishings and fresh linens. The older units are in great need of new decor.

Prepare to be pampered at the completely renovated spa, which offers shiatsu massage, aromatherapy, hydrotherapy, herbal wraps, salt scrubs, and facials. It's the perfect way to unwind after a leisurely bike ride along the quiet country roads of Salt Spring Island. **1460 North Beach Road; (250) 537-4111, (800) 665-0039; www.saltspring.com/saltysprings; expensive to very expensive; minimum-stay requirement.**

❧❧ **SOLIMAR, Salt Spring Island** A long, winding drive south brings you to one of Salt Spring Island's most secluded waterfront locations. Here, madrona trees reach for the water from rocky outcroppings and small islands dot the horizon. Solimar is Spanish for "sun and sea." Although we can't promise year-round sunshine as its name suggests, you can be assured of total seclusion at this cozy one-bedroom cabin perched just above the water's edge. Overstuffed floral couches, a full kitchen, and a private bath are modern touches in the otherwise very rustic cabin, which features exposed wood beams and dated artwork and fabrics. Guests can effortlessly appreciate the stunning water views through the cabin's windows or explore the property's waterfront acreage on foot. Breakfast fixings await in the refrigerator (provisions for other meals are up to you), and guests are allowed to pick vegetables and herbs from the owners' organic garden. Laundry facilities are available next door for guests' added convenience. **347 Bridgman Road; (250) 653-4418; expensive; no credit cards.**

❧❧ **WESTON LAKE INN, Salt Spring Island** One of the oldest professionally run bed and breakfasts on the island, Weston Lake Inn is also one of the more reasonably priced. Set on ten idyllic country acres, this contemporary home overlooks tranquil, forest-lined Weston Lake. Guests can best appreciate this view from the steamy warmth of a hillside hot tub located on a wooden deck just in front of the house.

The three small guest rooms are all quite comfortable, with private bathrooms, down comforters, skylights, and a mixture of contemporary and country touches. Our favorite is the Petit Point Room, which overlooks the lake and has a queen-size bed. An upstairs common room is warmed by a roaring fire in the hearth and furnished with contemporary overstuffed sofas and artwork by local artists. Downstairs, guests can pop in a video and lazily loll away the hours in the more casual TV room.

After a sumptuous morning meal of fresh fruit, warm scones and croissants, and herbed scrambled eggs or sockeye lox on a bagel, explore the inn's tranquil fishponds, noteworthy gardens, and acres of quiet forest. **813 Beaver**

Point Road; (250) 653-4311; www.bbcanada.com/172.html; moderate; minimum-stay requirement seasonally.

Restaurant Kissing

❤ **BOUZOUKI GREEK CAFE, Salt Spring Island** Bouzouki is harbored right on the water in the town of Ganges. "Romantic" isn't exactly the best word to describe this casual Greek cafe, but "authentic" is. Good lunch spots are hard to come by on Salt Spring Island, and the Greek food served here is superlative. Inside, the decor is simple and to the point. Photographs of Greece adorn the walls, and the windows are framed by cheerful blue trim and lace valances. When the weather cooperates, the outside deck overlooking the water is an ideal spot to enjoy pita bread and hummus, chicken wrapped in phyllo, beef souvlaki, and, for dessert, a gooey slice of baklava. **2104-115 Fulford-Ganges Road, in Grace Point Square; (250) 537-4181; inexpensive; lunch and dinner Monday–Saturday.**

❤❤❤❤ **HASTINGS HOUSE RESTAURANT, Salt Spring Island** One of the most expensive, exclusive places to stay on the west coast of Canada is HASTINGS HOUSE (see Hotel/Bed and Breakfast Kissing). If the cost of staying there exceeds your vacation budget but you want a taste of this regal style of living, make dinner reservations at its elegant restaurant. Several tables offer the ultimate in private dining. Our top choice is the solitary porch table, ideal for a summer evening. On a chilly night, request the living room table, where the two of you can fan the flames of love in front of the grand fireplace. Food lovers may want the chef's table, smack-dab in the middle of the kitchen—it's certainly not private, but the experience is memorable.

The sumptuous, five-course prix fixe meals feature tantalizing Northwest cuisine and produce harvested from the inn's meticulously maintained herb and vegetable gardens. Our superb roasted leg of Salt Spring Island lamb with grainy mustard demi-glace and the pan-seared wild sockeye salmon were models of perfection. Cap the evening with a Belgian white-chocolate parfait, adorned with locally picked strawberries. Regrettably, there is a dress code; men must wear jackets, which is fine if you remembered to pack one. If you didn't, don't fret. Hastings House can loan you one or you can dine in the more casual dining room below called SNUG, where jackets are not required. **160 Upper Ganges Road; (250) 537-2362; very expensive; reservations required; dinner daily.**

Romantic Note: The inn is devoted to its patrons and allows the public to partake of its sublime dinners only if the inn's guests haven't taken the limited reservations first.

❤❤❤ **HOUSE PICCOLO, Salt Spring Island** Once you've sampled House Piccolo's delicious fresh seafood and charming ambience, you'll understand why this dinner spot is touted as one of Salt Spring Island's best. Set in the heart of Ganges, the small blue and white farmhouse is wonderfully intimate. Tables covered in ivory and blue linens are scattered throughout two connecting dining rooms, each appointed with copper kettles, antique dishes, and local artwork. Everything on the Scandinavian-inspired menu is enticing, particularly the tender fillet of salmon, and the prawns Persillé sautéed with garlic and parsley and served with a tomato-herb sauce. Portions are small, but beautifully presented. The chocolate terrine Finlandia is a masterpiece of flowers painted in a sea of crème anglaise surrounding a layered chocolate gâteau. It's almost too pretty to eat . . . almost. **108 Hereford Avenue; (250) 537-1844; expensive; reservations recommended.**

Outdoor Kissing

❦❦ **ARTISAN SUNDAYS, Salt Spring Island** Sundays on Salt Spring Island are loosely organized but exceptionally interesting. Every Sunday the local craftspeople open their studios to the public for browsing and shopping. Every imaginable artistic mastery and innovation can be found in all kinds of hideaways dotted along forested hillsides and settled at the end of long, winding roads. Handmade candles, art glass, knitted items, paper art, ironwork, paintings, pottery, weavings, sculpture, baskets, quilts, and dried flowers are just some of the specialties you can discover during your journey. It might not sound romantic, but once you find a place that has created something you will share forever, it will be an affectionate memory for a long time to come. *Visit the travel information center in Ganges or Vesuvius for a map with addresses and other information.*

❦❦❦❦ **MOUNT MAXWELL PARK, Salt Spring Island** Endless views are just the beginning of what you will experience at the end of the bumpy gravel road that takes you to the top of Mount Maxwell. If you do nothing else on this island, you must witness the breathtaking panorama from up here and kiss passionately for at least a moment or two. It is hard to describe how magnificent and inspiring the scenery is from this vantage point. To the north are the snow-crowned mountains of the Canadian Rockies; to the south stands the glacial peak of Mount Baker; all around, for 360 degrees, are the forested islands and the sparkling, crystalline waters of the Strait of Georgia. Ahh, the sheer beauty of it all. Kissing isn't really mandatory, but you'll find it very hard not to indulge; the sensory stimulation is that potent. **Free admission.** *From the town of Ganges, take Lower Ganges Road south out of town and follow the signs to the park.*

Cost ratings for British Columbia listings are in Canadian funds. American travelers should check the exchange rate or ask an innkeeper to figure out the cost in U.S. dollars.

❦❦❦ **WELCOME ABOARD SAILING CHARTERS, Salt Spring Island** If you're in the mood for a seaworthy adventure and would like a waterborne look at the Gulf Islands, consider sailing on the sleek and elegant 36-foot *Malaika*. You can help crew the boat as much or as little as you'd like; we suggest snuggling up at the bow and nibbling on the provided cookies and hot chocolate. Lessons and a prepacked picnic lunch are available upon request for an additional charge. **Reservations through Weston Lake Inn, (250) 653-4311; $150 per party for a three-hour minimum, $450 per party overnight.**

Mayne Island

Mayne Island may be more populated than some of the other Gulf Islands, but its peaceful aura and natural beauty are intact, making it the perfect choice for a secluded vacation or extended day trip. There's no town center on the island, so restaurants and stores are few.

Hotel/Bed and Breakfast Kissing

❦❦ **A COACH HOUSE ON OYSTER BAY, Mayne Island** This bed and breakfast, tucked away on a quiet corner of the island, is supposed to resemble a turn-of-the-century coach house, although it looks more like a multidimensional West Coast–style home to us. Regardless of architectural interpretation, its waterfront location overlooking the Strait of Georgia can't be beat.

Two ground-level rooms in the main house are nicely furnished with contemporary art, brightened by neutral colors and big windows, and appointed with gas fireplaces, standard baths, and small patios. (Tall people: Watch out for the extremely short patio doors in the Cabriolet Room.) The third room, above the garage, is the most secluded (except in the morning—read on) and has a four-poster queen-size bed, fireplace, skylights in the bathroom, and a hot tub on its private patio. Although this suite is separate from the main home, it is attached to the guest lounge where breakfast is served. Sleeping in could be a problem, especially if some early bird starts playing a prebreakfast tune on the 165-year-old square grand piano, the lounge's centerpiece.

After a four-course breakfast, wander outside and explore the sandy tidal pools bordered by fascinating sandstone formations. Ideal places to rest include the hot tub, perched ten feet from the water, and the glass-enclosed gazebo, which was a work-in-progress when we visited, but looks charming. While parts of this home could use some sprucing up (most notably the stairway leading to the lounge and suite), the wonderful surroundings, pleasant innkeepers, and plenty of deer should make up for such shortcomings. **511 Bayview Drive; (250) 539-3368, (888) 629-6322; expensive; minimum-stay requirement on weekends and holidays.**

❦❦❦❦ **OCEANWOOD COUNTRY INN, Mayne Island** Enveloped by lush gardens, towering trees, and a sweeping view of Navy Channel, this large

Tudor home holds 12 magnificent guest rooms, several ultra-cozy common areas, and an elegant 30-seat country-gourmet restaurant. All rooms, except the Daffodil, have water views; eight have private decks and fireplaces as well as whirlpool or deep soaking tubs. We don't have space to list all our favorites, but the Lilac Room is certainly one of them; it boasts two levels of plush carpeting, a queen-size canopy bed, a deep soaking tub facing a wood-burning fireplace and window, and a private deck overlooking the water. The Fern Room is equally engaging, with a pretty yellow and green color scheme, vaulted ceiling, queen-size canopy bed, large soaking tub, wood-burning fireplace, and private deck that faces the water. For the ultimate in romance (and price), the top-floor Wisteria Suite comes with a deep soaking tub on the deck, sunken living room with fireplace, a queen-size bed, and a spacious bathroom with a private patio. If you can tear yourselves away from your room, you'll find the four common areas are just as wonderful. Two of the loveliest are the garden parlor, with a terra-cotta-tiled floor and floral-tapestried chairs (tea is served here at 4 P.M.), and the library, with soft couches and dozens of books. A double-sided fireplace warms both rooms. If the weather permits, soak in the outdoor hot tub or wander through the herb and flower gardens.

Breakfast (guests only) and dinner (by reservation) are served in the sunny downstairs dining room (see Restaurant Kissing), where you'll have front-row views of the water and the gardens. Your morning could very well begin with a fruit smoothie, fresh muffins and breads, waffles with raspberry purée, and freshly squeezed juices. Our earnest recommendation is that you pack your bags right this minute and take advantage of what this first-class inn has to offer. **630 Dinner Bay Road; (250) 539-5074; www.gulfislands.com/mayne/oceanwood; expensive to very expensive; minimum-stay requirement on weekends; closed December–February.**

Restaurant Kissing

❧❧❧ **FERNHILL LODGE, Mayne Island** This restaurant is a must for food connoisseurs. You'd never guess that feasts like this could possibly exist on a remote island. Every night between May and October, the menu lists four-course theme dinners based on a particular time in history. The Renaissance is evoked with slivers of smoked eel in fruit sauces, a garden-picked salad with quail eggs, barbecued lamb in sweet-and-sour citrus sauce, and sweet and spicy pear pie. A Roman motif is carried out with dates fried in honey and olive oil and sprinkled with pepper, barbecued pigeon with mustard and nut sauce, lentil-chestnut potage, and cheese and honey balls. The proprietors are moving toward lighter cooking with more adventurous sauces and international flavors, including a sprinkling of African-inspired dishes. Also, much of the food is grown on the property, in keeping with the owner's plan to make Fernhill a self-sufficient farm.

The small country-rustic dining rooms are somewhat austere, but they hold a handful of tables set near a warm wood-burning stove and windows that look out to the beautiful flower beds and forested surroundings. If you are in the mood for a particular cuisine, call ahead and put in your request. You may get lucky. **610 Fernhill Road; (250) 539-2544; moderate; call for seasonal hours.**

Romantic Note: FERNHILL LODGE (moderate to expensive) is also a bed and breakfast with three rooms decorated in ethnic motifs, including the aqua blue East India Room, filled with white wicker furniture. It's a fantasy style that seems out of place in the Northwest. While the rooms are certainly private, we just can't recommend them wholeheartedly.

❤❤❤ **OCEANWOOD COUNTRY INN, Mayne Island** Housed on the ground level of the impeccable OCEANWOOD COUNTRY INN (see Hotel/ Bed and Breakfast Kissing), this warm and intimate restaurant is bordered by a brick hearth on one side and a wall of windows overlooking lush gardens and sparkling Navy Channel on the other. Service is exemplary, and the continental prix fixe menu might include such delicacies as roasted garlic and chive flower soup, sun-dried tomato polenta cake with balsamic syrup, potato-crusted sea bass, or oven-roasted rack of lamb with yam lasagne and shallot jus. Top off your repast with the baked citrus meringue covered with fresh strawberries, lavender syrup, and whipped cream, and you'll have an evening to remember. **630 Dinner Bay Road; (250) 539-5074; expensive; call for seasonal hours.**

Saturna Island

Saturna Island is one of the more remote destinations in the Gulf Islands. Ferry schedules are tricky, but it's worth the effort to find yourselves this close to the middle of nowhere. Although the entire island is lush and forested, and wildlife abounds, **EAST POINT** offers particularly impressive views of neighboring Tumbo Island. From this vantage point you're almost guaranteed to see eagles diving and sea otters frolicking, and sometimes (if you're very lucky) a pod of orcas blowing and breaching on the horizon.

Hotel/Bed and Breakfast Kissing

❤❤ **SATURNA LODGE, Saturna Island** This French-style country inn overlooking Boot Cove is the most convenient place to stay on Saturna Island. Not only does it offer easy access to the ferry dock and nearby Saturna Vineyard, but it also houses the island's only kiss-worthy restaurant (see Restaurant Kissing).

Seven guest rooms sporting wine-inspired names are equipped with simple pleasures; most offer queen-size beds, down quilts, pine furnishings, en suite bathrooms, and views of either the cove or surrounding farmland. Sauterne, named for the sweet white wine, is considered the honeymoon suite; its private balcony affords views of the water, and the en suite bathroom holds a soaking tub. Sunny Aligot, reminiscent of vintages from the golden coast of Burgundy, features a four-poster queen-size bed, and an old-fashioned tub with commode sink in the en suite bathroom. Tokay's dormer ceilings, country wallpaper, and lovely view of Boot Cove make it a cozy option as well. Amorous couples should steer clear of Ambrosia (which has two twin beds) and Napa; they are usually rented together to groups or families and have detached bathrooms down the hall.

After a full day spent exploring the island, relax in the hot tub overlooking the gardens or hold hands in front of the fireplace in either of the two lounges. Mornings begin with a complimentary full breakfast for two, served either in the restaurant or on your own private patio (available in some rooms only). **130 Payne Road; (250) 539-2254, (888) 539-8800; www.saturna-island.bc.ca; moderate to expensive.**

❧❧ **STONE HOUSE FARM RESORT, Saturna Island** If you value romance, solitude, and relaxation, you would be wise to plan a sojourn at this 17th-century-style English country home surrounded by 25 acres of farmland and forest. Stone House Farm sits on the banks of Narvaez Bay, with a half mile of picturesque waterfront and sandy beach. As the name implies, the formidable tile-roofed structure is built from stone. Inside, the massive Tudor-style wood beams and handsome paneling are equally impressive.

Guests are encouraged to make themselves at home. Cuddle in the comfy sofa as you share a good movie in the upstairs TV room or challenge each other to pool, darts, or shuffleboard in the adjacent game room. You can also accompany the innkeeper (and his faithful canine companion, Flossie) as he tends to his chores, which include feeding his Highland cow and a well-tended flock of woolly sheep. The three guest rooms here are modest but comfortable; private balconies offer stunning water views, and private baths and plush down comforters are satisfying amenities. In the morning, an exceptionally hearty English breakfast is served in the dining room at your own private table. **207 Narvaez Bay Road; (250) 539-2683; www.bbcanada.com/55.html; moderate; minimum-stay requirement.**

Restaurant Kissing

❧❧ **SATURNA RESTAURANT, Saturna Island** Culinary options on Saturna Island are limited, to say the least. Local pubs offer standard salads, sandwiches, and burgers (which can be satisfactory if you're in the mood for fast food), but, until recently, possibilities for romantic dining were virtually nonexistent. We were pleased to discover this casual little dining room in the newly renovated **SATURNA LODGE** (see Hotel/Bed and Breakfast Kissing). The kitchen here serves up delicious Pacific Northwest cuisine, and the wine cellar offers a variety of B.C. wines to complement just about anything on the menu. When the neighboring winery brings forth its first vintage in 1999, local bottles of pinot noir, chardonnay, merlot, and gewürztraminer will further enhance the selection.

Each evening a prix fixe menu features seafood dishes, Saturna Island lamb, and organic produce. Dine inside surrounded by cheery yellow walls and large windows, or, when the weather cooperates, outside on the decks overlooking the bay. **130 Payne Road; (250) 539-2254, (888) 539-8800; www.saturna-island.bc.ca; moderate to expensive; reservations required; dinner daily.**

Galiano Island

For thousands of years, Galiano Island was frequented by the Coast Salish Nation, a native people who would harvest its wild berries, hunt in its forests, and comb its shores for food. Today, this exceedingly small island, known as "the jewel of the Gulf Islands," provides a handful of amorous options for island-hopping lovers.

Hotel/Bed and Breakfast Kissing

❧❧ **THE BELLHOUSE INN, Galiano Island** A donkey and a pasture full of sheep are the first to welcome you to the Bellhouse Inn. This turn-of-the-century farmhouse, situated on a quiet bay at the southern tip of Galiano Island, offers guests a peaceful setting in which to reflect upon matters of the heart. Watch for killer whales from the beach, or hold hands as you stroll among the fruit trees and manicured lawns surrounding the inn. All six acres are yours to explore.

Unfortunately, the accommodations here don't begin to match their lovely surroundings. An eclectic mix of antique and contemporary furnishings is over-powered by bright peach carpeting that winds throughout the common areas. Upstairs, three of the four guest rooms boast private balconies with water views, but we were disappointed to find that the rooms themselves have mismatched decor and dated touches. The best features are the beds: pretty floral duvets are filled with wool from the innkeepers' sheep—perfect for snuggling the morning away! Of the four, the large Kingfisher Room is worth requesting when making your reservations. French doors open to a private balcony with expansive views of Bellhouse Bay (the view is almost as good from the four-poster bed), and a Jacuzzi tub awaits in the bathroom. The remaining rooms have private baths (although one is located across the hall) and tend to be on the small side. A two-bedroom guest cottage is also located on the property and is best suited for families or groups who are willing to bring their own provisions.

For those staying in the farmhouse, a full, four-course breakfast is served each morning at an antique table in the dining room or outside on the deck if the weather permits. We prefer the latter option; views of the bay are sure to complement your meal of eggs Benedict, scones, cinnamon rolls, fruit, and homemade muffins. **Call for directions; (250) 539-5667, (800) 970-7464; www.monday.com/bellhouse; expensive.**

❀❀❀ **WOODSTONE COUNTRY INN, Galiano Island** Nestled in the hills of Galiano Island, this rural hideaway is surrounded by forests and farmland. Although the inn does not have shimmering water views, the lovely country setting hardly inhibits kissing. Curl up on one of the leather chairs or floral couches near the lobby's stone fireplace and take in serene views of the valley together. Or pull on a pair of boots, grab some binoculars, and head out for an afternoon of birding and other island adventures (rubber boots in varying sizes and binoculars are complimentary for guests).

Most of the 12 rooms have views of the forest and the rolling valley, where hawks float effortlessly in the sky and horses graze in distant corrals. Private porches are greatly appreciated in this setting, although a few face the parking lot. For the best views of the valley, we recommend corner units such as the Hawthorn and Wild Rose Rooms. Each unit at the inn radiates a great deal of warmth, and all are appointed with antiques and floral linens. Most have fireplaces, five offer large soaking tubs, and some boast extra-long king beds. Despite these amenities, the otherwise elegant rooms are marred by drab carpeting, unattractive artwork, and slightly mismatched decor. Still, you'll hardly notice after only a few hours in this lovely setting.

A complimentary breakfast is served to guests every morning at two-person tables in the charming dining room overlooking the valley. Fine dining options are limited on Galiano Island, so guests will appreciate that the inn's restaurant is the best on the island (see Restaurant Kissing). **743 Georgeson Bay Road; (250) 539-2022; www.gulfislands.com/woodstone; moderate to expensive; minimum-stay requirement on weekends seasonally; closed December–January.**

Restaurant Kissing

❀ **LA BERENGERIE, Galiano Island** A rustic, homegrown place like this would not normally have a place in a book like ours, but with such limited dining options on the island, you're bound to end up at La Berengerie sooner or later. This restaurant occupies the main floor of a wooden structure, almost hidden from the road by cedars and overgrown vegetation. The interior is far from elegant, but those with a taste for the eclectic may find it charming. Gingham, floral, and patterned tablecloths cover the tables in the single dining room, and faded Oriental rugs add warmth to the scuffed tiled floor. Colorful abstract art and painted vines adorn the yellow walls. The four-course, prix fixe menu might include red pepper soup, halibut in a lemon-ginger sauce, and Galiano-grown vegetables, followed by pear cake for dessert. **Montague Harbour Road; (250) 539-5392; moderate to expensive; reservations required; call for seasonal hours.**

❀❀❀ **WOODSTONE COUNTRY INN, Galiano Island** If you eat at only one place on Galiano Island, this should be it. Located on the ground floor of the **WOODSTONE COUNTRY INN** (see Hotel/Bed and Breakfast Kissing), this epicurean dining spot provides the perfect backdrop for a romantic evening. Well-spaced tables draped in pink and maroon tablecloths are scattered throughout this gracious, country-style restaurant, where guests partake of serene valley views through floor-to-ceiling windows. Here, excellent four-course dinners are presented by candlelight to the accompaniment of soft classical music. A surprisingly smooth cream of cauliflower soup precedes delectable entrées such as braised lamb shanks or baked shrimp and halibut with fresh dill and lemon butter sauce. We also recommend the vegetarian porcini ravioli: a delightful blend of marinated tomatoes, red peppers, mushrooms, and roasted garlic. Although you really can't go wrong with any of the desserts, the crème caramel is first-class. **743 Georgeson Bay Road; (250) 539-2022; www.gulf islands.com/woodstone; expensive; dinner daily.**

Gabriola Island

Although it is only a 20-minute ferry ride from the industrialized city of Nanaimo, Gabriola Island is a distinctly rural community of about 4,000 residents. Eagles frequently fly overhead, and deer nibble along roadsides (and in residents' gardens) all over the island. Similar in topography to the other Gulf Islands, Gabriola is lushly forested and has a rugged, rocky coastline. You'll find ample inspiring opportunities to pucker up on this tranquil island paradise.

Hotel/Bed and Breakfast Kissing

❦❦❦ **MARINA'S HIDEAWAY, Gabriola Island** Hidden away on an oceanfront bluff, this contemporary home commands views of the ocean through a stand of trees. Privacy is the emphasis here. All the necessities are provided to make you feel right at home, plus extras like chocolates on your pillows at turndown, fluffy robes hanging in the closet, and heated towel racks in the bathroom. The innkeeper is respectful of your space—a definite romantic advantage—although noise from the main part of the house has a tendency to drift into the guest rooms. Situated at one end of the home, the three suites have sliding glass doors that open onto decks with water views. Comfy down comforters and lacy white linens drape the king-size beds, and all rooms feature gas fireplaces, TV/VCRs (accompanied by a small selection of movies), and private entrances. The bottom-level suite feels less intimate than the others because of its full kitchen, separate sitting area, and location just steps away from the communal hot tub (available to guests in all suites). We recommend the top-floor suite, which has the most privacy and the best view.

Begin the day with a gourmet breakfast, served in the privacy of your own room, while taking in the view from your windowside table for two. You'll probably have difficulty finishing the more-than-generous portions, so be sure to ask for a "to-go" box and enjoy the leftovers on your trip back to the mainland. **943 Canso Drive; (250) 247-8854, (888) 208-9850; www. island.net/~gbrunell; moderate; minimum-stay requirement seasonally.**

❧❧ **SUNSET BED AND BREAKFAST, Gabriola Island** Those looking for an authentic bed-and-breakfast experience will appreciate the warmth and hospitality offered here. Perched on a residential hillside across the street from the water, this garden-fronted wooden home is as charming inside as it is outside. A fire crackles in the hearth and classical music sets a tranquil mood in the lovely living room, distinguished by hardwood floors, a sloped ceiling, skylights, and large picture windows with wonderful water views. A generous gourmet breakfast is served at one large table in the airy kitchen adjacent to the living room. Local and organic ingredients are used to create healthy entrées; the apple cloud, a delicious concoction made from Granny Smith apples, lemon juice, eggs, cinnamon, and pecans, is rumored to be a particular favorite.

Of the three guest rooms, the Wild Rose Suite offers the most romantic inspiration. Decorated with a mixture of contemporary and antique furnishings, this spacious suite enjoys beautiful water views, a fireplace, and the luxury of a soaking tub set in a beautifully tiled bathroom. Polished hardwood floors and solid oak accents add warmth to the suite's private sitting area. The other two rooms are much smaller (and consequently quite a bit cheaper), but don't offer much more than a comfortable night's sleep and quiet views of the home's meticulous landscaping.

On lazy summer evenings, guests are welcome to retreat to the backyard and relax on the red-tiled patio adjacent to two small ponds filled with koi. **969 Berry Point Road; (250) 247-2032; www.islandnet.com/~sunsetcl; inexpensive to moderate.**

Restaurant Kissing

❧❧❦ **LATITUDES AT SILVA BAY, Gabriola Island** Set at the east end of the island, in Silva Bay's bustling marina, Latitudes is the only romantic restaurant on Gabriola. Floor-to-ceiling windows command pleasant views of the harbor, and when the weather permits, guests can dine outside on the torchlit deck. Sloping wood ceilings, a fireplace, and Native Canadian wood sculptures lend a rustic, artistic touch to the dining room's otherwise plain interior. Though the tables are a little too large for real intimacy, a pianist playing soothing melodies at a baby grand in the corner creates a romantic atmosphere. Service here is exceptionally accommodating, and the usually reliable menu features seafood, meat, and pasta. Our favorite item was the appetizer of Camembert baked in puffed pastry and served with herbs and sautéed mushrooms. We were pleased to find clams on the menu, but were very disappointed to discover they were canned, not fresh. The tiramisu for dessert, however, was a smashing success and revitalized our taste buds. **Silva Bay; (250) 247-8662; expensive; call for seasonal hours.**

Outdoor Kissing

❀❀ **MALASPINA GALLERIES, Gabriola Island** Centuries ago, wind and sea sculpted the sandstone formations of Gabriola Island, and long before the first Spanish explorers arrived, the native people of the island claimed this spot as a spiritual site. Today the natural beauty of the Malaspina Galleries continues to inspire ethereal encounters of the heart as romantics pause, take in the panoramic views, and steal a kiss or two. A short trail at the end of a quiet street leads past a rocky cove to a mini-peninsula edged in sandstone. Here, you can explore the formations to your hearts' content or enjoy a picnic lunch sheltered by pines and madronas. Although this spot is surrounded on three sides by water, be aware that you're not entirely alone; the peninsula is in full sight of the nearby homes that dot the coastline. *From the ferry terminal at Descanso Bay, go north on Taylor Bay Road and then turn west onto Malaspina Drive. Follow this road until it dead-ends and look for the sign directing you to the entrance of the trail.*

Denman Island

Denman Island's collection of serene country roads, intriguing rocky beaches, abundant wildlife, and funky art galleries makes it a perfect spot for leisurely bike rides with the one you love. **BOYLE POINT PARK** offers a stunning vantage point for viewing the Strait of Georgia and the Chrome Island Lighthouse, and **FILLONGLEY PROVINCIAL PARK** has limited camping facilities and trails that wind through old-growth forests. Directions to these parks can be acquired at the general store in "downtown" Denman or by calling Denman/Hornby Tourist Services (250-335-2293). Although you'll find a handful of casual pubs and coffee shops here, we recommend bringing along a picnic lunch and spending the day exploring Denman's wonderful outdoors.

Hornby Island

A visit to Hornby Island is like a visit to Woodstock, New York, circa 1969. The dress, manner, and conversations in the Co-op Center, where most of the island activity takes place, will make you feel as if you've entered a time warp. Two rather good food stands here serve delicious vegetarian fare and decent espresso to boot. But it's the gorgeous sandy beaches, crystal-clear blue water, and gentle coves and bays that make Hornby Island a romantic destination.

Cost ratings for British Columbia listings are in Canadian funds. American travelers should check the exchange rate or ask an innkeeper to figure out the cost in U.S. dollars.

Outdoor Kissing

❦❦❦❦ **TRIBUNE BAY, Hornby Island** Soft sand under your feet, sparkling surf lapping against the shoreline, a thickly forested backdrop, and cool fresh breezes that blow your cares out to sea: Tribune Bay is the best place in south-western Canada to spend a summer afternoon. *From the Hornby Island ferry dock, follow Central Road to the small Co-op Center and follow the signs a short distance to the bay.*

Quadra Island

Although best known for its commercial and recreational fishing, this island at the northern end of the Gulf Island archipelago also boasts an abundance of wildlife and plenty of terrain worth exploring.

Hotel/Bed and Breakfast Kissing

❦❦ **TSA-KWA-LUTEN LODGE, Quadra Island** Set on a Native Canadian reservation, this handsome, upscale fishing lodge features a most impressive soaring entryway and an almost cavernous interior supported by massive log beams and pillars. Striking floor-to-ceiling windows, surrounded by bright salmon-colored walls, look out to a stunning view of the water and the mountains on the mainland. The rooms are hotel stylish, with high ceilings, tall windows, plain bathrooms (some with single-person Jacuzzi tubs), gas fireplaces, and comfortable, although sparse, furnishings.

The lodge offers several packages, some of which may include continental breakfast and/or dinner with your stay, so be specific when making reservations. Breakfast, lunch, and dinner are served in the glass-enclosed waterfront dining room just off the main lobby. Begin your evening meal with savory steamed butter clams, simmered in fresh herbs and white wine and served with garlic bread. Be sure to try one of the restaurant's specialty entrées; the orange cream prawns and scallops or the phyllo chicken Cordon Bleu are superb and perfectly prepared. **Lighthouse Road, at Quathiaski Cove; (250) 285-2042, (800) 665-7745; inexpensive to unbelievably expensive; call for seasonal closures.**

". . . kisses are a better fate than wisdom."

e.e. cummings

Sunshine Coast

The Sunshine Coast is accessible only by ferry from Horseshoe Bay, just past West Vancouver where Highway 1 meets Highway 99. A 40-minute ferry ride takes you through the mountain-ringed waters and islands of Howe Sound to Langdale. Ferries make eight sailings per day, approximately every two hours. For schedules and general information, call British Columbia Ferries (250-386-3431, 888-223-3779 in Canada) or visit their Web site at www.bcferries.bc.ca.

Whoever named this region was certainly an optimist (or perhaps just a good marketing person). It may not always be clear and sunny, as the name suggests, but this region does provide all the wonderful rugged sights and sounds you could want from the Canadian Southwest, and a multitude of other getaway opportunities you probably didn't know existed. Regardless of weather conditions—even on a cool misty morning or a wet afternoon—the Sunshine Coast is breathtaking.

You'll feel as though you've accidentally stumbled onto a remote, lengthy peninsula or a long skinny island, yet this geographically unique area is neither. This section of British Columbia, beginning at Langdale's ferry dock and ending at Powell River, is indeed part of the mainland, but because it is bordered on the north, south, and west by water and on the east by mountains, it is accessible only by ferry. While this keeps the area from becoming too crowded, more people are discovering this affordable getaway and the lines at the ferry terminal grow longer every year. Yet even when the ferry from Horseshoe Bay is packed and you have to wait awhile to board, the other cars seem to disappear once you get off and head north along the coast. It is unlikely you will encounter crowds again until you return to the Vancouver area. Do take advantage of the ferryboat ride: It is one of the most visually glorious excursions around. Get out of your car, walk outside, and breathe in the salt air; the ride is a perfect prelude to the magnificent sights ahead.

Romantic Note: For all its spectacular scenery, the Sunshine Coast is still a fairly remote destination. In other words, come here for the isolation and the incredible seascape, not for lively nightlife or four-lip restaurants and accommodations. Room rates are in keeping with the low-key atmosphere, making the Sunshine Coast one of the most affordable getaways in British Columbia (and in this book, for that matter).

Romantic Suggestion: If hiking and outdoor activities are part of your romantic itinerary, the Sunshine Coast is your kind of place. We highlight several of our favorite Outdoor Kissing spots throughout this chapter, but for more detailed information we wholeheartedly recommend purchasing *Sunshine and Salt Air: A Recreational Guide to the Sunshine Coast,* by Bryan Carson and Karen

Southern (Harbor Publishing). This handy guide details the type of terrain you will encounter, suggests hikes (and tells you how long each one is), and offers brief but vivid descriptions that will make you even more eager to reach your destination.

Bowen Island

Although it is just a 20-minute ferry ride from Horseshoe Bay, Bowen Island feels worlds apart. There is enough rural charm and serenity here to soothe even the most tense, city-weary traveler. Bowen Island is one of the less touristed of British Columbia's Gulf Islands (it's more of a bedroom community for Vancouver than a tourist destination); however, the remote location makes the trip here worthwhile, and the overall relaxed feel of the island provides unbeatable tranquillity. Even though the island is relatively undiscovered, a variety of low-key services and activities are available: There are sunset horseback rides to Mount Gardner and plenty of hiking trails for outdoor lovers. The 23 miles of coastline may be calling you—if so, consider a kayak excursion. One reliable company that offers affordable rentals and guided trips is **BOWEN ISLAND SEA KAYAKING** (604-947-9266, 800-60-KAYAK in Canada). Ask about renting a double kayak for a true sense of togetherness as you explore the island.

Hotel/Bed and Breakfast Kissing

❦❦❦ **ON THE SEA BED AND BREAKFAST, Bowen Island** Bowen Island is replete with rural charm as well as a few hidden treasures, and On The Sea is one of them. While a breathtaking ocean view may be the best reason to consider this bed and breakfast, it certainly isn't the only one. If you are looking for privacy, tranquillity, and a touch of elegance, you will find them here. This part of the island (on the northwest side) has a steep incline up to the homes resting on a cliff above the ocean. From the accessible beach below or from the floor-to-ceiling windows in your room, the effect is dramatic. A distinct romantic advantage is the surrounding quiet; since the house is relatively secluded, the only sounds you might encounter are sounds of the sea.

The lower level of this large home comprises two almost identical guest rooms, and each has its own private entrance. Both rooms include a small kitchenette where fresh juices and snacks are stocked. Plush cream-colored carpet, muted beige walls, and layered satin and floral drapes make the large rooms cozy and warm. Vases of fresh flowers are a sweet touch, as are the biscotti waiting on the lace pillows. Near the windows, a sunken sitting area

Cost ratings for British Columbia listings are in Canadian funds. American travelers should check the exchange rate or ask an innkeeper to figure out the cost in U.S. dollars.

filled with antiques, solid mahogany tables, and Victorian-style furniture provides a comfortable retreat. An entire wall of each room is devoted to windows overlooking the ocean, so you can enjoy watching cruise ships, regattas, and an occasional whale from your private deck, sunken living room area, or queen-size bed. A sense of peaceful serenity flows from the almost complete silence.

An elegant gourmet breakfast, served on bone china and accompanied by sterling flatware and crystal, arrives at your door in the morning. The aroma of a smoked-salmon omelet with a blend of cheeses or the French toast with fresh berries and cream will surely tempt you out of bed. After breakfast, and before heading out to explore, take a walk down a trail to the private rocky beach below, where you can kiss to your hearts' content. Just watch your step on the way down; the trail is very steep. **728 Taylor Road; (604) 947-2471; moderate to expensive.**

❦❦ **ORCHARD BED AND BREAKFAST, Bowen Island** This bed and breakfast consists of one sunny suite located directly above BEGGAR'S PURSE restaurant (see Restaurant Kissing). Only a few hundred yards from the ferry terminal, this is a convenient spot for those who choose to leave their car behind and explore the island on foot (not a bad idea, since almost everything you need for a romantic weekend is within walking distance). Head down to the marina and browse through the shops, kayak around the island in the afternoon, or have a quiet intimate dinner at the Beggar's Purse. When you're ready to retire for the evening, simply walk up the stairs to your suite.

Upstairs, French doors on the deck lead to a bright sitting room adorned with comfortable Old English–style furniture done up in a soft rose print. A gas woodstove keeps things toasty on cool evenings. An adjoining bedroom features a king-size sleigh bed with a fluffy comforter, plenty of pillows, floral lamps with white fringe, and an overstuffed chair in the corner for snuggling. The private bath has a sparkling tile floor and antique-style fixtures, including a claw-foot tub that is six feet long and perfect for a bubble bath. From the many windows in all three rooms, light seems to pour in from every direction.

Two romantic drawbacks here are the noise drifting up from the restaurant below, and the fact that if you choose to have breakfast included in your stay (it is optional), it is served in the busy café downstairs. We suggest you bring some muffins and juice up to your room for a more intimate morning repast. **Orchard Square, at Snug Cove; (604) 947-0550; moderate.**

❦❦❦ **THE VINEYARD AT BOWEN ISLAND, Bowen Island** If you fantasize about getting away from it all but have only a weekend to spare, then dream no longer. Nestled on the side of Cates Hill, just a few minutes from the ferry landing, the Vineyard at Bowen Island is a newly built bed and breakfast where your dreams of seclusion and tranquillity can come true.

As you might guess from the name, this bed and breakfast is associated with a working vineyard. Set on four acres, the guest house overlooks one rolling acre devoted to pinot noir and pinot gris grapes. Although the grape-vines may not look like much at certain times of the year, they will eventually bear thick, lush rows of precious fruit, and have been maturing in anticipation of the first pressing (1998 marks the first vintage). Separate from the winery, the guest facilities are ready year-round, and they are completely worth your affectionate consideration.

In the main house, plush couches sit beside a stone fireplace in the French country–inspired living room. Beyond, a sunny breakfast room has tables for two by windows that face the vineyard. Also overlooking the vineyard and neighboring forest is an expansive brick patio with a large pool and hot tub, located behind the house. Guest rooms are in a separate two-story building next door, and each of the six units has its own private entrance. Every room and suite is equipped with a gas-log fireplace, small kitchenette, rich Native Canadian–print linens, wrought-iron touches, and exquisite local artwork. Contemporary furnishings blend with warm color schemes, stylish accents, and natural wood to create modern, comfortable rooms. The two suites up-stairs overlook a little garden courtyard and include large bathrooms with hardwood floors and soaking tubs for two; king-size beds, superior views, and separate living and dining areas are additional amenities. Balconies off every unit survey the property and the surrounding hills.

Nightlife is pretty mellow on Bowen Island, but every room has its own TV/VCR, and you can borrow a video from the main house. In the morning, generous full breakfasts are served to individual tables in the breakfast room, or you may arrange to have breakfast delivered to your room. As much as we appreciate this couple-oriented option, we found the cheerful breakfast room sufficiently intimate. Wherever you end up eating, the smoked-salmon Bene-dict is outstanding. **687 Cates Lane; (604) 947-0028, (800) 718-9463; www. vineyard.bc.ca; inexpensive to very expensive; minimum-stay require-ment on holiday weekends.**

Romantic Suggestion: The owners offer dinners by previous arrangement, and we highly recommend that you make a reservation. Prices for this four-course, gourmet delight start at $60 per couple (not including wine).

Restaurant Kissing

❤❤❤ **BEGGAR'S PURSE, Bowen Island** There are only a few places to dine on Bowen Island, and most are exceedingly casual, so it was a wonderful surprise to discover this charming little restaurant with incredible food just a short walk from the ferry landing. Strangely enough, this restaurant has two distinct personalities. During breakfast and lunch, it's a busy café that goes by the name of Orchard Square. At night it is transformed into Beggar's Purse, a romantic candlelit bistro serving three-course gourmet dinners. The limited menu offers only three entrée selections, including one vegetarian dish. The tender lamb osso buco with potatoes and braised greens is prepared to perfection, and the seared chicken on lightly creamed spinach will practically melt in your mouth. Saving room for dessert is a must, considering the mouthwatering pear tarte à la mode and the creamy mocha fudge pudding. The latter is so rich and smooth, we recommend one dish with two spoons.

Round tables fill the dining room and are draped with white tablecloths and topped with fresh flowers and candles. Two cozy and intimate tables rest on a lower landing near the fireplace and are a warm choice on a cool evening. During the summer, seating is available outside on the patio. Considering the limited size of Beggar's Purse and the delicious entrées prepared nightly, it would be wise to make your reservations early. **Orchard Square, at Snug Cove; (604) 947-0550; moderate to expensive; reservations recommended; call for seasonal hours.**

Gibsons

Gibsons is the most densely populated town on the Sunshine Coast. If shopping and browsing are part of your vacation plans, you'll love this little village's array of shops and boutiques.

Hotel/Bed and Breakfast Kissing

❀❀ **BONNIEBROOK LODGE, Gibsons** Bonniebrook Lodge comprises four country Victorian guest rooms above **CHEZ PHILIPPE RESTAURANT** (see Restaurant Kissing) and three newly constructed suites in a separate building. The four cozy rooms above the restaurant have floral bedspreads, dormer ceilings, and striped wallpapers in varying color schemes. Only the Rose Room has a private bath; the other three share two detached baths (not exactly our idea of romantic, but we must say that the prices are quite reasonable). Unfortunately, the three rooms with shared baths have the best ocean views, while the Rose Room has a partial water view beyond the small parking lot. As with most guest rooms above a restaurant, noise from the dining room can be a problem (especially in the summer months, when Chez Philippe is extremely popular).

The newest additions to the lodge are three "Romance Suites," located in a separate building behind the main house and across from the beach. Each suite includes a queen-size bed, a private deck, and a marble soaker tub for two. These rooms are decorated in a simple, contemporary style with vaulted ceilings, yellow walls, and gas fireplaces edged in Indian slate. Giant pine armoires and wood furnishings add some warmth to the otherwise sparse decor.

A full breakfast of omelets, hash browns, fresh fruit, and muffins awaits each morning in the restaurant area of the main house. If the thought of lounging in bed all day is appealing, we recommend staying in one of the suites: Guests here have the option of having their morning repast delivered right to their door. **Gower Point Road; (604) 886-2887; www.bonniebrook.com; inexpensive to moderate; minimum-stay requirement on holiday weekends; closed January.**

❧❧ **MARINA HOUSE, Gibsons** This 1931 heritage home is located just down the beach from Molly's Reach (also known as the Gibsons Landing Marina and former site of a long-running Canadian TV show called *The Beachcombers*). The beach in front of the house offers safe moorage for boats and kayaks, and the area has miles of coastline that invite exploring, sailing, and diving. In addition, several restaurants, charming cafés, art galleries, and shops are within walking distance of the front door.

Perched on the top floor of the house, all three guest rooms feature private baths (although one room has a detached bath across the hall), floral country decor, and views of the water. Molly's Room is the most romantic, mainly due to the breathtaking views of the coast (you can see Shoal Channel, which runs between the Sunshine Coast and Keats Island), but also because of its hardwood floors, queen-size sleigh bed, and white lace curtains. Although all three rooms are small, they are beautifully decorated with pine furniture, plush bedding, and floral wallpaper. A common room is also available, with windows overlooking the water and a balcony for watching the sunrise. In the morning, head to the library to feast upon a four-pepper frittata or poached eggs served on three-corn bread with lemon sauce and smoked salmon, all accompanied by fresh fruit, muffins, and scones. **546 Marine Drive; (604) 886-7888, (604) 886-4906; www.bcbandb.com/whis/marina.htm; inexpensive.**

❧❧❧❧ **ROSEWOOD COUNTRY HOUSE, Gibsons** At first glance Rosewood looks like a renovated or beautifully maintained turn-of-the-century house, but it is actually a newly built reproduction of a 1910 Craftsman-style home. From the gabled detailing to the antique leaded glass windows, every aspect of this slate blue house is immaculate and authentic feeling. Lush flower gardens trim the home in brilliant color, and a charming gazebo is set near a spring-fed pond in the front yard. Tender loving care and attention to detail mark every inch of the Rosewood. And except for the third floor, where the innkeepers reside, the entire house is yours.

Polished hardwood floors, Oriental carpets, and gorgeous antiques adorn the interior, and an elegantly appointed sitting room provides a place to relax and savor the view of the ocean and mountains. The main floor holds one guest room (the Orchid Room) and a large suite (the Sunset Room); these two rooms can be rented as one unit for families or couples traveling together. The Orchid Room is small and attractive, with a queen-size bed in a contemporary bedframe, floral linens, a down comforter, pale lavender walls, and a detached bath. The Sunset Room is one of the absolute best amorous options on the Sunshine Coast, with its cushioned window seat where you can watch the sun make its dramatic daily exit. A tub is cleverly tucked beneath the window seat, so sunset soaks are a definite option. In addition, this opulent room features a private entrance, a gas fireplace in a brick hearth, a TV/VCR and CD player, a queen-size brass bed, lace appointments, and exquisite decor. The full en suite bathroom holds a double shower. A separate entertainment room available to all guests features a pool table, but such distractions hardly seem necessary in such a romantic setting.

At breakfast time, champagne, orange juice, warm croissants, and home-baked muffins accompany the health-conscious, filling meal served in the sunny breakfast room. All of the jams and jellies are homemade. In fact, ask your attentive hostess about the various gourmet delights she creates; her pantry is full of goodies that would put Martha Stewart to shame. **575 Pine Road; (604) 886-4714; web.idirect.com/~dneff/rose.html; inexpensive to moderate; no credit cards; closed January; recommended wedding site.**

Romantic Suggestion: The multitalented hostess can prepare a personalized romantic dinner for two on the picturesque balcony overlooking the gardens, pond, and gazebo. Arrangements and menu requests must be made a day in advance; the price is approximately $100 for two. Although this price does not include wine, you are welcome to bring your own bottle of wine or champagne if you would like to toast a special occasion.

Restaurant Kissing

❧❧❧ **CHEZ PHILIPPE RESTAURANT, Gibsons** What do you get when you combine a French restaurant, a Victorian inn, RV sites, and a tent campground? There is no punch line—the straight answer is Chez Philippe Restaurant at **BONNIEBROOK LODGE** (see Hotel/Bed and Breakfast Kissing). As strange as the combination may sound, all of these businesses operate on one property, offering something for every type of traveler. For those with romantic inclinations, however, we specifically recommend an evening at the restaurant.

Colorful flower gardens border the front patio of Chez Philippe, which occupies the first floor of a large 1920s home. Quiet country elegance best describes the two dining rooms, each with delicate stencilwork lining the walls, rich mustard-colored linens, and little oil lanterns at every table. Picture windows face the ocean across the street, and a crackling fire enhances the already intimate ambience.

Call ahead and reserve a sunset window seat—an exquisite place to witness the sun's daily curtain call. If you arrive a little too early for sunset, you can always linger over your West Coast–influenced French meal. Rack of lamb roasted with mustard and a seven-grain crust; red snapper pan-fried with cilantro and julienne of smoked salmon; and the fabulous seafood ragout with salmon, snapper, scallops, and prawns tossed in a garlic cream sauce are just a few of the items to choose from. If the sun hasn't set by the time you finish dinner, why not linger a bit over dessert? The profiteroles in warm chocolate sauce are a heavenly accompaniment to nature's heavenly show. **Gower Point Road, at Bonniebrook Lodge; (604) 886-2188; www.bonniebrook.com; moderate to expensive; reservations recommended; call for seasonal hours.**

Roberts Creek

Roberts Creek is a mere 15 minutes from the ferry dock in Langdale. While this town has several wonderful bed and breakfasts, it offers only a few restaurants and shops. We suggest visiting the oceanside regional park, with its newly constructed boardwalk; bring along a picnic lunch and walk hand in hand along the shore.

Hotel/Bed and Breakfast Kissing

❤❤❤ **THE COTTAGE ON DRIFTWOOD BEACH, Roberts Creek** Have you ever dreamed of having your own quiet little beach house? Well, even if it is yours for only a few nights, the Cottage on Driftwood Beach will make that dream come true. This modest cottage is set right at sea level; high tide is only 20 yards away, and guests have their own private walkway down to the beach.

Even with the owners' home right next door, you will find the cottage wonderfully secluded and private. A large stone fireplace, cedar interior, shelves full of books, and an eclectic mix of artwork and furnishings make the interior feel warm and cozy. There are plenty of extra blankets for snuggling on the couch and savoring the peaceful view. A large picture window in the sitting room allows for an incredible 180-degree view, and the sunsets here are mesmerizing. You'll also find a full kitchen, two bedrooms, and one bathroom. Two couples could easily share the facilities here, but for obvious reasons we think it is perfect for just one couple. One of the bedrooms has a bay window facing the ocean through tall trees, and the sound of waves lapping against the shore will lull you to sleep. Go ahead and leave the window open to let in the sea breezes—flannel sheets will help keep you toasty.

In the morning a full, hearty breakfast is delivered to the cottage. Every breakfast begins with fantastic fresh fruit yogurt made exclusively with berries grown on the property. After a filling meal of waffles and sausage, stroll along the stretch of sandy beach just steps away. If you sit very still and wait long enough, you might catch a glimpse of the eagle that regularly hunts from the ancient Douglas fir right in front of the cottage. Consider yourselves blessed; it isn't every day that you find a quiet spot like this. **3807 Beach Avenue; (604) 885-3489; www.bbcanada.com/841.html; moderate; no credit cards.**

❤❤❤ **COUNTRY COTTAGE BED AND BREAKFAST, Roberts Creek** Country Cottage Bed and Breakfast is a perfectly cozy retreat. Genuine Canadian country hospitality prevails here, from the congenial innkeepers to the hot tea and freshly baked scones offered upon your arrival. Although large sections of the property's two acres are wooded, the innkeepers have managed to create a small picturesque farm around their central farmhouse. You'll know that you have truly escaped the city after you've strolled through the gardens, stopped to visit the sheep, and watched the chickens busily moving around the henhouse.

Only two units are available here, which helps create a personal experience. The Cottage, adjacent to the main farmhouse, defines country charm. Colorful gardens and window boxes trim the exterior of this little cedar cabin. Hand-loomed throw rugs on the hardwood floors, mixed antiques, a patchwork quilt covering the queen-size bed, and a little woodstove are among the touches that make this an inviting environment.

More privately located at the back of the property is the handsome and rustic Cedar Lodge. Although it can comfortably accommodate up to three couples (which makes it a real bargain), we think it's a great choice for a twosome. You'll want to light a fire in the massive river-rock fireplace even on a warm day, just to give the knotty pine walls the proper luster. Hunter green and cranberry-colored Adirondack-style furnishings, fishing paraphernalia, and sleeping lofts with fine wool blankets and snug flannel sheets create an exceedingly cozy atmosphere that would fit right into an Eddie Bauer catalog. If you happen to be traveling with another couple, you can all have privacy. A tiny cabin, complete with a skylight, private bath, and sauna, is separated from the lodge by a deck and provides additional sleeping quarters.

Both the Cedar Lodge and the Cottage have full kitchens, so you'll need to venture out only if you desire an outdoor excursion. A hearty farm-fresh breakfast, served at one table in the kitchen of the main house amid vintage country collectibles, is included in your stay. A wood-burning stove crackles in the background as your gracious hostess serves up such delectables as whole-grain Belgian waffles with whipped cream and fresh fruit, or savory asparagus crêpes. Whatever the main course, you'll be more than adequately prepared for a full day of outdoor activity. **1183 Roberts Creek Road; (604) 885-7448; inexpensive to expensive; no credit cards; minimum-stay requirement on holidays.**

❧❧ **HUCKLEBERRY HOUSE BED AND BREAKFAST, Roberts Creek** Just steps away from Henderson Beach, this newly constructed cottage is a great place to spend quality time together (and, if your vacation time allows, a sizable quantity of time as well). Timber for the home was hand-selected from the surrounding woods, and attention to detail is apparent everywhere, from the fine wood trim around the French doors and windows to the potted plants and flowers that grow on the large wraparound deck. (At the time of our visit, plans were being made to construct a hot tub on the deck; if all goes well, this will be a relaxing spot to soak away life's stresses beneath a canopy of stars.)

The cottage is completely self-contained, with everything from a barbecue to a washer and dryer. While the style of the cottage is clean and simple, that doesn't exclude romantic possibilities; what the cottage lacks in coziness, it makes up for in seclusion and charm. You'll find a fully equipped kitchen; a large living room with a woodstove and vaulted ceilings and decorated with woven rugs, seascape pictures by local artists, and brightly colored throw blankets; and a comfortable bedroom with an antique dresser and a queen-size bed. Off the bedroom, the large white-tiled bathroom features a deep soaker tub and a separate shower.

A breakfast of warm home-baked croissants, a generous bowl of fresh fruit, and a delicious blend of coffee is delivered to the cottage each morning. Relax, enjoy the surrounding forest, and stay as long as you can. **1495 Henderson Avenue; (604) 885-0603, (800) 272-8206; www. huckleberry.bc.ca; moderate; minimum-stay requirement.**

❤❤❤ **WILLOWS INN, Roberts Creek** Willows Inn consists of just one little log cabin, and you are the only guests, so enjoy—it isn't often that you find seclusion like this. Colorful hanging plants and a well-tended yard separate the picturesque cabin from the owner's log home, enhancing the cabin's intimate potential. Inside, polished hardwood floors, scattered throw rugs, green floral fabrics, comfy rocking chairs, a woodstove set against a brick hearth, and bouquets of fresh flowers give the large, one-room cabin a fresh and simple country air. A fruit basket and chocolate-covered strawberries await you in the small kitchenette area.

In the morning, wake to sunlight streaming through the skylights overhead, and savor the abundant country breakfast brought directly to your cottage door at whatever time you choose. One morning you may find gourmet omelets with freshly baked scones; next morning's feast could include Belgian waffles with strawberry sauce and Canadian bacon. Once you've experienced the solitude and quiet splendor of this cozy retreat, located only a five-minute walk from the beach, you may not want to leave. **3440 Beach Avenue; (604) 885-2452; inexpensive; no credit cards; minimum-stay requirement on weekends seasonally.**

Restaurant Kissing

❤❤❤ **CREEKHOUSE RESTAURANT, Roberts Creek** What a wonderful surprise to discover that fine dining exists in this unassuming rural neighborhood. Windows along two walls of the modest dining room face lush greenery, while dark hardwood floors, potted plants, and high ceilings give the room a casual ambience. French cuisine with an emphasis on fresh local ingredients graces the menu, and the catch of the day is always excellent. We highly recommend beginning with the endive salad with roasted pecans and asiago cheese, which is served with apple slices and has a sweet, crisp, full flavor. Seafood crepes stuffed with shrimp, scallops, fresh fish, and spinach in a wine and cream sauce are one entrée option; pork tenderloin with a port sauce is an-

Cost ratings for British Columbia listings are in Canadian funds. American travelers should check the exchange rate or ask an innkeeper to figure out the cost in U.S. dollars.

other. Both dishes are exquisite. These and other delicious entrées may not leave you with room for dessert, but if you can force yourselves to be decadent, the chocolate mousse and fruit tarts are marvelous. Service is knowledgeable and friendly. **1041 Roberts Creek Road; (604) 885-9321; moderate to expensive; dinner Friday–Sunday.**

Outdoor Kissing

❀❀❀ **CLIFF GILKER PARK, Roberts Creek** A hiker's dream, Cliff Gilker Park features trails of varying distances leading through thick woods, fields of flowers, and magical waterfalls. Around every corner there is something new to discover, and you're bound to find a trail that perfectly matches your energy level. Trails are well marked and well maintained, so whether you are a hiker or just want to enjoy a light walk, don't miss this park. **Free admission.** *Located in Roberts Creek, just off Highway 101. Watch for signs.*

❀❀❀ **ROBERTS CREEK BEACH PARK, Roberts Creek** Driftwood benches line each side of this long, thin stretch of beach that juts into Georgia Strait. This is one of the best lookout points for viewing all of the marine wildlife of the Sunshine Coast. Diverse seabirds, bald eagles, seals, otters, and orcas are just a few of the creatures that enjoy the remote splendor of this coastline. You will surely join them in appreciation of this area's natural beauty and tranquillity. **Free admission.** *Follow Highway 101 to the Roberts Creek Road turnoff and turn north onto Beach Avenue.*

Sechelt

Located halfway up the Sunshine Coast, Sechelt is a small community with a handful of shops and art galleries, and the coast's only movie theater.

Hotel/Bed and Breakfast Kissing

❀❀ **PACIFIC SHORES, Sechelt** Pacific Shores offers one spacious guest room in the owners' large white beach home. Thankfully, a separate entrance offers some seclusion, and since you are the only guests, the beach is all yours. Inside you'll find fresh flowers, wicker furniture with floral cushions, a white brick fireplace, and generous pictures windows overlooking the beachfront yard. A tropical-print bedspread drapes the queen-size bed. Baskets and large plants fill the room, seashell plates with potpourri rest on night tables, and plenty of extra pillows allow for snuggling wherever you'd like. In such a charming atmosphere, it's difficult not to feel energized. Even when it's raining, Pacific Shores will put you in a sunny frame of mind.

A breakfast of fresh fruit and hot croissants, followed by a waffle and crisp bacon, is served to your room or outside on the patio when weather permits. The hospitality is wonderful, and you are afforded all the privacy you desire. A five-minute walk takes you to Sechelt, where you can browse through the shops and restaurants, or you can drive up to **EARL'S COVE** to catch the scenic ferry ride to Saltery Bay (see Outdoor Kissing). **5853 Highway 101; (604) 885-8938; moderate.**

❦❦❧ **TRANQUILITY BAY, Sechelt** Tranquility Bay—what a wonderful name for a romantic getaway destination! Actually, it is a bay east of Sechelt where the water is as smooth and still as glass. As the name implies, the bay is protected from the wind by the surrounding islands, making it a serene spot to kayak, hike, bike, or just relax on the beach. For those with subaquatic skills, the bay is considered one of the best diving spots on the Sunshine Coast.

Tranquility Bay is also the name of a newly opened bed and breakfast consisting of a main lodge and three cottages situated along this peaceful body of water. While the location is picture-perfect, these accommodations are geared more for outdoor enthusiasts than for amorous-minded couples. There's no shortage of amenities here (TVs, stereos, and hot tubs grace most of the units), but limited romantic touches give it a casual atmosphere. That's not to say you can't find romance at this beautiful spot; seclusion is possible if you choose the accommodation that best suits your needs and wants.

One cottage is located across the street from the bay and features two bedrooms (one with a pine sleigh bed), a living room, kitchen, and a private hot tub on the deck bordering the creek. Wood walls warm the exterior, and snuggly plaid comforters drape the beds. This cabin may be a little spacious for one couple, but relax and enjoy the fact that this is an incredible bargain. Another small cottage next to the main house features a queen-size bed, private bath, and cozy sitting room equipped with a woodstove. The furnishings are casual, but the cabin is exceedingly private, and right outside the front door you'll find a path that leads to the beach for late-night walks together. A third cabin, Upland Cottage, is located a few blocks up from the beach and is designed for larger groups and families, so it is not the most romantic option.

Last, but certainly not least, is the Sunset Suite, located in the main lodge. A large living room with a woodstove, pool table, bar, exercise equipment, and beautiful views of the bay is yours and yours alone. An antique cherry-wood bed awaits in the bedroom, which has been done up in rich shades of burgundy and green. Even the hot tub, situated just outside the sliding glass doors, is wonderfully private; if you prefer staying indoors, the bathroom has a large soaker tub.

Guests in the suite and the cottage next to the main house may partake in a full gourmet breakfast served in the main lodge each morning. (The other cabins have full kitchens, so guests in those units should bring their own provisions.) Tranquility Bay is a wonderful place for an extended stay, especially if you plan to take advantage of all the amenities. Packages are available, and may include your ferry ticket, lodging, and dinner at the **BLUE HERON INN** (see Restaurant Kissing). **7651 Sechelt Inlet Road; (604) 885-3442, (800) 665-2311; www.ewest.com/tranquility_bay; inexpensive to moderate.**

Restaurant Kissing

❤❤❤ **BLUE HERON INN, Sechelt** Pull into the driveway and head down to the water's edge, where the Blue Heron Inn fills the lower level of a family home. This contemporary dining room is adorned with bright floral table-cloths, fresh flower arrangements, and heron-inspired artwork. Luminous little lamps at every table and a fire burning in the large stone fireplace impart a soft golden glow throughout. A wall of windows faces the glassy waters of Porpoise Bay, and almost every table shares the magnificent vista. The house specialty is seafood, and unless you catch it yourself, seafood doesn't get much fresher than this.

Start with one of the wonderfully creative appetizers, such as artichoke hearts filled and baked with shrimp, crab, and Parmesan cheese, or Sambuca prawns sautéed in a garlic cream–Sambuca sauce. As a main course, we recommend the broiled halibut fillet topped with red onion and strawberry salsa, or the bouillabaisse with fresh fish, scallops, crab, and prawns, served in a lobster bisque. **Porpoise Bay Road; (604) 885-3847, (800) 818-8977; moderate to expensive; reservations required; call for seasonal hours.**

Halfmoon Bay

Hotel/Bed and Breakfast Kissing

❤❤❤❤ **HALFMOON BAY CABIN, Halfmoon Bay** A luxury log cabin may sound like a contradiction in terms, but Halfmoon Bay Cabin has everything, including complete privacy, and is wholly worth your romantic consideration. English country gardens, old-growth trees, and a large deck drenched in sunlight from dawn to dusk (at least on sunny days) surround this large cabin.

The cabin's two bedrooms feature queen-size feather beds, pine furnishings, and French doors leading to the deck. An entertainment center and a huge master bath with a Jacuzzi tub are welcome bonuses. In the living room, a giant stone fireplace would get all the attention if it not for the ocean view across the deck and through the trees. Snuggle up on the plush cream couch in front of the fire and enjoy a dinner you have prepared in the large furnished kitchen. Some walls in the cabin are solid yellow cedar, and a fresh woodsy fragrance fills the air.

A short walk takes you down to the sandy, driftwood-covered beach, where you can spend a leisurely day watching the waves lap against the shore. A cabana has been constructed on the beach with everything you could ever need: lounge chairs, a wet bar, full fridge, barbecue, and a wonderful cedar-walled shower.

Privacy, luxury, and every convenience are waiting for you at Halfmoon Bay Cabin. The only things you need to bring along are food and an appetite for love. **8617 Redroofs Road; (604) 688-5058; www.halfmoon-bay-cabin.com; expensive; minimum-stay requirement.**

Outdoor Kissing

❀❀❀ **SMUGGLER COVE, Halfmoon Bay** Dozens of spectacular and isolated watery enclaves adorn the Sunshine Coast, and Smuggler Cove is among the most easily accessible. A short drive off Highway 101 leads to the entrance of the cove, which is awesome in itself, but a short meander through a rain forest will bring you to a wondrous view that is provocative in any weather. A sunny day reveals an entirely private inlet, etched from assorted rocks and jagged coastal formations. Sailboats add to the picturesque beauty as they quietly pass along the outer edge of the bay. In the overcast opaqueness of a fall or winter day, you may imagine an English seaside underneath the clouds. Why not bring along some scones and a thermos filled with tea to snack on while you enjoy this haven? If by chance you hear some cries emanating from the water or islands, don't be surprised. You've probably happened upon a group of sea lions or otters lounging in the afternoon sun or playing in the evening tides. (Anyone for amending the name to *Snuggler* Cove?) *Signs clearly mark the trailhead to Smuggler Cove, in the town of Halfmoon Bay.*

Romantic Note: The walk to Smuggler Cove takes about 20 minutes each way. The trail is extremely well maintained by the B.C. Parks Department, but marsh-side portions of the path are sometimes covered with water. This usually happens only in winter and early spring, but you should be prepared for at least some muddy spots if there have been heavy rains—a not unlikely circumstance, even on the Sunshine Coast.

Earl's Cove

Outdoor Kissing

❀❀❀ **FERRY RIDE FROM EARL'S COVE TO SALTERY BAY, Earl's Cove** If you don't have a chance to become acquainted with the Sunshine Coast via your own boat or a chartered excursion, a ride on the ferry crossing from Earl's Cove to Saltery Bay is a must. An array of snowcapped mountains frames your tour through Jervis Inlet, where magnificent rocky promontories covered with trees jut into the water. The soaring peaks all around make you realize the sheer vastness of the area, and a view from the water affords an opportunity to truly understand what makes the Sunshine Coast unique and special. Many of the locals have compared this journey to traveling through the fjords of Norway and claim it is even more spectacular. Have your camera ready: Fabulous photo opportunities lie around every corner, and you never know when (or what) marine life might join you in your trip across the bay. *The ferry landing is at the northern tip of the Sunshine Coast, at Earl's Cove.*

Romantic Note: We suggest that you check the ferry schedule for departure information before making this winding trek up the coast. Sailings are fairly infrequent, particularly during the off-season, and once you're at the ferry terminal there isn't much to do (except wait). Be sure to call **BRITISH COLUMBIA FERRIES** (250-386-3431, 888-223-3779 in Canada) in advance for the current sailing schedule.

Egmont

Outdoor Kissing

❤❤❤❤ **SKOOKUMCHUCK NARROWS, Egmont** The Canadian Southwest and the Pacific Northwest are filled with more than enough natural wonders to impress even the most experienced world traveler. Skookumchuck Narrows is one of the more intriguing phenomena. Enormous energy passes through this thin portal and is so moving (figuratively and literally) that the experience is nearly indescribable. An easily accessible trail out to the narrows is enveloped by abundant foliage, the ground is often carpeted in autumn-colored leaves, and trees are wrapped in moss. The trail has recently been improved and widened, so there are fewer muddy areas. As you make your way out to the tip of the peninsula, you approach Sechelt Inlet. You can stand almost at the edge of the rock-bordered gateway to the narrows. Through this tiny opening, at high and low tide, the rush of water is so intense that the land actually shakes beneath your feet. This is one time and place when, without even kissing or touching, you really can feel the earth move.

Optimum viewing times are posted at the trailhead and in the local paper so you can be sure to witness Mother Nature's colossal show. You will need to allow about an hour to reach the narrows from the parking lot, and you may want to plan on arriving an hour before a high or low tide and staying for another hour after the tide changes. After the water violently rushes one way, the narrows flatten, but water rushes the opposite way soon after. Moments like these are worth waiting for. *The trailhead is located just off Highway 101, on the road to Egmont. Signs clearly indicate where to go.*

Romantic Suggestion: If witnessing the tidal surge through the narrows leaves you hungry for another superlative experience, you might want to stop at the **BACKEDDY MARINE PUB** (Egmont Marina Resort, Backeddy Road; 604-883-2298; www.egmont-marina.com; inexpensive). It's not exactly the most romantic destination, but it's reputed to have the best and biggest hamburgers in the world.

"Let him kiss me with

the kisses of his mouth:

for thy love is better than wine."

The Song of Solomon

Whistler and Environs

For awesome scenery and year-round outdoor sport action, there is no spot in the Pacific Northwest/Canadian Southwest quite like Whistler. When the first serious snowfall of the year blankets the slopes of Whistler and Blackcomb Mountains (elevations 2,182 and 2,284 meters—7,160 and 7,494 feet— respectively), skiers the world over gather to revel in miles of spectacular downhill skiing. The two mountains offer a total of 3,139 meters (10,300 vertical feet) of downhill skiing accessed by 28 chairlifts (nine of which are high-speed), and more than 200 marked cross-country skiing trails. And when we say that snow blankets the slopes, we are not exaggerating: The average snowfall at the top of both mountains is approximately 110 meters (360 feet) per year. Even during the summer, glacier skiing is available at the very top of Blackcomb Mountain. You won't find the mile-long runs of the winter season, but then again, in winter you can't wear your bathing suit on the slopes.

Whistler's year-round raison d'être is the enjoyment of every outdoor recreational activity you can imagine: alpine skiing, cross-country skiing, heli-skiing, kayaking, canoeing, windsurfing, white-water rafting, hiking, mountain biking, and golfing. The world-class resort facilities of Whistler Village and the surrounding area are unrivaled almost anywhere else in the world. If you like fast-paced fun and an easygoing party atmosphere amid high-altitude grandeur, Whistler delivers in the slickest, most impressive way possible.

The only drawback to this mountain holiday mecca is that the town of Whistler is growing so fast the area has a few disturbing elements of urban sprawl—functional for skiers, but not necessarily intriguing or charming. Designer homes, mountainside condominium complexes, chateau-style hotels, and an assortment of inns, bed and breakfasts, and lodges accommodate more than 1.7 million visitors to these slopes each year. Starting in April and ending when the first snows arrive sometime in October, you are more likely to hear the roar of development than the call of the wild. When we visited, new construction projects covered the resort like a fresh snowfall. However, if charming and remote are not at the top of your list of mountaintop necessities, you needn't be too concerned with the real estate explosion up here. Any time of year, you can find the romantic sparkle and secret solitude that still abound in this part of Canada.

Wherever you stay, be sure to ask about discount packages and special seasonal rates. Most places have several different price categories depending on the time of year you venture up here. While the rest of the world has four seasons, Whistler has up to eight, at least when it comes to rate changes. Sorting out when all those periods stop and start for different properties can get very complicated, but you can be assured of one thing: High season is definitely the last week in December and the first weeks in January as well as the summer months of July and August.

Ski lifts and properties on the mountain are open sporadically during shoulder seasons. For general information, call the **WHISTLER CHAMBER OF COMMERCE** (604-932-5528) or the **WHISTLER RESORT ASSOCIATION** (800-944-7853).

Romantic Warning: At some point during your visit to Whistler, or in the mail afterward, you are very likely to receive a sales pitch from a time-share development company. In exchange for sitting through one of their presentations, you will be offered a free or discounted stay during your next visit or a discounted meal at an associated restaurant. There is a great deal of consumer information about time-shares you should know before you deal with a provocative sales performance (and we mean provocative). Do your homework before you inadvertently sign on the dotted line.

Whistler

Hotel/Bed and Breakfast Kissing

N/A WHISTLER RESERVATION COMPANIES, Whistler Literally thousands of condominium units and dozens of homes are available in Whistler. From the most basic one-bedroom condominium units to elaborate log homes, the scope and variety are nothing less than staggering. This deluge of accommodations is due to the large number of nonresidents who buy property here for their seasonal getaways. Rather than leaving their places empty, and to help pay off the mortgage, many of these owners list them in a rental pool. Several management companies in the area handle the marketing, rental, and maintenance of these residences, and most represent the same complexes, but different units. Listed below are several of the area's largest management companies, which are responsible for many of the properties reviewed in this section. **Central Reservations: (604) 932-4222, (800) 944-7853. Powder Resort Properties: (604) 932-2882, (800) 777-0185; www.powderproperties.com. The Coast Resorts at Whistler: (604) 938-9666, (800) 565-1444. Whistler Chalets and Accommodations Ltd.: (604) 932-6699, (800) 663-7711; www.whistlerchalets.com.**

Romantic Warning: Checkout times for this rental pool of condominiums and homes can be as early as 10 A.M., and maid service may be limited to every three days or even just once a week. You will want to be crystal clear on these very important details when making final plans and arrangements. Also, it is hard to tell what type of decor you'll find, since each condo and home is individually owned. We saw everything from hotel-style furnishings to beautiful metal beds, pine armoires, and elegant Oriental rugs. If you're picky about such particulars, be sure to ask when making reservations.

Romantic Note: Whistler Chalets specializes in house rentals. Although this is not the only company to represent the larger free-standing homes, several of its outstanding selections deserve at least a four-lip rating. Our favorites are identified in Whistler Chalets' brochure as **NEW DELUXE LOG HOME WITH DEN** (V3257), **DREAM LOG HOME WITH PRIVATE HOT TUB** (F3514), **WHISTLER CAY HEIGHTS LOG HOME** (H6215), **LAKEFRONT HOME** (V3315), and **HORSTMAN ESTATES HOME** (K4965 or K4950). All of these are large, handsomely constructed, and beautifully furnished homes offering more than enough room for three couples. Everything that could possibly enhance your comfort awaits at these locations, including stone fireplaces, Jacuzzi tubs, stereos, TV/VCRs, designer kitchens, and views. Any of them will meet your affectionate needs, and then some.

❦❦ ALPINE GREENS, Whistler

❦❦❦ BLACKCOMB GREENS, Whistler

❦❦ GLEN EAGLES, Whistler

❦❦ LOST LAKE LODGE, Whistler

❦❦ THE WOODS, Whistler

Undeniably, golfers have their own sense of passion. Many are able to concentrate on kissing only after they've shot below par and successfully negotiated their way past (or out of) all sand traps. Any other outcome, and smooching may be out of the question. Depending on your point of view and temperament, golfing may not be the best way to spend romantic moments. Why, then, have we included five condominium complexes that frame the popular Chateau Whistler golf course? Because during the winter, when snow veils the area in white, some of the most immaculate cross-country ski trails you've ever seen are right out your front door.

Of these complexes, Blackcomb Greens is by far our favorite. The handsomely furnished two-level condominiums all have smart detailing, gas fireplaces, great floor-to-ceiling windows, single Jacuzzi tubs, double-headed showers, and very livable and open floor plans. The only slightly unappealing feature is the communal hot tub that's plopped in the middle of a plain-looking patio.

Alpine Greens and Glen Eagles are both nice Whistler-style condominiums, but their view of the golf-course-turned-snow-covered-meadow makes them first among equals. Comfortable and cozy, they are decked out with all the usual conveniences and amenities, including fireplaces, stereos, TV/VCRs, and designer kitchens; a few also have jetted tubs and double-headed showers.

As the name indicates, The Woods is tucked into the forest, so views consist mainly of trees, mountains, and, depending on your unit, rooftops. Some two-bedroom units have jetted tubs, double showers, and wonderful vaulted

---

Cost ratings for British Columbia listings are in Canadian funds. American travelers should check the exchange rate or ask an innkeeper to figure out the cost in U.S. dollars.

ceilings in the living rooms. One-bedroom units are cozy and can be a bit on the dark side, but overall are quite nice. Lost Lake Lodge, a new mountain lodge with studios and one- and two-bedroom suites, is at the top of the hill. The rooms don't have much going for them amenity-wise, but they are brand-new. Stay away from the studios (sofa beds and Murphy beds only) and book a room facing the wonderful O-shaped pool and hot tub. **Call one of the reservation companies listed on page 170; moderate to very expensive.**

❤❤ **BREW CREEK LODGE, Whistler** As you travel down the potholed road to this lodge, you might wonder what awaits at the end. You'll be pleasantly surprised when you see a rustic lodge, several cabins, pristine Brew Creek, and sprawling grassy lawns divided by wooden boardwalks. About 15 minutes south of Whistler, Brew Creek Lodge provides a retreat for couples who don't mind things rustic, very relaxed, and certainly serene. There are several options to choose from, including (in ascending order of cost) the private Trapper's Cabin, the roomy Executive Suite, and the faraway Brew House for big spenders. We are sorry to say that the furnishings in all the rooms and cabins are straight from the '70s. But there's also some fun whimsical art (as well as outdated macramé), and plenty of windows and wood accents. Even though the interiors aren't terrific, the grounds are gorgeous, and you'll truly feel like you're in the thick of nature (except for some ugly power lines). Birds, squirrels, mosquitoes, and rabbits visit daily, while a beaver or bear may pop in occasionally. Cinders, the innkeepers' cat, makes her home at the main lodge.

In the morning, a continental breakfast is served family-style in the lodge. You'll easily burn it off hiking to Brew Lake, swimming in the chilly pond, or playing ball on the lawn. Or just relax in the creekside hot tub and listen to nature. By special request (and advanced notice), the gracious innkeepers will cook you dinner with an authentic French flair (moderate). **1 Brew Creek Road; (604) 932-7210; moderate to expensive; recommended wedding site.**

Romantic Warning: On summer weekends, wedding parties often book the entire place. During the off-season, the lodge hosts corporate retreats, so you might have to share the facilities with business types. Don't worry, there's lots of space. Last, but not least, is a warning for women: Don't wear high heels here. The rough-hewn floors in the main lodge and the wooden walkways could be difficult to navigate.

❤❤❤❤ **CEDAR CREEK, Whistler** When a brochure boasts that a place offers "the ultimate in luxury," our first reaction is to assume that the management is stretching things a bit—after all, it's hard to be the ultimate in anything. However, when it comes to accommodations in Whistler, Cedar Creek is as lavish as it gets. The entire complex consists of only six units, and it is designer heaven from top to bottom. Astounding floor-to-ceiling windows fill the rooms with outdoor splendor, massive stone fireplaces cast a glow on the terra-cotta floors, and the artistic furnishings invite you to put up your feet and forget the rest of the world. These units are fully equipped in every sense: You can soak for hours in an oversize whirlpool tub or a private outdoor hot tub while listening to CDs on a state-of-the-art stereo. Follow that with a romantic movie on the TV/VCR. If your culinary talents need exercise, you can create a masterpiece meal for the two of you in a kitchen Julia Child would envy. Step outside your back door onto Blackcomb's Cruiser Run, and, in the summer, explore the small creek bordering the slope. In front, you'll find a small alpine rock garden and no obstacles to block your view of the mountains. **Call one of the reservation companies listed on page 170; unbelievably expensive.**

♨♨ **CHALET LUISE, Whistler** Whistler has several Swiss- or German-style pensions that cater to visitors who want a more reclusive, less hectic residence than a condominium complex in the heart of Whistler Village. Chalet Luise is just such a place, with a little bit of everything for couples who want to be close to the mile-long mountain runs. Pine accents and furnishings, Austrian decorations, a huge outdoor whirlpool protected from the elements by a gazebo, and all the extra comforts and crisp, clean detailing you would expect from a European-style bed and breakfast can be found here. Some of the quaint, exceptionally neat rooms are a bit on the snug side, two (Rainbow and Summit) have fireplaces, and a few offer views and balconies. All eight rooms are decorated in bright Laura Ashley fabrics, and all boast heated floors in the en suite bathrooms.

A buffet breakfast is served in a fireside lounge each morning; individual tables are placed around the room, allowing for a private morning repast of juice, pancakes or waffles, cereals, breads, and jams. Located in a residential neighborhood, Chalet Luise is only moments away from the slopes and cross-country ski runs (ski in, ski out), so once you arrive you may not need to use your car again during your winter stay. Best of all, you're guaranteed genuine European hospitality here since one of the innkeepers is Swiss. **7461 Ambassador Crescent; (604) 932-4187, (800) 665-1998; www.whistlerinns.com/chaletluise; moderate to very expensive; minimum-stay requirement seasonally.**

♨♨♨♨ **CHATEAU WHISTLER RESORT, Whistler** In a sea of condos, timeshares, and ordinary ski lodges, it is almost a relief to find a hotel of this quality and sophistication. Chateau Whistler's deserved reputation precedes it via the many accolades and laurels awarded by travelers the world over. For ski buffs the big attraction is location, and this one is ideal: right at the foot of the ski lifts. For a romantic, albeit super-expensive sojourn, skip the very nice but standard rooms (all 510 of them, to be exact), and head to one of the 53 Entrée Gold rooms or suites. Dubbed a "hotel within a hotel," these luxurious rooms give guests private check-in, concierge services, and their own lounge in which to enjoy complimentary evening hors d'oeuvres and continental breakfast. Furnished with an elegant country touch, all Entrée Gold accommodations have gas fireplaces and luxurious bed linens and duvets. The enormous marbled bathrooms will wow you: Special water jets in the Jacuzzi tubs give neck massages, and wall-mounted showerheads cover you with water from knees to neck.

The enormous lobby area, with its soaring glass windows, peaked ceilings, rock columns, and hand-stenciled walls, is by far the most exquisite in the area. Adjacent to this grand hall is the elegantly refined **MALLARD BAR,** which holds it own with picturesque windows, comfortable seating, and a handsome stone fireplace.

A notable Chateau Whistler attribute is **THE SPA,** where the excellent services include massage, Shiatsu, hydrotherapy, and skin and hair care. Take time off from the slopes to enjoy the indoor/outdoor pool, heated year-round to a very swimmable but warm 86 degrees. Or soak in the two large Jacuzzi tubs, one indoor and the other outside, both with powerful jets for muscle-sore skiers. Keep your ski legs in shape by working out on state-of-the-art equipment in the health club, then clear your head in the eucalyptus steam baths.

Chateau Whistler offers a four-star hotel experience with an exceptionally attentive staff and all the necessary services. But, like the mountain above it, this place is mammoth, and people are everywhere. Splurge and stay in the Entrée Gold rooms and suites for romance and privacy. Otherwise, the rooms aren't the most affectionate choice in town. **4599 Chateau Boulevard; (604) 938-8000, (800) 441-1414; www.cphotels.ca; expensive to unbelievably expensive; recommended wedding site.**

Romantic Note: A meal at **THE WILDFLOWER** (see Restaurant Kissing), the hotel's country-elegant restaurant, is an exceptional culinary experience, particularly for dinner. The chef makes passionate culinary use of a wide variety of local herbs and vegetables.

Romantic Suggestion: For a wildly romantic time, look into Chateau Whistler's Romance Package. Part of the profits go toward helping endangered species, most notably the beluga whale. Included in the package are strawberries, sparkling wine, turndown service, and a "Be my beluga" stuffed toy.

◆◆ **DELTA WHISTLER VILLAGE SUITES, Whistler** You can't miss this new hotel in Whistler Village—it takes up an entire city block! (Don't confuse this place with Delta Whistler Resort, its older cousin.) Most of the 207 condo-style suites are equipped with full kitchens, washer/dryers, fireplaces, balconies, TVs, and standard bathrooms. Guests also get all the benefits of a full-service hotel.

The one-bedroom suites, decorated in subtle Southwest tones with maple Craftsman-style furnishings, are quite cozy for a condo-style hotel room (and nicer than many condos we saw). The two-bedroom suites are oddly designed and much too big, while the tiny studios come with Murphy beds and kitchenettes. We can truthfully say that all rooms have mountain views (if you look up). However, because of the hotel's central locale, you'll also look down into a parking lot and/or shopping plaza. Choose wisely with room location. Several popular (read: noisy) bars and restaurants reside below many of the rooms.

Despite these shortcomings, the lobby is lovely, the staff friendly, and the heated indoor/outdoor pool and two hot tubs are worthy of a dip. **4308 Main Street; (604) 905-3987, (888) 299-3987, (800) 268-1133; www.deltahotels.com; moderate to unbelievably expensive.**

Romantic Note: Carnivores should try HY'S STEAKHOUSE (see Restaurant Kissing), a classical steak house on the ground level of the hotel.

❦❦❦ **DURLACHER HOF, Whistler** Top to bottom, the Austrian influence is strong at the Durlacher Hof. Elaborate breakfasts and cozy rooms are standard amenities, but where some bed and breakfasts stop, Durlacher Hof is just beginning. The innkeeper here serves a most bountiful morning meal that might include freshly baked breads with basil goat cheese, divine Danishes, homemade jams, a leek and zucchini frittata, plum crêpes, cold cuts with marinated vegetables, and fresh fruit—and that is just in the morning. Afternoon tea with fresh-from-the-oven cakes is also wonderful, as are the après-ski treats.

If you're smart enough to stay around for dinner, the Durlacher Hof offers five-course gourmet dinners (expensive) to hungry guests during the winter. Luckily for nonguests, special events such as seasonal winemakers' dinners (unbelievably expensive) are available for the public. Chefs from all over the world come to take part in these culinary productions. It makes for an incredible, exclusive evening without crowds or pretense. After indulging in such culinary extravaganzas, retreat to the tiled *Kachelofen* (an old-fashioned farmhouse fireplace) for rest and relaxation, or, in the summer, enjoy the outside patio embellished with hanging flower baskets.

All six rooms on the second floor are simply decorated, immaculate, and cheerful; some have spa tubs and balcony access, one has a gas fireplace, and all are quite spacious. In keeping with the Austrian theme, cute bouquets of alpine flowers are everywhere. Two romantic rooms await on the third floor, with Romeo and Juliet balconies, jetted tubs, cushioned reading alcoves, and skylights. The only drawback to this inn: Highway 99 is too close for comfort. But once the quiet of night embraces the area, it really doesn't matter. **7055 Nesters Road; (604) 932-1924; www.durlacherhof.com; moderate to very expensive; minimum-stay required on weekends; call for seasonal closures.**

❦❦ **EDGEWATER LODGE, Whistler** If only the rooms here were equal to the views, the two-lip rating for Edgewater Lodge would soar to a four-lip rating in a heartbeat. The expansive bay windows in each unit offer scintillating, unobstructed views of Whistler's resplendent scenery. Each of the 12 rooms is a front-row seat where you can be dazzled by towering snow-clad mountains that intertwine and overlap endlessly in flawless panoramic glory. An occasional floatplane or canoe momentarily breaks the calm surface of serene Green Lake, which fronts the vista. The same incredible scenery fills the floor-to-ceiling windows of the lodge's dining room, where you can enjoy a complimentary continental breakfast. Alas, the view and the 45 acres of surrounding property are the main reasons to stay here, besides the fact that this inn is located two miles from the hectic center of Whistler Village. The suites and rooms are strictly motel quality, with impossibly tiny bathrooms and stark, out-of-date furnishings. **8841 Highway 99; (604) 932-0688; www.whistler. net/accommodate/edgewater; moderate; minimum-stay requirement on weekends; recommended wedding site.**

Romantic Note: The petite **EDGEWATER LODGE RESTAURANT** (see Restaurant Kissing) serves delectable four-course dinners.

❦❦ **THE GABLES, Whistler** In addition to excellent ski runs and the latest in express chairlifts, Whistler is crammed with condos of every size, shape, and price. From the heart of Whistler Village to the base of the gondola that ascends Whistler Mountain to even farther out on the back roads, there are more than enough accommodations to suit the tastes and budgets of the hordes of winter-sports enthusiasts. The Gables stands out from the crowd as a fetching place to recover from a day of mountainous pursuits. This small, pleasant development is just a two-minute walk from the village and right across the street from the Wizard Express. Although well equipped and well located, the units are surprisingly sedate (and in need of some renovations). Each apartment has a small entry hall that nicely handles wet clothing and snow-laden boots. The living room is then entered through glass-paned French doors. All 12 units have fireplaces and full kitchens, and the bathrooms have small spa tubs. Cozy loft bedrooms overlook the living rooms. For the best views, be sure to request a unit that faces the mountain or the rushing creek at the back of the property. **Call one of the reservation companies listed on page 170; moderate to very expensive.**

❦❦ **THE INN AT CLIFFTOP LANE, Whistler** In a neighborhood of stately cedar-planked homes, this inn blends in beautifully. Yet it stands out in Whistler's B&B scene in that it caters solely to couples. With so many accommodations in town that are group and family oriented, this is a refreshing find.

A mishmash of objects from the innkeepers' travels furnishes each of the five rooms. You may find yourself sleeping in the dappled blue room with Indonesian furnishings or on a small antique French bed surrounded by complementary art. Regular comforts found in every room include en suite baths with jetted tubs, embroidered robes, TV/VCRs, and lovely linens. Some rooms are quite small and, due to the woodsy location, can be a bit dark. (This may prove refreshing in the hot months.) Our favorite is light and large Room 3, which has a private balcony and sitting area. In the inn's oddly shaped dining room—with an elegant Southwest-style stairway as its centerpiece—two-person tables are the norm. Enjoy a delicious three-course breakfast of fresh fruit, orange juice, coffee, baked goods, and such specialties as zucchini–Gruyère cheese crêpes. Outside, a covered hot tub (with no view) and a rustic gazebo built of logs invite affectionate attention. Entertainment is provided by Alfonse and Gaston, two Tibetan terriers who will delight you with their antics. **2828 Clifftop Lane; (604) 938-1111, (888) 281-2929; www.whistler.net/resort/cliffinn; moderate to expensive.**

Romantic Note: The inn is located about five miles south of Whistler Village, so plan on driving to the resort.

❀❅ **LE CHAMOIS, Whistler** This comparatively small 52-unit hotel has an unimpressive lobby, sparse furnishings, views in some rooms, a standard rooftop pool and hot tub, an impressive restaurant—and location, location, location. Just whiz from your room to Blackcomb's Wizard Express lift a few hundred feet away. As for a place to kiss, Le Chamois offers six attractive studios, each with an open floor plan, high ceilings, a kitchenette, and a stepup deep soaking tub that oddly enough borders the kitchen counter (at least in the room we saw). Surprisingly, these are the least expensive rooms in the hotel! During the summer they are incredible kissing bargains. **4557 Blackcomb Way; (604) 932-2882, (800) 777-0185; www.powder-properties.com; expensive to unbelievably expensive; minimum-stay requirement seasonally.**

Romantic Note: Le Chamois' restaurant, **LA RUA** (see Restaurant Kissing), is one of Whistler's more provocative settings for dinner. Sometimes its romantic ambience is smothered by crowded conditions and noise, but it is still an exceptional find, and the menu is a work of art.

❀❀ **LORIMER RIDGE PENSION, Whistler** Dignified details, majestic mountain views, and welcoming hosts make this bed and breakfast a preferred choice for every taste and budget. Set in a residential neighborhood away from Whistler Village, the eight modest, small, and exceptionally clean guest rooms are unadorned save for beautiful soft comforters, a picture or two, and handsome wood furnishings. Room 4 is our favorite because of the fireplace, pine sleigh bed, and private patio with mountain views. The large common rooms with wood-burning river-rock fireplaces, the sauna, the outdoor hot tub, and the generous buffet breakfasts will melt cold hearts regardless of the weather conditions. **6231 Piccolo Drive; (604) 938-9722, (888) 988-9002; www.whistlerinns.com/lorimerridge; inexpensive; minimum-stay requirement seasonally.**

❀❀❀ **MOUNTAIN STAR, Whistler** When we visited these ski-in, ski-out townhomes, the builders were just putting the finishing touches on the landscaping. These brand-new, gorgeous units on the side of Blackcomb Mountain are the king of the hill . . . at least for now. Nothing is above you except forest, and nothing below you obstructs the valley view (except for the other units). Luckily, these are multilevel places, so you're bound to get a good view from the tip-top master suites. We visited Unit 1, a corner unit, which is ideal for privacy. Classic wooden blinds, Shaker-style kitchen cabinets, vaulted ceilings, balconies, and granite fireplaces are standard in most units. No corners were cut when it came to providing small luxuries such as double shower heads and heated bathroom and kitchen floors. Hot tubs on the back decks of the upper units are some of the most private we've seen. For the best, most unobstructed views, book one of the lower units. But no matter where you stay here, you'll be surrounded by luxury. **Call one of the reservation companies listed on page 170; very expensive to unbelievably expensive.**

❤❤❤ **NORTHERN LIGHTS, Whistler** After a while, all the condominiums in Whistler start blurring together, with little to distinguish one from another. Even the appealing features seem to be repeated time and time again. Northern Lights is a bit of an exception, in part due to its location—high enough on the slopes to give a sense of being above it all. The building holds a mix of rental and residential units, each with a private garage. Inside these deluxe townhomes are designer kitchens, comfortable bedrooms, sunken living rooms, glowing fireplaces, attractive furnishings, and oodles of space. Most have decent views of the valley below from the soaring floor-to-ceiling windows. You can also enjoy that view from a private outdoor hot tub, some of which are romantically tucked into alcoves. Whistler Village and the slopes are a downhill walk from Northern Lights. However, what goes down must come up, in this case. And, if you're lugging ski equipment at the end of the day, you might be too tired for romance once you finally reach home. **Call one of the reservation companies listed on page 170; very expensive to unbelievably expensive.**

❤❤ **PAINTED CLIFFS, Whistler** Just a few years ago, this large condominium complex was tops, in regard to its location on the mountain. Now, however, a large hotel is its uphill neighbor, and even more new townhomes are perched above that (see **MOUNTAIN STAR**, reviewed above). Despite this, Painted Cliffs still feels less crowded than other condos. The one-bedroom unit we saw (No. 39) was just right for two people, although the view of the courtyard and next unit didn't excite us. These attractive units with ski-in, ski-out access from Blackcomb's Cruiser Run are attractive throughout, with single-person Jacuzzi tubs, fireplaces, and nice kitchens. Top units are larger, and also come with superior panoramic views, so you may want to splurge, depending on what you want to see. **Call one of the reservation companies listed on page 170; moderate to unbelievably expensive.**

❤❤ **THE PAN PACIFIC LODGE WHISTLER, Whistler** Whistler's newest hotel is sitting pretty at the base of both mountains. Consequently, guests have roll-out-of-bed access to the lifts, and, on the less desirable side, a lot of noise (especially on summer nights, when restaurants move seating outdoors onto the plaza). Famous for their international hotels, Pan Pacific has ventured into new territory with their first resort lodge. By the looks of things, it's a nice first.

Of the 121 suites, the one-bedrooms provide enough room for comfort, but close enough quarters for romance. The smaller studios will do . . . if you can make a Murphy bed your love pad. Two-bedroom suites, situated on the corners, dazzle the eye with vaulted ceilings and enormous windows. However, the large floor-to-ceiling windows in our one-bedroom proved panoramic enough, and cost less. Elegantly decorated with maple Craftsman-style furniture, each room has a granite-tiled kitchen and bathroom, beautiful gas fireplace, and balcony. Standard but large bathrooms feature soaker tubs and Aveda spa products. Book a mountainside room if possible, and the higher it is, the less noise you'll hear from the ski plaza below. If you run around in the buff, beware. Due to the hotel's configuration, you can often see into your neighbors' huge windows and vice versa. Exercise lovers can sweat it out in the health club's steam bath or small exercise room. A heated outdoor pool and two hot tubs overlook the ski plaza below and the mountain above. **4320 Sundial Crescent; (604) 905-2999, (888) 905-9995; www.panpac.com/hotels; moderate to unbelievably expensive; minimum-stay requirement seasonally.**

Romantic Note: Consider it the luck of the Irish if you happen to find THE DUBH LINN GATE (moderate) in the plaza level of The Pan Pacific. While the decor won't fan the flames of love, it certainly ranks high on authenticity. All furnishings and bar fixtures were imported directly from Ireland. There's excellent pub grub, too. To heat things up, head through the stained glass door to ARTHUR'S (see Restaurant Kissing), one of Whistler's most romantic hideaways.

❤❤❤ THE PINNACLE INTERNATIONAL HOTEL, Whistler

This 84-room hotel could be Whistler's most romantic small hotel, thanks to the many in-room comforts: seated showers for two, double Jacuzzi tubs with views of the fireplace, TV/VCRs, full kitchens, bathrobes, and wineglasses full of Hershey's Kisses. All rooms also have air-conditioning, a big plus on hot summer nights.

You may feel like you're in a fishbowl, but the corner rooms are the best due to their many windows, two balconies, and roomy surroundings. Other rooms are smaller, although those on the fourth floor have high ceilings. Balconies range in size from large to too tiny to stand on, so if outdoor access is important to you, ask ahead of time. Neutral colors open up the rooms, as do the mirrored walls, but overall the interior is just slightly above the standard hotel look. Our only complaint with the rooms are the bathrooms. They are very cramped, even for one person. We wonder how two people could possibly get into the shower? Also, we heard the rumble of our neighbors' Jacuzzi tubs at night, despite the concrete construction. Other than that, this hotel has a friendly staff, an outdoor pool and hot tub, tiny exercise room, and a central

---

Cost ratings for British Columbia listings are in Canadian funds. American travelers should check the exchange rate or ask an innkeeper to figure out the cost in U.S. dollars.

location surrounded by other hotels, condominiums, and nearby shops. Traffic noise could be a problem if you leave the windows open, but you can turn on the air-conditioning. **4319 Main Street; (604) 938-3218; (888) 999-8986; www.pinnacle-hotels.com; expensive to very expensive; minimum-stay requirement seasonally.**

Romantic Note: The Pinnacle has one of Whistler's most romantic Italian restaurants, QUATTRO (see Restaurant Kissing).

❦❦ **STONERIDGE, Whistler** Stoneridge is located in the Benchlands area of Whistler Village. Many of the amenities found in this small cluster of townhomes sound enticing: Floor-to-ceiling windows, vaulted ceilings, sharp detailing, wonderful kitchens, single Jacuzzi tubs, gas fireplaces, and private decks are all perfect for a mountain retreat. Unfortunately, the units are situated so that most of them face the parking lot or street, which is not desirable when the mountains are the main reason you are here. Try to reserve one of the units with a close-up view of the woods. The view adds to the privacy and makes the interior feel much more intimate. **Call one of the reservation companies listed on page 170; expensive to very expensive.**

❦❦❦ **SUNDANCE, Whistler** As you venture into Whistler on Highway 99, you pass the original ski-resort site of Whistler Mountain. Unfortunately, age and fashion have left the area a bit behind in terms of conveniences and polished accommodations, which is why Whistler Village, at the foot of Blackcomb Mountain, is the preferred destination. (Don't repeat that to any Whistler Mountain enthusiasts, who swear the slopes here are superior to Blackcomb's.) Regardless of your skiing preferences, there is romance to be found up in these hills.

The view units at Sundance (the ones that face the mountain or woods) are located along one of the ridges just to the south of the ski runs. These impressive condominiums have enormous vaulted ceilings, floor-to-ceiling windows, wood-burning fireplaces, and hot tubs on spacious outdoor decks. Like all of the condominium accommodations in Whistler, each is individually decorated, but the individual owners of these units have made them quite attractive and comfortable. Don't expect a lot of space; even the units with three bedrooms are more cozy than spacious. But the windows and decks add immeasurably to the sense of roominess. **Call one of the reservation companies listed on page 170; inexpensive to moderate.**

❦❦ **WOODRUN, Whistler** Woodrun was built before land in Whistler became super-expensive, so no expense was spared in spaciousness—at least in the rooms. There are two truly extravagant rooms here, each with cathedral ceilings, floor-to-ceiling windows, wonderful views of the mountains and ski area, a full kitchen, marble and hardwood floors, a gas fireplace, and a double Jacuzzi tub in the master bedroom. The furnishings are casual and plush, and the space is considerable. The communal outdoor swimming pool and large hot tub have a view (to console all those in rooms without a master-bedroom Jacuzzi tub). Woodrun is not a hotel, but it is a sizable lodge set up in the impressive Benchlands area (above the base of Blackcomb), with ski-in, ski-out accessibility and a front desk for check-in during limited hours. You can't splurge all the time, but when you do, you might as well go big. **Reservations through Powder Resort Properties; (800) 777-0185; expensive to unbelievably expensive.**

Restaurant Kissing

☙☙☙☙ **ARTHUR'S, Whistler** If an intimate, candlelit setting is what you crave at dinnertime, this restaurant delivers what few in Whistler can. Fewer than 15 tables dot the small room; some are tucked into cozy corners, and all are perfect for romance. As the lights dim and piano music fills the air, enjoy cuisine that draws on international flavors accented by French flair and preparation. If you've never sampled such delicacies as sweetbread spring rolls, frog legs in curry, or lamb carpaccio, try them here. With an exceptional chef in the kitchen, you can trust all will be excellent. Our meal was exquisite, from the pan-fried duck foie gras with polenta French fries to the outstanding black pepper–crusted wild caribou with blueberry sauce, wild rice, and fiddlehead ferns. **4320 Sundial Crescent, in the Pan Pacific Lodge; (604) 905-0525, (800) 387-3311; expensive to unbelievably expensive; reservations recommended; breakfast and dinner daily.**

☙☙❨ **BEARFOOT BISTRO, Whistler** Don't be put off by the bistro label or the out-of-the-way location. This restaurant's unique interior certainly sets it apart from other area restaurants. High-backed leather chairs and terra-cotta and light brown walls add a Southwest tone, while long rectangular windows, accented by blond wood, are reminiscent of Japanese shoji screens. Tables are spaced reasonably well apart, and on each beige tablecloth are artistic Swiss-made plates, more showpieces than functional serviceware. Empty wine bottles line the mantels and windowsills, while a wall of wine barrels skillfully divides and hides parts of the spacious dining room. Whimsical artwork is sprinkled here and there. A cigar lounge, done with a nod toward British colonial style, is located at the end of the restaurant; although it is outfitted with an air-ventilation door, some say it doesn't work that well.

The interior is relatively romantic, and locals are quite fond of this place, although some complain the portions are tiny. Wild Northwest Territories caribou is the house specialty, and the wine selection weighs in with some 5,000 bottles in stock. **4121 Village Green; (604) 932-3433; expensive to very expensive; breakfast and dinner daily.**

☙☙☙☙ **CHRISTINE'S ON BLACKCOMB, Whistler** Perhaps it's the fresh mountain air that makes your heart go pitter-patter. Maybe it's the breathtaking scenery. Whatever the cause, lunch at Christine's can be a heart-stirring experience. It will take a while for your eyes to adjust to the magnitude of the view from Christine's: It's at the top of Blackcomb Mountain. Summer months up here are filled with visual ecstasy. When the snow has melted (except for the perennial glacier patch at Blackcomb's summit), the sun shines on endless rugged mountain peaks. On the wildlife side of things, bears are a common sight on the slopes. In winter, be sure to make a reservation for lunch. It's the prime spot for watching ski bunnies, daredevils, and snowhounds.

The restaurant is open only for lunch in winter and summer, with patio dining when weather permits. Christine's used to be open for weekend sunset dining, but that has been suspended indefinitely. Too bad. The casual but gourmet menu changes to match the mood of the mountain. In summer, lighter, less expensive dishes make their mark, including the faux moose burger, smoked chicken salad, spicy lentil burger, and tofu udon soup. Comfort foods that warm the soul dominate in winter. The B.C. salmon with pistachio crumble is popular, as is their famous oyster, leek, and potato soup.

Regardless of what season you choose to journey up here, you're guaranteed a feast for the senses. And, besides all that, there's something about dining on a mountaintop that is wildly romantic. **On Blackcomb Mountain; (604) 938-7437, (604) 932-3141 (in Vancouver); moderate to expensive; reservations recommended; lunch daily during summer and winter.**

Romantic Note: Don't let a summer rain stop you from eating here. The Wizard Express chairlift, which transports you to Christine's, has covered seating.

❦❦ **CRÊPE MONTAGNE, Whistler** As the saying goes, good things come in small packages. Such is the case at this nine-table restaurant (one of the smallest in Whistler), unromantically located in the Village's hodgepodge of shops. However, the locale doesn't matter inside, where your senses will be entranced by the sweet smell of crêpes, the charming French-country decor, and the very romantic two-person booths tucked in back. You'll be even more delighted with the reasonable prices and substantial portions.

Crêpes aren't just for breakfast, as many Americans tend to think. And, although these savories have a French accent, the ingredients are far from foreign. You'll find an assortment of creations, ranging from popular seafood crêpes to vegetarian specialties. (A romantic alternative is the fondue for two; at around $30, this is one of the best dinner deals in town.) Dozens more choices include a sumptuous, sweet selection of fruit crêpes, ice-cream crêpes, and, most exciting of all, flambéd crêpes. Our fiery number came filled with strawberries, bananas, and oranges and was set aglow with Cointreau, an orange-flavored liqueur. Of course, you can still have crêpes for breakfast, including one with bacon and eggs for all you die-hards. **4368 Main Street, Unit 116, in the Market Pavilion; (604) 905-4444; inexpensive; breakfast, lunch, and dinner daily.**

❦❦❦ **EDGEWATER LODGE RESTAURANT, Whistler** Romantic dining is not exactly common in Whistler. The atmosphere of most dining establishments tends to be gregarious and sociable rather than intimate and cozy. That's not the case in the Edgewater Lodge's small dining room, which commands one of the most stunning views imaginable. Although the furnishings could be freshened up, the handful of tables, soft lighting, whimsical art accents, sweeping floor-to-ceiling windows overlooking Green Lake, and the exceptional cuisine more than compensate. Besides that, the setting—on 45 acres—is a refreshing change from the maddening crowds at Whistler Village. Local venison is the specialty here, and you can enjoy it in pâté as an appetizer or as medallions with shiitake mushroom sauce or as châteaubriand, a lavish treat for two, for an entrée. The signature B.C. salmon in a silky smooth béarnaise sauce and the rack of lamb are sheer perfection. There is little the kitchen can do wrong, so whatever the weekly offerings, dig in and enjoy. **8841 Highway 99, at the Edgewater Lodge; (604) 932-0688; www.whistler.net/accommodate/ edgewater; reservations recommended; moderate to expensive; dinner daily.**

❦❦❦ **HY'S STEAKHOUSE, Whistler** After a day of slicing up the slopes, head into town to do some carving of a different kind. Cut into thick steaks aged 28 days, rotisserie prime rib, and Australian rack of lamb at this classic and elegant steakhouse. Although part of a chain, Whistler's Hy's is a flagship restaurant with a lighter decor than its big-city cousins, which cater to heavy-duty business types. No expense was spared in creating an elegant, inviting, and romantic (in spots) restaurant. Glowing cherry wood covers all, from ceiling to shutters, and chairs are soft leather. On a down note, many of the white-linen-draped tables are too close to one another, and there's a TV in the bar area. Despite the electronic intrusion, the bar is a sight to see, with colorful liquor bottles backlit by the setting sun. While many two-person tables along the windows looked nice, we spotted several areas that were prime kissing spots. Our favorite is table 36, a tiny love zone by the fireplace. There's also a nice four-seater directly in front of the fireplace. Horseshoe-shaped booths, while big, could be cozy if you snuggle. A few more tables are hidden in an alcove near the wine cabinets.

You'll get straightforward fare here: steaks cooked correctly to order, and portions worth pondering. However, several steaks can be ordered in different sizes, a plus for those with a small appetite. Decadence demands you order the rich Gorgonzola filet mignon, a house specialty. There's also rotisserie prime rib and chicken. Even though this is cow country, the crab cakes proved excellent, as did the filet mignon covered in peppercorn sauce (a special request) and garlic mashed potatoes. (Don't worry about kissing later on—the potatoes aren't too garlicky.) **4308 Main Street; (604) 905-5555; expensive to very expensive; reservations recommended; dinner daily.**

❀❀❀ JOEL'S RESTAURANT AND FIREPLACE LOUNGE AT NICKLAUS NORTH, Whistler Dare we say this golf clubhouse restaurant, overlooking Green Lake and the 16th tee, is par excellence? Typically, golf club dining facilities lack a certain elegance associated with romantic dining. This one differs. Joel's succeeds at bringing the outdoors inside with floor-to-ceiling windows, gorgeous summer and fall colors, light maple furnishings, stately granite pillars, and leaf-mosaic lamps. A candle, fine silverware, and white linen adorn all tables, which are spaced far enough apart so no one can hear you discuss your golf score. An outdoor patio is perfect for summertime dining, while the very green lounge accented by a cozy granite fireplace is ideal for a wintertime warm-up.

Continental cuisine with a French flair is the name of the game here. Summertime specialties focus on light dishes, salads, and seafood. Barbecues are also big hits. Wintertime brings fondue and comfort foods to the menu, for a satisfying ending to a day of cross-country skiing on the course. During the greener months, dinner is the best time for a romantic meal as the sun sets over the mountain and the course quiets down. **8080 Nicklaus North Boulevard; (604) 932-1240; expensive to very expensive; reservations recommended; call for seasonal hours and closures; recommended wedding site.**

Romantic Suggestion: In conjunction with WHISTLER AIR (604-932-6615), Joel's offers a Fly & Dine special for lunch and dinner. Soar over the mountains in a floatplane, land on Green Lake, then stroll over to Joel's for a three-course gourmet dinner or lunch. The price ($125 per person for dinner flights) includes transportation to and from your hotel.

❀❀❀ LA RUA, Whistler La Rua's two handsome dining rooms are framed with brick-red walls, bold works of art, and beautiful wood paneling. Terra-cotta floors, soft lighting, black lacquered chairs, and white tablecloths in both rooms complete the striking, intriguing setting. We prefer the lakeside room with a mural behind the banquettes; the ambience there is warmer, cozier, and slightly quieter.

The interesting international menu has a noticeable West Coast flair, with plenty of local items, most notably B.C. salmon, fresh trout, and fallow deer. Our meadow greens salad tossed with edible flowers, a light pear vinaigrette, and oven-dried pear chips was remarkably light and refreshing. The menu's descriptions are on the humorous side, with the house specialty being Chilean sea bass with crazy herbs. While it sounds exciting, the dish didn't please our taste buds. The fish flavor was off, and those crazy herbs consisted of charred thyme and rosemary stuck into thick, rubbery fish skin. Luckily, other items do please, especially if you stick to dishes that incorporate local ingredients. Still, in spite of the occasional faux pas (and the kitchen owns up to its mistakes), you are likely to be pleased with your repast, and the view is one of the best shows in town. However, it should be noted that when the resort is busy, this restaurant can be crowded and very noisy. **4557 Blackcomb Way, at Le Chamois Hotel; (604) 932-5011; expensive; call for seasonal hours.**

Whistler and Environs

❀❀❀ **QUATTRO, Whistler** Tucked away on the main floor of **THE PIN-NACLE INTERNATIONAL HOTEL** (see Hotel/Bed and Breakfast Kissing), this Italian restaurant is warming up Whistler with a touch of the Mediterranean. The decor, modeled ever so subtly after a palace in Venice, brings elegance and class together in a manner that's inviting and comfortable. You'll find an open kitchen, two fireplaces, and floors and ceilings painted to resemble marble, accented by hand-painted chandeliers from Italy and solid mahogany tables.

The diverse menu mostly comprises traditional Italian entrées emphasizing flavor and limited calories (i.e., no heavy cream or butter sauces). From the pasta plates to the chicken, seafood, and venison, expect skillfully prepared dishes using fresh herbs, ripe tomatoes, and the perfect amount of garlic. **4319 Main Street, at the Pinnacle International Hotel; (604) 905-4844; www.pinnacle-hotels.com; expensive; reservations recommended; dinner daily.**

❀❀❅ **RESTAURANT ARAXI, Whistler** Restaurant Araxi is perhaps too large to be truly appealing for a cozy discourse over dinner (and the chairs a bit too uncomfortable for lingering), but the inviting interior and the superior northern Italian cuisine will warm your hearts and please your palates. Terra-cotta floors, oversize urns and casks, wooden tables, and sultry lighting give the room a contemporary but rustic flavor. And the food surpasses the decor. Exquisite appetizers such as baked eggplant stuffed with goat cheese, ricotta, spinach, and fresh tomato sauce, and roasted fresh mussels with an incredible vermouth, lime, and honey sauce, are nothing less than triumphant. And the entrées are just as wonderful. The penne with freshly smoked turkey in sage butter with roasted vegetables, and the West Coast fisherman's stew, an array of fresh fish and seafood in a rich saffron-tomato broth, are beyond reproach. You won't have room for dessert, no matter what you select, but force yourselves: This kind of indulgence is too good to pass up. **4222 Village Square; (604) 932-4540; expensive; reservations recommended; call for seasonal hours.**

❀❀❀ **THE RIM ROCK CAFE, Whistler** Ask any local to name the best seafood restaurant in Whistler and you are likely to be directed to the Rim Rock Cafe. It's situated outside the main village, but well worth the short drive. Two stone fireplaces fill the wood-paneled room with a blushing glow in winter. Booths in back provide the most privacy, although the two-seat tables in front of the fire are nice too. The open-beam ceiling and antique tables help establish a rustic setting, while halogen lamps, Hollywood caricatures, and linen tablecloths add elegance and class. During summer, sit on the front deck and watch the sunset (and traffic), or cool off on the shady, secluded patio in back.

The kitchen serves the freshest of fish, napped nicely with light sauces and accompanied by tender vegetables, all flawlessly prepared and beautifully presented. After a tiring day of skiing or hiking, or a lazy afternoon communing with nature, this is a handsome place to have dinner. Unfortunately, it is very popular and usually full (reservations are a must, sometimes a week in advance). **2117 Whistler Road, at the Highland Lodge; (604) 932-5565; moderate to expensive; reservations recommended; dinner daily.**

❤❤❤❤ **VAL D'ISÈRE, Whistler** The most exquisite French food in Whistler is served at Val d'Isère. The elegant, slightly conservative beige and blue dining room, aglow with the customary white tablecloths and gleaming china and crystal, is accented with mountain views as well as views of the shopping plaza below. The traditional French fare emphasizes rich sauces and succulent fresh fish. Our meal included a delicate tomato and gin soup, and arctic char pan-fried to perfection. You can't go wrong trying one of the house specialties, most notably the onion tart or the loin of fallow deer. Share savory kisses as you try to decide between the baked cheesecake or rhubarb Florentine with sabayon and fresh strawberries. **4433 St. Andrews Place, at St. Andrews House; (604) 932-4666; expensive to very expensive; dinner daily.**

❤❤❤ **THE WILDFLOWER, Whistler** Almost everything inside **CHATEAU WHISTLER RESORT** (see Hotel/Bed and Breakfast Kissing) is striking and eye-catching, including the Wildflower. Its radiant, bright feeling is enhanced by its warm red and peach color scheme, whimsical birdhouses, spectacular architectural pieces from an old church, and floor-to-ceiling windows that look out to the foot of the ski slopes. Service is attentive and considerate, without the slightest hint of haughtiness. In many ways this is one of the most soothing environments for dining in all of Whistler.

As your senses are being calmed by the surroundings, your appetite will be stimulated by the delectably varied menu. The versatile kitchen produces casual fare such as sandwiches and pizzas (the pie with grilled venison sausage and basil pesto is delicious), as well as formal entrées. The chef here is known for his skillful use of herbs and local fresh meats and fish, but he's also brilliant at meeting vegetarian needs. Our meal included a mixed-leaf salad laced with edible flowers and drizzled with an incredible watermelon-and-berry vinaigrette, a rich and flavorful baked tofu lasagne with three cheeses and grilled vegetables, and an ambrosial crispy duck breast with wild rice crêpes. **4599 Chateau Boulevard, at Chateau Whistler Resort; (604) 938-8000, (800) 441-1414; inexpensive to expensive; reservations recommended; breakfast, lunch, and dinner daily, brunch Sunday.**

Romantic Note: Breakfast here can be relaxing, but the food is disappointingly lackluster and bland. Thankfully, the Sunday buffet brunch is a cornucopia of nicely presented dishes, and the kitchen once again lives up to its reputation. The dozen-plus dessert selection is reason enough to try the brunch.

Outdoor Kissing

❤❤❤❤ **BLACKCOMB HELICOPTERS, Whistler** We cannot begin to describe to you the literally awesome landscapes you will witness during a helicopter flight over this magnificent realm. The experience will engulf your souls with images that will last a lifetime. Blackcomb Helicopters offers various ways to partake in the spectacle of true mountain alpine wilderness. You can sightsee on 20- or 30-minute flights or enjoy an eight- or 12-minute glacier tour from the top of Blackcomb Mountain. Adventurous souls can opt for guided heli-hiking excursions deep into the heart of this rugged, glacier-crowned terrain. Less strenuous but equally scenic is a heli-picnic that sets you down beside a pristine, untouched mountain stream or ridge where you can enjoy a tasty gourmet lunch. If you're planning to pop the question or, better yet, want to perform a special ceremony, custom-designed trips can be arranged to suit your romantic needs. **(604) 938-1700, (800) 330-4354; expensive to unbelievably expensive.** *Free shuttle service to the departure pad from anywhere in Whistler.*

Romantic Note: Other helicopter companies in the area provide tours as well: Call **PEMBERTON HELICOPTERS, INC.** (604-932-3512) or **TYAX HELI-SKIING** (604-932-7007, 888-HELISKI; www.tyax.com).

❧❧❧❧ **BRANDYWINE FALLS, Whistler** A brisk ten-minute jaunt through lush forest will bring you to a monument of natural construction that deserves a standing ovation. As you emerge from the pine trees, you arrive at a cliff with views of the top of Brandywine Falls. The water drops down a tube-like canyon into the river, which cuts through a valley of interlacing mountains and meadows. During the summer you can climb down to the rocky ledges under the falls and sit side by side beneath the surging waters as the spray cools your faces. *A few miles south of Whistler on Highway 99, you will see signs directing you to the falls.*

❧❧❧❧ **HIGHWAY 99, Whistler** The combination of perilously dropping cliffs, cerulean glacial flow, dramatic waterfalls, and uninterrupted, fragrant pinery forms the best of all outdoor worlds. The drive along Highway 99, nicknamed the Sea-to-Sky Highway, is so gorgeous that you'll actually be relieved when a curve takes you away from the view and lets you get your mind back on driving. That doesn't happen very often during the first half of your trip, so be sure to agree beforehand about who's going to drive, or else take turns. Both of you should get a chance to gawk at the wonders that line the 90 miles of curvaceous highway from Vancouver to Whistler. *From Vancouver, cross into West Vancouver via Highway 1 north over the Second Narrows Bridge, or via Highway 1/99 over the Lion's Gate Bridge. Follow the signs to Squamish and Whistler. Depending on the road conditions, this is about a one-and-a-half-hour drive. Winter driving conditions can be hazardous.*

❧❧❧ **SHANNON FALLS, Whistler** Highway turnouts are practical places to stop for a momentary respite from the road and to review where you've just been or where you're heading. What's nice about such sites is you don't have to hike anywhere, and the big-screen viewing begins the instant you stop. The Shannon Falls turnout is a view extravaganza.

Immediately after you pull off the main road into the parking area and silence the engine, you'll hear the thunder of a huge waterfall plummeting straight down the face of the mountain. One would expect to find such a spectacle at the end of a long, arduous trail and not in the middle of a rest area, but here it is nevertheless.

While hordes of camera-toting tourists stop here, there are some semi-secluded spots. The large lawns bordering the upper trail make excellent picnic spots where you can take full advantage of this very accessible, scenic paradise. *North of Vancouver on Highway 99, about halfway to Whistler on the east side of the road. Look for signs that identify Shannon Falls.*

❤❤❤ **WHISTLER RIVER ADVENTURES, Whistler** There's river rafting, and then there's river rafting through the stately snowcapped peaks of Whistler's rugged, supernatural terrain. Your memory of the thrilling, scenery-packed journey will linger for months and perhaps even years. It is truly that majestic—at least on a clear day. Several different water excursions are available, depending on your temperament and budget. Don't miss the excitement. **(604) 932-3532, (888) 932-3532; www.whistler-river-adv.com; moderate to expensive; open mid-May–early September.** *Call for directions and river conditions.*

Romantic Alternative: River expeditions don't have to be intense. Rather than touring a river roller-coaster style, you can navigate a canoe or two-person kayak down the River of Golden Dreams. This relatively peaceful, meandering river maneuvers calmly around and through some incredible scenery. Several companies provide canoes or kayaks; call the **WHISTLER ACTIVITY AND INFORMATION CENTRE** (604-932-2394) for more information.

Pemberton and Mount Currie

Twenty minutes past Whistler on Highway 99, you'll find the teeny towns (compared to Whistler) of Pemberton and Mount Currie. In many respects these villages are not much more than truck stops along the highway, yet Pemberton at least is slowly becoming a destination for those who feel Whistler has become a burgeoning suburb of Vancouver with ski runs. A lot of the locals up here feel Pemberton is what Whistler was 30 years ago. Visually stunning and bucolic, the town is nestled in a mountain valley dotted with farms framed by the snowy peaks of Mount Currie, which rises some 9,000 feet into the air. The town of Mount Currie, we are sad to say, is a slightly depressed area surrounded by spectacular scenery.

Cost ratings for British Columbia listings are in Canadian funds. American travelers should check the exchange rate or ask an innkeeper to figure out the cost in U.S. dollars.

For those in pursuit of real country living, it is worth the extra few minutes' drive due north. We urge you to consider making this trip sooner rather than later; civilization is on its way. Pemberton even has an 18-hole golf course, the **PEMBERTON VALLEY GOLF AND COUNTRY CLUB** (1730 Airport Road, Pemberton; 604-894-6197), and where there's a golf course, the accompanying tourists will follow.

Hotel/Bed and Breakfast Kissing

❦❦ **THE LOG HOUSE BED AND BREAKFAST INN, Pemberton** Some places are just too hard to describe because they are such a mixed bag, and the Log House is one such place. In some ways it is just a nondescript bed and breakfast set in a rather ordinary neighborhood cul-de-sac. In other ways it is a one-of-a-kind mountain getaway in the middle of a lovely country setting. As you drive up the otherwise drab street, an amazing, recently constructed log home seems to appear out of nowhere. Guests have the entire house to themselves, as well as use of a hot tub with views looking up to Mount Currie. Of the six rooms, our two favorites are Rooms 1 and 2. Equipped with private baths and beautiful wood accents, they are mirror images of each other. There's a comfortable reading loft on the second floor, but with Mount Currie staring down through the large window, you might just put that book away.

Breakfast is an enticing promenade of fresh fruits, pastries, and a main dish such as French toast stuffed with fresh berries or Midwestern eggs Benedict, made with cornbread and topped with a chili sauce. **1357 Elmwood Drive; (604) 894-6000, (800) 894-6000; inexpensive.**

Restaurant Kissing

❦◁ **THE SPIRIT CIRCLE, Mount Currie** Designed after a Salish longhouse, this building resides on what locals believe is sacred ground. "Spirit Circle" refers to the influence of Native Canadian (First Nations People) culture in the artifacts, books, and cuisine the restaurant dedicates itself to.

At first glance the menu comprises a simple assortment of lighter fare such as soups, sandwiches, and salads. On closer examination, especially when the daily specials are recited, an entire ethnic culinary event begins to unfold. Native foods such as bannock (Indian fried bread), wind-dried salmon, various salmon soups (a few have names with no written counterpart), buffalo, and swamp tea (made from wild herbs that grow alongside alpine lakes) are among the house specials, and they are remarkable.

Large communal wooden tables fill the bright dining area, which features floor-to-ceiling windows and French doors that open onto a deck for summer seating. Display shelves are lined with First Nations People books and art, which are there for your enlightenment. You may not get in many kisses here, but you will be all the more in love with the area you've discovered. **212 Main Street (Highway 99); (604) 894-6336; inexpensive; call for seasonal hours.**

Outdoor Kissing

❦❦❧ **THE ADVENTURE RANCH, Pemberton** This group of outdoor specialists offers a summer agenda that will suit your abilities and preferences with any of a dozen adventures. Horseback riding (including full-day rides), jet-boat river rides, white-water rafting, float-raft trips, kayaking, camping expeditions, and hiking excursions are all available. On the ranch itself, guests will find a swimming pool and a large patio for barbecues. There's little in the way of romantic ambience here, but once you get out in the wilds, watch out! Special trips can be arranged for twosomes, but many are group oriented. **1642 Highway 99; (604) 894-5200; moderate to expensive.**

WASHINGTON

Seattle and Environs

Microsoft, Boeing, Nordstrom, Starbucks, and some of the most magnificent scenery in the world have given Seattle a reputation as an innovative, attractive city (with the highest number of espresso stands per capita in the universe). It is a robust metropolis and growing bigger every day. But despite a handful of big-city ills, such as booming real estate prices, congested highways, and crowded restaurants, Seattle holds fast to a small-town mentality. Its many neighborhoods are fiercely individualistic, with distinct personalities reflected in the homes, shops, and people. What Seattleites have in common is a true passion for the outdoors. From bicycling, hiking, and in-line skating to boating, windsurfing, and skiing, outdoor recreation is a serious year-round pursuit here, although once the sun emerges, so do the locals—en masse. Any time of year, Seattle's striking setting amid lakes and bays, verdant hillsides, and rugged mountain peaks gives it a serene, beguiling environment with mesmerizing views, regardless of the weather.

Several popular movies, television shows, and national magazine articles have enhanced Seattle's reputation, but the city's recent population boom, fed by the growing software industry, has taken some of the glitter off this previously untarnishable gem; there are even days when smog hovers above the horizon. But those drawbacks can't diminish the honeymoon Seattleites have with their city—the ski slopes are only an hour's drive east of downtown; excellent theater, jazz, opera, dance, and comedy clubs abound; island getaways are an hour or two away; and the hiking is stupendous. There are enough kissing places here to keep two people preoccupied with romance for a lifetime.

Hotel/Bed and Breakfast Kissing

❀❀❀ **ALEXIS HOTEL, Seattle** When the Sultan of Brunei stayed at this 109-room historic downtown hotel, he did more than relax at the Aveda Spa or enjoy the wine tastings and four-star restaurant, **THE PAINTED TABLE** (see the Romantic Suggestion below). He redecorated his room in dark purples and grays and brought in a collection of world-class antiques. He came, he saw, he stayed—and then left almost everything to the hotel. So for $450 a night, you too can live like a sultan. If you want to *veni, vidi, vici* for less, however, Alexis' Fireplace Suites are ideal; each one features a king-size bed hidden behind Japanese screens, a large formal living room, a TV/VCR, tall windows, and a wood-burning fireplace. While you can't light a real fire in the spacious Spa Suites, the jetted tubs for two will do just fine for sparking romance. The one- and two-bedroom suites are elegant, but unimpressive. These converted condos still smack of residential living, with long hallways and boring kitchens. The contemporary European decor features muted yellows and oranges, along with fancy floral motifs, opulent fabrics, and striped patterns.

Unfortunately, the small, elongated lobby is nothing to write home about, and, despite the four-story hotel's location a few blocks uphill from Elliott Bay, views aren't a top attraction either. **1007 First Avenue; (206) 624-4844, (800) 426-7033; expensive to very expensive.**

Romantic Note: Ask about the Alexis' Unforgettable Romance package, which includes Aveda aromatherapy products, sparkling wine or cider, and handmade chocolate truffles. Enjoy a complimentary continental breakfast and newspaper in the morning.

Romantic Suggestion: No need to travel far from the Alexis for a nice breakfast, lunch, or dinner. THE PAINTED TABLE (206-624-3646; moderate to expensive; breakfast and dinner daily, lunch Monday–Friday) offers diners a contemporary setting warmed by apricot-colored walls, handsome wood paneling, and French doors overlooking a tiny flower-filled terrace. The restaurant's name comes from the colorful, hand-painted plates displayed throughout, and if you find one you like, you can buy it: They are for sale. A seasonal menu brings sophisticated dishes—both in taste and presentation—to your linen-covered table. The chef's trademark creations include a tower of crabmeat crowned with soft-cooked quail egg and the impressive stacked, herb-basted Chilean sea bass with Japanese eggplant and roasted poblanos.

❧❧ **THE BACON MANSION, Seattle** Edwardian style abounds in this classic 1909 Capitol Hill mansion. Despite the urban location, the surrounding lawn and flower gardens provide a sense of country relaxation; on nice days, guests can lounge outdoors on the patio and admire the fountain and the adjoining rose garden. The spacious, beautifully renovated interior, comprising over 9,000 square feet of living space, is divided into four levels, all accessed by a winding, maroon-carpeted staircase. Downstairs, the fir-paneled library, living room, and dining room are highlighted by leaded glass windows, pastel fabrics, and hardwood floors covered with Oriental carpets. Each morning, an extended continental breakfast is served in the dining room at a long, stately table beneath a sparkling chandelier.

The ten guest rooms are not exactly exceptional; they vary in size, and two lack private baths. Most of the rooms feature four-poster beds, wicker furnishings, large windows, and rather basic and old-fashioned tiled bathrooms (one with a claw-foot tub). Both antiques and contemporary furnishings are found throughout, creating a rather eclectic decor in some of the rooms. The largest unit, the Capitol Suite, offers a four-poster queen-size bed, a cozy sitting area next to the fireplace, and a view of the city. The Carriage House, which sits behind the mansion, is divided into two units; the downstairs suite is equipped with a kitchenette, wet bar, and a roomy walk-in shower in the tiled bathroom, while the upstairs unit is smaller, but very cozy, with a queen-size bed, sloping ceilings, and a view of the trees and the patio. **959 Broadway Avenue East; (206) 329-1864, (800) 240-1864; www.site-works.com/bacon; inexpensive to expensive; minimum-stay requirement on weekends.**

❀❀ **CHELSEA STATION ON THE PARK, Seattle** Wake up and smell the roses—literally!—at this charming bed and breakfast across from the Woodland Park Rose Gardens. Located ten minutes north of downtown Seattle, two 1920s Federal Colonial-style homes—separated by a carriage house—offer a rosy, cozy retreat from the city as well as easy access to Fremont, one of Seattle's most-loved neighborhoods.

The nine guest rooms all come with private, albeit standard, baths. (The exception is the soaking tub in the Honeymoon Suite.) Of all the rooms, we prefer the coral and cream Morning Glory Room on the ground floor across from the parlor. Hardwood floors, simple lace curtains, and a sunny sitting room add elegance, while an antique pump organ provides some foot-pedaling fun. Directly upstairs, the Sunlight Suite is a wonderful place for catching afternoon rays; this suite offers a four-poster queen-size bed and outstanding views of the Cascades. If you seek privacy, request the suite on the ground floor that has its own private deck entrance. Throughout both homes you'll find comfy Arts and Crafts furniture (made by the talented proprietor), along with Northwest-scene watercolors and period antiques. Silly-looking ornamental fireplaces—popular fixtures when these homes were built—are found in most suites. Just don't try heating up the night by turning on the electric log—fire codes don't permit it. Too bad, since Seattle nights can be chilly.

In the morning, wake up your palate with ginger pancakes complemented by lemon sauce, a baked grapefruit drizzled with honey, or eggs Florentine served alongside a tomato-apple salad. Guests sit family-style at the dining room table or at a parlor table. And, yes, since this is the coffee-drinking capital, a hot cup of java is always ready. **4915 Linden Avenue North; (206) 547-6077, (800) 400-6077; www.bandbseattle.com; moderate.**

Romantic Suggestion: If beautiful roses and that cup of caffeine have you ready for fun, take a walk to Seattle's most popular park, **GREEN LAKE,** where you can share a picnic by the lake or rent a canoe and rock the boat with a kiss. The **WOODLAND PARK ZOO** is only a hop, skip, and jump away, too.

❀❀❀❀ **FOUR SEASONS OLYMPIC HOTEL, Seattle** This ultra-posh downtown hotel features more than 450 guest rooms in a centrally located landmark building. The spacious accommodations (some with separate parlors and living rooms) are graciously decorated, but the focus on business travelers is all too apparent—the simple decor and sober beige color schemes certainly won't spark much romance. What will sweep you away are the restaurants, health club, myriad services, gracious concierges, opulent lobby, and boutiques, which are all simply sensational. Once you arrive at the Four Seasons, you'll have no reason to go anywhere else to fulfill your amorous requirements. After your morning workout at the complimentary health club—a lap pool, a 20-person spa tub (which never seems to be in use), and modest workout and weight rooms—you can arrange for fresh coffee, a daily newspaper, and eggs Florentine to be delivered to you pool-side or out on the sunny garden patio.

Located just off the lobby, the **GARDEN COURT LOUNGE** (moderate to expensive) is a radiant composite of tearoom, lounge, bistro, and ballroom. The immense hall, adorned with a bevy of trees, marble and carpeted floors, 40-foot-tall windows, and a petite waterfall cascading into a rock pond, offers well-spaced groupings of settees, cushioned chairs, and glass coffee tables. This prodigious dining room changes its agenda as the day progresses: Depending on the time and day, you can come here for a Sunday brunch, savory lunch, authentic afternoon tea service, evening cocktails, and late-evening dancing to a small band every Friday and Saturday. The hotel's main restaurant, **THE GEORGIAN ROOM** (see Restaurant Kissing), is one of the most stunning dining spots in Seattle. All in all, when you talk about grand accommodations in the heart of downtown Seattle, you're talking about the Four Seasons Olympic. **411 University Street; (206) 621-1700, (800) 223-8772; www.fourseasons.com; unbelievably expensive.**

Romantic Note: Ask about the different packages available. The Romance package offers one night in an executive suite, champagne upon arrival, and continental breakfast delivered to your door the next morning. The Honeymoon package is truly the epitome of romance; it includes one night in an executive suite, plus chocolate-covered strawberries, personalized robes, and continental breakfast in bed.

❤❤ **THE GASLIGHT INN, Seattle** Businesspeople weary of large hotels, as well as traveling romantics in search of rest and relaxation, enjoy staying at this appealing inn that is housed in two turn-of-the-century homes. The Gaslight Inn and the Howell Street Suites are located right next to each other on Capitol Hill's busy 15th Avenue.

Guests are sure to find a room that suits their fancy, with 16 unique accommodations spread out between the two homes. The Gaslight Inn holds nine homey, slightly worn rooms, each decorated with rich Northwest colors, bent-willow and Arts and Crafts–style furnishings, Native American art pieces, and handsome antiques. Unfortunately, only five of the rooms have private baths, but to make up for it, one room features a warm gas fireplace and two have decks that overlook the backyard pool area and downtown Seattle.

For romantic endeavors, reserve one of the Howell Street Suites. Although the building lost most of its old-world charm during its most recent renovation, the seven attractive self-contained suites are still spacious and airy. They feature warm carpeting, richly colored walls, full kitchens, private bathrooms, living areas with comfy couches, and large windows with views of the outdoor courtyard or surrounding neighborhood. We especially recommend Suite 6, which is exceptionally roomy and has a gas fireplace. Located on the top floor of the building, it also has a spectacular view of the Seattle skyline.

The innkeepers urge guests at both houses to unwind in the wood-paneled common rooms of the Gaslight Inn. Cozy sofas are set in front of a crackling fireplace in one room, while the other is distinguished by deep green walls and a mounted deer head over the couch. In the morning, follow the scent of fresh coffee and local teas to the main-floor dining room, where a continental breakfast is presented for all to enjoy. **1727 15th Avenue; (206) 325-3654; www. gaslight_inn.com; inexpensive to moderate; minimum-stay requirement on weekends.**

❀❀❁ HILL HOUSE BED AND BREAKFAST, Seattle

Recently under new ownership, Hill House Bed and Breakfast comprises two Victorian homes resting side by side, both renovated in an immaculate contemporary fashion. It is obvious that the new owners maintain a consistent level of excellence in every detail, from the lace curtains to the handsome furnishings throughout.

Upstairs in the original home are three petite but attractive guest rooms, two of which share a small standard bath. Eyelet-covered down comforters on the beds are a cozy extra. As well put-together and reasonably priced as these rooms are, they are really too small and too close for comfort to recommend wholeheartedly. However, the two garden-level suites have gracious appointments and room to spare. Striking hunter green and burgundy decor, enticing down comforters, separate seating areas with sofas, brightly tiled standard bathrooms, and private entrances guarded by a magnificent willow tree make these a welcome sight for loving eyes.

Two additional guest rooms take up the second level of the home next door, and offer a considerable amount of privacy. Both are furnished with lace-covered canopy beds, beautifully restored antique furniture, and large private baths.

A full gourmet breakfast is served in the dining room at a somewhat cramped shared table in the main house. It would be better if there were more space, but despite this shortcoming, mornings taste great at the Hill House. **1113 East John Street; (206) 720-7161, (800) 720-7161; www.seattlebnb.com; inexpensive to moderate; minimum-stay requirement on weekends and holidays.**

❀❀❁ HOTEL EDGEWATER, Seattle

If the Northwest lodge look is your style, you'll love the decor of this hotel. If not, the views alone may sway you into staying. The 238-room hotel prides itself on being Seattle's only waterfront hotel, and the unobstructed views of Puget Sound and the Olympic Mountains are truly outstanding. An inviting lodge-like lobby, heavy on fly-fishing themes and Northwest colors, soaks in the afternoon sun and is an excellent, but public, place to watch the sunset. If the day's gray, cuddle up on the couch beside the statuesque river-rock fireplace.

Request a waterfront room, otherwise you'll be staring up at skyscrapers and down into a parking lot. The small, standard-looking rooms hold handcrafted knotty pine furniture, comfy red armchairs, and king-size beds adorned with Ralph Lauren plaid comforters. Amoires hide the TV, which you won't want to watch anyway . . . the view from your small patio will provide enough entertainment. (In the past, guests fished from these balconies, but that messy tradition has floundered. Sorry, fisherfolk.) The ultra-expensive, two-bedroom Presidential Suite is the hotel's only concession to extravagance. Skylights jazz up the two-person Jacuzzi tub and double shower, while wall-to-wall windows let you sunbathe on the California king-size sleigh bed.

The touristy (and somewhat tacky) waterfront, downtown Seattle, and the exciting **PIKE PLACE MARKET** (see Outdoor Kissing) are a short walk (or complimentary shuttle ride) away. You can also hop on the waterfront trolley that stops right across the street and passes through Pioneer Square before ending in the International District. **2411 Alaskan Way, at Pier 67; (206) 728-7000, (800) 624-0670; expensive to very expensive.**

Romantic Note: The Northwest lodge look continues in the **RESTAURANT AT HOTEL EDGEWATER** (expensive). Antler chandeliers, knotty pine chairs, and forest green carpet don't make for a romantic ambience, but then again, you can't beat the views for breakfast, lunch, or dinner.

❤❤❤ **HOTEL MONACO, Seattle** The spectacular Mediterranean-style lobby of the Hotel Monaco offers a welcome escape from the busy streets of downtown Seattle. Let your senses come to life as you take in the boldly colored furniture, giant potted palms, gold-framed mirrors, and the large dolphin mural that spreads across the upper portion of the vaulted ceiling. Tied-back velvet curtains divide the main sitting area from a small alcove near the windows that holds the hotel's "kissing couch." (Unfortunately, you really can't kiss here unless you don't mind that passersby can see you through the windows). Tiered bronze and glass chandeliers, tasseled throw pillows in bright paisleys and stripes, several chaise lounges, and round portal mirrors complete this magnificent entryway. Return to the whimsical lobby in the evening to participate in the nightly wine reception.

The hotel's 189 guest rooms are definitely not for the faint-hearted. All the rooms have similar color schemes, with either vivid splashes of pink, yellow, and cream, or bold displays of red, green, and charcoal. Patterns layered upon patterns, striped walls, and a combination of cherry-wood and white-washed furniture create a dramatic effect. Plenty of amenities accompany each room, including TVs conveniently hidden away in armoires. Of the 45 suites, the Monte Carlo is the most romantic, with pinstriped curtains that separate the sitting room from the bedroom. We also like the Mediterranean Suite, which features a large jetted tub in its spacious bathroom. Perhaps the most interesting service offered is having a pet goldfish delivered to your room (in a fishbowl) upon request, to keep you company—not exactly romantic, but definitely unique.

If, after a day of exploring downtown Seattle, you'd like an altogether different experience, visit the hotel's New Orleans–style restaurant, **SAZERAC** (see Restaurant Kissing), located on the ground floor adjacent to the lobby.

1101 Fourth Avenue; (206) 621-1770, (800) 945-2240; www.monaco-seattle.com; very expensive to unbelievably expensive.

❀❀❀❀ **HOTEL VINTAGE PARK, Seattle** Romance and convenience come together at the Hotel Vintage Park, located just blocks away from fine boutiques, upscale department stores, colorful Pike Place Market, and the 5th Avenue Theater. Elegance and supreme comfort are the hallmark of this intimate downtown hotel. A winery theme plays throughout the hotel's 126 guest rooms, and the suites are named after Washington vineyards. Inside the rooms, stately cherry-wood furnishings, TVs hidden away in wooden armoires, tall ceilings and windows, richly colored tapestried sofas and chairs, sumptuous linens in deep plum and hunter green, and small but attractive bathrooms ensure that all your affectionate needs will be met. If your wallet can recover from the blow, you'll find that an especially amorous ambience flourishes in the Chateau Ste. Michelle Suite, with its gold and bright blue color scheme, wood-burning fireplace, canopied bed, and Jacuzzi tub for two. A competent staff provides attentive service to all guests.

Twenty-four-hour room service is available from the adjacent, lively, and well-regarded **TULIO RISTORANTE** (206-624-5500; moderate to expensive; breakfast, lunch, and dinner daily). Complimentary evening wine tastings next to a crackling fire in the cozy lobby make Hotel Vintage Park a premium addition to the Seattle area, and one not to be overlooked. **1100 Fifth Avenue; (206) 624-8000, (800) 624-4433; www.hotelvintagepark.com; very expensive to unbelievably expensive.**

❀❀❀ **INN AT THE MARKET, Seattle** Set on a slope in the heart of the colorful and intriguing **PIKE PLACE MARKET** (see Outdoor Kissing), this stylish inn surveys spectacular views of either the bustling city or Elliott Bay and the snowcapped Olympics. Guests can lounge on the rooftop patio and relish one of the best views in the city. On blustery, rainy days, the overstuffed sofa arranged beside a blazing fire in the common area makes a cozy refuge.

The decor in the 70 guest rooms is as fresh as the market's produce, with French country pine furnishings and neutral color schemes. Plump down duvets and thick terry-cloth robes add comfort. TVs are discreetly hidden in large wooden armoires, and the private bathrooms are roomy enough for two. Breakfast is not included in your stay, but a French bistro-style café downstairs offers hearty European repasts. We also recommend taking advantage of the fresh fruit and baked goods offered just steps away in the market, where you can have fun hand-picking the makings for your morning meal. **86 Pine Street; (206) 443-3600, (800) 446-4484; www.innatthemarket.com; expensive to unbelievably expensive.**

❀❀ **MAYFLOWER PARK HOTEL, Seattle** Convenience and charm are tastefully united in this downtown hotel. Actually, "convenience" is a bit of an understatement: The Mayflower is located one block from Nordstrom, three blocks from **PIKE PLACE MARKET** (see Outdoor Kissing), around the corner from the Monorail Terminal, and within easy range of more than a dozen espresso stands (a Northwest essential). Built in 1927, the historic structure has been renovated to resemble an intimate European hotel, and to some extent it succeeds. Terra-cotta detailing on the building's facade and the classic elegance of the common areas give the hotel an inviting warmth. In the lobby, huge bouquets of flowers accent dark mahogany tables, a 1776 grandfather clock holds court in one corner, and beautiful stained glass windows allow sunlight to play across the ceilings. The adjacent sitting room is perfect for amorous conversation or a quiet evening in front of the fire. Both the lobby and the sitting room are decorated in soothing greens and beiges, with subtle Asian touches that complement the European architecture.

It's a shame you can't sleep in the lobby, because it is the best room in the house! Although all 173 guest rooms have mahogany furnishings, plush color schemes, and conservative artwork, they lack the beauty and charm of the common areas. The so-called Deluxe Suites are standard rooms connected to a small lounge area with an extra bath. Disappointingly, the bathrooms, which probably haven't seen new fixtures or tiles since 1940, are crying out for renovation. Stiff floral bedspreads, bare walls, and a lack of personal touches make the rooms somewhat uninviting and impersonal.

Downstairs, **ANDALUCA** (see Restaurant Kissing) serves Mediterranean-inspired cuisine in an informal setting. Off the main lobby, **OLIVER'S** (inexpensive to moderate) is a stunning spot for refreshments and appetizers. Decorated in deep hunter green, Oliver's boasts magnificent towering windows that bring in sunlight during the day and afford views of Seattle's nightlife after dark. Take advantage of the complimentary hors d'oeuvres served weeknights, which include fresh fruits and cheeses, mini-pizzas, and wonderful spanakopita. **405 Olive Way; (206) 623-8700, (800) 426-5100; expensive.**

❧❧ **PLAZA PARK SUITES, Seattle** Standing tall amid apartment buildings on the eastern fringe of downtown, this high-rise hotel is hard to miss. Helpful, friendly staff greet guests in the small, sleek lobby. Although the hotel caters primarily to business executives, a vast majority of the 193 guest rooms have romantic amenities such as fireplaces, jetted tubs, and panoramic city views. Luxurious linens and down comforters are accented with decorative pillows, and the blond wood furnishings are both stylish and comfortable. Our favorite rooms are the corner Skyline and Grand Suites, encased by windows that showcase the cityscape. (The higher the floor, the more inspiring the views and the less audible the traffic noise from busy Pike Street.) Extra-spacious bedrooms in the Skyline Suites are a decisive romantic attraction; in contrast, dining tables that can seat up to six make the Grande Suites better suited for large groups. A private elevator gives rooms on the ninth floor an added sense of privacy. Plaza Park Suites prides itself on being a full-service hotel: Guests have access to a fitness center, heated outdoor pool and spa, steam room, and sauna. A complimentary continental breakfast is served in a cheery breakfast room just off the lobby. Couples eager to explore Seattle's thriving downtown will appreciate the hotel's complimentary shuttle bus service, which whisks guests to central downtown destinations, just minutes away. **1011 Pike Street; (206) 682-8282, (800) 426-0670; www.plazaparksuites.com; expensive to unbelievably expensive.**

❀❀❀ **SALISBURY HOUSE, Seattle** Located on a quiet, tree-lined residential street in an established Capitol Hill neighborhood, this inviting 1904 Prairie-style house is a peaceful oasis amid the area's colorful but sometimes overwhelmingly busy street scene. The handsome common rooms on the main floor are appointed with comfortable couches and chairs, polished maple floors, Oriental rugs, fireplaces, and leaded glass windows. On the second floor, a glass-enclosed sunroom filled with wicker furniture and plants overlooks the lush backyard, with views of the manicured lawn, trees, flower gardens, and brick courtyard below.

All five guest rooms have queen-size beds draped with down comforters, attractively renovated bathrooms (one has a six-foot-long claw-foot soaking tub), and a mixture of antiques and contemporary furnishings; two have cozy window seats. The decor is simple but surprisingly elegant. For complete privacy request the Suite, a spacious room located on the lower level of the home, which offers such romantic amenities as a private entrance, fireplace, whirlpool tub, and shower for two. A full vegetarian breakfast of eggs, pancakes, fresh fruit, juice, and coffee is served each morning in the formal dining room. **750 16th Avenue East; (206) 328-8682; www.salisburyhouse.com; inexpensive to expensive.**

❀❀❀ **SORRENTO HOTEL, Seattle** Very little about the Sorrento bears any resemblance to a typical city hotel: One visit will convince you of that. Built in 1909, the Sorrento Hotel reigned for years as the most romantic spot in the city. Time took its toll, but in 1981 the Sorrento was restored to its previous glory. Today, this Italianate Renaissance building on the western slope of First Hill has regained its romantic standing.

Of the hotel's 76 rooms, the suites are the best, with their plush furnishings, large windows, stereos, goose-down pillows, and formal fabrics. Muted yellow-and-green color schemes enhance the regal feel of the suites. Unfortunately, the bathrooms are dull and the standard rooms are just OK, but everything else is exemplary. On chilly nights, turndown service includes a hot water bottle placed under the sheets for a warm evening snuggle.

Live entertainment takes place most evenings downstairs in the **FIRESIDE ROOM**, where a stunning, albeit formal, assortment of settees, sofas, and chairs are arranged around an imposing hand-painted tile-and-stone fireplace. The polished Honduran mahogany paneling makes this an inviting spot for an early-evening conversation or an after-dinner cognac. The award-winning **HUNT CLUB RESTAURANT** (see Restaurant Kissing) serves consistently fine meals in a radiantly seductive series of mahogany-paneled rooms. **900 Madison Street; (206) 622-6400, (800) 426-1265; www.hotelsorrento; very expensive to unbelievably expensive.**

Restaurant Kissing

❦❦❦ **ADRIATICA, Seattle** Perched on a steep hillside overlooking Lake Union, this tall villa-style home seems out of place among its industrial neighbors. But when the sun has gone down and the surrounding area is obscured by nightfall, Adriatica looks regal and refined.

Romance and intimacy are the focus here, from the well-spaced tables dressed with classic white linens to the soft light shed by antique chandeliers and small table lamps. Unfortunately, recent construction has all but blocked the tranquil view of Lake Union that this restaurant used to showcase with pride. However, the soothing ivory walls, dark wood accents, lovely modern art illuminated by wall sconces, and soft jazz are more than enough to dazzle your senses. A small room at the rear of the restaurant gives patrons an added bonus: Three walls of windows are surrounded by dense trees and shrubbery, creating a serene greenhouse ambience.

In spite of the steep prices, the food here is almost always worth the splurge. If you're having difficulty deciding among the menu's many tasty items, we highly recommend starting with the heavenly grilled portobello mushroom or the fresh Penn Cove mussels with red pepper butter. The evening's risotto rarely disappoints, the grilled lamb chops are excellent, and the Spanish-style mixed seafood in zesty romesco sauce with peperonata and garlic aioli is a citywide favorite. After you have savored the last bites of your chocolate decadence or warm apple tart, pop up to the second-floor bar—a perfect spot for a quiet drink. Even on Saturday nights, very few people seem to make their way up here, and you are sure to find a secluded table where you can enjoy a long, divine kiss. **1107 Dexter Avenue North; (206) 285-5000; expensive to very expensive; reservations recommended; dinner daily.**

❦❦❦ **AL BOCCALINO, Seattle** If you're looking for fine Italian cuisine in a sophisticated atmosphere, Al Boccalino should be first on your list. Lunchtime can be boisterous, but the pace slows around dinnertime, making this tiny restaurant an extremely charming find. The vintage red brick building is typical of many in the Pioneer Square area. Inside the unassuming dining room, wrought-iron-caged windows are framed by floral curtains and white tablecloths are starched to perfection. Dignified turn-of-the-century lamps hang from the ceiling, spreading soft light throughout the room. Service is attentive and professional.

The menu is filled with classic and innovative southern Italian dishes. The risotto with scallops, prawns, calamari, clams, basil, plum tomatoes, and garlic in a white wine stock is excellent. We also recommend the potato gnocchi tossed in a tomato-basil sauce and baked with provolone, as well as the oven-roasted fillet of salmon stuffed with sun-dried tomatoes and oregano, and wrapped in grape leaves. *Mama mia!* Stop counting calories after the main course: The tantalizing desserts, featuring homemade ice cream and a sinful chocolate-espresso torte, are bliss inducing. **1 Yesler Way; (206) 622-7688; moderate; lunch Monday–Friday, dinner daily.**

❦❦❦ **ANDALUCA, Seattle** It seems as though everyone is jumping on the Mediterranean bandwagon these days, but Andaluca stands out from the crowd. This dark and lively restaurant, housed right downtown in the **MAYFLOWER PARK HOTEL** (see Hotel/Bed and Breakfast Kissing), holds an interesting mixture of old-fashioned wooden booths and tables in assorted sizes, accented by contemporary fixtures and colorful table accessories. Service is both friendly and helpful, but never intrusive. The creative menu is very small (you may feel annoyed at the lack of choices), but everything is excellent. We remember our meal as a progression of delicious dishes: crispy seasoned duck cakes with mango chutney, superb herb bread, and pan-seared salmon so tender it melted in our mouth. Our dinner was accompanied by fine wine and capped with truly memorable desserts; the lemon-mascarpone custard was elegantly rich, and sharing the warm liquid chocolate cake was a true test of love. **407 Olive Way, at the Mayflower Park Hotel; (206) 382-6999; expensive to very expensive; breakfast and dinner daily, lunch Monday–Saturday.**

Romantic Warning: The noise level can be overwhelming, which can help fill the conversational spaces if you're here on a first date. (Andaluca is an excellent choice is you want to impress someone with a good meal in an informal atmosphere.) But if you're planning some quiet cooing, go early to beat the crowds or come late, maybe after the theater, for dessert.

❦❦ **ANTHONY'S PIER 66, Seattle** Anthony's is part of a chain of seafood restaurants scattered throughout the Puget Sound area, but what makes this one stand out is its location. Perched right on Pier 66 at Seattle's waterfront, the second-floor dining room overlooks Puget Sound and its busy waters. Most Seattle eateries would sacrifice a sous-chef for such a view. Sit and sip a glass of wine on the casual outside deck as you watch ferries and sailboats pass by against the backlit majesty of the Olympic Mountains, or enjoy the same brilliant scene from the dining room, where immense windows capture the enchanting panorama. Anthony's shares the building with two other restaurants: the extremely casual walk-up **FISH BAR** (inexpensive), which serves delicious fish tacos, and the sit-down **BELL STREET DINER** (moderate; lunch and dinner daily), with a larger menu selection. Both are managed by Anthony's, and all three offer great food; however, the upstairs restaurant is most worthy of romantic consideration.

Due to its prime location and stylish interior, Anthony's Pier 66 is popular for special occasions and group gatherings. Large groups make the ambience less than tranquil and sometimes downright loud, but the view and the fabulous food more than compensate. Lacquer-coated wicker chairs and pine tables fill the dining room, and there are several high-backed booths that provide minimal privacy. Ever inventive and wonderfully fresh, the nightly fish specialties vary from char-grilled salmon medallions in sun-dried tomato–basil butter to grilled halibut with rhubarb coulis to seared mahimahi with mango–macadamia nut salsa. Service is attentive, presentations are impressive, and the seafood is always a sure thing. **2201 Alaskan Way; (206) 448-6688; expensive to very expensive; dinner daily.**

❦❦ **ASSAGGIO RISTORANTE, Seattle** A romantic meal here will depend on when you dine. Lunch packs in the suit-and-tie crowd, and the high ceilings don't help the noise factor. Try arriving early or later for dinner and, if possible, request a window table, adorned with white linen tablecloths and flowers. (These tables have more elbow room.) The interior, reminiscent of a classic Italian church with Michelangelo-inspired frescos, elegant archways, and stone statues, is warm and inviting, especially at night. Assaggio's owner, known for his graciousness, regularly greets diners and occasionally visits tables to make sure all is well.

Begin your meal with the antipasto plate, featuring house specialties, including the popular goat cheese–covered prawns—barbecued to perfection. The *pappardella boscaiola*, a wide-noodle dish with mushrooms, smoky prosciutto, and a touch of cream, leaves no long-lasting impression. However, the generous free-range veal chop stuffed with prosciutto, fontina cheese, and sage is fondly remembered. Desserts can be hit or miss: Our tiramisu had a peculiar, unappealing flavor, while the poached pear was just about perfect. **2010 Fourth Avenue, at the Claremont Hotel; (206) 441-1399; moderate to expensive; reservations recommended; lunch Monday–Friday, dinner daily.**

❦❦ **AVENUE ONE, Seattle** Transformed from its previous Victorian incarnation into a more dignified, upscale restaurant, Avenue One has been handsomely renovated to exude a New York state of mind while still retaining a Northwest preference. Glass doors swing open to reveal a sparkling interior replete with a small copper-topped bar area, towering ceilings, and peach- and saffron-colored walls framed by intricate moldings. Tables in the main dining area are a bit too close for comfort, but this doesn't detract from the welcoming atmosphere. The real destination here is the back room, where a handful of tables are warmed by a glowing fireplace and a view of Puget Sound and the Olympics in the distance.

Many interesting dishes are listed on the French country menu. Be aware that the kitchen often produces over- or undercooked entrées with slightly bland flavors. Our coriander-crusted salmon on couscous with wilted spinach was delicious; but we were disappointed with the stew of eggplant, tomatoes, currants, figs, chickpeas, and Moroccan spices, which proved relatively flavorless. Avenue One had been open only a few months when we visited, but we are confident that with a little time and attention, the cuisine will one day live up to the restaurant's heart-stirring ambience. **1921 First Avenue; (206) 441-6139; inexpensive to expensive; lunch Monday–Friday, dinner daily.**

❤❦ **CAFE DILETTANTE, Seattle** In Seattle, Dilettante has become synonymous with incredible chocolate (an important ingredient for any romantic encounter). Dilettante's chocolates are the stuff dreams are made of—rich, dark, complex, and deeply flavorful. A large display of truffles and treats tempts even the most devoted dieters at the café's entrance. Once inside, you'll discover that the menu is filled with exquisite mousse, heavenly tortes, and to-die-for layer cakes; all are as wonderful as they sound.

Due to its location on the main drag of Capitol Hill, this café is usually bustling and the mood changes very little in the evening, even when the fluorescent lights are dimmed and candles are lit at every table. Regrettably, the tables are tightly spaced and crowds often make it impossible to whisper sweet nothings. But once you take that first bite of vanilla ice cream drizzled with Dilettante's dark chocolate sauce, everything around you will melt away.

Extended hours allow you to drop in for a luscious treat after a movie or late dinner. The café stays open until midnight every day except Friday and Saturday, when it is open until 1 A.M. You can also purchase candies or truffles to go if you want to indulge later on. **416 Broadway East; (206) 329-6463; inexpensive to moderate; lunch and dinner daily.**

❤❤❦ **CAFE FLORA, Seattle** From both a decor and a dining point of view, Cafe Flora is utterly Northwest. Inside, this Madison Park restaurant manages to retain its neighborhood flavor without feeling commonplace or pedestrian. Surrounding windows reveal a handsome interior of stone floors, pine accents, and soft lighting. Plants abound in the atrium section of the restaurant, where tables are well spaced for intimate conversation. The atmosphere is congenial and comfortable throughout.

The 100-percent vegetarian menu uses locally grown produce and herbs. Luscious combinations, such as portobello mushroom "steaks" in a stunning wine sauce, and abundant burritos filled with brandy-soaked black beans and a rich chipotle sauce, are pleasing both to eye and palate. In every way Cafe Flora offers a premium, epicurean experience for heart-healthy lovers. **2901 East Madison; (206) 325-9100; inexpensive to moderate; lunch Tuesday–Friday, dinner Tuesday–Sunday, brunch Saturday–Sunday.**

❤❤❤ **CAMPAGNE, Seattle** Situated in Seattle's famous PIKE PLACE MARKET (see Outdoor Kissing), Campagne serves up superior dinners in an elegant, stately atmosphere. During summer, outdoor seating is available on the brick courtyard, where flickering candles give off a dreamy light. Inside, the simple, somewhat sparsely furnished dining room features hardwood floors, large fresh flower arrangements, white linens, and expansive windows looking out to

Post Alley and the blazing "PUBLIC MARKET" sign. There is no question as to exactly where you are, no matter where you sit. The coziest spot here is the lounge, with its floral upholstered chairs, muted gold tablecloths, and dark wood accents.

The creative French menu with Northwest overtones will satisfy even the most finicky palate. Your taste buds will be aroused by the inspired and interesting creations. An excellent choice is the wild rice risotto with roasted pumpkin, accompanied by grilled pears and sprinkled with fresh Parmesan. The sea bass, served atop lentils and simmered in a rich lobster, fennel, and tarragon broth, can definitely inspire a gourmet kissing experience. **86 Pine Street; (206) 728-2800; expensive; dinner daily.**

Romantic Note: CAFE CAMPAGNE (1800 Post Alley; 206-728-2233; inexpensive; breakfast, lunch, and dinner Monday–Saturday, brunch Sunday) is a casual, equally attractive first cousin to Campagne. Salad Nicoise (with fresh, deliciously rare grilled tuna), mussels precisely steamed in white wine, and a smooth country pâté are among the memorable, reasonably priced offerings. But be careful: Some of the specials are overpriced.

❧❧❧ **CANLIS RESTAURANT, Seattle** Perched high above Lake Union, just steps from the Aurora Bridge, the legendary Canlis Restaurant has served as a Seattle landmark since 1950. The steep (borderline extravagant) prices tend to draw in a wealthy clientele, and sleek limousines and high-end wheels are a common sight in the valet parking lot. But Canlis's long-standing reputation for fine service and superb cuisine is well deserved, making it worthy of a splurge for a special romantic occasion.

Recent renovations have dramatically improved the antiquated decor. The interior is reminiscent of a lodge, with dark wood beams, rugged rock walls, and earth-tone color schemes. Asian accents lend simple elegance to the dining room, where an entire wall of windows overlooks expansive views of Lake Union and the surrounding city. A fire blazes in a floor-to-ceiling fireplace, warming new arrivals in the front entrance. Dim lighting, tables cloaked in white linen, and candlelight are sure to inspire kisses, enhanced by the panoramic views and side-by-side seating arrangement at cozy, cushioned banquettes. A talented classical pianist fills the dining room with soothing background melodies.

The chef here is renowned for his use of regional, seasonal ingredients, and the menu is creative and impressive. Even the salads have a dash of the unusual, such as Mrs. C's Salad: mixed young greens, ripe strawberries, sweet basil, and a rice wine vinaigrette. We were partial to the forest mushroom pasta, handmade spinach fettuccine served with a forager's selection of flavorful mushrooms. We also enjoyed the light, crispy Dungeness crab cakes, which were complemented by an orange butter sauce, and the tender filet mignon. When ordering your entrée, be sure to put in an advance request for the dark chocolate lava cake with a molten interior, which can take more than half an hour to prepare. The Grand Marnier soufflé is another luscious dessert choice. If you're in the mood to spoil yourselves, you've found the right place to satiate your senses with the finer things of life. **2576 Aurora Avenue North; (206) 283-3313; expensive to very expensive; dinner Monday–Saturday.**

❦❦ **CASSIS, Seattle** If a trip to Paris isn't in the budget, you can still experience what a casual evening would be like in the City of Lights at this intimate yet casual storefront restaurant on Capitol Hill. Beige walls decorated with mirrors, tables clustered in partitioned groups, a compact but handsome bar, and high ceilings give the room austere French flair.

The brief menu focuses on bistro-style dishes. Begin with a hearty portion of the house pâté or one of the generous salads, followed by your entrée. The grilled rib-eye, served in a rich wine sauce, is flavorful but a bit too fatty; on the other hand, the Eiffel Tower of pomme frites that shares the plate deserves a medal for best use of a tuber. Grilled salmon is cooked with care, although the fennel celeriac rémoulade that accompanies it is oddly reminiscent of coleslaw. The limited wine list offers French and domestic vintages; in keeping with the informal atmosphere, tumblers are used instead of wineglasses. Save room for dessert; the chocolate bread pudding with crème Anglaise is a model of sophisticated simplicity. **2359 Tenth Avenue East; (206) 329-0580; moderate; dinner daily.**

❦❦❦ **CHEZ NOUS, Seattle** We were prompted to ring the doorbell of this vintage English tearoom after catching a glimpse of the picturesque interior from the sidewalk. Our curiosity paid off: Chez Nous is easily one of Seattle's most kiss-worthy dining rooms; in fact, it would be hard not to kiss here. Located in the heart of Seattle's vibrant Capitol Hill neighborhood, this contemporary private home is ensconced on an upscale, residential side street. Guests are ushered into a lavish reception area where overstuffed floral sofas sit in front of a fireplace. Pink carpeting and yellow walls invigorate the open, flowing parlor and dining room with a fresh country appeal. A handful of tables with floral tablecloths are surrounded by fresh flowers, country art pieces, more floral fabrics, and antiques.

High tea is a serious affair for the gracious owner, who is a professional chef. Everything on the menu is made from scratch, including the delicate smoked salmon and egg mayonnaise finger sandwiches, fruit scones with strawberry jam and double cream, petite chocolate eclairs, fresh seasonal fruit tarts, and traditional sherry trifle. The English Breakfast and Earl Grey teas are specially blended. A pianist plays soothing melodies at a white baby grand piano while guests savor these delicious English delicacies. Linger as long as you like in this cheerful setting; there is only one seating a day, so you won't be hurried out to accommodate other reservations. **723 Broadway Avenue East; (206) 324-3711; moderate; reservations required; high tea Tuesday–Saturday (one seating daily at 2:30 p.m.).**

Romantic Note: Chez Nous has one guest suite (moderate; minimum-stay requirement), situated on the home's basement level. Though it isn't nearly as lavish or as lip-worthy as the tearoom, the bright color schemes, green wicker furnishings, and crisp white linens are attractive. Sliding glass doors open onto a private outdoor patio. Guests also have exclusive use of a full kitchen, small standard bathroom, and TV/VCR.

❤❤❤❤ **CHEZ SHEA, Seattle** After you've walked through evening's deserted **PIKE PLACE MARKET** (see Outdoor Kissing) and quietly watched the vendors close up shop, climb the wooden stairs to Chez Shea for an unforgettable dinner. This charming restaurant continues to delight time and time again. We have never been disappointed with any aspect of dining here, except when the meal ends and we have to leave. Because the room is small, all tables share the view of Puget Sound and West Seattle. From this vantage point you can watch the sky turn from vivid blue to glowing crimson. If you sit right next to the towering windows you can also gain a clear perspective on happenings in the market below.

Dark wood floors, cinnamon-colored walls, white arched windows, and high ceilings set the stage for the ultimate romantic evening. The menu features several different five-course meals, which change every six to eight weeks to feature the best seasonal and regional ingredients. Lamb medallions roasted in a fennel-cumin crust drizzled with a lemon-olive sauce; chicken laced with sage, prosciutto, and mango cheese; scallops in champagne sauce served in a potato basket; and blackberry mousse are just a few of the creative culinary masterpieces offered here. Shea's Lounge, the restaurant's bar area, features a more casual bistro menu. Wherever you decide to sit, Chez Shea is the perfect place to take someone special. **94 Pike Street; (206) 467-9990; www.wet.net/ chezshea; moderate to expensive; dinner Tuesday–Sunday.**

❤❤❤ **DAHLIA LOUNGE, Seattle** Theatrical detailing lightens the formal atmosphere at this popular downtown restaurant. Outside, the entrance is marked by a humorous fluorescent sign of a chef holding a fish. Inside, a neon sign proclaiming "CAFE" is at the center of the elegant and sophisticated dining room, which is distinguished by tall ceilings, vivid red walls, large mirrors, papier-mâché fish lanterns, cushy booths, and a mezzanine level. The clinking of glasses mixes with the constant hum of conversation, a phenomenon that doesn't appear to slow down as the evening draws to a close.

The creative menu changes weekly and lists entrées such as pan-roasted salmon with crème fraîche mashed potatoes, and Vietnamese duck with egg noodle phó. We recommend the pepper-crusted ahi, which is seared rare and accompanied by baby beets, arugula, and a horseradish vinaigrette; however, the house-made papparadelle is less than spectacular. Portions tend to be on the small side but are always flawlessly presented. **1904 Fourth Avenue; (206) 682-4142; www.tomdouglas.com; expensive to very expensive; reservations recommended; lunch Monday–Friday, dinner daily.**

❦❦❦ **DULCES LATIN BISTRO, Seattle** Don't be fooled by the name: Dulces is no bistro. On the contrary, this quiet, sleek restaurant is elegant and upscale. White linens and candles top the well-spaced tables arranged alongside large windows that overlook a semi-busy street in Madrona, an eclectic neighborhood experiencing increasing gentrification. The terra-cotta-colored walls impart a feeling of earthy warmth, accented by a swag of red fabric that partitions off the open kitchen and absorbs most of the noise (but fortunately not the wonderful aromas). Track lighting in the entrance illuminates a large, sensual oil painting of a blossoming flower, reminiscent of Georgia O'Keeffe's work. The experience is enhanced by a relaxed and gracious wait staff that attends to your every need, and a guitarist who plays flamenco and classical music Wednesday and Sunday evenings. Best of all, the menu features superb Latin and French seafood and meat specialties, such as bouillabaisse teeming with shellfish and seasoned with paprika and saffron; filet mignon served in a reduction sauce of Madeira and truffle paste; and Mexican prawns sautéed in butter with dried chiles and a hint of orange. Served with a cilantro-tomatillo cream sauce, the red pepper ravioli was delightfully seasoned. We were also enamored with the special of the day: grilled breaded eggplant topped with caramelized onions, peppers, and savory grilled portobello mushrooms. Gelato for dessert adds a final, sweet touch. **1430 34th Avenue; (206) 322-5453; moderate to expensive; dinner Tuesday–Sunday.**

❦❦❦ **EL GAUCHO, Seattle** If you think dinner at a steakhouse can't be romantic, think again. El Gaucho is a seductive and stylish 1950s-style bar and grill, with deep blue tones and cozy couch seating. Even the food is bliss inducing. You'll soon see why this Belltown hot spot has become one of the trendiest restaurants in town.

The high-ceilinged, cavernous interior is dimly lit and exudes an aura of intrigue and class, enhanced by the stylishly tuxedoed wait staff. A small open kitchen with a flaming grill on one side of the restaurant and a full bar set away from the dining area provide a sense of action without being overly distracting. Live music is performed on some nights, but is soothing rather than loud.

Marvelously moist Dungeness crab cakes, enlivened by a roasted pepper pesto; fresh Northwest oysters on the half shell; and a spicy tuna tartare are among the excellent starters. While steaks, chops, and kebabs are El Gaucho's pride, the menu also lists ostrich, Cornish game hen, lamb, and a selection of fresh fish and lobster prepared a variety of ways—in some cases, flambéed with finesse at your table. Carnivorous couples can delight in the Châteaubriand for two, but even the most dedicated herbivores will find something of interest on the menu, including vegetarian cannelloni and wild mushroom risotto. The grand finale is a complimentary fruit and cheese platter, almost big enough to be considered an entrée in itself. If you still have room for some sweet stuff, the dense chocolate cake and the bananas Foster are certain to please. **2505 First Avenue; (206) 728-1337; www.elgaucho.com; very expensive; dinner daily.**

❤❤ **FULLERS, Seattle** An evening at this elegant restaurant, located in the heart of downtown Seattle, will be an evening to remember. We wish the atmosphere were a little more imaginative, but the delicious masterpieces coming your way will surely inspire a kiss or two. The dining room is decorated with beige and cream wallpaper, earth-tone carpeting, soft candlelight, and white tablecloths on every table. There really isn't a bad seat in the house, although the cozy cushioned booths that line the perimeter of the room are our choice for romantic dining.

Succulent starters include seared scallops in a light mushroom broth and the ultimate seafood sampler, with chilled oysters, gravlax, and smoked trout. Our favorites among the intriguing entrées are pancetta-wrapped monkfish in a tomato-saffron broth with sage gnocchi; grilled wild Alaskan salmon with picholine olives; and pan-seared tenderloin of beef with herbed bread pudding, asparagus, and red onion jam. Whatever you decide to order, you won't be disappointed. **1400 Sixth Avenue, at the Sheraton Hotel; (206) 621-9000; expensive to very expensive; reservations recommended; dinner Monday–Saturday.**

❤❤❤ **THE GEORGIAN ROOM, Seattle** Every facet of this distinguished dining room is luxurious and regal. Ornate crystal chandeliers, monumental floral arrangements, two-story Palladian windows, and subdued lighting create a captivating, sensual atmosphere. Breakfast is executed with enough style to make the Georgian Room the city's most luxurious place to greet the morning, but the evening is when the sparks fly. Posh dinners are beautifully presented with flawless kid-glove service. Although the formal style seems a bit out of place in Seattle, you will be completely taken with the menu selections, which reflect eclectic Pacific Rim and spa cuisine influences. Breast of duck with stewed figs, wild rice pancakes, and sweet Whidbey Island Liqueur sauce is as sensational as it sounds. The same can be said for the spiced whole pheasant ladled with port wine sauce and the roast rack of lamb with eggplant compote and creamed sweet onion mustard. For most budgets the Georgian Room is a splurge, but when you're in the mood to paint the town, this spot does it in brilliant full color. **411 University Street, in the Four Seasons Olympic Hotel; (206) 621-1700; expensive to unbelievably expensive; breakfast daily, dinner Monday–Saturday.**

❤❤❤❤ **HUNT CLUB RESTAURANT, Seattle** A hallowed Seattle dining spot for years, this seductively lit dining room oozes genteel romance. Honduran mahogany paneling frames the brick walls, cozy booths and white-linened tables are set beneath European-style windows, and wall sconces glow invitingly throughout the handsome interior. The wait staff performs with panache, and the kitchen lives up to the atmosphere with exceptionally creative and carefully prepared meals. Your every need, including privacy, will be obligingly met. Succulent Sonoma duckling, incredibly moist and delicious Alaskan king salmon, and remarkable sauces are highlights of this superlative dining experience. Breakfasts and lunches are more affordable, but still memorable. **900 Madison Street, at the Sorrento Hotel; (206) 622-6400; expensive to very expensive; breakfast, lunch, and dinner daily.**

❧❧❧ **IL TERRAZZO CARMINE, Seattle** On your first visit to Il Terrazzo Carmine, you may wonder about its location in an anonymous office building in a not-so-pretty part of Pioneer Square. But everything changes once you enter the candlelit dining room, replete with fresh flowers and gleaming crystal. High ceilings with exposed beams, walls decorated with Mediterranean art, and fringed Victorian-style lamps convey a sense of grandeur. Settle back in this serene atmosphere, and get set to sample some of Seattle's best Italian food.

Our appetizer, the spinach *soffritti*, was absolutely delicious; sautéed with lemon and garlic, this preparation would make Popeye proud. And don't overlook the interesting array of soups, which on our visit included cream of prawns with roasted peppers and fresh fish simmered in a light tomato broth. Pasta dishes are masterfully prepared, with choices ranging from angel-hair pasta with fresh basil and tomato sauce to fettuccine with smoked salmon, mushrooms, and cream. Among the more substantial entrées are a beautifully done roast rack of lamb with garlic and rosemary, dry-aged New York steak with peppercorn sauce, and sautéed chicken breast served alongside artichokes and black olives. Desserts are prepared daily.

The only thing that keeps Il Terrazzo Carmine from getting one more kiss is its service, which was unpleasant. We hope our experience was an isolated one, since the combination of food and romantic ambience make this place worth trying. **411 First Avenue South; (206) 467-7797; moderate to expensive; lunch Monday–Friday, dinner Monday–Saturday.**

❧❧❧ **ISABELLA RISTORANTE, Seattle** Low lighting and raspberry-colored walls spread a warm glow throughout Isabella's seductive dining room. Crisp white linens and a single votive candle top every table, and soft white curtains help block out the view of cars rushing by outside. Once you snuggle into one of the upholstered booths that line each side of the dining room, you will forget busy downtown even exists.

Classic Italian cuisine is the specialty here, and portions are more than generous. Hearty pasta dishes include penne pasta with peas, pancetta, and caramelized onions in a light cream sauce, as well as risotto blended with seasonal vegetables, mozzarella, and Parmesan cheese. A variety of excellent meat dishes are also offered, and the daily seafood specials are reliably fantastic. Service is attentive and knowledgeable, although we encourage you to let your server know if you are on a tight schedule. The atmosphere is far from rushed, which translates into plenty of time for the two of you to whisper sweet nothings between courses. **1909 Third Avenue; (206) 441-8281; moderate to expensive; lunch Monday–Friday, dinner daily.**

Romantic Note: The open bar adjacent to the main dining room hosts live music several evenings a week. The music here is surprisingly subtle, lending a pleasant tone to the glowing ambience of the evening.

❀❀❦ **KASPAR'S, Seattle** Harbored in Seattle's lower Queen Anne neighborhood, not far from the Seattle Center, Kaspar's subdued dining room draws crowds, but never to the point of distraction. Bamboo partitions and a latticed ceiling give the impression of an outdoor garden terrace in the front dining room, where a wall of windows overlooks leafy treetops. A single fresh flower graces each linen-cloaked table. Our favorite spot in the house is the corner banquette in the solarium, where you can snuggle up close and sneak in a few kisses between courses. Unfortunately, some of the other tables are arranged just a little too close for comfort. A second elegant dining room is decorated with hand-painted shoji screens; tables in this room are topped with glowing candles and feel a little more secluded.

Kaspar's owner/chef specializes in creative, contemporary Northwest cuisine. The menu features primarily meat and seafood items, including rabbit, Muscovy duck breast, Chilean sea bass, wild Coppper River salmon, and even whole Dungeness crab. We were impressed with the unusual but delicious cold cantaloupe soup with port wine and mint, and surprised but delighted by the unexpected touch of curry accenting the Penn Cove mussels. The portobello mushrooms served with linguine and grilled vegetables had just the right amount of savory sweetness. After trying to decide between the flourless chocolate cake with fruit sauce and the sorbet trio, we gave in and ordered both. A delicious compromise! **19 West Harrison Street; (206) 298-0123; www. kaspars.com; moderate to expensive; dinner Tuesday–Saturday.**

❀❀ **LA FONTANA SICILIANA, Seattle** Situated on the ground floor of a downtown brick apartment building, La Fontana offers a cozy atmosphere for romantic dining. A handful of well-spaced four-person tables, accented with small bouquets and candles or lamps, are arranged in each of the two dining rooms. In one room, artwork decorates the brick walls; in the other, a wooden wine rack is tucked to one side, and a mural of arches embraced by trailing grapevines covers an entire wall. Chandeliers hang from the intricately patterned white ceiling, and lace window treatments partially shield diners from the street. Classical music accompanies the Italian food, which is spectacular. The fresh black pasta in a smoked-salmon cream sauce is rich and delicious, as is the risotto with fresh herbs, olive oil, prawns, garlic, and tomato sauce. On nicer days and evenings, tables are placed outside in the courtyard, where you can enjoy pretty flower boxes and the namesake fountain in addition to each other's company. **120 Blanchard; (206) 441-1045; moderate; lunch Tuesday–Friday, dinner daily.**

❀❀❦ **LAMPREIA, Seattle** Located in the heart of busy, eclectic Belltown, Lampreia uses minimalism effectively. The mustard-colored walls are simply decorated with modern artwork, while candles, a wrought-iron chandelier, and wall sconces provide soft light. The dozen or so tables are topped with crisp white linens that set off the dark mahogany chairs and marble floor. Because the restaurant's ceiling is fairly high, the acoustics are poor and conversations tend to carry over to other tables.

The outstanding food is presented with simple elegance. Dishes, however, are on the pricey side, especially considering the minuscule portions. Start off with braised Dungeness crab and lobster mashed potatoes, a truly decadent concoction that will whet your appetite for entrées such as roast pheasant with couscous, seared lamb loin with herb crust, and halibut fillet with braised fennel. Indulge in the fried truffle and banana mousse for dessert. **2400 First Avenue; (206) 443-3301; expensive; dinner Tuesday–Saturday.**

❤❤❤ **LE GOURMAND, Seattle** Ballard is a neighborhood best known for its Scandinavian heritage, yet Le Gourmand is 100-percent French. This elegant little dining room is tucked away in a modest building that appears to be boarded up at first glance, but take a closer look—the windows are covered only to deflect the sight and sound of traffic outside. Inside, the setting is refined and completely charming. A whimsical pastel mural of a meadow with birch trees covers one wall, and pink crushed-silk pillows fill the bench that lines the perimeter of the room.

The appealing ambience is complemented by gracious service and fine French cuisine. Three-course meals are prepared from local organically grown ingredients, and the presentation is straightforward. Delectable starters include sole and shrimp mousseline, and blintzes filled with sheep's-milk cheese and covered with a chive butter sauce. The chicken stuffed with a medley of Northwest mushrooms and served in a savory grape sauce, and the poached king salmon fillet with a creamy sauce of dried salmon and fresh sorrel were unimprovable. However, we were disappointed with the poached golden-eyed rockfish, which we found surprisingly bland. The third course, a mixed green salad with edible flowers, marks the end of the meal—unless you have spared room for dessert. The homemade ice creams and sorbets are difficult to resist, and the profiteroles are *tres bien*. **425 Northwest Market Street; (206) 784-3463; moderate to expensive; dinner Wednesday–Saturday.**

Romantic Warning: Noise carries easily throughout the tiny dining room, especially when large groups are present.

❤❤❤❤ **LEO MELINA, Seattle** If you are wondering where the stars dine when they visit Seattle, look no further: Leo Melina's is the place, and for good reason. The entry of this beautiful restaurant leads you past the impressive glass-enclosed kitchen to the exquisite dining room, set aglow by majestic contemporary chandeliers and sconces. From any angle, the dining room has a dazzling, august personality. Live opera fills the restaurant Friday and Saturday nights as you dine amid golden angels, cloud-painted ceilings, and sultry lighting.

Some might describe the mood as celestial, but don't think the heavenly experience stops there; just wait until you savor one of the incredible entrées. Begin with the calamari, sautéed in a slightly spicy sauce of garlic, white wine, and fresh herbs. Follow that with baked sea bass accompanied by ravioli, or homemade pasta rolled and stuffed with crab, ricotta cheese, and spinach and topped with a tangy tomato–pine nut sauce. Both are excellent—just be sure to leave room for what could be the best tiramisu in the city. **96 Union Street; (206) 623-3783; moderate to expensive; lunch and dinner daily.**

◆◆◆◆ **MAXIMILIEN, Seattle** There are many reasons why Maximilien is one of downtown's most romantic restaurants, starting with its attractive location. The restaurant is tucked away in a quiet corner of **PIKE PLACE MARKET** (see Outdoor Kissing), so you can escape the crowds but still experience the vitality of this popular Seattle attraction. Inside, you are greeted by a panorama that takes in Puget Sound, Elliott Bay, West Seattle, and the Olympic Mountains, all framed by huge picture windows. Seen at the right time—during a summer's sunset or a sudden rainstorm—the view could even be called sublime.

Recent renovations have given new luster to the wood floors and a deeper hue to the green walls, which are hung with an imaginative variety of antique mirrors. Small tables covered in crisp white linens are brightened by fresh rosebuds and flickering candles. Second-floor seating offers more astounding views and the same intimate setting. The service is low-key, friendly, and not the least bit pretentious.

Unsurprisingly, considering the culinary bounty available at the Pike Place Market, the food is farm fresh and presented with wonderful panache. Vegetables, meats, and seafood are color-coordinated with garnishes and sauces. Start off with puff pastry stuffed with crab and Brie, or escargot with wild mushrooms. Among the entrées, bouillabaisse is a favorite, as is the assortment of seafood infused with herbs and wrapped in parchment paper. The restaurant also serves an excellent roast pork with sautéed apples and a beef tenderloin with foie gras and truffle sauce. Ice cream–filled cream puffs drizzled with chocolate end the meal on a sweet note. **81-A Pike Street; (206) 682-7270; moderate to expensive; breakfast Saturday, lunch and dinner Tuesday–Saturday, brunch Sunday.**

◆◆◊ **PALISADE, Seattle** It's no secret that Palisade is the place to come for celebrations. In fact, reservations are booked back-to-back almost every summer night and the numerous tables are crowded with boisterous groups and smiling couples. The huge amphitheater-like dining room is showy and a bit overdone. A man-made saltwater stream filled with live steelhead, starfish, and seashells meanders through the restaurant, starting at the reception area and passing near many of the tables. Polished Hawaiian koa wood, subdued track lighting, and glowing lanterns at each table enhance the sophisticated scene. As impressive as this is, the real thrill is the panoramic view from the picture windows. From some tables, the sparkling city is in full sight, with Mount Rainier in the distance. Other tables view Puget Sound and passing ferries beyond a marina full of sailboats, while still others enjoy a breathtaking view of the Olympic Mountains and awe-inspiring sunsets.

Relish the view together as you share bites from the generous Captain's Pupu Platter, a three-tiered presentation of teriyaki filet mignon tenderloins, wood oven–roasted tiger pawns, and crispy Dungeness crab–stuffed ginger wontons. Seafood is Palisade's specialty, and the chef skillfully combines various cuisines to satisfy every palate. Cedar plank–roasted salmon is a favorite, but the apple-wood rotisserie king salmon served atop roasted garlic mashed potatoes is also incredibly good. Mushroom-crusted halibut and tender prime rib are other promising options. By the way, if you are wondering whether your salmon came from the little "river" that cuts through the dining room, the answer is no—those lucky fish are there only for looks. **2601 West Marina Place; (206) 285-1000; expensive to very expensive; reservations recommended; lunch and dinner daily, brunch Sunday.**

❦❦❦ **PERCHE' NO, Seattle** Perche' No is located only a few blocks from the Seattle Center, home to major theater, symphony, opera, and ballet companies. The restaurant prides itself on being more than willing to work around your schedule—just tell the wait staff when the performance starts and you'll be out in plenty of time. But don't rush your meal here if you can help it; the ambience and food are worth admiring. Crisp white table linens, fresh flowers, and bottles of red Italian wine adorn an assortment of well-spaced small tables throughout the two cozy, dimly lit dining rooms. European artwork, dried flower arrangements, and strands of garlic decorate the walls, while floral drapes shield the restaurant from the busy street outside. A personal touch is added by the restaurant's pleasant owner, who stops by every table over the course of the evening to say hello and make sure guests are comfortable. Piano music accompanies meals every Friday and Saturday night.

The homemade pasta selections are all outstanding, including fresh fettuccine with scampi, cream, and fresh basil, and spaghetti made with aged-in-house prosciutto and tossed in a tomato cream sauce. Dessert is definitely worthwhile, especially the lemon eggless custard dressed with brown sugar sauce and fresh strawberries, an outstanding original recipe from Tuscany. Excellent entrées combined with a romantic setting make for a memorable evening here, so *perche' no* (why not) come here and find out for yourselves? **621 1/2 Queen Anne Avenue North; (206) 298-0230; moderate to expensive; lunch Tuesday–Saturday, dinner Tuesday–Sunday.**

Romantic Note: Perche' No offers a dinner/limousine package that includes round-trip limousine service within the Seattle metropolitan area and a four-course dinner ($60 per person, with a two-person minimum).

❤❤ **PHOENECIA AT ALKI, Seattle** Phonenecia takes full advantage of its location facing Alki Beach, with generous windows that look out to expansive views of Puget Sound. Just about every white-linened table in the small dining room has its share of the view. A striking black ceiling and warm yellow walls adorned with colorful rugs add pizzazz to the handsome setting. Mediterranean cuisine is featured here, handled deftly by the friendly, laid-back chef (who can get overly creative in the kitchen, so ask specifically what's in store or you're liable to be surprised and possibly disappointed). The hummus, Moroccan eggplant with penne, and broiled lamb are all authentic and tasty. **2716 Alki Avenue Southwest; (206) 935-6550; moderate; dinner Tuesday–Sunday.**

❤❤❤ **PONTEVECCHIO, Seattle** At first glance, Pontevecchio's location on a busy street in funky Fremont seems an unlikely spot for romance. A closer look reveals that Pontevecchio caters almost exclusively to couples. A sign posted in the intimate, dimly lit dining room says it all: "We reserve the right to refuse service to anyone not in love." (Not surprisingly, the evening we dined here we saw several starry-eyed couples.) Small and stark, the dining room is appointed with a sleek tiled floor, marbled brown walls, and artistic black-and-white photographs. The room holds a mere seven candlelit tables, arranged on opposite sides of the room to enhance privacy. You can't help but sit extremely close to one another at the tiny round tables. (The tables are so small, in fact, that we scarcely had room for our plates!) The gracious wait staff encourages long, leisurely meals. Fortunately, the vintage Italian cuisine is excellent, and you'll want to linger over every bite of your savory grilled antipasti, pasta entrées done to perfection, fresh seafood and chicken dishes, and homemade hazelnut gelato for dessert. **710 North 34th Street; (206) 633-3989; moderate to expensive; lunch Monday–Friday, dinner Monday–Saturday.**

Romantic Note: Pontevecchio's slow pace is enlivened on Wednesdays with live tango dancers and live opera music on Fridays.

❤❤ **PONTI SEAFOOD GRILL, Seattle** *Ponti* means "the bridge" in Italian, and this waterfront restaurant offers a view of one of Seattle's busiest. On warm summer days, you can lounge on the lovely outdoor patio, overlooking the ship canal, and watch the Fremont Bridge move up and down for passing boats. (While the sight is entertaining, the clattering warning bells and blasting air horns can seriously interrupt conversation.) Inside the stylish restaurant, other features take center stage, such as a gorgeous floral bouquet, artistic ceramic plates, and large champagne bottles encased behind a wall of glass.

Tables topped with white linens, turquoise napkins, and brilliant fresh flowers are set off by creamy beige walls and dark wood accents, while large windows frame views of the bridge. Even though the noise level can escalate as the closely placed tables fill up, the room remains surprisingly cozy and intimate.

Ponti's menu knows no boundaries, drawing upon culinary influences from India to Thailand to France. While a variety of pasta and meat dishes are available, fresh fish is what this restaurant has built its reputation on. We suggest beginning your meal with an alternative to Seattle's omnipresent crab cakes: Dungeness crab spring rolls served with a zesty lime-chile dipping sauce. Next move on to one of the restaurant's signature items, decadently rich Thai curry penne pasta with seared scallops, Dungeness crab, and ginger-tomato chutney. What makes the fish dishes so outstanding here are the sauces and toppings. When it's in season, try grilled halibut adorned with a roasted corn–mango salsa and swirled in a chipotle vinaigrette, or grilled salmon topped with an olive oil, soy sauce, ginger, and basil purée. Dessert didn't wow us as much as the entrées. Our peach pie—accompanied by two tiny scoops of vanilla ice cream—had no personality. Steer clear of that one and you're certain to be delighted by something else that's sweet. **3014 Third Avenue North; (206) 284-3000; expensive; lunch Monday–Friday, dinner daily, brunch Sunday.**

❤️❤️ **QUEEN CITY GRILL, Seattle** A well-known landmark in Belltown, Queen City Grill has been serving up delectable seafood for over ten years. The best seats in the house are the high-backed, polished wood booths, which provide ample privacy for intimate conversation. Tall windows edged in exposed brick, hardwood floors, a long antique bar, an open kitchen, and bare tables evoke early Seattle. If it weren't for the packed dining room and somewhat clamorous atmosphere, you could lose yourselves in imagining the surrounding neighborhood before all the hip bars, trendy eateries, and skyscrapers came along. However, the typical dinner crowd reminds you that you are in the middle of a modern cosmopolitan area.

If you can't decide between the many grilled seafood entrées, opt for the excellent mixed seafood grill, a combination of prawns, clams, mussels, and at least two varieties of fish. Chicken, beef, and grilled vegetables are also available, as well as those ubiquitous Dungeness crab cakes. Unfortunately, the kitchen seems to be overwhelmed on busy nights, and quality and attention to detail often suffer as a result. Still, desserts are consistently scrumptious and worth saving room for. **2201 First Avenue; (206) 443-0975; expensive to very expensive; lunch Monday–Friday, dinner daily.**

Romantic Warning: Unfortunately for nonsmokers, cigarette smoke is a problem—thankfully, cigar smoking has recently been restricted—and open windows often aren't enough to diffuse the scent.

❤️❤️❤️ **QUEEN MARY, Seattle** It is easy to drive past this small storefront restaurant and never notice it, which may be why it has remained such a special place over the years. Once inside, however, you will feel as if you've been transported to the English countryside. This exceedingly charming, polished restaurant has a beautiful interior; we couldn't resist the wood wainscoting, pleated floral fabric lining the walls and entrance, lace-covered windows, and comfortable wicker chairs placed around tables set for two. A couple of ring-necked doves coo softly from a glass-enclosed sanctuary near the entrance, while waitresses sporting black-and-white maid uniforms add the finishing touch to this formal setting.

Fastidious attention to detail and freshness marks every meal. Breakfast is an elaborate display of fresh pastries, granolas, and breads; midday brings light, flaky quiches and generous sandwiches. The cheese tortellini in a hazelnut cream sauce and the chicken breast with sautéed mushrooms are both sumptuous. High tea is also a daily offering, and you will be properly impressed with this ritual. But we've left the best for last: dessert. The most outrageous, luscious cakes, tortes, and mousses are made fresh here daily. Chocolate cake with amaretto mousse, marbled cheesecake, and fresh fruit tarts were only a few of the selections available on the night we fell in love at Queen Mary. **2912 Northeast 55th Street; (206) 527-2770; inexpensive to moderate; breakfast, lunch, and high tea daily.**

❤❤❤❤ **REINER'S, Seattle** Reiner's location, crammed between two city buildings and around the block from a large hospital, is not exactly romantic, but you'll forget that as you enter the lovely courtyard entryway shaded by trees. Inside the small dining room, every last corner is filled with polished details. The tables, draped in white linen and set beneath an arched dome ceiling, are surrounded by modern tapestries. Venerable antiques, crystal chandeliers, and lace-curtained windows convey a sense of refined intimacy. Although the tables are arranged somewhat snugly, the rich ambience seems to promote privacy. Dine on extremely fresh halibut, baked king salmon, or roasted rack of lamb. Whichever entrée you choose, a meal at Reiner's is sure to satisfy your palate and whet your romantic appetite. **1106 Eighth Avenue; (206) 624-2222; expensive; dinner Tuesday–Saturday.**

❤❤ **RISTORANTE SALUTE, Seattle** If you're in the mood for a taste of Italy's countryside, you can't do better than this casual eatery. White-and-red-checked linens cover the tables, and fishing nets, buoys, and rowboats hang from the ceiling in two intimate dining rooms adorned with pictures of Italy. While the tables in both dining rooms can feel a little too close for comfort when the restaurant is operating at full capacity (which is often), flickering candlelight and cozy two-person tables help to maintain an amorous mood. Check the chalkboard for daily specials; we especially liked the *fettuccini al salmone*, a pasta dish with smoked salmon, peas, brandy, and cream. Save room for Salute's tiramisu—undoubtedly one of Seattle's best. **3426 Northeast 55th Street; (206) 527-8600; moderate; dinner daily.**

❤❤❤❤ **ROVER'S, Seattle** An unassuming neighborhood setting, a discreet interior, subtle lighting, white walls covered with pastel art, and some of the most sumptuous continental cuisine you will ever taste are waiting for you at

Rover's. The decor is a bit too stark to be truly cozy or charming, but the flaw-less, elegant dinners more than compensate. Summer months allow for more intimate dining in the restaurant's fragrant garden courtyard.

The incredibly skilled owner/chef has a worldwide reputation as one of the region's best. This fact is proven night after delicious night with dishes such as roasted monkfish with smoked apple bacon and a rich red wine sauce; roasted squab with onion confit and a warm pecan vinaigrette; and venison medallions with chanterelle mushrooms in a remarkable Armagnac sauce. Unparalleled and outstanding! **2808 East Madison; (206) 325-7442; www. rovers-seattle.com; expensive to very expensive; reservations recommended; dinner Tuesday–Saturday.**

❤❤❤ **SALEH AL LAGO, Seattle** The simple decor of this Italian restaurant isn't an oversight. Rather, it illustrates the owner's philosophy that diners should concentrate on the food rather than the wallpaper. But is this place romantic? Absolutely, and the Italian dishes, spiced with Arabian specialties, are out-standing.

Enclosed by windows, the small interior offers peekaboo glimpses of nearby Green Lake as well as the busy street. Candle lanterns and fresh flowers add color to the two-tiered dining room, which is filled with linen-cloaked tables. Cushioned booths tucked in window alcoves on the lower level offer the most privacy. Behind the glass-enclosed kitchen the talented chef/owner works dili-gently on flawless entrées such as Northwest salmon topped with a black olive, red wine, and olive oil purée; wild mushroom and Gorgonzola ravioli with roasted garlic and tomato-butter sauce; and, representing that Arabian twist, the popular upside-down chicken. This fragrant cumin- and garlic-spiced con-coction layers boneless chicken and fried cauliflower with seasoned rice for a tasty treat. After you've lingered by candlelight over coffee and perhaps some gelato or crème caramel, walk hand in hand across the street and enjoy the bustling Green Lake setting. **6804 East Green Lake Way North; (206) 524-4044; moderate to expensive; dinner Monday–Saturday.**

❤❤ **SALVATORE, Seattle** Situated in the heart of the Roosevelt District, not far from the University of Washington, Salvatore is a local romantic favorite. Savory aromas (and, unfortunately, unsavory noises) drift from the open kitchen through the small dining room, which is filled with a handful of candlelit two-person tables positioned very closely together. If you look closely, you'll notice that people have pasted their pictures onto an Italian townscape painted on the dining room's largest wall. Not your typical mural, but this isn't your typical Italian restaurant. Everything here is wildly delicious, especially the *rigatoni ai peperoni*, a savory pasta dish with olive oil, bell peppers, garlic, and roma tomatoes. And the freshly baked desserts are sheer perfection. Our only hesitation about recommending this restaurant is the fact that reserva-tions are not accepted, which means you often have to contend with crowds and a long wait for a table. Also, because this place is so popular, service can be slow on busy nights. **6100 Roosevelt Way Northeast; (206) 527-9301; moderate; dinner Monday–Saturday.**

💋💋 **SAZERAC, Seattle** There isn't a Bourbon Street in downtown Seattle, but your taste buds can take a trip to the French Quarter when you dine at Sazerac. Located adjacent to the **HOTEL MONACO** (see Hotel/Bed and Breakfast Kissing), Sazerac will sweep you up with its high ceilings, dazzling contemporary chandeliers, and festive phrases painted on the walls. Tables draped with white tablecloths and topped with brightly painted salt and pepper shakers fill the large dining room, and spicy aromas drift from the open kitchen. Semicircular mahogany-colored booths, separated by tied-back velvet curtains, line the walls and provide a little extra privacy in this lively restaurant.

Named after a popular New Orleans cocktail, Sazerac displays its Southern flair with a Louisiana-inspired menu. We started off our meal with lemon-basil gravlax and hush puppies served with warm molasses. The hush puppies were a little dry, but the cured salmon, which was served with bitter greens and cumin crackers, was tender and flavorful. For our main course, we chose the delicious Dungeness crab–and–shrimp enchilada. We also enjoyed the unusual mixture of sweet and bitter flavors found in the butternut squash raviolis with leek fondue and candied cranberries. For dessert, we can't imagine a more Southern treat than sweet potato–pecan pie, drizzled with chocolate and caramel sauces. **1101 Fourth Avenue, at the Hotel Monaco; (206) 624-7755; moderate; breakfast, lunch, and dinner daily, brunch Sunday.**

Romantic Warning: While high ceilings, an open kitchen, and a bar area enhance the festive feel of Sazerac, they also contribute to the fairly high noise level. You cannot entirely escape the bustling atmosphere, but we suggest you request one of the booths along the wall or in the back corner to enjoy a more private dinner.

💋❤ **SERAFINA, Seattle** We are told that marriage proposals are a frequent occurrence at Serafina. That may sound romantic, but the reason this is common knowledge is because the proposer practically has to shout across the table just to get the proposee's attention. With many small tables placed very close together, don't count on your evening here being a private affair. Serafina is one of Seattle's most talked-about restaurants, so it is almost always crowded and reservations are a must. The room holds a certain amount of rustic Italian charm, with earth-tone murals and low lighting, but ultimately it is the food and not the clamorous atmosphere that makes the whole experience worthwhile.

The bruschetta topped with sautéed shrimp makes a delicious starter. Incredibly flavorful and interesting entrée selections include the tender chicken breast stuffed with vegetables and mascarpone cheese in a roasted chestnut-marsala wine sauce; and the Serafina Melanzane, thinly sliced eggplant rolled in ricotta cheese, fresh basil, and Parmesan, and then baked to perfection.

Although the menu changes seasonally, you can count on the skilled kitchen for inventive dishes, and the desserts are equally pleasing. Service, however, can be rushed on busy evenings. **2043 Eastlake Avenue East; (206) 323-0807; moderate; reservations recommended; lunch Monday–Friday, dinner daily.**

Romantic Note: Live music is performed at Serafina Thursday through Sunday, starting at 8 P.M. This would be a romantic plus if the restaurant weren't already so noisy, but as it stands now, the music makes whispering sweet nothings nearly impossible.

❀❀❀ **SOSTANZA TRATTORIA, Seattle** Madison Park is a charmingly urbane, entirely gentrified neighborhood, but it isn't so slick that you will feel out of place without your power suit; after all, this is still Seattle, despite the multimillion-dollar homes lining the area. Located around the corner from a row of very upscale shops and boutiques, Sostanza is a delightful dining spot with a tender blend of elegant and country-rustic touches. Amber stucco walls, a wood-beamed ceiling, soft lighting, a large gas fireplace, and nicely spaced tables fill this Italian trattoria with warmth and comfort. Upstairs, a second dining room features Caravaggio prints and an outdoor deck overlooking Lake Washington.

Everything on the menu is very good and richly flavorful, from smoked salmon to cappellini with sun-dried tomatoes, pine nuts, and capers. The quail, wrapped and grilled in pancetta, served on a bed of risotto with sage and shallots, and drizzled with a Chianti demi-glace, is as fabulous as it sounds. Kissing possibilities abound here for those who want to enjoy excellent cuisine near the shores of Lake Washington. **1927 43rd Avenue East; (206) 324-9701; moderate to expensive; dinner Monday–Saturday.**

❀❀❀ **SPACE NEEDLE RESTAURANT, Seattle** Of all the places to dine in Seattle, the Space Needle is without question the most touristy. As Seattle's most indelible trademark, it seems to be on the short list of must-see sites for millions of visitors every year. Why is this flying saucer–shaped tower so popular? Because on a clear day, all of the region's glories are astonishingly visible from up here, from the Olympics to the Cascades to the Puget Sound islands to the green-haloed local neighborhoods. Why are we recommending the Space Needle in a book like this? Because the service is excellent, and nothing compares to the ever-changing view as the restaurant makes a full revolution each hour. A summer sunset, candlelight, and fresh king salmon accompanied by this view are worthy of more kisses than we care to count.

Most agree that the kitchen relies on the incredible views to compensate for less than incredible cuisine. Portions are on the small side, especially considering the exorbitant prices, but quite satisfying. We enjoyed the Alaskan red king crab legs and the sake salmon special, served with a beurre blanc sauce and sprinkled with candied almonds. You'll know you've entered a tourist trap if you order the overpriced ice cream dessert known as "the Orbiter." Dry ice concealed in the serving dish emits a wave of "Seattle fog" that flows out of the bowl and onto your table as you eat. It also ends up covering neighboring tables; in order to maximize the view seating, tables in the two contemporary dining rooms have been arranged almost on top of each other. **219 Fourth Avenue North, at the Seattle Center; (206) 443-2150, (800) 938-9582; www.spaceneedle.com; very expensive; breakfast, lunch, and dinner Monday–Saturday, brunch Sunday.**

Romantic Note: You do not have to pay the usual fee for the elevator ride when dining at the restaurant. This sounds like a great deal because you also have access to the observation deck while waiting for your table or after dinner. However, when you see the prices on the menu (average $30 per entrée), you'll realize it isn't such a bargain after all.

❀❀❅ **SZMANIA'S, Seattle** Sometimes romantic ambience takes a backseat to incredible cuisine. At Szmania's, a stylish bistro in the upscale Magnolia neighborhood, the atmosphere is lively and not necessarily intimate, but the German-inspired cuisine is always remarkable. Casual outdoor seating is available in summertime; inside, the sleek interior features dropped lighting over each table and bar seating around the open kitchen. (It's fun to watch the chef and his skilled staff create the masterpieces that will soon grace your plate.)

Presentations are lovely, service is impeccable, and every dish is magnificently prepared, with each succulent, mouthwatering nuance intact. Delicious options include grilled tiger prawns on angel-hair pasta; and herb-crusted mahimahi, prepared with a pinot noir sauce and accompanied by oyster mushrooms and lobster mashed potatoes. The Caesar salad here is one of the best and most authentic in the city. Finish off your evening with the warm apple tart (it's actually shaped like an apple) drizzled with a sweet ginger-caramel sauce. The perfect crème brûlée, strawberry shortcake, or white and dark chocolate mousse can prove almost too wicked. But what's a little decadence between friends? **3321 West McGraw; (206) 284-7305; moderate to expensive; call for seasonal hours.**

❀❀❅ **UNION BAY CAFE, Seattle** The Union Bay Cafe offers a touch of casual elegance for dining romantics, although you'd never guess it from the restaurant's location on a heavily trafficked street not far from the University District. A cafélike entryway separates two cozy dining rooms that tend to fill up quickly on weekends. Colorful modern art, soothing color schemes of muted mustard and sage, soft music, and tables dressed in white linens and topped with simple votive candles help take your mind off the cars speeding by just outside the window. The experienced kitchen specializes in Northwest cuisine with Asian and Italian influences, and prepares a variety of meat, seafood, and pasta dishes. Calamari breaded with ground almonds and served with roasted garlic aioli makes a wonderfully light precursor to Dungeness crab cakes, rack of lamb, or portobello mushroom "chops." Desserts here are outstanding;

don't miss the rich pecan-chocolate-caramel tart, topped with a dollop of whipped cream. **3515 Northeast 45th Street; (206) 527-8364; moderate to expensive; dinner Tuesday–Sunday.**

Outdoor Kissing

❤️❤️❤ **ALKI BEACH, Seattle** The waterfront neighborhoods of West Seattle are only a few minutes from downtown Seattle. LINCOLN PARK, a large wooded tract just north of the Fauntleroy ferry, faces a spectacular view due west; but Alki Beach, with its northwesterly exposure, has the most expansive, sensational vistas of them all. This long stretch of sandy beach, backdropped by exquisite profiles of the snowcapped Olympics and the silvery waters of Puget Sound, is an incredible place to stroll hand in hand almost any time of year. Unfortunately, a warm summer day can change this flawless stretch of land into a mass of urban congestion, as cars cruise by and walkers, runners, and rollerbladers vie for space on the paved promenade. During the spring, fall, or winter, when things are quieter, couples can pass gentle moments here watching the sky and mountains change expressions with the passing hours. *Take Interstate 5 to the West Seattle Freeway exit and the West Seattle Bridge. Cross the bridge, follow Harbor Avenue to the beach, and continue around to Beach Drive.*

Romantic Alternative: HAMILTON VIEWPOINT in West Seattle, at the northernmost end of California Avenue Southwest, faces the downtown skyline of Seattle. In the evening you can watch as the city's twinkling lights are reflected in the cobalt blue water and the moon's golden glow dances over the surface. This is also a rare vantage point from which to watch the sun rise above Seattle. You won't be the only couple embracing in the moonlight, but you will probably be the only ones snuggling in the early light of dawn.

❤️❤️❤️ **"BHY" KRACKE PARK, Seattle** Unless you've read a previous edition of this book or live nearby, you may not have heard of this park with the funny name. As you drive through the unpretentious neighborhood, you'll probably think nothing of the small, unobtrusive playground on your left. But stop and take another look. "Bhy" Kracke Park starts off as an innocent playground, less than a block long, at the bottom of a hill. On either side of it, landscaped walkways angle upward, meet, then curve around and up, and around and up, to the top of the hill. As you climb, you'll find five tiers of grassy vistas; well-placed park benches, surrounded by dense hedges and vines, face a startling city view. Around each turn is another glimpse of the city, building up to what lies at the top. Unbelievable! **Free admission.** *Located on southeast Queen Anne Hill, north of downtown, at the intersection of Fifth Avenue North and West Highland Drive. It is also known as Comstock Park.*

Romantic Note: If you don't want to walk up, drive to the park entrance on Comstock Street at the top of the hill, and walk down one tier.

❀❀❀ **DISCOVERY PARK, Seattle** Snaking around the edge of Seattle's exclusive Magnolia neighborhood on the way to Discovery Park, **MAGNOLIA BOULEVARD** is blessed by a majestic wraparound view of Puget Sound. The cliffs along its southwest border showcase the city and the Olympic Mountains. As you follow the drive, you will notice several obvious places to pull off and park. The panoramas from these areas are spectacular, but, unfortunately, they lack privacy. However, if you walk from the grass-lined curb down to the edge of the cliff overlooking the water, the street is no longer visible.

Continue along the road to reach Discovery Park, an unusual area with an amazing variety of trails and terrain. You can hike through dense woods or along sandy cliffs above Puget Sound with unmarred exposure to everything due north, south, and west. Or take the wooden steps leading down through the woods to the shore and ramble along the driftwood-strewn rocky shoreline. While wandering through your new romantic discovery, look for the sand cliffs on the southwest side of the park. During the winter, when sundown occurs in the late afternoon, stand atop these golden dunes for an intoxicating view of day passing into night. **Free admission.** *Take the Magnolia Bridge exit off Elliott Avenue and stay to your left. At the first stop sign, turn left onto Magnolia Boulevard and follow it until it dead-ends at the park's southeast entrance.*

Romantic Warning: A sewage treatment plant is located adjacent to the beach and, unfortunately, there is a strong odor on some days that can stifle the most romantic inclinations. This problem exists only down on the beach (mostly on days when the air is still); a constant breeze helps to keep the air fresh on the cliffs.

❀❀❀❀ **HIGHLAND DRIVE/KERRY PARK, Seattle** This exclusive street, lined with mansions and classic older apartment buildings, offers enviable southwestern views from below the summit of Queen Anne Hill. In Kerry Park, a grassy knoll with benches offers sweeping, complete views of the city skyline, Puget Sound, and the Olympic Mountains. Just down the road, the intersection of Seventh Avenue West, Eighth Place West, and West Highland Drive affords an especially grand panoramic vista of the water and mountains. With a picnic basket in tow, you can spend an entire summer afternoon up here in each other's arms. **Free admission.** *From Roy Street on lower Queen Anne, turn uphill onto the steep part of Queen Anne Avenue North. Two blocks up, turn left onto West Highland Drive and follow it along the southwestern slope of the hill.*

Romantic Warning: Although it is located in a residential neighborhood, on warm, sunny days Kerry Park may be crowded with camera-toting tourists. You and your loved one might want to witness the spectacular view from this park on a cooler day, which will give you even more reason to cuddle.

❀❀❀❀ **HOT-AIR BALLOONING, Seattle** If you're thinking that a hot-air balloon ride sounds like a frivolous, expensive, childish sort of excursion, you're right. It is a Mary Poppins lift-off into fantasy land. After an evening balloon ride, the term "carried away" will suddenly have new meaning.

Depending on the weather, departures usually take place just before sunrise or just before sunset, and each ride lasts roughly an hour to an hour and a half. Floating over the beautiful Snoqualmie Valley, your first impression will be astonishment at the enormous mass of billowing material overhead and the dragon fire that fills it with air. As you step into the gondola, your heart will begin to flutter with expectation. Once you're aloft, as the wind guides your craft above the countryside, the world will seem more peaceful than you ever thought possible. You will also be startled at the splendor of sunset from way up here as twilight covers the mountains with muted color and warmth. A caress while floating above the world on a cloudless summer evening can be a thoroughly heavenly experience. **Balloon Depot: (425) 881-9699. Over the Rainbow: (206) 364-0995, (888) 346-8247. $130–$165 per person.** *Call for flight times and meeting locations.*

Romantic Note: Some balloon companies serve either a light dinner or a champagne brunch after the flight. Call for details.

❧❧❧ **PIKE PLACE MARKET, Seattle** Even though it becomes a zoo on summer weekends, there is absolutely no better place than the Pike Place Market for an authentic Seattle experience. Fresh seafood (some of the best crab and mussels you'll ever taste), colorful regional produce, gorgeous flowers, and locally made arts and crafts are just some of the bounty offered at the market. Some of the fish stands feature flying fish (when you select your fish, it is tossed raucously from one employee to another), and there are plenty of interesting restaurants (including Lowell's, where Tom Hanks and Rob Reiner discussed the intricacies of dating and tiramisu in the movie *Sleepless in Seattle*). We think visiting Pike Place Market is one of the most entertaining ways to spend a day in Seattle. Even though it can be crowded, there is still plenty of room for affectionate strolling. *In downtown Seattle, at Pike Street and First Avenue.*

❧❧❧❧ **WASHINGTON PARK ARBORETUM, Seattle** Many cities in the United States have an area they consider an urban paradise, an essential landmark that transports visitors into a world of greenery that erases the existence of city settings. San Francisco has Golden Gate Park, New York City has Central Park, and Seattle is blessed with the Washington Park Arboretum. This elysian realm is located just south of the University of Washington, near the neighborhoods of Madison Park and Madison Valley, and partly bounded by Lake Washington. Diverse foliage, stunning landscapes, meandering trails, and 5,500 different kinds of plants make this an oasis of beauty for city-stressed souls. This 200-acre living museum is filled with fascinating arbors and gardens. The fastidiously manicured areas include Rhododendron Glen, with different species and hybrids in a range of sizes; Woodland Garden, with two small ponds and many Japanese maples; Loderi Valley, featuring Loderi hybrids set among magnolias and conifers; and the spectacular Japanese Garden (admission $2.50), filled with tradition and home to formal tea ceremonies April through October, on the third Saturday of each month. Our favorite times of year for strolling through the arboretum are spring, when astonishing clouds of white and pink cherry blossoms overwhelm the senses, and autumn, when vibrant fall colors paint the scenery in ardent shades of red, gold, orange, and yellow. **Free admission; open daily 7 A.M. until dusk.** *From downtown Seattle, drive east on Madison Street to Lake Washington Boulevard East and turn left into the Arboretum.*

Romantic Note: Whether you venture here on foot or bicycle, please remain on the established pathways. This gem won't remain unspoiled for long if it is mistreated by careless humans.

❧❧ **WASHINGTON STATE FERRIES, Seattle** Utilitarian types may use the Washington State Ferry System only as a means of transportation to and from work, but we romantics take a different approach. What better way is there to get a sweeping view of the majestic mountains surrounding the Seattle area or the many islands scattered throughout Puget Sound? Granted, it's no *Love Boat*—the decor is tacky and privacy is lacking—but for very little money, you and yours can bundle up for a stroll on the open deck and enjoy a glowing sunset. The crisp salt air is bound to inspire some snuggling. Another option is to make a day of it: Bring a picnic, comfortable walking shoes, and a sense of adventure to explore some of the nearby ports of call, which include Bainbridge Island, Bremerton, Kingston, and Vashon Island. **(206) 464-6400, (888) 808-7977; www.wsdot.wa.gov/ferries; seasonal fares range from $3.60 (walk-on passenger) to $17.25 (car and driver).**

Romantic Note: The rating of this outing definitely depends on when you make it. During rush hour or peak tourist season, lines can be long and crowds can be abundant; at those times you may want to use the ferry only as a means of transportation.

❧❧ **WATERFALL GARDEN, Seattle** Discovering this gem among the brick and concrete of Pioneer Square is like a breath of fresh air—moist air, that is. Inside the urban atrium, a majestic 22-foot-high waterfall sends water crashing down on granite boulders (some 5,000 gallons of recycled water a minute, to be exact). Inside the elegant stone walls and wrought-iron gate that protect this secluded haven, the outside noise is muffled by the sights and sounds of nature. Japanese maples and enormous pink rhododendrons attract the eye while a peaceful fountain on the upper tier provides a gentle counterpoint to the waterfall's power. Being the only oasis in a concrete jungle, the park attracts the lunch crowd who sit at the small tables and on the stone benches. At any other time of the day you're likely to be alone. Grab a pastry at a nearby bakery and then come here to soak up the serenity . . . and the water vapors. **Near Pioneer Square; free admission; open daily during daylight hours.**

Just north of the Kingdome at the junction of South Main Street and Second Avenue South.

Romantic Warning: Pioneer Square is a lovely historic neighborhood, but it attracts some unlovely characters. Otherwise, we'd give this park another smooch.

Bellevue

It used to be that as far as Seattleites were concerned, east was east and west was west—and west was definitely best. Those east of Lake Washington came to Seattle for jobs, cultural events, fine restaurants, and downtown shopping, while Seattleites passed through the Eastside only on their way to the Cascades. The place was nothing more than a bedroom community, with little to attract nonresidents.

Well, things have changed. Today the Eastside is thriving, thanks in large measure to Bill Gates and Microsoft, as well as many other software companies, and the area is now known as the Silicon Valley of the Northwest. The two floating bridges that connect Seattle and Bellevue are busy with cars going both ways at all hours. Bellevue and its surrounding towns of Redmond, Kirkland, Issaquah, and Woodinville are no longer considered mere suburbs of Seattle. With a collective population of more than 200,000, these affluent communities now have a large selection of engaging restaurants, hotels, spas, shops, parks, and cultural attractions. We found many reasons to visit Bellevue and the Eastside if you have romance on your mind—whether you're from Seattle or beyond.

Romantic Note: We must mention that Bill Gates himself lives in the Medina area of Bellevue. His $54 million, 20,000-square-foot waterfront home isn't romantic (unless you live there, we guess), but it is a unique landmark that's worth noting. You can't see it from land, but this immense house is clearly recognizable from Lake Washington. If you know someone with a boat, ask for a ride past this Northwest-style mansion.

Hotel/Bed and Breakfast Kissing

❧❧❧❧ **BELLEVUE CLUB HOTEL, Bellevue** Attached to the Eastside's most exclusive health club, this 67-room boutique hotel proves that exercise isn't the only thing that can get your heart pumping. You'll see what we mean once you step into the elegant lobby, with its ceramic and glass artwork, contemporary Northwest decor accented by Oriental touches, subdued lighting, and crisp but warm earth tones. If that doesn't raise your pulse rate, the rooms will: They are a slice of designer heaven. You'll be enthralled with the impressive furnishings, from the radiant, handcrafted cherry-wood furniture to the original art and accessories that individualize each room. (In fact, guests often inquire about purchasing pieces, and the staff is happy to provide information on obtaining duplicates.)

In addition to being beautiful, the rooms are extremely spacious, with 12-foot ceilings that make them feel even larger. The handsome patio units on the ground floor are the most inviting, with terra-cotta tiles and attractive outdoor furniture. If you want to splurge, request the Wilburton Suite or the Fountain Suite; both are distinguished by a slate entry, a sitting room with fireplace, and jetted tub. For a truly special night, reserve the Rainier Suite, with its hardwood floors, double shower, and Roman bath. No matter which room you choose, all feature comfy beds with plump duvets and feather pillows. TVs are hidden within lovely armoires, but the opulent bathrooms, which feature soaking tubs, glass-enclosed showers, marble and granite surfaces, and a hedonistic array of toiletries, will tempt couples to ignore the late show in favor of some good, clean fun. Perhaps best of all is the unlimited use of the health club facilities, which include state-of-the-art exercise equipment, tennis and squash courts, an Olympic-size swimming pool, saunas, aerobic classes, a spa with massage service, and Jacuzzi tubs.

As sublime as all this sounds—and it is indeed sublime—the ambience is slightly marred by a nearby freeway. Chances are you won't even notice, because you will probably be on your own road to love. **11200 Southeast Sixth Street; (425) 454-4424, (800) 579-1110; expensive to unbelievably expensive; recommended wedding site.**

Romantic Note: The hotel's dining room, **THE POLARIS RESTAURANT** (expensive to very expensive; breakfast and lunch Monday–Friday, dinner Monday–Saturday, brunch Sunday), is open to hotel guests and club members only. It's an exceptional place for breakfast, lunch, or dinner, and the wine list features a number of premium Northwest bottlings.

Restaurant Kissing

❀❀❀ **AZALEAS FOUNTAIN COURT, Bellevue** Amid the glossy skyscrapers of downtown Bellevue resides an oasis of tranquillity and romance. This Eastside treasure, housed in a light green brick and clapboard cottage on a quiet side street, brings the warmth of a home to a fine-dining establishment. Inside, three small, understated dining rooms—two in front and one in back—are tastefully decorated with hunter green carpets, whimsical art pieces, and tables topped with crisp linens, candles, and fresh flowers. In summer, couples gather out back, where a bubbling fountain, ivy-covered walls, and a delightful mural add charm to the secluded and romantic courtyard.

The menu changes with the seasons to assure that the food, best described as Northwest eclectic with Asian and Southwest accents, is fresh and flavorful. In late winter you might start your meal with pot stickers stuffed with lobster, roasted red peppers, and tarragon, accented by a soy–green peppercorn vinaigrette; or peppercorn-encrusted lamb carpaccio served over a chilled mushroom salad with Bosc pears, Asiago curls, and a truffle-sherry vinaigrette. If you prefer a lighter repast, enjoy the vegetable Napoleon, or the tamale stuffed with roasted wild mushrooms and goat cheese complemented by a black bean and roasted corn ragout. Heartier appetites can feast on charbroiled ahi tuna with a tangerine, rum, and basil relish, or the braised lamb shank served with a grilled red onion marmalade and rosemary demi-glace. Desserts range from cool sorbets to down-home delights like cheesecake. **22 103rd Avenue Northeast; (425) 451-0426; expensive to very expensive; lunch Monday–Friday, dinner Monday–Saturday; recommended wedding site.**

Outdoor Kissing

❧❧ **BELLEVUE BOTANICAL GARDEN, Bellevue** Although downtown Bellevue may be dominated by cars, boring bank buildings, and large shopping malls, this green retreat offers 36 acres of woods, display gardens, and lawns. Stroll hand in hand as you admire the lush, colorful borders and see if you can find one of the secret paths leading through them for closer looks at the blossoms . . . you just might find that ideal kissing spot. A half-mile loop winds around the gardens, leading you by the Botanical Reserve, the Rhododendron Garden, and more. Before leaving, share a serene moment in the elegant Yao Garden, a sister-city project with Yao, Japan, and bless the hard work and foresight that make this special place possible. **12001 Main Street; (425) 452-2750; free admission; open daily.** *From Interstate 405, exit onto eastbound Northeast Eighth. Drive to 120th Avenue Northeast, turn right, and follow the street as it winds uphill. Turn left onto Main Street; the parking lot for the garden is several blocks up on the right.*

    Romantic Alternative: Picnicking is not allowed in the Bellevue Botanical Garden. If dining alfresco is your passion, take a basket and blanket to **BELLEVUE DOWNTOWN PARK**, located just west of Bellevue Way on Northeast Fourth Street. This 14-acre oasis of grass and trees, across the street from busy Bellevue Square, is surprisingly underused, which can be a romantic advantage. Futuristic-looking spheres and pylons mark a circular canal, and a cascading waterfall at the south end is a refreshing alternative to the sounds of nearby traffic. A scattering of wooden garden benches and a tiny rose garden are additional amenities.

Redmond

Restaurant Kissing

❧❧ **TROPEA RISTORANTE ITALIANO, Redmond** Ignore the unbecoming strip of shops that surround this tiny gem. As you sit at one of the intimate tables, surrounded by stucco walls painted to resemble a Mediterranean villa, and listen to your waiter describe the daily specials in a soft Italian accent, you can easily believe you have taken a magic carpet ride to Rome. And, as the saying goes, when in Rome, do as the Romans do.

Listen to beautiful arias while you share a basket of fresh bread accompanied by spicy extra-virgin olive oil. Follow this with the truly bountiful antipasto misto, featuring an abundance of grilled vegetables dressed in a light vinaigrette. Pastas are reliably good, and the *pollo limone*, tender chicken breast napped in a delicately creamy lemon sauce, is a definite palate-pleaser. One wall showcases a wide selection of Italian wines, in case you care to imbibe. Dessert is another possible indulgence: Will it be the spumoni or the tiramisu? Both? *Bene!* **8042 161st Avenue Northeast; (425) 867-1082; inexpensive to moderate; lunch Monday–Friday, dinner daily.**

Kirkland

Hotel/Bed and Breakfast Kissing

❤️❤️ **SHUMWAY MANSION, Kirkland** Built in 1909, this four-story, post-Victorian estate is a curious blend of bed-and-breakfast rooms and banquet facilities. Surrounded by ample parking (enough for 60 cars) and fronted by a busy street, the 10,000-square-foot mansion is surrounded by a nicely manicured lawn, pretty flower gardens, and an adjacent duck pond. Doors open from the downstairs ballroom onto a covered patio area and the backyard, where you'll find an arched trellis draped with climbing roses and a gazebo embraced by wisteria. The mansion is best known for its weddings: More than 150 weddings a year take place here. When the wedding party stays elsewhere, the guest rooms can be rented out to nonparticipants; however, the cozy, handsomely decorated common areas may be inundated with celebrants around the time of the ceremony.

The eight simple guest rooms are appointed with homey Victorian-style furnishings, patterned wallpaper, lace curtains, and dried floral arrangements. Unfortunately, the rooms are too dimly lit, even for romantics. Each room has a queen-size bed, and all offer private tiled bathrooms (one is detached). Antiques, such as the four-poster cherry-wood bed in the Redmond Room, add romantic appeal to the otherwise standard accommodations.

In the morning, a full buffet-style breakfast is served downstairs at one long table in the handsome dining room. **11410 99th Place Northeast; (425) 823-2303; www.websmithpro.com/shumway.com; inexpensive to moderate; recommended wedding site.**

❤️❤️❤️ **THE WOODMARK HOTEL, Kirkland** We wish we could rate this contemporary hotel purely on its common areas and stellar location. Situated on the eastern shore of Lake Washington, the hotel boasts an elegant lobby and a cozy library. In the lobby, overstuffed couches, a glowing fireplace, sumptuous color schemes, and tall windows framing lovely views of sparkling Lake Washington beckon you to idle the day away in style. The Library Room, with its comfy chairs, interesting Asian art pieces, and crackling fire, is an ultra-warm and inviting spot for a romantic nightcap. However, the guest rooms keep the

Woodmark from earning our whole-hearted approval (and four lips).

It's not that the guest rooms are unattractive; it's just that they are not as impressive as the rest of the hotel. The contemporary decor in the 100 guest rooms is engaging, with cream and beige linens, pretty watercolors, pine furnishings, and king-size beds. (We are particularly partial to the Petite Suites and the Parlor Suites, due to the extra space they provide.) The views differ from room to room, so be sure to ask for one with a full lake view or you may end up staring at the specialty shops across the street.

When making reservations, we also recommend asking about weddings. The Woodmark Hotel has become a premier Northwest wedding site, and from early May until late September there probably won't be a weekend without one. If you are staying here in the summer months, be prepared for a crowd. Luckily, the receptions take place on the bottom level of the hotel, so they are not hard to avoid if you and your sweetheart are not in the mood for droves of party-goers. **1200 Carillon Point; (425) 822-3700, (800) 822-3700; www.thewoodmark.com; expensive to unbelievably expensive; recommended wedding site.**

Romantic Note: Visit **WATERS LAKESIDE BISTRO** (moderate to expensive; breakfast and lunch daily, dinner Tuesday–Saturday), located in the hotel. It's the perfect spot to enjoy a fresh seafood entrée and each other's company. You can't go wrong with the seared tuna with pear wasabi and rice crisps, or the grilled king salmon with wild mushroom orzo. Those of you who love midnight snacks will appreciate that Waters opens up its kitchen at 11:30 P.M. so guests can help themselves to sandwich makings, several different kinds of bottled water, and delectable desserts.

Restaurant Kissing

❦❦ **BISTRO PROVENÇAL, Kirkland** If you and your beloved long for a taste of Provençal, head to Kirkland, where you can dine in an atmosphere that evokes the French countryside. Rustic beamed ceilings, a double-sided brick fireplace, and an assortment of copper utensils and hand-painted dishes adorn the two small dining rooms. Each room holds well-spaced tables draped with black-and-white-checked tablecloths and topped with an impressive complement of linen napkins, candles, wineglasses, and silver. The traditional Provençal menu is straightforward and simply executed. Classic, understated entrées such as lamb chops in two sauces (béarnaise and pepper) are cooked to order and attractively presented. The staff exudes Gallic charm while unobtrusively ensuring that your meal proceeds smoothly. If you have room, say *oui* to dessert. **212 Central Way; (425) 827-3300; moderate; dinner daily.**

❦❦ **THIRD FLOOR FISH CAFÉ, Kirkland** As the sun dips below the horizon, the lights in this Kirkland restaurant dim for optimal viewing of Seattle's skyline and the marina below. In fact, the best time for romance here is later in the evening, when the after-work crowds have dispersed and the place settles down with the night. Although window seats provide the best views, we can't recommend them for romance because they are out in the open in a high-traffic area. Instead, snuggle up in a high-backed booth on the less frantic upper level; views here are equally appealing.

We recommend the delicate pan-seared sturgeon adorned with a shiitake-ginger vinaigrette atop a rice cake kissed by coconut milk. The more robust grilled salmon served with a tomato-basil ragout, grilled eggplant, and cabernet jus is also excellent. While seafood highlights most of the menu, delicious alternatives include oven-roasted chicken, prime beef tenderloin, and braised veal osso bucco. Desserts here range from simple treats to rich, complex delights. **205 Lake Street South; (425) 822-3553; expensive; dinner daily.**

❀❀❀ **YARROW BAY GRILL, Kirkland** Sprinkled with sailboats and lavish yachts, Lake Washington's busy, blue waters taken center stage at this waterfront restaurant. Located at Carillon Point, one of Kirkland's most upscale business and shopping areas, this restaurant will please those with romance in mind. The interior is designed to showcase the view: all windows face westward, and each booth provides a certain degree of privacy as you watch the sun set over Seattle's distant skyline. Chocolate-colored walls, metal salmon sculptures, and large marble-slab-like artpieces add a contemporary touch to this very popular place. We highly recommend requesting a booth, ideally one near the center of the restaurant. Otherwise, you may be too close to the back room, where large groups tend to congregate.

The daily-changing menu offers an international feast for the palate, drawing upon Japanese, Thai, and Mediterranean influences. Appetizers such as Penn Cove mussels in a smooth red Thai coconut curry broth, and fire prawns bathed in a spicy Cajun broth will heat up your lips for later on. Fish figures prominently in nightly specials, and you can't go wrong with the sake king salmon, a house favorite, or the seared halibut cheeks finished with yellow and green Thai coconut curry. Top off the evening with a rich espresso crème brûlée or mango cheesecake. **1270 Carillon Point; (425) 889-9052; moderate to expensive; lunch Sunday–Friday, dinner daily, brunch Sunday.**

Romantic Note: For a more casual lunch or dinner, venture downstairs to **THE BEACH CAFE** (inexpensive to moderate; 425-889-0303; lunch and dinner daily), which serves up a less expensive, international array of seafood dishes, pastas, sandwiches, and so forth. If the sun shines, snag a table on the outdoor deck overlooking the marina.

Juanita

Restaurant Kissing

❀❀❀ **CAFE JUANITA, Juanita** The white brick house that shelters this welcoming dining spot is surrounded by tall trees and lush foliage, making the most of an otherwise dubious location. The modest, L-shaped interior is simply but beautifully decorated, with linen-covered tables, hardwood floors, lovely flower arrangements, and jewel-like prints of the Italian countryside. Equally appealing are the exceptional views of the gardens and creek out back. The open kitchen is a bit of a drawback, but surprisingly quiet. A fireplace in one alcove lends a cozy feel, and the congenial service is excellent.

Two blackboards list the day's entrées. Appetizers are not listed, but are nevertheless available. Start your meal with a serving of homemade pasta (the spaghettini with morels in a brandy sauce is top-notch), the hearty antipasto, or a savory bowl of mussels. Plan on sharing, because portions are generous. The main course is preceded by a small salad topped with crumbled Gorgonzola. Entrées are uniformly excellent. A mixed grill features two skewers of sausages, chicken, onions, and peppers; the braised lamb shank, cooked to tender perfection, is flavorful and rich. Fresh, precisely prepared fish is the restaurant's specialty, but many patrons are addicted to the *pollo pistacchio*, chicken breast in a creamy pistachio sauce. Café Juanita's desserts are worthy of several kisses alone. The crème caramel is exceptionally good, strawberry gelato captures the cool essence of summer, and the tiramisu is as light as a cloud. **9702 Northeast 120th Place; (425) 823-1505; moderate to expensive; dinner daily.**

Woodinville

Outdoor Kissing

❤️❤️❤️ **CHATEAU STE. MICHELLE WINERY, Woodinville** Built in the style of a French country chateau, this well-known winery offers visitors more than superior Northwest wines. The 87 acres of manicured grounds are ideal for lazy strolls after a complimentary wine tasting and a cellar tour, particularly during the fall harvesting season. The winery's shop offers meats, cheeses, exquisite wines, and chocolate truffles—all the essentials for a gourmet picnic; simply choose a sunny spot on the soft lawn or sit at a picnic table overlooking rows of grapevines and a small pond. A summer-long series of moderately priced performances, ranging from jazz to Shakespeare, attracts happy crowds to the outdoor amphitheater. **14111 Northeast 145th; (425) 488-1133; www.ste-michelle.com; free tours and tastings daily.** *From northbound Interstate 405, turn east at the Wenatchee/Monroe exit. Follow State Route 522 east and take the Woodinville exit. Keep right, and at the second stoplight turn right onto Northeast 175th. At the four-way stop, turn left onto Highway 202. Go two miles to the winery, which is on the right side of the road.*

Romantic Note: Directly across the street is the **COLUMBIA WINERY** (14030 Northeast 145th Street; 425-488-2776; www.columbiawinery.com; open daily, tours Saturday–Sunday). The setting here isn't nearly as pretty as its neighbor's, but Columbia's status as the oldest premium winery in the state makes it an interesting stop.

Bothell

Restaurant Kissing

❤❤❤❥ **RELAIS, Bothell** Housed in a converted home on busy Bothell Way, Relais is actually two restaurants under one roof: an informal but gracious bistro, known as The Bistro Next Door at Relais, and an elegant dining room. Both are thoroughly French. The bistro, located at the front of the house, offers an à la carte menu of classic soups, salads, and entrées. Tables feature linen cloths, fresh flowers, and an array of silver. Handsome chandeliers and wooden beams supply elegance; a brick fireplace lends warmth.

The dining room, which is located at the back of the house, is an equally romantic, but far more expensive, choice. Crystal chandeliers, dark wood beams, red walls adorned with gilded mirrors, and a double-sided marble-and-wood fireplace create a seductive atmosphere. The handful of well-spaced tables seem to be arranged with couples in mind, providing privacy as well as views of the tiny courtyard. (In good weather, tables are also set up outside.) The prix fixe menu lists three completely different four- to six-course options. First courses may bring to the table perfectly cooked mussels bathed in a delicious cream sauce or a delicate custard served in an eggshell and topped by caviar, followed by moist sea bass or a refreshingly light vichyssoise. A sorbet, perhaps pear–pink peppercorn, allows diners to prepare their palate for such entrées as succulent roasted guinea hen or a serving of duck and duck foie gras in a blood orange sauce. In European fashion, the salad follows the main course. A plate of mixed greens might appear, or an artichoke tart paired with a pouf of whipped goat cream. Dessert is included, *naturellement*. The Grand Marnier soufflé is as light and sweet as a first kiss; the chocolate sampler is downright sinful. **17121 Bothell Way Northeast; (425) 485-7600; bistro: moderate to expensive; dining room: very expensive to unbelievably expensive; dinner Tuesday–Sunday.**

Snoqualmie

Hotel/Bed and Breakfast Kissing

❤❤❤ **SALISH LODGE AND SPA, Snoqualmie** Salish Lodge and Spa has almost everything going for it: a respected name, a celebrated location at the top of Snoqualmie Falls, a full-service spa facility, and thoroughly romantic guest rooms. All 91 of the plush suites feature ample spa tubs, well-stocked wood-burning fireplaces, and comfortable furnishings that invite tenderness. As you might expect, the outstanding accommodations go hand in hand with outstanding tariffs that increase as the view of the falls improves. A major drawback to this stellar location is the throngs of tourists that invade the place day in and day out, particularly on weekends. (Thankfully, the guest wings are accessible only with guest room keys, so the tourists can't go everywhere.) Also, only a handful of these exquisite rooms have views of the falls; the rest look out to the road or the power plant upstream. **6501 Railroad Avenue Southeast (Highway 202); (425) 888-2556, (800) 826-6124; very expensive to un-believably expensive.**

Romantic Suggestion: If staying here requires an unreasonable dent in your pocketbook, you can still enjoy the extremely intimate, extremely popular SALISH LODGE DINING ROOM (expensive; breakfast and lunch Monday–Saturday, dinner daily, brunch Sunday). Although the steaks, seafood, and pasta dishes rank high in presentation, they sometimes miss the mark in terms of quality and flavor. The restaurant is elegantly appointed with handsome cherry-wood paneling, a wood-burning fireplace, and muted lighting. Almost every seat in the house has a view through floor-to-ceiling windows, but the very best tables are those directly beside the windows that face the falls. Reservations are recommended, so you might as well ask if any of those seats are available.

"The sound of a kiss is not so loud as

that of a cannon, but its echo lasts a

great deal longer."

Oliver Wendell Holmes

Puget Sound Area

Bellingham

Although best known for Western Washington University and its densely forested campus, Bellingham is much more than just a college town. Congenial neighborhoods, the historic Fairhaven District, and an overwhelming number of outlet stores are a few of the attractions that have made it one of the fastest-growing cities in Washington. Spectacular **CHUCKANUT DRIVE** and **BOULEVARD PARK** (see Outdoor Kissing), the sparkling waters of Lake Whatcom and Bellingham Bay, and the spellbinding slopes of Mount Baker (only an hour's drive to the east) make it a transcendent romantic destination. Luckily, Bellingham has a superlative selection of restaurants and inns, and retains a vast amount of pristine woods and waterfront for couples to explore.

Hotel/Bed and Breakfast Kissing

💋💋 **BIG TREES BED AND BREAKFAST, Bellingham** Talk about an escape from the city! Old-growth cedars and firs, sprawling green lawns, gardens teeming with wild and domestic flowers, berry bushes, and a flowing creek surround this stately gray Craftsman-style home. The eclectically decorated interior retains its handsome original woodwork, including a wood-beamed ceiling and built-in cabinetry framing a huge stone fireplace in the common area. Upstairs, the three guest rooms are appointed with fresh flowers, floral comforters or handmade quilts, plump feather beds, a variety of antiques and contemporary pieces, and TVs. Cedar and Rhodie each have their own private bathroom, and Rhodie's deserves special mention: Magazine pictures have been cut out by guests and pasted on the painted floral floor to create an ongoing collage. (As bizarre as this may sound, it's really quite an impressive work of art.) Maple, the third room, does not have its own bathroom, but is not rented unless two couples are traveling together.

Your full country breakfast is a veritable feast fit for royalty, perhaps including soy milk–mango smoothies, hot-out-of-the-oven pumpkin spice muffins, coffee cake, baked apples with pistachios, hot apple crumble, or Irish oat pancakes filled with orange and blackberry-cherry sauce. After this very filling breakfast, you may want to stroll the forested grounds with one of the innkeeper's lovable dogs or just sit on the veranda and take in the tranquil neighborhood setting. **4840 Fremont Street; (360) 647-2850, (800) 647-2850; www.nas.com/~bigtrees; inexpensive to moderate.**

💋💋💋 **SAIL THE SAN JUANS, Bellingham** Ahoy, mates! Come sail the San Juans for three days or an entire week aboard *Northwind*, a sparkling, 42-foot Catalina sailboat. This admirable floating getaway is a unique (although expensive) alternative to "stationary" hotels, inns, and bed and breakfasts. Guests have the opportunity to help create the week's flexible itinerary, yet are still pampered by having someone else do the cooking, shopping, and navigating. What could be more relaxing and romantic than sailing with your sweetheart through Bellingham Bay and the magnificent Strait of Georgia? During your tour, you'll stop at both remote and popular destinations in the San Juan archipelago. On occasion, porpoises, seals, and otters play near the boat, and orcas and minke whales are sighted about 50 percent of the time.

Couples traveling alone are provided accommodations in the bow, where you'll find a snug double bed, blue and white linens, teak accents, and a private head and shower. If you decide to travel with another couple (which is far more economical), you will stay in identical bedrooms in the stern, featuring nautical blue comforters, teak floors and walls, water views through small windows, and a shared head and shower. Although the rooms are snug (just enough space for the two of you and a bed), they are exceedingly romantic. *Northwind* is also equipped with fishing and crabbing equipment, TV/VCR, a CD player with an extensive library of CDs, a freezer, refrigerator, and foul-weather gear.

Gourmet meals, cooked by the crew, are served in the salon. Guests can look forward to a variety of creative dishes, such as crêpes, blintzes, scones, and fruit for breakfast; sandwiches, salads, and soups for lunch; and fresh-caught seafood and pasta dishes for dinner.

With the Olympic Mountains to the south, the Cascades to the east, and nothing but glistening waters and charming harbor towns in between, your sailing adventure will be nothing less than magical. **(360) 671-5852, (800) 729-3207; www.stsj.com; prices begin at $895 per person per week (all meals included), and vary according to season and number of passengers; minimum-stay requirement; closed November–March.**

❤❤❤❤ SCHNAUZER CROSSING BED AND BREAKFAST INN, Bellingham

After many years of operation, Schnauzer Crossing continues to set the standard for other bed and breakfasts in the Northwest. Two friendly but low-key schnauzers (the inn's namesakes) greet guests in the driveway, guiding them onto the beautifully landscaped property. Enveloped by one and a half acres of colorful gardens, well-groomed lawns, a small koi pond, and tall trees, the contemporary wood-and-glass home is a dream come true. Views of Lake Whatcom are visible from nearly every angle of the property. Every detail necessary for an intimate getaway is here, so you can relax in an atmosphere of comfortable luxury.

Schnauzer Crossing offers two guest rooms in the main house and an elegant self-contained guest cottage next door. Dubbed the King Room, the main-house master suite is comparable to a small apartment, with a private entrance from a tree-framed garden and a king-size bed with a floral down comforter. Its alcove sitting area is a perfect place to lounge and relax, complete with a CD player, TV/VCR, wet bar, and wood-burning fireplace. You will never want to leave this suite, especially after you see the huge bathroom with a Jacuzzi tub for two, roomy double-headed shower, and sumptuous terry-cloth robes. Not as big or as lavish, but just as lovely, the adjacent Queen Room is appointed with a crisp white down comforter on a queen-size bed, views of colorful rhododendrons, a closet library with a wonderful selection of books, and a private bathroom. Two sets of doors shut the Queen Room off completely from the rest of the home to ensure privacy.

Set amid lofty cedar trees next to the main house, the picture-perfect guest cottage is decorated in a subtle Asian motif. Views of Lake Whatcom are spectacular from a private wraparound deck that is exclusively yours. Hardwood floors and original Northwest artwork lend elegance, while a king-size bed covered with luscious linens and a warm gas fireplace provide comfort. A TV/VCR, CD player, and extensive movie and CD collection are some of the amenities offered in the cozy sitting area. In the lovely green-tiled bathroom, a large Jacuzzi tub awaits, bordered by thick, fluffy towels. A wet bar hidden away in the closet holds the makings for coffee, tea, and hot cocoa, along with an "I-forgot-it basket," filled with items you may have forgotten at home and fun things you never even knew you needed.

Breakfast is an impressive presentation of gourmet delights that might include sweet rhubarb crisp dribbled with hazelnut cream, triple sec French toast with three kinds of syrup, gourmet baked oatmeal, fresh muffins, and a fruit parfait. Breakfast can be served wherever you choose, including the privacy of your own suite. If you can pull yourselves away from your room or the breakfast table, take a bike ride on the nearby rural roads or go for a leisurely walk around Lake Padden. Afterward, you can have a good, long, steamy soak in the outdoor hot tub, tucked next to the house beneath the towering trees. **4421 Lakeway Drive; (360) 733-0055, (800) 562-2808; www.schnau zercrossing.com; moderate to very expensive; minimum-stay requirement on weekends and holidays.**

❦❦❦ **SOUTH BAY BED AND BREAKFAST, Bellingham** Technically located in the small town of Sedro Woolley but close enough to Bellingham to make it a convenient stop, this brand-new, premier establishment is surrounded by wilderness at the south end of Lake Whatcom. Built to serve as an inn, the sprawling, contemporary wood building is perched high on a supremely quiet wooded hillside above the lake. Outside, trails meander through five surrounding acres of old-growth cedar and many more acres of undeveloped park property. Inside, a fire roars in the fireplace in the comfortable, elegant common area, surrounded by windows that showcase the spectacular views. Here, guests can admire the resident wildlife close up with the help of a powerful telescope. A cushioned window seat in the glass-enclosed kitchen is a comfortable place to soak up the views while taking in the aroma of freshly baked bread.

The gracious innkeepers strive to create a professional but comfortable and welcoming ambience. All five of the handsome guest rooms are appointed with a mixture of antique and contemporary furnishings, and beds are smothered in opulent down comforters and luxurious linens. The absence of TVs and phones is purposely designed to shift your focus from the world at large to each other. Four of the guest rooms are located on the home's lower level. Trestle is the smallest, but still features a fireplace, floral linens, a private bath with shower, and large windows and doors that open onto an outdoor patio. Thistle and Trellis are similar to Trestle but have luxurious whirlpool jetted tubs set next to windows that open onto the bedroom areas with views of the water beyond. Terrace, the corner room, is slightly larger and beautifully appointed with warm wood accents. Upstairs, Tanglewood feels a little less private because it is located closer to the innkeepers' quarters. However, it too is lovely, with crisp white linens, a cozy window seat, and a large corner Jacuzzi tub that hugs the windows and their water views.

A hearty, healthy breakfast of fruit, coffee, juice, and savory baked goods is served to guests in the lovely breakfast room. After filling up on the innkeepers' gourmet fare, we recommend retiring to the porch swing outdoors, nestled between two tall trees in a quiet, shady grove. **4095 South Bay Drive; (360) 595-2086; www.southbaybb.com; moderate to unbelievably expensive.**

❤❤❤ **STRATFORD MANOR, Bellingham** Stratford Manor is the spitting image of a proper English countryside estate. Surrounded by rolling emerald pastures sprinkled with wildflowers and 20 acres of quiet woodland, the sprawling wood-and-brick Tudor mansion exudes a dignified atmosphere. Far removed from city life, the property is enfolded in country quiet, punctuated only by the croaking of bullfrogs who inhabit the nearby pond. Guests are greeted in the contemporary common area, where a wet bar is filled with complimentary refreshments, and a TV/VCR and well-stocked romantic movie library are arranged near a comfortable sofa. Other common areas and facilities located in the 6,500-square-foot inn include a bright terra-cotta-tiled sunroom, a large communal hot tub, an inviting library with floor-to-ceiling bookshelves, and an elegant formal living room with comfortable antiques.

Three of the four capacious guest rooms are located in a private wing of the manor. The exceedingly spacious Garden Room is the premier romantic draw. High ceilings enhance the sense of space, and the antique king-size four-poster bed is embraced by luscious white linens, a down duvet, and soft pillows. An enormous sunken hot tub looks out to an enclosed garden, and a gas fireplace provides glowing warmth. A double-headed shower is an added romantic feature in the roomy private bathroom. Located upstairs, the Sunrise and Hilltop Rooms are somewhat smaller but almost as lovely, with beautiful floral wallpapers, choice linens, slightly smaller Jacuzzi tubs, and Martha Stewart–style touches. The fourth room is available only in the summer and features the same amenities, including a king-size four-poster bed and Jacuzzi tub.

In the morning, a wake-up tray with fresh, warm muffins and coffee or tea is delivered to your door. An hour later, guests are invited to partake of a generous, delectable four-course breakfast of coffee, juice, fruit, pastries, cereals, and egg-based entrées, served around the large dining room table. What a romantic haven—our only complaint was having to leave. **1416 Van Wyck Road; (360) 715-8441; inexpensive to expensive.**

Restaurant Kissing

◈◈ CLIFF HOUSE, Bellingham Without a doubt, Cliff House has the best views of any restaurant in Bellingham. Perched high on a residential bluff, the circular glass dining room offers panoramic views of wooded **BOULEVARD PARK** (see Outdoor Kissing) and the water and islands beyond. In warm weather, dinner is also served on an outdoor deck overlooking the same spectacular view. What a shame the ambience and food are somewhat mediocre by comparison. Casual wooden tables give the place the appearance of a steak house, and the menu confirms the impression, offering a standard selection of steak and seafood combinations. The 360-degree views are still compelling, but best enjoyed over dessert and drinks, after you've eaten elsewhere. **331 North State Street; (360) 734-8660; moderate to expensive; dinner daily.**

◈◈◈ IL FIASCO, Bellingham Il Fiasco (meaning "the flask" in Italian) retains its reputation as Bellingham's premier dining location, and we can see why. The sophisticated yet intimate interior resembles an Italian country courtyard, complete with flower boxes, wooden shutters, and exposed brick. Overstuffed armchairs are arranged around well-spaced wooden tables topped with flickering candles. Soft lighting, tall ceilings with exposed air ducts, and sunny yellow walls with terra-cotta and black accents complete the picture.

We suggest beginning your meal with fresh Manila clams steamed with fennel, tomato, and garlic, and then moving on to risotto embellished with a medley of mushrooms, roasted root vegetables, red chard, sherry, and spiced hazelnuts. The menu also features unusual antipasti such as gingered crab and shrimp cakes with tangy jade sauce, and pasta delights such as cappellini entwined with sautéed prawns and sweet and hot peppers. Conclude with a heavenly dessert and a discreet kiss. **1309 Commercial Street; (360) 676-9136; moderate to expensive; dinner daily.**

◈◈ ORCHARD STREET BREWERY, Bellingham Famous for their penchant for gourmet coffee, Northwesterners have more recently become enamored with microbreweries and brewpubs. For this reason, it seemed appropriate for us to include a select few brewpubs that meet our strict tandards. Don't worry—we haven't changed our format to include just any old tavern. Traditional rowdy pubs and greasy fare do nothing to inspire romance. Instead, we set our sights on sophisticated, stylish pubs that can be counted on for a relaxing, enjoyable evening out together. Without a doubt, Orchard Street fits the bill.

Located at the end of an industrial strip mall, this popular brewery possesses a simple, modern interior with cement floors, bright red accents, exposed air ducts, an attractive open kitchen, and brewery equipment visible behind a solid glass wall. A large oil painting covers one wall, which is much appreciated since the only views are of the parking lot. The food, however, is the real reason to dine here. The wood-fired pizzas never disappoint, and the roasted vegetable turnover with wild mushrooms, artichoke hearts, and pine nuts is divine. Naturally, you can select a microbrew to accompany your meal, but if you are not a beer lover, you'll find plenty of other beverages to sip.

We wouldn't go so far as to say that this place is particularly intimate or romantic, but the food is exemplary. We just couldn't pass it up. **709 West Orchard Drive; (360) 647-1614; moderate; lunch and tours Monday–Friday, dinner Monday–Saturday.**

☙☙❧ **PACIFIC CAFE, Bellingham** Set in the heart of downtown Bellingham, this metropolitan restaurant draws a strictly business clientele on weekday afternoons. However, the mood changes dramatically in the evening, with the aid of soft lighting and flickering candles at every cozy table. A soothing combination of blond wood, contemporary artwork, and shoji screens fills the small dining room, which overlooks busy Commercial Street. Reservations are an absolute must, as locals and visitors compete for tables and the opportunity to sample Pacific Cafe's renowned cuisine. The menu is small but impressive, offering items such as smoky grilled portobello mushrooms and sweet-and-sour prawns topped with Hawaiian lemon sauce. Pineapple-mango chutney adds a sweet surprise to the Punjabi curry with Alaskan prawns, and the pork tenderloin and grilled beef are house favorites. Desserts change daily and are sure to satisfy your sweet tooth. **100 North Commercial Street; (360) 647-0800; moderate to expensive; reservations recommended; lunch Monday–Friday, dinner Monday–Saturday.**

☙☙ **PASTÁZZA, Bellingham** We were hesitant to try this casual eatery, nestled in a newly constructed shopping village just outside the heart of downtown Bellingham, even though it is much praised. Pastázza doesn't take reservations, and on weekend evenings the wait for a table averages at least half an hour. Don't let any of this deter you, however; Pastázza is a must for pasta connoisseurs. Although the ambience is casual and lively, the create-your-own pasta entrées are tremendous. Choose from a list of homemade pastas; vegetarian, meat, and seafood sauces; and special ingredients, all accented with garden-fresh salads and freshly baked focaccia. The eggless linguine with grilled portobello mushrooms and savory tomato-herb sauce is heavenly, as is the chocolate pâté, which comes drenched in tangy raspberry sauce. If your stomach is the way to your heart, Pastázza is guaranteed to inspire many kisses. **2945 New Market Street, Suite 101, in Barkley Village; (360) 714-1168; moderate to expensive; lunch and dinner daily.**

❀❀❀ **WILD GARLIC, Bellingham** Everybody is talking about Wild Garlic, and for good reason. Located in the heart of downtown Bellingham, in an inconspicuous strip mall, this restaurant at first glance may seem like an unlikely candidate for romance, but it won't take long to convince you otherwise. Green, cushioned banquettes border the dimly lit, upscale dining room, which has been embellished with rich green walls and etched glass. Black-and-white photographs adorn one brick wall, lending an artistic mood. An inscription on the small, gourmet menu describes its culinary philosophy: "A saucepan without garlic is like a kiss without love." It goes without saying that nearly every entrée is enhanced with garlic, from whole roasted cloves swimming in olive oil to fragrant garlic pizzas. We were partial to the Mediterranean linguine served with wild mushrooms, garlic, and sun-dried tomatoes, as well as the scampi with roasted garlic and beurre blanc. Cap your meal with one of the sweet, beautifully presented desserts to refresh your palate. **114 Prospect Street; (360) 671-1955; moderate to expensive; lunch Monday–Friday, dinner Monday–Saturday.**

Outdoor Kissing

❀❀❀ **BOULEVARD PARK, Bellingham** Bellingham boasts incredible views of Puget Sound and the many tree-covered islands that dot the endless horizon. Perched high on a bluff in the heart of Bellingham, Boulevard Park offers numerous vantage points to survey the area's arresting scenery. Park benches are strategically placed along the bluff, and tall trees shade walking paths that meander past lush greenery and gardens. Sunsets along this stretch of coast are simply glorious. **Free admission.** *Located between downtown Bellingham and the Fairhaven District. From downtown, follow State Street south toward the waterfront; Boulevard Park is on the west side of the street.*

❀❀❀❀ **CHUCKANUT DRIVE, Bellingham** From the moment you embark upon this landmark coastal drive, you'll be dazzled by visual delights. If you're heading south, the exhibition starts with forested cliffs that plunge down to the water's edge. On the horizon lies the silhouette of Lummi Island, and in the distance the rugged coastline of Chuckanut Bay. As you continue south, the varying patterns of islands, trees, water, and rocks form a breathtaking panorama. **LARRABEE STATE PARK**, eight miles south of Bellingham, is a perfect place to stop for a walk along the chiseled beach. *From Interstate 5, exit to State Route 11 outside of Bellingham or Burlington, and follow the signs for Chuckanut Drive.*

Lummi Island

Just north of Bellingham, follow the signs to the Lummi Island ferry landing and the Lummi Casino. The ferry leaves on the hour between 6 A.M. and midnight.

Accessible via a small ferry that docks just west of Bellingham, Lummi Island is a pastoral escape from the real world. Just nine miles long and less than two miles wide, Lummi has no real town to speak of, but does boast a church, library, post office, fire station, and general store. A coffee cart cleverly dubbed "Well Latte Da" serves espresso and gourmet sandwiches to commuters heading to or from the ferry dock. Because the ferries run so regularly, Lummi Island is ideal for a day trip (we suggest a quiet bike ride or afternoon picnic), although the lovely accommodations may entice you to spend the night.

Hotel/Bed and Breakfast Kissing

❀❀❅ **COTTAGE BY THE SEA, Lummi Island** The word is out. Although this remote seaside cottage is relatively new, reservations are already hard to come by—especially on weekends. If you are lucky enough to reserve a stay here, you'll have the entire place to yourselves. From its bluff-top location above the water's edge, this gray country cottage surveys spectacular views of Puget Sound and the San Juan Islands. Outside, a roomy deck juts out over the hillside, and a private stairway leads down to a rocky beach strewn with driftwood. Inside, a wall of large windows takes full advantage of the water views and serene setting. Fresh flowers and artistic tiles decorate the full kitchen, and an attractive but eclectic mix of furnishings and nautical touches adorns the living room. The two bedrooms are equally charming, appointed with antique beds, lovely linens, and fresh flowers. Fluffy blue towels accent the gleaming white bathroom, where a sunken two-person Jacuzzi tub is arranged beside a window with a panoramic water view. Breakfast provisions are up to you, which only adds to the sense of seclusion and privacy. **3869 Legoe Bay; (360) 758-7144; moderate to expensive; minimum-stay requirement on weekends.**

❀❀❀ **THE WILLOWS INN, Lummi Island** Enamored couples on the verge of saying "I do" vie for reservations at The Willows Inn, which has recently begun to cater more to wedding parties than to traveling couples. The setting couldn't be more perfect for nuptials. Embraced by rose arbors, vegetable patches, and scented herb gardens, this lovely retreat offers scintillating views of the Strait of Georgia and the forested hills of nearby Orcas Island. The innkeepers' white waterfront home is dedicated exclusively to wedding parties, and offers separate bride and groom dressing rooms upstairs.

Even if you don't have wedding plans in your near future, The Willows Inn offers two additional accommodations perfect for any occasion. Outfitted in a Scottish Highland theme, the two-bedroom Guest House is appointed with dark fir paneling, a wood-burning fireplace, TV/VCR, and CD player. A door off the living room opens to a private deck with distant water views. Both bedrooms in the Guest House, Heather and Thistle, have comfy queen-size beds, antique furnishings, and spacious bathrooms. (Thistle even has the luxury of a Jacuzzi tub.) Dark wood paneling in Thistle is somewhat overbearing, but the effect is almost cozy. The neighboring honeymoon cottage, aptly dubbed Piece of Cake, is adorable and serene, with its pink-hued interior and floral linens. Hardwood floors, a small bathroom with a claw-foot tub, and an antique love seat add vintage country charm. Other amenities include a full kitchen, TV/VCR, and a deck with impressive views of the water and surrounding colorful gardens.

Breakfast can be self-catered or, for a small extra charge, continental breakfast fixings can be stocked in the kitchen before you arrive. A complimentary basket of fruit and chilled juice is provided in both the Guest House and cottage. **2579 West Shore Drive; (360) 758-2620; www.pacificrim.net/~willows; moderate to very expensive; minimum-stay requirement on holidays; closed Thanksgiving–March; recommended wedding site.**

Bow

Hotel/Bed and Breakfast Kissing

❤❤❤ **SAMISH POINT BY THE BAY, Bow** It doesn't get more private than Samish Point, which comprises 43 acres of forested acres, fruit orchards, and sweeping lawns hemmed with colorful flowers. This spectacular rural property surveys panoramic views of Samish Bay and Puget Sound. More than 100 trails invite you to set off on your own amorous adventure, and private sandy beaches await discovery.

Samish Point offers four guest rooms in its two buildings. A single guest room is located in an immaculate, contemporary home, encompassed by gardens and trees, that guests share with the innkeeper. Guests staying here will be tempted to spend most of their time in the inviting common living room, embellished with Northwest accents, gleaming white furnishings, and wall-to-wall windows that offer impressive views of the water and gardens. The breakfast room is equally elegant, with dark slate floors, tall ceilings with skylights, a wood-burning stove, and more stunning views. Unfortunately, the private guest bedroom here lacks some of the splendor and luxury of the common areas, but the contemporary furnishings, queen-size bed, hardwood floors, private bathroom, and private entrance make it a comfortable and relaxing retreat. Your morning meal may include banana granola, pancakes with homemade berry syrups, omelets, French toast, and fresh fruit. Best of all, you'll have the breakfast room all to yourselves.

The other three guest rooms are located across the road in a cozy Cape Cod–style guest house bordered by a lush lawn, flower gardens, and trees, and guarded by a flock of grazing sheep. Inside, the cheery living room has hardwood floors, a river-rock fireplace, gingham couches, and sliding doors that open onto a wooden deck where a hot tub awaits moonstruck lovers. The white-tiled designer kitchen next to the living room is available for use only if you rent the entire house for yourselves. One guest room is located on the main floor and features a king-size bed and pine furnishings. Two more are found upstairs, each with its own private bathroom, a patchwork quilt or floral comforter, pine furnishings, and views of the pastoral landscape. In the morning, a breakfast buffet is set up in the kitchen, with cereals, pastries, quiches, and fresh fruit for all to enjoy. **4465 Samish Point Road; (360) 766-6610, (800) 916-6161; www.samishpoint.com; inexpensive to unbelievably expensive; minimum-stay requirement on weekends.**

Romantic Note: Unless you rent the entire guest cottage (an enticing but pricey option), you could be sharing common areas with couples you don't know. Because the cottage is so intimate and isolated, this may feel a bit awkward.

Restaurant Kissing

OYSTER BAR, Bow This refined and elegant restaurant is a culinary milepost along famous **CHUCKANUT DRIVE** (reviewed on page 243). Only 12 tables fill the pocket-size, cedar dining room upstairs, which is lined with floor-to-ceiling windows that frame breathtaking views of Samish Bay and the San Juan Islands. More tables are available downstairs, but the atmosphere there is far less warm and cozy. Unfortunately, service can be slow, but the presentations are always impeccable. The quintessentially Northwest menu features mostly seafood and shellfish. We ordered the grilled salmon with sautéed shiitake mushrooms and radicchio in a balsamic-lemon butter, and it was beyond reproach. The Oysters 222, six Samish Bay oysters with three different toppings, were perfect, and the chocolate-espresso decadence—rich chocolate cake accented with coffee and drizzled with warm dark and white chocolate sauces—was an early taste of heaven. **2578 Chuckanut Drive; (360) 766-6185; expensive to very expensive; dinner daily.**

OYSTER CREEK INN, Bow Only a minute's drive north of the OYSTER BAR (see above), but a far greater distance in mood and style, the casual and unassuming Oyster Creek Inn provides a relaxing environment for lunch or dinner. Because the wood-paneled dining room holds only a handful of tables, everyone has a chance to gaze out the huge windows at the towering trees and rugged cliffs. As you would expect, the classic Northwest menu features fresh seafood and shellfish, and the halibut, prawns, and oysters are flavorful and precisely prepared. Entrées are accompanied by your choice of oyster soup or a salad of assorted fresh greens, both of which are exceptional. **2190 Chuckanut Drive; (360) 766-6179; moderate; lunch and dinner daily.**

RHODODENDRON CAFE, Bow Set on the corner of a busy intersection along popular **CHUCKANUT DRIVE** (reviewed on page 243), the Rhododendron Cafe couldn't be more conveniently located. This tiny country café caters primarily to travelers who have worked up a hearty appetite after spending several hours being seduced by the spellbinding views from Chuckanut Drive's winding waterfront bluffs. Decidedly casual, the tiny cream-colored country home has a sparsely furnished but cheery interior, accented with country fabrics and a handful of peach-colored tables. The café doesn't rely on location alone, but strives to live up to its glowing (and ever-growing) reputation; the food here is simply outstanding. Specials change daily but always include garden-fresh salads, exceedingly fresh seafood and chicken, savory pasta entrées, and tantalizing desserts. **553 Chuckanut Drive; (360) 766-6667; moderate; call for seasonal hours; closed Thanksgiving–December.**

Anacortes

Anacortes is a well-known stopover for ferry-bound travelers heading to and from the San Juan Islands. Even if you've planned only a brief encounter with this Northwest port of call, unexpected ferry traffic could cause you to miss your boat. Not to worry—there are a few romantic locales where you can happily while away the hours (and possibly the entire evening) until the next boat arrives.

Hotel/Bed and Breakfast Kissing

❀❀❀ **ABC YACHT CHARTERS, Anacortes** Imagine touring the awe-inspiring Northwest islands aboard a private yacht chartered exclusively for just the two of you, and staffed with a skipper and crew to attend to your every need. A dream come true? Possibly, although the exorbitant price tag may come as a rude awakening and deter you from even daydreaming about such an endeavor. We're talking thousands of dollars for a chartered cruise, which, if you ask us, is going a bit overboard. However, if you do happen to live the lifestyle of the rich and famous, you should know that ABC offers three itineraries, including a seven-day cruise through the San Juan Islands, a seven-day cruise through Canada's Gulf Islands, and a 14-day cruise up to Desolation Sound. ABC's yachts are brimming with space and amenities, including double staterooms, full galleys (kitchens), good meals, washers and dryers, and entertainment centers, not to mention the ever-changing, always spectacular Northwest scenery. For the adventurous at heart with super-generous budgets, splurging on an ABC yacht will net you the adventure of a lifetime. Landlubbers with a moderate budget are better off seeking romance on the mainland. **Skyline Marina; (360) 293-9533, (800) 426-2313; www.anacortes.net/abcyacht; unbelievably expensive; minimum-stay requirement.**

❀❀❀ **CHANNEL HOUSE, Anacortes** Ferry-bound traffic speeds by the Channel House at all hours, but don't worry; this ceases to be a romantic distraction once you've stepped inside the lovely 1902 Craftsman home. Oriental rugs cover shiny hardwood floors, a fire roars in the wood-burning fireplace, and modest furnishings lend a cozy atmosphere to the home's main floor.

Of the six guest rooms, four are found in the main house; two additional suites are located in an adjacent cottage. Antique furnishings and lace curtains give rooms in the main house an authentic flavor, while fluffy down duvets and spacious private bathrooms ensure comfort. A stately four-poster canopy bed stands in the center of the aptly named Canopy Room, our favorite. The Island View Room surveys wide vistas of the water and passing ferryboats bound for the islands that dot the horizon. Grandma's Room features a comfortable queen-size four-poster bed, and the Garden View Room looks down from the second floor onto a flower garden enclosed by a white picket fence.

Outside, a walkway lined with flowers and plants passes by the not-so-private hot tub on its way to the Rose Cottage, where two large suites reside. Victorian Rose is equipped with a queen-size four-poster bed, whirlpool tub, warm wood-burning fireplace, and French doors that open to a private garden and views of the water. Country Rose boasts Laura Ashley linens, sunny yellow walls, a two-person Jacuzzi tub, and another wood-burning fireplace. These two suites are definitely Channel House's finest offerings.

Breakfast can be scheduled for any time, depending on which ferry you may be taking in the morning, and is guaranteed to delight hungry lovebirds. Homemade breads and muffins, a hot egg dish or French toast stuffed with cream cheese and pecans, plus plenty of seasonal fruit, are likely to get your day off to a good start. **2902 Oakes Avenue; (360) 293-9382, (800) 238-4353; www.channel-house.com; inexpensive.**

❦❦ **MAJESTIC HOTEL, Anacortes** It's hard to miss the Majestic Hotel, a grand four-story building built in 1889, standing tall in the midst of the industrial jostle of Commercial Avenue. French doors open to reveal a pleasant lobby with high ceilings and European decor. The 21 Victorian guest rooms have been restored over the years, though their color schemes vary significantly from one to the next. Room 404 is especially alluring, with rich red walls and lush inky black linens. Daylight streams into the fourth-floor Majestic Suites, which feature wet bars, marble bathrooms with large soaking tubs, and patios that look out to the courtyard and gardens below. Some feel a bit spartan, but most are delightfully detailed, with lovely antiques, fresh linens, new down comforters, attractive artwork, and warm wood accents.

As you climb the open, winding staircase to the mezzanine level for your continental breakfast of fresh fruit and pastries, don't miss the expansive stained glass skylight overhead. For the best views (and the best kissing), be sure to climb to the cupola at the top of the hotel, which is filled with antiques and surrounded by windows. The cozy English-style pub is another fun spot for a quick kiss and your favorite microbrew. **419 Commercial Avenue; (360) 293-3355, (800) 588-4780; inexpensive to very expensive.**

Romantic Note: THE SALMON RUN (see Restaurant Kissing), on the main floor of the Majestic Hotel, is an elegant and delightful place for a romantic dinner.

Restaurant Kissing

❤❤❤ **THE SALMON RUN, Anacortes** Located on the main floor of the MAJESTIC HOTEL (see Hotel/Bed and Breakfast Kissing), this elegant Victorian restaurant looks like it could have been transplanted from Victoria, British Columbia. Peaked cathedral ceilings soar over the two-tiered dining room, which is framed by a wall of floor-to-ceiling windows that look out to a serene garden courtyard and gazebo. White tablecloths drape well-spaced tables and soft gold- and green-marbled walls lend quiet elegance. The Northwest menu features an abundance of seafood and meat entrées, from baked oysters and pan-seared sea bass to Szechuan tangerine chicken. We especially enjoyed the savory pasta dishes, which are among the best in the region. Even if you've both eaten your fill, the dessert tray—loaded with chocolate delights—may prove too tempting to pass up. **419 Commercial Avenue, at the Majestic Hotel; (360) 299-2923; inexpensive to expensive; call for seasonal hours.**

La Conner

La Conner is the heart of the Skagit Valley's famous TULIP FESTIVAL, which takes place during the last weeks of March and first weeks of April. Its soul is the 1,500 acres of prime farmland that blanket the area with huge swatches of brilliant color. Although this area is assuredly *the* Northwest destination during the festival, every season blesses it with a romantic aura all its own. Hemmed in by mountain ranges and guarded by often-visible Mount Baker, this pastoral valley is also filled with waving cornfields, pastures, and acres of lush crops.

La Conner itself is a colorful, picturesque town, and a favorite spring and summer destination. Bordering the Swinomish Channel, it offers a remarkable selection of restaurants, boutiques, antique shops, and bed and breakfasts. The crowds and tour buses calm down in the late fall and winter, after the tulip lovers and vacationers leave, making La Conner a charming corner of Puget Sound for spending time together. For more information about the Tulip Festival and the area in general, call the LA CONNER CHAMBER OF COMMERCE (360-466-4778).

Hotel/Bed and Breakfast Kissing

❤❤ **THE HERON, La Conner** Set overlooking acres of cultivated farmland, the Heron shares a parking lot with its notoriously romantic neighbor, THE WILD IRIS (see below); in fact, the same competent management company oversees both properties. Although the Heron markets itself as a Victorian-style inn, the contemporary exterior and modern decor are not completely convincing. Antiques and new furnishings fill the pleasant common area and dining room, as well as each of the 12 guest rooms. Lace duvets and handmade quilts lend coziness to the attractive rooms, which have been accented with pine wainscoting, antiques, and country wallpapers. TVs set on tabletops give the rooms a subtle hotel flavor, but fireplaces compensate with warmth and style. For a slightly higher price, guests can reserve the special Honeymoon Suite, the only room with a private Jacuzzi tub set in a sunny corner. Guests in other rooms needn't despair, however; a large community hot tub awaits outdoors, surrounded by flower boxes and views of farmland, Mount Baker, and the Cascades.

A large continental breakfast buffet served in the inn's dining room features hot scones, cereals, cinnamon rolls, fresh fruit, and a variety of baked entrées. **117 Maple Avenue; (360) 466-4626; inexpensive to very expensive.**

❀❀ **HOTEL PLANTER, La Conner** Even though the rooms in this historic gray stone building are located directly above well-traveled First Street, the hotel's old-world charm makes this a worthwhile destination. Traffic noise is audible during the day, but the hubbub calms down at night, just in time for you to sink into a blissful slumber.

All 12 units boast plenty of country touches and modern amenities, including TVs hidden in custom pine armoires, dried flower arrangements, floral bedspreads atop double or queen-size beds, and wicker furnishings. Extra-tall windows and ceilings make every room feel quite spacious. Small private bathrooms accompany each room, embellished with old-fashioned tile and pedestal sinks. Three rooms look down on a flower-laden brick courtyard where a waterfall spills into a tiny pool and a communal hot tub awaits in a wooden gazebo. Our favorite room is the Queen Jacuzzi Room, which has a large Jacuzzi tub in the corner near the bed and a great view of the courtyard through lofty trees.

Meals are not included in your stay, but the hotel is a moment's walk from a number of excellent restaurants. **715 First Street; (360) 466-4710, (800) 488-5409; inexpensive to moderate.**

❀❀❀ **KATY'S INN, La Conner** Surrounded by a neatly trimmed lawn, colorful perennial gardens, a forested hillside, and a white picket fence, this 1876 Victorian bed and breakfast is conveniently located just blocks from downtown La Conner. Warmth and elegance envelop you in the main parlor, where antique furnishings and family heirlooms mix with tasteful contemporary accents. Upstairs, four small but beautiful guest rooms are chock-full of country-elegant comfort. Ashley's Room, the smallest of the four, features hand-painted French Provincial furnishings and an antique lace bed covering. Picture windows frame views of Fidalgo Island and the Swinomish Channel in the blue-and-white Garden Room. Pastel pinks and blues lend a peaceful air to the cozy Rose Room; and the Lilac Room, the most spacious of them all, holds a beautiful antique armoire and a cheery white wicker bed. The Lilac Room and the Garden Room have private bathrooms; Ashley's Room and Rose Room share one bathroom (located down the hall) with an antique chain-flush toilet and an elongated claw-foot tub. All four rooms open to a wraparound deck that offers views of the tranquil neighborhood and Swinomish Channel.

The newly added Honeymoon Suite is now the inn's premier romantic accommodation. Located on the main floor, this room is filled with impressive antiques and overlooks the verdant backyard, with its flowering trees and gardens. Cream-colored quilts, a bounty of pillows, and swaths of lace fabric ornament the elegant four-poster bed. A TV/VCR is accompanied by a delightful assortment of videos, including several classics. Warm yourselves by the gas stove or head outdoors for a soak in the enormous hot tub (available to all guests) set in a white gazebo—a perfect end to a day spent touring the area. Our only reservation about the Honeymoon Suite is its close proximity to the common areas, where guests sometimes like to lounge late into the evening or early in the morning.

The extremely friendly innkeepers offer afternoon refreshments in the lovely main parlor. A full gourmet breakfast of baked goods, fresh fruit, and a hot entrée such as French toast or a veggie omelet is served in the formal dining room each morning. If you find it too hard to leave the warmth of your cozy bed, breakfast can be delivered to your door on a silver platter. **503 South Third Street; (360) 466-3366, (800) 914-7767; home.ncia.com/katysinn; inexpensive to moderate.**

Romantic Note: Christian knickknacks are scattered throughout this bed and breakfast, and the morning meal is preceded by a Christian prayer led by the innkeepers.

❤❤❤ LA CONNER CHANNEL LODGE, La Conner

Owned by the same management company as the **LA CONNER COUNTRY INN** (see below), the Channel Lodge is our favorite of the two, boasting a choice location on the bank of the Swinomish Channel. The expansive dark gray shingled exterior is captivating. Inside, hardwood floors, a huge stone fireplace, boldly colored area rugs, and beautiful views distinguish the common area. The lovely antique-filled library and an outdoor patio overlooking the water are both ideal spots to relax and enjoy the quiet setting.

Charm and coziness alleviate the hotel feeling here, but the fire extinguishers and pay phones in the hallways, metal doors in every guest room, and standard bathrooms are hard to ignore. Even so, all 40 units are beautifully decorated and tastefully furnished with Northwest flair. The King Parlor Rooms are the most desirable, with tall ceilings, Jacuzzi tubs, large tiled showers, fireplaces, and decks that overlook the water below. The Queen Jacuzzi Rooms are also very appealing, with Jacuzzi tubs, tiled showers, wooden shutters, and Northwest prints. Polish off your relaxing stay with a light continental breakfast served in the lovely dining alcove. **205 North First Street; (360) 466-1500; www.laconnerlodging.com; moderate to very expensive.**

❤❤ LA CONNER COUNTRY INN, La Conner

Vines climb the exterior of this sprawling wood-shingled inn, located a block away from La Conner's main thoroughfare. Tired shoppers will appreciate the cozy common area, where antiques and comfy couches are arranged in front of a large stone fireplace. Housed in the main inn and an adjacent building, the inn's 28 rooms all have gas fireplaces and spacious but standard private bathrooms. Tall, wood-beamed ceilings and wood-paneled walls enhance the upscale hotel-style decor. Attractive floral bedspreads complement the brass or wooden beds, and wooden shutters on the windows help to muffle the noise from outside traffic. In the morning, enjoy a continental breakfast served in the common area by the warmth of the roaring fire. **107 South Second Street; (360) 466-3101; www. laconnerlodging.com; moderate to very expensive.**

❧❧ **RAINBOW INN, La Conner** This renovated turn-of-the-century Craftsman farmhouse is a mere five-minute drive from the busy town center of La Conner, but far enough away to offer refuge from the mobs of tourists. Although it sits on a heavily trafficked road, a perennial garden and a manicured lawn help shield it from too much noise. In this country setting, guests can enjoy sweeping views of the bucolic valley and Mount Baker, a stately old chestnut tree, and the nearby tulip and daffodil fields that blaze with color in the spring. (An outdoor hot tub set beneath a picturesque gazebo offers grand views of the tulips and daffodils when the season is right.) Inside this mammoth home, a snug parlor with a wood-burning fireplace beckons travelers to sit and relax.

Such lovely surroundings gave us high hopes for the guest rooms, but we found them a bit disappointing. Dated colors, fabrics, and carpets give all eight guest rooms an exceedingly homey flavor. The Daisy Room in particular, with its red-white-and-blue USA theme (complete with faded flag), is far from inspiring. Fortunately, most of the rooms survey lovely pastoral views, and nearly all have a private bathroom (with the exception of three rooms on the third floor that share just one bathroom). The Violet Room and the Heather Room share a large wraparound deck, an ideal spot for reading and sipping iced tea on hot summer days. Our favorite spot for romance here is the suite on the main floor, with a sunken Jacuzzi tub and comfortable four-poster bed.

A full gourmet breakfast featuring fresh baked goods, fresh fruit, and an ever-changing hot entrée such as brandied French toast or vegetable frittata is served on the enclosed sundeck. Intimate tables for two and walls of windows make this a lovely place to begin your day. **12757 Chilberg Road; (360) 466-4578, (888) 266-8879; www.rainbowinnbandb.com; inexpensive to moderate.**

❧❧❧ **THE WILD IRIS, La Conner** Every detail at The Wild Iris exudes country refinement and amorous bliss. Although the two-story Victorian-style inn overlooks a parking lot, the parlor and the 20 individually decorated guest rooms compensate with sheer elegance. The deluxe Jacuzzi King and Queen Suites are the most desirable, with elegant contemporary furnishings, plush down comforters, extra-roomy Jacuzzi tubs set near gas fireplaces, and views of the stunning mountains and sprawling valley. Some rooms have romantic white-veiled wrought-iron beds, others feature white wicker or contemporary pine furnishings, and all of the main-floor rooms sport private patios that look out to pastoral scenes. We were most impressed with the fanciful Cloud Room, which lives up to its name with blue rag-rolled walls, wooden columns, playful white cloud murals, and billowy white gauze draped above the king-size bed. Twelve suites have private Jacuzzi tubs, but guests booked in rooms without one can use the beautiful outdoor community hot tub, set on a deck overlooking quiet farmland.

A lavish complimentary breakfast is served at separate tables in the inn's country-style dining room, where rose-scented fruit soup, poached eggs *en croûte* with roasted–red pepper coulis, and homemade granola are just a few of the enticing dishes offered each morning. After a day of play, you won't have to go far for dinner (moderate to expensive). Simply head downstairs to the dining room to find delectable entrées such as the Shades of Spring capellini, made with garlic slivers, shiitake mushrooms, and asparagus. (Dinners are available for guests and nonguests on Friday and Saturday evenings.) With advance notice, portable picnics can also be packed for off-site lunches in the country. **121 Maple Avenue; (360) 466-1400, (800) 477-1400; www. ncia. com/~wildiris; inexpensive to very expensive.**

Romantic Note: The management company that oversees The Wild Iris recently took over **THE HERON** (see above), located next door. Though somewhat less luxurious, The Heron is still worth looking into if The Wild Iris is booked.

Restaurant Kissing

❤❤❤ **ANDIAMO, La Conner** Andiamo is owned by the same people who run the renowned **PALMER'S RESTAURANT AND PUB** (see below), so it's not at all surprising that the food, atmosphere, and service are so impressive. Although a parking lot across the street somewhat obstructs the panorama on busy summer evenings, views of the Swinomish Channel are still superb, especially from the upstairs dining room. Pale green sponge-painted walls are illuminated by sconces, and the handful of intimate tables are decorated with pink linens. Gracious and efficient, the wait staff go out of their way to ensure your comfort.

The menu is quintessentially Italian, with the exception of the store-bought bread sticks (our only complaint) brought to your table when you first arrive. Don't even bother to try them; instead, request the fresh-out-of-the-oven focaccia or roasted-garlic crostini, brushed with olive oil and garlic. Everything else on the menu is perfectly prepared and presented, such as the fresh spinach salad with candied walnuts; the oyster saffron bisque with white wine and shallots; and, best of all, the spicy linguine *puttanesca* with sweet cherry peppers, roasted garlic, fresh basil, and capers. Andiamo's cioppino is hard to pass up, but so are the baked gnocchi, fresh pasta with chicken, and the pan-grilled beef tenderloin with wild mushrooms, roasted garlic, diced tomatoes, and Marsala. Desserts are equally tantalizing, so come prepared to indulge your sweet tooth. **505 South First Street; (360) 466-9111; dinner daily.**

❤❤❤ **PALMER'S RESTAURANT AND PUB, La Conner** After visiting Palmer's, we understand why couples flock here on weekend evenings. Soft lights illuminate the wood-beamed ceiling in the upstairs dining room, where cozy tables are draped in mauve linens. The seafood, chicken, and pasta specialties are as pleasing as the ambience, from the steamed Pacific mussels to the penne rigatta served with wild mushrooms, garlic, capers, and sweet bell peppers. The dessert tray varies daily but always features something rich, chocolaty, and delicious.

If you want to save some money and enjoy a more casual ambience, visit the main-floor pub. The environment isn't nearly as appealing, but the service is quick and efficient, and the excellent food speaks for itself. **205 East Washington Street; (360) 466-4261; moderate to expensive; lunch and dinner daily.**

Mount Vernon

Set just off Interstate 5, the growing town of Mount Vernon seems almost like an extension of La Conner. We were impressed by its small but diverse selection of kissing locales.

Hotel/Bed and Breakfast Kissing

❤❤ **STORYVILLE BED AND BREAKFAST, Mount Vernon** Built in 1904, this stunning gray Victorian home is adorned with stately white columns and flanked by a manicured lawn. In the side yard, a communal hot tub is surrounded by dozens of newly planted rosebushes, Japanese maples, and brightly colored tulips. Traffic zips by at a quick pace on nearby Chilberg Road, but inside the noise is almost inaudible. The good-humored innkeepers, who strive to be low-key, pride themselves on a no-frills but professional approach to hospitality.

Located on the upper floor of the main house, four classic guest rooms boast four-poster beds draped in gorgeous linens and down comforters. Large picture windows allow ample light in the elegant Storyville Suite, while the Downey Room has been done up in lovely shades of blue and cream. The East and West Rooms have the disadvantage of a shared bathroom, though it is spacious and has a large Jacuzzi soaking tub. If privacy is a top priority, the self-contained Bungalow unit next door should be your first choice. Driftwood art pieces add a vintage Northwest flavor to the beautiful suite, which is outfitted with an inviting four-poster log bed, private bath, and TV/VCR.

In the morning, a full breakfast of seasonal fruit, homemade pastries, and delicious baked egg dishes is served in the comfortable dining room. Coffee connoisseurs will be happy to know that java drinks are made to order at the full espresso bar. **18772 Best Road; (360) 466-3207; (888) 373-3207; www.ncia.com/storyville; inexpensive to expensive.**

❀❀❅ WHITE SWAN GUEST HOUSE, Mount Vernon Productive fruit trees and lush flower gardens surround this picturesque yellow Queen Anne farmhouse, set on a quiet country road just six miles from La Conner's town center. Commanding poplars border the long gravel driveway that ushers you to the door of the home, where several friendly dogs welcome guests. The scent of freshly baked cookies permeates the kitchen and drifts into the cozy parlor, where antique couches and chairs are placed near a wood-burning stove. Upstairs, the three guest rooms (named for their color schemes) offer relaxing views of the tranquil rural surroundings. Sunny buttercup-colored walls and a thick yellow comforter decorate the Yellow Room; the Peach Room boasts a pretty patchwork quilt, and the Pink Room features a pale pink comforter and a snug sitting area in a window-lined turret. Unfortunately, all three rooms share just two bathrooms down the hall. Luckily, both bathrooms are quite spacious (one holds a large tiled shower, the other an elongated claw-foot tub), and they also afford lovely views of the brilliantly colored flower gardens.

For more private accommodations, choose the modest, self-contained Garden Cottage, set beneath huge silver maples at the edge of the property. Amenities include a cedar deck, a comfortable living room, full kitchen, spacious second-floor bedroom, and floor-to-ceiling windows showcasing views of the surrounding farmland.

A country continental breakfast begins with fresh fruit smoothies, seasonal strawberries, and homemade applesauce, followed by filling home-baked muffins. Guests staying in the main house are served breakfast in the brightly painted breakfast room; guests in the cottage have their morning repast delivered to their front door. **15872 Moore Road; (360) 445-6805; www.cnw. com/~wswan; inexpensive to moderate.**

Restaurant Kissing

❀❀❅ PALMER'S RESTAURANT AND BAR, Mount Vernon Much to the delight of local residents, Palmer's recently opened a second restaurant in the heart of Mount Vernon. Like its sibling in La Conner (reviewed on page 254), this restaurant is renowned for fine cuisine, soothing ambience, and gracious service. The stylish, metropolitan dining room is adorned with warm wood and French accents, and features a 30-foot cherry-wood bar. Etched glass panels separate the quiet bar area from the subdued dining room, where well-spaced tables are topped with candle lanterns, fresh flowers, and crisp white linens. A second dining room is bordered with red cushioned banquets and adorned with red-and-white-pinstriped wallpaper.

Every item on the small, gourmet menu is enticing; we especially like the organic baby pear tomato and fruit salad with toasted hazelnuts, and the penne rigatta with toasted walnuts, artichokes, kalamata olives, roasted garlic cloves, and spinach. Seafood and wild game specialties include Cajun-grilled Gulf prawns, smoked salmon and wild mushroom penne rigatta, roast duckling served with a wild berry demi-glace, and pan-grilled pheasant. Be sure to save room for a sweet denouement, such as fresh strawberries with cracked black pepper and balsamic vinegar over ice cream. **416 Myrtle Street; (360) 336-9699; moderate to expensive; lunch Monday–Friday, dinner Monday–Saturday.**

❤❤❤ **WILDFLOWERS RESTAURANT AND WINE MERCHANTS, Mount Vernon** Country charm is the last thing you'd expect to find anywhere near this commercialized strip of neon signs, food marts, and gas stations. Fortunately, you can escape the clamor and indulge your fantasies in the seclusion of this creamy white 1930s home. Pretty gardens surround the house, sheltering it from the busy street.

Inside, tables draped in dark blue linens are tucked into cozy alcoves in the home's original living and dining rooms. Tiny white lights in the corners and bold contemporary artwork add sparkle and color to the otherwise simple decor. The creative menu features innovative Northwest cuisine, such as onion soup baked beneath a puff pastry dome, fresh Samish Bay oysters, lamb shank roasted with red wine, Skagit Valley chicken, and perfectly done pasta entrées. Once you've shared bites of this wonderful cuisine, you're likely to forget about the traffic outside and focus on matters closer to the heart. **2001 East College Way; (360) 424-9724; moderate to expensive; dinner Tuesday–Saturday.**

Camano Island

Camano Island can be reached directly by car; simply follow the main thoroughfare through Stanwood.

Miles of flat farmland surround rural, tree-covered Camano Island. There isn't much here, but that is Camano's appeal. Spend a peaceful day exploring the island's relatively secluded waterfront and forested areas, then conclude with an elegant dinner.

Restaurant Kissing

❤❤❤ **RENEE'S ON CAMANO, Camano Island** Except for those who enjoy biking through Camano Island's well-preserved rural landscape, couples with a romantic agenda haven't had a reason to put Camano at the top of their list. Until now, that is. This newly opened, highly touted restaurant is drawing people from as far away as Seattle. Renee's award-winning chef performs magic in the kitchen, and meals are enhanced by the elegant ambience. A bronze carousel horse is the centerpiece of the upscale European-style dining room, where greenery and cushioned banquettes complement walls adorned with French etchings. Bronze statues of dogs stand guard beside a rock fireplace in the classic lounge and smoking room, near the back of the restaurant. (Don't worry, the smell of smoke is not detectable in the main dining area.) Crisp white and peach linens drape elegant tables, which are adorned with softly glowing green table lanterns. In the warmer months, meals are also served on an outdoor deck that overlooks a meadow of wildflowers and offers glimpses of a lake through tall trees.

The food here tastes as good as it sounds. Try chilled asparagus with green goddess dressing, apple salad with blackberry vinaigrette, Northwest cioppino, or seafood pappadella (a seafood sandwich accented with fresh herbs and sun-dried tomatoes). Renee's clam chowder is deservedly famous. Meat and seafood connoisseurs will appreciate the wide selection of options, including rack of lamb, filet mignon, cedar-planked salmon, and seafood crêpes. If you have the good fortune of arriving during brunch, the apple-vanilla crêpes and the cherry Napoleon are both absolute musts. **170 East Cross Island Road; (360) 387-0671; moderate to expensive; lunch Wednesday–Saturday, dinner Wednesday–Sunday, brunch Sunday.**

Whidbey Island

By ferryboat: Whidbey Island is accessible from Mukilteo, 20 minutes north of Seattle, and from Port Townsend on the Olympic Peninsula. By car: Reach Whidbey Island from Anacortes via the Deception Pass Bridge, 90 minutes north of Seattle.

Aside from being one of the most charming, easily accessible islands in the Seattle area, rural Whidbey Island is also the longest island in the continental United States. If you're looking for a quick escape from city life, Whidbey is an exemplary destination, offering an unusually large selection of engaging restaurants, wonderful bed and breakfasts, spectacular vistas, and idyllic forested parks.

Clinton

The Mukilteo ferry deposits passengers in the small, nondescript town of Clinton, which hosts an odd assortment of small businesses, gas stations, and convenience stores. Clinton itself has nothing to offer for a romantic sojourn, but we discovered some properties in the outlying areas that are undeniably ripe for kissing.

Hotel/Bed and Breakfast Kissing

❦❦❦ **FRENCH ROAD FARM COTTAGE, Clinton** Built in 1918, this quaint little cottage sits deep in the quiet countryside, next to several acres of vineyards. Rambling flower gardens and trees envelop the grounds, exuding privacy and peacefulness, while a hammock strung between two stately evergreens is the perfect spot for some late-afternoon tranquillity. The property is yours entirely, except for deer, fox, birds, and other wild residents that frequently pay visits. A vegetable garden provides guests with fresh zucchini and tomatoes, among other home-grown vegetables that you're welcome to pick.

Inside, the cottage is filled with an eclectic mixture of antiques. A sunroom filled with wicker furniture and plants leads to the living room, which has wood paneling draped with tapestries, a cozy couch placed in front of a wood-burning stove, and French doors that open to the lawn and a perennial garden. The bedroom is small and bright, with a queen-size bed, lace drapes, and French doors that open to a deck overlooking the vineyard. Perhaps one of the best features here is the large, airy bathroom, with its stone-tiled floor and seven-foot-long Jacuzzi tub set next to a window overlooking a flower-covered trellis.

Breakfast fixings, such as fresh fruit and baked goods, are left in a basket in the refrigerator of the full country-style kitchen. You can eat inside or enjoy an early-morning picnic anywhere on the gorgeous property. **3841 East French Road; (360) 321-2964; www.frenchroadfarm.com; very expensive; minimum-stay requirement on weekends.**

Romantic Note: The owners of French Road Farm have another property that may or may not be of interest, depending on your feelings about truly eclectic decor. Located at the end of a long row of nondescript waterfront homes, directly on the sandy beach of Useless Bay next to a 40-acre bird sanctuary, **HOME BY THE SEA COTTAGES** (2388 East Sunlight Beach Road, Langley; 360-321-2964; very expensive; minimum-stay requirement on weekends) offers heavenly quiet and endless views of vast Admiralty Inlet and the jagged Olympic Mountains. Although the property has two accommodations, we recommend only the Sandpiper Suite. Filled with a casual jumble of mismatched furniture and decor, the suite is nonetheless blessed with a fantastic location on the beach. If you are more interested in a gorgeous setting and the many romantic possibilities offered by miles of beach, you may want to give this location a try.

❤❤❤ **KITTLESON COVE, Clinton** Settled next to the gently lapping waters of Puget Sound, serene, secluded Kittleson Cove is made for romance. Its northeastern exposure affords a spectacular view of the Cascade Mountains and Mount Baker, providing ample evidence of the Pacific Northwest's magnetic beauty. Your privacy is assured in the property's two self-sufficient guest suites, both of which feature private entrances, private baths, decks overlooking the rocky beach, stereo systems (bring your favorite CDs), TV/VCRs, and well-stocked mini-kitchens that include pre-prepared and do-it-yourself breakfast treats. Binoculars are even provided to enhance your enjoyment of the remarkable scenery. If you'd like to keep civilization as far away as possible, bring dinner fixings and enjoy a waterfront repast.

Decorated with country-style pastel fabrics and floral linens, the Beachside Suite is cozy and comfortable. Our favorite aspect of this room is the private hot tub, set on the deck and enclosed by an ivy-covered trellis. In contrast, the three-room Cove Cottage has a beautifully rustic, earthy atmosphere. A stone fireplace warms the deep green and burgundy interior, while a profusion of throw rugs covers the quarried-rock floors. (We recommend bringing along slippers in the colder months.) A tall pine four-poster bed with a floral bedspread and matching canopy is lovely, but the bright red Jacuzzi tub in the bathroom is the decisive romantic touch. **4891 East Bay Ridge Drive; (360) 341-2734; www.whidbey.com/kittleson; expensive to very expensive; minimum-stay requirement on holidays; recommended wedding site.**

Langley

The town of Langley is five miles north of the Clinton ferry dock, on State Route 525.

Balanced on a bluff above the water's edge, the small town of Langley commands mesmerizing views of Mount Baker, the Cascades, and Saratoga Passage. Ice cream parlors, boutiques, and a two-screen movie theater lend old-time charm to the small-town streets. Langley maintains its Northwest look and style without compromising its virtues, which is precisely what makes it such a terrific getaway from life in the fast lane. In the outlying neighborhoods, an abundance of bed and breakfasts appeals to guests with romance and seclusion in mind.

Hotel/Bed and Breakfast Kissing

❤❤❤ **BOATYARD INN, Langley** Nestled in the Langley Marina and Boat Harbor, this aptly named inn resembles an old cannery structure, with corrugated metal roofs and siding. Despite the industrial exterior, the nine guest rooms are filled with straightforward Northwest style, including platform beds, blond wood furniture, knotty pine detailing, plaid bedspreads and upholstery, and wicker chairs. Each room is also equipped with a galley kitchen and a TV/VCR. A small balcony looks out to majestic views of Saratoga Passage and the Cascade Mountains, and a fire ignites at the turn of a switch in the gas fireplace trimmed with black marble. If you're looking for rustic yet elegant simplicity, your hearts will be more than content here. Fresh gourmet coffee is provided with your stay, but breakfast is not; fortunately, plenty of restaurants are just minutes away. **200 Wharf Street; (360) 221-5120; www. ohwy.com/wa/b/boatyard.htm; moderate to very expensive; minimum-stay requirement on weekends.**

❤❤❤❤ **CHAUNTECLEER HOUSE, Langley** Your worries will drift into oblivion the moment you set foot on this enchanting property. Six acres of lush green lawn and sprightly English gardens envelop this bluff-top house overlooking scenic Saratoga Passage. In the early spring, you're even likely to spot a pod of gray whales spouting and breaching on the horizon—a breathtaking sight!

The two-story Chauntecleer unit is utterly private and completely yours, from the large outdoor hot tub ensconced in the garden to the spacious deck with panoramic water views. Inside, large picture windows frame the water views, both upstairs and downstairs, and blond hardwood floors and soft yellow walls give the home's interior a crisp, contemporary look. English pine antiques are beautifully arranged in the living room, where overstuffed plaid couches flank a brick hearth. Wooden roosters, adorable ceramic piglets, and other country knickknacks lend warmth and creativity to Chauntecleer's immaculate design.

Take turns preparing gourmet meals in the ultra-modern full kitchen or enjoy the innkeeper's breakfast creations. (Fresh strawberries, muffins, and ready-to-bake omelets are stocked in the kitchen before you arrive.) Either way, you can savor your meals at a two-person table placed next to a bay window with stunning water views. Revel in the same panorama upstairs in the cozy bedroom, which is decorated in a nautical theme. Denim linens drape a sumptuous, pillow-laden bed where you can linger and watch the sun set. Other modern conveniences include a TV/VCR in the bedroom, a collection of CDs, and a double-headed shower in the beautifully tiled bathroom. You won't be the first guests tempted to extend a vacation at this supreme property. **5081 Saratoga Road; (360) 221-5494, (800) 637-4436; www.dove house.com; expensive; minimum-stay requirement on weekends.**

Romantic Note: At the time of our visit, the talented innkeeper was busy putting the finishing touches on a new adjacent cottage called the **POTTING SHED** (moderate). Set next to the English garden, the new unit promises to be as lovely and comfortable as Chauntecleer, although much smaller. It will feature a garden motif, a handmade twig bed, a woodstove, and a Jacuzzi tub with water views. This exceptional property also holds another beautiful cottage called the **DOVE HOUSE** (see below).

☙☙☙ CHRISTY'S COUNTRY COTTAGE, Langley Guests have exclusive use of this picturesque wood-shingled cottage, set beneath a stand of trees on a hillside overlooking a rural valley, the Olympics, and Useless Bay. Every detail of this handcrafted home is admirable, from the peaked cathedral ceiling and pine accents to the floor-to-ceiling brick hearth and expansive windows. Contemporary trappings abound, including a TV/VCR, CD player, a nice selection of movies and CDs, and a massive deck with an immense hot tub set beneath a canopy of stars at night (when it isn't cloudy). A modern, well-equipped kitchen overflows with snacks and breakfast goodies, such as fresh fruit, baked goods, and delicious homemade truffles. In the bedroom, a handsome four-poster is covered with a fluffy down comforter and an abundance of oversize pillows.

While these details are quite enticing, the main drawback is the property's close proximity to Whidbey Island's busy main road. One other kissing concern is the deck's exposure to the shared driveway, where intermittent traffic means privacy cannot be guaranteed. **2891 East Meinhold Road; (360) 321-1815; expensive to very expensive; no credit cards; minimum-stay requirement on weekends and holidays.**

❀❀❀ **COUNTRY COTTAGE OF LANGLEY, Langley** Conveniently located in a residential neighborhood just a few blocks from the town of Langley, this country-elegant farmhouse is surrounded by two acres of manicured lawns and colorful gardens. All five charming units have luxurious feather beds, down comforters, private entrances, TV/VCRs, stereos, refrigerators, and coffeemakers.

A small building that once served as a creamery has been remade into a quaint guest cottage, complete with pine floors, a white eyelet lace comforter, and Dutch doors. Two additional suites, Lynn's Sunrise and Sand N See (yes, it is "see"), share a gazebo-style cottage. Lynn's Sunrise has cheery yellow walls, plush yellow linens, beautiful antiques, and a shared deck with a magnificent view of the water (across the semi-busy street). Sand N See shares the same view and deck, but is decidedly more masculine, with a white and blue color scheme, denim linens, and seascapes.

Though all of the accommodations here are worth mentioning, the two newly renovated suites adjoining the main house are most deserving of romantic praise. The nautical Captain's Cove, decorated in blue, holds a beautifully made-up bed, covered with sumptuous linens and pillows, which directly faces the water. A large soaking tub tucked beneath a picture window overlooks a private deck, and a wood-burning stove provides warmth. Next door, the Whidbey Rose is exceedingly feminine but still impressive. The enticing four-poster canopy bed is covered with pink and maroon floral linens with lace accents, and a love seat with just enough room for two is set beside the gas fireplace. Stylishly decorated with Laura Ashley rose tiles, the large Jacuzzi tub takes center stage in this spacious designer suite.

In the morning, a gourmet multicourse breakfast may include coffee, fruit juice, fresh fruit, homemade bread or muffins, and hot entrées such as eggs Benedict, blueberry French toast, or salmon quiche. You can chose to eat either in the privacy of your own suite or at separate two-person tables in the lovely sunlit breakfast room in the main house, where a magnificent nature mural decorates the walls. **215 Sixth Street; (360) 221-8709, (800) 713-3860; www.virtualcities.com/ons/wa/w/wawc602.htm; moderate to very expensive; minimum-stay requirement for some rooms.**

❀❀❀❀ **DOVE HOUSE, Langley** You'd never guess that this self-sufficient cottage derives its name from its previous incarnation as a pigeon coop. Sheltered on six acres of gardens, ponds, and waterfront, the impressively renovated

Dove House is magazine material. Red geraniums peek from an antique wheel-barrow in front of this vintage island escape. Cedar walls, bright skylights, and terra-cotta floors give the cottage a rustic disposition. The home is enhanced with Southwestern fabrics and Native American artwork, and colorful hand-painted fish tiles adorn a cozy breakfast nook in the sunny, modern kitchen. Breakfast provisions are stocked prior to your visit and may include juice, fruit, coffee, fresh croissants, muffins, coffee cake, granola, and baked egg dishes. (Needless to say, you'll probably want to skip lunch!) In colder months, light a fire in the river-rock hearth in the airy living room, where shelves brimming with artifacts stretch from floor to ceiling.

A sculpted brass otter clings to the railing in the upstairs loft bedroom, which has been appointed with a handcrafted wooden bed covered with South-west-style linens. Here, large windows offer views of the nearby meadows and a tranquil pond. Pop in your favorite CD and cozy up side by side on the window seat or browse through the interesting collection of artwork and knick-knacks that fill every corner of the cottage. We can't think of a better place to seclude yourselves and enjoy the authentic beauty of the Pacific Northwest. **5081 Saratoga Road; (360) 221-5494, (800) 637-4436; www. dovehouse. com; expensive; minimum-stay requirement on weekends.**

Romantic Suggestion: Two additional enchanting cottages, **CHAUNTE-CLEER HOUSE** and the nearly completed **POTTING SHED**, share the same setting (see above).

❤❤❤ **EAGLES NEST HONEYMOON COTTAGE, Langley** Recently purchased by the owners of the **EAGLES NEST INN** (see below), this whimsical cottage is one of our favorite Langley locales. True to its old name, the cottage hugs a steep bluff overlooking Saratoga Passage and the Cascade Mountains: The view alone is worth a visit. Best of all, the cottage is rented to only one couple at a time, so the scenery is exclusively yours for the duration of your stay.

The cottage's simple exterior contrasts with the ultra-quaint interior. Antique dolls, angels, country relics, and handmade art pieces clutter the small but charming home. A cozy living room and full kitchen (complete with espresso maker and deluxe continental breakfast provisions) are enticingly arranged beneath a cathedral ceiling. A wood-burning stove and terra-cotta chimney ensure warmth in the winter months. Filled with more country trinkets and trimmed with an eye to romance, the separate bedroom and bath are accessible via a short hallway. In back of the house, beneath a covered porch, a bright red, heart-shaped Jacuzzi tub has scintillating views of the water. Adirondack furnishings adorn the deck, creating the perfect spot for long conversations. If you're in the mood for an adventure, descend a staircase to the shoreline below, where you can beachcomb to your hearts' content. **(360) 221-5331; www.eaglesnestinn.com; very expensive; minimum-stay requirement.**

❦❦❦ **EAGLES NEST INN, Langley** Aptly named for the eagles that roost high in the surrounding evergreens, this large, wood contemporary home rests on a hillside on the outskirts of Langley. Spectacular water views are visible from nearly every room in the elegant, comfortable home. A floor-to-ceiling stone fireplace and a pastoral mural lend Northwest charm to the inn's common area, where a grand piano beckons the musically inclined. Hand-painted images of wildlife appear around corners and on doorways throughout the home; this theme continues in the upstairs lounge, where guests can relax with books and enjoy complimentary refreshments.

Three of the four spacious guest rooms have stunning views of Saratoga Passage and Mount Baker, but views from the Eagles Nest Room are unsurpassed. This suite, set at the top of the house, is lined with windows that showcase a sweeping 360-degree view, which can also be enjoyed from the private deck. Plush linens and decorative pillows adorn a comfortable queen-size bed, and impressive wood eagle sculptures embellish the natural setting. The Saratoga Room enjoys similar views and the luxury of a private balcony and porch swing, although privacy is significantly diminished by the detached bathroom, located down the hall. Wood from storm-fallen trees has been transformed into furnishings in the Forest Room, where a plush down comforter and luxurious linens adorn a beautiful bed fashioned out of driftwood. A colorful outdoor garden is the focal point of the Garden Suite, located in the somewhat dim converted basement, which is still surprisingly roomy and comfortable. Adirondack furnishings contribute a rustic mood, and the four-poster bed covered with pretty floral linens is quite comfortable. Guests with seclusion in mind will also appreciate this suite's private entrance. All rooms feature TV/VCRs.

In the morning you can feast on a breakfast that may include a seasonal fruit plate, autumn pear pancakes with caramel sauce, and the innkeepers' famous wild blackberry coffee cake. Be sure to sample a freshly baked chocolate chip cookie and add to the ongoing cookie count. (At the time of our visit, guests had consumed more than 91,000 cookies!) **4680 Saratoga Road; (360) 221-5331; www.eaglesnestinn.com; inexpensive to moderate.**

Romantic Note: The innkeepers also own the endearing **EAGLES NEST HONEYMOON COTTAGE** (see above)—another undeniably romantic locale.

❦❦❦❦ **GALITTOIRE—A CONTEMPORARY GUEST HOUSE, Langley** Expect the unexpected at this contemporary wood-and-glass guest house, enveloped by a sloping green lawn and ten acres of tranquil woods. The meticulous owner, an architect turned innkeeper, has overlooked nothing in the design of this exquisitely detailed home that caters to the senses. A case in point: A couple concluding their honeymoon at Galittoire decided to take a last morning ramble in the woods. After walking several yards, they stumbled across a luxurious feather bed nestled in an enchanted forest grove, prepared just for them. Though we can't promise an exact duplicate of this experience, you get the idea.

Only two guest suites are available, located at opposite ends of the inn-keeper's house. The smaller (and less expensive) suite has elegant modern appointments, Japanese flower arrangements, and a bed covered with white linens and draped with white fabric. The Master Suite is more of the same, though its sensuality is enhanced by its location at the top of the house, where floor-to-ceiling windows look out to the sky and survey the property. Guests in this suite also have the exclusive use of a cozy wood sauna, triple-headed tiled shower, an exercise room, two-person Jacuzzi tub, *and* an immense hot tub. On rainy days, guests in either suite cuddle on a sumptuous white sofa in the elegant living room and enjoy the warmth of a fire blazing in the black glass-and-rock fireplace (a work of art in itself).

As if this isn't pampering enough, the talented innkeeper is a master chef and serves savory two-course gourmet breakfasts in the dining room or outside on a large patio. Kiss quietly and stay watchful if you're on the patio: you're likely to see deer. **5444 South Coles Road; (360) 221-0548; www. galittoire.com; very expensive; minimum-stay requirement on weekends; recommended wedding site.**

❤❤❤ **GARDEN PATH INN, Langley** Located a mere 20 steps from Langley's bustling First Street, the Garden Path Inn isn't exactly the path less traveled. Cloaked in wisteria and enveloped by nature's scents in springtime, a brick garden path leads away from the shop-clad street to the front door of this inn. In the midst of this busy setting, the soothing and luxurious accommodations will take you by complete surprise.

Windows in the spacious front suite look out to Saratoga Passage and downtown Langley. Skylights brighten the stately living room, filled with impressive antiques and ultramodern art. Artistic touches, such as a hand-carved chessboard displayed next to a love seat, give the room a boutique flavor. All the amenities required for a romantic getaway are at your disposal: a fireplace, Jacuzzi tub, TV/VCR, private kitchen, and separate bedroom with a four-poster bed covered with wonderfully luxurious linens.

On the opposite side of the building, a second, smaller suite faces the back parking lot and consequently offers a less engaging view. Still, the unit is lovely and immaculate, with a gracious daylight-filled sitting room and French country antiques. A wrought-iron chandelier casts a soft glow on the high-backed plaid chairs flanking a beautifully set table for two. Sunshine floods in through skylights in the fully equipped kitchen and small but cheery bedroom. A skylight also brightens the private bathroom, adorned with a hand-thrown ceramic sink and glass-enclosed shower.

Both suites are accompanied by a continental breakfast delivered to your door. You won't regret having chosen this path, which offers the perfect combination of a garden hideaway and the convenience of an island town. **111 First Street; (360) 221-5121; inexpensive to expensive.**

❧❧❧❦ **THE INN AT LANGLEY, Langley** For as long as we can remember, the Inn at Langley has been one of Whidbey Island's sleekest, most desirable, and best-known places to kiss. Set high on a bluff, the wood-shingled building overlooks Saratoga Passage, endowing each of the 24 rooms with glorious views of the mountains and water. Asian artwork and ultramodern furnishings lend elegant simplicity to the guest rooms, which also feature private decks, wood-burning fireplaces, and spacious tiled bathrooms. Deep two-person spa tubs, fronted by shower areas the size of small rooms, are precisely placed to face both the view and the fireplace. Thick comforters and crisp white linens make the cushy beds inviting. Two spacious new townhouse suites, located adjacent to the main building, offer more of the same polished decor and impressive amenities. Guests who are inspired by the views can access the beach below the main building, via a boardwalk.

The heart of the inn is its acclaimed formal country kitchen, which turns out generous complimentary continental breakfasts. You can enjoy your breakfast at a large table placed next to a river-rock fireplace or carry a breakfast tray back to the privacy of your room. (We recommend the latter, of course, if you've got kissing in mind.) A Northwest epicurean production is presented on Friday and Saturday nights to guests and visitors alike; these meals run $60 per person and reservations are required. **400 First Street; (360) 221-3033; very expensive to unbelievably expensive; minimum-stay requirement on weekends.**

❧❧❦ **ISLAND TYME BED AND BREAKFAST, Langley** Slow down, you're now operating on island "tyme." Tucked far away from the road and nestled on ten serene acres of woods and pastureland, this recently constructed, multicolored Victorian offers guests an abundance of space and privacy. Even the entryway deserves mention, with its life-size apple tree stenciled in the corner. The five guest rooms here, located on the main and second floors, feature private baths, queen- or king-size beds draped with beautiful comforters or charming patchwork quilts, and an eclectic assortment of antiques mixed with country touches. Though the decor borders on ordinary, the many romantic amenities make up for it. Glowing fireplaces and shared or private decks are found in three suites, and every room has a TV/VCR. Adorned in blue and mauve florals, the Heirloom Room has an antique fireplace and a private deck that overlooks the property's quiet wooded setting. The Turret Room features a windowed tower, two-person Jacuzzi tub, American pine antiques, and a shared deck. Masterpiece also has a spacious Jacuzzi tub and a king-size bed, as well as a semiprivate deck.

Morning brings a bountiful gourmet breakfast that may include poached pears, Dutch babies, quiches, gourmet waffles, pancakes, scones, and more, served family style in a sunlit dining room. After you've eaten your fill, you may want to explore the property and say hello to the pet pygmy goats. Those with a penchant for antiques should be sure to ask the innkeepers about their second business, Iron Horse Antiques, which features a wonderful collection of vintage furnishings and collectibles. **4940 South Bayview Road; (360) 221-5078, (800) 898-8963; www.moriah.com/island-tyme; inexpensive to expensive; minimum-stay requirement on weekends seasonally.**

❧❧ **LOG CASTLE, Langley** You've never seen a castle quite like this! Settled comfortably on a Saratoga Passage beach, this one-of-a-kind homegrown project has taken its owners 18 years to complete. Every piece of wood has an accompanying story of origin, which the owners readily share with all who ask—from the driftwood door handle to the wormwood staircase to the log breakfast table. Family pictures and heirlooms adorn the homespun and somewhat dated common area, where guests are encouraged to relax in front of the large stone fireplace and enjoy the water views.

The four cozy guest rooms, each named for one of the owners' daughters, are simple yet comfortable. Although the decor is very casual, our favorite is Ann's Room, set in an octagonal turret on the third floor. Here you'll find a small but cozy double bed, a 1912 wood-burning stove, and surrounding windows that survey panoramic views of Puget Sound and Mount Baker. A door opens to a private deck, offering prime views of mesmerizing sunsets and majestic eagles perched in the nearby trees. Marta's Suite is also engaging, with a king-size bed covered in a colorful patchwork quilt, a large bathroom with the only tub in the house, a tiny wood-burning stove, and a sundeck with a two-person porch swing. Lea's Room also has a porch with a hanging swing and wonderful water views. Glass French doors open onto a private patio in Gayle's Room, located on the main floor. Although the decor in all of the rooms could use some updating, the atmosphere is so warm and inviting, you probably won't mind.

The three-course gourmet breakfast is preceded by the mouthwatering aroma of cinnamon rolls and other freshly baked goods. After you've eaten, explore the beach and enjoy the quiet surroundings. **4693 Saratoga Road; (360) 221-5483; www.whidbey.com/logcastle; inexpensive to moderate; minimum-stay requirement on holidays.**

Romantic Note: Christian religious items placed throughout the inn may make some people feel uncomfortable. However, the ultra-accommodating innkeepers are never pushy about their beliefs.

❧❧❧ **THE PENTHOUSE, Langley** Those in search of a country escape will appreciate this property's quiet location just outside Langley's town center. Paths marked with stepping stones meander past birdbaths, blooming flower beds, and shady trees, inviting you to slow your pace. Lovingly landscaped gardens enfold the two-story wood-paneled Penthouse, designed exclusively for couples.

Set back on the property, the unassuming cabin surveys views of Saratoga Passage and Mount Baker through the surrounding trees. An outside stairwell leads to a snug but handsome apartment that boasts floor-to-ceiling windows, an assortment of quirky heirlooms, and an abundance of country charm. Enjoy the fresh pastoral breezes and water views from the outdoor deck furnished with handcrafted willow chairs. Velvet settees and other antiques adorn the sitting areas, which brim with colorful artwork and eccentric knickknacks. Hand-painted tiles ornament the small but complete kitchenette, which includes an espresso maker, imported Italian coffee, and a delectable array of breakfast items such as hearty mushroom quiches, pastries, breads, and fresh juices. A wood-burning stove provides abundant warmth in the winter. Upstairs, a loft bedroom holds a grand hand-carved king-size bed draped with luxurious linens and a down duvet. An enormous Jacuzzi tub awaits in the black-and-white-tiled bathroom, which is decorated with fun romantic touches, including a shower curtain decorated with Botticelli artwork. After a long soak in the Jacuzzi tub, guests can cuddle up in front of the fireplace or watch a video from the inn's extensive collection. **(360) 221-8857, (800) 243-5536; www.whidbey.com/edgecliff; very expensive; minimum-stay requirement.**

♥♥♥ SARATOGA INN, Langley Everything about this sprawling country inn would be sheer, immaculate perfection—if only it were on the other side of the street. The inn's spectacular views of Saratoga Passage are disrupted by the main thoroughfare leading into Langley, which can be heavily trafficked in the summer months. Otherwise, the professionally run inn is picture perfect, with its classic wood-shingled exterior and wraparound veranda. You'll feel right at home in the inviting and roomy common areas, which are filled with an elegant assortment of comfortable furnishings. Fourteen upscale guest suites fill the inn's two stories. The green and taupe color schemes are elegant and enticing, as are the plush floral-patterned linens, down comforters, and decorator pillows. Gorgeous watercolor paintings add even more color and style. Gas fireplaces warm up every room, and beautiful tiles embellish immense walk-in showers in the attractive bathrooms. Rooms on the top floor are especially appealing, with high cathedral ceilings and supreme water views.

If you really want it all (and you're willing to pay for it), book the adjacent, very private Carriage House Suite. Designed with couples in mind, this beautifully designed suite embodies romance. Oriental rugs cover gleaming hardwood floors, and a seductive claw-foot tub awaits in the spacious marble bathroom. A fluffy down duvet adorns a gorgeous king-size sleigh bed, and an enormous deck offers views of the water across the street. A TV/VCR, CD player, and large open kitchen are additional romantic features.

No matter which room you choose, a generous continental breakfast is included with your stay and can be delivered to your room or enjoyed family style in the dining room of the main house. **201 Cascade Avenue; (360) 221-5801, (800) 698-2910; www.foursisters.com/saratoga.html; moderate to very expensive.**

❤❤❤ **VILLA ISOLA, Langley** More than three and a half acres of towering pines and fastidiously maintained gardens envelop this romantic Italian-inspired escape. Chirruping frogs and a crowing rooster are the only neighbors you'll hear, and if you keep your eyes open, you just might glimpse resident deer or wild rabbits. If either of you has a sweet tooth, you've come to the right place: The scent of freshly baked goodies lingers in the air, and guests are invited to raid the fridge for biscotti, tiramisu, and other delectable treats in the evening. Baked pears in orange sauce, hazelnut French toast, French pastries, stuffed pancakes (Italian style), and double-chocolate cranberry bread are served for breakfast in a dining room that overlooks the flower-laden yard.

Guests can listen to their favorite CDs and lounge in the elegant, comfortable common areas or retire to the luxury of their own private suite. Named after Italian destinations, all seven guest rooms are spacious and exceptionally attractive. Three rooms are located in the main house. Facing the front lawn and gardens, the suave and sophisticated Torino Suite is accented with white linens, boutique pillows, and crisp white draperies. (Our only complaint about this room is the detached bathroom down the hall.) A Jacuzzi tub in the black-and-white-tiled bathroom and a beautiful wrought-iron bed are the highlights of the sleek Venice Suite. Downstairs, the Florence Room features a wrought-iron canopy bed draped with cascading fabric. Guests in this suite have exclusive access to an adjacent sitting room at the bottom of the stairs. (Although there are no other guest rooms on this floor, we should warn you that the sitting room does not have a door and is also accessible from the stairwell.) Even though none of the rooms have much of a view, that doesn't detract from their distinctive sense of style.

Guests who want more privacy will appreciate the two adjoining suites in a neighboring building. Though the decor is somewhat sparser, both suites are impeccably polished and feature luxuriously thick, pure cotton comforters. These units bask in the morning sun and share a deck overlooking the verdant backyard. Another option is the self-contained cottage decorated in a contemporary version of 1940s style, with a fully equipped kitchen (including an espresso machine for caffeine addicts), a wood-burning fireplace, a separate bedroom, and a spacious bathroom with a wonderful Jacuzzi tub.

Last but not least is the property's newest and most luxurious accommodation: the much-talked-about Grand Suite. Designed to look Mediterranean, the suite features a dramatic private entrance with cathedral ceilings and a wall of windows in the living room overlooking the pastoral setting. Sumptuous linens and draperies create a sense of luxury, as do such much-appreciated amenities as a fireplace, TV/VCR, CD player, kitchenette, and a full-size luxury bath with Jacuzzi tub. Guests here can keep to themselves all weekend or join other guests for an extravagant breakfast in the main house's cheery dining room. **5489 South Coles Road; (360) 221-5052, (800) 246-7323; www.villaisola.com; inexpensive to moderate; recommended wedding site.**

❤❤ **THE WHIDBEY INN, Langley** One of Whidbey Island's longest-established properties, the Whidbey Inn is easy to miss at first glance. Set in the heart of Langley's town center, it is bordered by shops on one side, and a pizza parlor operates above it. However, these drawbacks are all forgiven and forgotten once you step inside your room and take in the serene water views. Guests are greeted with a plate of delicious appetizers, and gourmet chocolates and decanters of sherry await in each of the six units. The three top-floor suites, although a bit austere in decor, are the most spacious and desirable options. The Saratoga Suite, with its bay windows, marble fireplace, and posh English furnishings, is wonderfully comfortable; the Gazebo Suite has a marble fireplace, floral linens, and its own private gazebo set outside in the trees; and the Wicker Suite is light and airy, with white wicker furnishings and a mint green comforter. The other three rooms are more standard, but still fine options for a peaceful night's rest. An expansive, weathered sundeck stretches the entire length of the building, facing the spectacular water.

A full gourmet breakfast is brought to your room in the morning, complete with a hot egg dish, fresh fruit plate, breads or muffins, and coffee and tea. **106 First Street; (360) 221-7115, (888) 313-2070; www.whidbeyinn. com; inexpensive to expensive; minimum-stay requirement on weekends seasonally.**

Restaurant Kissing

❤❤❤ **CAFE LANGLEY, Langley** Cafe Langley has been serving up reliably delicious Greek cuisine—and romance—for years. A handful of oak tables and chairs are scattered around the small dining room, which boasts white textured walls, wood-beamed ceilings, and terra-cotta floors. Though the ambience is more casual than intimate, the tables are spaced far enough apart for semiprivate discussions and a few daring kisses. Softly glowing candle lanterns adorn each table, enhancing the romantic mood.

The menu showcases vintage Mediterranean cuisine such as hummus and baba ganoush; daily specials feature fresh local fish and produce. Every dish is cooked to perfection, with plenty of Greek flair. The service is friendly and attentive; you will be thoroughly satisfied by the time you've finished dessert (the Russian cream is outstanding). Of course, due to the café's popularity you might have to wait for a table, but the wait is always worthwhile. **113 First Street; (360) 221-3090; inexpensive to moderate; call for seasonal hours.**

❤❤ **LANGLEY TEA ROOM, Langley** Hidden away on a side street in the heart of downtown Langley, this picturesque, one-room teahouse is filled with the aroma of freshly brewed teas. Three linen-draped tables fit perfectly in the airy, terra-cotta-tiled room, where knickknacks and whole-leaf teas are arranged on shelves. Fresh gingerbread is the highlight of the After School Tea, while the Afternoon Tea includes an assortment of finger sandwiches and delectable desserts. Crumpets with marmalade are the perfect accompaniment to a small pot of your favorite tea, brewed fresh to order. **112 1/2 Anthes Avenue; (360) 221-6292; inexpensive; afternoon tea Thursday–Tuesday.**

❧❧ **LANGLEY VILLAGE BAKERY, Langley** Magenta awnings mark the entrance to this modest bakery, tucked into a small array of specialty shops. In any other part of the world it would not be worth pointing out, but in the town of Langley it deserves a mention for its luscious fresh pastries, decadent homemade truffles, and piping hot espressos. If you want a quiet morning repast or have an afternoon sweet craving that needs attending to, this is the best location in town. **221 Second Street; (360) 221-3525; inexpensive; no credit cards; open daily.**

❧❧❧ **TRATTORIA GIUSEPPE ITALIAN RESTAURANT BAR AND GRILL, Langley** Harbored in a shopping plaza just off Whidbey Island's main highway (an unlikely spot for romance), Giuseppe's is well known throughout the island for its authentic Italian cuisine and heartwarming ambience. Cathedral ceilings with large skylights lend an open, cheerful feeling to the restaurant's three dining rooms. Chandeliers cast soft light on the yellow- and peach-colored stucco walls, and the snugly arranged tables (a little too snug for kissing comfort) are draped with yellow linens. Dried flowers, candles, pottery, and other knickknacks warm up the otherwise plain rooms. Noise from the open kitchen is a distraction, but the chef's tasty Italian cuisine rarely disappoints. Choices are difficult: Should you order the superbly fresh antipasto or the homemade minestrone, the wild mushroom ravioli with sun-dried tomatoes or the linguine with mussels, clams, and squid? The menu offers something for everyone, from grilled vegetable antipasti and fresh soups to hearty entrées such as roasted pork loin in prosciutto, and grilled New York steak. For dessert, tiramisu is a definite must, but so are the cannelloni: pastry shells filled with ricotta, chocolate shavings, and almonds. **4141 East State Route 525; (360) 341-3454; moderate to expensive; lunch Monday–Friday, dinner daily.**

Freeland

Hotel/Bed and Breakfast Kissing

❧❧❧❧ **CLIFF HOUSE, Freeland** Situated atop a towering bluff overlooking Admiralty Inlet and surrounded by forest, Cliff House is truly unparalleled in both location and design. It's easy to see why this contemporary timber home has won nine architectural awards. Floor-to-ceiling, wall-to-wall windows frame amazing water and forest views, which can also be enjoyed outside from the hot tub or hammock, depending on your mood. High open ceilings with wooden beams impart a sense of spacious ease, while the natural touch of stone floors, wood-paneled walls, and earth tones throughout is counterpointed by international antiques and modern furnishings. A 30-foot glass-enclosed atrium in the center of the house brings the elements safely inside for your observation. The house holds two upstairs bedrooms, several different sitting areas, a sunken living room with a couch and fireplace, and a full gourmet kitchen. To ensure total privacy, an abundant continental breakfast is stocked in the fridge before guests arrive.

Despite the fact that there are no interior doors (except on the bathrooms), every room maintains an abundance of privacy: The house simply flows effortlessly from one level to the next. We prefer the larger bedroom loft, featuring a sumptuous king-size feather bed covered with a down comforter and boutique pillows; a small Jacuzzi tub awaits in the adjoining bathroom. An extensive video and CD collection is also provided for your enjoyment. Though the price tag may seem steep, time spent here is well worth the splurge. Simply put, Cliff House is an island utopia built for two. **727 Windmill Drive; (360) 331-1566; www.whidbey.com/cliffhouse; unbelievably expensive; no credit cards; minimum-stay requirement.**

❀❀❀ **SEACLIFF COTTAGE, Freeland** Located a short distance from **CLIFF HOUSE** (see above), on the same bluff with the same premium view, Seacliff proves that the owners of these homes have a rare talent for creating remarkable places where you and your special someone can retreat from the world. Small and rustic, this cozy gingerbread cottage has wood-paneled walls, plush furnishings, a TV/VCR, and an impressive selection of movies. A wood-burning stove keeps the chill away, and the petite kitchen, appointed with weathered wood cabinetry, is stocked with continental breakfast delicacies each day. You won't want to leave the private deck, with its views of boat traffic navigating up and down Puget Sound. Enjoy a quiet meal for two at the picnic table, or pass the afternoon swinging serenely in a hammock. At night, retreat to the bedroom, where a comfy queen-size bed, cushioned window seat overlooking the water, and charming pink-and-yellow-striped wallpaper distinguish this blissful haven for two. Just before dusk, be sure to climb up to the newly built tree house—a perfect vantage point for watching the sun make its nightly descent—and make a toast to your loved one beneath the starlit sky. **727 Windmill Drive; (360) 331-1566; www.whidbey.com/cliffhouse; moderate; no credit cards; minimum-stay requirement seasonally.**

Greenbank

As you head north on Whidbey Island, past the town of Langley, you'll hardly notice when you've come to the town of Greenbank. More a scattering of residential homes than an actual town, Greenbank harbors one of our favorite places to kiss (see Hotel/Bed and Breakfast Kissing). While you're in the vicinity, we also recommend stopping by **MEERKERK RHODODENDRON GARDENS** (Meerkerk Lane; 360-678-1912; www.whidbey.net/meerkerk/gar

dens.html; $2 per person). This 43-acre wooded preserve is a testing site for different varieties of rhododendrons. Gardening buffs can gain valuable knowledge and even buy the rhododendrons in bloom. Those with kissing in mind can simply enjoy the quiet natural scenery while walking hand in hand.

Hotel/Bed and Breakfast Kissing

❤❤❤ **GUEST HOUSE LOG COTTAGES, Greenbank** Twenty-five acres of gorgeous meadow and forest enfold the five cabins, private suite, and luxurious log mansion that comprise this property. Straight out of a fairy tale, the authentic log cabins were designed with privacy in mind. Each is surrounded by shady trees and decorated with old-fashioned country touches. Patchwork quilts adorn the sumptuous feather beds, and the knotty pine walls and oak furniture are endearingly rustic. Petite kitchens, Franklin fireplaces, TV/VCRs, and private spa tubs in some of the cabins supply an abundance of charm and romantic potential. A new private suite has been added to the log cabin at the south end of the wildlife pond. Its French doors open onto a private deck that takes full advantage of the serene view, while inside a king-size bed draped with deluxe linens is a decidedly romantic touch.

Each cabin is stocked with a generous supply of fresh breakfast items, including eggs from the owners' chickens, fresh pastries, and ready-to-bake quiches. If you're able to pry yourselves out of bed, we encourage you to take the opportunity to explore the property's forested acreage or make use of the outdoor hot tub, heated swimming pool, and exercise room (available for all guests).

Serious romantics with a generous budget should sequester themselves in the spacious log mansion, custom designed for lovers and harbored at the edge of a duck pond. Cathedral ceilings soar above the rustic but elegant interior, where a fire crackles in an immense rock fireplace and floor-to-ceiling windows offer views of the pond. Upstairs, an enormous king-size bed covered with luscious white linens takes up most of the loft bedroom, which also has views of the pond. A full kitchen, TV/VCR, stereo, and *two* Jacuzzi tubs are additional amenities. We enjoyed examining the cabin's overflowing collection of fascinating antiques and relics, although the bear rugs and mounted deer head bring almost too much authenticity to the lodge-like atmosphere. Otherwise, the capacious home provides all the ingredients necessary for ultimate togetherness. **24371 State Route 525; (360) 678-3115; www.whidbey. net/logcottages; expensive to unbelievably expensive; minimum-stay requirement on weekends.**

Coupeville

"Why is *this* romantic?" you might ask yourselves, as we did on our way down Coupeville's commercial Main Street. You haven't gone far enough. Sitting directly on the water, the tiny one-street town of Coupeville is as picturesque and old-fashioned as they come. Browse the turn-of-the-century, harbor-style storefronts for antiques and trinkets, or stop for homemade ice cream in one of several sweet shops (sure to inspire kisses).

Hotel/Bed and Breakfast Kissing

☙❦ **ANCHORAGE INN, Coupeville** Built to look like a 100-year-old Victorian home, this rambling white inn is located near downtown Coupeville. Sporting a wraparound veranda decorated with white wicker furniture and potted plants, the exterior has a friendly and inviting feel. Inside, the six guest rooms feature quaint pastel floral wallpapers, lace curtains, wicker accents, an awkward mixture of antiques and imitations, and disappointingly standard motel-style bathrooms. Perhaps the best amenities are the water and mountain views from four of the rooms. In the morning a full gourmet breakfast is served downstairs in the handsome dining room. **807 North Main Street; (360) 678-5581; www.whidbey.net/~anchorag; inexpensive; closed mid-December–mid-January.**

☙❦ **COLONEL CROCKETT FARM BED AND BREAKFAST, Coupeville** Colonel Crockett Farm's claim to fame is that it was home to Danny DeVito, Michael Douglas, and Kathleen Turner for several weeks during the filming of *War of the Roses*. In spite of its popularity with celebrities, however, this Victorian bed and breakfast is anything but pretentious. Surrounded by two acres of beautifully tended grounds, the turn-of-the-century farmhouse hugs the edge of Admiralty Bay, overlooking acres of lush meadows that sweep down to the edge of the water. Inside, the inn features antiquated colors, old-fashioned decorations, and a variety of family photographs and other personal touches. Though it may be too old-fashioned for some tastes, the five guest rooms here offer simple comforts for those seeking refuge from the fast-paced life of the real world.

A series of small two-person tables that overlook the garden fill the small, countrified dining room. Luscious breakfasts feature sumptuous egg dishes, hot meat, an abundance of fruit, and heavenly fresh breads and muffins. **1012 South Fort Casey Road; (360) 678-3711; www.members.aol.com/crocket bnb; inexpensive; minimum-stay requirement.**

Romantic Note: A Christian prayer precedes breakfast.

Bainbridge Island

Bainbridge Island is accessible via car on Highway 305 from the Poulsbo area, or via ferry from Pier 52 in downtown Seattle. For ferry schedules and information, call Washington State Ferries (206-464-6400, 800-843-3779).

Though Seattleites commonly utilize Bainbridge Island as a gateway to the Olympic Peninsula, it possesses romantic interest of its own. Peruse the storefronts in tiny Winslow, and, if you're not in a particular hurry to get to the peninsula, stop at one of Bainbridge's several lip-worthy locations.

Romantic Warning: Because hordes of tourists use the Bainbridge Island ferry in the summertime and on most weekends during the rest of the year, be prepared to contend with horrendous ferry traffic and interminable delays. You can avoid much of the hassle if you leave your car behind; downtown Winslow is within easy walking distance of the ferry terminal.

Hotel/Bed and Breakfast Kissing

❤❦ **THE BEACH COTTAGE, Bainbridge Island** Picture windows in this private beachfront cottage look out to a marina full of sailboats and houseboats bobbing on the waves. Guests can lounge in the hot tub on the cottage's private outdoor deck while watching seagulls and ferryboats float by. In the backyard, large trees shade footpaths that meander past other cottages, a cluttered greenhouse, outdoor decks with water views, and a rushing, rocky waterfall.

Exceedingly timeworn, the small cottage's dated interior is nevertheless cozy and comfortable. Low ceilings and narrow hallways conspire to make you feel as if you're on a boat. A tiny bedroom overlooks the water and has a wonderfully comfortable bed covered with a fluffy white duvet. A breakfast of fruit and coffee, plus a bottle of complimentary wine for later, are stocked in the complete old-fashioned kitchen, and a fireplace warms the living room, where you'll also find a TV/VCR. This isn't the lap of luxury by any means, but simple comforts and water views aren't always this affordable. **5831 Ward Avenue Northeast; (206) 842-6081; moderate; no credit cards; minimum-stay requirement on weekends.**

❤❤ **BOMBAY HOUSE BED AND BREAKFAST, Bainbridge Island** A historic island landmark, the Bombay House is simply stunning. Perched on a grassy knoll, the immense gabled Victorian is surrounded by immaculately groomed lawns, trees, and flowering gardens. Continuing in the same gracious fashion, the common area inside features white oak floors, an enormous open brick hearth, eclectic antiques, and a working loom.

Sweet-smelling breakfast aromas scent the air, precursors of the award-winning baked dishes the innkeeper is known for. Savor such delectables as fresh fruit and nut breads, coffee cakes, bread pudding, pastries, homemade cereals, baked apples, and the specialty of the house—molded "Orange Butter." (Many of these recipes are featured in the innkeeper's published cookbooks.) This bountiful feast is served in a large country kitchen that looks out onto a deck with views of the water through tall leafy trees.

The five guest rooms are furnished with a mixture of modern and Victorian furnishings and knickknacks; only three of the five have private baths. Though privacy in the Red Room is diminished because of its detached private bath located down the hall, it is worth mentioning for its impressive collection of vintage antiques and richly colored red walls. Daylight pours into the King Room, where lovely antiques, a tin soaking tub, and hardwood floors create an elegant turn-of-the-century ambience. A beautiful antique queen-size bed is the romantic draw in the Captain's Suite, though the tub, shower, and toilet tucked in different closets are peculiar touches. Both the Morning Room and Crow's Nest are snug and countrified, but the shared bath is a romantic distraction. **8490 Beck Road Northeast; (206) 842-3926, (800) 598-3926; www.travelassist.com/reg/wa108s.html; inexpensive to moderate; recommended wedding site.**

❤❤ **ROCKAWAY BEACH GUEST HOUSE, Bainbridge Island** Rockaway Beach is literally just steps from the front door of this beautiful turn-of-the-century log home. Large driftwood logs separate the front lawn from the rocky beach, where guests can shed their shoes and explore tide pools or watch for blue herons and bald eagles. Seattle's twinkling cityscape can be seen on the horizon across the sound, backdropped by Mount Rainier and the Cascades. On chilly days, a fire crackles in the river-rock fireplace of the comfortable common area, an inviting place to curl up and enjoy the view.

Both guest rooms are simple but pleasant. Couples who demand complete privacy will be deterred by the detached bath of the smaller, pink-hued guest room, but the larger master suite is worth consideration. The mint green carpet in this unit seems out of place in a historic home, but is soon forgotten in favor of the view. A full wall of windows frames the beach, water, mountains, and city skyline, while a telescope enables you to get a bird's-eye glimpse of local wildlife. A colorful quilt and plump down duvet cover the comfy king-size bed, and the large soaking tub in the oversize bathroom is placed next to more windows with water views.

Wake to a creative and healthy full breakfast that features an abundance of fresh fruit, savory pastries, and hot egg dishes. Your morning meal is served either at one large table in the dining room or beneath shaded umbrellas on the beach in warmer weather. **5032 Rockaway Beach Road; (206) 780-9427; moderate to expensive.**

Restaurant Kissing

❤❤❤ **THE FOUR SWALLOWS RESTAURANT, Bainbridge Island** This picturesque 1889 yellow farmhouse is wonderfully romantic, which explains the weekend crowds. Elegantly appointed with turn-of-the-century antiques, lace curtains, dried flower arrangements, and leaded glass windows, the house's original living quarters now serve as a semi-casual dining room and adjacent antique store. Two-person booths fill the dining room, so you won't have difficulty finding a cozy spot where you can savor each other's company and sample scrumptious fresh Northwest cuisine. The seafood, meat, pizza, and pasta entrées are hearty and delicious, including spaghettini and baby spinach, seasoned with extra virgin olive oil, shaved garlic, basil, pine nuts, and lemon zest. Desserts change daily but are always tantalizing. **481 Madison Avenue; (206) 842-3397; inexpensive to moderate; dinner Tuesday–Saturday.**

❦❦ **SAWATDY THAI CUISINE, Bainbridge Island** Owned and operated by a local family that has lived on the island for years, Sawatdy serves up some of the best Thai cuisine in the region. Reservations are an absolute must at this popular restaurant, which always seems to have a line of people spilling out the door. Although Sawatdy's location next to a convenience store in a shopping complex is far from romantic, the one-room restaurant is painted deep green inside and boasts a wall of mirrors embellished with statues and art pieces from Thailand. White tablecloths embroidered with Thai designs cover the closely arranged tables and booths, and a large pagoda encloses several floor-level booths in the back. Although the restaurant is often too crowded for serious romancing, the soft track lighting sets a gentle, affectionate tone, and the service and superb food never disappoint. Choosing from the enormous menu can be a challenge, but the gracious wait staff can help you select just the right dish. Selections include traditional Phad Thai; deep-fried tofu topped with the chef's special chile-peanut sauce, served on a bed of sautéed fresh spinach; Asian eggplant sautéed with fresh mushrooms, bell peppers, Thai basil, and chile garlic sauce; and hot and sour soup made with beef or tofu, lemongrass, roasted-chile paste, and exotic spices. **8770 Fletcher Bay Road; (206) 780-2429; moderate; reservations recommended; lunch Tuesday–Friday, dinner Tuesday–Sunday.**

Outdoor Kissing

❦❦❦❦ **THE BLOEDEL RESERVE, Bainbridge Island** Bloedel Reserve embraces more than 150 acres of meticulously maintained gardens, so you're sure to find a peaceful haven for an afternoon interlude. The reserve is a place where the artistic splendor of sculpted plants brings pleasure to the senses. Wander through the bird sanctuary, verdant woods, and Japanese gardens; pause at the reflecting pool; or admire the dense moss garden. All of it is divine. As the brochure for the Bloedel Reserve plainly states, "Man's first recorded home was a garden, no sooner known than lost—and we've been trying to return ever since." This might not be Eden, but it is the next best thing. **7571 Northeast Dolphin Drive; (206) 842-7631; $6 entrance fee; reservations required; open Wednesday–Sunday by reservation only.** *From Seattle, take the Winslow ferry to Bainbridge Island and follow State Route 305 six miles to the north end of the island. Turn right onto Agatewood Road, which becomes Northeast Dolphin Drive. This road leads to the estate. Call for reservations; access is limited to a specific number of people each day.*

Vashon Island

Vashon Island is accessible via ferry, from West Seattle (at the Fauntleroy ferry dock) or Southworth to the island's north end, or from Tacoma (at Point Defiance) to the island's south end. For information on schedules and directions, call Washington State Ferries (206-464-6400, 800-843-3779). The trip takes less than 30 minutes, so hurry to the bow of the boat and stand watch on the deck to fully enjoy the scenic crossing.

In spite of the fact that Vashon Island is a quick escape from the city, it remains relatively quiet and undeveloped, with an abundance of rural and residential countryside. Fortunately, it has a wide assortment of captivating places to stay, because you'll want to come back over and over again to explore everything this rustic island has to offer.

Hotel/Bed and Breakfast Kissing

❤❤❤ ARTIST'S STUDIO LOFT BED AND BREAKFAST, Vashon Island
Surrounded by five acres of beautifully landscaped gardens, ponds, footpaths, and lush green pastures, the second-story Aerial Cottage Loft truly feels like an artist's studio. Stained glass windows (the artist's handiwork), modern art, a wood-burning fireplace, ceiling fans, and brightly colored beams add personality to the imaginatively furnished room. Oriental rugs lend color to the parquet floors, and lengths of fabric accent a four-poster canopy bed covered with lush linens. A small kitchen, private bath, TV/VCR, and large deck are exclusively yours, and plush robes are provided if you choose to use the sizable outdoor hot tub snuggled into a gazebo (it's also available to other guests). A complimentary breakfast is served directly to your doorstep, and mountain bikes are available for your use. All of this for an exceptionally reasonable price!

Downstairs, the small Ivy Room has just as much character, although it's quite different in nature. Mexican saltillo tiles on the floors and peach-colored sponge-painted walls give this room a Southwestern flavor; dried flower wreaths, local artwork, and contemporary linens are additional affectionate touches.

Recent updates have increased the romantic allure of the private Master Suite, situated above the owner's home. Pretty floral linens and piles of pillows adorn the queen-size bed, and the bright, airy bathroom has the convenience of double sinks. This suite also has a TV/VCR. A generous continental breakfast of freshly baked scones or muffins, creamy fruit compote, cereals, coffee, tea, and juice is served in the owner's cozy kitchen to guests staying in the Ivy Room and Master Suite. **16529 91st Avenue Southwest; (206) 463-2583; www.asl-bnb.com; inexpensive to moderate; minimum-stay requirement on holidays and weekends seasonally.**

❤❤❤ BETTY MACDONALD FARM GUEST COTTAGE, Vashon Island Betty MacDonald was a best-selling children's author renowned for her beloved *Mrs. Piggle Wiggle* books, so it's no wonder her enchanting guest cottages are so much like those found in storybooks. Couples in the mood for a romantic adventure will best appreciate this property's absolute uniqueness. A creaking staircase climbs past empty rooms with open rafters to an unusual but enticing suite situated on the top floor of an old barn. Oriental rugs and an eclectic array of antiques and modern appointments clutter the spacious suite, which features knotty pine walls, fresh flowers from the surrounding gardens, and a deck that juts out over the hillside to survey magnificent views of the trees and water. Near the back of the suite you'll find a wooden four-poster bed covered with a thick down comforter and plenty of pillows. Other amenities include a TV/VCR, CD player, and a rustic but functional private bathroom. On cold winter days, the innkeeper has a fire burning in the woodstove when guests arrive. Year-round, the full kitchen is stocked with delicious breakfast items that can be enjoyed privately at your leisure.

A second option, an all-cedar cottage, is also available for guests, offering somewhat less rustic ambience and more space. A large woodstove cranks out heat in the country-style, two-bedroom cabin. In the master bedroom, a fluffy down comforter covers a queen-size bed that faces majestic views of the water, trees, and mountains. A TV/VCR and well-stocked full kitchen are exclusively yours for the duration of your stay. On spring mornings, the roomy outdoor deck enfolded by country quiet is an ideal spot to sip your morning coffee and enjoy the spectacular setting. This unit can also be rented for weeks—and even months—at a time.

Be sure you save time to explore the farm's six wooded acres, complete with flower and herb gardens, a greenhouse, and paths that lead to the beach below. Trail bikes are available and can be used to explore Vashon's inviting countryside and beaches. A stay here is sure to inspire a few stories of your own. **12000 99th Avenue Southwest; (206) 567-4227; moderate.**

❀❀❀❀ **HARBOR INN BED AND BREAKFAST, Vashon Island** Looking out of place in a quiet waterfront neighborhood on Vashon Island, this English Tudor–style bed and breakfast is a refined change of pace. Dark woodwork, towering windows, and fine antiques fill the innkeepers' home with a handsome allure. Admiring the sensational views of Quartermaster Harbor from this vantage point is heart-stirring, to say the least. No matter which of the three guest rooms you choose, it is possible to admire each morning's sunrise right from your pillow. Be sure to nudge your significant other awake to savor the magic together.

The largest guest room here is breathtaking. A king-size four-poster bed sits on lush, deep green carpet, a gas-log fireplace provides warmth, and bay windows front an entire wall. The white-tiled bathroom with pink accents continues in the same spirit of seduction: Bay windows and mirrors surround a deep two-person Jacuzzi tub where you can scrub each other's back by candlelight. Though the remaining two guest rooms are somewhat smaller and do not have Jacuzzi tubs, they are equally stylish and comfortable, with the added bonus of being considerably less expensive.

In the morning, allow the skillfully prepared omelets, French toast, pancakes, fresh fruit, juice, coffee, tea, and other delicious surprises to settle; then borrow mountain bikes supplied by the innkeepers to explore miles of enchanting forest trails in nearby **BURTON ACRES PARK**. It is seemingly undiscovered, so you may have the whole area to yourselves. **9118 Southwest Harbor Drive; (206) 463-6794; moderate to expensive.**

❀❀ **MANZANITA HOUSE, Vashon Island** If privacy is at the top of your priority list, you can't do much better than Manzanita House. Shaded by tall evergreens, this contemporary cedar and glass rental home can be exclusively yours for a shockingly reasonable price. Though it lacks amenities like a VCR or hot tub, the architecturally impressive house compensates with abundant space and serene quiet. Large picture windows let in ample natural light and showcase glimpses of the nearby water peeking through the trees. Don't expect any frills: The modern appointments are attractive but exceedingly sparse and utilitarian. Guests can make use of a fully equipped gourmet kitchen (provisions are your responsibility), a spacious dining room, and three different bedrooms and bathrooms. "Leave it as you found it" is standard operating procedure here, which means guests are expected to make their own beds with the linens provided and clean up after themselves before departure. Not your typical lazy vacation, but with this much space and privacy at such reasonable rates, who minds? **10402 Southwest 268th; (206) 633-4230; moderate; no credit cards.**

Romantic Note: Much to our disappointment, the lot next door has recently been developed, which somewhat reduces the sense of isolation in this otherwise rural wooded area.

❀❀❀ **MIMI'S COTTAGE, Vashon Island** Walking into Mimi's small country-style cottage is like walking right into a copy of *Country Living* magazine. Nestled on a wooded residential hillside, the self-contained private bungalow has distant water views and, when the weather is clear, magnificent vistas of Mount Rainier. Knotty pine floors and exquisite woodwork add rustic charm to the cabin's lovely interior, which is accented with antiques, a mismatched assortment of Oriental rugs, a woodstove, and a hand-sewn patchwork quilt draped over the bed.

A cozy lower-level unit aptly dubbed "The Snug" has recently been added. Just large enough for a bed and a small sitting area, this charming hideaway is adorned with soft yellow walls and warm wood accents. A plump yellow-and-blue down comforter covers the inviting bed, and stained glass windows open to an adjacent flower-scented courtyard. The beautifully tiled bathroom features a glass-enclosed shower with room for two. Guests in each suite are greeted with a large bowl of fresh fruit and chilled bottled water; both units also have TV/VCRs.

The innkeeper (who lives right next door) serves a full gourmet breakfast complete with fruit, cereals, and delightful egg dishes in her pleasant dining room with water views. Or, if you'd rather, the innkeeper will deliver a tray to your door, which you can serve to your sweetheart in bed. **7923 Southwest Hawthorne Lane; (206) 567-4383; inexpensive to moderate; minimum-stay requirement.**

❤❤❤ **OLD MILL COTTAGE, Vashon Island** Slow down your frantic urban pace and revitalize your senses with the sights and sounds of nature at picturesque Old Mill Cottage, where gentle trails wind through ten acres of quiet woods. A hammock sways invitingly between two trees, urging you to stop in your tracks completely. Secluded and self-sufficient, the yellow Cape Cod–style cottage faces the owner's home across a vast expanse of lawn. Tranquillity and seclusion are the focus here. Colorful rugs are scattered across hardwood floors in the cottage's mismatched interior decor, while puzzles, a TV/VCR, CD player, and an eclectic assortment of books provide sufficient entertainment on rainy days. Upstairs, a stark sleeping loft with a slanted ceiling holds a four-poster wooden bed covered with blue-and-white linens and a warm down comforter. The most luxurious spot in the house is the spacious tiled bathroom, where you'll find a large sunken Jacuzzi tub that overlooks a shady grove of trees.

You certainly won't go hungry here—the kitchenette is stocked with fresh fruit, gourmet coffee, baked goods, and juice. Rain gear and bikes are available for guests' use, and the innkeeper will be happy to guide you to some of the best nature trails on the island. **24603 Old Mill Road Southwest; (206) 463-1670; moderate; minimum-stay requirement.**

❤❤ **SEA LOTUS DAY SPA BED AND BREAKFAST, Vashon Island** Guests here don't have to bother bringing their car over from the mainland; Sea Lotus is a mere five-minute walk from the Vashon ferry terminal at the north end of the island. (This is a tremendous advantage and a time saver on busy summer weekends.) This blue-and-white country home serves as both a day spa and a one-unit bed and breakfast. Seagulls and eagles soar overhead, and waves lap at the front yard of the small property. Overgrown with moss, the weathered cabin's exterior is somewhat rundown, contrasting with the surprisingly pretty interior. Swaths of fabric and lush down linens adorn the bed, French country antiques lend quaintness, and a beautifully set two-person table is arranged beside a window that frames views of the waves crashing onto the beach. A propane stove and plush robes ensure warmth on even the coldest of nights and a small kitchenette stocked with freshly baked scones and muffins will ward off hunger.

The beach is at your fingertips, but when the tide is high you can still enjoy the waterfront setting from cozy Adirondack chairs on the spacious sundeck. Guests are encouraged to take advantage of the spa next door (for an additional fee), which offers everything from throat treatments and European facials to Swedish and deep massage. The price is hard to beat, and the location couldn't be more convenient. **10823 Vashon Highway Southwest; (206) 567-5565; www.mistyisle.com/sea-lotus.htm; inexpensive.**

Restaurant Kissing

♥♥ **EXPRESS CUISINE, Vashon Island** Nestled among storefronts on the main thoroughfare in Vashon's town center, this small dining room holds several large communal tables set adjacent to the lively open kitchen where the expert chef is hard at work. Diners order at the cash register, then sit and chat while they wait for their express orders. So, what's the draw? You won't find better food on the island, from freshly baked breads, garden-fresh salads, and perfectly seasoned pasta, chicken, and seafood dishes to vegetarian Phad Thai and creamy tiramisu. The communal seating arrangement prohibits amorous encounters, but couples with discriminating palates will be impassioned by the food alone. Your best bet for romance is a to-go order, which can be enjoyed at the beach or by candlelight in the privacy of your own room. **17629 Vashon Highway; (206) 463-2125; moderate; no credit cards; dinner Wednesday–Saturday.**

♥♥ **SOUND FOOD RESTAURANT AND BAKERY, Vashon Island** What a perfect name for this casual gourmet eatery that serves up freshly baked pastries and hearty island fare seven days a week. Large windows look out to the serene backyard garden, where you may catch a glimpse of a colorful resident rooster. The garden views brighten the rustic but cozy wood-accented dining room, creating a soothing countrified ambience with plenty of kissing appeal. Although the setting is somewhat casual, the semiprivate booths and corner window tables are ideal spots to sit close and soak up Vashon's rural scenery.

Service here is casual and notoriously slow, especially on weekend mornings. If you have a ferry to catch, your best bet is to get a pastry to go. If you're not on a schedule, you're guaranteed plenty of time to savor the subtleties of your meal, indulge in a second helping of fresh bread, and treat yourselves to a delicious homemade dessert. The warm apple pie, decadent brownies, thick cookies, and tasty cinnamon rolls are done to perfection. **20312 Vashon Highway Southwest; (206) 463-3565; inexpensive to moderate; breakfast and dinner daily, lunch Monday–Saturday.**

Federal Way

We know what you're thinking: Coming to the Seattle area and staying in Federal Way is like visiting Manhattan and staying in Queens. How could we possibly have found any romantic destinations in this less-than-desirable suburb? Surprisingly, we have. And they're well worth a visit.

Hotel/Bed and Breakfast Kissing

❤❤❤❤ PALISADES BED AND BREAKFAST, Federal Way Elegance and

luxury accent every room of this wood-shingled home, located in the attractive Dash Point neighborhood and surrounded by myriad trees and views of Puget Sound and the Olympic Mountains. Beautiful contemporary furnishings grace the formal living room, where the honey-colored walls, cathedral ceiling, and tall arched windows create an exquisite spot for lounging in front of the wood-burning fireplace. From the pretty, airy parlor, step through French doors to the veranda, where views of the water through lofty trees are awe inspiring. Outside, a private gazebo looks out to the magnificent grounds and a sandy beach beckons to be explored.

Privacy and opulence await guests in the only suite in the house, located on the second floor. Soft cream carpeting blankets the entire space, which includes a study with a small library and writing desk, a large bathroom with an emerald green marble Jacuzzi tub and a double-headed shower, and a sumptuous bedroom equipped with a gas fireplace and wonderful views. The queen-size canopy bed is adorned with lush beige and cream linens and a fluffy down comforter; a floral couch rests beneath a hand-painted domed ceiling, creating a very cozy sitting area; and an antique armoire hides the TV/VCR. Fresh flowers and two fluffy robes await beside the bed.

In the morning, a full breakfast (for just the two of you) is served in the terra-cotta-tiled breakfast room at a lovely wood table set beside a warm stone fireplace. You can look forward to breakfast goodies such as baked Brie in puff pastry with honey walnut sauce, and that's just the appetizer. Your meal may also include vanilla granola, blueberry scones, poached pears in raspberry sauce, fresh fruit juice, and espresso. **5162 Southwest 311th Place; (253) 927-1904, (888) 838-4376; www.bbonline.com/wa/palisades; expensive to very expensive; recommended wedding site.**

Restaurant Kissing

❤❤ THE DASHPOINT LOBSTER SHOP, Federal Way Located in what

used to be a small neighborhood post office, this small, wood-shingled restaurant is an appetizing spot to enjoy fresh, local seafood. Beige vinyl booths and small tables, each adorned with white linens and a single votive candle, crowd the casual interior. Each table affords views of the water and the nightly sunset. A skilled staff prepares consistently delicious dishes. Start your meal with lobster bisque or the sampler platter, which includes Dungeness crab dip, poached prawns, curried calamari, and jalapeño peppers with three different dipping sauces. We highly recommend the pan-fried oysters lightly breaded in panko bread crumbs; the seafood fettuccine with clams, mussels, prawns, and scallops tossed in a garlic-cream sauce; and the Australian rock lobster tails, oven roasted with butter. **6912 Soundview Drive Northeast; (253) 927-1513; expensive; dinner daily.**

Tacoma

Once known only for the "Tacoma aroma" (generated by the local pulp mills), this city has blossomed into a desirable place to stop on your way up or down the I-5 corridor. Tacoma offers a surprising number of attractions, including the **TACOMA ACTORS GUILD** and the **PANTAGES THEATER,** the **TACOMA ART MUSEUM,** the **WASHINGTON STATE HISTORY MUSEUM, POINT DEFIANCE ZOO AND AQUARIUM,** and a number of charming waterfront areas and gracious neighborhoods. Tacoma also boasts several heartwarming, impressive accommodations and choice restaurants conducive to romantic interludes.

Tacoma is linked to the Kitsap Peninsula by the second Tacoma Narrows Bridge. (The first one, better known as "Galloping Gertie," collapsed in 1940.) Bordered by Commencement Bay, Tacoma enjoys awesome ringside views of Mount Rainier.

Romantic Suggestion: Travel west over the aforementioned bridge to the picturesque town of **GIG HARBOR,** where boutiques, views, and leisurely strolls are the reason to visit.

Hotel/Bed and Breakfast Kissing

❤❤❤ **CHINABERRY HILL, Tacoma** Another world awaits inside this proud 1889 Victorian, sitting on a flowering hillside in a bustling residential area. Playful eccentricities and cluttered, rustic touches add intrigue to the home's old-world luxury and elegance. The oak- and fir-lined main foyer and breakfast room are peppered with historical artifacts and original art pieces, and the hardwood floors are blanketed with antique Oriental rugs. Rich red velvet curtains (remnants from the old Pantages Theater) drape the entrance to the comfortable guest parlor, which features a sizable fireplace, stunning antiques, and an expansive literary collection.

Wind your way up the open oak staircase to three of the five guest rooms, each appointed with earth-toned color schemes, wonderfully restored antiques, and sumptuous custom-designed Victorian Renaissance linens festooned with velvet, fringe, and tapestry accents. Fluffy robes and en suite bathrooms assure pampered privacy. Tall ceilings soar above a queen-size bed draped with beige, cream, and gold linens in the Pantages Suite. On clear days, the large windows in this suite offer distant views of Commencement Bay, Brown's Point, and the islands beyond. In the beautifully tiled bathroom, you'll find a sitting area complete with an antique desk, an impressive antique armoire, and our favorite feature: an enormous, gold-accented Jacuzzi tub tucked in the corner. The Wild Rose is equally stunning, with a queen-size four-poster rice bed set in the center of the room, and a gas fireplace to warm your toes on cold nights. A large Jacuzzi tub and stall shower are set in a pretty tiled bathroom accessible through sexy purple velvet curtains. Large picture windows in this room showcase leafy treetops and peekaboo glimpses of the water and Mount Rainier.

The Garden Suite, the smallest of the three upstairs rooms, is also lovely, with a cream painted floor, a pretty private bathroom, and tall ceilings. The only disappointment is that traffic noise from the busy street below is audible in all upstairs guest rooms. Fortunately, the luxurious surroundings will keep you focused on matters of the heart.

Located just behind the main house, the Carriage Suite and the Hayloft afford the most privacy. Housed on the lower level of what was originally the estate's carriage barn and stable, the Carriage Suite feels both elegant and cabin-like, with its four walls of dark wood wainscoting. Historic memorabilia, such as an original carriage door, a kerosene pump, a 200-year-old hand-carved trunk, and a hay chute that has been turned into a shower for two, add interest to this cozy, upscale retreat. In the center of the room sits a dramatic eight-foot curved iron queen-size bed, with ribbons and silk roses entwined in the canopy. A convenient kitchenette is set just off the bedroom, and a Jacuzzi tub for two is a decisively romantic bonus. Upstairs, the Hayloft is awash in white and beige and holds a quaint sitting area, a bedroom with an antique French queen-size cane bed, and a bathroom with an antique claw-foot tub, shower, and pedestal sink.

Your stay at Chinaberry Hill is complete only after you've savored the multicourse country breakfast, which can be served at separate tables in the cheery breakfast room or delivered directly to your room. Chinaberry Hill is more than just a place to stay—it's an experience. **302 Tacoma Avenue North; (253) 272-1282; www.wa.net/chinaberry; inexpensive to expensive; minimum-stay requirement on weekends seasonally.**

COMMENCEMENT BAY BED AND BREAKFAST, Tacoma

Set in a quiet residential neighborhood on a gentle hilltop that overlooks Commencement Bay and stunning evening sunsets, this stately white Colonial home offers solace to couples in search of rest and relaxation. A mixture of contemporary and antique furnishings fills the comfortable interior, which is further enhanced by dramatic water views. Three traditional guest rooms are available on the second floor, each with a private bath and comfy floral linens. Myrtle's Room boasts the most impressive views of Puget Sound, Mount Rainier, and Mount Baker, in addition to a wooden four-poster queen-size bed covered with a floral comforter. Jessie's Room, our second favorite, also has a lovely water view and a queen-size bed covered with a handcrafted patchwork quilt. Laurie's Room has warm yellow walls, a white iron-and-brass bed, and partial views of the garden and bay. All rooms feature TV/VCRs, and guests can choose from a large selection of romantic videos.

After you've lounged in front of the fire in the common area or had your daily workout in the small exercise room (mountain bikes are also available), you'll want to relax in the semiprivate outdoor hot tub. In the morning, awake to the sound of soft harp music that accompanies a multicourse gourmet breakfast of custom-blended orange juice, homemade pastries, and a variety of egg dishes or baked main courses served in the dining room at one long table. **3312 North Union Avenue; (253) 752-8175; www.bestinns.net/usa/wa/cb.html; inexpensive to moderate; minimum-stay requirement on weekends seasonally.**

❧❧ **DEVOE MANSION, Tacoma** Enclosed by tall trees and a white wooden fence, this grand Colonial mansion stands out in an unassuming residential neighborhood. Built by the DeVoes in 1911, the mansion boasts a fascinating history. Emma Smith DeVoe helped the women of Washington state achieve the right to vote—ten years before all women in the United States were granted that right. The home is teeming with historical references and intriguing memorabilia. A mixture of antiques embellishes the somewhat simple living room, where floral sofas are arranged near an enormous marble fireplace. Historical books, board games, and puzzles fill the shelves, and a piano is tucked in one corner. Complimentary hot drinks are available to guests at all times. Colorful Oriental carpets cover the hardwood floors in the elegant dining room, where baked goods and omelets or French toast are served in the morning. After breakfast, stroll the lovely, tree-covered grounds or enjoy a steamy soak in the outdoor hot tub.

The inn's four rooms are named after Emma's friends, and all have private baths, although two are detached. The Carrie and John Henry Rooms are nicely decorated but have the disadvantage of detached baths, located down the hall. In the Susan B. Anthony Room, the focal point is a hand-carved oak antique bed draped with plush purple and green linens. Emma's Room, on the opposite corner of the house, is equally alluring. All of the beds here are queen-size, and all are covered with lush linens and down comforters, and embellished with darling stuffed rabbits.

Devoe Mansion is a wonderful place to unwind and share an interesting history lesson, and the reasonable prices are an extra incentive. **208 East 133rd Street; (253) 539-3991; www.wolfenet.com/~devoe; inexpensive; minimum-stay requirement on holidays.**

❧❧ **THE GREEN CAPE COD BED AND BREAKFAST, Tacoma** Aptly named, this green Cape Cod–style home is nestled in a tranquil neighborhood just blocks from the quaint boutique-lined Proctor district. The common areas, breakfast room, and three small guest rooms with private baths are filled with restored American antiques and attractive contemporary furnishings. After you've seen your room, you'll want to return to the living room and stake out one of the comfy bent-willow couches so you can cuddle up in front of the warm, crackling fire. Guest quarters are located on either the main or the second floor, and appointed with either a king- or queen-size bed. Soothing beige and white envelop the Gibson Girls Room on the main floor, which features turn-of-the-century drawings on the walls, fluffy green robes in the closet, and crisp white linens draped over the king-size bed. A color TV sits out on a stand, and a detached but private white-tiled bathroom lies just outside the door. Upstairs, two snug but engaging guest rooms offer floral and white linens, sea green or white walls, more timeless antiques, and private baths. The Iris Room, tucked under the eaves, is especially cozy.

A full country breakfast awaits in the morning, or you can opt for an informal light continental breakfast if you're in a hurry to begin your day. **2711 North Warner; (253) 752-1977; www.tribnet.com/adv/bb/green capecod; inexpensive to moderate.**

Romantic Note: Ask the innkeeper about the honeymoon packages available. They may include special touches such as sparkling cider, fruit, cheese, and chocolates set in your room at turndown time and, in the morning, a full or continental breakfast delivered to your door.

❀❀❀❀ **THORNEWOOD CASTLE, Tacoma** You'll want to pinch yourselves to see if you're dreaming when you catch your first glimpse of Thornewood. A bona fide English Gothic Tudor castle (Thornewood's original owner imported all of the building materials from Europe, and much of them came from a 15th-century castle), this spectacular three-story brick mansion dates back to the turn of the century and boasts over 30,000 square feet of old-world opulence and elegance. Outside, four green acres of pristine lakefront property harbor old-growth firs and a restored sunken "secret garden" enclosed by a brick wall and filled with blooming roses. Inside, you could literally spend hours exploring the lavish, museum-like rooms. Vintage oil paintings adorn the walls in the antique-filled parlor, where a fire provides radiant warmth. A priceless collection of more than 100 rare Gothic stained and painted window panels spread light and color throughout the stately manor. Thick Oriental carpets bedeck the hardwood floors, and chandeliers illuminate the high ceilings, rich old-world fabrics, and art pieces.

Each of the five suites available in this 54-room castle is authentic and inviting, and all have private baths. On the main floor, the Lakeside Suite has a windowed alcove that overlooks the sweeping lawn and sparkling lake beyond. Lush linens and boutique pillows cover the queen-size bed, and the bathroom is almost as large as the bedroom, with tall stained glass windows and hardwood floors. Across the hall, the Garden Suite is furnished with similar grandeur, and surveys the front grounds. A massive wood staircase winds upstairs to the other three suites. The Bridal Suite couldn't be more perfect for your wedding night: The four-poster bed is topped with sumptuous linens, a fire glows in the hearth, and a whirlpool tub awaits in the spacious bathroom. Chester's Room is the smallest guest room available, but still cozy and elegant. A second staircase climbs to the Penthouse Suite, where guests can reserve the entire top floor of the mansion. This suite features more turn-of-the-century charm and elegance, and a claw-foot tub promises satisfying soaks in the lovely bathroom.

You'll fill up quickly on the bountiful breakfast of fresh fruit, bread with homemade jam, hot entrées, fresh gourmet coffee, and tea or juice. Breakfast baskets are available upon request to enjoy in the garden; gift baskets and massage therapy can also be provided for an additional fee. The prices here are shockingly reasonable, but we recommend booking your reservation soon. As soon as the word gets out, reservations are going to be hard to come by and the prices may justifiably go up. **8601 North Thorne Lane Southwest; (253) 584-4393; www.thornewoodcastle.com; moderate; closed December; recommended wedding site.**

❀❀❀❁ **THE VILLA, Tacoma** This white stucco Italianate mansion capped with a red-tiled roof is so authentic-looking you can imagine it being airlifted here straight from the coast of the Mediterranean. Gardens, fountains, and even a palm tree adorn the grounds, adding to the illusion. Built in 1925 and located in a quiet, upscale residential neighborhood, this vintage Italian villa is brimming with opulence and vibrant color; Oriental carpets cover gleaming blond hardwood floors throughout the mansion. An elegant open stairwell bordered by tall white pillars is a dramatic focal point on the main floor. Fine antiques, artwork, and artifacts from exotic lands fill the spacious living room, where comfy overstuffed sofas sit in front of a stone fireplace. Cathedral ceilings, dried flowers, and an extra-long antique wooden table adorn the elegant pink-hued breakfast room. An adjacent window-lined solarium is outfitted with cheery white wicker furnishings and a collection of thriving plants.

Each of the six guest rooms has its own unique appeal. Four are located upstairs. A private staircase climbs up to the cozy Ravello Suite, awash in white, with a king-size bed, hand-crafted headboard, down duvet, and floral linens. A gas fireplace turns on at the flick of a switch, and the pleasant white-tiled bathroom holds both a claw-foot soaking tub and a sexy, glass-enclosed walk-in shower. Best of all, this suite offers views of Puget Sound and the Olympics. The Cimbrone Suite has bright fuchsia walls, a spacious tiled bathroom, and a fluffy comforter draped atop the queen-size bed. The adjacent sitting area, with its cozy couches, a gas fireplace, and a writing desk, is the perfect spot for devouring—or composing—some romantic poetry. In the Napoli Room, a beautifully carved four-poster queen-size bed commands center stage. By far the most engaging of the four is the Sorrento Suite, which features deep olive green walls with white trim, a king-size bed seductively draped with a soft white veil, a veranda overlooking the neighborhood, and fluffy white couches covered with boutique pillows and placed in front of a gas fireplace. Distant views of the Olympics and Puget Sound are splendid from this vantage point.

Two additional suites are located in a separate wing on the main floor. Yellow brightens the handsome Amalfi Room, where a handmade green four-poster bed is decorated with contemporary linens. A large soaking tub and glass-enclosed shower are romantic features in the pretty bathroom. In the Caserta Room, bright fuchsia accents and floral fabrics impart colorful flair.

Rich linens cover a queen-size white iron bed warmed by a gas fireplace, and the black-and-white-tiled bathroom holds a Jacuzzi tub for two.

Awake to a full country breakfast of stuffed French toast, fresh fruit, and delicious baked goods, served in the spacious breakfast room, where colorful gardens peek through tall arched windows. A weekend here will help you understand why Italy is famous for love. **705 North Fifth Street; (253) 572-1157, (888) 572-1157; www.villabb.com; inexpensive to expensive; call for seasonal closures.**

Restaurant Kissing

❤❤❤ **CLIFF HOUSE, Tacoma** If you have any hesitations about kissing in Tacoma, the Cliff House will soon set you straight. Poised high atop a steep cliff on Browns Point, the upscale, glass-enclosed dining room surveys panoramic views of the Port of Tacoma and surrounding hillsides. The interior is arranged to take full advantage of the view: Nearly every seat in the house is angled toward the water. Crisply ironed white linens drape tables topped with candle lanterns, and wood and brass detailing adds elegance. Stylish green-and-cream-pinstriped chairs hug intimate tables, while circular wooden booths offer ample privacy for couples who want to sit close.

Even during the busy lunch hour, the service and food are impressive. The steamed clams served in a Thai-inspired lemongrass-basil broth with red curry oil were fresh and flavorful. We were also delighted with the grilled brochette of spring vegetables served with marinated portobello mushrooms and crisp potato cake, accented with basil Thai miso oil. Unique and delicious! **6300 Marine View Drive; (253) 927-0400, (800) 961-0401; expensive; reservations recommended; lunch Monday–Friday, dinner daily.**

Romantic Note: GUIDO'S (inexpensive), a casual lounge/café on the lower level, shares the Cliff House's impressive view and talented chef. Unfortunately, the blaring television and thick cigarette smoke are romantic distractions.

❤❤ **LUCIANO'S, Tacoma** This quaint Italian dinner spot is situated on Tacoma's popular waterfront, which is also home to a number of unromantic night spots and chain restaurants. Tables are draped with deep maroon and black tablecloths and embellished with fresh flowers. In the background, Italian music lulls diners into a state of tranquillity. Guests seeking authentic Italian delights will not be disappointed with Luciano's new menu: Pasta and seafood are the specialties here. Wonderful antipasto choices include polenta topped with Gorgonzola cream sauce, and toasted Tuscany bread topped with fresh Roma tomatoes, garlic, and basil. We also recommend the seafood linguine, brimming with mussels, clams, and calamari in a plum tomato sauce. Ask your server about the evening's dessert selections—one of them will be the perfect finale to a very romantic evening. **3327 Ruston Way; (253) 756-5611; moderate; lunch and dinner daily.**

❦❦❦ **THE OLD HOUSE CAFE, Tacoma** Set in Tacoma's charming Proctor district, this old house turned café is a delightful setting for an intimate lunch or a romantic dinner. Floral linens drape small tables in the main-floor and upstairs dining rooms, and the crisp white walls in both rooms are accented by pretty floral window treatments. You'll have no chance to forget about dessert here because the host will walk you by the dessert case before showing you to your table; you'll have chocolate decadence imprinted on your brain throughout your meal. For a main course, we highly recommend baked Hood Canal oysters layered with dill, garlic, basil, cream, and bread crumbs, or pasta with fresh mushrooms, sun-dried tomatoes, red onions, and garlic, tossed with a creamy herb sauce. **2717 North Proctor; (253) 759-7336; moderate to expensive; lunch and dinner Tuesday–Saturday.**

Lakewood

Outdoor Kissing

❦❦❦ **LAKEWOLD GARDENS, Lakewood** Once a private estate, Lakewold Gardens is now open to the public, and its ten acres of manicured lawns and gardens are a beautiful setting for a romantic stroll. Exquisitely crafted waterfalls, several shady Japanese maples, and one of the largest collections of rhododendrons in the Northwest make this a horticulturist's dream come true. Bring a picnic and sit beneath the mammoth Wolf Tree, or just pick a path that looks empty and steal a kiss amid the brilliant colors. **12317 Gravelly Lake Drive Southwest; (888) 858-4106; $5 general admission; call for seasonal hours; recommended wedding site.** *From Interstate 5, take Exit 124 and go west on Gravelly Lake Drive about a mile. The park entrance is on your right.*

Parkland

Restaurant Kissing

❦❦❦ **FROM THE BAYOU, Parkland** Due to its proximity to Pacific Lutheran University, you might expect this place to be a traditional college hangout, and from the street it does appear rather modest. Inside, however, it's a completely different story. Operated by four young men from Louisiana, From the Bayou dishes up large helpings of Cajun cuisine and Southern charm in a stylish setting. A hand-laid stone-tile floor, wood walls lined with pictures of Louisiana homes, vases of fresh daisies, cozy wood booths, and an eclectic selection of candles adorn the dining room. Any seat here invites you to be swept up in the chic atmosphere, while happenin' music creates an ever-changing mood. Couples seeking ultimate togetherness will delight in the "chill room," a private alcove with a single table, an overstuffed couch, deep green walls, and an assortment of games. Strings of white holiday lights illuminate this secluded room, where the wait staff serves up private, extraordinary meals for two.

Start your meal with crawfish tails baked in a seasoned cheese sauce and served with warm peasant bread. The house salad with a tangy basalmic vinaigrette dressing will prepare your palates for taste sensations like crab-stuffed halibut topped with a spicy pepper sauce. If you prefer a little extra bang in your bite, three bottles of Louisiana pepper sauces augment the salt and pepper on each table. End your meal on a sweet note with a freshly baked dessert—perhaps praline cream pie, or New Orleans cheesecake with caramel and pecans. **508 Garfield Street; (253) 539-4269; moderate; lunch and dinner Monday–Saturday.**

Olympia

Unless you've got a penchant for politics or an affinity for beer, Olympia's legislative buildings, courthouses, and prominent brewing company don't stimulate your romantic inclinations. But Washington state's capital, harbored on Puget Sound's Budd Inlet, can be a lip-worthy destination as long as you know where to go.

For starters, a walking path along the west side of serene **CAPITOL LAKE** meanders past **TUMWATER FALLS** and the **OLYMPIA BREWERY**. Farther on, there are viewpoints from which you can appreciate the Legislative Building's landmark marble dome ascending above a wooded hillside. After your walk, you can take refuge from Olympia's busy city center at the **YASHIRO JAPANESE GARDEN** (Plum and Union Streets; 360-753-8380; free admission). Very small, but lush and beautifully manicured, the garden is replete with Japanese stone lanterns, an 18-foot pagoda, and footpaths that wander past a bamboo grove, streambed, pond, and miniature waterfall.

Hotel/Bed and Breakfast Kissing

❤❤ **HARBINGER INN BED AND BREAKFAST, Olympia** Budd Inlet laps at much of the Olympia shoreline, and at the Harbinger Inn guests can admire engaging views of the inlet's east bay and quiet marina. The inn is set atop a steep hillside across the street from the water. Expansive balconies and white columns fortify the majestic turn-of-the-century home, built of gray ashlar blocks and trimmed in yellow and gray. Manicured gardens surround the entire Mission-style structure, and in the backyard a spring-fed waterfall trickles down the foliage-covered hillside.

Visitors are encouraged to kick back and relax at this comfortably refurbished home, appointed with hardwood floors, antiques, Oriental rugs, and bookshelves brimming with novels. Upon arrival, a complimentary presentation of tea and cookies is offered. Five guest rooms are available here, each with a private bathroom and views of the water or the neighborhood. Timeless antiques fill our favorite room, the Honeymoon Suite, which features a queen-size bed, private sitting room, and distant views of the Olympic Mountains. Once you've tasted the fresh breads and pastries in the morning, you'll understand why guests rave about the innkeeper's scrumptious and generous continental breakfasts. **1136 East Bay Drive; (360) 754-0389; inexpensive to expensive.**

Romantic Note: A short-term rental unit called the **BUDD BAY BUNGALOW** (unbelievably expensive; minimum-stay requirement) is also available. Although too spacious and pricey for a single couple—the cabin features four bedrooms and four bathrooms—this would be an affordable and roomy option for families or large groups. And its location right on the bay can't be beat.

Romantic Suggestion: After breakfast, head several miles north to **PRIEST POINT PARK,** situated on a bank overlooking Budd Inlet. Handfuls of picnic tables are sheltered beneath evergreens, and privacy abounds on the myriad walking paths that traverse the park's wooded acreage.

Restaurant Kissing

❀❀❀ **SEVEN GABLES RESTAURANT, Olympia** Enveloped by colorful gardens, this light blue, gabled 1893 Victorian looks more like a private home than a restaurant. Closer inspection reveals that the entire first floor has been converted into a charming dining area, where cozy tables draped in mismatched linens are tucked into corners and alcoves of the home's original living and dining rooms. For romantic purposes, the two front dining rooms are preferable, due to the smaller number of tables and the distant views of the water and city. When weather permits, guests can relish the hilltop setting at several tables placed in the shade on the wraparound veranda.

Tantalizing menu items include baked Alaskan halibut with a dill cream sauce; avocado seafood crêpes filled with crab, shrimp, and Asiago and Swiss cheese; scallops with ginger and red pepper; and chicken breast sautéed with apples, caramel, lemon juice, and cream. Reservations are hard to come by as a result of the restaurant's popularity, so it's best to call in advance. **1205 West Bay Drive; (360) 352-2349; moderate; reservations recommended; dinner Wednesday–Sunday.**

"A kiss can be a comma,

a question mark or an

exclamation point.

That's basic spelling that every

woman ought to know."

Mistinguett

San Juan Islands

Several of the islands are accessible by ferry from Anacortes, one and a half hours north of Seattle. For information on departure times, call the Washington State Ferries (206-464-6400, 800-843-3779). The Victoria Clipper (206-448-5000 in Seattle, 250-382-8100 in Victoria, 800-888-2535) also provides access to San Juan Island and Orcas Island from either downtown Seattle or Victoria's Inner Harbour. Call ahead for departure times and fares.

There are 172 islands in the San Juan archipelago, each one characterized by its own distinctive terrain. As you circumnavigate the most popular island grouping—Orcas Island, San Juan Island, Lopez Island, and Shaw Island—by ferryboat, you may be reminded of the island-dotted Caribbean, a notable difference being that the San Juans are much more spectacular in their topography. Of course, you won't see any palm trees here, and because you're about as far north as you can go in the continental United States, the blush on your cheeks will be from the cold and not the equatorial heat. But so much the better: Cool cheeks give you a snuggling advantage.

Deciding on one ideal destination won't be an easy task. You can opt for the convenience of the more populated islands, or, if you have access to a boat, you can homestead on one of the lesser-known islands, setting up camp for a more back-to-basics holiday. Wherever you put down roots, you'll be more than happy with what you discover.

Romantic Note: To save a lot of time and frustration, check with the VISITOR INFORMATION CENTER (360-468-3663). They can give you good recommendations for outdoor activities and campgrounds. Always check seasonal hours and rates whenever you choose a restaurant or island accommodation.

Romantic Suggestion: During summertime and holiday weekends, the ferry wait can range anywhere from two to eight hours. In warmer weather many folks avoid the ferry hassle by leaving their cars behind and traveling by bike on the island of their choice. It would be great if the roads were wider, to safely and easily accommodate bikes alongside the cars, but cycling is a great way to enjoy the San Juans if you are up for it. All islands, except Shaw, have bike rental outfits, although not all of them are within walking distance of the ferry terminals. You can also board on foot, since many bed and breakfast owners will gladly pick up guests from the ferry with prior notification.

Romantic Alternative: How else can you travel to the San Juan Islands besides on a ferryboat? An exciting (albeit more expensive) alternative is to be flown here in an intimate seaplane. KENMORE AIR (425-486-1257, 800-543-9595; www.kenmoreair.com) offers transportation to San Juan Island, Orcas Island, and Lopez Island, plus a variety of other lip-worthy destinations within the Northwest. Departures are from Lake Union in Seattle or from Kenmore at the north end of Lake Washington. Call for prices and a detailed schedule.

San Juan Island

San Juan Island is nothing less than a vacation paradise. It is the largest and most developed of the San Juan Islands, and the westernmost destination in the Strait of Juan de Fuca. Replete with restaurants, bed and breakfasts, hotels, and enough shoreline to satisfy any nature lover, it is an island escape par excellence. San Juan Island is also in such close proximity to Vancouver Island that you can often see its interior mountains and Victoria's city lights twinkling in the distance.

Hotel/Bed and Breakfast Kissing

❧ **ARBUTUS LODGE, San Juan Island** Three cats and two large dogs comprise the welcoming committee here. Just watch out for one friendly canine, who gets nosy in all the wrong places. Tucked away off a country road, this two-room bed and breakfast is modeled after a contemporary Northwest lodge. The sprawling common room sports high ceilings, fir beams, cushioned window seats, the proprietor's office, and plenty of windows for watching birds (sorry, there's no TV). Outside, lounge in the hammock or follow a grassy pathway to one of the sitting spots on the six-acre property.

While both second-story guest rooms are pleasant, only one is worthy of a kiss: the Robin's Nest, with its cathedral ceilings, queen-size bed, Shaker-style furnishings, wood-burning fireplace, and oversize tub and shower.

One of the innkeepers is a professional massage therapist and can help you unwind with a Swedish relaxation massage (an appointment is necessary). Come morning, you'll be further refreshed by cantaloupe soup, smoked salmon with eggs, or hazelnut pancakes, served in the common room. **1827 Westside Road North; (360) 378-8840; www.karuna.com/arbutus; expensive.**

❧❧ **ARGYLE HOUSE BED AND BREAKFAST, Friday Harbor** Located in an appealing residential neighborhood, this 1910 Craftsman-style home is just minutes from the ferry dock and downtown Friday Harbor. Both the main house and the adjacent private cottage are bordered by shady trees and colorful wildflowers that blanket the rear meadow during spring and summer. Inside the main house, hardwood floors, figurine and plate collections, and a wood-burning stove fill the common area, while large windows spill sunlight into the light pink breakfast room. Upstairs, all three rather small guest rooms have attractive floral linens, queen-size beds, contemporary furnishings, plush carpeting, and private bathrooms (one is detached).

Directly behind the main house is the most private accommodation option: a self-contained cottage fronted by a wooden deck that overlooks a grassy lawn. The simple cream and green interior includes a queen-size bed, standard bath, and mini-kitchen, all brightened by an overhead skylight and a wall of windows. Bonus: After 10:30 P.M., guests of this cottage have exclusive use of the hot tub, just steps from the door.

Your stay is complete only after you've indulged in the five-course breakfast served in the main house. A hot egg dish such as smoked salmon quiche or French toast with fruit, rolls with orange glaze, and a giant fresh fruit plate are among the possible delectables that will keep you going until dinnertime. **685 Argyle Street; (360) 378-4084, (800) 624-3459; www.pacificws.com/sj/argyle.html; moderate to expensive; minimum-stay requirement seasonally.**

❀❀ **DUFFY HOUSE BED AND BREAKFAST, San Juan Island** This bed and breakfast, housed in a 1920s farmhouse, is definitely the king of the hill. Grassy hillsides, a colorful English flower garden, and a fruit orchard share its unobstructed water view. The window-lined common room and dining room are decorated with Native American pottery and Navajo rugs, white leather furniture, a wood-burning stove, and elegant curved ceilings.

Hidden away on the main and second floors are five traditional guest rooms, all of which have queen-size beds and private, standard bathrooms located either in the rooms or down the hall. An extra touch of coziness is added by the innkeeper's handmade quilts, which adorn the beds and other areas of the home. The Panorama Room offers a direct water view and an antique bed. Sunset, a small suite outfitted with antique furnishings and the only bathtub in the home, has a peekaboo view of the water—and a parking lot. Check out the resident eagles in their aerie from the small room appropriately named Eagle's Nest.

In the morning, wake up your taste buds with such delicacies as strawberry-rhubarb coffee cake, cheesy egg strata, fruit smoothies, and melon balls with mint. Afterward, walk up the ridge behind Duffy House for a spectacular view, or climb down to the private pebbled beach and comb the ground for sea treasures. If you're lucky, Mr. Duffy, the owners' bright orange cat, will accompany you. **760 Pear Point Road; (360) 378-5604, (800) 972-2089; www.san-juan.net/duffyhouse; moderate; minimum-stay requirement on weekends seasonally.**

❀❀❀❀ **FRIDAY HARBOR HOUSE, Friday Harbor** You could spend all day in Friday Harbor without noticing this exquisite inn perched on the hillside. And that's the way it should be. There's no need for this inn to compete with its beautiful surroundings; instead it concentrates on offering a welcoming, private, and subdued setting for relaxation and romance.

Handsome slate floors, a stylish water fountain, and whimsical driftwood furniture accent the small lobby where guests receive their first taste of the understated elegance that distinguishes Friday Harbor House. In most of the 20 rooms, floor-to-ceiling windows showcase unparalleled views of the water and the bustling marina below. On clear days, Orcas Island's Mount Constitution can be seen in the distance. (As with most places, the more you pay, the better the view. Some less expensive rooms have parking lot peekaboo views.) Romance-friendly features in all rooms include gas fireplaces, dimmer switches, TVs, queen-size beds, and spacious bathrooms with Jacuzzi soaking tubs. Some rooms are lucky enough to have tiny balconies, while others have an open Jacuzzi area so you can view the glowing fireplace while you soak the night away. Each room is a study in refinement, touched with light taupe and sand accents, Craftsman-style furnishings, and Northwest finishes, including wooden fish, beach rocks on the fireplace mantle, and paintings of San Juan scenes.

A complimentary continental breakfast is served to guests in the hotel's stunning dining room (see Restaurant Kissing). Served buffet style, the generous assortment may include butter and currant scones, several types of breads, yogurt, granola, fruit juices, and cereal. If the weather's nice, have your breakfast on the grassy patio and watch the ferries come and go. **130 West Street; (360) 378-8455; www.karuna.com/fhhouse; very expensive to unbelievably expensive; minimum-stay requirement on weekends seasonally.**

❧❧ **FRIDAY'S HISTORICAL INN, Friday Harbor** Built in 1891, this gray three-story hotel was a youth hostel before its attractive reincarnation as an island bed and breakfast. Due to its location in the heart of Friday Harbor, noise from the bustling streets and restaurant below can pose a problem for guests seeking quiet refuge; but all will be forgiven once you set foot in the luxurious top-floor Eagle Cove Room. It is hard not to feel pampered here, as you bubble away in the large two-person Jacuzzi tub set in a beautiful green-and-maroon-tiled bathroom accented with glass blocks and wood trim. Vaulted ceilings, a king-size bed backed by a unique driftwood headboard, a modern-looking kitchen, and the harbor views from the private balcony easily take your mind off the busy town life below.

All of the remaining ten guest rooms at Friday's feature TVs and similar accoutrements. However, six rooms share baths, and some rooms are on the first floor, adjacent to the large common room where a continental breakfast is served buffet style in the morning. Two new ground-level suites—the Wine Cellar and the Chart Room—with queen-size beds, kitchenettes, sofa sleepers, TVs, and computer hookups, are options if you have to travel with your whole family. The Wine Cellar's name is fitting: It is dark like a cellar, and punctuated with an unappealing array of patterns. Book the Chart Room instead, with its double Jacuzzi tub. If romance is at the top of your list, though, you will definitely prefer the Eagle Cove's extravagance and seclusion, and if your budget can handle its slightly steeper tab, you will be elated with what it has to offer. **35 First Street; (360) 378-5848, (800) 352-2632; www.friday-harbor.com/lodging.html; inexpensive to very expensive.**

❧❧ **HARRISON HOUSE SUITES, Friday Harbor** All five suites at Harrison House deliver views (neighborhood or partial water), private bathrooms (some with jetted tubs), sitting areas, and either full kitchens or small kitchenettes. Still, the accommodations in this classic 1905 Craftsman home, perched above the Friday Harbor ferry landing, are mostly designed to be shared by more than two people. However, there are exceptions. One spacious but slightly outdated two-bedroom suite features hardwood floors, Persian rugs, comfy couches, a wood-burning stove, TV/VCR, whirlpool tub, intricate antiques, and a full kitchen. The homey honeymoon suite, similarly furnished, has a private deck and whirlpool tub. The private cottage, located across from the main house, could be romantic, but the mismatched furnishings and cramped quarters make it seem more claustrophobic than cozy. The other suites, including a 1,650-square-foot unit, are too big to qualify as romantic. If you're on a budget, book the downstairs suite, which boasts a queen-size bed tucked away in a loft and lots of windows. Hundreds of flowers, a king-size outdoor Jacuzzi tub (open to all guests), and a charming little stream await outside.

Next to the home, a nicely decorated café serves breakfasts and inexpensive dinners (dinners by reservation only) for Harrison House guests. The amorously inclined can even book a private dinner exclusively for two here. The talented innkeeper—who grows his own vegetables and flowers, catches his own fish, prepares gourmet meals, and plays the piano—is eager to please and can certainly cook up a way to make your stay memorable. **235 C Street; (360) 378-3587, (800) 407-7933; www.rockisland.com/~hhsuites; inexpensive to very expensive; minimum-stay requirement.**

❀❀❀ **HILLSIDE HOUSE BED AND BREAKFAST, Friday Harbor** Attractive landscaping, a small pond, and a trickling fountain welcome guests who wander up the path to this contemporary bed and breakfast, located in a residential neighborhood. Six guest rooms occupy the upper main floor and daylight basement, and a seventh option, a spectacular suite, is perched on the top floor. All rooms have a contemporary country look, with dried flowers, quaint sitting nooks with comfy pillows, private bathrooms (either in the room or down the hall), and plush floral linens on raised beds. Several rooms offer a bird's-eye view into an atrium/aviary, which was a work-in-progress during our visit. While the upstairs and downstairs rooms are almost identical, we recommend the upstairs rooms for their abundance of natural light. But for the fairest room of all, check into the expansive Eagles' Nest Suite. Large windows toss lots of light into this third-floor loft that has a private entrance and stairway, cathedral ceilings, a king-size bed, and a huge jetted tub with a skylight view. A private deck, just right for two, overlooks the immediate neighborhood and Friday Harbor in the distance.

The warm, amiable, and casual hosts encourage guests to relax in their comfortable living room and on roomy outside decks with distant water views. When the birds start to sing, sit down to a bountiful, vegetarian-oriented buffet breakfast in the bright dining room or on the deck when weather permits. **365 Carter Avenue; (360) 378-4730, (800) 232-4730; rockisland.com/**

~hillside/house.html; moderate to very expensive; minimum-stay requirement on weekends seasonally.

❀❀❅ **LONESOME COVE RESORT, San Juan Island** Have you always wanted a waterfront retreat? Lonesome Cove offers you a chance to live out that dream, if only for a short while. Located on the northernmost part of the island, the resort's six delightful cedar-log cabins with red-trimmed windows are nestled between a small pebbled beach and a forest full of wildlife. Deer leisurely forage for fallen apples on the manicured lawn; beyond the beach cormorants dive for their dinner; and several resident ducks waddle here and there looking for handouts. On a hill above the cabins, sit in solitude on a wooden bench beside a trout-stocked pond, or follow the half-mile-long gravel driveway for a wonderful and quiet walk through the woods.

A surprising amount of romance and coziness awaits within the cabins. Their prime assets are huge stone fireplaces, exposed log walls, full kitchens, and private decks that overlook Speiden Island and the turbulent channel. While the homespun decor is a blast from the past, and the linens are just average, everything is clean and in good condition (except our cabin's door locks, which didn't work, but that's not a big deal out here). Be sure to stock up on groceries, barbecue supplies, and personal items at Friday Harbor or nearby Roche Harbor, because once you arrive, you won't want to leave. By the way, the name of this resort is misleading; with the right someone, you won't experience any lonesomeness here. **5810-A Lonesome Cove Road; (360) 378-4477; moderate to expensive; minimum-stay requirement.**

❀❅ **MOON AND SIXPENCE, San Juan Island** Skip the accommodations in the main house here (they're best for large groups), and journey through a green pasture dotted with colorful gardens to a unique island hideaway—a renovated 1902 post-and-beam water tower (one of only a handful still standing on the island). For couples who don't mind a few cobwebs in unreachable locations, this fairy-tale place has plenty of charisma. Antique furnishings accented with homey country touches fill the three small levels. The ground level holds a wet bar and a bathroom with a stall shower. A barn-wood staircase leads up to the bedroom, where a queen-size bed draped in a pretty patchwork quilt is tucked into a tight space. From the bed, you have wonderful views into the marsh and grass fields below. A trap-door ladder offers access to the tower's top floor, where you can read in the small sitting area and catch glimpses of the main house and the on-site weaving studio. When daylight arrives, you'll have to come down from your little perch and journey to the main house—a 1902 classic revival farmhouse—for a self-serve continental breakfast. **3021 Beaverton Valley Road; (360) 378-4138; www.rockisland.com/~moon6p/ inn; inexpensive to moderate; no credit cards; minimum-stay requirement.**

❀❀❅ **OLYMPIC LIGHTS BED AND BREAKFAST, San Juan Island** Generally, we hesitate to recommend a bed and breakfast where the rooms share baths, for all the obvious unromantic reasons. But Olympic Lights is worth making an exception for. Island tranquillity is practically guaranteed in this picturesque 1895 Victorian farmhouse. The pale yellow exterior contrasts with the surrounding green fields and purple, blue, and pink wildflowers. To the south, the Strait of Juan de Fuca and the Olympic Mountains occupy the horizon. While strolling the five-acre farm, you might spot one of the resident cats on patrol, and you're bound to hear the chickens and roosters. Occasionally, a bald eagle makes an appearance overhead.

Inside, the sunny parlor, common area, and five guest rooms are appointed with simple decorations, ivory tones, and fresh flowers. Only one room is located on the main floor off the kitchen pantry, and some say it's the most desirable due to its private bathroom and garden view. We'd agree. The four second-story rooms have queen-size beds with fluffy comforters and share two spacious bathrooms, each with a tub/shower, double vanity, and a bouquet of fresh flowers. A no-shoes policy is in effect upstairs because of the creamy white carpet; bring your own slippers, as the proprietors do not provide any. And while we're on the subject of clothing, robes are not provided for that bathroom dash across the hall either; pack accordingly. Morning sunlight pours in through the many windows of the room called Ra (named after the Egyptian sun god), which sparkles in cheery shades of cream and white. The Olympic room affords the best views of the water and the Olympic Mountains, and is a picture of beauty with its white linens and floral accents.

Thank the resident chickens for the wonderful breakfasts, which focus on (what else?) egg dishes, including soufflé-like oregano eggs filled with mushrooms and fresh chives. Blueberry scones, buttermilk biscuits, fresh fruit, and frothy fruit smoothies round out the rest of the vegetarian meal, which is served family style in the sunny kitchen or sitting room. **4531-A Cattle Point Road; (360) 378-3186; www.ohwy.com/wa/o/olyligbb.htm; inexpensive to moderate; no credit cards; minimum-stay requirement seasonally and on holiday weekends.**

❀❀❀ **PANACEA, Friday Harbor** Panacea means "a cure-all," and if you're in need of a magic potion for romance, this bed and breakfast may do the trick. Located in a residential neighborhood across from a school, the early Craftsman-style home, complete with wraparound porch, spacious lawn, and four bedrooms, is one elixir that goes down nice and smooth.

Each room has enticing floral appointments, classic architectural touches, a private entrance, and private bath. A king-size bed, a two-person Jacuzzi tub inlaid with hand-painted tiles, a wood-burning fireplace, and Native American art highlight the cozy and peaceful Veranda Room. However, the next-door Trellis Room, which also boasts a large Jacuzzi tub, is the nicer and more romantic of the two king rooms. (However, we wonder why no window blinds cover the side windows? Lace curtains don't allow for much privacy.) Both these rooms open onto the covered veranda—an ideal place for sunset viewing. The two queen rooms have garden patios, but lack the amenities, space, and charm of the king rooms.

The innkeeper, a former professional caterer, cooks up dishes that are plentiful and delicious. Be prepared for wonderful afternoon refreshments (homemade brownies, cookies, etc.) as well as evening desserts and cordials. When you awake, you'll find an outstanding breakfast served in the living room. The seasonal menu might feature island eggs Benedict topped with mango salsa for a light summertime special or walnut-pecan pancakes for a wintertime warm-up. The innkeeper also offers an impressive, but expensive, breakfast-in-bed option, with a choice between caviar with blini and molded eggs Florentine or lobster medallion Benedict with ham and cheese muffins.

While parts of the home and lawn need touching up, we are confident the new innkeeper's enthusiasm, determination, and organizational skills will help shape up this place in no time. Besides, the food is so good that such shortcomings can be easily overlooked. **595 Park Street; (360) 378-3757, (800) 639-2762; www/friday-harbor.net/panacea; expensive to very expensive.**

❤❤❤ **SAN JUAN REAL ESTATE COMPANY, Friday Harbor** There's no place like home—especially when home sits on an immaculate stretch of waterfront set amid pines on idyllic San Juan Island. If you are fortunate enough to have a week-long holiday (or a weekend in the off-season), these vacation rental homes may be right for you. Dispersed all around the island, the homes vary in style and character and each has totally different amenities and settings. Fortunately, San Juan Real Estate Company provides a detailed brochure and photos containing all the information you will need to make a decision. Below we list just a few of the homes that struck our fancy as romantic island retreats.

ROCHE HARBOR RABBIT FARM (No. 5) is perfectly suited for couples. As the name suggests, it is located close to Roche Harbor. Set in the woods with water views through the trees, this fairly new home looks like a weathered old country cottage. A loft bedroom holds a queen-size four-poster bed, and the sunny little bathhouse has a claw-foot tub with shower. The eclectic decor won't please everyone, but we found it quite charming, with hardwood floors, an open-beam ceiling, antiques, a piano, and a bright yellow rabbit-crossing sign. It may sound odd, but if you are interested in something fun and different, this home is a wonderful option, and the easy beach access is an additional bonus.

YACHT HAVEN (No. 36), another excellent getaway, is also near Roche Harbor. Decorated in a more upscale fashion, with cream-colored leather couches and elegant country touches, this two-bedroom waterfront home has fabulous views of Haro Strait, immediate beach access, and a huge front deck with a Jacuzzi tub. Sunsets from this vantage point will leave you speechless, and stargazing is just as wonderful.

Orcas are the stars of the show at **WHALE WATCH COTTAGE (No. 1)**. High above the hills on San Juan Island's southwest side, this cozy honeymooners' cottage has all the essentials: a queen-size bed, standard bath, woodstove and, most important, a telescope for watching orcas. Be careful driving up to this remote spot. The loose gravel roads offer tricky traction, especially when wet.

You won't be moored near any million-dollar yachts if you rent **OTTER MAGIC (No. VR49)**, but living aboard this customized houseboat is great fun. The boat's exterior isn't picturesque—it's surrounded by fluorescent pink bumpers, two aging boats, and one eyesore of a building above—but the inside is nautical-cozy, private, and has somewhat of a view. The marina, which wasn't crowded when we visited, is a few blocks north of Friday Harbor. A crab pot and a dinghy come with the package.

If you like a cabin that's tucked into the cedars and find that dim-even-during-daytime interior appealing, try the **WATERFRONT BUNGALOW (No. 10)**. Perched on the northernmost part of the island, this rounded A-frame captures that quintessential Northwest cozy-dark feel. Inside, the furnishings are a game of mix and match, including contemporary couches, an avocado-green fridge, and a mirrored kitchen. An upstairs loft holds the bedroom; the large front porch overlooks spectacular views of the waterfront.

One of the nicest homes we saw was **CARTER BEACH (No. 77)**. The front is all window, and the interior is light, elegant, and simple. The slate blue, three-bedroom home lets nature put on the show, and complements its surroundings with simple furnishings, natural colors, Ansel Adams prints, a black-lacquered piano, and a light blue tiled kitchen. A private dock and a hot tub hidden underneath the madronas complete the picture.

Staying in a vacation home (or houseboat) is an entirely different experience than staying in a hotel or bed and breakfast. At first you may feel like an intruder in someone else's home (you'll find family photos and personal mementos belonging to the owners in most of the houses). By the end of your week, however, you will feel like residents of these precious islands, and you probably won't want to leave. **285 Blair Avenue; (360) 378-5060, (800) 992-1904; www.sanjuanrealestate.com; moderate to very expensive; no credit cards; minimum-stay requirement seasonally.**

Romantic Note: Considering that most of these vacation rentals have two or more bedrooms, they do make wonderful getaways for several couples to share. When split between more people, most of San Juan Real Estate Company's homes fall into the inexpensive to moderate range—you need only find other couples who can take a weeklong vacation.

☙☙ **TRUMPETER INN BED AND BREAKFAST, San Juan Island** Set in the middle of a gigantic lawn and surrounded by grassy meadows and a goldfish pond, the Trumpeter Inn allows for quiet moments in a calming, country atmosphere.

The cheerful exterior is inviting; inside, the aroma of freshly baked cookies wafts through the six attractive guest rooms and two comfortable common areas. Each guest room boasts a private bathroom, a fluffy down comforter in a pretty cover, and a view of the garden or meadow. We have two favorite rooms. For romantic features, book the second-floor Bay Laurel, with its gas fireplace, private deck overlooking the pond, and king-size bed covered by a burgundy plaid duvet. While the Sage Room doesn't have such amenities, it's a charming, private corner room with a queen-size bed, excellent views, and plenty of morning sun.

The pleasant and friendly innkeepers prepare a delicious morning meal that might include pear soufflé, smoked salmon quiche, or the famous strawberry pancake basket. Top that with homemade breads, granola, and other goodies and you'll be set to explore the island all day until dinner. If you tire, you can hang out in the hammock; come evening, don't miss taking a dip in the outdoor hot tub. Just be sure to turn off the jets for a moment and listen to the night sounds. **420 Trumpeter Way; (360) 378-3884, (800) 826-7926; www.karuna.com/trumpeter; inexpensive to expensive; minimum-stay requirement seasonally.**

❀❀❀❀ WESTWINDS HARMONY COTTAGE, San Juan Island

Spectacular sunsets, whale watching, and sublime seclusion—what more could you ask for on San Juan Island? High above it all on the rugged southwest side of the island sits this cottage built for two. What isn't glass is lovely red cedar surrounded by a covered, wraparound porch. And what isn't forest is unbroken water views. Everything is here to keep you happy: a full kitchen where you can cook all your meals, a gas fireplace, contemporary furnishings, terry-cloth robes, a deep soaker tub, and a well-stocked library. (There are even phones for those poor souls who must communicate with the outside world.) In the upstairs loft, rest your head on the queen-size bed and stare out through large triangular windows. Down below on the deck, use the binoculars to spot orcas during the summer. You won't see another soul up here, so everything is for your eyes only. **Hannah Road; (360) 378-5283; www.karuna.com/westwinds; expensive to very expensive.**

❀ WHARFSIDE BED AND BREAKFAST, Friday Harbor

This is not your run-of-the-mill bed and breakfast in any way, shape, or form. Wharfside Bed and Breakfast is a docked, beautifully restored 60-foot ketch named the *Jacquelyn*. Anyone familiar with boats will not be surprised by the compact size of the two guest rooms here, but for the less nautically aware, we must explain that these rooms are a lot smaller than any on-land bed-and-breakfast rooms you have ever seen.

Polished hardwood adorns both below-deck rooms, and portholes look out to passing boats and ferries. The Forward Stateroom is rather narrow, with an elongated double bed, patchwork quilt, down comforter, and bunk beds. A detached bathroom, located across the main salon, is tiny, with just enough room for a sink, toilet, and shower. (The shower is shared with the other guest room.) The low-beamed ceiling in the Aft Stateroom is deceiving, but this room is actually larger than the other. A velvet settee and a queen-size bed with a burgundy bedspread and down comforter are about all that fits in here. A bathroom with a toilet and sink is tucked into one corner.

Homemade (or should we say boat-made?) breakfasts are served on the deck during sunny weather, or in the snug salon, with its skylight, woodstove, and nautical paraphernalia and furnishings. Life aboard the *Jacquelyn* is a cozy and unique adventure. If you think of the tight quarters as a way to be closer to one another, this is also one of the most affordable options in Friday Harbor. **Slip K-13, Port of Friday Harbor; (360) 378-5661; www.san-juan-island.net/wharfside; inexpensive; minimum-stay requirement seasonally.**

Romantic Suggestion: Seafood fresh from the local waters is available just down the dock at **FRIDAY HARBOR SEAFOOD** (Main Dock, Port of Friday Harbor; 360-378-5779; inexpensive). Purchase some precooked crab or shrimp and enjoy the catch of the day right on the *Jacquelyn*'s deck.

Restaurant Kissing

☙☙☙❧ **DUCK SOUP INN, San Juan Island** Duck Soup Inn is the restaurant of choice for hungry lovebirds on San Juan Island. Tucked into a forest, the wood-frame building overlooks a tranquil duck pond. Country accents, cozy wood booths, and walls accented by local artwork create a wonderfully rustic yet elegant setting.

If your taste buds and hearts long for savory fresh Northwest cuisine with a French touch, you've come to the right place. All dinners start with soup and salad, including such treats as creamy tomato-saffron soup and generous greens topped with lovage dressing. (How appropriate for a romantic dinner!) Continue on with such offerings as steak Diane with roasted rosemary potatoes, applewood-smoked oysters (the most delicious you'll ever taste), duck cakes, or steamed local clams in a garlic–tarragon–brown mustard sauce. Desserts can be as light as mango sorbet or as indulgent as lemon-coconut cheesecake or pear-almond pie. Be assured that, from start to finish, nothing is less than divine. **3090 Roche Harbor Road; (360) 378-4878; moderate to expensive; call for seasonal hours; closed December–March.**

☙☙☙❧ **FRIDAY HARBOR HOUSE RESTAURANT, Friday Harbor** Located on the main floor of **FRIDAY HARBOR HOUSE** (see Hotel/Bed and Breakfast Kissing), this polished dining room is an elegant, refined place in which to enjoy a superior meal. Because the small space is able to hold only a handful of tables, intimate moments are guaranteed. Floor-to-ceiling windows frame views of the picturesque marina, while soothing yellow walls, dark slate floors, fresh flowers at every table, and a glowing fireplace enhance the simple, tasteful surroundings. On warm evenings, the grass patio overlooking the marina is a terrific place to dine on appetizers.

Guests will enjoy the Northwest-accented fare. We went wild for the Westcott Bay oysters baked with sweet red pepper butter, the breast of chicken baked with chanterelles and tomatoes, and the halibut bathed in a ginger-soy glaze accompanied by wasabi mashed potatoes. A trio of handmade ice creams—most noteworthy being the luscious lemongrass—put the perfect finishing touch on a wonderfully romantic evening. **130 West Street, at Friday Harbor House; (360) 378-8455; expensive; reservations recommended; call for seasonal hours.**

❀❀❀ **THE PLACE NEXT TO THE SAN JUAN FERRY, Friday Harbor** Don't expect to cruise in here for a quick bite before you catch your ferry. That's what all those other places around the ferry landing are for. When you dine at this waterfront restaurant, plan on enjoying a quiet dinner while you watch everyone else rushing to board the boats.

Perched on pilings, this restaurant features three walls of windows that give diners excellent views of the ferry terminal and marina. White holiday lights are draped around each window, black wooden chairs complement tables covered by thick white cotton tablecloths and bouquets of fresh flowers, and the light wood paneling softens the effect. Local art, ranging from amateurish to professional, adds plenty of spice.

The refined Northwest cuisine is worth skipping the ferry for. We couldn't get enough of the mushroom sauté appetizer served with garlic crostini and herbed goat cheese. Dishes such as the Dungeness crab and roasted corn cakes, shrimp sauté, pork tenderloin medallions, and grilled halibut drizzled with a roasted hazelnut and basil butter are equally inspired. The four-chocolate fantasy cake, made with rich European cocoa, is a dream come true for chocolate lovers. **One Spring Street; (360) 378-8707; moderate to expensive; call for seasonal hours.**

❀❀ **ROCHE HARBOR RESORT RESTAURANT, Roche Harbor** Roche Harbor is San Juan Island's second most popular port of call (Friday Harbor sees the most water traffic). This scenic, historic harbor and marina, protected by a tiny barrier island, is a yachting and tourist playground. Every inch of the resort and marina that isn't lined with boats is covered with gazebos, rose gardens, sculpted hedges, ivy-laden buildings—and people. As you follow the winding brick pathways that weave around the crisp white and dark green New Englandesque buildings, you may feel as if you have stepped back in time.

Bright flower boxes line the waterfront deck of the Roche Harbor Resort Restaurant. Patio furniture placed around the deck allows you to enjoy the sun and the harbor view at the same time. The breakfast and lunch menus offer typical fare—pancakes and omelets, sandwiches and fries—but well-prepared seafood is the specialty at dinnertime. After you've eaten, spend some time wandering the grounds—the gardens are truly lovely, and the harbor scene is ever-changing. In addition, you can book guided kayak tours, whale-watching excursions, and day trips to Victoria's Butchart Gardens here. Stop by the information booth at the resort or call the resort's main number (see the Romantic Note) for information. **4950 Tarte Memorial Drive, at Roche Har-**

bor Resort; (360) 378-5757; www.rocheharbor.com; **moderate to expensive; call for seasonal hours.**

Romantic Note: Overnight accommodations are available at the 20-room HOTEL DE HARO (360-378-2155, 800-451-8910; expensive to very expensive). Be forewarned! This hotel looks charming on the outside, but the inside is scary (literally), with sagging ceilings and floors, rickety stairways, dark Victorian decor, bathrooms with exposed plumbing, and doors that don't shut properly. If you must stay here, the spartan, two-bedroom COMPANY TOWN COTTAGES will do for sleeping purposes. Their best asset is unobstructed harbor views; just be sure to ask for a front-row unit. Waterfront condominiums are also available but are not recommended.

❀❀❀ **SPRINGTREE GRILL, Friday Harbor** Located in the heart of Friday Harbor, the Springtree has one of the most charming courtyards on the island. Bordered by other buildings and framed by an immense 130-year-old Camperdown elm, this spot is shady, sheltered from the street, and sometimes, depending on the season, the most popular place in town. Guests can dine on this pleasant outdoor patio when weather permits; when it doesn't (which is more often than Northwesterners care to admit), they can dine inside. Floor-to-ceiling windows brighten the restaurant's casual interior. Terra-cotta-colored walls adorned with local art, and well-spaced wooden tables lit by single votive candles, set the mood for an enjoyable evening.

Only fresh local ingredients are used in the creative seafood entrées, and the impressive kitchen consistently turns out one delight after another. We highly recommend the Dungeness crab cake and the grilled lamb chops, and we can't say enough about the blackened sea bass, which may be the most flavorful fish dish on the island. **310 Spring Street #C; (360) 378-0858; inexpensive to moderate; call for seasonal hours.**

Outdoor Kissing

❀❀❀❀ **AMERICAN CAMP, San Juan Island** The heavily forested terrain in the northern section of San Juan Island gives way to windswept trees carpeted with poppies, wildflowers, wild rabbits, and waving waist-high grass at the island's southern extremity. Once you arrive at American Camp, you can walk down to the enormous sandy beach and investigate the shoreline or meander through spacious meadows composed of sand hills and sea grass. The many opportunities for ducking out of sight into secluded and sheltered coves make this a perfect site for lovers. You'll be mesmerized by views of the Olympic and Cascade Mountains (both ranges are visible from this spectacular park). Find your own personal beach, then watch the sun's procession from morning to dusk as it bathes the hills in a rainbow of colors. *From the ferry, exit onto Spring Street and turn left on Argyle Road. Argyle jogs around to become Cattle Point Road; from here, turn left again and proceed directly to American Camp.*

❤❤❤ **ENGLISH CAMP, San Juan Island** If you have the energy and a good pair of hiking shoes, don't miss climbing the beautiful uphill trail from English Camp to **YOUNG HILL**. Travel though tree-canopied pathways and madrona forests to reach the majestic windswept top. There are plenty of spots up here to catch your breath and then lose it again to the view (or a kiss). Give yourselves at least an hour for this round-trip jaunt, and bring a picnic, because once you're on Young Hill, you'll want to stay at the top as long as possible. *To reach English Camp from Friday Harbor, travel northwest on Roche Harbor Road to West Valley Road. Turn left and follow the signs to English Camp.*

❤❤❤ **WHALE WATCH PARK, San Juan Island** While you're on San Juan Island, be sure to visit Whale Watch Park on the western shore. Several pods of whales make regular trips through this area, and it is from this spot that you're most likely to see these enormous creatures searching for food or cavorting in play. Even if you don't catch a glimpse of them here, you'll probably see a bald eagle or witness a sensational sunset with the strait in the foreground and the white-capped Olympic Mountains in the distance. There are flocks of folks here in the summer, but at other times you and the seagulls may be the only ones about. **Free admission.** *On West Side Road near Deadman Bay.*

Romantic Suggestion: For an even closer look at the island's wildlife, consider a nautical cruise with **SAN JUAN BOAT TOURS** (360-378-3499, 800-232-6722; www.san-juan.net/whales; prices start at $45 per person). This is the chance of a lifetime to come face to face with harbor seals, bald eagles, or a pod of orcas, among other magnificent creatures. Many other whale-watching companies are based on San Juan Island; look for the flyers posted all over the ferry landing. We suggest calling around to get the exact price and experience you're looking for. Also, be sure to dress warmly.

Orcas Island

Horseshoe-shaped Orcas Island, the northernmost of the touristed San Juan Islands, offers a pleasing blend of rural scenery, mountain wilderness, and several small communities. Eastsound, at the central northern portion of the island, is the largest town. If you need groceries, gas, or a quick lunch, or if you simply want to spend some time wandering through gift shops and little boutiques, this is the place to do it. Beyond Eastsound is Moran State Park, Washington's fourth-largest park, which takes up a good portion of the eastern half of the island and is home to one of the most frequently visited points on all of the islands, **MOUNT CONSTITUTION** (see Outdoor Kissing). There is an abundance of hiking terrain and enough campsites to please any outdoor enthusiast. A good number of esteemed accommodations and restaurants also call Orcas home—and maybe you should too (at least for a while).

Artists of all types are drawn to these islands because of the natural inspiration found in every direction. Orcas Island has become particularly well known for the wealth of talented potters who reside here. Studios, many of which are extensions of the artists' homes, are scattered around the island, and they are worth visiting. The abundance and variety of fantastic local artwork and crafts (pottery, paintings, jewelry, and sculpture, to mention just a few) make it fairly easy to find a unique souvenir of your sojourn in this incredible part of the world.

Hotel/Bed and Breakfast Kissing

❤❤❣ **THE ANCHORAGE INN, Orcas Island** Sitting on 16 acres of wooded beachfront land, the Anchorage Inn is far removed from civilization; the only neighbors you'll find here are other guests and the innkeepers (who built their dream home next door).

A gravel road takes you to a plain, two-story brown home. While the building is somewhat bland in appearance, the forested surroundings and blue water more than compensate. The three suites are simply but pleasantly decorated, and each is equipped with a private entrance, queen-size bed, fireplace, standard bath, and kitchenette. Sit on the cedar deck and look out through the trees to water and the distant lights of Eastsound. Below the home is a wonderful hot tub; a lighted path marks the way to its waterfront location. Be sure to spend some time beachcombing or kissing down on the secluded pebbled beach, which is hidden from the home. In the morning, a breakfast basket is delivered to your door. **Sunderland Road; reservations through The Old Trout Inn, (360) 376-8282; www.oldtroutinn.com; very expensive; minimum-stay requirement seasonally.**

❤❤ **BAYSIDE COTTAGES, Orcas Island** This waterfront hideaway, located on ten acres near the town of Olga, offers several overnight possibilities. The two-room Mount Baker Suite, located on the top floor above the garage of the main house, has a private entrance, large deck, full kitchen, queen-size bed, TV/VCR, and plenty of space. While the views are terrific, this suite is more gigantic than romantic.

We preferred the three cozy cabins—two of which were under construction when we visited. The most isolated of the threesome is the Bayside Cottage. Built many years ago and located down by the beach, this cabin stands alone, with only the trees to keep you company. The inside resembles the curvaceous cover of an old-fashioned rolltop desk with curved pine ceilings and pine wainscoting. The full kitchen, woodstove, TV/VCR, one bedroom with a queen-size bed, and full bath complete the picture. Windows aren't big, so it's a bit dark (which might be a romantic plus, depending on how you look at things). The two new one-room cabins, located on the hillside closer to the home, look promising. Take the one to your right as you face the water if you like light. (We can't figure out why they made the water-view windows in the other cottage so small.) Both have nice-size decks, full baths and kitchens, and plenty of privacy. Bring your own food: Breakfast is not provided. **Mount Baker**

Lane; (360) 376-4330; www.pacificrim.net/~jenelson/cottage.html; moderate to expensive; minimum-stay requirement.

❦❦❦❦ CABINS-ON-THE-POINT, Orcas Island When you see the two Cape Cod cottages perched on the point, you won't be surprised to learn that couples frequently rent them for weeks at a time. Why not? If you get bored with lounging around, you can dig for clams on the private beach, kayak to Skull Island, pick flowers, picnic on the lawn, or take a quick dip in the chilly water. (We prefer a long soak in the waterfront hot tub, nestled beneath a madrona, fir, and old cedar.)

For the ultimate in romance, book the Heather Cottage, a beautifully renovated 100-year-old cabin perched on the bluff. Inside, you'll find hardwood floors, comfortable antiques, a full, slightly rustic kitchen, and a wood-burning stove harbored in an old rock fireplace. Best of all, the cozy bedroom holds a queen-size bed that has been tucked into a window-trimmed alcove overlooking the water. It's one of the nicest bed nooks we've seen. There are not many places like this—where you can lounge in bed and watch fiery sunsets linger right above the tips of your toes. If you tire of staying in this bed, move to the comfy captain's bed in the front room.

A smaller cabin, Primrose, is nestled among fir trees farther back from the water. Although its setting is not quite as spectacular as the Heather Cottage's (few settings are), this is still an incredibly cozy little unit. Cedar-planked walls and hardwood floors lend rustic charm to the bedroom/sitting room. A queen-size canopied bed outlined in white holiday lights adds to the ambience, and a tiny woodstove in the corner provides warmth. Down several steps is a petite, fully equipped kitchen with skylights and a separate private bathroom with a shower. A covered porch with patio furniture provides a place to sit and savor the quiet, and a brick pathway leads to a grassy knoll with fantastic views of Westsound. A new cabin, Willow, was undergoing renovation when we visited. Done in a 1920s beach cottage theme, the two-bedroom cabin is more suitable for small families than kissing couples.

Herb gardens on the property provide the perfect seasonings for a romantic breakfast or dinner; however, meals are not included in your stay. Be sure to bring your own groceries or journey 15 minutes to Eastsound for meals. After a few days at this waterfront retreat, you'll wish you could stay here forever. **Route 1, Box 70; (360) 376-4114; www.islandcabins.com; expensive; no credit cards; minimum-stay requirement.**

Romantic Note: HIGHLANDS HOUSE (very expensive; minimum-stay requirement) is another retreat operated by the same innkeepers. Located near Moran State Park, the private home is geared for two couples traveling together; the two very private bedrooms feature four-poster, peeled-log queen-size beds, down comforters, and private baths with Italian stone-tiled floors. The 30-foot-high cedar-and-glass living room offers a fieldstone fireplace, a full kitchen, and wonderful views of the water. An outside deck holds the hot tub. Unlike the Cabins-on-the-Point, Highlands House is equipped with a TV/ VCR, movie collection, and CD player.

When we visited, the innkeepers were also refurbishing a little waterfront studio called the **DAISY CABIN** (very expensive), located elsewhere on Orcas Island. It looked quite promising for couples seeking 24-hour privacy and peace. A queen-size bed, tucked into tall bay windows, overlooks Mount Constitution and the waters of Eastsound. The solar-powered cabin also features skylights above the two-person shower, a full kitchen, TV/VCR, and CD player. Best of all, there's a pathway leading down to a rocky shoreline where you can rest in the hammock, eat lunch at the picnic table, or cuddle up next to the outdoor fire pit (when fire bans are not in effect).

❦❦❦❦ **CHESTNUT HILL INN, Orcas Island** This inn is one of the most exquisite and romantic accommodations to be found anywhere in the San Juan Islands. As you drive along a gravel road, you'll spy a yellow Victorian farmhouse set atop a hill among the chestnut trees. The wraparound veranda overlooks green fields, a red barn, a small rowing pond, and a charming country chapel. Inside the farmhouse, Persian rugs, polished hardwood floors, plush couches, French country furnishings, and a marble gas fireplace in the parlor set a casually elegant tone.

There are just five guest rooms here, each one a testament to comfort and beauty. Lavish appointments include plush feather beds and down comforters, four-poster or canopied beds, fine linens, and gas-log fireplaces. The most romantic room is the new Chestnut Suite. Live the life of luxury with a four-poster canopy bed, fireplace, TV/VCR, stereo, wet bar, fridge, and French doors that open to the garden. The bathroom—one of the best amenities—holds a double Jacuzzi tub bordered by a huge glass-block shower.

The remaining rooms are romantically equal; it's the color schemes and views that differ. The Garden Room, decorated in country style with subtle blue tones, has a private entrance and is located next to the Suite; the other three are upstairs. Deep rose-colored walls, a lace-canopied bed, and dark wood furnishings make the Stable Room a cozy retreat. The Chapel Room features a double-headed glass-brick shower, a massive canopied bed, and, as you may have guessed, a view of the little chapel. Yellow floral linens brighten the four-poster canopied bed in the Pond Room, which also boasts a clawfoot tub.

Tables for two fill the main-floor dining room, where a full country breakfast may include an artichoke frittata; cranberry-orange buttermilk scones; eggs Benedict layered with polenta, sautéed spinach, and poached egg; and a yogurt-apple-oats dish that gave us a whole new appreciation of oatmeal. In the summertime, additional tables with comfortable wicker chairs are set on the front veranda overlooking the bucolic landscape. **John Jones Road; (360)**

376-5157; www.chestnuthillinn.com; expensive to very expensive; minimum-stay requirement on weekends and in the Chestnut Suite; recommended wedding site.

Romantic Note: Depending on the time of year, different meals and services are available at the inn. November through April, a wonderful, three-course dinner is served here ($30 to $40 per person). In the summer, pre-order a gourmet picnic basket and row across the pond to the little island with its one weeping willow tree.

Romantic Suggestion: Why say "I love you" when you can say "I do"? For those wanting to speak those two magic words, the inn offers an Elopement Package, which includes flowers, cake, champagne, and a photographer. You choose from a list of ministers who can help seal the deal. There's even a cute little chapel on the adjacent property for the ceremony. (Wedding parties are limited to ten people.) This is only one of many fun and romantic packages available; call for details.

❀❀❀ FOXGLOVE COTTAGE, Deer Harbor Renting a fully equipped cottage is an ideal way to get a true feeling for the San Juan Islands: You can settle in and live by your own vacation schedule (or opt for no schedule at all). Foxglove Cottage, next to Deer Harbor, is an adorable little waterfront cabin. The fresh white exterior is accented by crisp green trim, and the contemporary country-style interior is just as immaculate. Although it is petite, once you step inside you may never want to leave. The modern white-tiled kitchen is perfect for cooking up a dinner for two. Share your repast outside on the private deck overlooking the harbor or in the cozy living room warmed by a wood-burning fireplace. Afterward, you may want to take a walk—and, lucky for you, the beach is just a few steps away.

THE RESORT AT DEER HARBOR (see below) is in your backyard, as is a road. Luckily, most of the cottage's windows face the water or trees, so privacy is possible. Also, the convenience of having the resort so close means you can spend less time running to the store and more time focusing on each other. (800) 522-7072; www.orcasisland.com/foxglove; very expensive.

❀❀❀ THE OLD TROUT INN, Orcas Island From inside this home, all you'll see through the large windows is water. A large, lovely trout pond wraps around the house, allowing water views from most rooms. The large cedar home resembles a West Coast lodge on the outside, while inside the decor is contemporary and inviting. From the living room, dining area, and large deck, look out across the pond to acres of lavish green meadows, a bubbling rock water fountain/waterfall below, and Turtleback Mountain in the distance. Interior decorations include collections from the innkeepers' travels, as well as a sprinkling of antiques and a glass chess table with two white chairs.

The inn offers three guest rooms in the main house and a detached cottage. Best for privacy is the self-sufficient Water's Edge Cottage, with a kitchenette, gas fireplace, and, perhaps most enticing, a hot tub overlooking the pond. The main house holds a two-bedroom suite, the Pond Suite, and the Greenhouse Suite. The latter two are both good choices, but may be a bit noisy. The Pond Suite, a huge lower-level suite, is equipped with a fireplace, wet bar, and jukebox. Down here you can dance for as long as you like, and maybe, if it's not too late, two-step on the terraced deck that descends to the pond. Did we mention there's also a private outdoor hot tub, a four-poster queen-size feather bed, and a walk-in sauna? The light, window-filled Greenhouse Suite is off the dining area, but has the advantage of a semiprivate deck and a glassed-in sitting area facing the pond. It shares a hot tub with the two-room suite (geared for couples traveling together).

Whichever unit you choose, you'll have wonderful views, and a full country breakfast in the morning. **Horseshoe Highway; (360) 376-8282; www. oldtroutinn.com; expensive to very expensive; minimum-stay requirement seasonally; main house closed November–April.**

❦❦ **ORCAS HOTEL, Orcas Island** The stately Orcas Hotel is probably the first thing you will see as the ferry pulls into the Orcas Island landing. "Hotel" is really a misnomer here, since that term often conjures up an image of a sterile building with identical rooms and basic detailing, none of which applies to this striking Victorian inn trimmed by a white picket fence and a flowering English garden. The view from the wraparound windows in the dining room and lounge—and from many of the rooms upstairs—is striking. From this vantage point you can watch the comings and goings around busy Harney Channel and Shaw Island across the water.

Unfortunately, the majority of rooms in this 1904 landmark hotel are shared- or half-bath specials. In terms of kissing-preferred accommodations, we can recommend only two of the 12 rooms here, both of which fall into the very expensive category during high season (not exactly a bargain compared with other island accommodations that offer a lot more privacy and style). These two units, dubbed the Romantic Rooms, have French doors opening to a shared sundeck, private bathrooms with two-person whirlpool tubs, queen-size feather beds, and stained glass windows created by a local artist.

You have two choices come breakfast time. If you crave omelets, pancakes, and other big beginnings, eat in the dining room (which you pay for). Our preferred choice is to grab a delicious fruit scone or other bakery treats along with a latté in the outstanding bakery/café. Breakfast here is on the house if you're a guest. **Orcas Ferry Landing; (360) 376-4300; inexpensive to very expensive.**

Romantic Warning: Since this hotel is located at the foot of the ferry dock, it is affected by the exceptionally heavy tourist and car traffic during the summer. The downstairs public rooms can get crowded when there is a delay in boarding the ferry.

☙☙❧ **OTTERS POND BED AND BREAKFAST, Eastsound** This is one of the most bird-friendly places we've ever visited, for both lovebirds and the wild variety. The backdrop for this two-story country home is Otters Pond, which looks like something out of a Monet masterpiece. It's home to hundreds of birds, including plenty of red-winged blackbirds, which dominate the numerous bird feeders on the porch and subsequently leave lots of birdseed scattered about.

What can we say about the inside, other than it's overpowered by the outside? With a pond so spectacular in your backyard, why compete? Everything inside is contemporary, comfortable, cozy, and spic 'n' span clean. The huge deck overlooking the pond harbors one of the most charming hot tubs on the island. This little hot pot is housed in a Japanese-style cottage complete with shoji screens for privacy.

Of the five guest rooms, three have private baths. (Plans are in order for the other two to be similarly blessed.) Our favorites are the expensive Swan Room and the more moderate Chickadee Room. Located upstairs, the light and airy Swan Room has a spectacular pond view, king-size bed, elegant country furnishings, and plenty of skylights. An extra-long claw-foot tub and double shower overlook the woods and creek. Although it's on the main floor, off the living room (not a choice location), the Chickadee Room is as cute as its namesake, with a four-poster queen-size bed, fluffy down comforter, and pond view. The antique bathroom is replete with authentic fixtures, a claw-foot tub, and water closet.

Mornings are busy times here with all the bird life about, so prepare yourselves for some singing outside. A five-course breakfast will keep your stomachs satisfied all day. **Six Pond Road; (360) 376-8844, (888) 893-9680; www.otterspond.com; inexpensive to expensive; minimum-stay requirement seasonally.**

☙ **THE OUTLOOK INN, Eastsound** The brochure states that the Outlook Inn has been welcoming visitors since 1888, and the decor might lead you to believe nothing has changed since then. We'll be blunt: Avoid the inexpensive rooms in the main building unless you want to sleep in a tiny room with gloomy Victorian decor or share a bathroom with the sweaty bicyclists who flock here. (A few rooms in the east wing have private baths, but their decor is just as tired.)

Although the new, nearby Bay View Building resembles a suburban apartment complex, the suites here are nicer, brighter, and have such romantic perks as jetted tubs, gas fireplaces, king-size beds, sunken living rooms, and private, albeit small, patios. Depending on your room, views vary from satisfactory to very good. Unfortunately, these accommodations cost megabucks and, compared with other places on the island, are not worth the price. **Horseshoe Highway; (360) 376-2200, (888) OUT-LOOK; inexpensive to unbelievably expensive; closed January.**

☙☙☙ **THE RESORT AT DEER HARBOR, Deer Harbor** Changes are happening fast at this longtime island resort, and all look romantically promising. The recent renovation of all rooms, along with the construction of 11 new cottages, has boosted this resort's kiss rating to three well-deserved smooches. There are now many room choices here—waterfront suites, historical cottages, executive suites, etc.—but we highly recommend the new cottages. Built with an eye toward Craftsman simplicity, these charming and roomy accommodations offer partial to full water views and are decorated in light greens and blond woods, accented by whimsical Northwest art. Best of all, each one features two wonderful places to soak together: a hot tub that sits on the deck (perfect for sunset watching, but with no privacy), and a two-person jetted tub that resides in the slate-covered bathroom. A romantic fireplace can be viewed from the king-size bed, tub, or sitting area. Top all this off with a wet bar, CD player, and TV/VCR, and you won't want to leave. The only downside is that some cottages are close to the road. Luckily, cars are few and far between.

The historical clapboard cottages, used by apple pickers in the 1930s, are quite small, slightly rustic, but cozy, with a pot-bellied stove inside and a hot tub outside on the deck. For those who want lots of space, two private beachfront homes are also available. When we visited, the final touches were just being put on the executive suites (nice views, but the cottages are better) and the surrounding landscaping.

Don't miss the sunset wine and cheese reception at the resort's main office or dinner at Deer Harbor's new restaurant, **SEAN PAUL'S AT DEER HARBOR** (see Restaurant Kissing). In the morning, a continental breakfast is delivered to your door. **200 Deer Harbor Road; (360) 376-4420, (888) 376-4480; www.deerharbor.com; expensive to unbelievably expensive; minimum-stay requirement seasonally.**

Romantic Warning: Although the resort is adults-only, kids from the Deer Harbor Marina can use the pool. If you're in a nearby cottage, be prepared to hear screams of "Marco Polo" one time too many.

☙❮ **ROSARIO RESORT, Orcas Island** Rosario has become a community unto itself, and at its heart is the landmark Rosario Resort, where the historic Moran mansion proudly sits at the edge of Cascade Bay. Picture a sparkling white mansion, manicured grounds, and a luxurious interior with teak floors, rich mahogany paneling, and Arts and Crafts–style furnishings.

Now, picture no guest rooms in this lovely place. Too bad, too, since this is the resort's best feature. Instead, guests are housed in condo-style buildings near the mansion or far away on the hillside. Needless to say, the rooms with direct water views are highly desirable and highly expensive. But don't think you'll be getting a better deal by being tucked away on the hillside. Those rooms can be equally expensive.

Out of the 130 rooms here, some are better suited for romantic encounters than others. Rooms in the 1100, 1200, and 1300 buildings are choice options since they are near the water, the mansion, the three pools, and the luxurious spa. Now, how do we describe the room decor? Perhaps by what it is not: It's not Northwest, West Coast, French country, English country, or anything from any other country. There was a moment of silence when we opened our door. Pale blue, yellow, and cream are the reigning colors on the heavy, striped curtains and matching bed skirts. The same colors are picked up in the animal-motif bedspreads and animal-motif shower curtains, which resemble a three-ring circus gone on safari. The orangey taupe-and-white checkerboard motif in the bathroom couldn't clash more. Despite the chromatically contradictory appointments and peculiar patterns, all rooms have comfy furnishings, patios, and wet bars, and some have deep jetted tubs.

What's the secret to enjoying Rosario? Go big here or go home (where you can define the decor). If forking out the funds for the ideal waterfront room near the mansion isn't a problem, you probably won't be disappointed with your stay. **One Rosario Way; (360) 376-2222, (800) 562-8820; www. rosarioresort.com; very expensive to unbelievably expensive; minimum-stay requirement on weekends.**

Romantic Note: Rosario is extremely popular in the summertime, and getting a reservation can be difficult. Even if you do not stay here, you may want to visit the resort for a meal (see Restaurant Kissing) or to tour the Moran Museum, which takes up the second floor of the mansion. You can walk through rooms originally used by the Moran family, who built this mansion as their summer residence. A massive pipe organ fills the music room; during evening historical presentations in the summer this grand instrument is played, followed by a slide show. Call the resort for additional information.

❦❦❦❦ **SPRING BAY INN, Orcas Island** Start with a sea kayak built for two. Add to that a pristine coastline, the early-morning stillness of the water, a friendly and informative guide, and plenty of wildlife. What do you have? A morning at Spring Bay Inn. Rain or shine, this adventure is offered daily at this unique and wonderful wilderness hideaway. And who better to run this nature lover's paradise, surrounded by wilderness, wildlife, and hiking trails, than two former park rangers? Completely sheltered from civilization by 137 acres of forest, the Spring Bay Inn is two miles away from the tiny town of Olga. On your way to the inn, it may seem as if you've taken a wrong turn, but hang tight, watch out for deer, and don't mind the potholed road—the treasure that awaits is worth the bumpy ride.

This lodge-like house fits in so well with its surroundings that it looks as if it might have grown here alongside the towering cedars. Inside, the main-floor common area is grand yet cozy, with a 14-foot-high exposed-beam ceiling, two river-rock fireplaces, and comfy couches that just beg to be cuddled upon. Also begging (for a game of catch or a tummy rub) are Carson and Radcliff, the two extremely friendly resident retrievers. Expansive windows along one wall look out to a glorious scene of fir trees, the sheltered waters of Spring

Bay, and a trail leading to the pebbled beach, where a large hot tub awaits. Private soaking times can be reserved so you can luxuriate while you enjoy each other and the natural beauty around you.

Upstairs, four generous guest rooms share the same forest and water views through six-foot-high windows. All of the rooms are decorated with stylish Northwest simplicity, showcasing nature photography, local artwork, and a mix of antique and contemporary furnishings. (A good example of the inn-keepers' ingenuity is the driftwood mantel in one room.) Every room also features such amenities as a patchwork quilt, plush feather bed, wood-burning fireplace, and tiled private bath with a claw-foot tub and separate shower, to ensure a comfortable stay. The two larger rooms at either end of the house have private decks, excellent for stargazing or just enjoying the calm bay and tranquil surroundings.

The main-floor Ranger Suite is the largest of all. This grand room boasts the same 14-foot ceiling as the living room, an antiqued brass queen-size bed, a glassed-in reading solarium, a wood-burning fireplace, and its own private entrance. Best of all, it features a private little courtyard that holds a deep soaking tub with low-speed jets. Getting comfortable here is not the least bit challenging. And if you think all this sounds great, just wait, there's more.

As we mentioned, mornings start with a two-hour kayak tour. Not only is this a great deal, considering that kayak rentals elsewhere on the island start at $35 per person, but it is an incredible way to start your day. (If you can pass a basic skills test, you may be able to rent a double kayak for later.) Through interesting stories and descriptions, the informative hosts will give you a new appreciation and understanding of Orcas Island and its spectacular wildlife. After an easygoing paddle, it's back to the inn, where a hearty and healthy brunch is served family style. You'll have no trouble devouring a marionberry smoothie, carrot juice, fruit soup, vegetarian sausage, and multigrain pancakes topped with hot applesauce. After breakfast, hike along one of the trails on the property. With former rangers as trail builders, you can be assured these pathways are well maintained and well marked, and lead to wonderful places—maybe even a romantic spot. **Obstruction Pass Trailhead Road; (360) 376-5531; www.springbayinn.com; very expensive (includes kayak tour); minimum-stay requirement seasonally.**

Romantic Suggestion: For some real local flavor at dinnertime, ask for directions to nearby Buck Bay Shellfish Farm and buy a dozen oysters or clams. Return to Spring Bay Inn, light up the barbecue out back, grill those bivalves until they burst open, and slurp away on the beach.

❀❀❀ **TURTLEBACK FARM INN, Orcas Island** When the sun begins to warm the air and the colors of the countryside come alive with the glow of daybreak, Turtleback Farm Inn is a delightful place to be. The pastoral setting—80 acres of hills, pastures, ponds, and orchards in the breathtaking Crow Valley—is the farm's best asset and worth a walk around.

Every corner of this turn-of-the-century farmhouse has been painstakingly renovated by people who clearly were sensitive to the surrounding landscape. The seven rooms, all with private baths, range from charming to more charming (though the less expensive rooms are rather small). Polished hardwood floors, fir wainscoting, and fluffy lamb's-wool comforters endow every room with elegant simplicity, and white muslin curtains and floral bedspreads lend a crisp country touch. Every bath is outfitted with a porcelain and silver antique replica claw-foot tub, a pedestal sink, and a water closet, along with a modern-day shower. The welcome omission of TVs and phones in the rooms guarantees a quiet country getaway.

A new addition to the farm is the Orchard House, a two-story barn-like building that houses four of the most private (and expensive) rooms. Like the popular Valley View Room in the main house, each Orchard House room is done up with taupe walls, shiny hardwood floors, and tall windows. A king-size bed, gas fireplace, and private deck overlooking the orchard are additional romantic assets. Best of all, breakfast can be delivered in your room via a two-way pantry. Although new, the house doesn't seem to have much soundproofing. We recommend the two top rooms for noise reasons.

We will preface our description of breakfast by saying that perhaps we were expecting too much from an innkeeper who has published a cookbook. Our in-room breakfast was mediocre. Although the Northwest egg dish was tasty, the thrown-together fruit bowl, granola, and dry homemade toast were nothing special. Be sure to ask who is cooking, because on this day the cookbook author wasn't. Still, for the price you pay here, you should expect more. Guests in the main house have their own table in the window-enclosed dining room. If peaceful seclusion and a leisurely pace sound appealing, and you can curb your breakfast expectations, you will be pleased with your stay here. **Crow Valley Road; (360) 376-4914, (800) 376-4914; www.turtlebackinn. com; moderate to very expensive; minimum-stay requirement holidays and seasonally.**

❦❦ **WINDSONG BED AND BREAKFAST, Orcas Island** Built as Westsound's first schoolhouse in 1917, this brick-red home is now a welcoming bed and breakfast. Friendly innkeepers and three friendly dogs greet you at the door and set the tone for the relaxing time to come. An eclectic mix of furnishings fills the comfortable, gold-carpeted main-floor living room, which is open for guest use; a glass-enclosed hot tub area is located off to one side. Hand-painted walls decorate many rooms in the house. The common room's walls are adorned with vines and birds, the foyer offers a panoramic picture of Madrona Point, and each bedroom (and one bath) is an individual creation.

All of the modest rooms feature antique furnishings, down comforters, robes, and private baths (although the bath for the Concerto Room is detached). Our favorite room is the upstairs Rhapsody, with its alder headboard, queen-size bed, corner gas stove, and a whimsical hand-painted mural in the bathroom—depicting a female version of the wind blowing out sweet messages of love. The nearby Concerto also has a gas wood stove, and the skylight above the bed is great for stargazing, but the mismatched furnishings are a little too eclectic for our tastes.

Thankfully, the innkeepers go out of their way to make sure you are comfortable. In fact, they make everyone feel welcome—outside near the road they have a water stand for bikers and hikers who pass by. A multicourse, gourmet breakfast is served under two whimsical tin fish, which float above the dining room table. Windsong is by no means fancy, but if you can forgive some of the decor's shortcomings, the quiet setting is wonderful. **Deer Harbor Road; (360) 376-2500, (800) 669-3948; www.pacificws.com/windsong; expensive; minimum-stay requirement on weekends.**

Restaurant Kissing

❤ **BILBO'S FESTIVO, Eastsound** Generally speaking, Mexican restaurants are rarely romantic—the focus tends to be on good food, generous portions, and a fun atmosphere. Bilbo's Festivo is no exception to this trend, but we must say that it does have a unique character. Carved wooden benches surround a blazing fire pit on the outdoor deck, and a foliage-covered lattice conceals the patio from the road. A stone fireplace and soft lighting embellish the charming interior, which could be romantic if it weren't for the noisy bustle of the big groups and families who also frequent Bilbo's. The food is light and mildly spicy, with generous portions and remarkably fresh seafood. This is a local favorite, so reservations are a good idea. **North Beach Road; (360) 376-4728; inexpensive to moderate; reservations recommended; call for seasonal hours.**

❤❤ **CAFE OLGA, Olga** Want to experience island dining at its most realistic? Travel a few miles south of Mount Constitution to this charming remodeled 1936 strawberry packing plant turned rustic café, art gallery, and gift boutique. As laid-back and casual as the atmosphere is, the food is anything but. Items from the eclectic, health-oriented menu include Sicilian artichoke pie; creamy, rich manicotti with walnuts; Moroccan salad brimming with couscous, dates, almonds, and spices; and a Mediterranean plate with hummus, Greek olives, pepperoncinis, and an assortment of fresh vegetables. Breads, soups, and irresistible desserts are always fresh and homemade. In fact, locals wait for months to sink their teeth into the luscious blackberry pie. As you leisurely dine, you'll have plenty of time to share your thoughts and get to know each other a little better. If you have to wait (which is often the case), browsing in the art gallery can help pass the time. **Horseshoe Highway; (360) 376-5098; inexpensive to moderate; brunch, lunch, and dinner daily; closed January–February.**

❤❤❤ **CHRISTINA'S, Eastsound** Critics from all over the world have been raving about Christina's inventive Northwest specialties for years. The trick is to make sure that Christina herself, the chef and owner, is in the kitchen, since she is the one with the magic touch. Sadly, those days are very limited; Christina usually comes in during off-hours for sauce preparation, menu planning, and so forth. Despite her frequent absence, her unique touch has been passed on to the chef in charge. The fresh local clams, superb salmon, creamy pasta dishes, and vegetarian items served here are sheer heaven.

Set on the second floor of a gas station and little store, the Craftsman-style dining room is adorned with oak tables and chairs, hardwood floors, and wildflower arrangements; the effect is island elegant—not too fancy, but tastefully done. The building is right on the waterfront, and views of the mountains surrounding Eastsound's inlet are fantastic, particularly from the sunporch. On sunny summer evenings, the rooftop terrace is an alluring alternative for dinner, and the views up here are even better. For a real taste of the Northwest, Christina's is the place to come. **No. 1 Main Street (Horseshoe Highway); (360) 376-4904; moderate to expensive; call for seasonal hours; closed two weeks before Thanksgiving.**

❤❤ **ORCAS WINE COMPANY AND OYSTER BAR, Eastsound** Oysters are a lot like wine. Their character differs depending on where they are grown. To taste what local waters produce, visit this oyster bar/restaurant/wine shop on the waterfront. What this place lacks in romantic ambience, it makes up for with some of the freshest oysters we've tasted. Actually, the waterfront restaurant has an outstanding view, but the furnishings—green plastic chairs and tables, lattice walls thick with grapevines, and an old piano—are a bit cheap looking. But you won't care once you slurp down Buck Bay's best or Judd Cove's finest. If you think raw is repulsive, try the pan-fried Cajun oysters or, better yet, the baked oysters Asiago or oysters Beaubien (broiled with sun-dried tomatoes, olives, and herbs). Wash it all down with a glass of the special Dry Oyster White Wine, available only on Orcas Island. Dinner features other dishes besides bivalves: New York peppercorn steak, oven-roasted salmon, and special pastas. Wine tastings are available any time of the day (four samples for 50 cents). Sip your wine, savor your oysters, and enjoy the view. What more could you ask for? **Main Street (Horseshoe Highway); (360) 376-6244, (800) 934-7616; inexpensive to expensive; call for seasonal hours.**

❤❤❤ **ROSARIO RESTAURANTS, Orcas Island** Rosario has two restaurants designed for romantic encounters: the casual **ORCAS DINING ROOM** and the intimate **COMPASS ROOM**. Both dining rooms are located on the main floor of the historic waterfront Moran mansion, so diners can take pleasure in the remarkable views and watch plenty of water traffic—from seaplane landings to sailboats breezing by.

Perhaps the hardware store was having a special on yellow paint the day they painted the Orcas Dining Room. From the walls right down to the tablecloths, everything is bright buttercup. Add some sunlight to this scene and you'd better wear shades. Luckily, high ceilings and colorful ceramic plates add some diversion. Window seats are obviously choice spots, but three walls of windows and the room's terraced layout allow excellent views wherever you are seated. An elaborate seafood buffet is available every Friday, and the Sunday brunch here is wonderfully extravagant. Otherwise, the menu offers typical Northwest fare, including the largest Caesar salad we've ever seen. Service is a bit poky and amateurish, but friendly. Reports on the cuisine range from good to excellent; you be the judge.

Open for dinner only, the Compass Room is a more formal, intimate setting. This area was once the resort's lounge, and all the tables are lined up alongside arched windows, so you really can't go wrong anywhere you sit. Beautifully presented dishes worthy of recognition include pan-roasted king salmon with zinfandel-stewed morels, oven-roasted duck breast with leek and sweet potato hash, and roasted chicken. You might have to ask the waiter to explain some of the desserts, since their names are a bit odd. **One Rosario Way, at Rosario Resort; (360) 376-2222, (800) 562-8820; www.rosarioresort.com; moderate to expensive; reservations recommended; Orcas Dining Room: breakfast and lunch daily, dinner seasonally, brunch Sunday; Compass Room: dinner daily.**

Romantic Note: Rosario is probably the most well-known establishment on the island, so reservations are highly recommended, although we should add that reaching the dining room via phone can test your patience. Dress is resort casual, but management asks guests not to wear tank tops or shorts in the Orcas Dining Room or the Compass Room. A more casual restaurant, **CASCADE BAY CAFE** (inexpensive; lunch and dinner daily), is near the water front for the underdressed or those wanting a quick nibble.

❤❤ **SEAN PAUL'S AT DEER HARBOR, Deer Harbor** The complete renovation of **THE RESORT AT DEER HARBOR** (see Hotel/Bed and Breakfast Kissing) did more than just provide a much-needed upgrade to the area. It also added a new restaurant to the island's dining scene. Overlooking the Deer Harbor Marina, this modest restaurant's best aspect is its large outside deck, which makes for wonderful sunset watching. If the day is gray, the bright honey-colored interior will cheer you up with its blond wood chairs, black-and-white photographs on the walls, and fresh roses and large candles on the tables. Windows are draped with delicate white fabric, allowing in as much light as possible.

The menu has a bit more zest than the decor. Seasonal Northwest cuisine with some Southwest influences makes up most of the menu. A real treat is the strawberry and spinach salad, pepped up with a paprika dressing. Chicken tandoori, oven-roasted halibut with garlic cream sauce, and grilled sea bass with black bean and tomato salsa are among the more outstanding choices. The grilled lamb chop proved satisfactory, although the accompanying deep-fried wild mushroom risotto cakes could have been lighter. Desserts suit the seasons. During our summer visit, the strawberry and key lime napoleon was as refreshing as the cool breeze off the water. A mango mousse, swirled in a chocolate-coated cocktail glass, was equally delightful. **200 Deer Harbor Road, at The Resort at Deer Harbor; (360) 376-7030; expensive; call for seasonal hours.**

❧❧❧ SHIP BAY OYSTER HOUSE, Eastsound

Deer often graze in the orchard leading up to this large yellow restored farmhouse, setting the mood for a splendid evening to remember. Ship Bay Oyster House is nestled on a grassy lawn only yards away from a shimmering bay, so request a window seat and watch the sun set behind the trees.

Many of the home's original features, including cobbled tin walls, a fireplace, and an ornate ceiling, have been painted in shades of taupe, and pictures of tall ships dot the walls. While desirable, the few window seats here are quite close together. Tables farther back tend to get less light, but that might add to the romantic mood.

As for the menu, it's standard surf 'n' turf specials, with charbroiled steaks, fish, and chicken included on the long lineup. Since this isn't cow country (our steak was fatty), avoid the moo and savor the local stars—oysters (served a variety of ways) or the bucket of clams. Stay in local territory with dessert too. The Lopez Island Creamery makes ice cream in such wonderful flavors as cinnamon, mango, and Skor coffee. Such sweet endings are always wonderful. **Horseshoe Highway; (360) 376-5886; expensive; call for seasonal hours; closed December–February.**

Romantic Note: The renovated barn out back is for weddings and conferences, in case you wonder about that mammoth structure. When we visited, plans were being made to add guest quarters, including suites with jetted tubs. No word on how they'll look, but most likely they'll have great views.

Outdoor Kissing

❧❧❧❧ MOUNT CONSTITUTION, Orcas Island

From Mount Constitution's vantage point of 2,409 feet, the highest elevation on the San Juan Islands, a breathtaking view stretches to unbelievable distances. On a clear day, you can see Mount Baker, Mount Rainier, the Olympics, the Cascades, and the Gulf Islands, not to mention the 171 other islands in the San Juan archipelago and the coastal towns across the water. The easily attained summit boasts a historic stone lookout tower well above the treetops. Even though this site is typically awash with tourists, a visit is well worth your while: The view simply cannot be rivaled. Unquestionably, Mount Constitution is a must-see for any island visitor. (Even if you are staying on a different island, it is worth the daytrip to Orcas Island.) **Moran State Park; (360) 376-2326.** *From the Orcas ferry landing, go north on Horseshoe Highway and follow signs toward Eastsound. After taking the turnoff into Eastsound, stay on the main road and pass through town. Continue south on this road and you will come to the* *massive white arch that marks the entrance to Moran State Park. The six-mile road to Mount Constitution is clearly marked, on the left.*

Romantic Option: On the way up the mountain, you will see a turnout on the right for **CASCADE FALLS.** A short, easy hike leads to a fern-lined stream and cascading waterfall. This scene provides a great photo opportunity and could also inspire a kiss or two.

Romantic Suggestion: If you would like to bring along a picnic for a mountaintop meal, stop at **ROSES BREAD AND SPECIALTIES** (at the back of Eastsound Square, just off A Street in Eastsound; 360-376-5805; inexpensive to moderate). Gourmet meats and cheeses, fresh homemade European-style breads, Northwest wines, delicious bakery goods, and a variety of other locally made items are available for your afternoon feast. If you ask, they'll pack it all up in a bag with all the necessary utensils.

❤❤❤ **QUARTER MOON CRUISES, Deer Harbor** Riding the ferry from Anacortes to the San Juan Islands is a magnificent prelude to a romantic getaway. However, spending this brief time on the water surrounded by so many other vacationers will probably leave you longing for a private, relaxed cruise around the islands. Quarter Moon Cruises may provide just what you are looking for.

Imagine an excursion on a deluxe 55-foot motor yacht. Gourmet lunch or dinner cruises last approximately three and a half hours, and the menu always includes fresh local seafood, homemade pastas, soup, salad, fresh bread, dessert, and a complimentary Northwest microbrew, Washington wine, or other beverage. On warm summer days, this feast is presented outside on the deck. Even if the weather is uncooperative, the view can be enjoyed from the comfortable, window-lined main salon. Up to six people may join you for the ride, but two-person excursions can also be arranged (for an additional fee, of course). **(360) 376-2878; www.orcasisland.com/cruises; $1,100 per day for six people (meals included).**

Romantic Option: Quarter Moon Cruises also offers bed-and-breakfast cruises. This type of trip begins with a yacht cruise, during which lunch is served. In the afternoon, the boat sets anchor just offshore and you can paddle in a rowboat to one of the islands. On-island transportation is provided for whichever activities you like, and you are then transported to a bed and breakfast, where you spend the night. After breakfast, it's back to the yacht for more cruising around the archipelago. Prices vary depending on which bed and breakfast is included, but rates start at $1,100 per day for two to six people for a two-night, three-day cruise. This is not exactly inexpensive, but keep in mind that the price includes sailing through the islands for three days, activities such as crabbing or fishing, three lunches, two nights at a bed and breakfast, and any transportation necessary. Bon voyage!

❤❤❤❤ **SEA KAYAKING, Eastsound** There is something quite remarkable about propelling yourselves in a two-person kayak through the open waters around the forested islands of the San Juans. It's exciting to be part of nature's aquatic playground, where eagles and gulls swoop down across the water's surface, a variety of seabirds dive underwater, otters and seals dart in and out of the current, and, on rare occasions, a great orca effortlessly glides by. There are no words to describe the sensation of watching the world from this vantage point, and the strength of your arms (or lack of it) has little bearing on the quality of the experience. All kinds of special trips are possible, some of which include time for picnicking, sunbathing, and island exploration. Whichever one you choose, you won't regret the experience. **Osprey Tours: (360) 376-3677, (800) 529-2567; www.fidalgo.net/~kayak. Shearwater Adventures, Inc.: (360) 376-4699. Prices start at $39 per person; reservations required; closed January–February.**

❦❦❦ **WHALE WATCHING CRUISES, Orcas Island** Orcas Island's name suggests that it is *the* place to view a majestic orca, but San Juan Island is much better known for onshore whale sightings. If you are able to get out on the water, however, everything changes, and you just may be lucky enough to catch a glimpse of one. What inspires these incredible creatures to put on such a show is not known, but their behavior includes tail-lobbing, in which they wave their sleek black tails above the surface; spy-hopping, in which their heads peek out of the ocean and they seem to observe the activity around them; and breaching, in which they propel their entire bodies out of the water and then splash with awesome force. Even when they are just gracefully gliding along with their massive dorsal fins cutting through the water, it is a sight to see. Witnessing such a performance could change your life. Even if you aren't graced by the presence of orcas, you may see porpoises, seals, various seabirds, or bald eagles, and just being out on the water is a wondrous experience. **Deer Harbor Charters: Deer Harbor; (360) 376-5989, (800) 544-5758. Orcas Island Eclipse Charters, Inc.: Orcas Ferry Landing; (360) 376-4663, (800) 376-6566. Prices start at $45 per person; reservations required; closed November–January.**

Lopez Island

Although Lopez Island is one of the better-known islands in the San Juan archipelago (it's one of the four on the ferry run), it still seems untouched, with its miles of farmland, rolling tundra, and roaming rabbits. It's also regarded as the friendliest island. Don't be surprised if passersby wave to you from their cars; everybody does. By the end of your relaxing stay, you may acquire the habit of waving in return. Lopez Island is also bicycle friendly, thanks to its easygoing terrain and lonely backcountry roads. Bike rentals are available on the island; if you bring your own two-wheeler, you'll be glad to know many bed and breakfasts are just a few miles' ride from the ferry terminal.

Hotel/Bed and Breakfast Kissing

❤❤❧ **BLUE FJORD CABINS, Lopez Island** A little Swedish Dala horse statue displaying the word *Välkommen* (welcome) introduces you to this lovely and remote place. Two secluded Nordic chalets—appropriately named Sweden and Norway—are sequestered beneath groves of cedar and fir trees, and are perfect for those seeking to escape everything but each other. Sunlight filters through skylights in both of the simply decorated, modified A-frame cabins, appointed with open-beam ceilings and cedar paneling. Those craving coziness and sleep-ins should stay in Norway, hidden among the cedars. More exposed Sweden catches the morning light—perfect for early risers. Even though the furnishings are plain and the colors stuck in the '70s, the queen-size beds, full kitchens, large decks with forest views, and privacy on all sides more than compensate.

Near the innkeepers' house some seashells mark the beginning of a short nature trail (a five-minute walk) that descends to a "mini-fjord" in Jasper Bay. Savor the stillness as you relax in the private gazebo on the beach, with a stunning view of Mount Baker in the distance. You may also catch a glimpse of your only other neighbors (besides the owners): bald eagles, blue herons, and a cluster of sea otters.

Since this isn't a bed and breakfast, you're on your own for meals. Stock up in Lopez Village before arriving. **Elliott Road; (360) 468-2749, (888) 633-0401; inexpensive; no credit cards; minimum-stay requirement.**

❤❤❤ **EDENWILD INN, Lopez Island** The Edenwild Inn may fool you a bit, but in a good way. It resembles a grand old Victorian home, but actually it's a recent replica. Perhaps it's the attention to detail that does the trick: Worn hardwood floors, antique replica light fixtures, and antique furnishings are found throughout the large home. Unlike many authentic Victorian homes, however, this one has eight large bedrooms with private baths. Despite being in the center of Lopez Village, there's a country feel about this place thanks to its large lawn and herb garden, wraparound porch draped with clematis, and an encompassing arbor accented with antique white roses and wisteria.

All rooms are simply but beautifully appointed with antiques, dried flowers, artwork, and beveled glass windows. Some have fireplaces and water views. Rooms 5 and 6 are especially choice. Both large rooms have perfect sunset and water views, queen-size beds, and sitting areas. While Room 5 is more our style, with taupe-colored walls, contemporary art, pounded copper–topped tables, and a bay window sitting area, Room 6 (the official honeymoon suite) tempted us with its fireplace and claw-foot tub. But, unless bright forget-me-not blue is your favorite color, the walls can be a bit overwhelming.

A three-course breakfast is served in a simply decorated dining room that overlooks the brick patio. The proprietor, an award-winning chef, whips up such delectable delights as poached egg in cheddar-port sauce served in a puff-pastry shell, and blueberry-stuffed French toast topped with blueberry sauce.

Two-person tables let you enjoy breakfast without interruption. **132 Lopez Road; (360) 468-3238; www.edenwildinn.com; moderate to expensive; minimum-stay requirement on holiday weekends; recommended wedding site.**

Romantic Suggestion: Want to be whisked away in grand style? With advanced notice, the Edenwild Inn's staff can pick you up from the ferry terminal or airport in their classic Checker Aerobus. The cream-colored vehicle is 20 feet long, seats 12, and beats a taxi any day.

❧❧ FISHERMAN BAY GUEST HOUSE, Lopez Island

We are reluctant to reveal the location of this one-room hideaway, because people get the wrong impression when you say it's above a garage. If you can shift those stereotypes into neutral, you'll be delighted by this large, light room with a wood-burning stove and hardwood floors. As for the noise factor, the proprietor doesn't use the garage when guests are in residence.

Between the detached garage and matching buttercup yellow farmhouse awaits a delightful flower and herb garden bedecked with whimsical ornaments. Follow the geranium pots and frog statues lining the wooden stairs to your private deck overlooking Fisherman's Bay, the marina, and some flotsam and jetsam near the pier. Tall rectangular windows face the water, and skylights flood the high-ceilinged room with natural light. The eye-catcher here is the queen-size bed with a white picket fence headboard. Behind it, a painted garden mural winds upward to a gigantic circular window with views of the road and nearby horse pastures. Breakfast is not included with your stay; however, the stocked mini-kitchen should satisfy your snacking needs, and Lopez Village and its restaurants are a short walk away.

Although the bathroom is small and the decor eclectic (including a Peruvian chest, a blue kitchenette, souvenir plates, and antique cabinets), this room above the garage is a suitable place to park yourselves for romance. **2612 Fisherman Bay Road; (360) 468-2884; www.rockisland.com/~ralphndoris/ fbguest.html; expensive.**

❧❧❧❧ INN AT SWIFTS BAY, Lopez Island

The pineapple, a symbol of hospitality, is a fitting icon for this Tudor home nestled near Swifts Bay. The innkeepers' keen eye for detail is borne out in all aspects of the food, service, and surroundings, creating a retreat well suited for our favorite three Rs: relaxation, refreshment, and romance.

Tucked among the cedars just minutes from the beach, the inn fills almost every affectionate requirement. Make a selection from their unique tea library (over 40 choices) and sip your tea in the comfortable common room adorned with rich colors, floral fabrics, and a wood-burning fireplace; lounge in the backyard courtyard that's popular with the wild birds; or stargaze from the very private hot tub. (You can reserve the hot tub to ensure total privacy.)

All five guest rooms are appointed with soothing colors and comfortable furnishings. Only three of the five rooms have private baths, but even the two rooms that share a bath are beautifully endowed with luscious linens and lovely antiques. Romance seekers should head to one of the two attic suites, particularly desirable for their skylights, queen-size beds with goose-down comforters, double-headed showers, gas fireplaces, private decks, and private entrances.

If the day is rainy, put on the portable headphones and watch a movie (from a library of over 300 videos) or exercise in the small but mighty workout room separate from the home. It comes complete with a selection of exercise tapes, a sauna for two, and an alfresco shower—a rare find in this neck of the woods.

The locals say the inn's breakfasts are the best on the island, and there's no disputing that. Can any breakfast top fresh pear muffins, fruit smoothies, and a torte layered with red pepper, spinach Florentine, herbed eggs, ham, and Gruyère cheese sprinkled with translucent potato chips? By the way, as a repeat guest, you'll never have the same breakfast twice (unless you request it). A computerized guest-breakfast tracking system guarantees you'll savor a different morning delight each time you visit. How's that for detailed service? **Port Stanley Road; (360) 468-3636; www.swiftsbay.com; inexpensive to expensive; minimum-stay requirement on holiday weekends.**

❧❧❧❧ LOPEZ FARM COTTAGES, Lopez Island To check into one of Lopez Farm's charming cottages is to step into an oasis of privacy. Indeed, the sweet solitude starts when you leave the main thoroughfare and drive down a gravel road to the 20-acre farm. There's no official check-in: just pick up your key (and a list of housekeeping details) in a little hut near the 1907 Craftsman-style farmhouse. With your luggage in a pushcart, walk along the lighted gravel path to your cottage nestled between the cedars. It's pure privacy, plain and simple.

Four nicely spaced cottages overlook a tranquil field of green grass, punctuated by four glacial boulders (and plenty of bouncing bunnies). It's evident this place has been designed strictly for couples—from the two Adirondack chairs in front of each unit to the double-headed showers in the bathrooms. Combining elegant Scandinavian simplicity with rustic Northwest flair, the cottages are one-bedroom wonders. While similar on the outside, with light cedar siding and white-trimmed windows, the interior of each has its own character, expressed through colors (such as lavender and coral), fabric choices and patterns, and flower arrangements. All have hardwood floors, classic Craftsman-style furnishings and lighting, kitchenettes, queen-size beds, high ceilings with fans, and enough windows and French doors for light to flow freely. The decor is pleasingly simple, and so is life on this farm. There are no TVs or telephones, just you two, so dim the lights, prop up the pillows, and enjoy the fireplace in front of you. On warm evenings, sit outside and watch deer graze in the meadow. For ultimate relaxation, and a few wet kisses, visit the jetted hot tub hidden in a cedar grove and surrounded by old barn panels for privacy.

A breakfast basket of fruits and baked goods arrives in the early evening, so there's no hurry getting up in the morning. Get a little taste of farm life by feeding the adorable sheep that live in a nearby pasture. You'll soon have several instant friends. **555 Fisherman Bay Road; (360) 468-3555, (800) 440-3556; www.lopezfarmcottages.com; expensive.**

❦❦ **MACKAYE HARBOR INN, Lopez Island** Kayakers, beachcombers, and romantics alike can find a haven for their hearts and hobbies in this gracious farmhouse and carriage house overlooking MacKaye Harbor. Each of the five cozy guest rooms in the Colonial-style farmhouse is adorned with a mismatched blend of antiques and country furnishings; some offer full or partial water views. Unfortunately, only two of the rooms in the main house have private bathrooms. One such room is the Harbor Suite, which boasts a wood-burning fireplace, queen-size bed, and unobstructed views of the bay from a private covered deck. The Blue Room also has a private bath and almost the same view as the more expensive Harbor Suite. Adjacent to the main home, the Carriage House Studio is well suited for romance, appointed with a private bathroom, white wicker furnishings, Laura Ashley fabrics, and a small but modern kitchenette. The next-door Master Carriage House is geared for larger groups.

Roll out of bed and you're almost on the beach, which makes MacKaye Harbor House an ideal getaway. After a gourmet breakfast of Finnish pancakes, aebleskiver, or another wonderful recipe from the innkeeper's published cookbook, you can rent a two-person kayak and paddle off to sea in romantic synchronization. Complimentary mountain bikes are also available for guests' use. **MacKaye Harbor Road; (360) 468-2253; www.pacificrim.net/~mckay; moderate to very expensive.**

Restaurant Kissing

❦❦❦ **BAY CAFE, Lopez Island** It's a shame the Bay Cafe serves only dinner—we would gladly come here for breakfast and lunch too. Colorful, whimsical local artwork and Fiestaware are displayed on the walls, a wooden kayak hangs overhead, and an agreeable mixture of European and American furnishings imparts a casual, eclectic atmosphere. The menu is just as eclectic, with innovative, multiethnic fare. Excellent choices include wild Mexican prawns grilled with Thai lime dipping sauce; hoisin-glazed, peanut-encrusted pork medallions; and, for tastes from the deep, wonderful seafood tapas. Whatever you do, you must try dessert. The chocolate gâteau and coffee nudge crème caramel with a hint of cognac should not be missed. **Lopez Village; (360) 468-3700; moderate to expensive; reservations recommended; call for seasonal hours.**

Shaw Island

The smallest of the ferry-served San Juan Islands, Shaw Island is also the least populated and least developed. The only business establishment here is at the ferry terminal, where a little general store is run completely by nuns (the nuns—dressed in full habit—even rope in the ferryboat). From the moment you step off the ferry, utter tranquillity surrounds you and you begin to slow your quick city pace. What is the best way to explore Shaw's natural surroundings, rural country roads, secluded beaches, and nightly sunsets? Pack up a picnic, hop on your bikes, and ride to your own private grassy field. You'll have to share the space only with the occasional deer or blue heron. A day on Shaw Island, with no distractions other than the birds' sweet songs and the pleasant company of each other, will make for a day to remember.

"Where kisses are repeated

and the arms hold there is no

telling where time is."

Ted Hughes

Olympic Peninsula

Taking the 40-minute ferry ride from Seattle to Bainbridge Island is one of the more popular ways to begin a trip to the Olympic Peninsula. From Bainbridge Island, cross the Agate Pass Bridge, drive north up the Kitsap Peninsula, and then head over the Hood Canal Bridge. You can also take the ferry from Edmonds, just north of Seattle, to Kingston, located on the Kitsap Peninsula, and follow the signs west and north to the Hood Canal Bridge. A longer route is to take the ferry from Seattle across the sound to Bremerton and then continue on north to Hood Canal Bridge. The bridge is a gateway to the Olympic Peninsula, where the Northwest's largest national park and some of the state's most spectacular scenery await you.

Bremerton

Hotel/Bed and Breakfast Kissing

❀❀❀❀ **ILLAHEE MANOR, Bremerton** Attention to detail and a multitude of amenities make this one of the finest bed and breakfasts we've encountered. Resembling a small castle, the main house sits on a landscaped bluff above the sparkling waters of Puget Sound. (A hot tub on the large deck shares the splendid view.) Majestic trees, an apple orchard, and two separate vacation homes are spread out on the sur- rounding six acres.

The five suites in the main house are appointed with gas fireplaces or wood-stoves, beautifully restored antiques, and private bathrooms. The second-story Penthouse Suite has enough space to live in and enough enchantment to make you never want to leave. Richly colored furniture and a woodstove add warmth to the inviting living room. Just beyond, high ceilings and beams slope down to form arches that separate different areas of the suite. In one alcove, a giant Jacuzzi tub near the king-size bed is surrounded by plants and affords views of the water below. A full kitchen, separate bath, and lounging area with a stereo are part of this suite deal. Although the Penthouse is extraordinary, the other four rooms are amazing in their own right. Even the Library Room on the main floor, which has a detached private bath, is exceedingly romantic, despite the walk across the hall. Its enormous bath contains skylights in the two-person shower, a huge spa tub, and a sauna.

Separate from the main house, the spacious Honeymoon Cabin and the Beach House are actually best suited for families or couples traveling together. We especially liked the Honeymoon Cabin, which has been done up in country-style furnishings and features a deck overlooking Puget Sound.

Nothing here will disappoint, including the gourmet breakfasts. Apple-rum griddle cakes, peach melba croissant French toast, and strawberry granola sundaes will entice you to leave your room—at least long enough to enjoy the view from the wood-paneled dining room, with its dramatic vaulted ceiling. If you prefer total privacy in the morning, the innkeepers will gladly deliver breakfast to your suite. **6680 Illahee Road Northeast; (360) 698-7555, (800) 693-6680; www.comstation.com/illaheemanor; moderate to very expensive.**

Belfair

Hotel/Bed and Breakfast Kissing

❀❀❀ **SELAH INN, Belfair** There aren't many deluxe accommodations on the north shore of Hood Canal, but Selah Inn is clearly an exception. Prime beachfront property, beautiful guest rooms, gourmet breakfasts, and dinners featuring fresh Northwest seafood make this a premier romantic destination.

Nine guest suites are available in two different buildings, all with private baths and extra soundproofing to ensure privacy. In the main house, the King Room features a green marble fireplace, double Jacuzzi tub, and a large deck with a view of the canal. The best views, however, are from the Front Room in the adjacent beach house (which is closer to the water). Here you'll discover warm colors, a fireplace, Oriental carpets, a step-up tiled Jacuzzi tub, and a private glass-enclosed deck with inviting hammock-style chairs. No matter which one you choose, all the rooms feature first-class beds with luxurious linens. Unwind in the inn's common areas, which include a library, a tiled sunroom, and a comfortable modern living room with a massive stone fireplace.

Breakfast is included in the price of your stay; lunch and dinner are available at an additional cost. Between meals, you're welcome to dig for clams on the beach (shovels are provided) and then grill them over the outdoor fire pit until they pop open: a delicious afternoon snack. If you choose to eat dinner at the inn, you're sure to enjoy the remarkably fresh salmon stuffed with crab and shrimp, followed by homemade peach pie. **Northeast 130 Dulalip Landing; (360) 275-0916; www.selahinn.com; moderate to expensive.**

Romantic Note: Don't be surprised to find yourselves involved in a religious discussion during your stay; one of the owners is a former pastor of a Christian church and enjoys sharing her faith.

Seabeck

Hotel/Bed and Breakfast Kissing

❀❀❀❀ **WILLCOX HOUSE COUNTRY INN, Seabeck** We're in full agreement with those who think that the Willcox House is one of the premier places to kiss on the Kitsap Peninsula. What we found here exceeded our wildest imaginings. The drive from Bremerton leads you through 14 miles of towering evergreens and rolling countryside to the turnoff for the house, where the road takes a steep turn down to the water and passes beneath a dramatic log and stone archway. The enormous copper-roofed mansion with terra-cotta tiles is a magnificent sight, resting on a forested bluff with superb views of Hood Canal and the Olympic Mountains. Wisteria climbs the trellis in the backyard, where walking paths wind through palatial gardens, past a swinging hammock, a swimming pool, and a goldfish pond.

A visit to the Willcox House will take you back in time to the romantic Hollywood of the 1930s: The home's original owners ran in the same circle as Clark Gable, who often stayed here as a guest (one of the rooms is even named after him). Restored at a cost of more than $300,000, the 10,000-square-foot interior is a masterpiece of Northwest architecture and extravagant decor (although a bit on the eclectic side). This place has to be seen to be believed! There are almost as many common areas as there are bedrooms. You can tinker with the grand piano in the wood-paneled guest parlor, amuse yourselves with darts in the large game room, or socialize with other guests over wine and cheese in the upstairs library overlooking the water. A small, elegant movie theater is the perfect spot for late-night cuddling.

All five guest rooms have been diligently renovated and feature gorgeous linens, copper-framed fireplaces, walnut paneling, and wood parquet floors. Some offer views of the sweeping lawn and gardens, mountain peaks, and water; two have Jacuzzi tubs; and one has a private balcony.

Breakfast is a remarkable presentation of fresh fruits, granola, and crêpes topped with strawberry-blueberry syrup, served in a glass-enclosed dining room with impressive views. **2390 Tekiu Road; (360) 830-4492, (800) 725-9477; www.willcoxhouse.com; moderate; minimum-stay requirement weekends and seasonally.**

Romantic Suggestion: On Saturday evenings, the innkeepers at Willcox House serve a formal four-course dinner (expensive) that is available to guests as well as to the public. This is a meal you will thoroughly appreciate. Baked Brie with pineapple-mango chutney, a salad with 20 different greens and edible flowers, alder-smoked fresh salmon or chicken, and asparagus with kumquat butter are a few of the menu's savory delights.

Silverdale

Hotel/Bed and Breakfast Kissing

HEAVEN'S EDGE BED AND BREAKFAST, Silverdale Pictures of the view from Heaven's Edge have graced the cover of many travel guides, Northwest magazines, and a local cookbook. And no wonder. After witnessing a breathtaking sunset from the deck of this lovely home, it is not presumptuous to say that this is the best panoramic view on the Kitsap Peninsula.

Besides the wondrous view, an additional romantic plus is the fact that the only suite here can be yours and yours alone for the duration of your stay. A garden path leads you to your three-room suite. Here you'll find a nicely decorated private bath, as well as a sitting room containing a white leather love seat, an entertainment center, and vases of fresh flowers to brighten the interior. Rich shades of red and green in the bedroom create a cozy atmosphere, and the queen-size bed is adorned with feather pillows and a fluffy down comforter. This bedroom is designed to be your cuddling destination after an evening walk down to the private pebble beach below the property. Guests are also welcome to use the game room, located down the hall, featuring a pool table, comfortable leather furniture, a large TV, and a wood-burning stove.

Breakfast at Heaven's Edge is a bountiful feast that begins with fresh fruit and decadent scones filled with white chocolate and fresh berries. You might want to wrap these up and save them for a midmorning snack; that way you'll have room for the three-cheese and bacon quiche or a frittata made with spinach, onions, and fresh mushrooms. Breakfast can be served in your suite, in the game room, or on the patio when the weather permits. **7410 Northwest Ioka Drive; (360) 613-1111, (800) 413-5680; www.kitsap.net/business/ bnb/heaven; moderate to expensive; minimum-stay requirement on weekends seasonally.**

Poulsbo

This tiny waterfront town is best known for the charming (admittedly touristy) Scandinavian motif of its coffee shops, restaurants, and storefronts. You'll certainly be drawn in by the tantalizing aroma of fresh apple-cinnamon bread wafting out the door of the popular **SLUYS BAKERY** (18924 Front Street; 360-779-2798; inexpensive). Once you've selected your pastry (this is easier said than done), head for the boardwalk at **LIBERTY MARINA PARK**. The scenery here is sure to inspire a kiss or two. Poulsbo has much more to offer than is first apparent from its ersatz facade, and its distinctly romantic destinations, concealed in the countryside, are not to be missed.

Hotel/Bed and Breakfast Kissing

❀❀❅ **EDGEWATER BEACH BED AND BREAKFAST, Poulsbo** Bald eagles, blue herons, otters, sea lions, pheasants, and songbirds frequent this location, which might be incentive enough to pack your bags and leave city life behind. If it isn't, this should help: 3,000 square feet of this 4,800-square-foot renovated 1920s beach house are dedicated exclusively to guests. This space includes comfortable (albeit somewhat eclectic) sunlit common areas with views of Hood Canal and the ascending Olympic Mountains. Your privacy is further ensured by the fact that there are only three guest rooms here, so the meandering garden paths and the winding trail that leads down to the beach are likely to be yours alone.

Gas fireplaces, CD players, antique beds draped with down comforters and cut-lace duvets, private baths, and eclectic country furnishings adorn the two smaller guest rooms. The most expensive room (yet still affordable) is the Olympic Suite, which is the best reason to stay here. Oriental rugs grace gleaming hardwood floors in this airy suite that is accented with a hand-thrown pottery sink, a five-headed shower, and a cheery sitting area that affords views of Hood Canal and the Olympic Mountains. The color blue, in varying shades and prints, seems to be the recurring theme in all the guest rooms, so if you have an aversion to an overuse of it, this is probably not the place for you. (Everything is blue including the furniture, sinks, carpets, and bedding—we are really talking blue here.)

Pastries and other breakfast goodies are delivered to your room each morning in a basket. In addition, you'll find meats and cheeses, fresh fruit, and chilled refreshments already stocked in your refrigerator. **26818 Edgewater Boulevard; (360) 779-2525, (800) 641-0955; members.aol.com/edjh2obe; moderate to expensive.**

❦❦ LOMAS' MURPHY HOUSE BED AND BREAKFAST, Poulsbo

Lomas' Murphy House is a great getaway for couples who don't want to get too far away from it all. Conveniently perched on a residential hillside in the heart of town, the home sports Poulsbo's casual Scandinavian theme and overlooks views of neighboring houses, Liberty Bay, and the Olympic Mountains. The seven guest rooms here are all filled with a homey mixture of modern and country furnishings. Five have private, albeit standard, bathrooms, and several rooms have small private patios with views. Couples with kissing on their agenda should request either of the two largest rooms in the house; both feature king-size beds, lovely linens, and distant water views. An affectionate bonus: The comfortable common areas offer ample space for snuggling. In fact, we actually preferred the cozy library, brimming with books and games, to some of the bedrooms. Guests also have access to a handy kitchenette, TV/VCR, and a large selection of movies.

A full breakfast of cream cheese croissants, Amish bread, and crab quiche is served in a spacious common area that is warmed by a fireplace and replete with water views. **425 Northeast Hostmark Street; (360) 779-1600, (800) 779-1606; www.bbonline.com/wa/murphy/index.html; inexpensive to moderate.**

Restaurant Kissing

❦❦ JUDITH'S TEA ROOM, Poulsbo

If you are in a mood to share a confection at a cozy table for two, Judith's Tea Room will suit you to a tee. The small country-style dining rooms here provide a charming setting in which to enjoy decadent desserts served daintily on hand-painted china. If you're willing to ignore the adjacent busy street, opt for one of the two-person tables set outdoors on a lovely brick patio enclosed by brass gates. Don't miss the house specialty, Black Forest soup, a hearty concoction of meatballs, potatoes, cabbage, and sausage. If you find yourselves strolling through town in the evening, you may want to inquire about the dinner theater in the back dining room, where live theater is performed on summer evenings. **18820 Front Street; (360) 697-3449; inexpensive to moderate; lunch and afternoon tea daily.**

❦❦ **MOLLY WARD GARDENS, Poulsbo** Surrounded by organic gardens, this interesting restaurant is alive with sounds and scents. The dining room takes up the ground floor of a large home and doubles as a dried flower shop, so if you glance upward at the ceiling you will see flowers everywhere. Dine at an eclectic mix of tables, either inside the dining room or out on the patio, while live jazz fills the air. Soft lighting and a quiet, relaxed atmosphere set the mood for romance.

The menu changes each evening at the whim of the owner; you can count on a fresh seafood entrée, but the other two options are anyone's guess. Choices are written on a blackboard in the dining room, or you can call ahead to find out the selections. All meals begin with either a salad made with fresh greens from the garden or a cup of fabulous homemade soup. Rosemary-infused rack of lamb and fresh halibut with a mango-tomatillo-papaya salsa were available the night we stopped by, and both were perfection. **27462 Big Valley Road; (360) 779-4471; moderate to expensive; lunch Tuesday–Sunday, dinner Wednesday–Monday, brunch Sunday.**

Port Ludlow

Mainly a destination for Northwest golf enthusiasts, Port Ludlow is a sprawling little community that still feels close to nature and is highlighted by awesome views of Puget Sound and the Cascades. Construction of new homes along the water is increasing, but the surrounding area is extremely pleasant, and is a good central location from which to tour the rest of the Olympic Peninsula.

Hotel/Bed and Breakfast Kissing

❦❦❦ **HERON BEACH INN ON LUDLOW BAY, Port Ludlow** Perched at the mouth of Port Ludlow Bay, this stately inn resembles a New England estate, with its clapboard siding, cedar shingles, and wraparound porch. All of the amenities necessary for a romantic interlude are at your fingertips here. Creative Northwest cuisine is served in the relaxed yet sophisticated restaurant on the main floor; upstairs, 37 comfortable, refined guest rooms await your pleasure. Each room has a gas-log fireplace, Jacuzzi tub, cozy bathrobes, and a plush down comforter. Mission-style furnishings, wood shutters, minimalist decor, and black-and-white accents create an elegantly simple ambience. The Bayview Suites, which we consider the most romantic, offer vaulted ceilings, king-size beds, and unobstructed water or mountain views. In the morning, an ample continental breakfast of homemade scones and muffins, fresh fruit, and Northwest coffee is presented in the cheerful sunroom on the main floor. **One Heron Road; (360) 437-0411; very expensive to unbelievably expensive; dinner Wednesday–Sunday; minimum-stay requirement on holidays.**

Romantic Note: The gracious comfort level found here comes as no surprise, since the management company that created this inn specializes in exclusive retreats. One of the inn's sister properties is the highly acclaimed, incredibly romantic **INN AT LANGLEY** on Whidbey Island (reviewed on page 265). While the professionalism and decor found at both properties are comparable, we must say that the property and setting here do not measure up to the Inn at Langley's. Townhomes closely border one side of the Heron Beach Inn, and the landscaping has not yet matured.

❀❀❀ **THE NANTUCKET MANOR, Port Ludlow** The appropriately named Nantucket Manor, with its weathered cedar exterior and stately architecture, looks as if it belongs on a New England seashore. Luckily for Northwesterners, it is located just west of the Hood Canal Bridge. Gorgeous landscaping, a charming gazebo, and abundant gardens grace the yard, and white wicker chairs are set on the front patio, where you can sit and gaze out at the Olympic Mountain Range, Mount Rainier, and the waters of Hood Canal.

Upstairs, this same view can be appreciated from three of the five simple but comfortable guest rooms. All five rooms boast private bathrooms and either queen- or king-size beds covered with plush down comforters. Nantucket is a bright room with dainty rose wallpaper, a king-size four-poster bed, white linens, wicker furnishings, and French doors that open to the expansive front balcony. Pretty antiques and a canopied queen-size bed in the Manor Room are quite inviting, and sage green wallpaper and whitewashed furnishings in the Seaview Room are wonderfully soothing. The Manor and Seaview Rooms also have French doors leading to their balconies. To help compensate for the lack of water views, the two remaining rooms, which overlook the gardens, have larger bathrooms with soaking tubs.

A spa tub off to one side of the house is available for all guests, as is the main-floor parlor, with its glowing wood-burning fireplace. In the morning, before you set out to explore the area, savor a full breakfast, served at one large table adjacent to the parlor or out on the covered veranda. Enjoy fresh fruit and gourmet omelets, followed by strawberry cheesecake for dessert. **941 Shine Road; (360) 437-2676; www.olympus.net/nantucket; expensive to very expensive; recommended wedding site.**

Romantic Suggestion: Wanting to forgo the 30-minute drive to Port Townsend, we asked the innkeepers about a local place to dine. At their suggestion, we went to the **AJAX CAFE** (271 Water Street, Port Hadlock; 360-385-3450; www.olympus.net/ajax; dinner Tuesday–Sunday; closed January), only ten minutes away. It isn't the most romantic restaurant in the area, but it's one of the most interesting and fun, and worth mentioning for its eclectic charm and fabulous food. The entry is decorated with the front end of an old Cadillac, while the dining room is filled with brightly painted chairs and funky decorations. (An assortment of hats adorn the walls of the rest rooms; diners are welcome to pick out a hat to wear during their meal.) Live music (usually jazz, blues, or folk) most nights, large portions of steak and fresh seafood, and a view of the water add up to a memorable evening.

Outdoor Kissing

❤❤❤ **OLYMPIC MUSIC FESTIVAL CONCERTS IN THE BARN** A rustic turn-of-the-century barn is the setting for the Olympic Music Festival, where members of the highly acclaimed Philadelphia String Quartet perform brilliant chamber music every summer. You can sit on hay bales and padded church pews in the barn or spread a blanket outside on the lawn and picnic while classical music fills the air. Come early, before the 2 P.M. performance, and explore the festival grounds. Country paths crisscross the 40-acre farm, which is home to donkeys, cows, pigs, and goats. Although the rural setting may sound like an unlikely venue for passionate renderings of works by Brahms and Mendelssohn, among others, the experience is thoroughly exquisite. **(360) 732-4000; ticket prices start at $10 per person; open weekends from late June through early September.** *From the Hood Canal Bridge, travel west ten miles on the main road (State Route 104). Exit at the "*OLYMPIC MUSIC FESTIVAL*" sign and turn right onto Center Road. The festival entrance is a half mile to the right. Parking is free.*

Romantic Note: Children under six are not allowed in the barn, but they are admitted on the lawn at no charge. If you wish to enjoy the music without the sounds of children scurrying about, the added expenditure for seats in the barn is worth it—and you can still picnic on the lawn before the performance if you'd like.

Marrowstone Island

This idyllic, summer home–clad island, connected to the mainland by a small bridge, is only a 20-minute drive from Port Townsend. Simply follow Highway 116 east to Port Hadlock and cross the bridge to Indian Island. Pass the naval base and continue on Highway 116 east to Marrowstone Island. This is one place even most Northwesterners don't know about.

Hotel/Bed and Breakfast Kissing

❦❦❦ **HONEY MOON CABIN ON MARROWSTONE ISLAND, Marrowstone Island** Seclusion and quiet beauty combine to make the Honey Moon Cabin a spectacular romantic destination. Its six surrounding acres of woods are filled with paths to explore, and a short walk reveals a rocky beach with remarkable views of the Olympics and Puget Sound. The cabin itself is essentially one large room filled with lovely furnishings, attractive antiques, and plenty of cozy comfort. An oak-trimmed gas fireplace warms the sitting area, and an entertainment center with a selection of movies is available for guests. Two impressive murals, painted by a local artist, reside high on the cabin's walls beneath a cathedral ceiling, and the beautiful four-poster bed is covered in fluffy soft floral linens. Almost as big as the main room, the spacious bathroom has a slate-colored tile floor, glass-block shower, and a giant Jacuzzi tub. Outside, the wraparound deck is the perfect spot for barbecuing or simply savoring the surrounding tranquillity.

If your idea of a getaway means staying put, you're in luck: The cabin also features a full kitchen and a washer/dryer, so you could easily stay here for a week. If you do venture out, stop by **NORDLAND GENERAL STORE** (7180 Flagler Road; 360-385-0777) to pick up a picnic lunch (we recommend the fresh oysters). You can also rent a kayak or canoe for exploring nearby Mystery Bay. **1460 East Marrowstone Road; (360) 385-4644; www.marrowstone.com/honeymooncabin/index.htm; expensive; minimum-stay requirement on weekends.**

Port Townsend

Port Townsend, a small town at the extreme northeast corner of the Olympic Peninsula, was originally settled in the 1800s. Authentic and lovingly restored period architecture is this town's trademark. Its beautifully cared for, gingerbread-trimmed, Victorian homes are perched on a bluff overlooking the waterfront. Nearby parks, boutiques, antique shops, and restaurants project an aura of charm and tranquillity. A favorite weekend getaway for Seattleites escaping hectic urban life, Port Townsend is relatively slow-paced all year long. A walk around the waterfront district and the bluffs above will give you outstanding views of the Olympic Mountains, Admiralty Inlet, and island-dotted Puget Sound.

Over the years, Port Townsend has earned a reputation for being the hub of cultural activity on the Olympic Peninsula, with diverse events scheduled from spring through fall. A management company called **CENTRUM** (360-385-3102, 800-733-3608) handles many activities in Port Townsend and the surrounding area, including the Port Townsend Blues Festival, the Festival of American Fiddle Tunes, Jazz Port Townsend, and the Theater Festival. The Wooden Boat Festival in early September has gained international attention and offers tours and boat races. The nearby **OLYMPIC MUSIC FESTIVAL** (reviewed on page 336) is another favorite summertime event. For general information about local events, you can also contact the **PORT TOWNSEND CHAMBER OF COMMERCE VISITOR INFORMATION CENTER** (2437 East Sims Way, Port Townsend, WA 98368; 360-385-2722, 888-ENJOYPT; www.olympus.net/ptchamber) or drop by on your way into town.

Hotel/Bed and Breakfast Kissing

❦❦❦ ANN STARRETT MANSION BED AND BREAKFAST, Port Townsend

Port Townsend's luxurious past has been beautifully and authentically revived in this ornate 1889 Victorian home. Settled on a quiet resi- dential corner, the Ann Starrett Mansion is a sight to behold. A Gothic octagonal tower is the focal point of the mansion, and rich red-and-green-gabled detailing adorns the exterior. The outstanding architectural elements continue inside. Just off the foyer, a free-hung, three-tiered circular staircase spirals up the tower. Be sure to look up at the eight-sided dome ceiling, where beautiful frescoes depict the four seasons and the four cardinal virtues (which are justice, prudence, fortitude, and temperance, if you were wondering).

Classic Victorian elegance throughout the mansion embraces you in stunning splendor. All nine guest rooms in the mansion are plush yet comfortable, with rich color schemes, original period furnishings, antique brass and canopied beds, and lace curtains. Honeymooners have been known to disappear for entire weekends in the Gable Suite, located at the top of the tower. This room is especially grand and private, with a king-size bed, skylights, views of the water, and a two-person soaking tub. As with many renovated Victorian homes, the bathrooms were formerly closets and thus are rather small, albeit private. Downstairs, the carriage house–level rooms are a real romantic bargain if you don't mind a detached bath in some and the lack of a water view. These rooms are still extremely pleasant and cozy, with exposed brick walls, snuggly floral down comforters, and a burbling fountain in the garden just outside.

Right next door is an additional building, the Starrett Cottage, which holds two more rooms. Although they are not quite as grand as the neighboring mansion rooms, both two-room suites offer the ultimate in privacy and spaciousness. The Upper Cottage unit, on the second floor, is boldly decorated in flamboyant, sumptuous Victorian style, with red walls, chandeliers, a gas fireplace, and a Jacuzzi tub for two; the Lower Cottage Suite has a more subtle color scheme, a river-rock gas fireplace, and antique oak furnishings. It won't be easy to leave your room, but the award-winning full gourmet breakfast, served in the elegant dining room of the main house, really is worth getting out of bed for. **744 Clay Street; (360) 385-3205, (800) 321-0644; www. olympus.net/starrett; inexpensive to very expensive; minimum-stay requirement on weekends seasonally.**

Romantic Note: One of the main reasons people come to Port Townsend is to appreciate the architecture, and no such tour is complete without a stop at the Ann Starrett Mansion. Be aware that the mansion is open for self-guided tours before guests are able to check in. If you are staying for more than one night, the inn can feel like a museum filled with passing visitors for a few hours during the day. Most likely, though, you will be out touring Port Townsend and the Olympic Peninsula by day, and by the time you return, the tourists will have cleared out and you can delight in the private opulence of this magnificent Victorian as if it were your own.

☙❦ **BAY COTTAGES, Port Townsend** These two cabins are casual, inviting, and full of charm. If you are looking for a homey escape with access to a private sandy beach, the Bay Cottages are an appealing choice. Built in the 1930s, these cabins have low ceilings and a slightly weathered appearance; however, they are exceedingly comfortable, with handsome country-style furniture and sumptuous feather beds. Brass bedframes, claw-foot tubs, and private decks lined with clematis vines add to the welcoming atmosphere. The surrounding rose gardens are fragrant, and the views of Discovery Bay and the Olympics are stunning.

Both cabins feature full kitchens stocked with snacks and beverages. Meals are up to you, so bring along all the necessities for a light breakfast and perhaps a picnic lunch on the beach (picnic baskets are supplied) to take advantage of this premium location, only six miles outside Port Townsend. **4346 South Discovery Road; (360) 385-2035; inexpensive to moderate; minimum-stay requirement on weekends.**

☙❦ **BLUE GULL INN, Port Townsend** Recent restoration efforts have transformed this Gothic Victorian home into a pleasant bed and breakfast. Wood floors, brightly colored rugs in a mix of florals and checks, and a grand staircase painted deep green command your attention in the entry. Unfortunately, the owners have invested most of their time and energy refurbishing the building's exterior and guest rooms, leaving the common areas aching for cozy details.

All six guest rooms are nicely decorated, although only three have real amorous potential. The Angel Room features cream-colored satin bedding, angel pictures, and views of Admirality Inlet and Port Townsend; its large private bathroom with Jacuzzi tub shares the same view. Clouds painted on the ceiling create a dreamy mood in the Garden Room, nicely appointed with wicker furniture, green wood floors, vine trim on the iron bed, and a private bath. Grandma's Room is decorated with handmade quilts and antiques, and has a small sunporch overlooking the flower garden. The remaining three rooms are not spacious or private enough to recommend wholeheartedly.

A full gourmet breakfast including fresh fruit and giant Belgian waffles topped with strawberries and cream is served in the dining room. Given more time and attention (work was still in progress when we visited), the Blue Gull Inn could evolve into a truly romantic destination. **1310 Clay Street; (360) 379-3241, (888) 700-0205; inexpensive to expensive; minimum-stay requirement during festivals.**

🌸🌸 **THE CABIN, Port Townsend** There is a wide range of romantic options for those seeking accommodations in Port Townsend. At one end of the spectrum are elegant Victorian mansions brimming with antiques and filled with history; at the other end is the Cabin, an *extremely* small cottage set in the woods outside of town. If your hearts desire a remote, memorable spot, this is the place for you. Country decor, a full kitchen, and the fluffiest feather bed you'll ever encounter are all tucked into this rustic, one-room unit.

A short walk from your front door leads to a cliff towering above Puget Sound. Snuggle together on the small bench set near the edge as you take in the panoramic view that sweeps from Vancouver Island to Mount Baker. Guests at the Cabin also have access to a hot tub, located at the owner's home near the beach. For a more private way to unwind, however, we recommend watching the stars alone together from your cabin's wraparound deck.

Blackberry scones, fresh fruit, and juices are stocked for your morning enjoyment. Bring along something to barbecue on the outdoor fire pit and you will have no reason to leave this private retreat. **839 North Jacob Miller Road; (360) 385-5571, (800) 929-7444; inexpensive.**

🌸🌸🌸 **CHANTICLEER INN BED AND BREAKFAST, Port Townsend** Chanticleer Inn is elegant but not imposing. Every detail of this 1876 Victorian cottage radiates luxury and comfort. Pale hardwood floors, cream-colored furnishings, and fine antiques grace the sunny main-floor parlor, and neatly pressed linens, down comforters, feather beds, antique accents, and private baths are found in every guest room. Three of the main house's four guest rooms are located upstairs; two are quite snug, but one has a Jacuzzi tub and the other has a stunning, intricate antique bedroom set. We recommend Countess, the largest upstairs unit, with its king-size bed, pink and mauve accents, lace curtains, and, best of all, a private balcony with sweeping mountain and water views. Breakfast can be delivered to this suite and enjoyed privately while you savor views of the Olympics, the Cascades, Mount Baker, Admiralty Inlet, and Puget Sound.

On the main floor, the opulent, creamy white Duchess Room has a crystal chandelier and a bed with an antique lace half-canopy. French doors connect this room to the dining room and adjacent parlor, so you can enjoy the common areas as if they were your own in the evenings. In the morning, though, if sleeping in past breakfast is your plan, you will be out of luck. But why would you want to pass up a breakfast like this? A menu is posted to whet your appetite for the creative multicourse gourmet extravaganza, which is served on fine china and sterling silver and accompanied by live harp music every morning. **1208 Franklin Street; (360) 385-6239, (800) 858-9421; www. northolympic.com/chanticleer; inexpensive to expensive; minimum-stay requirement.**

Romantic Note: An apartment in the adjacent guest house is best suited for families, and the decor there is much more casual. If you are spending more than a few nights and want the option of cooking your own meals, this unit offers a lot of space for a couple to really move in and be comfortable. Just don't expect the same level of luxury found in the main house.

❧❧❧ **COMMANDER'S GUESTHOUSE, Port Townsend** Resting on Admiralty Inlet Beach, Commander's Guesthouse offers a multitude of outdoor activities, from beachcombing the 2,000 feet of nearby beaches to exploring the wildflower gardens to participating in outdoor games like badminton and croquet. All this, and we haven't even mentioned that you are within walking distance of Port Townsend's marina and shop-filled downtown.

This handsome seaside mansion combines romance with a subtle nautical theme and pulls it off quite well. The home itself is tastefully decorated with antiques, richly colored Oriental carpets, and sea-inspired knickknacks such as the owners' collection of miniature ships and a captain's wheel. The three guest rooms, all with private baths, are adorned with down comforters and offer views of the surrounding islands and mountains. We found the Lighthouse Suite to be the most romantic and spacious, with its green and cream color scheme, standing candles, and handsome wood furnishings, including a beautiful cedar hutch.

Breakfast is a gourmet feast served in the dining room, at a table set with gold-trimmed china and sterling silver platters. Begin with fresh fruit, yogurt, and granola, but be sure to save room for giant Belgian waffles with strawberries and cream. **400 Hudson Street; (360) 385-1778, (888) 385-1778; moderate to expensive; minimum-stay requirement on holidays and seasonally.**

❧❧❧ **HOLLY HILL HOUSE, Port Townsend** This lovely Victorian bed and breakfast, located in the heart of Port Townsend's Historical District, has recently undergone extensive restoration and redecoration. We are happy to report that the dedicated efforts of the innkeepers have paid off: The result is a peaceful setting for encounters of the heart.

Surrounded by rose gardens and ancient holly trees, the home boasts a main-floor parlor filled with antiques and warmed by a glowing fireplace. Upstairs, three guest rooms are dressed in handsome Victorian appointments. The spacious Colonel's Room, with its striped navy blue wallpaper, custom-built headboard, and deep soaking tub, overlooks Admiralty Inlet and the Cascades in the distance. Billie's Room also features a water and mountain view, and has a pretty blue floral duvet, brass lamps, and a shower in the private bath. A queen-size bed, an additional twin bed, and views of the garden are among the charms of Lizette's Room. Behind the main house, two more guest rooms are in the Carriage House. Skyview is a favorite because the large skylight above the bed allows moonlight to beam in, but Morning Glory is also a cozy option. Both Carriage House rooms open to the back patio, where flowerpots and wonderful gardens abound. Tea or lemonade and other treats are served each afternoon in this pleasant setting. Be sure to take a look at the Camperdown elm off to one side of the yard; this unique tree actually grows upside down (you will have to see it for yourselves) and produces enough lush foliage to create a private little alcove that's perfect for shady summer kissing.

In the morning, a bountiful breakfast is served family-style at two tables in the sun-filled dining room, or out on the back patio on warmer days. Home-baked muffins, fresh fruit, and a hot dish such as a cheese soufflé with mild chiles and olives are served, along with a detailed history of the 1872 home. **611 Polk Street; (360) 385-5619, (800) 435-1454 (outside Washington state); www.acies.com/hollyhill; inexpensive to expensive; minimum-stay requirement on weekends.**

Romantic Note: Twice a year Holly Hill House hosts a mystery dinner. Fabulous entrées, plenty of clues, and a whodunit atmosphere make for an entertaining evening. Call for reservations and more details.

❧❧❧❧ **JAMES HOUSE BED AND BREAKFAST, Port Townsend** This striking Queen Anne home—lovingly filled with re-covered and refinished period pieces and intricate handcrafted wood moldings—is as Victorian as they get in Port Townsend, and that's saying a lot. Of the 12 guest rooms scattered along a labyrinth of hallways, ten have private baths, and all are brightened by fresh flower arrangements. The elegant Bridal Suite, with its massive antique furnishings and crisp white linens, is by far the most grand. It features bay windows with unsurpassed water and mountain views, as well as subtle lighting, a wood-burning fireplace, and complimentary champagne delivered at your request. Both the Bay and Chintz Rooms also have fabulous views of Admiralty Inlet and Whidbey Island across the water. (Since the James House is set right on the bluff overlooking town, the stunning view is totally unobstructed.) The Gardener's Cottage, set right behind the main house, is another romantic option due to its private entrance and quaint patio that looks out to the verdant lawn, well-tended gardens, and water in the distance.

No matter which room you choose, there are plenty of cozy alcoves designed for snuggling. Freshly baked cookies in the afternoon and complimentary sherry are nice extras, but the real treat is the full sit-down breakfast. Your morning repast may include fresh scones, a baked pear with a walnut-fruit filling, and a tasty egg-filled croissant dish. **1238 Washington Street; (360) 385-1238, (800) 385-1238; www.jameshouse.com; moderate to expensive.**

Romantic Option: Right next door, a modest brick house holds another extremely romantic lodging option: **A BUNGALOW ON THE BLUFF** (very expensive). This private, petite unit is managed by the James House, but the style, decor, and setup are dramatically different. It is run more like a self-sufficient vacation rental than a bed and breakfast, although a generous continental breakfast is left for you in the small fridge. Reminiscent of a 1950s bungalow, the room has black and tan furnishings, a wood-burning fireplace, and a picture window overlooking the port and town below. In the spacious slate-tiled bathroom, a corner Jacuzzi tub for two is set beneath a skylight. Kissing here is inevitable.

❦❦❦ **LIZZIE'S BED AND BREAKFAST, Port Townsend** The abundance of fine Victorian bed and breakfasts in Port Townsend makes our job easy, because you can hardly go wrong here. Lizzie's is a lovely option and will surely meet all of your amorous requirements. The seven wonderfully spacious units are all equipped with fluffy down comforters and private baths. The bed and breakfast's namesake, Lizzie's Room, is the most regal, with a high ceiling, dark green floral wallpaper, a half-canopied queen-size bed, claw-foot tub, wood-burning fireplace, and a cozy sitting area beside a bay window. Sarah's Room has a bay window seat with supreme views of the water and mountains, and French doors that lead to a claw-foot tub in the bathroom. Daisy's Room is beautifully opulent, with cream-colored wallpaper, a stylish king-size art nouveau bed, and a view of the sunrise over the bay.

The friendly hostess serves a generous full breakfast at a large oak table in the country kitchen, or on the patio when the weather allows. Enjoy such delicious treats as freshly baked apple strudel and almond pastry, accompanied by creative egg dishes and hot porridge. **731 Pierce Street; (360) 385-4168, (800) 700-4168; www.kolke.com/lizzies; inexpensive to expensive; minimum-stay requirement on holidays.**

❦❦❦❦ **OLD CONSULATE INN, Port Townsend** If you're smitten with the idea of pampering yourselves in an atmosphere of days gone by, but with modern creature comforts, the Old Consulate Inn is exactly right for you. This venerable red Victorian inn boasts a music room with an antique organ and grand piano, a fireplace-warmed study, a reading nook in the front parlor, and a billiards and game room in the basement. You won't want to miss the handsome wood-paneled breakfast area where tea (or lemonade on sunny days) and cookies are served in the afternoon and an assortment of liqueurs and luscious desserts await in the evening. Elegant period antiques abound, and the parlor is filled with collectible dolls and porcelain unicorns.

At the top of the grand oak staircase you'll find eight spacious private rooms, each with its own bath. Cozy alcoves, turret lookouts, canopied king-size beds, and expansive views of the waterfront are among the amenities offered here. Especially alluring (and considerably more expensive than the other rooms) is the Master Anniversary Suite, with its antique wood-burning fireplace and four-poster canopied bed. The lacy Tower Honeymoon Suite is also one of our favorites, with water views from the pillow and a claw-foot tub in the bedchamber. Still, each room is such a wonderful retreat that you'll want to leave only for a soak in the outdoor hot tub, which is set in a gazebo overlooking the bay—and for breakfast, of course.

The morning meal, served banquet-style, is a gastronomic fantasy come true. The inn proudly presents its own blend of designer coffee along with seven courses: fresh fruits, liqueur cakes, pastries, gourmet egg dishes, and homemade granolas, to name a few. Savor the relaxed luxury of the Victorian era while you are here—you will return to the real world soon enough. **313 Walker Street; (360) 385-6753, (800) 300-6753; www.oldconsulateinn. com; inexpensive to very expensive; minimum-stay requirement on weekends.**

❦❦ QUIMPER INN, Port Townsend The five guest rooms at this grand Georgian-style retreat are handsomely adorned in unfrilly Victorian style, and three have private baths. Michelle's Room features a queen-size brass bed surrounded by bay windows that face Admiralty Inlet and the Cascades, and a huge bathroom with a six-foot-long claw-foot tub and a pedestal sink. Harry & Gertie's Suite offers extra kissing space, with two rooms separated by French doors. Attractive antique furnishings, blue velvet furniture, and wonderful bay windows facing the water and mountains make this suite the best amorous choice. The cozy Library Room on the main floor has shelf upon shelf of books lining the walls. If sharing a bath doesn't bother you, Christopher's Room and John's Room are attractive and quite a bargain.

An outside deck on the second level is lined with colorful flower boxes and provides a common area where everyone can indulge in the view. The bountiful breakfasts here feature baked ham and eggs, fresh fruit, and homemade muffins served family-style in the formal dining room. **1306 Franklin Street; (360) 385-1060, (800) 557-1060; www.olympus.net/biz/quimper/quimper.html; inexpensive to expensive; minimum-stay requirement during festivals.**

❦❦❦❦ RAVENSCROFT INN, Port Townsend The stately Southern-style architecture of Ravenscroft sets it apart from the other bed and breakfasts found in the Historical District of Port Townsend. In a town inundated with Victorian homes, this clapboard house with white trim and a long porch is a welcome change of pace. Inside, the entire inn is carpeted, creating a less staccato environment than the standard hardwood floors of other inns in the area. Furnishings here are a casual mix of wicker and antiques, and each room is distinguished by individual character and style.

All eight guest rooms at the inn are supremely delightful. Many of the lovely suites have French doors that open onto a balcony with views of the bay and mountains; some have spacious sitting areas, canopied beds, and brick fireplaces. Every room has an immaculate, attractive bath, plush down comforters, unlimited privacy, and room to spare. The least expensive accommodations, which instantly won our hearts, are the three secluded garden-level rooms with exposed brick walls, floral linens, and smaller windows that view greenery rather than the water. One room also has a fireplace; all of them offer a cozy and affordable option for budgeting lovers.

The top-of-the-line Admiralty Suite is a wonderful romantic splurge. Decorated in whimsical blue and yellow, this choice unit has a gas fireplace, a soaking tub, and a fabulous six-foot window seat overlooking the water and distant mountains. The recently remodeled Mount Rainier Suite shares this incredible view and has a gas fireplace and soaking tub for two, while the Fireside Room has a canopied queen-size bed, a wood-burning fireplace, and French doors leading to the expansive second-story veranda. All three have our seal of approval.

An imaginatively decorated dining area borders the inn's open kitchen, and a brick fireplace warms the cheerful room where breakfast is served. A baby grand piano is set off to one side. The host is a professional pianist, so live music accompanies such creations as frappés made from frozen berries, bananas, and yogurt; puff pastries filled with sun-dried tomatoes, artichoke hearts, onions, and cheese; Cointreau-drenched French toast; and fresh coffee cake. Sheer perfection! **533 Quincy Street; (360) 385-2784, (800) 782-2691; www.ravenscroftinn.com; inexpensive to very expensive; minimum-stay requirement on weekends and holidays.**

❦❦ **WINDRIDGE COTTAGE, Port Townsend** Nestled in the woods about ten miles south of Port Townsend, this self-contained getaway surveys wonderful views of Beausite Lake and the Olympic Mountains. One hundred and forty acres of majestic trees surround the cottage, creating a peaceful setting that is sure to enhance a country-quiet frame of mind.

Inside, amenities such as a TV/VCR, stereo, and fully equipped kitchen add comfort to charm. Why not take advantage of all this seclusion and snuggle up on the couch in front of the free-standing woodstove? Or slip outside to do some late-night stargazing on the large deck overlooking the lake and mountains. The cottage also contains a king-size bed in the bedroom; a full bath; and fresh coffee, juices, and other assorted goodies stashed in the kitchen. **2804 West Valley Road; (360) 732-4575; www.olympus.net/biz/getaways/WC/index.htm; moderate.**

Restaurant Kissing

❦◗ **THE BELMONT, Port Townsend** The exposed brick and wood interior, lofty ceilings, and unhindered water views at the Belmont will lure you to stay for lunch or dinner, despite the rather standard menu (burgers and fries, and pasta and seafood dishes that are fine but certainly not the best in the area). The wooden booths nestled near the entrance offer the most privacy, but you'll want to request window or outdoor seating to partake of the heavenly waterfront views. If gourmet dining isn't your top priority, the friendly service, reasonable prices, and magnificent view make this a great romantic choice. **925 Water Street; (360) 385-3007; inexpensive to moderate; lunch and dinner daily.**

🌸🌸 **BLACKBERRIES RESTAURANT, Port Townsend** Located in Fort Worden State Park, Blackberries isn't like any other state park concession you've ever seen. This interesting dining room is decorated with willow branches arranged halfway up the walls and trimmed with stencils of blackbirds nibbling on the fruits of blackberry vines. Historic local photographs adorn the walls and little lamps above tables for two provide a romantic glow. The attractive decor was inspired by the casual style of resorts popular a century ago, when Fort Worden was constructed. Innovative Northwest cuisine featuring local ingredients is the focus here, and you certainly will not be disappointed. The delicate halibut-and-salmon braid with tangy salal-berry sauce is absolutely grand; and the whiskey-pepper steak, coated with cracked peppercorns and flamed with Jack Daniels, is thoroughly satisfying. Try the blackberry-orange Charlotte for dessert—a rich concoction of ladyfingers and blackberry-orange custard. Yum! **200 Battery Way, in Fort Worden State Park; (360) 385-9950; www.geocities.com/~blkberries; moderate to expensive; dinner Wednesday–Saturday, brunch Sunday; closed November–April.**

Romantic Suggestion: Before or after dinner, you might want to explore the bunkers and beachfront that are part of historic **FORT WORDEN STATE PARK** (360-385-4730). Richard Gere and Debra Winger found plenty of places to kiss while filming *An Officer and a Gentleman* here, and you can too.

🌸🌸 **THE FOUNTAIN CAFE, Port Townsend** If we awarded stars or chef's hats, the Fountain's consistently excellent food and pleasant service would easily earn the highest rating. To earn an equally high lip rating, however, other criteria must be met. Although we'd be the first to admit that we oohed and aahed with pleasure during our meal, fine food alone doth not a romantic dinner make—atmosphere counts too.

The super-casual Fountain Cafe's dimly lit, tiny dining room is usually packed with people. Green walls and closely arranged tables draped with colorful, funky tablecloths and topped with little bouquets and candles impart a familiar Northwest coffeehouse feel. The creative, delectable dishes cooked up by the talented folks in the kitchen are what make the Fountain so much more than the sum of its parts. You can't go wrong when ordering seafood here—it is always fresh. You might want to start with Penn Cove mussels steamed with saffron, fresh herbs, and tomato, and then move on to the locally smoked salmon, topped with a cream sauce and a hint of Scotch, garnished with caviar, and served with fettuccine. Desserts are just as interesting and delicious—in particular, the warm homemade gingerbread cake on a bed of custard—so try to save room! **920 Washington Street; (360) 385-1364; inexpensive to moderate; dinner Wednesday–Monday.**

❧❧❦ **LANZA'S RISTORANTE, Port Townsend** Italian restaurants are known for being a little noisy, but even on busy weekends Lanza's is intimate and romantic. This could be due in part to the kitchen's location, hidden behind a thick oak door inset with stained glass, or to the subdued lighting and cozy booths. With a smoky gray interior and one wall of exposed brick, Lanza's is reminiscent of a New Orleans jazz club. Live music Friday and Saturday nights reinforce this impression, but rest assured that the music is soothing and the atmosphere right for romance.

We recommend one of the fabulous pasta dishes, such as the *pollo bolognese* with chicken, prosciutto, and provolone in a marsala cream sauce. A seafood lover's favorite is the Seafood Lorraine: scallops, clams, mussels, and shrimp tossed in a pesto wine sauce with tomatoes and green onions. Both of these dishes are flavorful and filling. If you feel like having dessert (after all, you are on vacation), share a serving of Lanza's rich and decadent tiramisu. **1020 Lawrence Street; (360) 379-1900; moderate to expensive; dinner Monday–Saturday.**

❧❧❧ **LONNY'S, Port Townsend** Step into another world at Lonny's—a world of relaxed elegance and Mediterranean ambience. Tawny stucco walls, soft track lighting, and intimate booths help set the mood for a memorable evening. This restaurant is the talk of the town, and for good reason. Not only is the ocher interior warm and welcoming, but the food is outstanding.

The scent of Italian specialties wafts across the dining room from the copper-accented open kitchen. We especially liked the tender fresh halibut with a pistachio crust, and the linguine with fresh scallops tossed in a *puttanesca* sauce. Fresh organic produce, free-range chicken, and local seafood highlight the menu, and the service matches the flawless presentations. **2330 Washington Street; (360) 385-0700; moderate to expensive; dinner Wednesday–Monday.**

❧❧ **MANRESA CASTLE RESTAURANT AND LOUNGE, Port Townsend** Manresa Castle is one of Port Townsend's most recognizable landmarks. Proudly roosting on a hill overlooking town, this impressive building was built in 1892 to resemble a Prussian castle. From the 1920s until the 1960s, Jesuit priests used the castle as a training college, but since 1968 it has been operated as a guest inn and restaurant. The castle really does not offer the best romantic accommodations in town; the rooms are rather tacky and small. The restaurant and lounge, meanwhile, are loaded with affectionate ambience; regrettably, the quality of the food is not up to the surroundings.

The stately cocktail lounge is a most irresistible setting for a romantic interlude, and next to it is an unpretentious dining room where tall, lace-covered windows, soft lighting, and handsome wood furniture create a charming, inviting, country-Victorian atmosphere. Although a new chef has taken charge here, the fare has garnered mixed reviews. The dishes are neither inventive nor interesting, with only a few exceptions, such as the curried chicken Casimir accompanied by chutney, raisins, and grated coconut; or the seafood cakes with salmon, cod, bay shrimp, scallops, and herbs. Steak, deep-fried prawns, and standard chicken dishes round out the menu. **Seventh and Sheridan Streets; (360) 385-5750, (800) 732-1281 (in Washington state); www.olympus.net/ manresa; moderate to expensive; call for seasonal hours.**

Romantic Note: Self-guided tours of the castle are encouraged. The history is fascinating, the architecture is lovely, and, depending on the time of day and occupancy, you can judge the guest rooms for yourselves.

◆◆ **SILVERWATER CAFE, Port Townsend** Please do not misunderstand the relatively low lip rating for this café: It has nothing to do with the quality of food or service here, which are actually quite good. However, the casual ambience does not exactly tug at the heartstrings. Still, our lunch was so tasty that we must at least mention this special little café.

Local artwork and brick walls lend character to the room, along with the high ceiling, numerous hanging plants, hardwood floors, and unadorned wood tables. Everything here is made from scratch, and the menu is surprisingly wide ranging: The homemade hummus and tabbouleh plate, served with fresh, soft pita bread, is perfect for a light lunch, and the seafood is consistently fresh and fabulous. One especially inventive and wonderful dish is the Oysters Bleu: fresh oysters, bacon, and spinach in a light blue-cheese sauce, presented on fresh black-pepper linguine. **237 Taylor Street; (360) 385-6448; inexpensive to moderate; lunch and dinner daily; closed the first two weeks of January.**

Outdoor Kissing

◆◆◆◆ **CHETZEMOKA PARK, Port Townsend** There are parks and then there are parks, but there is only one Chetzemoka. This ocean-flanked patch of land makes picnicking a treasured outing for two people, particularly a couple looking for surroundings that enhance the aesthetic appeal of bread, cheese, fruit, and wine. Here you can wander through scattered pinery along a cliff with an eagle's-eye view of Admiralty Inlet and Whidbey Island. Thick grass, a children's swing set, a footbridge spanning a babbling brook, and a few well-spaced picnic tables make this traditional, picturesque park a standout. Take the arbor walk to the gazebo overlooking the water or follow the paths past the gardens and waterfall; either way, this place will touch your heart. Whether your penchant is for a playful or a peaceful diversion, you will be pleased by Chetzemoka Park. **Free admission.** *As you head north into Port Townsend on Highway 20, turn west onto Kearney Street and travel approximately 500 yards to Lawrence Street; then turn north. Lawrence Street goes through Port Townsend's upper business and residential district, then curves to the left (where it becomes Jackson Street); the park is a few blocks farther, on the right.*

Port Angeles

Port Angeles is more a stopover than a destination. Most of the people who come here aren't looking for a special place to stay, but are only passing through on their way to Victoria or Olympic National Park. For this reason, budget motels and hotels have sprouted up along the main drag through town like pesky weeds. Thick traffic clogs the roads, and "NO VACANCY" signs continually glow in the summertime air. Only a few innkeepers have capitalized on the romantic potential Port Angeles has to offer.

Hotel/Bed and Breakfast Kissing

❤❤❤❤ **DOMAINE MADELEINE, Port Angeles** Exotic Asian art and French Impressionism are an unlikely combination, but Domaine Madeleine manages to blend these two worlds with elegance, imagination, and style. Nestled behind tall Douglas firs, this contemporary home perched on a bluff above the Strait of Juan de Fuca offers incredible water and mountain views. The grounds are covered with rhododendrons, flowering perennials, maples, cedars, pines, and an intriguing replica of Monet's garden specially designed by the resident botanist/innkeeper.

Domaine Madeleine goes above and beyond the romantic call of duty when it comes to comfort and hospitality. Expansive windows throughout the main house allow you to enjoy the captivating view. Hardwood floors, high ceilings, and an impressive basalt fireplace in the living room give the inn a distinguished Northwest feel, while Asian and European antiques add international flair. All four sumptuous guest suites, as well as the private little cottage, are supplied with fresh flowers, a fruit basket, chocolates, and an array of French perfumes. Jacuzzi tubs or showers for two, scented candles, remote-controlled gas fireplaces, and magnificent views make each sensuous room an extraordinary lovers' retreat. The Ming Suite, which occupies the entire upper floor, includes a free-standing fireplace, a king-size bed, and a 30-foot balcony from which you can watch the sun both rise and set. The Monet Room is decorated in Impressionist style, with pastel tones and windows that face the garden, while the sunny cottage feels entirely private since it is detached from the main house.

If the smell of fresh French bread and remarkable French cuisine weren't so tempting, it would be nearly impossible to get out of bed in the morning. But force yourselves and follow your noses! You don't want to miss seafood omelets, chicken tenderloins in a port wine mushroom sauce, or rich strawberry cream tarts. This four- or five-course extravaganza is served at one large table in the dining room of the main house. The enthusiastic innkeepers are eager to please and will make you feel right at home—only much more pampered. **146 Wildflower Lane; (360) 457-4174, (888) 811-8376; www. doma inemadeleine.com; expensive to very expensive; minimum-stay requirement on weekends seasonally; recommended wedding site.**

❤❤ **THE SEA SUNS, Port Angeles** Surrounded by gardens, this Dutch Colonial home is a welcome addition to the few romantic accommodations Port Angeles has to offer. This grand white house with a large porch and pillars will capture your attention and draw you into the inviting living room, where a mix of antiques, built-in glass shelves, and a fireplace await.

The four guest rooms (two with private baths) are named after the Dutch words for the four seasons and are decorated correspondingly. Zoner (summer) features warm floral wallpaper and bedding, and a beautiful marble-topped desk along with other fine antiques. A jetted tub in the private bath is an extra bonus. Herfst (autumn) has hardwood floors, a golden color scheme, and a private bath, and sits above the rose garden so fresh scents waft up to your room. By far the grandest room, Winter (spelled the same in both languages) welcomes you with deep red and green bedding, rugs, and curtains. A brass bed with white linen creates a lovely contrast to the Christmas colors. This room includes a small dressing room and a separate sitting room with comfortable wicker furniture; its only drawback is the shared bath. Lente (spring) is less impressive, with slightly mismatched decor and a shared bath.

Breakfast is a gourmet feast of Dutch babies with fresh fruit, smoked-salmon frittata, and custard and apples baked in a cinnamon pastry. Afterward, stroll along the covered walkway or relax near the property's waterfall and goldfish pond. **1006 South Lincoln; (360) 452-8248; www.northolympic. com/seasuns; inexpensive to moderate.**

❤❤ **TUDOR INN, Port Angeles** The Tudor Inn is a good place to rest your weary bodies after a day of hiking in Olympic National Park or touring nearby Victoria. The friendly hosts lived in Europe for ten years and have re-created a bit of European comfort in this historic Tudor home set in a residential neighborhood. Of the five choices here, the Country Room holds particular romantic interest, with its cathedral ceiling, pastoral mural, fireplace, and French doors that open to a private balcony with views of the Olympics in the distance. The Tudor Room, appointed with peach walls, dark woodwork, and a four-poster bed, features a down comforter and antique lace bedspread. The remaining three rooms are on the snug side, but each has a private bath, and the rates are quite affordable.

Graced by intricate European antiques, the lovely main floor provides several comfortable places to relax; we especially liked the living room, with its grand piano, white stone fireplace, and plush red velvet couch. A bountiful three-course breakfast is served family-style in the formal dining room. **1108 South Oak Street; (360) 452-3138; www.tudorinn.com; inexpensive to moderate; minimum-stay requirement on weekends seasonally.**

Restaurant Kissing

❤❤ **BELLA ITALIA, Port Angeles** Located on the basement level of a health food store, Bella Italia is a casual retreat. High-backed booths provide a small measure of privacy and wood-paneled walls impart a feeling of cozy warmth. Service is attentive without being intrusive, and the Italian menu lists a variety of pasta, pizza, and seafood dishes. Unfortunately, the kitchen can be inconsistent. The night we were there, the crab cakes accompanied by linguine drizzled with a white wine–garlic sauce were delectable, but the crab ravioli were napped in a lemon cream sauce that was full of lemon seeds (not exactly tasty to bite into). Thankfully, the classic tiramisu was smooth and creamy, so our dinner ended on a deliciously sweet note. **117-B East First Street; (360) 457-5442; www.northolympic.com/bella; moderate; lunch Monday–Saturday, dinner daily.**

❤❤❤ **C'EST SI BON, Port Angeles** C'est Si Bon, Port Angeles's only fine French restaurant, is at the tip of every local's tongue when asked about where to have an enamored evening interlude. The bright turquoise, pink, and purple exterior is slightly garish, but inside the ambience is wonderfully elegant. A massive crystal chandelier hanging from the vaulted ceiling casts a warm glow upon rich fuchsia walls. Upholstered chairs provide comfortable seating, and silk flower arrangements are placed around the room and on every linen-draped table. The effect is quite grand, and the room becomes most lovely after the sun sets and the lights dim. A table by the window is best, where you'll view either colorful rose gardens, spouting fountains, or the flower-lined brick patio.

The owner insists on preparing each entrée personally, so on busy weekend nights the wait can be lengthy; once the food arrives, however, it is worth the wait. Our Cornish game hen with mushroom stuffing and rich brown sauce was tender and savory, and the filet mignon with crabmeat in a rich cream sauce was sinfully delicious. Service seems to fluctuate between eccentric and entertaining, and can also be slightly intrusive, especially if you are enjoying a quiet tête-à-tête. Still, our evening was quite pleasant—it is just that when an establishment is known as *the* place to go for a romantic dinner, expectations run high. **23 Cedar Park Drive; (360) 452-8888; www.north olympic.com/cestsibon; expensive to very expensive; dinner Tuesday–Sunday.**

❤❤ **CHESTNUT COTTAGE, Port Angeles** For years locals have had a love affair with the **FIRST STREET HAVEN** (see the following Romantic Alternative), and this little brick cottage, under the same management, has become just as popular for a reliably good breakfast or lunch. The casual dining room exudes country charm, with its honey-colored wood interior, well-placed plants, arched windows, and antique plates and pictures decorating the walls. The menu emphasizes a combination of California-style cuisine and down-home cooking, expressed in flavorful dishes such as grilled salmon with hollandaise sauce, or California pizza with sun-dried tomatoes, sautéed mushrooms, artichoke hearts, homemade pesto sauce, and three cheeses. The Caesar salad is another popular item, but we found the dressing a bit heavy. A sweet espresso drink might serve as the meal's finale, but it never hurts to look at the dessert tray and be seduced into a chocolate love affair. **929 East Front Street; (360) 452-8344; inexpensive to moderate; breakfast and lunch daily.**

Romantic Alternative: FIRST STREET HAVEN (107 East First Street; 360-457-0352; inexpensive; breakfast and lunch daily) is a tiny café that is usually extremely crowded. The hearty breakfasts and flavorful lunches explain why customers keep coming back for more. Jump-start your day with Haven veggie browns (potatoes sautéed with green peppers, onions, zucchini, and mushrooms, and topped with Swiss and cheddar cheeses). Refuel at lunchtime with a variety of burgers, sandwiches, and salads. The First Street Haven's baked goods are always great: If you will be trekking around the peninsula all day, you should take an apricot-walnut scone for the road, or make that two—you don't want to fight over who gets the bigger piece.

❦❦❦ **TOGA'S, Port Angeles** With a name like Toga's, you might expect a sheet-clad staff or at least a Greek menu, but you won't find either here—nor will you find a run-of-the-mill small-town restaurant. Toga's (named after the young entrepreneurial chef) is a modestly adorned, family-managed, fine-dining establishment that boasts the most creative menu in town. If only the overhead lights in the dining room were dimmed after dark, the small brass lamps, cream tablecloths, and softer lighting would succeed in creating an intimate mood.

European sauces and techniques are combined with fresh local ingredients to produce rich, inventive dishes such as baked prawns stuffed with crab and topped by Jarlsberg and Gruyere cheeses, broiled salmon and scallops served with a mustard-dill beurre blanc, and classic beef Stroganoff served in a crock pot with buttered noodles. A house specialty that you won't find anywhere else on the peninsula is "Jägerstein": the wait staff brings to your table an extremely hot stone, on which you prepare meat or seafood that you have selected. The concept is similar to fondue, except that you use the hot stone to cook the food instead of using a pot of hot liquid. As strange as this sounds, it is a fascinating dining experience. Desserts are just as decadent as the rest of your meal, so be sure to bring along a hearty appetite—you won't want to skip the famous Black Forest cake. **122 West Lauridsen Boulevard; (360) 452-1952; expensive; dinner Tuesday–Saturday; call for seasonal closures.**

Outdoor Kissing

❦❦❦ **DEER PARK, Port Angeles** Our recommendation to make the drive to Deer Park comes with a serious warning. The countless switchbacks and sharp turns you'll encounter on this predominantly unpaved road are hair-raising. With conditions like this, you need to be guaranteed that there's a payoff at the end. Rest assured that there is, but suffering this road's indignities is best with the appropriate car (we suggest a sport utility vehicle). The reward on a clear day is an enthralling view deep into the heart of the Olympics. And because of the road conditions, you are likely to find yourselves quite alone. Most everyone else takes the paved road to **HURRICANE RIDGE,** due south of Port Angeles just off Highway 101. The purple mountain majesty of Deer Park will be all yours. **Olympic National Park. Free admission.** *Deer Park is southeast of Port Angeles, in Olympic National Park. From Highway 101, turn south at the sign for Deer Park. The park is at the end of a 17-mile drive.*

Romantic Note: Ask at the Deer Park ranger station (open in summer only) about the short hike up Blue Mountain. Even your sore legs will thank you for the view at the summit.

❧❧❧❧ **OLYMPIC NATIONAL PARK, Port Angeles** Trying to describe the wonder and natural beauty of Olympic National Park in a paragraph or two is an impossible feat. Doing this scenery justice would take an encyclopedia, and even then details would be lacking. Really, there is so much to experience throughout this nearly 1,500-square-mile park that it is hard to know where to begin. The arresting splendor of every topographical area beguiles the senses. At the top of **HURRICANE RIDGE,** snowcapped peaks extend up to forever; in the forested territory below, old-growth evergreens reach heavenward to mesmerizing heights; deeper into the woods, the **HOH RAIN FOREST** is a mystical Eden draped in moss and shadows; and finally, in a stupefying climax, the powerful Pacific Ocean explodes against the western shore of the peninsula. To call this area exalted is an understatement. It is a must-see for anyone venturing to the Northwest.

Specific beaches, walks, and sites that are particularly conducive to affectionate moments are highlighted throughout this chapter under Outdoor Kissing, but it would be hard to find any place in Olympic National Park that does not inspire kissing and endless romantic adventures. **(360) 452-0330; www.nps.gov/olym; free admission.** *Olympic National Park comprises most of the central part of the Olympic Peninsula.*

Lake Crescent

Approximately 20 miles west of Port Angeles, Lake Crescent is Olympic National Park's deepest lake. This distinction makes it an enticing Northwest destination, enveloped by mountains and endless sky. Unfortunately, access to the lake is limited to just a few areas: the small East Beach, which is usually crowded on summer days, a few boat-launch areas, and the shore fronting the **LAKE CRESCENT LODGE** (see Hotel/Bed and Breakfast Kissing).

Hotel/Bed and Breakfast Kissing

❧❧ **LAKE CRESCENT LODGE, Lake Crescent** A sunny day here may wreak havoc with your senses and emotions. The drive around the perimeter of the lake is a monumental treat (unless you're inclined to car sickness—there are lots of curves). Take time to see the whole thing, and refresh yourselves with a chilly swim in summer or an energetic hike in the nearby forest at other times of the year.

Lake Crescent Lodge rests on the bank of its enormous namesake, and from your somewhat rustic cabin—heated by a woodstove or a stone fireplace—you can view this glassy stretch of water as it curves around forested mountains that ascend magnificently in the distance. Breath deeply in the fragrant air that permeates this epic landscape. The bond you and your loved one forge amid all this beauty will be strong and everlasting.

The most romantic accommodations at the lodge are the Roosevelt Fireplace Cottages. Some might call the furnishings dated, others would say they give the rooms character, but all of these cottages have wood-burning fireplaces and are close to the water's edge, which might make up for the lackluster decor. If a Roosevelt Cottage is not available, you may want to consider a Singer Tavern Cottage. Lined up near the main lodge, these units are close to one another and foot traffic passes by between them and the lake, but the peach walls, hardwood floors, and plain interiors make for adequate accommodations. Overall, this property has seen better days, but the rates are not outrageous, and if you want to spend some time thoroughly enjoying Olympic National Park, this is a good place to call home for a few nights. **416 Lake Crescent Road; (360) 928-3211; inexpensive to expensive; call for seasonal closures.**

Romantic Note: If you're just passing through, stop at the lodge's attractive restaurant (moderate to expensive). Here you'll find traditional mountain breakfasts with robust fresh coffee, wholesome lunches, and a selection of dinner entrées ranging from Hood Canal oysters in a smooth remoulade to king salmon.

Neah Bay

Outdoor Kissing

☙☙☙☙ **CAPE FLATTERY, Neah Bay** We aren't sure why the northwestern tip of the continental United States is called Cape Flattery, but perhaps it is because visitors have only words of praise about this absolutely exceptional location. For years, travelers braved a treacherous muddy trail to reach the magnificent edge of the mainland, but now there is a wonderful, easy-to-navigate boardwalk that leads through an old-growth forest to unbelievable vistas.

Tatoosh Island is the only piece of land in sight as the ocean seems to stretch forever from this clifftop point. The wind really whips around out here at times, which only makes the scenery more dramatic as waves crash below you on the rocky shore. One hundred percent guaranteed: A sunset here is an astounding experience you will never forget. *Highway 101 intersects State Route 112 a few miles west of Port Angeles. Take SR 112 west along the coast to the town of Sekiu. Twenty miles west of Sekiu is Neah Bay, and Cape Flattery is eight and a half miles northwest of there.*

❤❤ **HOBUCK BEACH PARK, Neah Bay** Outdoor enthusiasts weary of campsites that are merely parking lots with modern amenities for motor homes can find refuge in this tiny piece of paradise stretching along the outer reaches of the Pacific Ocean. Located in the heart of the Makah Native American reservation, this private oceanfront property attracts few tourists. Take your pick of the campsites, which are set back from the ocean (you can't pitch a tent on the beach) and secluded by trees and brush. Each has an expansive view of the empty beach. Share a solitary sunset that will surround you in hues of orange and pink. If you keep your eyes open long enough, you might glimpse the village horses running together across the beach or deer wandering near the campsites looking for tidbits. For those who don't want to rough it, three weathered cabins (inexpensive; minimum-stay requirement) are also available, complete with showers and kitchenettes. These cabins, however, are not next to the water and offer much less privacy. **(360) 645-2422; $10 per tent per evening; closed September–mid-June.** *Call for directions to this private campground.*

Romantic Warning: Keep in mind that this area does not cater to tourists. Consequently, the campground office, cabins, and surrounding village are in a state of disrepair. Also, don't leave any of your food unstored or unattended; the crows will carry it away!

La Push

Outdoor Kissing

❤❤❤ **THIRD BEACH, La Push** If you want to sense the power of the ocean, make the trip to Third Beach. Watching the waves crash into these rocks as they have done unceasingly for thousands of years is a humbling experience. Although this is one of the more tumultuous areas of coastline, there are plenty of surf-bared logs dotting the beach offering nooks of protection. You can snuggle close and feel the salty air caressing your face and lips. Two miles of coastline enclose the surf-pounded beach, where hidden caves and rock formations await your exploration. At low tide, you can climb onto what at high tide are islands and marvel at tide pools full of trapped sea life. As is true with any vacation outing, day's end will come too soon; be sure to enjoy the fresh air while you can. *Follow the signs on Highway 101 to La Push, on the northwestern coast of the Olympic Peninsula. There is only one road that goes south of La Push along the coast. Two miles down this road is a small, barely noticeable "THIRD BEACH" sign and an unmarked parking area at the trailhead. A three-quarter-mile walk on a forest path brings you to the beach.*

Romantic Warning: Beware of the tide, especially on these beaches, where you could easily get trapped if you try to hike around a point or headland during an incoming tide. Know when the tides occur (buy a tide table or copy the times from the newspaper). Mere guesswork could get you in trouble if you are trying to beat the water.

Kalaloch

Hotel/Bed and Breakfast Kissing

☙☙ **KALALOCH LODGE, Kalaloch** The Pacific Ocean is Kalaloch's front-yard entertainment and the primary reason to be here. During low tide, take a long, sandy hike along the shore, accompanied by seagulls drifting overhead. At high tide, the roar of the ocean surf resounds. If you would like enough time to enjoy all the tidal phases, stay overnight in the eclectic assortment of accommodations at Kalaloch Lodge. The main lodge has nine adequate rooms and a mediocre oceanside restaurant (moderate; breakfast, lunch, and dinner daily). Farther down, on a bluff overlooking the ocean, are 16 weathered cedar cabins and six older, rustic log cabins. Several of these have wood-burning fireplaces, and most have views of the sovereign sunsets and ethereal seascape. Unfortunately, even in rooms that have been recently renovated, the decor is merely hotel standard, and the few units that have kitchens are not adequately equipped for much cooking. Still, this is about the only coastal option on Washington's northern shore, and the setting truly is magical. If you plan to spend most of your time outdoors, you may not mind the less-than-inspiring interiors. In the evening after dinner, light a fire, turn the lights down low, and launch into a night of ghost stories, giggling, and cuddling. **157151 Highway 101; (360) 962-2271; www.kalaloch.com; inexpensive to very expensive.**

Romantic Warning: Due to its remote location, Kalaloch Lodge occasionally experiences power outages. Candlelight may be romantic, but the loss of your refrigerator, stove, and hot water isn't.

Outdoor Kissing

☙☙☙☙ **HOH RAIN FOREST, Kalaloch** The Hoh Rain Forest demonstrates what Mother Nature can do when she has an abundance of moisture to thrive on (150 inches of rain annually). Every inch of ground, including decaying trees, is covered with moss, lichens, mushrooms, ferns, and sorrel. You will also see some of the largest spruce, fir, and cedar trees in the world. Some of evergreens here are 300 feet tall and 23 feet around. Silence surrounds you as all traces of sky disappear under the canopy of moss-covered trees. On a rare sunny day, streams of light penetrate the thick foliage in a golden, misty haze. Don't even try to restrain the joy and excitement you'll feel with every step. And since you can't avoid the moisture that oozes from the ground, wear waterproof shoes. **(360) 374-6925.** *On Highway 101 south of Forks, on the northwest side of Olympic National Park, look for signs directing you to the*

Hoh Visitor Center, which is 18 miles east of the highway. Inquire there about hikes suitable for your skill level.

❧❧❧ **RUBY BEACH, Kalaloch** An easy walk on a well-maintained trail leads down to Ruby Beach. This pebbly stretch of coastline is graced with majestic sea stacks jutting from the ocean. The beach is named for the rosy sand, which contains tiny garnets, and we did find a number of red-speckled rocks along the shore. Although they do not exactly resemble rubies, they are part of the natural treasure that makes this beach so spectacular. *Off Highway 101, approximately nine miles north of Kalaloch.*

Quinault

Hotel/Bed and Breakfast Kissing

❧❧ **LAKE QUINAULT LODGE, Lake Quinault** Set in the heart of the Olympic Rain Forest, overlooking serene Lake Quinault, this lodge is a grand cedar-shingled building with hunter green shutters. A massive stone fireplace warms the lobby, and windows face the lake beyond a manicured front lawn that is edged by rhododendrons and hydrangeas. Add to this quiet setting a variety of intriguing hikes nearby and the opportunity for a lake cruise just before sunset, and the result is an incredible Northwest getaway.

Originally built in the 1890s, then destroyed by fire and rebuilt in the 1920s, Lake Quinault Lodge has seen many visitors come and go. Unfortunately, the lodge has also seen better days. Recent remodeling efforts included new carpeting, bedspreads, and curtains, but the overall effect is a confused combination of rustic wood-paneled walls, wood and wicker furniture, odd lamps, and brass beds. The rooms that seem the most pulled together are the pastel-appointed Lakeside Units, but they are located in a separate, more motel-like building, so the lodge feeling is totally lost. Consider a rustic little room in the main lodge so you can at least appreciate the history and authenticity of the place.

If you can focus on the natural wonder of the area, it should be easy to forgive the interior designer here, and you may even forget which way lies civilization. Sometimes you don't need fancy accommodations to find true romance; sometimes all you need is a remote location like this, and your certain someone. **345 South Shore Road; (360) 288-2571, (800) 562-6672 (in Washington and Oregon); www.visitlakequinault.com; moderate to very expensive.**

Romantic Suggestion: The Restaurant at Lake Quinault Lodge (moderate to expensive) has a captive audience due to the remote location. Thankfully, the kitchen does an impressive job with hearty breakfasts, basic lunches, and traditional Northwest cuisine at dinnertime.

"Kissing power is stronger

than will power . . ."

Abigail Van Buren

Southern Washington Coast

The southern Washington coast offers myriad possibilities for nature lovers as well as lovers in general. Nestled along this rugged coastline are forested hillsides, beautiful and isolated beaches, and secluded wildlife refuges. The northern and southern sections of this region have their own distinct personalities. To the north, between Hoquiam and Moclips, the coastline is almost untouched by development; this wild and pristine stretch is a tempting option all year-round. However, the lack of tourists and developers also means romantic accommodations are hard to come by.

To the south, between Leadbetter Point and Chinook on the Long Beach Peninsula, wide expanses of dramatic shoreline are bordered by mile after mile of motel-style properties and condominiums. Although less populated than tourist meccas like Ocean Shores or Cannon Beach, this area is fast making a name for itself. The crowds can be overwhelming during the summer —especially if it's a quiet retreat you're seeking. Still, small portions remain relatively undeveloped, and quite attractive to beachbound couples.

Hoquiam

Admittedly, this small industrial town is the last place you might think of going for romance. However, Hoquiam's **LYTLE HOUSE** (see Hotel/Bed and Breakfast Kissing) offers a welcome alternative to the chain-style motels in and around Ocean Shores.

Hotel/Bed and Breakfast Kissing

❀❀❀ **LYTLE HOUSE, Hoquiam** Set on a hill overlooking Grays Harbor and surrounded by lush gardens, this restored Queen Anne Victorian provides a pleasant refuge from the industrial feel of the surrounding lumber town. Much of the 1898 house has been kept intact—from the original kerosene lamp chandeliers to the stained glass windows and lacquered fretwork. Its circular second-floor sundeck, majestic front porch, variously shaped windows, and peaked awnings look much as they did at the turn of the century. One of the home's four parlors even displays a mural that was painted for the bride for whom the house was first built.

All but two of the eight guest rooms have private baths, but even those with shared or detached baths are pleasant (robes are provided) and offer something unique: For instance, the third-floor shared bathroom has a claw-foot European tub filled with live goldfish—and a separate shower of course. Done up in shades of red and accented with floral motifs, the richly appointed

Balcony Suite features lovely antiques, a claw-foot tub nestled in the corner, and a private balcony overlooking the fragrant rose garden. Delicate lace and a lovely floral motif decorate the sunny Rose Room. One of our favorites is the Windsor Room, with its potbellied stove, well-stocked bookcase, and private balcony surveying views of Grays Harbor; its only drawback is the detached bath down the hall. The other rooms also have details that make them special, such as antique sewing machines, tailor's dummies dressed in period clothing, and intricate tapestries.

Breakfast is served in the dining room at three separate lace-covered tables to ensure privacy. Guests have a choice of a continental buffet or specialty items such as oven-baked French toast, English shirred eggs, and baked omelets. The owners also provide desserts in the late afternoon to evening hours. **509 Chenault Avenue; (360) 533-2320, (800) 677-2320; www.lytlehouse. com; inexpensive to expensive.**

Copalis Beach

Hotel/Bed and Breakfast Kissing

❧❧ **IRON SPRINGS OCEAN BEACH RESORT, Copalis Beach** This 100-acre resort is so close to the Pacific Ocean, you're guaranteed to hear the surf from inside each cottage. Nestled among spruce trees on a low-lying bluff, the 28 cottages are spaced far enough apart to ensure privacy. Each cabin —from the one-bedroom studios to the two-bedroom cottages—is equipped with a wood-burning fireplace, a full kitchen, and cooking supplies (provisions are your responsibility). The interiors are simply decorated with brass lamps, throw rugs, and comfortable couches, while large picture windows let in the sunshine and provide wonderful views of the ocean and surrounding woods.

Although there is no direct beach access from the cottages themselves, a short trek along a nearby trail leads down to the shoreline. Those not daring enough to brave the ocean's cold can take a dip in the heated indoor pool, play a game of badminton, or hike along the trails that meander through the woods around the resort. If you get hungry, treat yourselves to homemade cinnamon rolls and clam chowder, available in the gift shop near the registration office; take these tasty treats back to your cottage to share in privacy. **3707 Highway 109; (360) 276-4230; www.irsonspringsresort.com; inexpensive to expensive; minimum-stay requirement on weekends, holidays, and seasonally.**

Romantic Warning: A possible drawback to this resort is its popularity with families in the summertime. Your cabin should provide enough privacy so that the only sound you'll hear is the gentle roar of the ocean. But just in case, consider coming only in the off-season to ensure complete tranquillity.

Moclips

Hotel/Bed and Breakfast Kissing

❤❤ **OCEAN CREST RESORT, Moclips** Although this resort looks much like your basic hotel from the outside, the romance factor improves considerably once you set foot inside the rooms. The 45 units range from two-bedroom apartments with a full kitchen to large studios with a fridge, and all offer either a fireplace or woodstove. Most offer little more than typical hotel decor except for the studios in Building 5, which have attractive cedar paneling and newer furnishings. Whichever building you choose to stay in, we recommend requesting a unit with an ocean view; you may pay a little more, but it's definitely worth it, especially since most of the rooms here feature large windows and decks.

For indoor recreation and relaxation, visit the resort's sauna, hot tub, swimming pool, and massage parlor. These facilities are located across the street in a contemporary wooden building with vaulted ceilings, skylights, and three tiers of windows. Because the building is open to all guests, privacy may be hard to come by here. For a better option, descend the bluff via a beautifully constructed 133-step staircase through a wooded ravine to the beach. From here, the sandy shoreline extends for miles in either direction. If you get tired on the way back up, stop and share a kiss in the shade on one of several benches along the way; these perches were seemingly made for just this purpose.

We recommend the Ocean Crest's dining room (moderate) for breakfast, lunch, and dinner. Its bay windows reveal the area's spectacular sunsets, and both the seafood and the service are superior. **4651 Highway 109; (360) 276-4465, (800) 684-8439; inexpensive to moderate; minimum-stay requirement on weekends and holidays.**

LONG BEACH PENINSULA

The thought of 28 miles of practically deserted beaches has drawn many visitors to this area over the years. Despite numerous developments and a seemingly endless succession of shops, motels, and gas stations along the Pacific Highway, the Long Beach Peninsula is still a marvelous destination to get in touch with nature and the sublime power of the ocean.

Chinook

Restaurant Kissing

❤❤❤ **SANCTUARY RESTAURANT, Chinook** There's no way around it: Eating here can be a heavenly experience. Set along Highway 101, this 92-year-old building was formerly the Methodist Episcopal Church of Chinook; today it retains the hushed, echoed atmosphere one would expect from such reverent beginnings. Most of the structure and appointments in the dimly lit interior are intact, and perfectly offset by the vaulted ceilings and polished wood floors. Original stained glass windows, angel sconces, a pump organ, and leaded glass door insets can be admired from the wooden pews, where diners sit at white-linened tables.

The food here is divine, from the fresh local seafood to the Scandinavian specialties. For starters, try the *kottbullar* (Swedish meatballs) or the clam bisque. Move on to entrées such as the crisp panko-dusted jumbo prawns and crab cake or the chicken roulade with prosciutto, Jarlsberg cheese, and herbs. Kudos to the impeccable rack of lamb, well seasoned and smothered with an herb crust before being oven roasted. For dessert, try the famous lemon cream sherbet or indulge in *krumkake,* waffle-like cones filled with whipped cream and topped with a light berry sauce. Such heavenly food, combined with the distinctive setting, may inspire you to pledge your vows all over again. **Highway 101 and Hazel Street; (360) 777-8380; moderate to expensive; reservations recommended; call for seasonal hours.**

Ilwaco

Outdoor Kissing

❤❤ **SCENIC ILWACO LOOP, Ilwaco** This three-mile scenic loop at the southern end of the Long Beach Peninsula begins at the town of Ilwaco. (While Ilwaco itself is not exactly romance inspiring, you may find the town's centennial murals interesting.) Stay in your car until you reach the parking lot for the **NORTH HEAD LIGHTHOUSE.** A short walk along a lightly wooded trail is rewarded by an astounding view of both the Pacific Ocean and the entire Long Beach Peninsula. Be it high noon or sunset, views from this vantage point, with the picturesque 100-year-old lighthouse in the background, are sure to inspire a kiss or two. For a small fee, you can climb to the top of the lighthouse for a short tour.

Continue driving south along the loop, pass through an entrance to the U.S. Coast Guard Station, and look for the path that leads to **CAPE DISAPPOINTMENT LIGHTHOUSE.** The hike up is steep, but worth it for a view of this historical lighthouse that has been guiding sailors into the Columbia River's entrance since 1856. Other highlights along the loop include **BENSON BEACH,** which is closed to car traffic and has a view of both lighthouses; **FORT CANBY STATE PARK,** with its 16 miles of hiking trails; the **ILWACO HERITAGE MUSEUM;** and the **LEWIS AND CLARK INTERPRETIVE CENTER,** which also offers a wonderful view of the Columbia River. *Take Highway 103 to the southern part of the Long Beach Peninsula. At the town of Ilwaco, follow signs to the loop.*

Seaview

Hotel/Bed and Breakfast Kissing

❦❦❦ **THE SHELBURNE INN, Seaview** When you first drive into town and realize that we have recommended an establishment that is right on the main street (and awarded it three lips, no less), you may wonder if we have allowed our requirements to become more lenient. Well, we haven't—establishments are still partially rated on their "surrounding splendor"—but The Shelburne Inn has managed to create enough surrounding splendor *inside* the guest rooms that we nearly forgot the road right outside. Noise is really not a problem here unless you open the windows.

This Victorian/Craftsman-style retreat is filled with antique pieces, original moldings, and ornate tapestries. The original owner built the home in 1896 to serve as a boardinghouse and named it after a grand hotel in Dublin. Since then, four major phases of refurbishing and construction have been completed, resulting in one of the region's premier country inns.

The 15 small, comfortably elegant rooms and suites are furnished with beautiful antiques, down comforters, lace pillows, handmade patchwork quilts, crocheted bedspreads, private bathrooms, marble-topped dressers, and plenty of country-Victorian charm. Many also feature either a balcony or deck. Of course, not all rooms are created equal. Some have queen-size beds while others have doubles; some face the charming garden, while others offer less inspiring street views (partially screened by frosted windows). The two suites are quite large, but our favorite is the pretty corner suite with a sitting area, leaded glass French doors, and an old-fashioned claw-foot tub. Guests in the Honeymoon/Anniversary Suite have the option of having breakfast delivered to their room in the morning.

For all other guests, breakfast is served family-style downstairs in the dining room at one large oak table. The Shelburne's artistic gourmet breakfasts are designed to please both the eye and the palate. Feast on treats like razor clam fritters, stuffed French toast, potato and lamb hash with a coddled egg, or Hangtown Fry—an open-face omelet with bacon, oysters, cheese, and spinach. Plates are beautifully decorated with edible flowers and herbs, while homemade pastries, fresh fruit, juice, and freshly ground coffee complete the picture-perfect meal. After this indulgence, you'll be ready to hike through a series of dunes to reach the long, smooth beach. Long Beach is vast enough that even when a lot of other people are out enjoying the sand and surf, it doesn't seem nearly as crowded as many other Northwest beaches. **4415 Pacific Highway (Highway 103); (360) 642-2442, (800) INN-1896; www. theshelburneinn.com; moderate to expensive; minimum-stay requirement on weekends.**

Romantic Suggestion: When you book your stay here, we suggest that you also make a reservation for dinner at **THE SHOALWATER RESTAU-RANT** (see Restaurant Kissing), located on the inn's main floor.

Restaurant Kissing

❤❤❤ **CHERI WALKER'S 42ND ST. CAFE, Seaview** Ask the locals about good food and they'll direct you toward Cheri Walker's 42nd St. Cafe. Formerly the chef at the renowned **SHOALWATER RESTAURANT** (see below), Cheri Walker has opened her own establishment, and her culinary wizardry is as potent as ever.

This modest restaurant may not look like much from the outside; in fact, it's housed in a building that was once Coast Guard barracks, moved from Fort Canby Station to this location after World War II. Inside, 15 tables are arranged around the dining room, which is reminiscent of a country kitchen. Lace half-curtains shield the view of the busy highway traffic outside, while dried and fresh flowers and colorful tablecloths brighten up the room.

If you're here for lunch, indulge in unusual offerings such as the chèvre fondue with apples, the smoked-salmon Caesar salad, or the fried green tomatoes with cumin-orange mayonnaise. We also highly recommend the halibut and shrimp cake with parsley-caper mayonnaise. The dinner menu offers a little bit of everything, from hand-cut spinach ravioli stuffed with three cheeses and roasted vegetables, to charbroiled meats livened up with cranberry barbecue sauce or mesquite butter. Finish up with homemade lemon dainties, chocolate and ancho chile brownies, or cranberry bread pudding with walnut crème anglaise. The service is cheerful and efficient. **4201 Pacific Highway (Highway 103); (360) 642-2323; moderate; breakfast, lunch, and dinner daily.**

❤❤ **MY MOM'S PIE KITCHEN, Seaview** Housed in a Victorian cottage with plenty of windows, My Mom's Pie Kitchen has a dainty tearoom feel with its royal blue tablecloths, lace curtains, and overall floral theme. Seating is offered in three petite dining rooms and outside on the patio, although busy highway traffic makes the latter a less-than-pleasant option on most days.

The menu features basic soups, seasonal salads, and sandwiches. House specialties include chicken almond pot pie, a perennial favorite, and a delightfully cheesy crab quiche accompanied by a refreshing cranberry ice. However, the kitchen is best known for (you guessed it) pies. All are handmade with a delicate, flaky crust, and you can smell them from the parking lot if you're lucky enough to arrive when they're cooling. Fruit pies include apple, rhubarb, and the ever-popular marion blackberry. Lemon meringue, banana whipped cream, chocolate almond, peanut butter, and sour cream raisin make up the cream pie selection. Sheer indulgence! **4316 Pacific Highway (Highway 103); (360) 642-2342; moderate; call for seasonal hours; closed December.**

❤❤❤❤ **THE SHOALWATER RESTAURANT, Seaview** Can food be wildly romantic? At the Shoalwater, the proof is in the pudding, or perhaps we should say it's in the rose-geranium sorbet. No matter what you choose from the imaginative and wide-ranging menu, it will be utterly fresh, delicious, and beautifully presented. Asian-style crab and shrimp cakes are kissed with sesame oil and ginger, plump Cajun-style Willapa Bay oysters are blackened to perfection, and a rich roast duck breast is gently enhanced with a drizzle of pomegranate juice and shallot sauce. The wine list here is so extensive that some bottles have to be stored off-site, and the desserts are definitely worth the extra calories. All this is accompanied by friendly and accommodating service.

Even if the food at the Shoalwater were merely ordinary, the setting alone would warrant at least a kiss or two. The restaurant takes up most of the main floor of a turn-of-the-century house that has long been **THE SHELBURNE INN** (see Hotel/Bed and Breakfast Kissing). Inside, leaded and stained glass windows are crowned by high ceilings and accented with soft candlelight at night. Crisp white linens adorn each of the well-spaced antique tables in the warm, country-Victorian dining room. **4415 Pacific Highway (Highway 103), at The Shelburne Inn; (360) 642-4142; moderate to expensive; lunch and dinner daily.**

Romantic Alternative: The owners of the Shoalwater also operate **THE LIGHTSHIP RESTAURANT** (409 West Tenth Street, Long Beach; 360-642-3252; inexpensive to moderate; lunch and dinner daily), located at the top of a budget motel right near the beach. Very different in ambience, this casual restaurant offers astounding views of the ocean and the coast from its vantage point.

Long Beach

Hotel/Bed and Breakfast Kissing

❤❤❤ **BOREAS BED AND BREAKFAST INN, Long Beach** Just as Boreas, the god of the north wind, brought clear weather to the Greeks, this bed and breakfast that bears his name is sure to bring gales of memories for amorous couples. You can unpack your bags and take refuge in this quaint beach house ensconced in grass-covered dunes, with sweeping, undisturbed views of the Pacific Ocean. The home is tightly tucked between other houses, but once inside, you will hardly notice the close neighbors. Unwind in comfortable common areas filled with an eclectic assortment of antique furnishings, potted plants, and a glowing marble fireplace. Listen to a favorite recording from the owners' extensive music collection or, if you're in the mood to serenade your sweetheart, tickle the ivories on the white baby grand piano. Done up in attractive tiles, the pleasant kitchen is open to guests, who can help themselves to tea and coffee or fresh brownies at any time during their stay.

Choose from five gracious guest rooms, three of which have ocean views. The newly constructed Dunes Suite has been endowed with many windows and a skylight, making it a remarkably bright and airy retreat. Its sage and cream color scheme is enhanced by a mural of the North Head Lighthouse, a regional landmark, that was painted by a Northwest artist. This suite also features a comfy queen-size bed and French doors that open onto a deck with views of the ocean (only a five-minute walk away). A jetted tub in the bathroom is the ultimate way to soak your cares away in privacy. Also on the main floor is the Garden Suite, which is filled with plenty of old-world charm. Delicate gold and rose brocade adorns this room, which looks out to a small, picturesque flower garden. Upstairs, the Pacifica offers skylights, a vaulted ceiling, and a spectacular view of the ocean; this is the perfect spot for storm watching or savoring gorgeous sunsets. The Stargazer has a similar view and Battenburg lace accents, while the attic-style Hideaway Suite offers a king-size feather bed, a small balcony, and a round window that affords a great mountain view on clear days. All five rooms have private bathrooms.

After a day of play head out to the dunes, where an enclosed cedar and glass gazebo houses a state-of-the art spa. Simply light one of the provided candles and place it in the window to stake your claim to this secluded spot. Since the gazebo and spa are reserved for one couple at a time, you can cherish your sunset soak in supreme privacy, with only the gentle rustle of beach grass to distract you from each other.

In the morning, a delicious full breakfast is served family-style at the dining room table. Jump-start your day with a cup of the innkeepers' organic coffee, followed by a main dish such as an omelet, frittata, smoked salmon, or ginger pancakes with fresh lime sauce, accompanied by homemade breads and pastries. After savoring your morning meal, take a walk through the dunes to the water's edge or along the nearby boardwalk. **607 North Boulevard; (360) 642-8069, (888) 642-8069; www.boreasinn.com; inexpensive to expensive; minimum-stay requirement on weekends.**

Romantic Note: Next door you'll find a rustic, family-style cabin available for rent. Although sparsely furnished and not nearly as charming as the bed and breakfast, it offers three bedrooms, a kitchen, and a fireplace. It's a great getaway for those seeking affordable, roomy, and exclusive privacy with beach access.

❦❦ SCANDINAVIAN GARDENS INN BED AND BREAKFAST, Long Beach

Set in a nondescript residential area, Scandinavian Gardens is a comfortable, affordable bed-and-breakfast option. Simple, albeit slightly worn, accommodations are enhanced by white Berber carpeting and a mix of antique and contemporary furnishings. Each of the four guest rooms—appropriately named Finland, Iceland, Denmark, and Norway—has its own distinct color scheme, a queen-size bed imported from Sweden, and a private bath. Although the rooms are a bit on the austere side, they are complemented by colorful throw rugs and wall hangings by local Finnish artists. The two-room Swedish Honeymoon Suite is incredibly spacious and includes a soaking tub for two set in an alcove beneath a skylight. The inn's homey common area is adorned with a piano, fireplace, and the owners' doll collection. After a day at the beach, check out the indoor spa area, with its large Jacuzzi tub and cedar-lined sauna.

A five-course breakfast is served family-style at one large table in the cheerful dining room. Begin with fresh fruit, creamed rice and fruit soup, homemade pastries and granola, and sorbet, followed by a delicious entrée such as blueberry French toast or a smoked-salmon omelet. **1610 California Avenue South; (360) 642-8877, (800) 988-9277; www.aone.com/~rdakan; inexpensive to expensive.**

Ocean Park

Hotel/Bed and Breakfast Kissing

❤❤❤ **BLACKWOOD BEACH COTTAGES, Ocean Park** Don't be dissuaded by the loosely graveled driveway leading to these cottages or the RV park right next door. Once you arrive at your oceanside getaway, you'll be pleased to discover the world of privacy that awaits. Five cheery red cottages trimmed in white are set literally a stone's throw from the beach on four acres of woodland. Tastefully designed and decorated, each spacious cottage is fronted by a porch and contains a living room, a fully equipped kitchen, a bedroom, and a bathroom. Plush carpeting and soft throw cushions in the living room invite snuggling by the gas fireplace. In the bedroom, a down comforter and a mound of fluffy pillows transform the queen-size bed into a guarantee of a good night's sleep. Each cottage is also stocked with cookbooks, gourmet chocolates, and board games, as well as garden shears for visits to the owners' nearby herb garden.

Color schemes and themes differ from cottage to cottage. Pine adorns the interior of Spinnaker; florals and denim tastefully come together in Beachcomber; Mystic is done up in sunny yellows and blues; and Klipsan Queen features vintage 1920s decor. The Sandbar, set a little higher than the others, is dressed in soothing deep green with wicker furnishings. At the time of our visit, three more cottages were being built in the woods, two of which will have gas fireplaces.

Bring along breakfast provisions so you can whip up a morning meal for your sweetheart. If your idea of a vacation means staying out of the kitchen, consider ordering a specialty food basket of brandied cranberries, French toast mixes, and smoked meats, available to guests at an additional cost. Whatever you decide to eat, be sure to take in the sweeping ocean view from your cozy breakfast nook.

Start and finish each day with a stroll on the beach, less than a minute's walk over rolling sand dunes. (If you're lucky, you may even meet Danny, the resident pheasant, along the way.) Steal a kiss in the glorious herb and vegetable garden, where rows of fennel, lovage, arugula, and chives are nestled next to lavender and three kinds of mint. A pond with a resident family of ducks completes the serene setting. With all this privacy and tranquillity at your fingertips, returning home may be harder than you think. **20711 Pacific Way; (360) 665-6356, (888) 376-6356; www.willapabay.org/~opchamber/ blackwood; inexpensive to expensive; minimum-stay requirement on weekends seasonally.**

❧❧❧ CASWELL'S ON THE BAY BED AND BREAKFAST INN, Ocean Park

This recently built Queen Anne Victorian sits proudly at the edge of Willapa Bay, lending it a certain grace even at low tide. Tall trees, a manicured lawn, hanging flower baskets, and colorful gardens trim the stately yellow home and its circular driveway, while the tidelands are an ever-changing backdrop. Unlike a traditional Victorian, this house is bright and airy inside, with high ceilings, plenty of windows, and excellent soundproofing.

The common area is tastefully done up with antique wicker furniture and has a fireplace to heat up those chilly winter evenings. A lovely sunroom faces nearby Long Island and provides the perfect spot for sharing afternoon coffee, catching glimpses of the local wildlife, or just curling up with a book from the well-stocked library. The owners plan to build a gazebo by the water, which will be an ideal kissing spot once it is completed.

Five comfortable guest rooms are located on the second floor. Private modern baths, handcarved antique pieces from different periods, and pleasant sitting areas are found in each room. Two rooms have wonderful views of the bay, and the rest overlook the garden. Additional amenities include ornate antique bedroom sets, down comforters, the owners' personalized brand of soaps and lotions, and designer sheets and towels. Of particular romantic interest is the Terrace Suite, which has plenty of windows facing the bay, a lovely patio, and an ornate French oak bedroom set from 1793. Breakfast can be delivered to this room, if you wish to enjoy an intimate morning meal for two. Otherwise, guests can feast on a full gourmet breakfast at one large table in the main-floor dining room. Orange-pecan French toast, hash brown quiche, buckwheat pancakes, and a variety of frittatas, cobblers, and homemade pastries are delicious ways to begin your day. **25204 Sandridge Road; (360) 665-6535, (888) 553-2319; www.site-works.com/caswells; inexpensive to expensive; minimum-stay requirement on weekends; recommended wedding site.**

❧❧ COAST WATCH BED AND BREAKFAST, Ocean Park

City dwellers often forget how beautiful a sunset or a star-filled sky can be, but a weekend at the Coast Watch never fails to reacquaint guests with nature's abundant splendor. Escape to one of two spacious, modestly appointed suites in this weathered gray-blue cabin set in the dunes, only yards from the ocean. Both suites are full of sunlight and provide breathtaking views of the pounding surf and rolling dunes. With such views, you'll hardly notice the somewhat dated carpeting and furnishings. The West Suite has a deck overlooking the ocean, perfect for enjoying a sunset or spending quiet time together; inside, a telescope makes stargazing a treat. The North Suite is slightly smaller, but still pleasant.

The conscientious hostess takes pride in the smallest of details, from fresh flowers adorning your suite, to roses left on your pillow, to the in-room stereo complete with romantic tapes and CDs. She has also been known to drive for miles to find high-quality items for breakfast, which she will deliver to your room at the time you specify. Homemade cinnamon rolls and roasted nectarines with raspberry-walnut sauce are just a sampling of the goodies she prepares.

This unique bed and breakfast has no common areas for guests outside of their individual suites, so privacy is guaranteed. And because there are only two suites, you'll feel as if the broad beach and grass-covered dunes are yours for the taking. Stroll at dusk and let the waves wash over your feet, or wait until the sun has set and let the stars above enfold you. The only drawback to a weekend at the Coast Watch is returning to the real world. **(360) 665-6774; www.willapabay.org/~kmj/cw; inexpensive; minimum-stay requirement on weekends.**

Romantic Warning: Coast Watch is located on an unmarked street and may be difficult to find; call ahead to get detailed directions before beginning your sojourn.

❀❀❀ THE DOVESHIRE BED AND BREAKFAST, Ocean Park
An acre of immaculate park-like grounds at the DoveShire provide a serene setting for lovebirds of the human variety, as well as a dovecote for the feathery kind. The Gothic-style main house is spacious and airy, with a common area filled with games and books, and a pretty breakfast area embellished with bay windows and a plethora of plants. Separate glass-topped tables in the breakfast room afford guests some privacy during the expanded continental buffet meal of homemade granola, fresh muffins, and a hot fruit dish.

Separate from the main house, the four guest rooms are arranged in motel fashion around the parking lot. Inside, they feature private baths, vaulted ceilings, queen-size beds, down comforters, handmade duvet covers, and TV/VCRs discreetly hidden away. All are decorated with a mix of family heirlooms and contemporary furniture, and open onto a deck overlooking the pristine lawn. **21914 Pacific Highway (Highway 103); (360) 665-3017, (888) 553-2320; www.willapabay.org/~doveshire; moderate.**

Romantic Note: If your sweetheart's cooing has won you over, you needn't venture far from your love nest to say "I do"; one of the owners is ordained and can perform weddings. A gazebo was under construction at the time of our visit, and from the look of things, this will be lovely spot in which to seal your vows with a kiss.

❧❧❧ **THE WHALEBONE HOUSE BED AND BREAKFAST, Ocean Park**
History and romance come alive at this restored 1889 Victorian farmhouse. Fronted by colorful gardens and an enclosed sunporch, the aloe green home is an architectural blending of Northwest and Maine influences. The property is bordered by a white fence made from the vertebrae of a whale that washed up on shore in the early '50s (hence the inn's name). Inside, a collection of modern and antique furnishings adorns the cozy common area on the main floor.

Antiques, family heirlooms, and private baths, as well as lessons in local history, distinguish the inn's four guest rooms. Named after the home's architect, the S. A. Matthews Room on the main floor features floral wallpaper, a claw-foot tub, and a hand-carved bed covered with a handmade quilt. Upstairs, romantic possibilities abound in the large Louise Rice Room, with its skylights, beautiful antique pieces, and queen-size bed topped with cream-colored linens and a down comforter. (This room was named for the woman whose efforts earned the home a place on Washington state's Register of Historic Places.) The Sou'wester Room is bright and cheery; its whitewashed wood paneling is offset by a hand-painted wooden beach chair and other knick-knacks reminiscent of coastal Maine. Here you can snuggle by the box-bay window while taking in views of the garden below. Artesmia's Parlor, named after the architect's wife and done up in a blue and white color scheme, was once the home's second-floor parlor. Details of its past remain today, including its high dormer windows and a plate rail that runs the length of the room.

Mornings at the Whalebone bring a full breakfast served at a long table in the dining area. Enjoy homemade muffins and scones, as well as the inn's Whalebone hash, containing smoked salmon, capers, potatoes, and sour cream. **2101 Bay Avenue; (360) 665-5371, (888) 298-3330; www.willapabay.org/ ~whalebone; inexpensive; minimum-stay requirement on holiday weekends.**

Romantic Warning: Although the inn is conveniently located, equidistant from Willapa Bay and the Pacific Ocean, it's situated on a main thoroughfare in Ocean Park, which may distract from the overall privacy.

Nahcotta

Hotel/Bed and Breakfast Kissing

❧❧❧ **OUR HOUSE IN NAHCOTTA, Nahcotta** Set in a residential area, this cedar-shake Cape Code–style home sits on an incline and is surrounded by abundant foliage and flower gardens. Inside, the three-story building is filled with treasures from the owner's antiquing expeditions. The two units here are both completely private and wonderfully spacious. With its floral accents and Victorian pieces, the First Floor Suite resembles an English country getaway. Bay windows look out onto the garden, and a short claw-foot tub is the highlight of the small private bath. The Second Floor Suite is decorated in a subtle, rustic Italian theme, with hardwood floors, a rich mustard and hunter green color scheme, and hand-painted plates. If two couples are traveling together, the owner will open up the third floor, which has a wood-paneled French country–inspired bedroom, a charming sitting area, and a bathroom with a skylight above the tub. Otherwise, there are no shared facilities, and the sitting area may be used as a reading nook.

Breakfast is an expanded continental affair highlighted by cinnamon rolls or sour cherry–rice pudding. Then it's time for the sun and surf and perhaps dinner at **THE ARK RESTAURANT** (see Restaurant Kissing), which is within walking distance of the inn. **268th and Dell Streets; (360) 665-6667; www.willapabay.org/~kmj/ohn; inexpensive to moderate; minimum-stay requirement.**

Restaurant Kissing

❀❀❀ **THE ARK RESTAURANT, Nahcotta** Locals and tourists alike tend to rave about the view and the food here, all in the same breath. Don't be distracted by the nearby oyster farm's industrial equipment, trucks, and buildings; once you're inside the small red-painted building that juts out into Willapa Bay, you'll be glad you came. With views of the water on all sides, the restaurant has a wide selection of window tables from which to choose. The wood and brick interior provides a comfortably casual dining atmosphere, warmed by a large stone fireplace. Colorful flags and knickknacks hang from dark wooden beams overhead.

The Ark is considered one of the finest restaurants on the peninsula. You really can't go wrong with any of the fresh local seafood selections. Try the salmon, pan-fried with a splash of scotch and orange juice, laced with Drambuie, and garnished with a touch of crème fraîche. Or chose the traditional Ark oyster feed; the lightly breaded, grilled oysters are harvested right from Willapa Bay. After your meal, order a specialty tea or a cup of espresso made from locally roasted beans as you decide between the seductive dessert choices presented on a silver tray. Then sit back and watch as the twinkling stars emerge from the sky beyond your window. **273rd Street and Sandridge Road; (360) 665-4133; moderate to expensive; call for seasonal hours.**

Romantic Note: Before The Ark closes for winter, be sure to ask about its popular summer Garlic Festival. Reservations for this epicurean festival are accepted only after midnight on Valentine's Day (after all your romantic kissing is done). Appetizers, entrées, and, yes, even desserts are prepared with more garlic than you can imagine. Just be sure to do all your kissing beforehand.

Outdoor Kissing

❀❀❀❀ **LEADBETTER POINT STATE PARK, Long Beach Peninsula** There are many romantic places to walk hand in hand on this peninsula, the most obvious being the beach and dunes. Other options include hiking to **NORTH HEAD LIGHTHOUSE** or **CAPE DISAPPOINTMENT LIGHTHOUSE,** although the latter is a somewhat steeper proposition (see the review of the **SCENIC ILWACO LOOP** on page 362). For assured privacy throughout the year, consider going to Leadbetter Point State Park, at the northern tip of the Long Beach Peninsula. The drive to the park is peaceful, and that sense of seclusion is enhanced as you pass beneath a canopy of shady trees marking the park's entrance. You can wander all day and not run into anybody. But don't wander too far; people have been known to get lost in the marsh up here. Also, the seasonal appearance of large, aggressive black flies can yield an unforeseen kissing obstacle. **Free admission.** *Take Sandridge Road north past the town of Nahcotta. Turn west onto Oysterville Road and follow the signs to the park.*

Washington Cascades

The most popular and accessible route through this region is the Cascade Loop, a series of connecting highways that passes through the northern section of the mountains. Begin the loop just south of Everett, where Highway 2 heads east across Stevens Pass to the town of Leavenworth on the east side of the mountains. Just before Wenatchee, take Alternate Highway 97 north past Chelan to Pateros, where you continue heading north on Highway 153 toward the towns of Twisp and Winthrop. From there take Highway 20 west toward Mazama, heading back across the Cascades to Interstate 5. (The loop officially continues out to La Conner and down through Whidbey Island, finishing with a ferryboat ride to Mukilteo, just south of Everett.)

Washington's stretch of the Cascade Range is nothing less than spectaclar. To the north, Mount Baker's glacial peak stands guard near the U.S.-Canadian border. South of Mount Baker lies a 300-mile expanse of mesmerizing wilderness that includes national forests, parks, and mountain passes, offering startling views of the range's volcanic giants: Mount Rainier, Mount St. Helens, and Mount Adams. This chain of mountains is liberally supplied with old-growth evergreens, snow-covered cliffs, and countless plummeting waterfalls and spirited rivers. In contrast to the wet, vivid greenery on the west side of the Cascades, the east side of the mountains is authentic Marlboro country—awash in hues of gold, bathed in hot sunshine in summer, and blasted by snowy cold in winter. Almost every square foot of this expanse is magnificent.

Driving is the fastest, but not the most intimate, way to experience this area. There are also stimulating hikes to consider. To request an informational packet and a catalog from which you can order hiking maps of the area, contact the **NORTH CASCADES NATIONAL PARK** (2105 State Route 20, Sedro Woolley, WA 98284; 360-856-5700). A network of graveled dirt roads branches off the main highways and leads to paths less taken. These treks of the heart will bring you pleasure and adventure.

Leavenworth

In some ways, the town of Leavenworth is a contradiction. The village's pervasive, tourist-attracting, ersatz Bavarian motif overwhelms most of the storefronts that line Leavenworth's all-too-authentic streets. Even the local McDonald's and Dairy Queen sport European facades. The alpine influence is almost quaint (and actually lovely in winter, when snow softens the effect)—that is, if you don't mind crowds and if you happen to love Wiener schnitzel. Whether or not this environment is conducive to tender snuggling and quiet moments depends entirely on your affinity for things German.

What most people don't realize is that there is more to Leavenworth than meets the eye. Accommodations in Leavenworth are second to none. Concealed in a valley and surrounded by the towering Cascades, Leavenworth has a setting so incredibly gorgeous that even a real Bavarian town would envy it. Just beyond the crest of the bordering foothills lies the astounding **ALPINE LAKES WILDERNESS** (see Outdoor Kissing), well known for its abundant lakes and vast stretches of stunning mountain terrain. The region is also encircled by thousands of breathtaking acres of evergreen forests in the **WENATCHEE NATIONAL FOREST** (see Outdoor Kissing). In addition, the **STEVENS PASS, MISSION RIDGE, LAKE WENATCHEE,** and **LAKE CHELAN** recreation areas are close at hand. If your vision of romance includes the great outdoors, you couldn't select a better place to visit. Here you can enjoy hiking, cross-country skiing, sleigh rides, white-water rafting, bird-watching, or just simply being together in the masterpiece of nature.

Long months of exceedingly hot, dry weather in the summer of 1994 led to forest fires that swept through this region's forested mountains. Structural damage was kept to a minimum, thanks to the vigorous efforts of firefighters from all over (who deserve medals of honor and plentiful praise). None of the establishments included in this publication were affected in any way. The fires were primarily located in undeveloped forestland; hiking trails suffered the most damage, but because of nature's abundance here, options for wilderness exploring still remain unlimited.

All of this is to say that Leavenworth is alive and well. In fact, it's probably better than ever, due to the community's resilience and renewed efforts to make Leavenworth an enticing, worthwhile destination.

Hotel/Bed and Breakfast Kissing

❧❧❧❧ **ABENDBLUME PENSION, Leavenworth** You'll find this newly built inn sheltered at the base of the Cascade Mountains on a flat residential plain. The white stucco and wood exterior, hemmed by a soft green lawn and myriad colorful flowers, is reminiscent of other properties found in Leavenworth, but that resemblance goes only as far as the facade.

Handcarved, arched double doors open to reveal a limestone foyer; a curved wrought-iron staircase winds upward beneath a stained glass skylight to six exquisite guest rooms (the seventh one is on the main floor). Even the least expensive rooms are special, with pencil-post beds, down comforters, TV/VCRs, and tiled private baths. Soft lounging robes are provided for your comfort, and in-room therapeutic massages for two can be arranged upon request.

For a little extra, you can stay in the lap of luxury in one of the inn's two deluxe suites. Relax in the two-person Jacuzzi tub, or enjoy a water massage in the two-headed shower with four body sprays, found in each of the suites' large Italian marble bathrooms. Even the bathrooms' floor tiles are heated for extra comfort. With the flick of a match, a prearranged bundle of wood ignites in the fireplace, warming your snow-white canopy bed. In each room, flower boxes create splashes of color that peek through every window, and views of the valley and distant mountains can be enjoyed from a cozy window seat or a secluded private deck or patio.

There is no shortage of good places to kiss at Abendblume. We suggest the outdoor Grecian spa inlaid with Italian tiles, or the sumptuous common area where you can snuggle up in front of a crackling fire on one of the overstuffed floral couches. Others may feel that the ultimate place to share a kiss is over dessert, served every evening to guests by candlelight at intimate, two-person tables in the knotty pine dining room. In the morning, a hearty German breakfast featuring sweet breads, a hot entrée, and an assortment of meats and cheeses is served in the same dining room, minus candlelight. **12570 Ranger Road; (509) 548-4059, (800) 669-7634; www.abendblume.com; inexpensive to expensive; minimum-stay requirement on weekends and holidays.**

Romantic Note: The hosts at Abendblume are eager to please and are dedicated to romance. Upon request, they will have champagne and chocolates or wine and cheese waiting for you in your room. They can even put a red rose on your pillow, dim the lights, and have your favorite soft music playing on the in-room CD player. Ask and you shall receive.

❀❀❀❁ **ALL SEASONS RIVER INN, Leavenworth** Positioned on a bluff overlooking the Wenatchee River, this country-elegant bed and breakfast caters to those seeking a romantic refuge in the Cascade Mountains. The spacious living room, filled with country touches and a river-rock fireplace, showcases views of the surging river and natural surroundings through expansive windows. Throughout the home, teddy bears tumble over couches in the common areas and sit atop beds in the lovely guest rooms. Snowcapped Wedge Mountain peeks through the windows in the upstairs game room, and a separate TV room offers floral upholstered couches perfect for snuggling upon.

Deliciously thick down comforters drape queen-size beds in all six enticing guest rooms. Most rooms have private decks or patios, gas fireplaces, Jacuzzi tubs, tasteful wall stenciling, and sitting areas furnished with restored antique love seats. Recent renovations have been a grand success: Three new two-room suites, complete with river views and cozy window seats, make elegant retreats for any occasion. Our favorites are the spacious Evergreen and River View Suites, which feature two-headed showers and soothing color schemes. The third two-room suite, River Bend, offers serene views of the river from its Jacuzzi tub, nestled in a cozy nook next to a large window in the bathroom.

Breakfast in the morning is a sumptuous spread of homemade granola, fresh zucchini bread, a kiwi–peanut butter parfait, Mexican tamale pancakes, savory sausage, and German potatoes. Ask for the innkeeper's recipe book if you'd like to try this unforgettable morning meal at home. **8751 Icicle Road; (509) 548-1425, (800) 254-0555; www.allseasonsriverinn.com; moderate to expensive; minimum-stay requirement seasonally and on weekends.**

❤❤❤ **FEATHERWIND'S BED AND BREAKFAST, Leavenworth** This country getaway is a quintessential rural retreat, about 15 miles from the heart of busy Leavenworth. You'll feel as if you've arrived at the middle of the Cascade forest after you finish the winding road that brings you here, but surrounding quietness and natural beauty is what you've come for, right? Tall trees and wildflowers surround the entire property of this picturesque, wood-shingled farmhouse. Once you step inside, you'll see that old-fashioned comfort is the focus here. Each of the three guest rooms offers a mixture of country and modern accents, as well as cushioned window seats, private baths, TV/VCRs, and old-fashioned feather beds that swell upward beneath pretty floral comforters. Our favorite room is located on the main floor; it boasts sumptuous linens and a whirlpool tub set beneath corner windows in the sunny bathroom.

There are plenty of activities to keep you occupied all year-round. In winter, cross-country ski along a mile-long trail or explore the property's nine wooded acres. In summer, explore the area on complimentary bikes, lounge in the large outdoor spa, or swim under the small waterfall that splashes into the outdoor pool. After you've worked up an appetite, you'll appreciate the complimentary dessert served every evening to guests. In the early morning, the aroma of piping hot coffee set just outside your door will make it that much easier to get out of your warm bed and enjoy the generous breakfast served in the main-floor dining room. **17033 River Road; (509) 763-2011; www.rightathome. com/featherwinds; inexpensive to moderate; minimum-stay requirement on holiday weekends.**

Romantic Note: Two new guest accommodations have cropped up at Featherwind's: the Country Garden Guest Lodge and the Cascade Berry Bunk House. Because these homes can sleep between 12 and 16 people, they are just too large to recommend for only one couple. However, if you are traveling with another couple or with your family, you'll be thrilled with the cathedral ceilings, pine accents, propane fireplaces, spacious full kitchens, sitting areas, and cozy bedrooms in these lodgings.

❤❤❤ **HAUS LORELEI ON THE RIVER, Leavenworth** Although Haus Lorelei is conveniently located near Leavenworth's town center, you'll find no evidence that the village is only steps away. This European-style mansion is set at the edge of the Wenatchee River and encircled by evergreens; private basketball and tennis courts are nestled among the trees near the property's entrance. With such relaxation close at hand, the stresses of the world are bound to fade into oblivion.

Homey accoutrements and family pictures adorn the common area, where a massive beach-stone fireplace and a pink 1886 billiards table reside. Each of the ten guest rooms is named after a different German fairy tale, but only eight can be wholeheartedly recommended. (The two less charming rooms are furnished with multiple beds and are obviously geared toward families.) Among the remaining eight pleasant rooms, our favorites are the ones on the main floor that face the Wenatchee River. Featuring magnificent antiques imported from Germany, private bathrooms, and lace-canopied or four-poster beds covered with down comforters and eyelet spreads, these three rooms make wonderfully romantic retreats.

An elegant breakfast is served in the dining room, overlooking a sweeping lawn and the tumultuous Wenatchee River. After breakfast, you can follow the stone trail to the river's edge or cherish the scenery from the luxurious outdoor hot tub. Your hostess is eager to accommodate you and, upon request, will help you plan a rewarding day. **347 Division Street; (509) 548-5726, (800) 514-8868; www.hauslorelei.com; inexpensive to moderate; no credit cards; minimum-stay requirement on weekends.**

❀❀ HAUS ROHRBACH PENSION, Leavenworth Haus Rohrbach is a quintessential European-style hotel. Those looking for authenticity will love it; those seeking romance will simply have to choose their accommodations carefully.

Ensconced on the forested hillside of Tumwater Mountain, this white stucco and pine Bavarian lodge affords sprawling views of the surrounding landscape. Eight guest rooms in the main lodge have down comforters with pretty floral duvets; unfortunately, their simple decor and shared baths make them feel more like hostel accommodations than luxurious retreats. Thankfully, there is one exception here: the Wildflower Suite. Its gas fireplace, whirlpool tub, French doors that open to a private deck, and beautiful linens set it apart.

Two additional Alm Suites, Snowberry and Larkspur, are housed in a white stucco structure just up the hill from the main lodge. These have the most romantic inspiration of all the rooms on the property. Each suite is spacious with a gas fireplace set in a rock hearth, cathedral ceilings, a cozy sitting area, and a wall of windows overlooking a private wood deck with views of peaceful farmland. You can play your favorite CD and soak in the oval tiled Jacuzzi tub, snuggle under a thick floral comforter, or prepare a snack for your sweetheart in the convenient kitchenette.

Upon request, the innkeepers will bring a breakfast of Dutch babies, sourdough pancakes, or cinnamon rolls to guests staying in the Alm Suites; those staying in the main lodge partake at long wooden tables in the modest common area. After your morning meal, take a dip in the outdoor pool surrounded by beautiful views and colorful flowers. **12882 Ranger Road; (509) 548-7024, (800) 548-4477; www.hausrohrbach.com; inexpensive to expensive; minimum-stay requirement on weekends and holidays.**

❀❀❀ HOTEL PENSION ANNA, Leavenworth The Bavarian exterior of this bed and breakfast is one more cliche in a town full of cliches, but its immaculate and comfortable interior will be appreciated even by those who think Leavenworth puts out too much of a good thing. Even the less expensive suites have thick down comforters, down pillows, stately armoires, and wood accents. (Plus, these rooms are a steal at $80 a night.) The pricier suites are really not all that pricey, considering that they feature the same European detailing in addition to spa tubs, pretty half canopies, sitting areas, and wood-burning fireplaces. All the rooms are named after valleys in Germany, and the common areas showcase colorful Bavarian mementos and antiques.

Our two favorite rooms here are found in an unconventional location. They reside in an old Catholic chapel, adjacent to the main building. Although both are celestial havens, we prefer the opulent chapel suite over the smaller parish nook. The sumptuous chapel suite has 15-foot cathedral ceilings, rich burgundy carpeting, and a two-person Jacuzzi tub set beneath leaded Gothic windows in the sitting room. Detailed tapestry adorns the wall above the ornate king-size bed, and a staircase leads to what was once a choir loft but is now a second sleeping area. Appropriately, the appointments are baronial and plush; without a doubt, this is a very sexy place to kiss. Unless, of course, you start feeling the need to confess something.

In the morning, all guests are welcome to enjoy a German-style continental breakfast of cheeses, sausages, fresh fruit, and breads. Breakfast is served in a congenial dining room at tables for two placed around a wood banquette, or may be delivered to your room if you happen to be staying in one of the suites. **926 Commercial Street; (509) 548-6273, (800) 509-ANNA; www. pensionanna.com; inexpensive to very expensive; minimum-stay requirement on holiday weekends.**

❧❦ **LEAVENWORTH VILLAGE INN, Leavenworth** At first glance this appears to be just another Swiss-style motel, and for the most part it is, with a balcony-and-shutter facade and standard rooms situated around a central parking lot. Of the 18 rooms at the inn, only the three two-room luxury suites are worthy of romantic consideration, so be specific when making reservations. If these suites are already reserved when you call, we recommend moving on; the other rooms here will leave your hearts and lips wanting.

A hunter-green and burgundy color scheme prevails in each of the two-room luxury suites. A gas fireplace warms up the comfortable living room, and the adjacent dining area is conveniently equipped with a microwave and small refrigerator. After a day of exploring downtown Leavenworth, sink into your own private jetted tub, which is encased in marble and framed by a columned structure in the corner of the large bedroom. King-size, four-poster beds also grace the bedrooms; however, their drab comforters seem out of place and made us yearn for plusher snuggling material. Views from here aren't at all interesting, but if you don't open the curtains, you can find plenty of romance and solitude inside your suite.

A light continental breakfast of fruit, cereals, and fresh pastries is served buffet-style each morning in the sunny breakfast room next to the lobby. **1016 Commercial Street; (509) 548-6620, (800) 343-8198; www.kimmyco.com/ lvipag~1.htm; inexpensive to expensive.**

❤️❤️❤️❤ **MOUNTAIN HOME LODGE, Leavenworth** If seclusion and romance are your hearts' desires, you'll find plenty of both at Mountain Home Lodge. Over the course of the two-mile drive up a steep gravel road that leads to the lodge, Mountain Home's isolation becomes increasingly apparent. In the winter, the lodge's privacy is further enhanced by the fact that the only way to reach it is via a Sno-Cat (a huge snowmobile) driven by one of the innkeepers. The slow, half-hour trip up the mountain is breathtaking, offering views of the snow-blanketed valley. This adventuresome ascent is part of the appeal of this unique bed and breakfast.

Once at the top, you can revel in the wondrous mountain playground and be comforted in the massive cedar lodge, cradled in the center of a sprawling meadow. You'll be graciously welcomed by the friendly innkeepers, who strive to ensure each guest's comfort and privacy. A massive stone fireplace warms the Great Room, where redwood couches and wall-to-wall windows give guests a front-row seat from which to witness the drama of the changing seasons.

Each of the ten recently renovated guest rooms is cozy and attractively furnished with Northwest themes, log or pine-peeled beds, and restored antiques. All rooms have private bathrooms and views of the tranquil surroundings. Our favorite is the Cabin Suite, which features a gas fireplace, rustic bent–vine maple furniture, plush robes, and a lovely Jacuzzi tub.

Whichever season you choose to visit, there is never a shortage of activities. In the winter, cross-country skiing, snowmobile rides, snowshoeing, and sledding are all at your doorstep. During the summer, even though Mountain Home Lodge is more easily accessible, it remains just as private and exciting. Explore your surroundings on foot or by mountain bike (40 miles of trails wind throughout the area), or stick around the lodge for a game of badminton, volleyball, or tennis. The heated outdoor pool and hot tub are available to guests all year-round.

Evenings are warm and enjoyable, with hors d'oeuvres and wine served next to the stone fireplace. An adjacent dining area with two-person tables is a cozy spot to enjoy gourmet meals served up by the lodge's talented chef (see Restaurant Kissing). **8201-9 Mountain Home Road; (509) 548-7077, (800) 414-2378; www.mthome.com; moderate to very expensive; minimum-stay requirement on weekends and holidays.**

Romantic Note: Don't be alarmed to discover that the rates here are significantly higher in winter than in summer. Due to the fact that guests are snowbound (a fact that ensures plenty of secluded time together), winter rates include transportation to and from the lodge, all meals, and unlimited use of recreational equipment like snowshoes, sleds, and cross-country skis.

❤️❤️ **MOUNTAIN SPRINGS LODGE, Leavenworth** We are the first to admit that conference centers are hardly conducive to amorous inspirations, but we just couldn't pass up the two new suites recently constructed at Mountain

Springs Lodge. Romance-minded couples need not even consider the other accommodations here; they are geared for corporate gatherings and large groups who flock here for hayrides and barbecues in summer and sleigh rides and snowmobiling in winter.

If you don't mind the action going on around you (or if you'd like to join in yourselves), check out the two sumptuous suites occupying the second floor of Beaver Creek Lodge, a new pine structure near the property's entrance. These suites mirror each other, with only a few differences in decor. Mountain Retreat is decidedly more masculine, with a plaid and denim comforter on the king-size bed and a hunting theme that includes old-fashioned guns displayed around the room. Northwest Territory is more elegant, despite its subtle dog-sledding theme. Cream linens and sage-colored throw pillows dress up the four-poster king-size bed, and sunlight pours into the room more readily than in the neighboring suite.

Pine interiors lend a definite Northwest flavor to both rooms, and vaulted ceilings provide a sense of spaciousness. Full baths, enormous river-rock fireplaces, and pine furnishings are additional amenities. Breakfast is not provided, and unfortunately the wet bars allow for very limited culinary preparations on your part. After a full day of enjoying the endless recreational activities at Mountain Springs Lodge, you'll appreciate the luxury of a Jacuzzi tub nestled in the corner of your suite. What you won't appreciate is the noise coming from downstairs. This can put a damper on quiet time together. When making reservations, we recommend asking if the ground level of Bear Creek Lodge will be in use during the time of your stay so you'll know whether or not to bring along your earplugs. **19115 Chiwawa Loop Road; (509) 763-2713, (800) 858-2276; www.mtsprings.com; expensive.**

❦❦❦ **NATAPOC LODGING, Leavenworth** About 15 miles outside the bustling town of Leavenworth, with the surging Wenatchee River literally at your doorstep, seven private log and pine cabins await your arrival. These cabins are tucked among 20 acres of tall pines and brilliantly colored wildflowers, so privacy here is ensured. Named after Native American words for flowers and trees, each one has its own private driveway and path down to the river. Unfortunately, most of the accommodations here sleep many more than just two people (the largest cabin sleeps up to 21), so they are just too big to recommend for only one couple.

But don't worry. We wouldn't tell you about this stellar location without giving you at least one romantic option. A wonderfully private honeymoon cabin named Stuchin (after the lily flower) offers much comfort and style, and is perfectly sized for just two people. Your spacious porch provides a front-row seat from which to view the rushing river. Barbecue equipment, a bubbling hot tub, and comfortable deck chairs make this the perfect spot for long hours of stargazing with your sweetheart. Inside, a woodstove warms the living room and the full kitchen on the main level. Climb up the open wood staircase to the master bedroom, which holds a queen-size bed draped with a beautiful Native American wedding ring quilt. A pretty stained glass window allows morning sunlight to filter through and wash the room in subtle color.

Because this is not a bed and breakfast, you'll need to bring along your own morning goodies; however, coffee and tea are provided to help you jump-start your day. **12338 Bretz Road; (509) 763-3313, (888) NATAPOC; www. natapoc.com; expensive; minimum-stay requirement on weekends and holidays.**

♨♨❀ **PINE RIVER RANCH, Leavenworth** If you're looking for some quiet country romancing, look no further than the Pine River Ranch. This charming 1940s ranch house is located about 14 miles west of the town center, which makes it feel worlds away from the tourist-filled streets of downtown Leavenworth. Although the ranch no longer operates as a dairy farm, the old barn remains intact and horses and llamas graze in an adjacent pen. (Ask Sadie, the friendly goat, to give you a tour of the property and she will gladly accompany you.)

Five guest rooms offer visitors a wide range of accommodations to choose from, so be sure to specify when making reservations. Steer clear of the two-room unit upstairs; it needs serious updating, and therefore cannot be wholeheartedly recommended. Apple Blossom, situated on the main floor, is quite snug and has been done up in a pretty red-and-blue color scheme. Your best option in the ranch house is the more spacious Wildflower Room, which has been tastefully decorated with a black wrought-iron bed and floral linens. A wall of windows frames a lovely pine hearth and gas fireplace in this room.

Two outstanding suites, the Ponderosa and its kissing cousin, Lodgepole, are set in a small white stucco building adjacent to the ranch house. We highly recommend these for their supreme privacy. Named after the lodgepole pine trees in view from its many windows, Lodgepole features a unique bedframe crafted from unfinished branches, and Ponderosa showcases distant views of the mountains. Both these suites boast vaulted ceilings, richly colored linens draped over mammoth log beds, spacious tiled Jacuzzi tubs nestled in cozy corners, and river-rock hearths with gas fireplaces. Private entrances and small kitchenettes (complete with espresso machines) ensure your sense of self-sufficiency and seclusion.

The best part about staying in the suites is that you don't have to leave your room until checkout time; a full breakfast is delivered to your doorstep in the morning, or you can join the other guests over at the main house for Cascade Mountain–stuffed French toast or smoked-salmon quiche. In the evening, take time to relax in the communal hot tub, set on a deck in front of the main house, or explore the property's 32 acres, which include hiking and cross-country skiing trails with access to nearby Mason Creek. **19668 Highway 207; (509) 763-3959, (800) 669-3877; www.lakewenatchee.com; inexpensive to expensive.**

❧❧❧❧ **RUN OF THE RIVER BED AND BREAKFAST, Leavenworth** This used to be a hidden jewel, but it isn't so hidden anymore. Word has gotten out that Run of the River is one of the finest bed and breakfasts in Leavenworth. Every romantic and practical detail has been attended to with great care and discernment, creating an exceptional place to spend treasured moments together.

Set along Icicle River and surrounded by colorful wildflowers, the expansive contemporary log home achieves a perfect balance between rustic and elegant. Vintage bicycles peek out of corners and hang from ceilings throughout the common areas, while handhewn log love seats invite you to curl up and take in the view. Dried flowers accent the inviting rooms, and antique quilts cover handcrafted log beds in each of the six distinctive guest rooms. Romantic amenities include soft robes, cozy cuddling nooks, private decks with wood swings, and binoculars for wildlife watching. Three rooms have Jacuzzi tubs, and two have woodstoves. Guests have access to a common deck with spectacular close-up views of the winding river and Cascade Mountains. Guests also share a large hot tub set in a log pavilion near the river.

Breakfast, served at one large table in the dining room, is a bountiful presentation that may feature fresh fruit or creative fruit smoothies, vegetable frittatas, organic sausages, and apple cobbler. **9308 East Leavenworth Road; (509) 548-7171, (800) 288-6491; www.runoftheriver.com; moderate to expensive; minimum-stay requirement on weekends and holidays.**

Romantic Suggestion: Take advantage of the in-room massage service, sure to put the finishing touches on a wonderfully relaxing time together. Also, don't hesitate to ask the innkeepers more about what this area has to offer. They are very knowledgeable about outdoor activities such as scenic drives, hikes, and mountain bike trails. Maps and information are available to guests, as is complimentary use of mountain bikes.

Restaurant Kissing

❧❧ **CAFE MOZART, Leavenworth** Tucked away on the upstairs level of Leavenworth's main shopping street, Cafe Mozart is an elegant retreat where guests can enjoy a romantic and substantial lunch or dinner. Pastel pink linens drape small tables set off in quiet corners, while white walls with pine wainscoting create a perfect backdrop for an assortment of classical paintings. At center stage is a wall stencil of the restaurant's namesake. Mozart's sonatas play in the background, and a harpist serenades dinner guests most Friday and Saturday evenings.

The menu specializes in authentic Bavarian fare with a twist. You'll find such menu items as Wiener schnitzel, which is lightly breaded and pan-fried veal, served with homemade German potato salad; Schwabenteller, pork tenderloin medallions presented with a mushroom sauce, spätzle, and fresh vegetables; or Kutwickerln Bayrische Art, a homemade stuffed cabbage roll in its own natural sauce, served with a side of freshly whipped potatoes. The creations served here are items Mozart himself would be proud to sample. **829 Front Street; (509) 548-0600; moderate to expensive; lunch and dinner daily.**

❦ **HOME FIRES BAKERY, Leavenworth** Locals and visitors alike make their way here most mornings, drawn by caffeine cravings and the aroma of fresh cinnamon rolls, coffee cakes, and warm loaves of bread. Located just outside Leavenworth's downtown area, this tiny bakery doubles as a gift store with country knickknacks displayed around the knotty pine interior. A small garden area outside is a lovely place to enjoy a cup of espresso and quiet conversation. If you can stop yourselves from buying everything in sight (it helps if you don't arrive with an empty stomach), you'll find the perfect assortment of tasty lunch items to pack along and sustain you during a day of exploration in the mountains. **13013 Bayne Road; (509) 548-7362; inexpensive; open Thursday–Monday.**

❦❦ **LORRAINE'S EDEL HAUS, Leavenworth** An anomaly in a town of faux Bavarian chalets, this charming country home turned restaurant is a welcome change of pace. Bright red paint trims the white stucco house, which is hemmed by colorful flowers and trees. Inside, the dining room's simple decor is inviting, with hardwood floors, linen-draped tables, and accents of dried twigs entwined with twinkling white lights. Outside, the patio dining area is embraced by more trees and is softly lit with torches in the evening. The ambience is more casual than elegant both inside and out, but that shouldn't detract from a romance-filled dining experience. What does detract is the fact that the food here can be inconsistent, even within the same evening. Our meal began on a delicious note with the portobello mushroom and goat cheese appetizer with roasted red bell peppers atop herbed crostinis. Unfortunately, the grilled Northwest king salmon, glazed with an oyster ginger sauce and wasabi crème fraîche, was a less than spectacular entrée, and the balsamic marinated grilled vegetables were disappointingly ordinary. When it came to dessert, however, the kitchen managed to redeem itself with the deliciously smooth Swedish cream topped with a blackberry port sauce. **320 Ninth Street; (509) 548-4412, (800) 487-EDEL; moderate to expensive; call for seasonal hours.**

Romantic Note: Lorraine's Edel Haus also has overnight accommodations that we would call "bed and lunch/dinner" (inexpensive to moderate). Breakfast is not provided, but you get a 50 percent discount off either lunch or dinner at the restaurant. Despite their affordable price tags, the three upstairs rooms don't offer much romantic potential, and noise from the dining room is a definite distraction. A better option is the self-contained cabin with private Jacuzzi tub, located on the ground floor with its own entrance. This modest spot is yours for $105 a night. Restaurant and road noise are still potential disturbances, but you probably won't mind as much, in light of the amenities you get for the low price.

❦❦❦❦ **MOUNTAIN HOME LODGE, Leavenworth** "1000 feet closer to heaven" is the catchphrase used to describe the Mountain Home Lodge, and we couldn't agree more. Not only are you elevated to Leavenworth's supreme mountain viewing spot, but the food and accompanying ambience are simply divine. Guests staying overnight at the lodge (see Hotel/Bed and Breakfast Kissing) receive priority seating, so be sure to make reservations in advance if you will be making the two-mile journey from downtown. (In winter, the lodge is accessible to outside diners only via the innkeepers' snowmobile.)

Before dinner unwind in the Great Room, where appetizers and a complimentary glass of wine are served in front of a crackling fire. The adjacent dining room houses a handful of cozy tables for two. Soft lighting, white tablecloths, and soothing music set the mood for romance, but nature itself has provided the crowning touch. Expansive panoramas of the snowcapped Cascades are showcased by large windows and are close enough to make you feel part of the scenery.

Perfect preludes to a gourmet Northwest meal include the apricot Brie in phyllo purses and the basil crostini. Only one entrée is prepared each evening, but that just makes your job easier: How could one decide between applewood-smoked breast of duck with marionberry compote and the incredibly tender grilled yellow-fin tuna? Luckily the decision has been made for you, so all that's left to do is focus on the spectacular view and each other. **8201-9 Mountain Home Road; (509) 548-7077, (800) 414-2378; www.mthome.com; moderate; reservations required; dinner daily.**

❦❦❦ **RESTAURANT ÖSTERREICH, Leavenworth** In a place like Leavenworth, where German-inspired cuisine appears on every menu in town, Restaurant Österrich has managed to make a name for itself. The skilled Austrian-born chef consistently serves up hearty Bavarian fare that will satiate every appetite. Menu choices consist of mostly seafood and game dishes, with everything from Viennese beef goulash to sautéed spätzle to charbroiled Angus beef tenderloin. We thoroughly enjoyed the delicious grilled pork chops, served in a large black skillet with cabbage and a bread dumpling on the side. After such generous portions, we found it nearly impossible to consider dessert, but if you do manage to find some room (or if your sweet tooth is calling), try the chocolate decadence cake or the apple strudel—you can't go wrong with either one.

The restaurant's location is a definite kissing advantage. Although the address will point you toward Front Street (read: tourists galore), Restaurant Österrich is actually hidden away from sight in the lower level of the Tyrolean Ritz Hotel. Descend the stairs and pass through a tiny cavernous room with an iron gate to the dining area, kept dark and cool by a lack of windows. In such dim lighting, you'll easily forgive the slightly tacky wall paintings of alpine scenes, chalets, and beer kegs in the two main dining rooms. A bar area resides in a third, smaller room where the only windows in the restaurant allow limited sunlight to filter in. No matter where you sit, tables are well-spaced for privacy and topped with maroon linens, white and green napkins, dried flowers, and candles. Service is attentive and friendly, but never intrusive. **633A Front Street, at the Tyrolean Ritz Hotel; (509) 548-4031; www. leavenworthdining.com; expensive; call for seasonal hours.**

Romantic Note: Live accordion music accompanies diners most Saturday nights. (We'll leave it up to you to determine if that's romantic or not.)

Romantic Suggestion: For some casual summer fun, visit the restaurant's Bier Garten (inexpensive; lunch Friday–Sunday in summer) located on a grassy plateau overlooking the nearby river and mountains. It's not exactly the most romantic option around, but it's difficult to resist the aroma of sizzling sausages wafting upward to tempt passersby on Front Street. Take a seat at one of the plastic lawn tables and enjoy the view as you down your sausage, beer or soft drink, and ice cream.

Outdoor Kissing

❀❀❀❀ ALPINE LAKES WILDERNESS AND WENATCHEE NATIONAL FOREST, Leavenworth

You don't even have to step out of your car to get the full effect of this region's stunning natural beauty. As you follow the Icicle River into the mountain wilderness, you'll feel as if the gates of heaven have swung open to receive you. Evergreens flourish on towering mountains that ascend in sheer majesty, their rocky snow-covered peaks cutting into the clear sky above. Those interested in traversing this glorious terrain on foot have unlimited options. Park your car alongside the road and follow one of the many marked trails that wind through the mountain landscape, revealing alpine lakes, meadows, and thriving wildlife. *From Highway 2, drive west on Icicle Road, which leads directly into the Alpine Lakes Wilderness and Wenatchee National Forest.*

❀❀❀ HORSE-DRAWN CARRIAGE SERVICES OF LEAVENWORTH, Leavenworth

On a crisp winter evening, when snow has covered the town in muffled splendor and Christmas lights illuminate the storefronts along Front Street, you and your sweetheart can take in the magic of Leavenworth from a horse-drawn carriage. Cuddle close as a well-cared-for Percheron clomps through the snow with you in tow. Carriages can hold up to four people, but we think two is perfect. You can easily steal a kiss or two while your amiable guide is busy pointing out the town's landmarks along the way. Tours are offered almost every day during the summer and on festival weekends; winter tours require advance reservations.

If you're willing to spend a little more, call ahead to request a gourmet picnic basket to share on your leisurely ride. A lunch basket ($30) includes croissant sandwiches filled with smoked turkey, Swiss cheese, and sprouts, plus two slices of pound cake with berry sauce and sparkling cider. The contents of the dinner basket ($35) vary from day to day. Our favorite option is the dessert basket ($25), which includes ingenious "tortes in a bag" with raspberry frappé sauce and a bottle of champagne, accompanied by cloth napkins and crystal. **1003 Commercial Street; (509) 548-6825; prices range from $25–$50; call for seasonal hours.**

❤❤ **ICICLE OUTFITTERS AND GUIDES, Leavenworth** A great way to explore this area is to take a trek on horseback. Icicle Outfitters and Guides provides everything from one-hour rides to overnight pack trips. Overnight journeys come complete with meals, pack horses, saddle horses, a well-seasoned wrangler, a cook, tents, and the entire camp setup necessary for a two- to seven-day expedition. This is one unbelievable adventure. You'll cross unspoiled wilderness where pure mountain lakes and streams glisten in the sunshine, the wind rushes through the trees, hawks soar overhead, and snowcapped peaks tower above. As you warmly snuggle by the roaring campfire at night, relaxing after a hearty dinner, you will find yourselves at peace with each other and the world. **14800 State Park Road, on the south shore of Lake Wenatchee; (509) 784-1145, (800) 497-3912; prices vary; call for a brochure, reservations, and directions.**

Romantic Alternative: EAGLE CREEK RANCH (7951 Eagle Creek Road; 509-548-7798, 800-221-7433; www.eaglecreek.simplenet.com; prices vary) is another full-service horse ranch that offers sleigh, buggy, hay, and trail rides as well as back-country hiking journeys. The hours of operation can be frustratingly inconsistent, so be sure to confirm your reservation before you make the trip out here.

Cashmere

Aplets and Cotlets are notoriously sweet confections that stick to your teeth and help dentists send their kids to college. They are also Cashmere's claim to fame. Even if you're not partial to Aplets and Cotlets, Cashmere is worth a quick look. This quaint little town is reminiscent of a western frontier town, with old-fashioned balustrades and streets lined with restaurants and antique, sweet, and gift shops.

Restaurant Kissing

❤❤ **THE PEWTER POT, Cashmere** Despite its storefront location along Cashmere's main street, you'll find a glimpse of the English countryside at The Pewter Pot. The cozy interior is slightly cramped and overdone, with outdated red carpeting and tables dressed in maroon and floral linens. Luckily, the overall effect has been softened by decorative swaths of lace draped from the ceiling and lovely window treatments that shield diners from the street. A collection of pewter dishes, tea pots, and other knickknacks warm up the white walls.

Despite all its English charm, The Pewter Pot offers traditional American fare consisting mostly of specialty salads and sandwiches. Try the smoked chicken and pineapple sandwich, served on a Kaiser roll with a mild curry sauce, or enjoy a shrimp salad alongside a cup of soup. The deep-dish marionberry pie is beyond delicious, and large enough for two. Authentic English tea is served every afternoon, and the fresh tarts and pastries are excellent. **124 1/2 Cottage Avenue; (509) 782-2036; inexpensive to moderate; lunch and afternoon tea Tuesday–Saturday.**

Wenatchee

Outdoor Kissing

❀❀❀ **OHME GARDENS COUNTY PARK, Wenatchee** It's hard to believe that what is now the lush Ohme Gardens was once desolate hillside. Over 60 years of painstaking work has transformed a dry, rocky wasteland into the fertile mountain splendor visitors enjoy today. The gardens are set high on a bluff, and footpaths wander through nine acres of flower beds, splashing waterfalls, and luscious alpine meadows. Natural rock formations emerge from tranquil pools set among evergreens, while views of the Columbia River and Cascade Mountains add to the idyllic setting. A miniature Garden of Eden, this would be paradise on earth if it weren't for the thousands of tourists who have discovered it. Though the scenery is apt to inspire some passionate kisses, the crowds will certainly inhibit your romantic inclinations. **3327 Ohme Road; (509) 662-5785; www.ohmegardens.com; $5 admission per adult; closed mid-October–mid-April; recommended wedding site.** *Just north of Wenatchee, near the junction of Highway 2 and Alternate Highway 97. The gardens are up on the bluff; watch for signs.*

Chelan

Hotel/Bed and Breakfast Kissing

❀❀ **A QUAIL'S ROOST INN, Chelan** A quiet hillside above the town of Chelan provides the setting for this pale yellow Victorian home turned bed and breakfast. Manicured lawns and colorful flowers border the historic 1902 residence, and its wraparound porch provides the perfect spot to linger over an iced tea on a hot summer night. Restored antiques mingle with homey touches in the common area, breakfast room, and each of the three guest rooms (located on the second floor).

The Rose and Wicker Room is our favorite; it is decorated in a French country theme, with white wicker furnishings, roses and ivy stenciled on the walls, a full bath, and a private porch that overlooks the sparkling lake.

Gramma's Room is also lovely, with its unique lace-canopy bed and patchwork quilt. Its private bathroom, which the innkeepers refer to as the "bird bath," boasts a wall mural of a garden scene. The Sewing Room is appointed with floral linens, Danish oak furnishings, and antique sewing machines. Hand-stenciled wisteria adorns the detached, private bath across the hall.

Each morning a full country breakfast is served in the antique-filled breakfast room or outside on the deck at green, wrought-iron tables. Guests can look forward to eggs with Havarti cheese, fresh fruit, country potatoes with rosemary, and strawberry-and-cream French toast. **121 East Highland Avenue; (509) 682-2892, (800) 681-2892; www.lakechelan.com/quailsinn; inexpensive to moderate; minimum-stay requirement on holidays.**

Stehekin

Following the North Cascades Highway, take Highway 20 east toward the towns of Twisp and Winthrop and continue heading south on Highway 153 toward Pateros. From here, take Alternate Highway 97 south to the towns of Manson and Chelan. From the greater Seattle area, take Highway 2 to Wenatchee and head north on Alternate Highway 97. At Manson and Chelan, catch the Lady of the Lake, the Lady Express, or the new high-speed catamaran to Stehekin. For information on scheduled departures from either place, call the Lake Chelan Boat Company (509-682-4584), Lake Chelan Tours, Inc. (509-682-8287), or the Lake Chelan Chamber of Commerce (800-4-CHELAN), or visit the web site www.ladyofthelake.com. Flights are also available on Chelan Airways (509-682-5555). For the backpacking route to Stehekin, hikers will want to check with the North Cascades office of the North Cascades National Park (360-856-5700).

Otherwise known as "the Enchanted Valley," Stehekin is a geographically unique town, accessible only by ferryboat or plane from the towns of Chelan and Manson, or via high-country trails that pass through the Cascade Mountains. (You have to be hardy and well prepared to take the latter route.) Once you're here, it's easy to see why the Skagit Indians of long ago gave this river valley the name Stehekin, meaning "the way through," as they searched for a passage through the glacier-laden Cascades Mountain range.

Today, this small community with its one-room schoolhouse is situated at the northernmost tip of Lake Chelan and is celebrated for its glorious, dramatic scenery and abundant wildlife. (Watch out for bears!) Many establishments in Stehekin don't even have telephones; locals are often seen pedaling on bicycles to a centrally located pay phone. Jagged mountains line the 55-mile fjord-like lake and are breathtakingly reflected in the cool blue of its glacier-fed waters.

The ferry ride takes between one to four hours, depending on which boat is running. Although both the ferry and the town of Stehekin tend to be a bit crowded with tourists on summer afternoons, most people stay only for the day, and even fewer visit in winter. Once the boat departs for Chelan in the late afternoon, Stehekin's exquisite scenery and hushed seclusion are yours for the taking, and you are sure to find the experience sublime.

Meal options are limited here, to say the least. Your choices include **STEHEKIN VALLEY RANCH** (509-682-4677; inexpensive to moderate), which serves a buffet-style dinner beneath tent-cabins near the far end of the valley, and the **NORTH CASCADES STEHEKIN LODGE DINING ROOM** (509-682-4494; moderate), located above the ferry dock and open for breakfast, lunch, and dinner daily. For a sweeter option, bicycle to the nearby bakery, **STEHEKIN PASTRY COMPANY** (open summer only), where you can stock up on freshly baked goodies to share at your leisure. If you really want to feel prepared, we recommend bringing your own food—there are no grocery stores out here, only what the locals call an "inconvenience store" that sells overpriced beer and candy.

Hotel/Bed and Breakfast Kissing

❦❦❦ **FLICK CREEK HOUSE, Stehekin** If you thought the town of Stehekin was an isolated destination, just wait until you see this secluded retreat! Your definition of privacy will never be the same. Hidden away along the shore of Lake Chelan, this post-and-beam cedar home is accessible only by boat, float plane, or trail, a fact that pretty much guarantees you will have the property's seven acres to yourselves. Depending on the season, the daily passenger boat can drop you off and pick you up at your own private bay; just be sure to call ahead to find out if this is an option during the time of your visit.

Embraced by towering pines and fronted by a large deck, the two-story wood cabin is comfortably rustic, with modest furnishings and two bathrooms. Breathtaking views through the trees of the Cascades and McGregor's Peak are showcased by large picture windows and a towering ceiling. The view is no less phenomenal in the master bedroom upstairs, where a unique bedframe made from Stehekin lumber elevates the bed for advantageous viewing.

Although the cabin sleeps up to ten people, we recommend renting the entire space for yourselves. A second bedroom upstairs is oriented more for kids, but the third bedroom on the main floor features a four-poster bed and serene views of nearby Flick Creek. Also on the main level, a pretty blue-and-white kitchen offers modern appliances and a cozy love seat for two; all you need to bring is a week's worth of provisions and an appetite for romance.

If you'd like to venture into town, follow the Lake Shore Trail two and a half miles into Stehekin, or make arrangements with the owners for boat transportation ($15 per trip). Also at your disposal are a private sandy beach, a barbecue and fire pit overlooking the water, and a complimentary

12-foot row boat for quiet moments on the lake. Gorgeous sunsets each evening are compliments of Mother Nature. After so much time away with the one you love, you may never want to return to civilization. **(509) 884-1730; www.lakechelan.com/stehekinrentals; very expensive; minimum-stay requirement.**

❤❤❤ **SILVER BAY INN, Stehekin** Silver Bay Inn is a Northwest must for those who want to escape the world at large. Sheltered on the tip of a tiny peninsula dotted with nondescript homes, the inn offers isolation and wondrous mountain and lakeside views that are thoroughly compelling. A hammock overlooking the placid lake sways lazily under a stand of trees, and the manicured grounds and gardens conceal a roomy waterside hot tub, at night lit only by moonlight and shooting stars. Complimentary canoes and bicycles are available, giving guests mobility to explore the surrounding waterways and wilderness.

Part of the inn is a wooden solar home dedicated exclusively to guests (the innkeepers live next door); it is rented as a single unit and sleeps up to five people. Antiques, local artwork, and country accents convey a feeling of comfort and warmth in the homey parlor and glass-enclosed sunporch overlooking the water. Patchwork quilts and wood detailing add charm to the two bedrooms, particularly the upstairs room with its large soaking tub and private lake-view deck. A full kitchen is at your disposal, so be sure to stock up on groceries before you arrive. (The closest grocery store is in Chelan.)

Attached to the main house is the smallest and least expensive option (available in summer only). Guests in the River View Room make use of their own private entrance, deck, and detached kitchenette.

For the most privacy, we recommend the two neighboring lakeside cabins, comfortably furnished and complete with full kitchens and baths. They also feature cozy sleeping lofts, woodstoves, propane barbecues, and wraparound cedar decks with expansive water views. Breakfast is do-it-yourself, so come prepared with plenty of fixings. There's a five-night minimum-stay requirement for the cabins during the summer. After you're first night here, you'll understand why: One evening just isn't long enough at a place like this. **10 Silver Bay Road; (509) 682-2212, (800) 555-7781 (in Washington); www. seattlesquare.com/silverbay; moderate to expensive; minimum-stay requirement; call for seasonal closures.**

Pateros

From Highway 2, travel north on Highway 97 on either side of the Columbia River; Pateros is about 25 miles north of Chelan. From Highway 20, turn south onto Highway 153; the town of Pateros is about 40 miles south of Winthrop.

Hotel/Bed and Breakfast Kissing

❦❦ **AMY'S MANOR, Pateros** Perched on a hilltop overlooking the Methow Valley, this lovely 170-acre property is a wonderful spot for an outdoor wedding. In fact, the entire event can be catered by your hostess (a former chef), with hors d'oeuvres seasoned with herbs from her well-tended garden and wedding cakes made completely from scratch. Even if you're not tying the knot, a stay here will allow you to undo all those tension knots and simply enjoy the towering trees and handsomely landscaped gardens. Relax in the swinging hammock, or snuggle up together on one of the wooden benches while taking in spectacular views of the valley below.

Thick floral bedding and oak furnishings adorn the three beautifully decorated rooms, and each one offers a view of the valley. The largest room is wonderfully spacious, with a sheer white veil adorning the bed, an oak rocking chair, and dried flower arrangements. The only romantic hurdle to Amy's Manor is not the home or the guest accommodations, but the fact that the rooms share a bath. However, once you experience the surrounding splendor, comfortable guest rooms, and delicious breakfasts, you'll soon forgive this drawback.

As should be expected, breakfasts here are outstanding and may include fresh-squeezed apple cider, egg dishes (with eggs provided by the free-range chickens raised on the property), and fresh fruit from the hostess's organic garden. Dinners are available by advance reservation (expensive). Meals at Amy's Manor are a culinary delight you are sure to remember. **435 Highway 153; (509) 923-2334, (888) 923-2334; www.amysmanor.com; inexpensive to moderate; recommended wedding site.**

Outdoor Kissing

❦❦❦ **RIVER RAFTING, Pateros** River rafting doesn't get more visually exciting or relentlessly tumultuous than on the Skykomish, Klickitat, Methow, White Salmon, Toutle, and Chiwawa Rivers. If you're in an adventurous mood, several river-rafting companies in the Northwest will provide professional guides to take you down the river of your choice. River Riders is a good, safe company that will give you reliable information as well as an unforgettable adventure.

Once you've decided which river you want to negotiate, the rest is, if you will, all downstream. As you follow the tendril-like course the water has etched through the land, each coiling turn exposes a sudden change in perspective on the landscape. One turn reveals grassy woods adjoining the quiet flow of peaceful water; another magically manifests a rocky tableau penetrated by a bursting mass of energy called white water. The raft's roller-coaster motion accentuates the thrill and glory of the scenery. The sensation of cold water against your skin as you wildly paddle over and through a whirlpool can make your hearts pound and your senses spin.

As wildly romantic as all this sounds, river rafting has its labor and dress rules that may leave some wondering why they paid someone to go through all this. Helmets and thick, cumbersome wet suits are mandatory, and weight distribution considerations may leave you sitting next to someone you don't want to kiss. Another issue is the bailing and paddling. Everyone in your raft shares the responsibility of getting down the river safely and that requires cooperation and use of your muscles. **River Riders, Inc.; (206) 448-RAFT, (541) 386-RAFT, (800) 448-RAFT; www.riverrider.com; expensive.** *If you are interested in rafting on any of the rivers in the region, call for information and directions on where to rendezvous with your guide.*

Okanogan

Outdoor Kissing

❤️❤️❤️❤️ **OKANOGAN NATIONAL FOREST, Okanogan** The Okanogan National Forest encompasses an impressive 1,706,000 acres of northern Washington wilderness, bordered by numerous national parks and recreation areas. Nature lovers will marvel at this region's diverse topography and botany, which range from grasslands in the lowest elevations to ponderosa pine forests in the mid-elevations and glades of Douglas firs in the higher elevations. Some of the more popular ways to enjoy the enchanting countryside are white-water rafting, hiking, snowmobiling, cross-country skiing, and heli-skiing. For more information about white-water rafting, call **OSPREY RIVER ADVENTURES** (Twisp; 509-997-4116, 800-997-4116). For information about heli-skiing, contact **NORTH CASCADE HELI-SKIING** (Mazama; 509-996-3660, 800-494-HELI). **Okanogan National Forest Supervisor's Office; (509) 826-3275; www.fs.fed.us/r6/oka.** *The Okanogan National Forest is reached from the north and south by Highway 2 and Highway 97. From the east and west, State Route 20 provides access to the forest.*

❤️❤️❤️❤️ **PASAYTEN WILDERNESS, Okanogan** If you own a reliable sport utility vehicle or a sturdy four-wheel drive car, embark on a two-hour round-trip adventure up the steep, bumpy gravel road to **HART'S PASS**. After winding through flower-laden alpine meadows and towering evergreens, you'll reach **SLATE PEAK**, the highest point accessible by car in Washington state. From this heavenly 7,500-foot vantage point, snowcapped mountains rise in succession in every direction, and the only audible sounds are bird songs and the gentle murmur of wind sweeping through the trees. A kiss here is likely to take your breath away, if it doesn't change your lives altogether.

Hart's Pass serves as a primary trailhead for hikers using the **PACIFIC CREST NATIONAL SCENIC TRAIL**. If you are interested in more information about day or overnight hikes in this area, contact the **OKANOGAN**

NATIONAL FOREST SUPERVISOR'S OFFICE at the number listed below. **Okanogan National Forest Supervisor's Office; (509) 826-3275; www.fs. fed.us/r6.oka.** *From west State Route 20, turn left onto Mazama Road and left again onto Lost River Road. Follow this until you see signs for Hart's Pass, which will lead you to the top of Slate Peak.*

Winthrop

Hotel/Bed and Breakfast Kissing

❤️❤️ **EAGLE PINE CHALETS, Winthrop** Those wishing to hibernate for a few days with their loved one need only venture two miles outside Winthrop to these cozy chalets. Each cabin is surrounded by wildflowers and boasts a studio-style layout with a reading loft, fireplace, kitchenette, and private deck. Although small, the two chalets are handsomely decorated and completely isolated; you won't find any phones or TVs to distract you from each other. Perhaps the best part about staying here is the price: These cabins are unbelievably inexpensive. As an additional bonus, the Winthrop Trail cuts across the back part of the forested property, offering 108 miles of groomed trails for hiking or mountain biking in the summer, and cross-country skiing in the winter. If you are planning to take advantage of all the area's outdoor activities, and only require a private place to snuggle in after an adventurous day, then Eagle Pine Chalets are a wonderful choice. **345 Twin Lakes Road; (509) 996-2109, (800) 422-3048; www.methow.com/~eagle; inexpensive; minimum-stay requirement.**

❤️❤️ **RIVER'S EDGE RESORT, Winthrop** The picturesque Chewuch River serves as the backdrop for the six custom cabins that comprise River's Edge Resort. Each cabin offers ample space and privacy, along with easy access to Winthrop's downtown shops, restaurants, and small brewery. At first glance, these cabins might seem rather large for just the two of you, but since the rates are based on occupancy, you'll soon realize that you're getting quite a kissing bargain.

Unique furnishings, full kitchens, and decks with shared hot tubs (one for every two cabins) make these cabins romantically viable. There are three bedrooms to choose from in each cabin, but the master sleeping loft is the obvious choice, thanks to its knotty pine ceiling and log bed embellished with a fluffy quilted bedspread and lace pillows. Polished hardwood floors and a woodstove warm up the living room, although the bare walls and lack of special touches may hinder romantic inclinations. We suggest you spend your evenings out on the large deck, taking in views of the Chewuch River from your hot tub. Once you witness the power and beauty of the rushing river, you won't want to leave your peaceful retreat. **115 Riverside Avenue; (509) 996-8000, (800) 937-6621; expensive.**

❦❦❦❦ **SUN MOUNTAIN LODGE, Winthrop** Every aspect of Sun Mountain Lodge is extraordinary, starting with the majestic drive to the mountaintop resort. Sweeping views of rugged, sculpted peaks and the golden Methow Valley below dazzle the eye and set the stage for romance.

Composed of massive timbers and stone, the original lodge has been beautifully renovated, and the lobby's interior is graced with immense wrought-iron chandeliers, stone floors, and rock-clad fireplaces. All rooms in the main lodge display a Northwest influence, with textured log walls and ceilings, bent-willow furniture, handmade quilts, and local blacksmith-styled sculpture. Twenty-four rooms have luxurious Jacuzzi tubs, and most rooms offer views of the dramatic mountain panorama. (We should mention, however, that some rooms also overlook the roof and, consequently, retain a hotel-like feeling.)

Two newer buildings across from the lodge house 36 impeccable suites. Sliding glass doors open to stone patios that survey mesmerizing views. Each unit has its own fireplace, elegant willow furnishings, and lush comforters; in winter, you can cross-country ski out your back door. In the Mount Robinson wing, you'll discover the most luxurious accommodations, featuring whirlpool tubs, beautiful sitting areas, and king-size beds with down comforters.

Couples with privacy in mind will also appreciate the four newly constructed cabin Loft Suites situated at the edge of Patterson Lake. You'll want for nothing in these sizable suites, which include two bedrooms, full kitchens, and private decks with wonderful lake views.

Sun Mountain Lodge offers every imaginable amenity: two heated pools and an outdoor hot tub, hiking trails, horseback riding, white-water rafting, a golf course, sailboats, sleigh rides, exercise equipment, and mountain bikes. Not to mention the totally outrageous, thoroughly intoxicating heli-skiing packages available for both downhill and cross-country skiers. Ski down untouched powder runs that will leave you breathless for months to come. At the end of the day in the warmth of your room, cuddle very close and review your feats of athletic prowess. **1000 Patterson Lake Road; (509) 996-2211, (800) 572-0493; www.sunmountainlodge.com; inexpensive to unbelievably expensive; minimum-stay requirement on weekends and holidays; recommended wedding site.**

Romantic Note: You don't have to leave the property in search of satisfying cuisine. The **SUN MOUNTAIN LODGE DINING ROOM** (see Restaurant Kissing) is a consummate place to savor spectacular views and Northwest cuisine.

❦❦ **WOLFRIDGE RESORT, Winthrop** There's plenty to do on the 60 acres that comprise this resort. When the summer sun shines, take to the trails for hiking and mountain biking; when snow blankets the ground, put on your skinny skies and venture into the vast white wilderness. Whatever the season, bring your camera because the Methow Valley always affords breathtaking views of the North Cascade mountains. When you do venture back to the peaceful riverside setting of WolfRidge Resort, you'll discover a heated pool and a spa enclosed in a glass and log gazebo, perfect for soothing those sore muscles.

Although spacious and comfortable, the 17 units don't quite compare to the beautiful setting. The rooms feature oil paintings by a local artist, exposed log walls, handcrafted wood furniture, and private standard baths. For those who want to be alone in the wilderness, check out the Cabin in the Woods, which offers a bedroom, loft area, kitchen, and pellet stove. No matter where you stay, cathedral ceilings are the norm, and private decks let you enjoy the best feature of this resort—the great outdoors. **412 B Wolf Creek Road; (509) 996-2828, (800) 237-2388; www.wolfridgeresort.com; expensive.**

Restaurant Kissing

❀❀❀❀ SUN MOUNTAIN LODGE DINING ROOM, Winthrop Even if you've decided not to take advantage of the premium accommodations at **SUN MOUNTAIN LODGE** (see Hotel/Bed and Breakfast Kissing), at least stop for a meal at the restaurant, housed in the original section of the lodge. Here the developers wisely left well enough alone: This part of the lodge has always been flawless. A wall of windows allow you to feast your eyes on surroundings that are truly food for the soul. Wrought-iron chandeliers hang from log-ceiling beams and illuminate cozy two-person tables and booths. The menu is equally impressive, and the service is prompt and gracious. Award-winning cuisine includes a porterhouse pork chop with garlic mashed potatoes and a pear-mustard, and a rib eye steak with a cabernet demi-glace and sourdough onion rings. (All beef served in the restaurant comes from the lodge's own organically fed, free-range cattle.) Also famous for its fresh seafood and hickory- and applewood-smoked duck, not to mention its exquisite desserts, the kitchen lives up to its stellar reputation time and time again. **Patterson Lake Road; (509) 996-2211, (800) 572-0493; www.sunmountainlodge.com; inexpensive to expensive; breakfast, lunch, and dinner daily; recommended wedding site.**

Mazama

Hotel/Bed and Breakfast Kissing

❀❀❀ FREESTONE INN AND CABINS, Mazama Set in the Methow Valley and surrounded by beautiful evergreen-covered hills and snowcapped mountains, this large log inn provides everything you need for a Northwest getaway. The main lodge is perfectly inviting, with its sweeping front porch, outdoor hot tub, and serene views of Freestone Lake. (During summer, the trout-filled lake attracts fly-fishers; in winter it freezes over to become a large ice-skating rink for guests.) Inside the lodge, Northwest rustic decor has been attractively rendered. Hand-forged iron fixtures, rustic antiques, and comfortable country furniture adorn the high-ceilinged Great Room and the adjoining library. A massive, stone fireplace divides the sitting area from the restaurant, where a complimentary continental breakfast is served each morning.

The 17 guest rooms and four suites in the main lodge are decorated in muted tones with iron and pine appointments. Each room comes equipped with either a private deck or patio, a kitchenette, TV/VCR hidden away in an armoire, and a gas-burning fireplace for those chilly evenings. Comfy wool blankets cover the king-size bed. In the suites, shutters open between the bedroom and bathroom, affording views of the lake and woods from your soaking tub.

If you prefer supreme privacy over luxurious accommodations, consider renting one of the 15 Early Winters Cabins. Located on the banks of a creek just a short distance from the main lodge, these knotty pine cabins are fully furnished with gas stoves, hardwood floors, and comfortable country furnishings. The walls are rather bare, but the cabins themselves are secluded, and each one features a private deck overlooking the tranquil creek.

The property also holds two spacious Lakeside Lodges situated along the shores of Freestone Lake. Although not as cozy as the other accommodations, these spacious retreats offer fully equipped kitchens and plenty of space, which make them more suited for families or couples traveling together. **17798 Highway 20; (509) 996-3906, (800) 639-3809; www.freestoneinn.com; moderate to very expensive.**

Romantic Note: For information about outdoor activities in the area, visit JACK'S HUT AT FREESTONE INN (509-996-2752). The helpful folks here can tell you all about horseback riding, fly-fishing, mountain biking, hiking, and white-water rafting. You can rent ice skates in winter and mountain bikes in summer, and even sign up for fly-fishing lessons.

❀❀ **MAZAMA COUNTRY INN, Mazama** Mazama Country Inn (and the town of Mazama, for that matter) is literally out in the middle of nowhere, which makes it ideal for those seeking to escape the crowded cities and suburbs. Set among evergreens at the foot of a mountain, the main lodge offers 14 exceedingly simple units, each with a private bath. Most inviting are the recently renovated rooms featuring patchwork quilts, new carpet, and private decks. Despite these improvements, the rooms' austerity would be a romantic drawback if it weren't for the property's sensational location and abundant outdoor activities. There is something for everyone here: horseback riding, heli-skiing, cross-country skiing, mountain biking, windsurfing, and sleigh riding. There's even a communal sauna and hot tub. Breakfast, lunch, and dinner are served daily at the country-style restaurant (see Restaurant Kissing); during the winter, three full meals are included with your room in one reasonably priced package. **42 Lost River Road; (509) 996-2681, (800) 843-7951 (in Washington); www.mazama-inn.com; inexpensive to moderate; minimum-stay requirement for the cabins.**

Romantic Alternative: Three is a crowd when it comes to romance, but people traveling in groups will appreciate the inn's six additional rental cabins that can sleep up to six people. Amenities vary from cabin to cabin (as do the prices), but many include fully stocked kitchens, wood-burning stoves, TV/ VCRs, stereos, and even washers and dryers.

Restaurant Kissing

❤❤ **MAZAMA COUNTRY INN DINING ROOM, Mazama** Even if you're not an overnight guest at the **MAZAMA COUNTRY INN** (see Hotel/Bed and Breakfast Kissing), you'll want to partake of the area's spectacular views and hiking terrain. Dinner here is a perfect way to conclude an exhilarating day in the mountains. A floor-to-ceiling stone fireplace keeps the dining room toasty warm in the colder months, and the soothing interior has a view of gently swaying boughs through tall windows. Although the menu is limited, you won't be disappointed with the tiger prawns sautéed with tomatoes, red peppers, and mushrooms in a lime-orange white wine sauce. Daily pasta selections, such as the mesquite-smoked chicken and bow-tie pasta in a light cream sauce, are prepared by an efficient, adept kitchen staff. **42 Lost River Road; (509) 996-2681, (800) 843-7951 (in Washington); www.mazama-inn.com; moderate to expensive; call for seasonal hours.**

Rockport

Outdoor Kissing

❤❤❤ **EAGLE WATCHING, Rockport** Bleak gray skies, negligible daylight, and the Northwest mist can make the heart of the Cascades relatively dreary during the winter months. Despite the inclement weather, winter is made vibrant by hundreds of bald eagles that migrate to the Skagit River during salmon-spawning season. (Salmon die after spawning, which makes the river an eagle's picnic ground.) All along its banks, eagles soar overhead or perch in clear sight on exposed alpine branches. With 1,500 acres, the Bald Eagle Wildlife Preserve is one of the largest in the continental United States. Sightings are possible from many points along the road and from eagle-viewing-oriented rafting excursions. By mid-March, after all the fish have disappeared and the eagles have dispersed, the Cascades are once again ready for spring renewal. **Watchable Wild Life Program; (360) 902-2200.** *Viewing is possible along State Route 20 between the towns of Concrete and Marblemount November– February.*

Mount Rainier

Hotel/Bed and Breakfast Kissing

❤❤ **NATIONAL PARK INN AT LONGMIRE, Mount Rainier** Located six miles inside the southwest entrance of **MOUNT RAINIER NATIONAL PARK** (see Outdoor Kissing), this inn operates as a bed and breakfast in the winter and a standard hotel in the summer. Although it has a less commanding view of the mountain than the park's other lodge (see below), the National Park Inn offers nicer accommodations and a beautiful woodsy setting. The 25 small guest rooms here are standard in their furnishings, but special touches like log furniture, soft quilted bedspreads, and oak-framed mountain pictures make them inviting and snug. Of course, the best reason to stay here is to enjoy the national park and the majesty of Mount Rainier.

A complimentary breakfast, served in the casual dining room downstairs, is included in your stay during winter, and ski packages are also available this time of year. The dining room is also open to the public year-round for breakfast, lunch, and dinner (inexpensive to moderate). While hardly gourmet fare, the restaurant's sandwiches, salads, and burgers are sure to satisfy hungry hikers and skiers. **Mount Rainier National Park; (360) 569-2275; www. guestservices.com/rainier; inexpensive to moderate.**

❦❦ **PARADISE INN, Mount Rainier** Recent renovations in excess of one million dollars have been made to update the guest rooms of this historic lodge. Unfortunately, one million dollars doesn't go as far these days as it once did. Our hopes for a newfound romantic mountainside retreat were dashed as soon as we stepped inside the guest rooms. Even with new carpeting, draperies, and bedding, the rooms still leave much to be desired. Don't be fooled by the inn's stately lobby, which is an impressive, airy, open-beamed room built from massive logs. Large fireplaces and cozy tables and chairs are scattered throughout, providing many tempting places to snuggle up together with a hot drink. The rooms, however, are an entirely different story. Situated along dismal hallways, all 117 rooms are claustrophobic, with small windows and standard, motel-style furniture. It's a shame that the management hasn't done more with this prime property, but the lack of competition for this awesome summer destination has let them get away with mediocre accommodations for years.

Despite the dreary guest rooms, its unparalleled location on Mount Rainier makes Paradise Inn worth a visit. The views up here truly defy description—this is purple mountain majesty in all its awe-inspiring glory. Romantically speaking, your best bet may be a daily excursion to **PARADISE** (see Outdoor Kissing) to take in the spectacular views, followed by nightly accommodations in the valley. **At Paradise in Mount Rainier National Park; (360) 569-2275; www.guestservices.com/rainier; inexpensive to moderate; closed October–mid-May.**

Outdoor Kissing

❦❦❦ **CHINOOK PASS, Mount Rainier** On a fall afternoon, Chinook Pass is almost too glorious for words. You'll be so excited by the scenery that you might finish touring and forget to kiss. Take a moment to memorize the image of the golden light bathing hills and lakes. Notice the vivid shades of red and amber that embellish the trees and meadows. Feel the fall air brush your skin while the sun's heat tempers the chill. This is a visual gift to share with each other. **Mount Baker–Snoqualmie National Forest; (360) 569-2211.** *If you're in the Mount Baker–Snoqualmie National Forest on the east side of Mount Rainier, Highway 410 will take you through the pass.*

Romantic Note: The drive through the pass is loaded with vista turnouts, hikes with dizzying switchbacks, and meadows that you can explore hand in hand. Just be sure to travel prepared. Comfortable hiking shoes, plenty of munchies, a water bottle, bug repellent, tissues, and a day pack will make Chinook Pass an unsurpassed experience. Also, be considerate of the wilderness. Trails are for people; the rest of the area is for the animals and plants. Responsible behavior on the part of all visitors will keep the beauty intact for many years to come.

❦❦❦ **MOUNT RAINIER NATIONAL PARK, Mount Rainier** Using poetic words to describe Mount Rainier is best left to the laureates. For the kissing purposes of this book, suffice it to say that almost every inch of this mountain is romantic and outrageously exquisite. From its dormant volcanic heart to its eternally glacier-covered summit, Mount Rainier is guaranteed to provide superlative panoramic views, memorable hikes, and lasting memories. If it's Northwest drama and passion you yearn for, this mountain has it. **(360) 569-2211; www.nps.gov/mora; $10 entry fee per vehicle, $5 entry fee per bicycle.** *From Enumclaw to the north or Yakima to the east, take Highway 410 into the park. Highway 12 from both the southeast and southwest intersects with Highway 123, which will also take you into the park. On the southwest side of the park, Highway 7 intersects with Highway 706 at the town of Elbe. Highway 706 goes into the park and takes you straight to Paradise, both literally and figuratively.*

Romantic Note: Several park roads, including some of the main routes onto the mountain, are closed during the winter, so always check for seasonal accessibility. Excellent hiking books about this region are available from **The Mountaineers Books;** write for a catalog or call for more information (1001 Southwest Klickitat Way, Suite 201, Seattle, WA 98134; 206-223-6303, 800-553-4453; www.mountaineers.org).

❦❦❦❦ **PARADISE, Mount Rainier** Driving on the road to Paradise is certainly a journey of beauty. As your car climbs upward, the sky is lost through the lush old-growth evergreens and the spellbinding roar of waterfalls, and singing birds create a special symphony heard only up here. Deer foraging for greens at the side of the road, brightly hued blue jays darting from tree to tree, mountain goats peering from rocky cliffs and ledges, eagles soaring overhead, and wildflowers of all kinds continue to impress. Then, amid all this splendor, Mount Rainier suddenly looms before you, draped in majestic snowy white, growing larger and more magnificent the closer you drive up the windy curves toward its peak. Take advantage of the various scenic stops, with vantage points of the surrounding park and the mountain beyond. Get out of your car, carefully look over the stone railings, and marvel at the heights to which you've come together. Sunset over the valley of trees below is astonishingly surreal. When you come to the end of the road, you'll know why they call this Paradise. **Mount Rainier National Park; (360) 569-2211.** *Nineteen miles inside the southwest entrance of the park.*

❀❀❀❀ **SUNRISE, Mount Rainier** If you've always wondered what it must be like at the top of the world, come to Sunrise and fulfill your fantasy, for this is as close to the top as you can drive on Mount Rainier (elevation 6,400 feet). Once you arrive, there are so many inspiring trails (ranging from relatively easy hikes to death-defying expeditions to the summit) that choosing the right one for you might be more difficult than you'd imagine. Your day hike can be a level, leisurely stroll or a strenuous trek up a mountain path, far away from everyone and everything except each other, accompanied by endless views of miraculous landscapes. There are few places in the United States where you will hear such silence or witness such beauty. **Mount Rainier National Park; (360) 569-2211.** *From the north or east, take Highway 410 into Mount Rainier National Park and follow the park map to Sunrise.*

Ashford

Hotel/Bed and Breakfast Kissing

❀◖ **ALEXANDER'S COUNTRY INN, Ashford** Nestled at the edge of old-growth forest (and, unfortunately, next to the two-lane highway that leads to Mount Rainier), this quaint, blue country inn is surrounded by a lush green lawn with winding walkways and wooden benches. Beyond the main house is a small, peaceful trout pond, rippled by a dazzling waterfall and surrounded by evergreens.

Upstairs, the inn's spacious common room has a fireplace but is still somewhat disappointing due to its sparse furnishings, pink walls, and dim lighting. Some of the 12 guest rooms are much the same, even slightly gloomy, but there are two rooms occupying the tower that you'll be sure to appreciate. First is the Upstairs Tower Suite, a double-decker room with a bright sitting room, furnished with attractive antiques. Carpeted stairs lead to the loft bedroom and sunlight filters through the suite's large windows. In the bottom half of the tower is a second two-room guest suite; its octagonal bedroom has redwood paneling and wraparound windows. All of the inn's rooms have unique stained glass windows that add a colorful flair to otherwise drab accommodations.

Complete your evening with a soak in the intimate hot tub, sheltered in a half-enclosed gazebo that overlooks the pond. Watch the trout jump across the water's surface, and enjoy the sweet-smelling forest air. **37515 State Road 706 East; (360) 569-2323, (800) 654-7615; moderate.**

Romantic Note: Alexander's also offers a fully equipped house and chalet just down the road. Furnished with modern appointments, both accommodations are family-oriented and can accommodate up to six people. Although these units are designed more for groups, they would be ultra-private, preferred places for two.

Romantic Suggestion: Before you settle into a room, you might opt for dinner in the restaurant downstairs (moderate to expensive; call for seasonal hours). Cozy up in a casual wooden booth with soft cushions, savor the warmth of the wood-burning fireplace, and peek out of the lace-curtained windows that overlook the old wooden waterwheel and surrounding yard (and, in the distance, traffic). Request fresh trout, typically caught the same day in the backyard pond, or try hearty stuffed green peppers. The excellent entrées are accompanied by fresh sourdough bread, and the service is attentive. At the end of your meal, satiate your sweet tooth with a chocolate torte covered in a light raspberry sauce.

❤❤❤ JASMER'S AT MT. RAINIER, Ashford

A sublime way to enjoy Mount Rainier National Park would be to have your own private retreat. Luckily, Jasmer's provides just that. Choose between an A-frame cabin on the property or several cottages located throughout Ashford. Most are within a five-mile drive of the park entrance, and all provide enough privacy and refinement to satisfy your romantic wants.

Jasmer's A-frame cabin has two separate, affordable units known as the Bed-and-Breakfast Rooms. Both feature queen-size beds, down comforters, private baths, and wood interiors. One has a fireplace, bay window, and a shower for two. Although the hot tub, tucked away in the woods, is shared by both units, you can reserve private time for an evening soak. Breakfast, consisting of pastries and fresh fruit, is already stocked in your kitchenette so you can sleep in as long as you'd like.

The other accommodations consist of individual cabins. The largest and most secluded is Big Creek Cabin, located on a stream bank and surrounded by old-growth forest. A woodstove, full kitchen, Northwest-style country furniture, and an entertainment center provide all the creature comforts you could desire. Best of all, there's a hot tub on the large deck—the perfect place to soak and stargaze. There are seven other unique cabins to choose from, each individually decorated with its own romantic draw. Just be sure to make reservations ahead of time . . . this place fills up fast. **30005 State Route 706 East; (360) 569-2682; www.az.com/~syscon/jas.html; inexpensive to expensive.**

❤❤ MOUNTAIN MEADOWS INN BED AND BREAKFAST, Ashford

Located six miles from the entrance to Mount Rainier National Park, this bed and breakfast offers a mountain of outdoor activities. From roasting marshmallows over the bonfire to exploring (on foot or skis) the 11 wooded acres surrounding the inn, you and your sweetheart will find much to do in these great outdoors.

Six guest rooms are available, all with private baths. Two rooms are located in a separate house and are more family oriented than romantically appropriate. We recommend staying in the main house, where you'll find spacious guest rooms filled with beautiful antiques and romantic furnishings. Our favorites are the Sunnybrook Room with its bright wicker furniture and 19th-century brass bed, and the spacious Chief Sealth Room with Native American artwork and an antique trunk and armoire. This room also has large windows overlooking the garden.

Don't oversleep or you'll miss the bountiful breakfast prepared by the owner/chef. Homemade muffins, berry scones, and fresh fruits whet your appetite for the fabulous main dishes that follow: Quiche Huntington with artichoke hearts, fresh basil, and cheese; smoked-salmon omelet; and Belgian waffles topped with fresh strawberries and cream are just a few of the delights that await. **28912 State Route 706 East; (360) 569-2788; www.bbhost.com/ mtnmeadow_mt.rainier; inexpensive to expensive.**

Stevenson

Hotel/Bed and Breakfast Kissing

❦❦ **SKAMANIA LODGE, Stevenson** Although Skamania Lodge is geared to convention-goers and business retreats, the surrounding splendor is enough to attract twosomes seeking romance. The lodge overlooks the magnificent Columbia River and offers nearly five miles of nature trails. Although walking hand in hand is one option, try exploring the 175-acre property via an alternative form of transportation: horseback. Whether you decide to walk or ride, take a dip in the pool and outdoor hot tub afterward. Inside the lodge, the massive main-floor Gorge Room provides a wonderful fireside spot for relaxing and savoring the view. Many of the 195 rooms have sensational river views enhanced by Northwest artwork and pine furnishings. Unfortunately, the gray undertones in the bedspreads and carpet create an austere atmosphere. Some rooms have fireplaces to help warm things up a bit, but it would take a lot more than a crackling fire to drown out the murmur of voices heard through the thin walls. **1131 Skamania Lodge Way; (509) 427-7700, (800) 221-7117; www.skamania.com; moderate to very expensive.**

Romantic Note: Dining options are limited in the town of Stevenson. Thankfully, **THE DINING ROOM** at Skamania Lodge (moderate to expensive; breakfast, lunch, and dinner daily, brunch Sunday) offers outstanding Columbia River views and excellent regional cuisine. The tender Potlatch chinook salmon is one of the restaurant's signature dishes; however, other entrées are also enticing. Meat lovers won't want to miss the grilled filet mignon with truffle butter and wild mushrooms, served with three-grain risotto and green bean salad. Tables along the windows are obviously preferred, and the polished oak interior with vaulted ceilings is quite attractive (albeit too large to feel intimate). The coziest area in the lodge is the **RIVER ROCK LOUNGE** (inexpensive to moderate). Although the menu here is limited, gazing out to the river through floor-to-ceiling windows is heavenly. Or you can gaze at each other (equally heavenly) and bask in the glow of a fire in the huge river-rock fireplace.

❤❤❤ **THE TIMBERS, Stevenson** The Columbia River Gorge is sure to take your breath away with its majestic cliffs carved by wind, water, and time. With rolling hills and beautiful countryside bordering the river, this is a perfect location for hiking or mountain biking. And, with powerful winds whipping up the waves every afternoon, some of the best windsurfing in the world takes place on the Columbia. Luckily for amorous-seeking, action-loving couples, Timbers provides cozy accommodations for resting your head after a day of play.

Timbers features seven private units housed in three log cabins. All are decorated in an eclectic, country style and come with gas fireplaces, kitchens, and river views. Upper units are your best bet for romance with private double Jacuzzi tubs in the bathrooms. Hot tubs dot the decks of each cabin; however, only the Front Timbers Cabin has one that can truly be called private. This cabin is our romantic pick, thanks to a spacious interior and an ideal location directly on the water's edge.

Breakfast is not included in your stay, but a bistro (inexpensive) on the property serves coffee drinks, pastries, and giant waffles with strawberries and whipped cream. In the summer, enjoy your morning meal outside on the patio at brightly colored tiled tables. **200 Southwest Cascade; (509) 427-5656; www.timbersinthegorge.com; moderate to very expensive.**

Husum

Outdoor Kissing

❤❤❤❤ **WIND RIVER CELLARS WINERY, Husum** On your way to or from Mount Adams, be sure to stop at the Wind River Cellars Winery. A stroll through the vineyards treats you to exquisite views of the valley and idyllic surrounding countryside—particularly from June through October, when abundant foliage blankets the land. Visit the large wood-frame building with enormous wooden doors that serves as the tasting room, and then head outside to sit beneath the lush grape arbor. This is the perfect spot in which to sip your favorite vintage, breathe the fresh air, and enjoy each other's company. Take time for this one; your eyes, palates, and hearts will be forever grateful. **196 Spring**

Creek Road; (509) 493-2324; open 11 A.M.–5 P.M. daily; call for seasonal closures; recommended wedding site. *Nine miles north of White Salmon on the way to Trout Lake. Just off Highway 141, near milepost 9, turn west onto Spring Creek Road and follow it two miles to the winery.*

Trout Lake

Located about 25 miles north of the Columbia River, Trout Lake is a quiet agricultural community at the base of Mount Adams. For some reason, Mount Adams isn't lauded as much as the other sights in the Cascades, yet this inactive volcano is in a unique position at the south end of Washington state, juxtaposed between the green, lush forests of the western half and the arid flatlands of the eastern half. This is part of Washington's wine country, so the base of the mountain is dappled with graciously manicured vineyards. Whether you are a snow bunny or prefer the long, hot days of summer, the endless recreational opportunities in this region will provide all the outdoor entertainment you need for a Northwest escape.

Hotel/Bed and Breakfast Kissing

☙☙❧ **SERENITY'S, Trout Lake** Isn't everyone searching for a little serenity? For romantic-minded folk the answer to that question is obvious, so we're here to tell you that serenity resides inside four newly built A-frame chalets near Trout Lake. Set amid tall firs and ponderosa pines, these self-sufficient little hideaways have everything you need for a peaceful mountain getaway. Gas-log fireplaces warm the knotty pine interiors; comfortable, contemporary living rooms provide a place to relax; and each unit has a kitchenette where you can prepare your own breakfasts (provisions are your responsibility). Some units have Jacuzzi tubs, while the larger ones have loft bedrooms. Serenity's chalets are not frilly or fancy, but they are an extremely comfortable and private option for couples enamored with the great outdoors and, of course, each other. **Highway 141, Milepost 23; (509) 395-2500, (800) 276-7993; w3. gorge.net/serenitys; inexpensive to expensive.**

Romantic Option: Serenity's also operates a relaxed little restaurant (moderate; dinner by reservation only) inside a wooden barn adjacent to the cabins. Sample such continental cuisine selections as baked Icelandic cod fillet served with drawn butter or chicken Kiev with wild rice dressing as you soak in distant views of Mount Adams.

White Salmon

Unlike the Oregon village of Hood River (see the Oregon Cascades chapter), the towns on the Washington side of the Columbia River Gorge are mostly residential areas where logging and agriculture, not tourist dollars, keep the economy rolling. As in so many small Northwest towns, however, the demand for logging here is decreasing, so perhaps the focus will shift in the coming years. Until then, White Salmon remains a fairly quiet, nondescript stop along the Columbia River.

Hotel/Bed and Breakfast Kissing

❀❀ **INN OF THE WHITE SALMON, White Salmon** A testimony to the fruits of a little T.L.C., this remodeled 1937 two-story brick hotel welcomes you with comfortable warmth. The Inn of the White Salmon exudes old-world charm; the lobby and hallways are decorated with refurbished Victorian lamps, framed turn-of-the-century photographs, and period wallpaper. The 16 cozy rooms are said to remind guests of Grandma's house, and with good reason. Most have TVs placed at the foot of the bed and some of the carpeting needs replacing; however, several rooms have been endowed with affectionate touches that make them conducive to romance. The Honeymoon Suite features plush new carpeting, an enormous king-size bed covered in lush white linens, and a cozy sitting room lit by an intricate metal Victorian lamp. All the rooms have private baths, and several have attractive wood paneling.

In the backyard, follow a wooden walkway past a little hillside bursting with colorful terraced gardens. Dip your toes in the spacious nearby hot tub, well lit at night and enclosed in an attractive latticework fence.

Now for the real highlight of a stay here: An incomparable repast awaits every morning in the sunny dining room, highlighted with lace tablecloths, lace curtains, and bright floral wallpaper. More than 20 European-style pastries and breads, including baklava and strudel, are set out buffet-style, and you can choose from six savory baked egg dishes, including an artichoke frittata with marinated artichoke hearts, Jack cheese, green onions, black olives, and fresh tomato. Even if you aren't guests at the inn, you are invited to enjoy this culinary extravaganza (inexpensive)—it is a great way to start a day of touring and exploring the Columbia Gorge National Scenic Area. **172 West Jewett; (509) 493-2335, (800) 972-5226; www.gorge.net/lodging/iws; inexpensive to moderate.**

Bingen

Restaurant Kissing

❀❀❀ **THE WILD MUSHROOM, Bingen** When we discovered The Wild Mushroom restaurant in this remote area of the Columbia River Gorge, we were about as excited as a fungi forager who finds that prized morel. This isn't exactly the place one expects to find a fine dining establishment serving up romance, along with an inventive selection of entrées. But luckily for sweethearts and gourmands alike, such a restaurant has popped up on Bingen's main street. Its stucco interior is painted with soothing yellow, green, and rose hues, and small tables adorned with cream linen tablecloths are illuminated by candles placed in purple glasses. Such a blend of colors only reflects the vivid combination of flavors that await in the entrées.

Begin coloring your palate with the Northwest shiitake mushroom salad enhanced by an apple essence and topped with Gorgonzola cheese. Paint a festive picture for your taste buds with the roasted pumpkin seed–crusted halibut with an apple, served atop arugula angel-hair pasta, or try the enormous portion of stir-fry chicken in a pineapple-tarragon-ginger sauce. Be sure to end your dinner on an equally brilliant note: The interesting chocolate fettuccine with pear and raspberry sorbet will delight and dazzle. **Corner of Steuben and Ash; (509) 493-8566; moderate to expensive; call for seasonal hours.**

Goldendale

Set in a peaceful valley below the Simcoe Mountains, Goldendale is a quiet town with an abundance of antique shops and historic homes. This city is also home to the **MARYHILL MUSEUM OF ART** and the **GOLDENDALE OBSERVATORY** (see Outdoor Kissing).

Hotel/Bed and Breakfast Kissing

❦❦ **TIMBERFRAME COUNTRY INN, Goldendale** Can you imagine a home built without nails? Years ago, German builders used only pegs, dowels, and interlocking beams to make solid farm homes. Timberframe was built this way, with rugged red fir timber and red oak pegs. Your hostess will gladly give you a tour of the entire house, which is not only architecturally interesting, but is also filled with eclectic treasures from around the world. Outside, the inn is surrounded by acres of pine, fir, and oak trees.

Two units are available to rent, the Tree Top Room and the Ponderosa Apartment. Private stairs lead to the Tree Top Room and its secluded deck with hot tub. Inside is a queen-size brass bed, pale pink walls, and pink furnishings. Don't worry about the profusion of pink; the overall effect is not too frilly or feminine. Other extras include a TV/VCR, a kitchenette, and a wonderful tiled shower set beneath a skylight. The Ponderosa Apartment is basically one giant room containing a king-size bed, full kitchen, and a sitting area with comfortable furniture and a woodstove. A hot tub is also included outside the apartment in front of the main house. Although the apartment is much larger than the Tree Top Room, we found it a bit too dark to recommend wholeheartedly.

A full country breakfast is served in the main house dining room. Fresh fruit and muffins are followed by a serving of peppered bacon, scrambled egg enchilada, and a fantastic strawberry shortcake that's sure to sweeten the rest of your day. **223 Golden Pine; (509) 773-3660, (800) 861-8408; inexpensive to moderate.**

Outdoor Kissing

❀❀❀ **GOLDENDALE OBSERVATORY, Goldendale** If you want to wish upon a star, you won't have to wander far in Goldendale. Situated on a hilltop just outside town, this observatory houses one of the largest publicly owned telescopes in the nation. It's a wonderful spot for amateur astronomers or romantics with stars in their eyes. If you can stay up, don't miss the midnight shows, which are open to the public. This doesn't mean you will encounter a large group; in fact, on any given night it is entirely possible that the two of you will be the only guests. When you feel this close to the stars, you definitely won't have to wish on one for more romance. **1602 Observatory Drive; (509) 773-3141; free admission; open Wednesday–Sunday.**

❀❀❀ **MARYHILL MUSEUM OF ART, Goldendale** Who would expect a world-class museum way out here, literally in the middle of nowhere? Well, right along the majestic Columbia River you will find the Maryhill Museum of Art, one of Washington state's historic treasures. This regal mansion, perched upon grassy acres at the river's edge, was originally built in 1914 as railroad magnate Sam Hill's "ranch house." It really is an architectural masterpiece, and now it is home to a surprising number of exhibits, including an extensive collection of Rodin sculptures. An ornate group of valuables that once belonged to Queen Marie of Romania, who was a devoted friend of Sam Hill's, is also displayed. **35 Maryhill Museum Drive; (509) 773-3733; www.maryhillmuseum.org; $6 admission fee; closed mid-November–mid-March.**

Romantic Suggestion: About three miles farther east along Highway 14 is another interesting site. Set on a windy bluff above the river is a replica of England's Stonehedge. Sam Hill built this monument as a tribute to the local men who died in World War I.

"Soul meets soul on lovers' lips."

Percy Bysshe Shelley

Yakima Valley

For some, the Yakima Valley conjures up images of dry, rolling hills and roadside fruit stands rather than romantic inspirations. But 300 days of sunshine a year, countless recreational opportunities (including river rafting, golfing, and skiing), and more than two dozen world-class wineries attract adventurous couples to this agricultural Eden just two hours southeast of Seattle. Although the city of Yakima may be a study in urban sprawl, amorous-minded couples will find some charming spots in this region. The countryside stretching from Selah to Benton City offers mile after scenic mile of lush orchards, cultivated fields, green-aisled hop yards, and pampered vineyards, set off by rolling hills and a network of rivers and canals. Spring is an especially lovely time of year here, when clouds of blossoms give the valley an ethereal beauty; summer brings high temperatures, dry winds, and red cheeks on apples. Whatever the season, you'll return home with a few bottles (or cases) of wine and happy memories of your wine-country getaway.

Wine Kissing

Yakima Valley winegrowers like to point out that their vineyards share the same latitude as the renowned wine regions of France. There's certainly no denying that the grapes thriving here produce a variety of wines, from chardonnay to riesling to merlot, with intense flavors that compare favorably to some of the best in the world. Surprisingly, wine touring in this area is only just beginning to catch on, and because the wineries are spread out along the 50 miles between Wapato and Benton City, tasting rooms remain relatively free from crowds during most of the year. However, be aware that special-event weekends bring hordes of tourists to participating wineries, especially during the last weekend of April when the Spring Barrel Tasting attracts more than 1,500 visitors. Other wine-related special events include Red Wine and Chocolate, held Presidents' Weekend in February, and Thanksgiving in the Wine Country, held the Friday, Saturday, and Sunday following Thanksgiving. Normally the winemakers are happy to have visitors and enjoy discussing their wines, but the overall experience becomes less enjoyable when the scene resembles a free-for-all.

The Yakima Valley has been pivotal in the history of wine in Washington state. If you would like to educate yourselves before you go, or if your interest is piqued over the course of your tour, pick up a copy of *The Wine Project: Washington State's Winemaking History*, by Ronald Irvine with Walter J. Clore, available at bookstores, wine shops, and several wineries. It describes many of the area's wineries and winemakers, past and present, and will add depth to any visit.

Most of the valley's wineries are easily reached from Highway 12, which parallels Interstate 82 between Wapato and Prosser; the rest are accessible from Exit 96 on Interstate 82. Helpful signs alert tourists about where to turn. A map highlighting the area's wineries is available from the **YAKIMA VALLEY WINEGROWERS ASSOCIATION** (800-258-7270). Additional information on individual wineries throughout the state can be found in a brochure published by the **WASHINGTON WINE COMMISSION** (206-667-9463). Call to receive a copy of these publications before your trip, or pick them up at hotels, B&Bs, restaurants, wineries, and other locations throughout the region.

The Yakima Valley appellation encompasses more than 30 wineries, and, like wine itself, each one has its own distinct personality. The list of wineries presented here is not meant to indicate which wines are best (a highly subjective matter in any case); instead, we have highlighted places that hold special interest for couples seeking idyllic wine-country moments. Cheers!

🌸🌸 **BONAIR WINERY, Zillah** After you've sipped your way through the selections at this English-style winery, linger awhile in the small adjacent yard, complete with a koi pond, gazebo, and several benches; this serene setting has been known to inspire marriage proposals as well as kisses. Visitors are also welcome to stroll hand in hand through the nearby vineyards.

Bonair Winery can help you celebrate a wedding, anniversary, or other significant events in your lives with specially labeled bottles of wine, available in several styles. Dates, names, and even photographs can personalize a case of any wine you select. It's guaranteed to put you in high spirits; just be sure to place your order two weeks in advance. **500 South Bonair Road; (509) 829-6027; www.bonairwine.com; open 10 a.m.–5 p.m. daily, open 10 a.m.–4:30 p.m. on weekends in winter.**

🌸🌸 **CHINOOK WINES, Prosser** Three well-spaced picnic tables sit in the cherry orchard behind the charming farmhouse that holds Chinook's sleek tasting room. Bring along lunch or other goodies to share in this timeless country-garden scene. Despite the fact that a freeway passes nearby (and out of sight), you can slow down, raise a glass to the nearby vineyards, and toast the good life. **Wine Country Road at Wittkopf Road; (509) 786-2725; open noon–5 p.m. weekends May–December.**

🌸🌸🌸 **COVEY RUN WINERY, Zillah** Perched atop a green hillside, this handsome Northwest-style building features a large tasting bar, a lovely gift shop, and a viewing area showcasing the large-scale winemaking facilities. Outside, picnic tables and a deck with additional seating open to the glorious vista of surrounding vineyards and orchards. Kissing just seems to be the right response to all this pastoral splendor. **1500 Vintage Road; (509) 829-6235; open 10 a.m.–5 p.m. daily spring–fall, open 10 a.m.–4:30 p.m. daily in winter; recommended wedding site.**

❀❀❀ **HYATT VINEYARDS WINERY, Zillah** Wooden picnic tables scattered on a lawn outside this winery offer pleasant views of rolling hills blanketed with orchards and vineyards. A huge windmill offers a rustic touch and beautiful flowers add colorful refinement. Vintage moments are guaranteed here. **2020 Gilbert Road; (509) 829-6333; call for seasonal hours; closed January.**

❀❀ **KIONA VINEYARDS WINERY, Benton City** Kiona's tasting room and gift shop are located in the vine-stenciled basement of a modest family home. After sipping to your hearts' content, head outside to relax on the vast lawn, spread out your lunch on one of the tables scattered about, or challenge each other to a game of croquet (wickets are in place; mallets and balls are set out). Sagebrush, vineyards, and endless quiet surround you. **44612 North Sunset Northeast; (509) 588-6716; open noon–5 p.m. daily.**

❀❀❀ **STATON HILLS, Wapato** Stone gates and neatly labeled rows of well-tended grapevines line the driveway to this modern winery perched on a small hill. The stone building features massive carved wooden doors, a splendid tasting section, and a large sitting area. Outside, the scene is pure romance: The manicured grounds are dotted with lovely flowers and shrubs, and concrete picnic tables and benches, arranged on a pleasant slope and shaded by canvas umbrellas, offer inspiring views of the surrounding hills and valleys. **71 Gangl Road; (509) 877-2112; open 11 a.m.–5:30 p.m. daily March–October, open noon–5 p.m. daily November–February.**

❀❀❀ **TERRA BLANCA VINTNERS, Benton City** Terra Blanca is an exceptional place to kiss. Stone and iron gates mark the entrance to this brand-new facility, and a large wooden deck off the tasting room overlooks a spectacular view of trees and sagebrush, valleys, and mountains. Don't miss a visit to the man-made caves, sunk deep into the hill and lined with giant barrels where the wine can age at a consistent temperature and humidity. Landscaping is young but promising, and accented by huge rocks; a waterfall will be installed soon, and plans call for adding elaborate doors to the caves. **34715 North Demoss Road; (509) 588-6082; www.terrablanca.com; open noon–6 p.m. weekdays, open 11 a.m.–6 p.m. weekends, open by appointment only Christmas–Valentine's Day.**

Selah

Hotel/Bed and Breakfast Kissing

❀❀❀ **CHERRY HILL MANOR, Selah** You might not believe your eyes when you drive up to Cherry Hill Manor. Surrounded by working farms, ranches, and orchards, this huge new home looks like it's been transplanted from an upscale suburban development, complete with a smooth swath of bright green lawn. Interior spaces are equally grand, and filled with all sorts of eclectic accessories. Guests can make themselves at home in the regal yet comfortable living room or in the library filled with decoys and hunting trophies. Also on the main level is the 1950s room, with a checkerboard floor, ice cream parlor–style tables and booths, soft-drink memorabilia, and a jukebox loaded with golden oldies. A real soda fountain will be installed here soon; in the meantime, if you're inclined to snack, you can enjoy some popcorn from the movie-house popper.

The four large guest rooms upstairs are immaculately furnished with well-cared-for antiques and handmade crafts; all feature private baths and modern conveniences such as telephones, TVs, and coffeemakers. The frilly Bing Room, done up in shades of peach and green, is decorated with an antique wedding dress, hat boxes, and old-fashioned toys; it shares a veranda with the green and burgundy Lambert Room, which is decorated year-round in a Christmas theme. A king-size four-poster bed is the highlight of the Rainier Room, while the Cherry Hill Suite has a sitting area with sofa and chairs, and a jungle-theme bathroom. Central air conditioning keeps everything cool during the sweltering summer months.

Pack your swimsuits: An outdoor swimming pool provides cool fun in the hot sun. Bring along your appetites too; breakfast is a procession of home-made baked goods, blueberry pancakes, yogurt, fresh fruit, and California croissants (pastry filled with avocado, tomato, bacon, and eggs, all topped with béarnaise sauce), served each morning in the antique-filled dining room. Drinks and hors d'oeuvres are offered between 5:30 P.M. and 7 P.M. each evening. **81 Mapleway Road; (509) 697-8686; moderate to expensive.**

Yakima

Hotel/Bed and Breakfast Kissing

❤❤❤❀ **BIRCHFIELD MANOR, Yakima** Birchfield Manor is a family business run by hospitality professionals. The husband-and-wife owners left the Seattle area, where the husband taught culinary arts at a local community college, to open a fine restaurant (see Restaurant Kissing) that later expanded to become this very romantic inn. The result is an engaging getaway that offers two ways to spoil yourselves—with culinary delights and country-style luxury.

The five guest rooms in the original 1910 building are individually designated with women's names; all are decorated with enviable antiques and lovely wall coverings. Victoria features a queen-size brass bed, pot-bellied stove, and a window seat. Elizabeth, with its dusty rose color scheme and a king-size bed, overlooks the garden and has a separate dressing room with an additional bed. At the time of our visit, a double Jacuzzi tub and a double-headed shower were being added to the room named Allison. Jenny and Anne, both located in the front of the home, offer sunshine by day and pleasing views of the valley lights at night. All of the guest rooms have private baths and air conditioning, but phones and TV have been banished to a common area on the second floor.

The recently constructed annex next door holds six more rooms, with all sorts of modern amenities, including TVs and private phone lines. Our favorite rooms are the two oversize Penthouse Rooms on the top floor, both with gas fireplaces, double Jacuzzi tubs, mini-refrigerators, and steam sauna showers that can really heat things up. Snazzy climate-control units in the rooms are equipped with a remote control for ultimate convenience. Private decks overlook a pastoral scene, which includes a pond that is home to muskrats and herons. The same view is afforded to the four guest rooms on the main floor, which feature private patios (the patios belonging to the two rooms at the front of the annex have ingenious portholes that let in the view while preserving privacy). Rooms 3 and 4 feature fireplaces, double Jacuzzi tubs, and double-headed showers. All of the rooms are immaculate and individually decorated with themes ranging from subdued florals to vines and wines to a bold purple and green fishing and hunting motif.

Outdoors it's as serene and relaxing as indoors. A lush garden provides fresh herbs for Birchfield Manor's kitchen, and a small pool promises to help you cope with Yakima's searing summers. Begin your day with a hearty breakfast of fresh fruit, granola, baked goods, and a savory entrée such as a Spanish omelet or a crêpe stuffed with chicken and mushrooms. Guests staying in the main house eat at private tables in the charming dining room, while Annex guests can choose to have breakfast delivered to their room. **2018 Birchfield Road; (509) 452-1960; inexpensive to expensive.**

Romantic Option: Ask about the Birchfield's special packages. The Romantic Getaway includes hors d'oeuvres, a box of chocolates made in-house, chilled champagne, and two souvenir champagne flutes.

❦❦ **ORCHARD INN BED AND BREAKFAST, Yakima** Sequestered in the midst of a prolific cherry orchard, this relatively new inn takes country seclusion seriously. The guest rooms feature simple pine furniture, restrained country decor, queen-size beds covered with fluffy down comforters, and private baths equipped with jetted tubs. All three are located in a wing that extends off the main house, so guests can come and go privately. Your hostess has made every effort to make your stay as comfortable as possible: In the rooms, beds are outfitted with custom-made mattresses, and at the table custom-roasted and -blended coffee is guaranteed to perk up your mornings; the culinary creations are made from hand-milled flour. Air conditioning keeps things cool in hot weather, and a sitting room set aside exclusively for guests features a TV/VCR, books, games, and a refrigerator stocked with cold drinks. There's even a washer and dryer if for some reason you really must do laundry.

Cherries are in season year-round here, at least when it comes to the decor. The three guest rooms—Rainier, Lambert, and Bing—are named for different varieties, a cherry motif appears on napkins and tablecloths, curtains hang from cherry branches, and breakfast is served on china adorned with (you guessed it!) cherries. You may be wondering if the owners have taken this fruit-inspired theme too far, but not to worry; it's executed with plenty of good old-fashioned country charm.

Make sure you wake up with an appetite. Breakfast possibilities include fresh peach and caramel French toast, sausage and cheese quiche in a potato crust, or baked apple porridge with vanilla ice cream, plus seasonal fruits and scones. The country-style dining room is a friendly place to enjoy your morning repast. Weather permitting, you can eat breakfast on a deck bordered by cherry trees. (When the cherries are ripe, guests are invited to augment breakfast with these juicy, sweet treats.) If you prefer privacy, simply ask to have breakfast delivered to your room. **1207 Pecks Canyon Road; (509) 966-1283; (888) 858-8284; inexpensive.**

❤❤❤ **A TOUCH OF EUROPE BED AND BREAKFAST, Yakima** If you're in the mood for a tranquil, pampered stay in charming surroundings, book a room at this lovely bed and breakfast. The Queen Anne Victorian home is embraced by a curvaceous wraparound porch and accented with an octagonal turret. Built in 1889 by well-to-do Yakima pioneers, the home was once visited by Theodore Roosevelt; today, the friendly innkeepers happily devote themselves to making your stay just as memorable.

All three guest rooms offer an array of thoughtful amenities, private bathrooms, down-filled comforters, freshly ironed sheets (a sensuous bonus), vases filled with fresh flowers, and lovely antiques. Wall-to-wall carpeting and a slight amount of traffic noise from the street are among the few anachronistic touches. The small Victorian Walnut Room holds twin beds, a romantic minus for most couples, although these hand-carved beauties date back to the early 1800s. Lace curtains, period lighting fixtures, a fainting couch, and dignified mahogany antiques, including an early 1800s queen-size bed, make the spacious Princess Victorian Mahogany Room picture perfect; its handsome private bathroom is detached and located right next door. The Prince Victorian Mahogany Room, also furnished with elegant mahogany pieces, is the largest of the three, and boasts a gas fireplace, a view of the backyard, and a private bathroom. Fresh fruit, homemade cookies, and juice are set out in each room so guests can unwind with a snack upon arrival. In keeping with the point of a getaway, radios and TVs are absent.

Downstairs, the home's common areas are beautiful, and several, including the cozy book-lined library, feature elegant wallpaper that covers both the walls and ceilings. The front parlor, with its bay window, Victorian lamp, European antiques, and crushed-velvet seating, is a lovely space for quiet conversation. A doorway decorated with gingerbread millwork leads into the pale rose–colored parlor, where breakfast is served at one of the Duncan Phyfe tables adorned with lace tablecloths, silver candlesticks, lovely china, fine crystal, and fresh flowers. (If you absolutely must have privacy in the morning, let the innkeepers know and they will seat the other guests in the dining room and close the door between the two rooms.) Later in the day, spend quiet time in the tiny, lace-curtained sitting room upstairs in the turret, relax on the shady porch, or explore the property's acre of trees and flowers.

Breakfast is the high point of any stay here. You might sit down to a plate of fresh fruit accompanied by goat cheese and prosciutto, half a grapefruit sprinkled with chocolate shavings, and heavenly popovers served with home-made apple-pear and apple-apricot jam. Orange juice and tea or coffee are replenished unobtrusively. This bounty may be followed by a creative egg dish, perhaps a Brie and chive omelet garnished with slices of kiwi. But don't leave the table just yet. Another course follows, such as delicate apple crêpes comple-mented by a homemade berry sauce and topped with mango. Your hearts will be thoroughly won over at this point, so don't be surprised if you find your-selves discussing your next "European" holiday. **220 North 16th Avenue; (509) 454-9775, (888) 438-7073; inexpensive to moderate.**

Romantic Suggestion: Gourmet picnic baskets are also available and highly recommended if you are planning a day of wine touring. Four- to seven-course dinners can also be scheduled in the stunning Victorian dining room (see Res-taurant Kissing).

Restaurant Kissing

❧❧❧❦ **BIRCHFIELD MANOR, Yakima** Dinner at Birchfield Manor is wine-country dining at its best. Local wines from the well-stocked cellar perfectly complement the delicious French-accented entrées prepared by the talented chefs. Poultry, fish, and meat dishes, all enhanced with herbs from the adja-cent garden, are consistently excellent; desserts are memorable, especially the puff-pastry swan filled with cream and drizzled with fresh raspberry sauce.

The country-elegant dining room is appointed with floral carpeting, well-spaced wooden tables and chairs, a fireplace, and a variety of intriguing knick-knacks and antiques. A crystal chandelier sheds soft light that enhances the romantic ambience. Service is both professional and relaxed, and because seating is limited to 50 people, diners are unlikely to feel either crowded or rushed. A long, solitary table in the wine cellar is available for couples who want to share a vintage evening in complete privacy. **2018 Birchfield Road; (509) 452-1960; moderate to expensive; dinner Thursday–Saturday.**

❧❦ **DELI DE PASTA, Yakima** Don't be fooled by the name of this place: Deli de Pasta is no delicatessen, and it offers more than pasta. This tiny, unassuming restaurant in downtown Yakima consistently serves up delectable Italian cui-sine, and everything is made from scratch by the talented chef/owner. Begin with smoked-salmon ravioli, topped with a basil-cream sauce, followed by lemon chicken or lasagne with its five layers of mouth-filling flavor. The night we dined, the evening's special of seared salmon with a red pepper crust was simply outstanding. The Pick-a-Pasta section offers a choice of six types of homemade pasta and seven sauces. Soups, salads, and sandwiches round out the options. The wine list features mainly local bottlings.

Romantically speaking, the modest, plant-adorned interior does not measure up to the high quality of the meals, although the small linen-draped tables are pleasantly adorned with candles and flowers. We recommend holding hands across the table, gazing into each other's eyes, and letting the superb food arouse your passions. **7 North Front Street; (509) 453-0571; moderate; lunch Monday–Friday, dinner Monday–Saturday.**

❧❧❧ **GASPERETTI'S RESTAURANT, Yakima** Despite its less-than-stellar location on a busy street lined with motels and tattoo parlors, this formal Italian restaurant is where the valley's upper crust comes for a special night out. The parking lot full of Mercedes and other expensive vehicles was our first indication that this place had more to offer than first meets the eye. Inside, the two dining rooms display quite distinct personalities; one is filled with tables and banquettes and has a somewhat lively atmosphere, while the other is decorated with frescoed walls that suggest a quiet Mediterranean villa. Tables in both rooms are set with silver and crystal and topped with flowers and small lamps. Service is friendly and professional.

Begin your meal with a plate of fried calamari, accompanied by an irresistible spicy dipping sauce. Local produce provides much of the inspiration here: One bite of our cream of asparagus soup and we knew that these vegetables had originated in a nearby field earlier that same day. We were also impressed with the succulent halibut, served in a red and yellow pepper sauce that was astonishingly intense and flavorful. The poultry, veal, beef, and pasta dishes that round out the menu are equally good. In addition, Gasperetti's prides itself on its well-stocked cellar. Washington wines are the main event, but bottles from Italy and California are also highlighted. **1013 North First Street; (509) 248-0628; lunch Tuesday–Friday, dinner Tuesday–Saturday; moderate to expensive.**

❧❧❧❧ **A TOUCH OF EUROPE BED AND BREAKFAST, Yakima** Without question, the most romantic dinners in the valley are served at this charming bed and breakfast (see Hotel/Bed and Breakfast Kissing). That's why we've listed it in the restaurant section of our book, even though this place isn't officially a restaurant. Both guests and nonguests of the inn can enjoy exquisite meals here if they plan ahead. Dinners are by special arrangement only, and calling early definitely pays off. (The first party to reserve an evening gets to choose the courses and select the time; additional parties may reserve a place as well.) If you're lucky enough to be the first caller, the vivacious and talented chef will work with you to plan an unforgettable meal.

Be prepared to go back in time to a distant age of gracious, formal romance.

When you arrive for your meal, you will be ushered into the antique-filled front parlor, where you can relax to classical music and spend a few moments together reviewing your day. Next, you will be led to your table in the magnificent Victorian dining room, complete with a box-beamed embossed ceiling, built-in cabinets fronted with leaded and stained glass, a cast-iron fireplace, floral carpet, and antique tables and chairs. Plants, flowers, and china are on display, and the garden is visible through large windows. The other seating option is the charming adjacent parlor, where lace-covered tables are adorned with lovely crystal and silver, fresh flowers, and candles. (The parlor can be shut off from the other dining room if you would like total privacy.)

As gourmet dish follows gourmet dish, you will sigh with pleasure. The chef works with local growers and suppliers to make sure everything is of the highest quality. We thoroughly enjoyed the lamb, which was served in a red wine sauce; this dish was hearty without being heavy, with every flavor in perfect balance. Homemade condiments provide additional nuances. And the desserts! Their only failing is that they mark the conclusion of a wonderful dining experience. **220 North 16th Avenue; (509) 454-9775, (888) 438-7073; expensive to very expensive; reservations required; dinner and other meals by special arrangement only.**

Romantic Note: Guests are responsible for bringing their own wine to accompany dinner, although the hosts are happy to uncork and serve it for you.

❦❧ **TRATTORIA RUSSO, Yakima** Attention to detail is what distinguishes this relatively new addition to Yakima's Italian restaurant scene. Located on the second floor of a downtown building, the large, informal dining room features wooden tables and chairs, brick walls covered with artwork, and an open kitchen that is surprisingly unobtrusive. Potted plants, a small fountain, and twinkling white lights add a romantic touch, and the piano that sits against one wall gets a workout on Friday and Saturday nights.

The menu is filled with tempting choices. Will you begin with the mammoth portobello mushroom stuffed with risotto and blue cheese or the clams bathed in a garlic and basil broth? It's a tough decision, but you'll have to make even more difficult ones as the evening progresses. Choose between ravioli, linguine, penne, and angel hair, topped by your choice of a dozen or so sauces. Are you in the mood for something light, such as cioppino, swordfish, or eggplant lasagne, or a heartier dish like lamb steak with grilled vegetables in a rosemary-chianti sauce? Should you come back again? That's easy: Your hearts will say yes. **315 East Yakima Avenue; (509) 577-0360; moderate to expensive; call for seasonal hours.**

Romantic Warning: Avoid the seating on the outdoor balcony. Tables here overlook a traffic-infested street, making for a noisy meal with a side order of exhaust fumes.

Grandview

Hotel/Bed and Breakfast Kissing

❤❤❤ **COZY ROSE BED AND BREAKFAST, Grandview** One hundred rose-bushes decorate the grounds of this exuberant, whimsical country retreat, located on a blissfully quiet road that threads past the farms, vineyards, and hop yards of Grandview. Two farmhouses on the property hold the four spacious guest accommodations. Each suite offers a private deck and private entrance, a large bedroom, separate living room, well-equipped cooking facilities, and indoor and outdoor eating areas. The furniture and decor are country comfortable and somewhat eccentric, but delightfully unpretentious, with several truly romantic touches. The Irish House, occupying the entire first floor of one farmhouse, features a queen-size bed bedecked with floral sheets and crowned with an ethereal veil. Stenciled walls, lace curtains, and a Franklin stove help make this a completely desirable retreat. Upstairs, the Country Hideaway Suite is slightly smaller, but equally delightful, with a private deck that overlooks the surrounding countryside. The Rose Room, located in the adjacent farmhouse, offers a king-size bed and a living room with both a wood-burning Franklin fireplace and big-screen TV (something of a mixed romantic message, but worth extra points if you enjoy snuggling in front of the tube). The attached Mother-in-Law Room can be rented with the Rose Room in case you're traveling with another couple; this room holds a queen-size featherbed covered in white lace. (The Mother-in-Law Room is never rented separately.) This farmhouse also holds the Secret Garden Suite, billed as "the ultimate retreat," with its double Jacuzzi tub, deluxe stereo system, and king-size "wonder bed," which can be adjusted to change positions. (This bed even vibrates for those who want to put their love in motion.)

In the morning, guests are treated to a full breakfast that is delivered to their room. Huckleberry pancakes, homemade applesauce, ham, and home-grown fruits are typical of what you can expect. If you wish to dine in at night, but don't want to go to the trouble of cooking, the host will prepare a gourmet dinner for an additional cost. He can whip up entrées as simple as pasta or as extravagant as steak with caviar (price varies; advance notice required). **1220 Forsell Road; (509) 882-4669; inexpensive to moderate; recommended wedding site.**

Romantic Note: Guests are asked to leave pets at home, but animal lovers who want to take a walk in the country accompanied by a four-legged friend can take one or both of the owners' pet llamas with them (Saturdays only).

Romantic Option: Ask about the Cozy Rose's Honeymoon and Anniversary packages. A bottle of wine, a dozen baby roses, "rose-petal turndown," and other romantic extras will surely set your hearts aglow.

Restaurant Kissing

❧ **DYKSTRA HOUSE, Grandview** Fast-food joints, small-town cafés, and an array of authentic but unromantic Mexican eateries fill the Yakima Valley. Special places where a couple can share a peaceful meal in an environment conducive to affectionate discourse are as rare as skyscrapers here. That's why this low-key restaurant housed in a historic 1914 building is a welcome find. The best seating is on the main floor, either on the screened-in sunporch or in the dining room. Tables are covered with floral tablecloths, sheer curtains dress the windows, and papered walls and antiques complete the scene.

Lunches are nothing special, with a lineup of the usual suspects—soups, salads, and sandwiches—as well as a daily chef's special. Your best bet is to hold out for the prix fixe dinners, served on weekends only. The menu is Italian on Fridays, and features a triumvirate of beef, chicken, or fish on Saturdays, when a fire is lit in the tile fireplace for extra romantic ambience. As is only fitting in this area of the world, local wines are highlighted. **114 Birch Avenue; (509) 882-2082; inexpensive; lunch Tuesday–Saturday, dinner Friday–Saturday.**

Prosser

Restaurant Kissing

❧ **WINE COUNTRY INN, Prosser** This pleasant oasis on the bank of the Yakima River is a fine place to enjoy an unrushed lunch or dinner. The interior of the house that holds the inn is divided into several dining rooms and decorated with country charm and simplicity. Here, diners sit at cozy tables draped with tablecloths and encircled by wooden chairs. Additional tables are located outside on the riverside deck, a choice spot for a romantic interlude on warm days. The highway is nearby, but thankfully it is not a major distraction.

Lunches are simple, featuring soups, sandwiches, salads, a stir-fry, and a daily special. Dinners are more ambitious, with an array of Italian entrées on Wednesday and continental dishes served Thursday through Saturday. Rigatoni with ratatouille, chicken Parmesan, and linguine with clams and garlic in a cream sauce are among the Mediterranean-accented creations. Later in the week, set your taste buds for selections like duck with spiced Madeira sauce, New York steak with spicy wild mushrooms, or halibut with a lemon-pepper crust. As you might expect, local wines take top billing. **1106 Wine Country Road; (509) 786-2855; inexpensive to moderate; lunch Monday–Saturday, dinner Wednesday–Saturday.**

Romantic Suggestion: Call ahead if you would like the cook to prepare a picnic lunch to take with you as you tour the valley.

Romantic Note: Wine Country Inn also offers bed-and-breakfast rooms, but they lack romantic appeal and are not recommended.

"Every kiss provokes another."

Marcel Proust

OREGON

Portland

Once you visit Portland, you are likely to become a devotee of the City of Roses. This growing municipality has two distinct personalities—one urban and the other rural. There is an impressive amount of greenery here, and an amazing variety of terrain for walking, hiking, and exploring. Gardens, parks, forests, and rivers blanket the landscape, and all are meticulously maintained. Then there's the urban side of Portland's character: the upscale charm of Nob Hill, a refurbished neighborhood teeming with restaurants and shops; the growing downtown, dotted with art deco buildings and glass skyscrapers; a restored old-town area with all its vintage charm left intact; and the affluent, urban-chic riverfront area called RiverPlace. Portland's two personalities are in perfect balance, which is part of what makes the city so remarkable. Whether you are visiting for a day or a week, Portland's earthy appeal is bound to make a lasting impression.

Romantic Suggestion: Portland is home to one of the largest open-air markets in the country. The **PORTLAND SATURDAY MARKET** (503-222-6072) is open every Saturday and Sunday, from March through Christmas Eve. More than 200 booths feature a wide variety of handcrafted goods, from herbal soaps to ceramics to plenty of Polar Fleece wearables. If strolling around gets your stomach growling, stop by one of the dozen or so food booths, which dish out such delectables as sugar-coated elephant ears and mouth-watering Greek gyros. The market extends from the west end of the Burnside Bridge to the Fire Museum, between Front Street and the MAX trolley tracks. Besides the eating and shopping, the market is the ideal place to share a taste of city life together.

Hotel/Bed and Breakfast Kissing

❀❀ **THE BENSON HOTEL, Portland** This grand old hotel has one of the most massive, ornate lobbies in the Northwest. The Austrian crystal chandeliers, Italian marble floors, and the building's original Circassian walnut paneling are truly awe inspiring. This lobby is a hard act to follow and remains the most impressive part of the Benson.

All 286 rooms are comfortable enough, with cherry-wood furnishings, standard baths, and king-size beds covered with big, plush pillows. Compared to the fabulous lobby, however, the rooms are a bit of a letdown. The color schemes are fairly conservative (different shades of taupe, cream, and gray), and we were hard-pressed to find many heart-stirring qualities.

If you're willing to splurge, consider one of the two Grand Suites. Each has a step-up Jacuzzi tub and a double-headed shower in the bathroom; a king-size sleigh bed; and a sitting area lavishly appointed with chandeliers, beautiful window treatments, a gas fireplace, and your very own baby grand piano. These suites are excessively spacious (and should be, for the price you are paying) and are best suited for a party, rather than for two people seeking an intimate time together. **309 Southwest Broadway; (503) 228-2000, (800) 426-0670; www.citysearch.com/pdx/bensonhotel; very expensive to unbelievably expensive.**

Romantic Warning: Breakfast is not included with the price of your stay. And for tariffs this steep, that's simply unforgivable. Fortunately, breakfast, lunch, and dinner are available downstairs in the LONDON GRILL (see Restaurant Kissing). In addition, the hotel's downtown location allows easy access to a myriad of eating establishments in the area.

☙☙❧ THE GOVERNOR HOTEL, Portland

You don't have to be a governor or any other kind of politician to appreciate the stellar accommodations at this refined, historic downtown hotel (although a politician's pocketbook might help). A harmonious mixture of turn-of-the-century decor and modern appointments fills the grand, elongated lobby. Fascinating hand-painted murals pay tribute to Lewis and Clark and the Native Americans they encountered while exploring the Oregon Territory. The soft straw-colored hues, oversize chairs and massive fireplace, and original mahogany furnishings make for a warm introduction to your romantic interlude.

Each of the 100 rooms has slightly different decor but all are fairly traditional, with matching upholstered furniture in subtle tones of peach or beige with touches of Northwest and Asian-influenced art. Superior Guest Rooms, which are the least costly but still in the very expensive price range, lack decent views and have queen-size beds rather than kings. Deluxe Guest Rooms, which are slightly more expensive, offer considerably more comfort, with separate sitting areas, fireplaces, tall ceilings, and the same dignified decor. The hotel's suites are the most luxurious and feature amenities such as gas fireplaces, cozy love seats, jetted tubs, abundant space, and skylights that fill the rooms with sunshine. Some have balconies overlooking the nearby rooftops.

For a nominal fee, guests can take advantage of the full-service athletic club located on the hotel's lower level. There's just about everything you could ever need to stay buff, including a lap pool, whirlpool, track, weight room, saunas, and an aerobics room. After a good workout, visit JAKE'S GRILL (503-220-1850; moderate to expensive) on the ground floor for breakfast, lunch, or dinner. It's hardly intimate, but the carved wood columns, original tilework, and polished mahogany bar impart a historic warmth. Plus, Jake's has one of the most extensive menus we've seen, heavy on meat and potatoes, as well as soups, salads, and even a blue-plate special. Try to snag one of the old-fashioned booths near the windows: it's your best bet for privacy. **611 Southwest Tenth Avenue; (503) 224-3400, (800) 554-3456; www.govhotel.com; very expensive to unbelievably expensive.**

☙☙ THE HEATHMAN HOTEL, Portland

It's not quite a museum or an art

gallery, but the Heathman Hotel prides itself on a strong commitment to the arts. From Andy Warhol's "Endangered Species" series, which adorns the lobby and restaurant walls, to original works displayed in each room, art is at the forefront here. (Not only does the hotel display seasonal exhibits on its mezzanine level, but it also donates a portion of its proceeds to benefit Portland's artistic community.) Geometric and Asian artwork and marble detailing contribute to the small lobby's distinguished and striking appearance. The mood changes in the cozy and richly appointed **TEA COURT**, where tea is served each afternoon and jazz is performed three nights a week. The classic decor, expansive French canvases, rare eucalyptus paneling, large fireplace, and genial quiet make this a suitable place for an afternoon of thoughtful conversation and loving gazes. Upstairs, the Heathman Mezzanine Library, located next to the hotel's bar, has cozy sofas and chairs to snuggle in.

These alluring oases are all the more welcome because the accommodations themselves aren't particularly stunning. The 150 rooms are handsome, with all the pertinent amenities, but very small (unless you spring for a suite). Warm tones of vanilla accented by light woods, marble fixtures in the standard bathrooms, and original Northwest artwork help enrich the basic hotel style of the understated rooms. If your pocketbook needs emptying, why not go all out and stay in the hotel's Grand Suite? This two-bedroom suite is decorated in shades of yellow and cream, with views of the city from its many windows. Features include mahogany floors, a fireplace, and an inviting king-size four-poster bed in the master bedroom. A glass-enclosed three-headed shower and large whirlpool tub are luxurious additions to the marble-clad bathroom. This is definitely the most romantic room in the hotel. **1001 Southwest Broadway; (503) 241-4100, (800) 551-0011; www.holog.com/heathman; very expensive to unbelievably expensive.**

Romantic Note: To see and taste some culinary artwork, visit the hotel's sophisticated and stylish restaurant located on the ground floor (see Restaurant Kissing).

❀❀❀❀ **HERON HAUS, Portland** Bed and breakfasts are known for being cozy, warm, and congenial. Nothing is quite so affection-producing as a stay in a home where the owners diligently tend to their guests' hearts and senses with such niceties as the aroma of freshly baked morning pastries, the warmth of a roaring fire, lots of sitting nooks to snuggle up in, handmade quilts and oversize pillows, and a conspicuous amount of tender loving care. The Heron Haus has all this and more.

This English Tudor home is a huge, attractively furnished mansion in Portland's northwest hills. Features include a solarium and a pool, and the six spacious sun-filled suites—each given a different Hawaiian name—include cozy sitting areas. Many of the rooms have lovely pastel-colored walls, and all have contemporary decor, fireplaces, sitting areas, TVs, phones, and private baths. Some bathrooms are so spectacular that you may decide to stay in yours and forget about returning to bed. The Kulia Suite has an ample spa tub where you can soak while gazing into the glowing fireplace. In the Ko Suite's bathroom, a shower with seven nozzles will cover every inch of you (or both of you) with pulsating water. Above it all is the Mahina Room, the perfect hideaway, with a king-size bed and terrific views of Mount Hood and Mount St. Helens.

A continental breakfast of croissants, pastries, fresh fruit and juice, and coffee or tea is served in the refined dining room, which is filled with fascinating art from the innkeeper's travels. You probably won't be eager to leave this peaceful setting, but if you have a heartier breakfast appetite, you're just up the hill from Nob Hill, home to some of Portland's finest eateries. In this city of few parking places, off-street parking at the Heron Haus makes coming and going easy. **2545 Northwest Westover Road; (503) 274-1846; www.europa.com/~hhaus; expensive to very expensive.**

❤❤❤ **HOTEL VINTAGE PLAZA, Portland** If you think the brick exterior and Romanesque architecture of this historic building are impressive, wait until you get inside. The open lobby envelops you in classic, elegant style. More like a living room than a lobby, it is decorated in rich jewel tones with dark wood paneling, marble pillars, grandiose fresh bouquets, a warming marble fireplace, and sumptuous sofas. As you lift your eyes skyward, take notice of the upstairs hallways and wraparound balconies. A solarium roof many floors up draws in sunlight and gives the entire expanse an airy distinction.

You can escape the city in amorous style with any of the 107 rooms, each named after a different Oregon winery. The standard guest rooms are just that—standard. If stellar accommodations are more your style, check into one of the nine Starlight Rooms. Located on the top floor, each of these rooms has a breezy conservatory motif, with pastel color schemes and cozy sitting areas. Best of all are the solarium-style windows that allow you to gaze at the sky from the comfort of your plush bed, swaddled in pastel linens and a fluffy down comforter. (The corner Starlight Rooms afford the best views.) Some Starlight Rooms look into nearby office buildings, so close the automatic blinds if you want privacy during business hours. If space is a necessity, the nine two-story townhouse suites are also lovely, with loft bedrooms, winding staircases, full kitchens and living rooms, and private entrances for both floors; some also have two-person jetted soaking tubs.

In keeping with the hotel's wine theme, start your evening with the complimentary sampling of Oregon wines served nightly in the lobby, a decidedly warm overture to a quiet evening in the lap of luxury. In the morning, a complimentary light continental breakfast is served here as well. **PAZZO RISTORANTE** (503-228-1515; www.pazzo.com; moderate to expensive) is adjacent to the hotel's ground floor and serves breakfast, lunch, and dinner daily. The mood here contrasts sharply with the refined elegance of the hotel, embracing you instead with vivid colors and patterns, numerous tables, and steady, lively chatter. Even so, the service is prompt and the northern Italian cuisine is of the finest quality. **422 Southwest Broadway; (503) 228-1212, (800) 243-0555; www.vintageplaza.com; very expensive to unbelievably expensive.**

Romantic Suggestion: Ask about the hotel's romance packages. Amorous extras may include a chilled bottle of champagne, rose petals scattered over your sheets at turndown time, and continental breakfast delivered to your room in the morning.

❤❤❤ **THE LION AND THE ROSE, Portland** Even from a distance it is evident that this grand Queen Anne home holds something special inside. Established in a residential neighborhood on Portland's northeast side, it is conveniently, although not romantically, located near a busy arterial. But from the lofty cupola and turrets to the grand portico entrance, this is a classic Victorian bed and breakfast through and through, with all the appropriate details and decor. Historically accurate furnishings fill every corner, but in a tasteful, uncluttered manner.

Five guest rooms, two with shared baths, are found on the second floor. These spacious, richly decorated rooms exude a sense of comfort and warmth. Standard, snug bathrooms are a drawback but easy to forgive, given the other stylish enhancements: wrought-iron and oak beds, cascading draperies, handsome chandeliers, down comforters, and oversize pillows abound. The loveliest room upstairs is Lavonna, with its original leaded glass windows; white wicker furniture accentuated by a light violet, green, and white color scheme; and a romantic sitting area tucked into the home's tower. Unfortunately, you'll have to do the down-the-hallway dash to reach the bathroom. Although it's off the main living room, the downstairs Rose Room is perfect for those who want to soak in the home's only Jacuzzi tub.

Upon arrival guests are presented with a dessert tea; in the morning, a delicious breakfast is served around a large formal table in the stately dining room. Served on fine china, specialties include strawberry-banana French toast, a Spanish scramble, and baked ginger-pear pancakes.

In almost every aspect The Lion and the Rose is impressive, especially the attention given to keeping the home authentic, not to mention livable. If you have a penchant for the past, there are many reasons to choose this side of town for your comings and goings. **1810 Northeast 15th Street; (503) 287-9245, (800) 955-1647; www.lionrose.com; moderate.**

❤❤ **MACMASTER HOUSE, Portland** Inside and out, this turn-of-the-century mansion is reminiscent of grand old-world living. The formal facade, with its Doric columns and Palladian leaded glass windows, is impressive but welcoming. Inside, everything is grand and stately, although some areas (like the staircase and walls upstairs) are in need of cosmetic touch-ups. The antique-filled parlor is a vortex of Victoriana, so much so that it borders on cluttered. (While everything is spic-and-span, we do feel sympathy for the person who has to dust it all.) The abundance seems to spill over into the dining room and guest rooms as well.

All seven rooms are furnished with a variety of European antiques, four have fireplaces, and most have separate sitting areas. We recommend the two rooms with private baths, one of which is the McCord Suite. This two-bedroom suite is the largest and most attractive room, decorated with a safari mural and enhanced by a deck with a city view. Less extravagant, but more private, is the top-floor Artist's Suite. Reminiscent of a Parisian garret, this sloping-ceiling room features a queen-size old-fashioned iron bed, Swedish fireplace insert, and claw-foot soaking tub.

Every morning the on-staff chef cooks up generous, creative, and (sometimes) award-winning breakfasts. Her pear and B&B liqueur clafoutis recently took the grand prize in a magazine's recipe contest. If you can rise from the breakfast table, venture into the private gardens (which are in need of a manicure) or settle on the veranda, where the buzz of traffic is unlikely to distract you from each other. **1041 Southwest Vista Avenue; (503) 223-7362, (800) 774-9523; www.macmaster.com; inexpensive to moderate; minimum-stay requirement for suites on weekends.**

❤❤❤❣ **PORTLAND'S WHITE HOUSE, Portland** There's no need to venture to Washington, D.C., to see the splendor and elegance of the White House. Portland has its own version, albeit smaller and free from party politics. Built in 1890 by a lumber baron who spared no expense, this stately, gleaming white Greek Revival home exudes grandness, with its original mahogany doors, dozens of leaded crystal windows, oak-inlaid floors, and one-foot-thick walls. The new innkeepers have honored that attention to detail in remodeling and refining the home. Each room is equipped with such luxuries as handmade soaps, 250-count cotton sheets and pillowcases (pressed and starched), and fluffy monogrammed robes.

Guests pull up the circular driveway and enter the home beneath a portico supported by Greek columns. The grand entrance hall dazzles the eye with a cascading staircase and hand-painted murals. To the right, the inviting parlor, with its creamy yellow walls, is an excellent place to catch the afternoon sun and admire the elegant Victorian furniture and Chinese porcelain vases.

The six guest rooms (all with private baths) in the main home are delightful, especially the bright Baron's Room and the Canopy Room (which has a two-person claw-foot tub). Although a bit dark, the Balcony Room is blessed with a private patio underneath the portico—a perfect place for a smooch at night. With the exception of the Hawley Room, all quarters here have claw-foot tubs. For romance, we highly recommend the Carriage House, situated next to the main house. This restored building holds three guest rooms, each with a private bath and separate entrance. By far, our favorite is the downstairs Chauffeur Quarters, done up in shades of cream and periwinkle. You'll want to spend all day in this large room, complete with a king-size four-poster bed, French blinds, a double-headed shower, and Jacuzzi tub.

Remember those *Masterpiece Theatre* dramas where everyone dines in opulence? Breakfast is just that at the White House—but without the need for formal clothing. Seated at the 12-person table in the exquisite dining room, surrounded by a magnificent mirrored buffet, silver tea sets, chandeliers, and flower arrangements, you'll realize that such luxury exists outside of TV. While there are no butlers to serve you, breakfasts are lavish. The house specialty, Native American French toast, made with dark molasses bread, sautéed in orange juice, and topped with Northwest apples and maple syrup, is worthy of an extra lip rating. **1914 Northeast 22nd Avenue; (503) 287-7131, (800) 272-7131; www.portlandswhitehouse.com; moderate to expensive; recommended wedding site.**

❤❤ RIVERPLACE HOTEL, Portland While the riverfront location is wonderful, this first-class urban inn tends to cater to suit-and-tie types more than cuddling couples. But don't despair: The RiverPlace Hotel does have some romantic aspects to complement its views of the Willamette River. However, as Portland's only waterfront hotel, it also has the luxury of commanding unreasonably high prices for such views.

Of the hotel's 84 rooms and suites, the junior suites and two-room parlor suites are the most interesting in layout, but the bathrooms are just standard. Spring-like colors of robin's-egg blue, butter yellow, and creamy beige adorn each room in different combinations. No room stands out as more romantic than the others, except for the fireplace and grand suites, both with price tags that will drain your wallet.

Whichever room you call home, make a reservation to visit the private spa with sauna and two-person jetted tub. Dim the lights and enjoy this room together. Or opt for a "Do Not Disturb" romance package that delivers chilled champagne to your door and breakfast the next morning from **THE ESPLANADE RESTAURANT** (see Restaurant Kissing). A reservation in the spa is also included. The hotel's courtyard, tucked away on the second floor, is a perfect, but not necessarily private, place for a kiss. (Rooms that don't have a waterfront view offer either courtyard or city views.) If a healthy dose of patriotism gets your hearts pounding, book a room overlooking the flag pavilion. Upon request, the hotel will fly your country's flag in your honor. **1510 Southwest Harbor Way; (503) 228-3233, (800) 227-1333; www. riverplacehotel.com; very expensive to unbelievably expensive.**

Restaurant Kissing

❤❤ ALEXANDER'S, Portland Although Portland's Hilton Hotel may not be a best place to kiss, its restaurant is worth a visit. High above the city, Alexander's affords incredible views of the Northwest's snowcapped mountains: Mount Hood, Mount St. Helens, Mount Rainier, and Mount Adams are all within sight on clear evenings. The L-shaped dining room is nicely put together, with plush gray carpet, potted plants, and cherry-wood accents. Draped in scarlet linens and topped with fresh flowers, the tables are beautifully inviting, although they are arranged a bit more closely than true romantics might prefer. Choose from a variety of seafood dishes, stuffed quail, and filet mignon. Then sit back, enjoy the company, and take in the panoramic view of the city. **921 Southwest Sixth Avenue, on the 23rd floor of the Hilton Hotel; (503) 226-1611, ext. 2190; dinner Tuesday–Saturday.**

❤❤❤❤ **ATWATER'S RESTAURANT AND BAR, Portland** We are happy to report that Atwater's is one rooftop restaurant where the quality of the food equals the quality of the view. Both are excellent. High atop Portland's tallest building, the dining room resembles an exclusive uptown residence. From the Oriental accents to the silver serviceware, plush carpeting, and other extravagant touches, it is clear that this is an ultra-formal dining establishment. In the center of the room stands a glass-enclosed wine display, skillfully etched with vines and grapes, as a tribute to the region's wine-growing achievements. Pale green walls are accentuated by blond wood, and tables are draped with white linens and set aglow by candlelight. Two-person window seats are the best vantage point for watching the setting sun spread shades of yellow, pink, and violet over the evening sky. On cloudy days, watch the city lights flicker to life below you.

Atwater's offers a tempting and ever-changing selection of Pacific Northwest seafood, artistically presented. Try an innovative appetizer such as peppered prawns with mint, lime, and lentil salad, or choose a more traditional starter like the Dungeness crab bisque. It's difficult to decide between the dinner entrées; however, the honey-cured pork loin, the ahi tuna with artichoke risotto, and the wild mushroom cannelloni are as delicious as they sound. Top off the view with a terrific dessert, including panna cotta surrounded by succulent strawberries. **111 Southwest Fifth Avenue, on the 30th floor of the U.S. Bancorp Tower; (503) 275-3600; www.atwaters.com; expensive to very expensive; dinner daily; recommended wedding site.**

Romantic Note: Wednesday through Saturday nights, enjoy live jazz in the nearby bar area. Although it can get a bit smoky at times, the wood-accented bar offers the same spectacular view as the restaurant and is an attractive spot for a nightcap.

❤❤❤❤ **CAFÉ DES AMIS, Portland** Café des Amis, an effective blend of Northwest atmosphere and gourmet French cuisine, is considered one of the best dinner spots in Portland. And, with a name that means "café of friends," it's the perfect place to bring someone you're friendly with. Behind the ivy-covered facade are two small, simply appointed dining rooms. Well-spaced tables, sparse cream-colored walls, and starched white linen tablecloths, along with a no-music policy, offer nothing to distract you from what is truly important: each other.

A sophisticated wait staff delivers intricate entrées to your candlelit table. The pâtés are delicious; the duck, lamb, and salmon are perfectly prepared; and the New York steak is the thickest and most tender you may ever experience. Go ahead and try the succulent "40 cloves of garlic" chicken breast. Baking subdues the garlic and adds a sweetness that won't require breath mints later on. Our only complaint about this wonderful restaurant is the inconsistency in portion sizes, which range from hearty (the braised lamb shanks were a meal and a half) to skimpy (coin-sized crab cakes). However, the delectable desserts, including a pot de crème du jour, are sure to make your heart go pitter-patter. **1987 Northwest Kearney Street; (503) 295-6487; expensive; dinner Monday–Saturday.**

❤❤❤❤ **COUVRON, Portland** Blink and you might miss the small, unassuming entrance to this fabulous French restaurant. Only a blue awning over the door and an unobtrusive window sign invite you inside; but once there, you'll be delighted to discover that the subtle theme continues. Weave past the tiny entry and small kitchen into one of two dining rooms. Both have antique-replica mirrors; soothing blue and beige tones; and a handful of tables that are closely arranged, but not uncomfortable. Delicate drapes diffuse outside lights and commotion, while light classical music complements the softness of the interior. On the walls, vintage postcards and photographs of the French town of Couvron illustrate life in the old country.

Sample the contemporary French cuisine by either indulging in a seven- to eight-course seasonal tasting menu or choosing à la carte items. The house specialty is fresh foie gras, served a variety of ways, including topped with crayfish and bathed in a lobster–port wine sauce. Other notables include the ravioli of wild mushrooms bathed in a crème fraîche and sweet pea sauce, and the Oregon fallow venison. Thoughts of sweet endings start halfway through your meal. Around appetizer time, place your order for a dessert soufflé. Simple and light, this dessert will leave you floating on cloud nine. **1126 Southwest 18th Avenue; (503) 225-1844; very expensive; dinner Tuesday–Saturday.**

❤❤❤ **THE ESPLANADE RESTAURANT, Portland** The Esplanade just may be the most romantic locale along the RiverPlace boardwalk. Tucked into the **RIVERPLACE HOTEL** (see Hotel/Bed and Breakfast Kissing), the Esplanade sets the scene for romance with large windows, cloud frescos on the ceiling, and sienna-colored walls seasoned with large, modern artwork. Comfortable burgundy chairs accent blue tablecloths topped with fresh flowers. For a romantic evening, the Esplanade has that quintessential "corner table." However, the semi-enclosed space is near the entrance and large enough to seat six, so everyone gets a glimpse of the two of you. No matter where you sit, most tables offer unobstructed views of the marina below, the Willamette River, and the lighted Hawthorne Bridge at night.

Celebrate the ambience with grilled salmon accompanied by yellow pepper coulis and roasted garlic butter, or try the smoked mushroom ravioli tossed in extra-virgin olive oil, feta cheese, garlic, and fresh Roma tomato purée. Across the hotel's lobby in the bar, cozy up to the fireplace and listen to live jazz Wednesday through Sunday evenings. **1510 Southwest Harbor Way, at the RiverPlace Hotel; (503) 295-6166, (800) 227-1333; expensive; breakfast and dinner daily, lunch weekdays, brunch Sunday seasonally.**

❤❤❤❤ **GENOA, Portland** Genoa has the distinction of being rated one of the best dining experiences in Portland. That's easy to understand once you step from busy Belmont Street into this cozy, candlelit restaurant with only ten tables. The decor is simple, with chocolate-brown walls, a charming copper pot collection, and a handwoven Persian rug spanning the back wall. Best of all, the restaurant is romantically lit and pleasantly quiet. No music distracts you from your food or your tablemate.

For more than two decades, Genoa has served seven-course Italian dinners, and there are no plans to change this tradition. Chefs rotate the menu biweekly, highlighting such delicacies as mushroom-stuffed quail, striped bass topped with baby artichokes, and tenderloin steak sautéed with a caper sauce. Dessert showcases Italy's best, including a coffee crème brûlée that tastes like that perfect creamy cup of java. An enormous bowl of exotic fruit finishes the meal.

We found the two-person staff friendly, professional, and informative. While the menu is presented verbally in Italian, a detailed description in English follows. **2832 Southeast Belmont Street; (503) 238-1464; very expensive; dinner Monday–Saturday.**

Romantic Suggestion: For a before- or after-dinner drink, venture to the Victorian parlor tucked in the back of the restaurant. There's plenty of culinary literature to browse through, but a kiss may be more entertaining.

❤❤❤ **HEATHMAN RESTAURANT, Portland** A contemporary interior of teak and marble sets the stage at this lively, three-tiered downtown restaurant. Black leather booths, tables draped with white linens, and Japanese vases with fresh flowers fill the dining room, while the glass-enclosed exhibition kitchen lets you see the chefs at work. Glass sectional dividers and large windows, etched with stylish art deco designs, allow light to flow effortlessly about the space. One of the restaurant's most notable features (besides the food) is the artwork decorating the walls; Andy Warhol's "Endangered Species" series brings color to the otherwise understated decor, and continues into the lobby of the adjacent hotel (see Hotel/Bed and Breakfast Kissing). A small bar area next to the restaurant is a cozy spot for an after-dinner drink. The only drawback here is the business conversations taking place around you.

Attentive service and skillfully prepared French dishes make for a memorable evening of fine dining at the Heathman Restaurant. Just about anything on the menu will be worth your while. Tempting entrées include duck confit on a lentil salad, grilled halibut piccata, and smoked-salmon fettuccine. Breakfasts are as elegant and carefully created as the dinners. **1001 Southwest Broadway, at The Heathman Hotel; (503) 241-4100, (800) 551-0011; moderate to expensive; breakfast, lunch, and dinner daily.**

✿✿⁴ HIGGINS RESTAURANT AND BAR, Portland

Looking for a special dinner spot after a busy day in the city? Look no further than Higgins. Unwind in the simple elegance of this modestly appointed downtown restaurant. The main dining area is tastefully adorned with purple and green swaths of fabric, decorative vases, and potted plants, and polished wood accents throughout lend the interior a glowing warmth. Two floors of dining rooms are filled with white linen–covered tables and booths, set beneath tiny triangular lamps. A lower, separate room is more intimate, with dark wood paneling and candlelight.

Seafood at Higgins is always fresh and skillfully prepared. We recommend the pan-fried Alaskan razor clams or the broiled pavé of Alaskan halibut presented with olive and garlic mashed potatoes, basil vinaigrette, and vegetables. A honey-glazed loin of pork served with grilled Walla Walla onions, ginger-plum chutney, and almond couscous is a wonderful alternative to fish, and desserts are superb. **1239 Southwest Broadway; (503) 222-9070; expensive; lunch Monday–Friday, dinner daily.**

✿✿⁴ IL FORNAIO, Portland

Although its name means "the baker" in Italian, this upscale eatery is not your average bakery. Sure, it has a deli area, the *panetteria*, which offers a wide selection of fresh breads and pastries, sandwiches, salads, Italian coffees, and beverages; but it's better known for its dining accommodations. Il Fornaio caters to diners' ever-changing romantic moods with casual, lighthearted lunches or quiet romantic dinners.

The pale yellow exterior matches the sunny disposition of the interior. Skylights and abundant windows allow sunlight to stream in unhindered, while clusters of dried flowers, garlic cloves, hanging baskets, and copper pots adorn the walls. To the right is a casual area peppered with little wooden tables for two. Maroon booths line a curved wall of windows, and next to the bustling kitchen area is an open bar hosting twin television sets. For more intimate interludes, you may wish to sit in the formal dining area to the left of the entrance. Here, black-and-white photographs have been enlarged to fill the red brick walls. White linens, elegant sconces, and views of lush greenery create a more refined setting in which to enjoy the zesty Italian cuisine. Better yet, there's the enclosed brick patio out back, with a roof that opens to let in the night sky and a fireplace to keep you toasty.

Both lunch and dinner feature superb entrées ranging from pizza to pasta to rotisserie duck, rabbit, and poultry. Try the ravioli filled with fresh Maine lobster or the pasta shells stuffed with smoked mozzarella, eggplant, tomato, and spices, all baked in the wood-burning oven. Cool off the evening with a scoop of creamy Italian gelato. No matter what kind of romantic mood you're in, Il Fornaio fits the bill. **115 Northwest 22nd Avenue; (503) 248-9400; moderate; lunch and dinner daily.**

☙☙❧ **LONDON GRILL, Portland** An elegant refuge from the city streets, the London Grill's plush dining room is a den of refinement. Crystal chandeliers, large floral arrangements, ornate wall sconces, and finely upholstered armchairs help set a formal, sophisticated mood. Visitors dine by candlelight beneath an arched ceiling, surrounded by lovely wood paneling. Although extremely tasteful and polished, this dining room is almost too formal to be considered cozy or intimate.

Interesting menu choices range from fresh ahi tuna, sautéed with garlic and ginger and served with a lemon Szechuan sauce, to London Grill steak Diane, prepared tableside with mushrooms, garlic, shallots, and a hint of brandy. Specialty Northwest items, such as Oregon-raised ostrich, round out the continental menu. At one time, *Glamour* magazine listed the London Grill as one of the six most romantic restaurants in the United States. We're not nearly that enthusiastic, as our lip rating indicates, but you certainly should give it a try and compare notes. **309 Southwest Broadway, at the Benson Hotel; (503) 295-4110; expensive; breakfast and dinner daily, lunch Monday–Saturday, brunch Sunday.**

☙☙❧ **MARRAKESH MOROCCAN RESTAURANT, Portland** Eating with your fingers has never been more entertaining or romantic than at this Moroccan restaurant. Don't let the dark windows detour you from entering; once inside you'll be quickly swallowed up in an inviting darkness. Here, the aroma of Moroccan spices ignites the air, dissonant music dominates, and, on weekend nights, belly dancers entertain. Sitting in the room is like being in a plush tent: Every inch of the interior is draped with intricate Moroccan tapestries and rugs, including billowing fabrics on the ceiling. Cushy couches line the perimeter of the dining room, while small, beanbag-like cushions and leather pillows are strewn about knee-high tables. Big baskets throughout serve as decoration while holding warm homemade bread.

Before you begin dinner, a waiter pours warm water over your hands and presents you with a big towel. Choose from an à la carte menu featuring shish kabobs, lamb dishes, and couscous with vegetables, or indulge in the five-course feast with a choice of several dishes. Don't worry about hand holding after a meal eaten with your fingers. The waiter performs the warm-water ritual one more time before the grand finale—fresh mint tea and Moroccan pastries. **1201 Northwest 21st Avenue; (503) 248-9442; moderate; dinner daily.**

Romantic Note: We hate to spoil the fun, but yes, utensils are available upon request.

☙☙ **PALEY'S PLACE, Portland** Portland's Nob Hill is blessed with many lovingly renovated neighborhood shops and restaurants, several of which are among the best Portland has to offer. Paley's Place lives up to this area's reputation with its dedication to fine cooking in a relaxed setting. The attention given to maintaining an attractive, unpretentious place is reflected in the modest interior, which is filled with white linen–covered tables, hardwood floors, large art pieces, and such whimsical knickknacks as a door-handle collection. Past the bar area is a cozy back room with four tables that allow more private dining.

The menu offers well-prepared and graciously served Pacific Northwest cuisine with a regional and seasonal twist. Begin your meal with a goat cheese salad or the soup of the day. Dinner entrées range from pasta to duckling confit to braised halibut. Save room for dessert here, for the soufflés will sweep you off your feet. **1204 Northwest 21st Avenue; (503) 243-2403; www. citysearch.com/pdx/paleysplace; expensive; lunch Tuesday–Friday, dinner Tuesday–Saturday.**

❀❀❀ **PLAINFIELDS' MAYUR CUISINE OF INDIA, Portland** Very few dining rooms double as art galleries. Yet this fine-dining Indian restaurant manages to be both in an elegant and inviting manner. Resembling a mini-museum, the interior features large art pieces depicting characters from Hindu mythology who dance and pose sensuously. Simple white satin drapes, white walls, and English-style tables and chairs spaced comfortably apart do nothing to distract the eye from the exotic works.

A feast of Indian delicacies, from curries to tandoori chicken, is presented on fine European bone china. As you dine, watch chefs prepare and then bake food inside the tandoori ovens, which reach temperatures of 1,000 degrees. After dinner, cool off upstairs in the Indian art gallery (no dining) featuring everything from small hand-carved bookmarks to museum-quality masterpieces. **852 Southwest 21st Street; (503) 223-2995; moderate to expensive; dinner daily.**

❀❀❀ **TABLE FOR TWO, Portland** Lunch reservations for two are the only kind accepted here, and windowside seating is a given. Inside this small home, which houses a catering company, the dining room has just one table, two chairs, and one large window. However, obtaining such desirable reservations any time of year can be difficult if you don't plan three months ahead. Flexibility counts, as there are sometimes cancellations.

Butter-colored walls, low lighting, high ceilings, floral linens, and mismatched china create a cozy feeling. The single table is adorned with a vase of fresh flowers and is set by a window looking out onto a sunporch that's in need of a paint job. A divider-screen shelters your eyes from the chaotic kitchen, but delicious aromas drift freely through the house.

What arrives at your table is the chef's choice. Most likely the garden's herbs and seasonal ingredients will be integrated in such creative dishes as grilled salmon wrapped in grape leaves, sautéed asparagus with fresh fennel, luscious strawberry tartlets, and kiwi sorbet. Spend hours enjoying the four-course lunch with a chef-recommended wine. After eating at this house, you might not want to go home. **Briggs and Crampton Caterers; 1902 Northwest 24th Street; (503) 223-8690; expensive; reservations required; lunch Tuesday–Friday; call for seasonal closures.**

❧❧❧ **ZEFIRO, Portland** Sleek, modern, and minimalist describe the decor of this popular Nob Hill bistro. Simple black chairs and white tablecloths set off by celadon walls create an atmosphere that's soft and subtle. Black track lighting crisscrosses overhead, looking like abstract tree branches. The bar area is more informal but no less sophisticated, with round copper tabletops and geometric wall designs. Throughout the restaurant, the color scheme is further enhanced by black-and-white photographs on the walls. A taupe-colored curtain frames the back wall and provides a backdrop for a row of cozy black booths where friends and couples can convene.

Drawing on Mediterranean and Asian influences, the menu tantalizes taste buds with an avocado, mango, and watercress salad in a ginger-lime vinaigrette; salmon carpaccio served with a spicy citrus salad; and Moroccan chicken tagine. For the grande finale, go tropical with a trio of lemongrass, ginger, and coconut ice creams or satisfy the "Coffee or tea?" question all at once with chai ice cream in espresso. **500 Northwest 21st Avenue; (503) 226-3394; expensive; lunch Monday–Friday, dinner Monday–Saturday.**

Outdoor Kissing

❧❧❧ **CRYSTAL SPRINGS RHODODENDRON GARDEN, Portland** If pink and red are the traditional colors of love, then love's a-bloomin' here. Located at the back of the Eastmoreland Golf Course, this lovely seven-acre garden contains an outstanding collection of red, pink, and white rhododendrons as well as colorful azaleas and other plants and trees.

Stroll past the waterfall along shaded pathways to brilliantly clear Crystal Springs Lake. An abundance of waterfowl feed and nest here, including mallards, buffleheads, and the easily overlooked pied-billed grebe. There are also flocks of little kids who delight in feeding the ducks. For some solitude, venture to the northern end of the park where a quiet lagoon awaits with plenty of lakeside benches. Unfortunately, a wire fence around the lake detracts a bit from the beauty. Regardless of such an eyesore, the rhodies are delightful and all those romantic colors just might set you in the mood for love. **Southeast 28th Avenue, north of Southeast Woodstock Boulevard near Reed College; (503) 771-8386; $2 entrance fee March–Labor Day, free admission Tuesday–Wednesday; open daily; recommended wedding site.** *From downtown Portland, take Highway 99 east and turn west onto 28th Avenue. Watch for signs to the garden.*

❀❀❀❀ **ELK ROCK GARDEN, Portland** Elk Rock Garden is hard to find and equally hard to forget. Designed for strolling hand in hand, the private garden has plenty of gravel pathways weaving in and out of dense forests and across grassy lawns. A stately gray home, modeled after a Scottish manor, resides on the premises, along with 35 magnolia trees—favorites of a past owner. Other interesting trees include giant sequoias, Spanish firs, and Oregon oaks. Follow the trail along the cliff, past the fish pond, and out to a point that offers lovely views of the Willamette River and Elk Rock below. If you are lucky, the two of you might have this green gem all to yourselves. **11800 Southwest Military Lane; (503) 636-5613; donations accepted; open daily.** *From downtown Portland, take Highway 43 south past the Sellwood Bridge. Turn left onto Military Road, go 20 feet, turn right onto Military Lane, and follow it to the end.*

❀❀❀❀ **INTERNATIONAL ROSE TEST GARDENS, Portland** William Shakespeare once wrote, "Of all flowers methinks a rose is best." Agree? Then journey to these terraced gardens where row upon row of "the best" await. After sniffing your way through the fragrant and colorful petals and enjoying views of Portland, journey down to the Shakespearean Gardens. Here, tall hedges enclose a delightful grassy garden filled with graceful trees, perennials, annuals, and two wooden benches. Roses aren't necessarily the centerpiece here, but romance can be. **400 Southwest Kingston, in Washington Park; (503) 823-3636; free admission; open daily.** *From downtown Portland, drive west on Burnside Street. Turn left onto Tichner Drive and then right onto Kingston. The gardens are on the left in Washington Park.*

❀❀❀❀ **THE JAPANESE GARDENS, Portland** These outstanding gardens are the ultimate place for rest and reflection. Five and a half acres of lush lawns, forested alcoves, moss-covered pagodas, and carefully sculpted shrubs blanket a hilltop in Washington Park, at a place where heaven and earth seem to meet. Considered one of the most authentic Japanese gardens outside Japan, this oasis of greenery remains relatively secluded from the rest of the park. Don't miss the flat garden—a sea of raked sand outlining islands of greenery. Small streams and ponds sparkle throughout, and a magnificent waterfall tumbles over moss-covered boulders into a koi pond. Take in the sights of Portland and distant Mount Hood from the pavilion's deck or find one of the hidden benches, tucked among the trees, and soak in the sounds of serenity. **611 Southwest Kingston Avenue, in Washington Park; (503) 223-1321; $6 entrance fee; open daily except major holidays.** *From downtown Portland, drive west on Burnside Street. Turn left onto Tichner Drive and then right onto Kingston. The gardens are on the right in Washington Park.*

❀❀❀❀ **MACLEAY PARK, Portland** Macleay Park is really a park within a park, as well as a gorgeous example of nature's ability to thrive in the midst of a metropolis. This lush green wilderness is strewn with 152 acres of surging creeks and hiking trails. Visit some of the wildlife viewing areas or, if you're really ambitious, follow the Wildwood Trail approximately 13 miles to **PITTOCK MANSION** (see below). Macleay Park is just one of the almost limitless doorways into Forest Park. This immense park rests on the northeast face of the Tualatin Mountains and is the largest city wilderness in the United States. It affords so many kissing places that if you're not careful, you might just get tired out. **Free admission.** *Enter Macleay Park off the Thurman Bridge near Franklin and 32nd Street Northwest, or at the end of Forest Park in northwest Portland off Cornell Road.*

Romantic Note: Another doorway into Forest Park is **COLLINS' SANCTUARY** (5151 Northwest Cornell Road; 503-292-6855), run by the Portland Audubon Society. This area of untamed landscape is not very well known, even though its secluded beauty lies near the heart of the city. Intriguing trails and paths lead to private corners of this 67-acre wildlife area.

❧❧ **PITTOCK MANSION, Portland** This stately home, replete with beveled glass windows and a red-tiled roof, is essentially a museum. A walking tour through the 1914 mansion reveals its regal interior, ornately appointed with embossed wallpapers, hardwood floors, velvet furniture, and Oriental rugs. Among the handsome rooms are a wood-paneled library, a grand old parlor, and an elegant dining room eternally set for a formal occasion. While the interior is fantastic, do spend some time exploring the mansion's manicured grounds and wooded pathways. It's here that you'll find beautifully framed views of Portland through the trees, as well as a place to kiss. **3229 Northwest Pittock Drive; (503) 823-3624; $4.50 entrance fee; open daily.** *From downtown Portland, drive approximately two miles west on Burnside Street, following signs to the mansion.*

Romantic Note: Almost hidden from sight amid the foliage surrounding Pittock Mansion, the **GATE LODGE RESTAURANT** (503-823-3627; inexpensive) is a delightful place for lunch or afternoon tea. The interior pales in comparison to the Pittock Mansion, but it's a pleasant place to enjoy a quiche or hot crab sandwich. Call for reservations.

❧ **RIVERPLACE, Portland** RiverPlace doesn't seem the least bit romantic to us. How can a half-mile-long arcade of condominiums, stores, and restaurants be intimate and endearing? But so many couples can be seen strolling hand in hand along this Willamette River development that we can't ignore its apparent romantic appeal. Enough options are available here to offer something for everyone, regardless of taste or budget.

RiverPlace begins with the **RIVERPLACE HOTEL** (see Hotel/Bed and Breakfast Kissing) at the northern tip of the walk. This is a European-style building with overpriced, hotel-like accommodations. We do, however, encourage you to try the distinctive, much-admired restaurant adjacent to the lobby, called **THE ESPLANADE** (see Restaurant Kissing).

As you continue walking, you'll have a view of the water on one side and a series of handsome condominiums on the other, along with a dozen or so boutiques and eateries. Farther down, you'll pass more restaurants with water views. The constant hum of traffic is not exactly tranquil but, romantic or not, RiverPlace is worth a stroll—and perhaps a stop somewhere along the way for a glass of wine, a cappuccino, or whatever else may catch your fancy. *From downtown Portland, take Southwest Market Street east to the river, where it dead-ends at RiverPlace.*

❤❤❤ **SAUVIE ISLAND, Portland** When you feel the need for wide-open empty space, drive to this vast pastoral oasis. Sauvie Island is a popular Portland getaway, but its size ensures that you'll never feel crowded. You can enjoy relatively isolated beaches and numerous hiking trails through wetlands, pastures, oak woodlands, and spotty sections of coniferous forest. More stretches of sandy beach can be found on Oak Island, a much smaller land mass connected to the northeast end of Sauvie Island by a natural bridge. *Take Highway 30 north to the Sauvie Island Bridge, about 11 miles from downtown Portland.*

Romantic Warning: Sauvie Island can be shrouded in fog when other parts of the area are clear. Check the horizon before setting out. Also, you should be aware that gasoline and drinking water are not available on the island.

❤❤❤ **TRYON CREEK STATE PARK, Portland** This 645-acre state park is small enough for an afternoon walk, but large enough that you can be alone with your love. Well, somewhat alone. All sorts of critters live in this dark, dense forest, from noisy jays to silent deer. Douglas firs dominate the forest's upper reaches, while wildflowers and ferns blanket the mossy ground. There are 14 miles of trails to explore, some of which are muddy, so be prepared. Pick up a trail map at the Nature Center so you don't wander too far away. **11321 Southwest Terwilliger Boulevard; free admission; open daily.** *Head south from Portland on Interstate 5 to the Terwilliger exit. Travel two and a half miles due south on Southwest Terwilliger Boulevard to get to the park.*

"You are always new. The

last of your kisses was ever

the sweetest . . ."

John Keats

Willamette Valley

A 30-minute drive southwest from Portland brings you into the Willamette Valley, home of the famous Oregon wineries. Embraced on the west by the gentle countenance of the Coast Range and on the east by the glacial peaks of the Cascades, this area has much to treasure. You could call this region the Sonoma Valley of the Northwest, but that wouldn't do it justice. The Willamette Valley has smaller, family-owned wineries and a few corporate giants, and the wineries, although young, offer an acclaimed selection of wines any enophile would appreciate.

Numerous wineries are scattered throughout this picturesque area, each with its own attitude regarding the art of winemaking. Many of them feature vineyard-draped hillsides, a rathskeller-style tasting room, or a restful country setting. Still others are plain roadside buildings that make up for their lack of atmosphere with the excellence of their wines. Whether you choose to visit one or all, whether you choose to consume or not, your entire winery-hopping tour will be an intoxicating joy. And if you're pleased by what you taste, purchase a bottle or two for a toast to happy memories of a vintage visit.

To better acquaint yourselves with the myriad wineries in the region, contact the **OREGON WINE ADVISORY BOARD** (1200 Northwest Naito Parkway, Suite 400, Portland, OR 97209; 800-242-2363). Its excellent yearly publication, *Discover Oregon Wineries,* will help you with your tour. **GRAPE ESCAPE WINERY TOURS** (503-282-4262) provides transportation from Portland and offers full-day or afternoon tours of several wineries in the Willamette Valley. Appetizers, a gourmet sit-down lunch, and dessert are included in the tour price ($75 per person). Tours are customized to what guests want to see and sip. Call for more details. If you'd like to explore the area by less conventional means, book a hot-air balloon flight with **VISTA BALLOON ADVENTURES, INC.** (503-625-7385, 800-622-2309) out of Newberg. Flights depart at the crack of dawn and conclude with a champagne picnic lunch. A ride in the sky is serenity and exhilaration all wrapped into one . . . much like a kiss.

Wine Kissing

Considered the most sensual and satisfying of all wines, pinot noir is the Willamette Valley's shining star. Unlike its big, bold cousins merlot and cabernet sauvignon, a glass of pinot noir is delicate and full of nuances. Such characteristics spill over into Willamette's grape-growing region. A mild climate, influenced by the nearby Pacific, provides a long, warm, and gentle grape-growing season in the valley. And what's good for the grapes is also good for the visitor. Such mildness makes any season a wonderful time to tour the Willamette Valley. There are more than 50 wineries to choose from and, like wine, some have more character than others. Go on your own romantic expedition or try out these places for a kiss.

❦❦❦ **CHATEAU BENOIT, Carlton** From this hilltop winery, pastoral views and exquisite sunsets over the Coast Range complement a glass of wine. There are plenty of picnic tables in front of the French-style chateau, which doubles as a tasting room and facade for the wine warehouse. Sample their famous Müller-Thurgau, a light, easy-to-sip wine that's almost as sweet as a kiss. **6580 Northeast Mineral Springs Road; (503) 864-2991, (800) 248-4835; open 10 a.m.–5 p.m. daily; recommended wedding site.**

❦❦❦❦ **MONTINORE VINEYARDS, Forest Grove** After driving up a road lined with 100-year-old oak trees you'll come upon what we consider one of the loveliest wineries around. Montinore's grand Victorian mansion graces a hilltop surrounded by expansive manicured lawns and flanked by a pool house (sans pool), tennis courts, and a sitting area. However, the secret romantic spot here is the grotto. With a bottle of wine in one hand and your sweetheart's hand in the other, find your way to this tree-enclosed hideaway behind the tennis courts. Sit within a thatched gazebo and listen to wind chimes, the bubbling of the small pond, and the bamboo rustling in the breeze. **3663 Southwest Dilley Road; (503) 359-5012; open noon–5 p.m. daily April– December, open noon–5 p.m. weekends January–March.**

❦❦❦ **REX HILL VINEYARDS, Newberg** Picture terraced plateaus of grass divided by railroad ties descending into a forest of firs. Such is a snapshot of Rex Hill's lawn and garden located below the hillside vineyards. While wonderful for picnics and sunbathing, the grounds don't offer much privacy. Oh well, one must sacrifice something for such surroundings. If the weather is blah, venture inside the delightful tasting room, which features a massive stone fireplace, antiques, tapestry rugs, and wine barrels displayed in a brick-lined cellar. For a new perspective, Rex Hill Vineyard offers champagne breakfast/ hot-air balloon rides from late spring to early fall. After getting up with the birds, you'll be soaring with them. **30835 North Highway 99W; (503) 538- 0666; www.rexhill.com; open 11 a.m.–5 p.m. daily.**

❦❦❦ **TORII MOR WINERY, Dundee** Sometimes the most difficult search yields the greatest reward. Such is the case with this small winery hidden high in the hills. But once you've dusted off from the long gravel-road ride, a delightful Japanese garden—complete with a small rock garden, grassy alcoves, and moss-covered pathways—awaits. Best of all, you'll most likely have the place to yourselves, along with your bottle of pinot noir, of course. Walk over to the vineyard, where spectacular views will take your breath away. Samples of Torii Mor's high-end wines can be sipped in a Japanese-style tasting room adjacent to the garden. **18325 Northeast Fairview Drive; (503) 538-2279; open noon–5 p.m. weekends May–November.**

❦❦ **TUALATIN VINEYARDS, Forest Grove** Sip to your hearts' content in the pine-paneled tasting room, or sit outside in the picnic area shaded by cherry trees that overlook the valley and 85 acres of vineyards. **10850 Northwest Seavey Road; (503) 357-5005; open weekends Memorial Day–Thanksgiving.**

Hotel/Bed and Breakfast Kissing

Newberg

❦❦ **THE PARTRIDGE FARM BED AND BREAKFAST, Newberg** There's nothing fancy about this small farmhouse, and that suits us just fine. In keeping with traditional country decor, this three-bedroom inn is simple, unassuming, and charming. Two suites have a sitting room, but the single bedroom seems more spacious. All have a private bath, a quilt-covered queen bed, and a sprinkling of antique furniture. The TV/VCR can be found in the small downstairs parlor.

Breakfasts are farm fresh . . . literally. The proprietors pick berries, fruit, and herbs from the garden for muffins, pancakes, and other home-baked sweets. Plans are in the works to raise chickens for eggs, too. Enjoy it all in the dining area accented with a small wood-burning stove, farm artifacts, and dried flowers hanging from the rafters. In summer, breakfast is served on the slightly rundown backyard patio. In fact, the entire exterior needs a little freshening up and a new coat of yellow paint. However, the five acres of gardens and trees—tended to by a master gardener—might turn your attention away.

The Partridge Farm is affiliated with **REX HILL VINEYARDS** (see Wine Kissing), just a half mile up the road; the owners will occasionally break open a bottle for summertime tastings. **4300 East Portland Road; (503) 538-2050; moderate.**

Romantic Warning: The farm borders traffic-happy Highway 99W. Tall trees block some, but not all, of the noise.

❦❦❦❦ **SPRINGBROOK HAZELNUT FARM, Newberg** A Craftsman-style farmhouse, nestled among 10 acres of lawn dotted with enormous old trees, is the centerpiece of this working hazelnut farm. The home itself is extraordinary, with a bright yellow entryway opening onto a terrace overlooking the grounds. While the four rooms and upstairs suite here are pleasant, they are most appropriate for couples traveling together or serious wine connoisseurs who are more interested in sips than lips.

For the ultimate in romance and privacy, however, the Carriage House and Cottage take the cake (hazelnut, of course). The two abodes are similar in design, with Craftsman-style furnishings creating a timeless touch. Both have fir floors, large windows, and charming tiled kitchens with glass-front cabinets and big butcher-block tables. Other similarities include gas fireplaces, queen-size beds, and cream-colored walls with forest-green trim. Those who need space will want to book the Carriage House, which holds a large bathroom, complete with claw-foot tub, and a spacious bedroom and living room.

But is bigger better? We like the quaint, cozy cottage just a little more, with its rose garden, terra-cotta-tiled bathroom, and dining room designed for two. Best of all, the bathroom, bedroom, and dining room overlook a field of daffodils and a duck pond ringed with yellow irises. If you're lucky, you might see the resident blue heron or hear the call of red-winged blackbirds. What you won't see or hear are turbo tubs, telephones, or TVs in either hideaway.

Since privacy is a priority at both the Carriage House and Cottage, breakfast is already in the fridge when you arrive. But just try waiting until morning to devour the hard-boiled eggs, croissants, scones, fresh fruits, and the asparagus, ham, and cheese crêpes. Be sure to grind up the coffee beans and pour a little hazelnut flavoring into your brew.

We were tempted to stay inside the scrumptious cottage all day, but the grounds beckoned. Stroll through the hazelnut orchard to the adjacent Rex Hill Vineyards; lounge by the pool or plant yourself in the Adirondack chairs, which dot the estate; and get a little nutty while nibbling on hazelnuts—compliments of Springbrook. Also, be sure to ask to see the surprise in the barn. Words can't describe it. **30295 North Highway 99W; (503) 538-4606, (800) 793-8528; moderate to expensive.**

Romantic Warning: Highway 99W runs nearby, but luckily the traffic diminishes as night progresses; besides, this farm is so enchanting, you won't notice it.

Restaurant Kissing

❀ **THE COFFEE COTTAGE, Newberg** Need a coffee fix while in wine country? Stop by this small cafe (right off busy Highway 99W) for a java fill-up. What this place lacks in romance, it makes up for in interesting drinks such as the Razzamatazz (espresso, raspberry syrup, and chocolate) or the Iced Mocha Tree Climber—a blend of spicy chocolate, coconut, and espresso over cold milk and ice. Don't pass up the pastries, soups, sandwiches, and desserts either. The cottage also doubles as a book- and card store, although the merchandise looks like it was added as an afterthought.

Like all coffee places worth their salt, the Coffee Cottage opens at 6 A.M. Monday–Saturday for early birds. **808 East Hancock; (503) 538-5126; inexpensive; open daily.**

Dundee

Restaurant Kissing

❀❀❀ **RED HILLS PROVINCIAL DINING, Dundee** If Craftsman homes are your fancy, this restaurant is a lovely example of the wonders of restoration and reuse. Two dining rooms, appointed with linen-covered tables and fresh flowers, highlight the beauty and functionality of the home's original design features, including a built-in buffet and drawers (in the front room) and leaded crystal windows throughout. Chocolate and cream-colored walls add to the warmth of this home. Unfortunately, the Red Hills location, right above Highway 99, leaves a bit to be desired.

Crab cakes were generous, but please, hold the mayo in the sun-dried tomato aioli. Our rare filet mignon with diable sauce arrived in perfect condition and thoroughly heated, but why the delicious roast pork tenderloin with caramelized onions and olives arrived at a tepid temperature remains a mystery. End your meal with a sweet slice of pecan pie. **276 Highway 99W; (503) 538-8224; moderate; lunch Tuesday–Friday, dinner Tuesday–Sunday.**

Unrated TINA'S, Dundee Locals rave about the food here, and we did too in our last edition. But when we arrived this year, Tina's was under renovation. In fact, only the building's outer walls existed. Hopefully, the cooking won't undergo any renovations and once again diners will be in for mouthwatering entrées served in a new, larger space. **760 Highway 99W; (503) 538-8880; expensive; lunch Tuesday–Saturday, dinner daily.**

Dayton

Hotel/Bed and Breakfast Kissing

❤❤❦ **WINE COUNTRY FARM, Dayton** Spend some time walking around the 13-acre estate or swinging in the cool shade of the pavilion. Relax on the porch of this renovated 1910 French stucco farmhouse and take in the magnificent views of the valley, mountains, and Wine Country Farm's vineyards. With such outstanding scenery, it's understandable that the interior of this bed and breakfast pales in comparison. Outdated furnishings and an abundance of knickknacks prevail throughout.

All seven rooms have private baths, down comforters, and views ranging from average to extraordinary. Four upstairs rooms are nothing to write home about, but two recent downstairs additions are noteworthy. The Courtyard Room holds a king-size canopy bed, fireplace, sitting area, and private entrance. Next door, the smaller Willamette Room entices with a queen-size bed, bay windows, and a wonderful view. Both, however, are near potentially noisy spots: the living room and front door.

The real retreat here is the Vineyard Suite, a two-room, simply adorned alcove above the tasting room that offers a queen-size bed, standard bath, and all the privacy you need at night. However, come daytime, visitors sample the wines in the rustic, yet charming downstairs tasting room between 11 A.M. and 5 P.M.

A hearty farm breakfast is served in the sunny dining room; Belgian waffles, plenty of egg dishes, baked breads, and other treats are sure to satisfy. Don't forget to ask for some carrots, too: Several Arabian horses make their home in the stable and love visitors carrying vegetables. Plenty of cats and dogs roam the grounds as well. **6855 Breyman Orchards Road; (503) 864-3446, (800) 261-3446; inexpensive to expensive; minimum-stay requirement on holiday weekends; recommended wedding site.**

Romantic Suggestion: A private picnic here is easy as pie. On arrangement, the proprietor will pack a gourmet lunch—complete with wine, silverware, and a big blanket—and will take the two of you via horse-drawn buggy into nearby orchards where you can be alone for as long as your hearts desire.

Restaurant Kissing

◕◕◕◕ **THE JOEL PALMER HOUSE, Dayton** Don't be surprised to find this famous restaurant way off the beaten path in the middle of the countryside: Soils that produce fine grapes also produce a bounty of wonderful fruits and vegetables. That's one reason the restaurant's owner, a world-famous chef and mushroom collector, set up shop in the tiny town of Dayton. He chose one of Oregon's most famous historical homes, the Joel Palmer House, as the backdrop to showcase his culinary creations.

Inside the 1857 Southern Revival–style home, three cozy dining rooms are decorated in accordance with that bygone era. The interior—delicate lace curtains, linen-covered tables with fresh flowers, and a sprinkling of period antiques and artwork—is nice and simple, so you can concentrate on the food.

While ingredients are mostly Northwest, the cooking is freestyle. Drawing from Mexico, Thailand, Poland, and India, dishes are delicious, and some are a bit daring. Try the matsutake wonton soup with a wakame- and lemongrass-infused broth and matsutake duxelles-filled wontons. Joe's Wild Mushroom Soup, a local favorite, is a Polish-style soup made from puréed suillus mushrooms. Seafood lovers will savor the fresh halibut bathed in a wild ginger cream sauce, topped with chanterelles and (surprise!) seaweed, which you eat with your fingers. For dessert, you can't go wrong by indulging in a flourless chocolate torte made with locally grown hazelnuts.

If you missed visiting your favorite winery on your Willamette Valley tour, don't worry. The wine cellar here stocks more than 5,000 bottles of wine, all made from Oregon grapes. **600 Ferry Street; (503) 864-2995; expensive; dinner Tuesday–Saturday; recommended wedding site.**

McMinnville

Hotel/Bed and Breakfast Kissing

◕◕ **GAHR FARM BED AND BREAKFAST, McMinnville** Nature lovers will go wild over this place. There's plenty of animal activity near this three-room cottage located on a 350-acre farm surrounded by wetlands and forests. During our short stay, we spotted a herd of elk, red-winged blackbirds, a pair of pheasants, and a solitary hawk.

You might be too busy looking through the binoculars to notice that the cottage decor is a bit dated. But, despite the '70s-style television set, country knickknacks, and all, it's cozy. There's a wood-burning stove (with instructions on fire building for all you city slickers), a queen-size bed, and a covered front porch overlooking the wetlands, nearby hills, and, unfortunately, the main house 600 feet away. While the latter is a bit of an eyesore, it's not worth fussing over: You're here to enjoy the privacy, nature, and each other, not the architecture.

Breakfast is cooked to order by the proprietor, who comes to the cottage at a pre-arranged time. In your kitchen she whips up biscuits, baked eggs, and fruit dishes and serves them at the table set for two.

Be sure to explore the wetlands, which are home to several species of endangered plants and animals, or take a romantic stroll (or vigorous hike) along the grassy trails that weave throughout 150 acres of woodland. **18605 Southwest Masonville Road; (503) 472-6960; inexpensive.**

Romantic Warning: Hundreds of frogs inhabit nearby wetlands, and their nighttime "ribbit-ribbit-ribbit" racket can be distracting. Bring earplugs and do have some sympathy—this croaking chorus is only the cry of love-starved amphibians.

❦❦❦ **MATTEY HOUSE, McMinnville** Coming upon a stately 1892 Queen Anne Victorian positioned between a vineyard and orchard is a pleasant and unexpected discovery. Who wouldn't be wowed when turning the corner of a dirt road to discover this two-story house with its colorful stained glass windows and inviting wraparound porch amid towering trees?

All four upstairs bedrooms of this impressive home are appointed with period antiques, patchwork quilts, and antique light fixtures, and are painted in shades of pink, rose, and burgundy. We like the small Riesling Room or, more specifically, its claw-foot tub with views overlooking the orchards. There's even a rubber ducky (just in case you want more company). The only problem is the supposedly charming antique bed, which is about as small as a pillow. The Chardonnay and Pinot Noir Rooms, which have queen-size beds, are not as charming, but it's your choice: cozy quarters or spacious comfort? One's enjoyment of the brightest room of all, the Blanc de Blanc, may be diminished a bit by its private hallway bathroom, but this room (with another small antique bed) is reputed to be the most popular. The best upstairs feature is a patio above the front entrance. It's the ideal place for two people to enjoy views of the vineyard.

We adore the sunny sitting room bright with white wicker furniture and delicate lace curtains, but piles of games and books throughout the living room lend a lived-in look, and some worn parts of the house could use a pick-me-up. Breakfasts are served family-style in the country-style dining room. The English proprietors dispel the rumor that British food is boring by turning out such indulgences as baked peaches filled with raspberry jam, Italian frittatas, or poached pears topped with cream cheese, honey, and vanilla.

Last, but not least in romance, are the grounds. Curl up on the porch swing, kiss underneath the magnificent copper beech, or find the secluded cedar grove marked by a white, arched entryway. If you can ignore the barn (a work in progress) and the dilapidated milk shed by the orchard (which some say is rustic), the outside is pucker-up perfect. **10221 Northeast Mattey Lane; (503) 434-5058; moderate; minimum-stay requirement on holiday weekends; recommended wedding site.**

❦❦ **STEIGER HAUS, McMinnville** Steiger Haus looks as if it belongs in the Swiss Alps instead of in the residential neighborhood where it sits. Rich colors, plants, and natural wood throughout the house create a warm atmosphere, while bay windows and skylights allow sunlight to flood in. All five guest rooms have private baths, but our favorites are the Fireside and Treetop Suites. The Fireside Suite feels somewhat tucked away from the other rooms and has a private deck and wood-burning fireplace. The Treetop Suite, as the name suggests, is on the top floor. It is appointed with a Quaker-style pine bed, bay windows overlooking the grassy yard and healthy gardens below, and a large soaking tub set beneath a skylight in the bathroom. Also worth a mention is the two-room Merino Morning Sun Suite with a whirlpool bath, sitting area, mini-kitchen, and access to the yard. It is located in the basement, but seems to live up to its namesake.

In the morning, dine on raisin-bran muffins, fresh fruit, and a hot entrée such as quiche in the wood-accented kitchen. **360 Southeast Wilson Street; (503) 472-0821, (503) 472-0238; inexpensive to moderate.**

❦❦❦ **YOUNGBERG HILL VINEYARD BED AND BREAKFAST, McMinnville** Climb a little closer to heaven at this magnificent bed and breakfast. A mile-long, uphill driveway takes you through rolling fields, oak forests, and finally acres of pinot noir grapes that surround the large, two-story Craftsman-style farmhouse. Prominently perched on a hill, the home is visible for miles down in the Willamette Valley.

Once you've made it to the top, sit on the wraparound deck with a glass of Youngberg Hill's "young" pinot noir and enjoy the breathtaking views of the green, pastoral (and misnamed) Muddy Valley below. At night the distant lights of McMinnville illustrate just how far removed you are from civilization.

All five rooms feature simple but elegant Victorian decor, private standard baths, queen- or king-size beds with down comforters, and outstanding views; two have fireplaces. Furnishings include antique replica furniture and carved wooden headboards set against pleasing plum, sage, and buttercup yellow hues. The first-floor Gamay Room charms guests with its wood-burning fireplace and, best of all, a private deck overlooking the vineyard. Its only disadvantage: The front door is across the hallway. While the views from every room are noteworthy, we recommend the front-facing Jura Room for 180 degrees of oohs and ahhs.

Watch the morning fog roll into the valley below as you dine on baked apple pancakes, raspberry bread, fruit covered with a sweet poppyseed sauce, and sausage with apples and potatoes. Then spend the day hiking nearby trails, sitting on the porch watching the wildlife, or playing with Pantaloon, the lively black-and-white cat. **10660 Southwest Youngberg Hill Road; (503) 472-2727; www.youngberghill.com; expensive; recommended wedding site.**

Romantic Suggestion: From anniversaries to birthdays, a number of packages can help you celebrate a special occasion. The proprietors also have a nicely stocked wine cellar with recent and older vintages of Oregon's hard-to-find wines.

Restaurant Kissing

❤❤ **NICK'S ITALIAN CAFE, McMinnville** As the name suggests, Nick's is a casual place, but a meal here (typically lasting two and a half hours) is a serious dining experience. While the menu changes nightly, it is always a five-course Italian extravaganza that features the best local markets have to offer. Among the seasonal specialties are handmade pastas; rabbit braised in Oregon pinot gris; a pesto, chanterelle, and hazelnut lasagne; salt-grilled chinook salmon; and grilled fresh asparagus.

Nick's has two dining rooms, but for romance choose the front room that has private little wooden booths. A single candle tops every table, and low lighting makes the wood interior glow. **521 East Third Street; (503) 434-4471; moderate to expensive; dinner Tuesday–Sunday.**

❤❤❤ **THIRD STREET GRILL, McMinnville** Do you believe in love at first bite? We do, now that we've experienced a meal at this restaurant. Begin your evening with an appetizer of wild mushrooms and Brie baked in a puff pastry. Entrées are prepared with the freshest seasonal ingredients and explode with delicate flavors. We recommend the hazelnut-crusted halibut with citrus butter and wild rice pilaf, and the seared Yamhill pork tenderloin stuffed with sun-dried cherries and a sweet bourbon sauce. Top it all off with profiteroles for dessert.

Located next to the old train station, this 100-year-old house is neatly trimmed with flower boxes and a white picket fence. Its gray exterior only hints at the subtle refinement inside. Taupe walls, cherry-wood accents, and thick gray carpet conspire to set the mood in the three dining rooms on the main floor. Linen-draped tables are topped with fresh flowers and candles, and encircled by cushioned chairs. Burgundy and floral curtains frame the windows. A similar dining room upstairs, fronted by a lovely sitting room, is reserved for private parties and overflow. In good weather, more informal dining is available outside on the patio, though the view isn't much to rave about. **729 East Third Street; (503) 435-1745; expensive; lunch Monday–Friday, dinner Monday–Saturday.**

Romantic Note: In conjunction with the fine wine and food experience, Third Street Grill has opened a wine shop on site that specializes in hard-to-find, premium wines from local wineries.

Eugene and Environs

Eugene

College towns tend to radiate a casual atmosphere, where serious romancing takes a backseat to football games and lively bar scenes. Eugene is *the* quintessential college town, with a distinct spirit left over from the 1960s. Who would think that romantic accommodations could be found here? In the past, there wasn't much in the way of kiss-worthy destinations for us to send loving hearts in this direction (which is why the Eugene area has been absent from previous editions of this book). We are pleased to announce that things have changed! When it comes to matters of the heart, there are now a handful of heart-stirring locales that shouldn't be overlooked. Whether you're kissing your way to the coast, completing the last leg of the Willamette Valley Scenic Loop, or simply rejoicing in being together, Eugene offers something for everyone.

Eugene, together with its neighbor Springfield, comprises the second-largest metropolitan area in Oregon; however, with a combined population of only 180,000, this area easily retains a small-town feel. Home to the University of Oregon, Eugene attracts a combination of students, athletes, and nature lovers who have a passion for the Northwest and the lush greenery of the surroundings. Jogging and biking paths, including the groomed **PREFONTAINE TRAIL**, wind along the Willamette River and through Eugene's many parks. Hike up to the lookout at **SKINNER'S BUTTE PARK**, peruse the shops and crafts booths at the **FIFTH STREET PUBLIC MARKET**, or drop by the **SATURDAY MARKET** on Eighth Avenue and Oak Street to experience downtown's weekly open-air bazaar (open April through December). Don't miss the internationally acclaimed **OREGON BACH FESTIVAL** (541-682-5000, 800-457-1486), which takes place here late June through early July each year; this festival is sure to end any getaway on a beautiful note.

Hotel/Bed and Breakfast Kissing

❀❀❀❀ **THE CAMPBELL HOUSE, Eugene** Embraced by trees in Eugene's historic district, this 1892 Victorian home has been lovingly renovated to become the number-one place for romance in the city. The large white home is set squarely on an acre of landscaped grounds, embellished with colorful gardens and a charming gazebo (a prime kissing spot). Although the Fifth Street Public Market and Skinner's Butte Park are within walking distance of the inn, the sounds of the city are pleasantly muffled by the surrounding residential neighborhood. The occasional rumblings of a passing train are your only indications that city life is just moments away.

Complimentary tea, coffee, and wine are served in the Victorian parlor each evening. Lovely mauve and green couches, hardwood floors covered with area rugs, and large picture windows make this a perfectly inviting place to unwind. Adjoining the parlor is the library, filled with books, games, and an extensive video collection available for guests' use. Throughout the home, a few quirks lend an aura of authenticity and remind us of its recent transformation: Uneven flooring in the corridors distinguishes different wings, and unusual-shaped rooms and dormer ceilings create some extremely cozy quarters. Regardless of their size and shape, all 13 rooms in the main house feature private bathrooms, TV/VCRs, and terry-cloth robes. Some have claw-foot tubs and select rooms offer romantic amenities such as gas fireplaces, jetted tubs, and four-poster beds covered in pretty floral comforters.

Although the main-house guest rooms are endearing, it's the newly constructed Carriage House suites that won our hearts. All five suites are lavishly decorated with enticing color schemes and offer wet bars, spacious sitting areas, and whirlpool tubs in the upscale bathrooms. Each one has either a private deck or patio; some overlook a tiny outdoor waterfall, but all are overshadowed by the towering retirement complex next door. Fortunately, the outside world will hardly matter once you've cozied up in your attractive suite. With a flick of a switch, the gas fireplace sets the room aglow. Sumptuous linens piled high on the queen- or king-size four-poster bed will make you want to turn in early or sleep late (or both).

A complimentary breakfast is served each morning in the main-house dining room, where tables for two are draped with burgundy linens near windows overlooking the landscaped grounds. Plan your day as you feast on mini-Belgian waffles, pear pancakes, or a chile cheese egg dish, accompanied by scones or croissants. **252 Pearl Street; (541) 343-1119, (800) 264-2519; www.camp bellhouse.com; inexpensive to unbelievably expensive; recommended wedding site.**

❧❧❧ **THE SECRET GARDEN, Eugene** Despite its name, this bed and breakfast is no secret; the white three-story home and its abundant garden are proudly displayed on a residential corner two blocks from the University of Oregon. Built in 1918, the home has undergone several additions and an incarnation as a sorority house, all the while retaining its colorful gardens and stately interior.

Outside, the abundant greenery is bordered by hand-laid stone and sheltered by a canopy of birch trees. At the heart of the secret garden is an outdoor shower and hot tub, disguised by wattling and shielded from the street by abundant foliage. (If you do head outside for a soak, please note that this area can be seen from some of the upstairs guest rooms.) Inside, the decor leans heavily on the whimsical, sometimes to the point of overshadowing the home's collection of European antiques and Asian artwork. Still, the place comes off as elegant, despite some very eclectic touches. An exquisite bouquet of flowers greets you in the Great Room, where the home's original hardwood floors are covered with area rugs, plush curtains frame the generous windows, and a baby grand piano invites you to tickle the ivories; however, the small gift shop here seems out of place. Coffee and tea are available all day long in the second-floor sitting area called Daphne, where a wall painting depicts the room's namesake.

All ten guest rooms feature private baths, robes, piped-in music, TV/VCRs, small refrigerators, and, for those chilly evenings, electric bed warmers. An abundance of windows fill the airy rooms with plenty of light. Whimsical touches create a garden-theme in each room, from the literary quotes painted on the doors (i.e., "The weed is a flower in disguise") to views of the gardens, to linens and fabrics accented with flowers, bees, and ferns. Our favorite room is Apiary, distinguished by its French country style. It boasts a gas-fireplace in the sitting area, a king-size bed with a gorgeous antique headboard, and a European soaking tub.

Morning light streams through the windows in the dining room, illuminating the elegant spread of delights before you. Your full breakfast may include French toast or an egg dish, accompanied by freshly baked breads, juices, and fruit, not to mention that everpresent cup of coffee. As you would expect, the garden theme prevalent throughout the home also extends to the dining room: Bright floral place mats add a splash of color to the two dark wood tables set side by side to accommodate guests. **1910 University Street; (541) 484-6755, (888) 484-6755; www.secretgardenbbinn.com; moderate to very expensive.**

Restaurant Kissing

❀❀❀ **ADAM'S PLACE, Eugene** If a candlelit dinner at *your* place just won't do, head over to Adam's Place for an evening of romance. The atmosphere often borders on bustling, especially at the handsome bar near the entrance, but luckily this area is separated from the main dining room by a half wall. Polished mahogany wainscoting gives the sophisticated dining room its warm glow, while a fire in the brick hearth keeps things toasty in winter. We prefer the intimate upholstered booths (perfect for pre-meal snuggling), although the small tables topped with votive candles and fresh flowers are also cozy spots. Live music spills over from the bar area Friday and Saturday nights, but don't worry, it won't put a damper on whispering sweet nothings.

You won't go wrong with any of the menu selections. An excellent blend of flavors and textures come together in the butternut salad topped with dried cranberries, peaches, and toasted walnuts in a subtle cranberry vinaigrette dressing. Entrées are skillfully executed and beautifully presented. Seafood lovers will have a difficult time deciding between the sesame-encrusted Hawaiian ahi accented by a light Asian sauce, and the North Atlantic salmon served over farfalle and accompanied by wilted baby spinach. Seared medallions of pork tenderloin tempt carnivores, as will the Australian rack of lamb with a 12-garlic-clove demi-glace (just bring along those breath mints for later). Sweets for your sweetheart include the maple crème brûlée in a praline cup, accented by fresh orange segments, and the Tuscan cappuccino mousse with rum-soaked sponge cakes. After your place, Adam's Place is the next-best spot for romance in Eugene. **30 East Broadway; (541) 344-6948; expensive; lunch Monday–Friday, dinner daily.**

❤❤❤ **CHANTERELLE RESTAURANT AND LOUNGE, Eugene** Set near the Fifth Street Public Market, Chanterelle offers a heart-stirring locale for those with refined palates and romantic inclinations. The small dining room is quite modest, with exposed wood beams, hanging plants, and a handful of tables topped with white linens and tiny candles. The gentle rumblings of a passing train and its occasional *toot-toot* add a dash of excitement without disrupting conversation. Chanterelle's only windows are situated too high above diners' heads for viewing, but this just makes the interior more cozy and seductively dark. Besides, there's no need to be reminded of the outside world when you have your special someone sitting right across the table.

An evening of sophisticated flavors unfolds as flawless French cuisine emerges from the tiny, single-chef kitchen. Begin with either classic escargots bourguignon or a bowl of old-fashioned baked onion soup. When choosing an entrée, don't miss the tender tournedo of beef that seems to melt in your mouth. The rack of lamb provençale is splendid, and the night we dined, enticing seafood entrées like poached salmon and sautéed prawns maison also graced the small menu. No evening here would be complete without dessert. The Bavarian silk chocolate cake is smooth as silk and deliciously divine; however, sharing a slice should only be attempted by those deeply in love. **207 East Fifth Avenue, Suite 109; (541) 484-4065; expensive; dinner Tuesday–Saturday.**

❤❤ **EXCELSIOR INN RESTAURANT AND LOUNGE, Eugene** Bright and airy, the small dining room at the Excelsior Inn serves up classic Italian cuisine and tempting desserts. A polished parquet floor gleams beneath formal white-linened tables, accented with glowing candles and arranged near a large fireplace. Pretty floral chairs and booths are offset by the room's pastel green wainscoting. Whether you're coming here to pop the question or simply celebrating the weekend, request what the owner fondly refers to as "the engagement table." Tucked next to a floor-to-ceiling window overlooking the front courtyard, this intimate table for two is the best seat in the house. An indoor terrace offers diners a more casual dining option, but is not recommended for encounters of the heart; outdoor seating beneath the stars is also available when weather permits. **754 East 13th Avenue; (541) 342-6963, (800) 321-6963; www.excelsiorinn.com; moderate to expensive; breakfast, lunch, and dinner daily, brunch Sunday.**

Romantic Warning: Fourteen small guest rooms (inexpensive to very expensive) also comprise the red 1912 building that holds the restaurant. More dorm-like than intimate, these rooms won't inspire much in the way of romance with their cramped accommodations, undisguised heaters, standard baths, and uninspiring views. Only the two most expensive suites with whirlpool tubs and sleigh beds are worth a second look.

❀❀ **SORÍAH CAFÉ AND BAR, Eugene** Despite its unattractive setting (look for the bright pink building next to an auto repair business), Soríah Café is Eugene's only reputable Middle Eastern/Mediterranean restaurant. On any given night, the aromas of tantalizing spices and curries are enough to draw you in for some casual romancing. Good thing too, because the ambience isn't exactly heart-stirring. Ignore the bar/bistro area at the front of the restaurant and head to the modest dining room in back, where wood tables are simply adorned with fresh flowers in tiny glass vases. A few mirrors hang around the room, while photographs of nature scenes are the only splashes of color against the stark white walls. When weather permits, outdoor seating is available on the cramped patio near a small, bubbling fountain. Wherever you sit, feast on hummus, stuffed grape leaves, spanakopita, Greek salad, or lamb curry. Don't miss the chicken gaza, chicken that has been dipped in hot spices and baked, then topped with pomegranate, white wine, and garlic sauce. And the crowning touch? Peaches flambé will warm up your lips for kissing. **384 West 13th Avenue; (541) 342-4410; moderate; lunch Monday–Friday, dinner daily.**

❀❀❀ **WILLIE'S ON 7TH STREET, Eugene** Although busy Seventh Street passes by right outside, this restored 1820s Victorian home holds enough charm (and soundproofing) to make you forget the outside world. An inviting front porch draws you into the cream-colored home where well-spaced tables are spread throughout the two dining rooms, each adorned with green-and-white-striped wallpaper. Floral upholstered chairs are coupled with tables dressed in white linens and topped with green napkins and fresh flowers. Tasteful watercolors embellish the walls and lacy, white half curtains frame the windows. Before or after dinner, head upstairs to the casual banquet room for a drink at the polished mahogany bar.

Willie's eclectic menu allows you to eat your way around the globe without leaving your seat. Begin in China with the Szechuan prawn appetizer, followed by a trip to Lebanon for a fattoosh salad consisting of Romaine lettuce with tomatoes, cucumbers, onions, and toasted pita croutons tossed in a sumac-lemon-garlic dressing. For the main course, choose a classic Italian dish such as cheese-filled ravioli or fettuccine alfredo. If traveling doesn't appeal to you, then stay home; fresh chinook salmon will give you a taste of the Pacific Northwest. **388 West Seventh Avenue; (541) 485-0601; moderate to expensive; lunch Monday–Friday, dinner Monday–Saturday.**

Outdoor Kissing

❀❀ **HENDRICKS PARK, Eugene** Leave your worries behind as you head east out of the city to this green oasis. Walking paths meander through dense forest and ten acres of rhododendrons to a sheltered picnic area. Eugene's oldest park offers a world of muffled quiet where you can focus on the finer things in life: each other. **Free admission.** *Head east out of the city on 19th Avenue and follow signs to the park, at the intersection of Summit Avenue and Skyline Drive.*

❀❀❀ **OWEN MEMORIAL ROSE GARDENS, Eugene** What do Charisma, French Perfume, and Golden Slippers have to do with romance (besides the obvious)? These are some of the varieties of roses abloom at the Owen Memorial Rose Gardens. The Portland Rose Garden this is not, but if you're looking for a sweet-smelling spot where your love can blossom, you've come to the right place. This small garden hugs the shore of the Willamette River, and is marred only by noise from the nearby freeway. Wander hand in hand among rows of brilliant color or share an afternoon snack; stone picnic benches near the parking lot are set beneath open trellises entwined with greenery. Whatever the time or season, you're sure to find Love blooming here (the rose variety anyway). **Free admission.** *From downtown, head west on Eighth Avenue. Pass beneath Highway 105 and immediately turn north onto Jefferson; follow this street toward the river to the gardens.*

Springfield

Most visitors come here to fish or white-water raft along the McKenzie River, hike to the summit of **MOUNT PISGAH,** or just unwind in the serene, forested setting. Whatever the reason, Springfield offers one heart-stirring destination that is sure to put you in the right frame of mind for romance.

Hotel/Bed and Breakfast Kissing

❀❀❀ **MCKENZIE VIEW, Springfield** Where can you unwind along the banks of the McKenzie River, snuggle together on a hammock beneath towering Douglas firs, or share a kiss among perennial flower gardens? You'll find all this and more at McKenzie View bed and breakfast. Only a 15-minute drive from downtown Eugene, this large contemporary home and surrounding six acres feel a million miles away from civilization.

Of the four guest rooms, we prefer the ground-floor Woodland Suite. This spacious room has been nicely decorated in soothing blues and whites, from the formal armchairs to the displayed vases to the gas fireplace edged in decorative tiles. A cherry-wood headboard crowns the queen-size bed, and French doors open to a private porch affording serene forest views. Its large private bathroom features a wonderful sunken tub with a separate tiled shower. Although not as impressive as the Woodland Suite, the three rooms on the second floor offer the best views of the rushing McKenzie River. Coburg is decidedly snug, with dormer ceilings and a tiny bath, and boasts an attractive sage and cream color scheme. The Moonlight Suite can be shut off from the rest of the home by a set of doors and consists of three separate rooms: a bedroom, bathroom, and sitting area. While the extra space and privacy are appealing, the suite suffers from antiquated colors and unattractive artwork. Riverbend is a bit too homey for our tastes and offers two twin beds that can be joined to form a king-size bed.

Blue walls and cherry-wood furnishings in the dining room create a regal setting in which to enjoy a delicious breakfast, presented at one long table by your gracious hosts. After breakfast, curl up in the parlor in front of a crackling fire if the day is gray; if not, lounge outside on the newly constructed cedar deck near the river's edge. If you can't kiss in this serene setting, you can't kiss anywhere. **34922 McKenzie View Drive; (541) 726-3887, (888) McK-VIEW; design-web.com/mckenzieview; inexpensive to very expensive.**

Outdoor Kissing

👄👄👄 **WHITE-WATER RAFTING, Springfield** From its inception near the Cascade Mountains, the scenic McKenzie River winds its way past Springfield to join with its cousin, the Willamette River, just north of Eugene. Known for some of the best white-water rafting in Oregon, the McKenzie will capture your heart with its breathtaking scenery. Old-growth forests on either side of the river are crowned by the snowcapped peaks of the Cascades in the distance. If the surrounding splendor doesn't get your heart pumping, the sensation of cold water against your skin definitely will. Paddle through whirlpools and rapids with your special someone by your side and your experienced guide navigating your raft downstream. This roller-coaster ride is one journey together you won't soon forget. **The Oregon Paddler; (541) 741-8661, (800) 267-6848; www.rio.com/~paddler; rates and packages vary.**

"Women still remember

the first kiss

after men have

forgotten the last."

Remy de Gourmont

Oregon Coast

It is probably safe to say that no other state has a span of highway quite like Highway 101 in Oregon. This winding coastal highway runs the length of the state, and almost every mile is filled with awe-inspiring scenery that will take your breath away. Thank goodness for the many turnoffs, parks, trails, coves, and inlets where you can stop and drink in the view at your own leisurely pace.

Constant, temperamental mood swings in the weather enhance the boundless drama of this area. At times the mixture of fog and sea mist creates a diffuse screen through which the world appears like an apparition. Other moments bring a haunting quiet as a tempest brews on the horizon, where ocean and sky converge. Yet even on the calmest summer days, the unbridled energy and the siren song of the waves unleashing their power against beaches, headlands, and haystack rocks have a spellbinding impact. Time shared on the Oregon coast can rekindle your relationship with the world—and with each other.

Not only is the scenery stupendous, but the two of you can also indulge in a multitude of activities here, such as hiking through coastal rain forest, beachcombing, hunting for agates, clamming, exploring tide pools, kite flying, and whale watching. Until you've attempted each of these, you haven't truly experienced the Oregon coast.

After whetting your appetite with all these heartfelt images, we must warn you about one major drawback: Summers and most weekends can be maddeningly crowded, with traffic jams reminiscent of a big city and beaches overflowing with people. All of the places we recommend take the concept of solitude and seclusion quite seriously, but there is only so much they can do. It is essential that you keep the popularity of the area in mind when planning your getaway. This way you have a better chance of getting away from it all instead of finding it all there when you arrive.

To receive a free pamphlet highlighting scenic stops along this 360-mile stretch of coastline, and request the *Pacific Coast Scenic Byway* guide (888-628-2101). Call for information on **OREGON PARKS AND RECREATION AREAS** (503-378-6305). For up-to-the-minute camping information from March through Labor Day, call **RESERVATIONS NORTHWEST** (503-731-3411, 800-452-5687). Be sure to bring along proper beach attire and gear: bathing suits in the summer, jeans and warm sweaters all year long (just in case—after all, this is the Northwest), as well as plenty of towels, a blanket or two, and a bucket with shovel for clamming or agate hunting. Hundreds of secluded, totally accessible beaches line the road; be prepared, so that when the mood strikes to splash in the surf or walk hand in hand along the sand, there won't be anything stopping you.

Romantic Warning: Although this might sound like an exaggeration, it isn't: There is an almost interminable procession of motels bordering the coast and abutting Highway 101. Most of these are appropriately labeled "motel," but some facilities are described as "inns," "cottages," or "resorts." Several of them do have alluring views, real fireplaces, and efficient kitchens, but they are still motels—assuredly decent places to stay, but by the standards of this book not the least bit romantic. If you would like a list of these places for the entire state (and you might if you will be traveling with children and/or pets), contact the **OREGON LODGING ASSOCIATION** (12724 Southeast Stark Street, Portland, OR 97233; 503-255-5135) and ask for their concise guide, *Where to Stay in Oregon.*

Astoria

Occupying a peninsula near the mouth of the swelling Columbia River, the town of Astoria is the oldest United States settlement west of the Rocky Mountains. It became well known when John Jacob Astor's fur traders established a trading post here in 1811. During the early 1800s, Astoria operated as a port for the North West Company and the Hudson's Bay Company, and eventually grew into the bustling commercial port it remains today. The town's historical landmark, the Astoria Column, stands tall on Coxcomb Hill as a tribute to Lewis and Clark and other explorers who traversed this region long ago. Ascend the spiral staircase to the top of the column for sweeping views of the river and the four-mile Astoria-Megler Bridge that connects Oregon and Washington. Unfortunately for romantics, an industrial atmosphere permeates the town, overshadowing even the lovely Victorian buildings clustered on its hillsides.

Romantic Note: We were hard-pressed to find a restaurant in Astoria that would please both the palate and the heart. You may want to fill up on breakfast and then head south down the coast for more amorous dining options.

Hotel/Bed and Breakfast Kissing

❦❦❦ **ASTORIA INN BED AND BREAKFAST, Astoria** Although the Astoria Inn is only minutes from downtown, its location above the city provides two kissing advantages: expansive views of the Columbia River and good old-fashioned peace and quiet. Perched high on a grassy knoll in a residential neighborhood, this gray-and-white home is fronted by a small veranda. Inside, dried flowers, Victorian antiques, and contemporary furnishings greet you at every turn.

All four guest rooms are cozy retreats with private baths, inviting comforters, and lovely window treatments crowned with dried flowers. Three rooms are located on the second floor and share a small common area. The rooms named for Cape Lookout and Cape Meares face the river and afford the best views. Our favorite, however, is Cape Virginia, with its dark green walls and a whimsical canopy above the bed; stained glass windows, a claw-foot tub, and a pedestal sink embellish the modest bathroom. The fourth room is situated off the dining room, which could make sleeping through breakfast an impossibility if other guests prove talkative in the morning. You won't want to miss breakfast, though. What better way to start off your day than with warm Dutch babies, French toast, or homemade quiche—besides a kiss, of course. **3391 Irving Avenue; (503) 325-8153, (800) 718-8153; inexpensive.**

🦋🦋 FRANKLIN STREET STATION BED AND BREAKFAST INN, Astoria

Although the Franklin Street Station isn't situated in the most attractive of neighborhoods (mortuaries and apartment buildings are hardly conducive to romance), the interior of this 1900 Victorian home will surely set the mood for encounters of the heart. A stately grandfather clock and an old-fashioned settee, among other lovely antiques, grace the parlor, and the adjacent breakfast room is a sunny place to begin your day over Belgian waffles and fresh fruit.

All five guest rooms are cheerfully decorated in pastel colors with pretty floral wallpapers. Each room has a different combination of amenities, including partial river views, private entrances, mini-decks, wet bars, claw-foot tubs, and charming bed-frames. A queen-size bed with an unusual woven canopy is the centerpiece of the Lewis and Clark Room on the main floor, while the Astor Suite upstairs has a separate sitting area with a trundle bed (geared more for children) and frilly white drapes. The best room in the house is in the attic, accessible via a private staircase. Called the Captain's Quarters, this room has its own fireplace, TV/VCR, stereo, wet bar, tiny sitting area, and partial glimpses of the Columbia River. Amorous extras like satin sheets and breakfast in bed are available for all guests at an additional charge. **1140 Franklin Street; (503) 325-4314, (800) 448-1098; inexpensive to moderate.**

Romantic Note: The basement section of the house has recently been converted into a vacation unit that may be rented on a daily, weekly, or monthly basis (inexpensive). Breakfast is not included with this rental.

🦋🦋🦋 ROSEBRIAR HOTEL, Astoria

Astoria's oldest established bed and breakfast sits on a hillside overlooking the town center. Recognized as a historic landmark, this magnificent 1902 neoclassical home has been beautifully restored to retain much of its charm while offering modern-day comfort. The stately white building rises above a landscaped garden, and a small veranda fronts the columned entrance. Inside you'll find a fir-paneled front desk and a cozy parlor with overstuffed floral couches, elegant window treatments, and a fireplace with a handsome wooden mantel.

Adjacent to the hotel and its courtyard, the 1885 carriage house offers the most privacy as well as a kitchenette, fireplace, soaking tub, and stained glass windows. Upstairs in the main building, ten additional guest rooms are handsomely decorated with sage walls, mahogany furnishings, and elegant moldings. Generous windows grant sunlit views of the Columbia River that are only slightly obstructed by the town below. Several of the larger rooms have fireplaces and soaking tubs, as well as couches and chairs covered in plush burgundy and refined beige. However, after serving as a convent for 20 years, the Rosebriar could use some warming up; the rooms are a bit too spartan and sterile. What was once the chapel area now serves as a small reception room, complete with stained glass windows and French doors.

In the morning, seductive aromas will lure you to the dining area, where you can take your place at one of the tightly spaced tables. Feast upon such goodies as Finnish pancakes, baked pears, or a salmon frittata. A large, three-course breakfast is served every Sunday. **636 14th Street; (503) 325-7427, (800) 487-0224; www.oregoncoastlodgings.com/rosebriar; inexpensive to expensive.**

Warrenton

Outdoor Kissing

❤❤ **FORT STEVENS STATE PARK, Warrenton** Thirty-five hundred acres of parkland are yours to explore at Fort Stevens. This enormous park encompasses the northwest corner of Oregon and offers something for everyone: picnic areas, paved bike trails, dense forests, nature trails, a freshwater lake, a large campground area, and miles of virtually undiscovered beaches. Small lakes and historical sites punctuate the vast wilderness. (History buffs may want to check out the remains of the *Peter Iredale*, which was shipwrecked here in 1906.) If the day is overcast, drive to the **SOUTH JETTY**, Oregon's northwesternmost point, for some incredible storm watching. Witness the tumultuous union of the Columbia River and the Pacific Ocean from the safety of the lookout tower. Rocky outcroppings separate the waves from the windswept brush along most of **CLATSOP SPIT**. Because there is so much space for roaming, even in the throes of summer you're bound to find a secluded spot for a kiss or two. **(503) 861-1671; free admission, day-use fee for parking in some areas.** *From Highway 101, take Fort Stevens Highway near the town of Warrenton and follow the signs to the park.*

Gearhart

What distinguishes the seaside town of Gearhart from all the other communities hugging this end of the Oregon coast? We think it's the picture-perfect Northwest-style homes lining the quiet residential streets and the expansive beaches that go on for miles, where you can literally drive onto the sand and find your own secluded stretch of heaven. Northwesterners want to keep this area a secret. Well, it still is, because we won't tell anybody, right?

Romantic Note: Romantic accommodations are scarce in the town of Gearhart, so look for lodgings in nearby Seaside instead. Gearhart is more suitable for day trips to the beach than for overnight getaways.

Restaurant Kissing

❦❦❦ **OCEANSIDE RESTAURANT, Gearhart** In this town of breathtaking beaches and fabulous seaside homes, the only place that even vaguely resembles a tourist attraction is the sprawling condominium vacation complex directly behind the weather-worn Oceanside Restaurant. Fortunately, once you enter the restaurant you won't be aware of anything except the exhilarating beach panorama. The window-enclosed dining room—complete with brick-faced walls, oversize chandeliers, and a vaulted cedar-beamed ceiling—faces wind-swept sand dunes and the sparkling Pacific Ocean in the distance. What a view! And our dinners, fresh salmon and the angel-hair pasta with fresh crab and shrimp in a rich pesto sauce, were served with a wonderful sunset on the side. **1200 North Marion Drive; (503) 738-7789; www.pacifier.com/ ~oceansid; expensive; call for seasonal hours.**

❦❦ **PACIFIC WAY BAKERY AND CAFE, Gearhart** If you want to taste absolutely sensational baked goods, this unassuming, rustic café is the place to order hot espresso and fresh cinnamon rolls for two. The cheerful yellow exterior is set off by a green-striped awning. Inside, cranberry-colored tables with hunter green chairs surround a wood-burning fireplace. An eclectic array of old-fashioned knickknacks and photographs decorate the walls, and a small brick courtyard offers outdoor seating next to an Italian fountain. In spite of the laid-back nature of the staff, everything is immaculate and nicely presented. Lunch is superior, with generous sandwiches, delicious soups, fresh breads, and exact seasonings. Dinners feature Mediterranean dishes accentuated by fresh herbs.

The café's sunny disposition spills over into the quaint bakery next door, where two glass pantries display an assortment of tasty temptations, from rustic breads to French-style pastries. On warm summer days, place an order to go or linger over ice cream at one of the tiny marble tables set near the windows. All this, and the expansive empty beaches of Gearhart only a stone's throw away. **601 Pacific Way; (503) 738-0245; moderate; call for seasonal hours.**

Seaside

At first glance there is almost nothing romantic about Seaside, a town where much of the ocean has been obscured by hyperactive motel developers with little sensitivity for the landscape. In the summer, families flock here by the thousands to frequent the arcades, mini-malls, and popular beachfront. Fortunately, you can still find plenty of space to breathe and kiss on the vast beaches at the north and south ends of town. In the off-season you might even find yourselves alone on Seaside's famous Prom, a mile-and-a-half-long cement trail that meanders along the beachfront near the thundering surf. You'll also find plenty of romantic inspiration at many of the newer properties that have sprouted up over the past few years. Stay away from the video arcades and the kid-lined streets of the town center and you may actually find Seaside an enchanting locale, especially when school is in session and there is nary a child in sight.

Romantic Warning: Seaside's restaurants leave much to be desired, and we strongly recommend that you head just a little farther south to Cannon Beach for a truly romantic repast. Nevertheless, if you just don't feel like getting in your car, we can recommend one affectionate spot in the heart of town (see Restaurant Kissing).

Hotel/Bed and Breakfast Kissing

◆◆ **FOUR WINDS MOTEL, Seaside** Compared to the economical and somewhat rundown properties in the surrounding neighborhood at the north end of Seaside, the Four Winds Motel gleams like a diamond in the rough. This beige contemporary building offers 12 spacious rooms and a quiet refuge from the downtown crowds. Many of the rooms have ringside views of the grassy sand dunes that stretch to the water's edge. Here, seagulls' cries rise above the roar of the surf and the nearby promenade invites you to take a sunset stroll or early-morning bike ride.

In addition to stellar views, each guest room features a gas fireplace, wet bar, and private deck or porch. Whitewashed wood furnishings and fresh flowers give the otherwise standard interiors an upscale feel. **820 North Promenade; (503) 738-9524, (800) 818-9524; www.fourwindsmotel.com; inexpensive to moderate; minimum-stay requirement on weekends.**

Romantic Alternative: Couples looking for even more space will find it at the **BOOTH BROS. APARTMENTS** (inexpensive to expensive), which are owned and operated by the Four Winds Motel. Located a few blocks closer to downtown, these contemporary accommodations consist of two deluxe apartments, two houses, and one bungalow.

◆◆◆ **GILBERT INN, Seaside** A white picket fence surrounds this picturesque yellow Victorian, located one block from Seaside's popular beachfront. In the height of summer, when throngs of tourists are a force to be reckoned with, the inn's location on a corner intersection in the heart of town can feel like a disadvantage—until you step inside, that is. Once you've checked in, you'll find that Seaside's crowds simply fade into oblivion. Tongue-and-groove fir paneling lends rustic elegance to the spacious common areas, where comfy, overstuffed sofas hug a brick hearth.

Even the smallest of the inn's ten guest rooms have plenty of comfort and charm. Fluffy down comforters and armfuls of pillows embellish antique beds in every room. Fir paneling gives homespun appeal to rooms in the older wing, where we discovered our favorite room of all: the Turret Room. A circular wall of windows allows ample sunlight in this cozy room, which is furnished with an inviting four-poster cherry-wood bed. The newer wing contains a series of brightly done suites with wicker furniture, handsome wood armoires, country fabrics, and private bathrooms.

Raspberry French toast or blueberry pancakes might be featured in the generous morning meal, which is served at individual white wrought-iron tables tucked in a lovely pink breakfast nook on the main floor. **341 Beach Drive; (503) 738-9770, (800) 410-9770; www.clatsop.com/gilbertinn; inexpensive to moderate; minimum-stay requirement on weekends and holidays.**

Romantic Note: If you plan to stay in Seaside for a significant period of time, ask about the weekly rates at the inn's four next-door units. These private hideaways, separated from the inn by a lattice fence, feature full kitchens, hand-hewn fir beds, and contemporary decor.

❧❧ **RIVERSIDE INN, Seaside** Before we tell you why the Riverside Inn is such a kissing bargain, several romantic warnings are in order. First, this historic 1907 inn is harbored on one of Seaside's busiest thoroughfares. Second, the stores and rundown houses in the surrounding neighborhood leave much to be desired (not to mention the unattractive motel sign at the entrance). Third, most of the rooms here are much too small and homey for kissing comfort.

Here's the good news: the Riverview Annex. Set behind the main building, the Annex overlooks the peaceful Necanicum River. The four suites in this building have small kitchens and semiprivate decks with beautiful, and surprisingly quiet, river views (just past the parking lot). Vaulted ceilings and skylights in the two upstairs suites are especially enticing. For close-up views of the river, seek out the nearby communal deck perched at the edge of the river—it's a great place to catch up on those long discussions you've been too busy to make time for.

You don't have to worry about any interruptions in the morning. A hearty complimentary breakfast is included with your stay and can be delivered directly to the privacy of your room. Or, during the warmer months, you can choose to partake of berry French toast or ginger pancakes on the deck overlooking the river. **430 South Holladay; (503) 738-8254, (800) 826-6151; www.riversideinn.com; inexpensive; minimum-stay requirement on holidays.**

❧❧❧ **SEA SIDE INN, Seaside** One of Seaside's celebrated landmarks is the paved promenade bordering the enormous sandy beach that stretches alongside the ever-changing Pacific Ocean. As exceptional as this sounds, the beachfront is marred by a series of rather bland, timeworn motels near the town's center. Nevertheless, in the midst of this aesthetic lapse, we found a splendid, recently constructed inn that pampers guests who have a flair for the unusual. Views of the sprawling dunes and crashing surf appear to be within arm's reach of the inn's eclectic lobby, which is engagingly appointed with vividly colored modern art and a hodgepodge of trinkets. Guests can relax with a microbrew or a glass of wine in this comfortable ocean-view setting, which also doubles as a sometimes noisy local bar.

Eccentricities continue throughout the inn. Each of the 14 guest rooms has a personality all its own; the only trick is finding the one that best matches yours. The Logo Golf Ball Room features a miniature putting green, while the Rock 'n' Roll Room holds a bed made from a '59 Oldsmobile. Our three favorite suites are less peculiar and more romantic. In the Northwest Timber Room, cathedral ceilings soar above an immense four-poster king-size log bed crowned with a crocheted canopy. An open staircase climbs to a loft bathroom, where you'll find the best surprise of all: a green-tiled soaking tub and a sexy glass-enclosed shower. A gas fireplace and full-on ocean views complete this picture-perfect setting. Next door, the Clocktower Room features similar luxuries: a cathedral ceiling, fantastic ocean view, spa tub, and gas fireplace. A large round bed distinguishes this room from its neighbor. Last but not least is the Bubble Room—the brightest room in the house and our special favorite. Here, colorful fish accent a blue-tiled spa tub and glass-enclosed shower cozied in the corner; this mini-suite also has spectacular ocean views. (If you adjust the blinds just so, you can actually bathe or shower while watching the surf!)

A full, bountiful breakfast is served in the large common room, made remarkably inviting by floor-to-ceiling windows and a beach-stone fireplace. Tables topped with bright tablecloths and fresh flowers add to an already colorful setting. **581 South Promenade; (503) 738-6403, (800) 772-7766; www.seasideinnbandb.com; moderate to very expensive.**

Romantic Suggestion: Depending on reservations and the season, you can enjoy a four-course prix fixe dinner at the Sea Side Inn (moderate to expensive). If you're lucky enough to find the chef in, you will be treated to a country-fresh meal that is flavorful and rich. The fresh salmon, stuffed trout, and fresh shrimp are all delicious.

Restaurant Kissing

❤️❤️ **VISTA SEA CAFE, Seaside** Renowned for its gourmet pizza, the Vista Sea Cafe inhabits a bright yellow turn-of-the-century storefront several blocks from the beach. Hungry diners congregate in cushioned booths in the airy dining room, which features yellow walls, hardwood floors, and potted ferns. Lacy white curtains shield patrons from the crowds passing by outside. You won't want to miss the homemade beer bread, which accompanies bowls of soup, zesty salads, and a variety of specialty dishes. Design the pizza of your dreams with a vast selection of gourmet toppings and after one bite you'll understand why this charming cafe has become so famous. **150 Broadway; (503) 738-8108; inexpensive; call for seasonal hours.**

Cannon Beach

As you approach Cannon Beach, you may not believe your eyes. The cliffs and ocean here seem to stretch out to infinity, and massive rock outcroppings dot the shoreline. More than seven miles of firm sand and rolling waves beckon dreamers and lovers to roll up their jeans, hold hands, and stroll at the edge of the churning surf. At low tide you can stand at the base of a free-standing monolith called Haystack Rock, the third largest of its kind in the world and a true natural wonder, and feel humbled by its towering dimensions.

Evenings here provide another chance to appreciate the glory of the sea and the sky. The Oregon coast has been nicknamed the "Sunset Empire" for good reason. As the sun begins to settle into the ocean, brilliant colors radiate from the horizon, filling the sky like a golden aurora borealis. At first the light penetrates the clouds as a pale lavender-blue haze, transforming suddenly into an intense yellow-amber, and culminating in a blazing red that seems to set the sky on fire. Then, as dusk finalizes its entrance, the clouds fade to steely blue-gray and the sky changes its countenance to cobalt blue and then to indigo. Slowly the moon takes a central place in the evening heavens, and its platinum rays seem to dance on the surface of the water. When the moon and weather cooperate, this performance occurs nightly at Cannon Beach and along the entire Oregon coastline.

Of course, there is more to Cannon Beach than gorgeous beaches. Boutiques, gift shops, and restaurants entice tourists into the charming weathered storefronts that run the length of the town, and local artists display their handiwork in working studios and impressive galleries.

Romantic Warning: On warm summer days, Cannon Beach can be overwhelmed by tourists, traffic, and congestion that seem out of place in such a serene, tranquil setting. Farther south along the coast, the quiet towns of Manzanita and Oceanside (both reviewed later in this chapter) are excellent alternatives to Cannon Beach on crowded summer weekends.

Hotel/Bed and Breakfast Kissing

❦❦ **ARGONAUTA INN, Cannon Beach** While some of the appointments at the Argonauta are more secondhand than homey, its beachfront location makes it well worth a visit. Poised at the ocean's edge, this bright blue seaside complex comprises three small apartments and two homes. Although they lack ocean views, the two Lighthouse units are cozy little hideaways you can call your own for a weekend. Both boast plush down comforters and gas fireplaces; however, the airy upper unit is the more attractive, with its kitchenette, vaulted ceilings, and skylights. The spacious three-bedroom Beach House, which can accommodate up to ten people, is geared more toward families. Whether you bring along the kids or another romantically inclined couple or keep the space all to yourselves, you'll be mesmerized by the panoramic ocean views showcased on the glass-enclosed sundeck. You'll also appreciate the convenience of a full kitchen, the romance of a stone fireplace, and the seclusion of a private deck and lawn. Our only complaint is the dated and worn furniture, which turns up in full force in the neighboring Chartroom (not recommended). A final unit, the two-story Town House, offers two bedrooms and glass doors that slide open to an ocean-view deck. **188 West Second Street; (503) 436-2601, (800) 822-2468; inexpensive; minimum-stay requirement seasonally.**

❀❀❀ **CANNON BEACH HOTEL AND RESTAURANT, Cannon Beach** If only the Cannon Beach Hotel were situated directly on the beach, it would be a rare find. Instead, it is located on busy Hemlock Street, and as a result can get quite noisy. This turn-of-the-century building was once a boardinghouse for loggers, but it has been renovated, at least on the inside, to resemble a European-style hotel. The exterior retains a Northwest feel, with weathered shingles, green awnings and shutters, and striking white trim. Inside, the formal yet inviting lobby is done up with taupe walls, pine accents, and comfortable chairs that face a marble fireplace.

All nine rooms are quite handsome, with polished wood furnishings, Italian duvets, muted color schemes, and original local artwork. Some of the more expensive rooms have couches, small dining tables, gas fireplaces, king-size beds, and single-person spa tubs. In Rooms 7 and 8, the spas are tucked away in private alcoves, and an extra set of windows helps brighten the rooms. Despite all this classic elegance, the European formality and somewhat sparse decor may seem a bit too sterile for a true Northwest experience. In addition, light sleepers will not appreciate the rumblings of the hotel's water system every time a neighboring guest decides to draw a bath.

Each morning freshly baked scones, seasonal fruit, and a hot beverage of your choice are delivered to your room in a French market basket and left for you to savor in privacy. **1116 South Hemlock Street; (503) 436-1392, (800) 238-4107; www.oregoncoastlodgings.com; inexpensive to expensive; minimum-stay requirement seasonally.**

Romantic Note: Adjacent to the Cannon Beach Hotel is a European-style cafe called **JP'S AT CANNON BEACH** (503-436-0908; moderate to expensive; lunch and dinner Monday–Saturday). Sit outside on the patio or at one of the mahogany tables in the sunny bistro area, or snag a couple of bar stools near the counter. Wherever you end up sitting, this is a lively spot for a casual lunch or dinner.

❀❀ **CANNON BEACH VACATION RENTAL HOMES, Cannon Beach** If privacy is as important to you as being near the ocean, these are the people to call. Seclusion is the specialty of this property management company, and they will be more than happy to set you up with the private home of your dreams—at least for a while. The 20 homes in their rental pool range from modest to spectacular; their price tags do too. Some are so close to the ocean that the surf practically rolls through your front door. Those without ocean views are within walking distance of the beach and offer tranquil seclusion in peaceful forested settings. Even the smallest rental homes are equipped with all the amenities you could ever want: TV/VCRs, stereos, CD players, washers and dryers, full kitchens with dishwashers, wet bars, and queen-size beds. Some have whirlpool or Jacuzzi tubs, and one condo even features an indoor swimming pool! The only romantic drawback we encountered was the mismatched and dated decor in several of the more modest homes. Each property is unique, so be sure to get a good description when you call to book a reservation and specify exactly what you are seeking. **(503) 436-2021; www.cbpm.com; expensive to unbelievably expensive; no credit cards; minimum-stay requirement.**

❧❧❧ **THE COURTYARD, Cannon Beach** More like a group of attractive apartments than a hotel, The Courtyard offers a world of privacy and contemporary elegance. This two-story, wood-shingled building surrounds a lovely brick courtyard with potted plants and a burbling fountain. Seekers of solitude will be delighted to find that the front desk, located a block away at the Cannon Beach Hotel, is conveniently out of sight and out of mind. With all this privacy, you'll have no choice but to cuddle up and enjoy your time together.

Each unit has a private entrance via the central courtyard, and all 13 are tastefully appointed with teak furnishings, modern kitchenettes, gas fireplaces, Jacuzzi tubs, and tiny patios. Thick Italian down duvets, dust ruffles, and large fluffy pillows grace the beds, while colorful oil paintings add a finishing touch to the taupe walls and subdued color schemes. A continental breakfast is delivered to your doorstep each morning for you to enjoy at your leisure. When you've had your fill of peace and quiet, venture a short block to the beach or relax in the common area on the first floor. No matter how you decide to spend your time, The Courtyard offers a secluded haven in which to explore the desires of your heart. **964 South Hemlock Street; (503) 436-1392; inexpensive to expensive.**

❧❧ **HALLMARK RESORT, Cannon Beach** This sprawling clapboard complex, set high on a hill above the crashing surf in the heart of Cannon Beach, takes full advantage of its prime location. Spectacular water views of this caliber rarely (if ever) come at such affordable rates, making this otherwise very standard hotel worth checking into—literally. Dated fabrics, linens, and furnishings lend a motel flavor to most of the property, but fireplaces, fully equipped kitchens, and tiled Jacuzzi tubs are decidedly romantic touches in many of the suites. Private decks with ocean views outside nearly every room provide further kissing incentive. As its name implies, the Hallmark Resort offers everything you would expect from a full-scale resort, including an indoor recreation center with a heated pool, whirlpool spas, dry sauna, exercise room, wading pool, and even guest laundry facilities. **1400 South Hemlock Street; (503) 436-1566, (888) 448-4449; www.hallmarkinns.com; inexpensive to very expensive; minimum-stay requirement seasonally.**

❧ **HEARTHSTONE INN, Cannon Beach** This weathered wood cabin would look more like a residence than an inn if it weren't for the obtrusive, motel-style sign in the front yard. Inside are three studios and one suite, all with vaulted cedar ceilings, beach-rock fireplaces, skylights, fully equipped kitchenettes, and down comforters with denim covers. Unfortunately, the decor is somewhat dated and the furnishings are modest at best. Nevertheless, this rustic cottage is a refreshingly private place to stay, as long as you don't mind the traffic noise from Hemlock Street. If spending quality time together is your main objective, you can't get much closer to each other than at the cozy Hearthstone Inn. **107 East Jackson Street; (503) 436-1392; inexpensive to moderate; minimum-stay requirement seasonally.**

❦❦❦❦ **STEPHANIE INN, Cannon Beach** When it comes to indulgent beachfront accommodations, look no further than the Stephanie Inn. After an evening here, you'll understand why this sprawling, contemporary inn has become so popular. The surf practically laps at the foundations of the New England–style inn and its adjacent Carriage House, offering couples the romantic escape of a lifetime. A fire is always aglow in the river-rock hearth in the front parlor, where comfortable overstuffed sofas, impressive wood detailing, and hardwood floors create an inviting but elegant ambience. Help yourselves to a handful of saltwater taffy or fresh cookies (available at all hours) on your way to the elegant fireside library, which overlooks spectacular ocean views through a wall of bay windows. Aperitifs, wine, and hors d'oeuvres are served here in the early evening, accompanied by delicious sunsets. A complimentary breakfast buffet is presented in the inn's mountain-view dining room every morning.

The inn's 46 sophisticated rooms are all equipped with plush terry-cloth robes and four-poster beds draped with beautiful floral linens, and nearly every room has a private deck, gas fireplace, and a corner Jacuzzi or whirlpool tub in the spacious bathroom. Chocolates left on your pillows with the evening turndown service make you feel extra pampered. The Mountain View rooms are the least expensive, but also the least romantic because they face the parking lot. If you can, splurge for an Ocean Front room; the views of the vast sandy beach, crashing surf, and jagged sea stacks are indescribably beautiful. Tucked away in the two-story Carriage House next door, four recently constructed oceanfront suites offer all the amenities found in the main house, but with a distinct country flavor. **2740 South Pacific; (503) 436-2221, (800) 633-3466; www.stephanie-inn.com; expensive to unbelievably expensive; minimum-stay requirement on weekends seasonally.**

Romantic Note: The Stephanie Inn will do almost anything to make your stay special. Ask about "special occasion" packages, which can include everything from surprising your beloved with a birthday cake upon check-in to sprinkling flower petals on the bed at turndown. (Do keep in mind that there is an additional fee for these extras.)

Romantic Suggestion: Dinner at the Stephanie Inn (expensive) is a lingering four-course, prix fixe affair that can take several hours. The chef will sometimes greet you personally at your table and describe in advance the culinary wonders you are about to encounter. Though the dining room itself does not face the ocean, ample windows showcase mountain views (across the parking lot), and crisp linens and candlelight create an opulent dining atmosphere.

❀❀❀ **SURFSAND RESORT, Cannon Beach** You'd never guess the Surfsand was once a Best Western motel, at least not if you have the good fortune of staying in one of the property's newly constructed luxury suites harbored right on the beach. Every one of these rooms is appointed with maple-wood accents and elegant contemporary furnishings. Private decks or patios showcase panoramic views of the ocean and Haystack Rock, gas fires blaze in every hearth, and the pounding surf resounds throughout the building. We are especially partial to the rooms on the fourth floor, which offer peaked ceilings, wet bars, gorgeous corner Jacuzzi tubs, and seductive glass-enclosed showers. You'll be so enthralled with your surroundings that you'll easily forgive the motel-flavored linens on the king-size beds. A kitchenette in nearly every room is a convenient extra for those who are willing to plan ahead and bring their own provisions.

Unfortunately, the remaining rooms in the older building still show signs of the property's past. Dated color schemes, linens, and furnishings are functional but not impressive, and views of the ocean are obscured by neighboring buildings and a very large parking lot. The rooms with fireplaces and Jacuzzi tubs offer some romantic potential, but pale in comparison to the property's newer units. Whether you decide to stay in a room or a suite, take advantage of the property's indoor pool and hot tub located in the main building. **Oceanfront at Gower Street; (503) 436-2274, (800) 547-6100; www. surfsand.com; expensive to very expensive; minimum-stay requirement on weekends and holidays seasonally.**

Romantic Note: Surfsand Resort also manages several oceanside rental properties in the area (moderate to unbelievably expensive). Some of these homes are the most enviable places to stay on the coast. Imagine a handsome, traditional Oregon coast home that fronts the crashing surf, with scintillating views of the incredible scenery. Now imagine yourselves sharing blissful solitude. Anything else you imagine is between the two of you.

Romantic Suggestion: If you and your loved one hear wedding bells in the not-so-distant future, check out the **HAYSTACK GARDENS**, located across the street. Owned and operated by the Surfsand, this gray-and-white building houses a tastefully decorated reception room that also serves as the entryway to a secluded garden area. An acre of grassy lawn spreads out before you, punctuated by roses, trees, and occasional fountains, and cement paths meander throughout the property. What a perfectly wonderful place to say "I do."

❀❀❀ **TURK'S LODGINGS, Cannon Beach** A recent $30,000 renovation has restored Turk's reputation as one of the Oregon coast's most extraordinary places to kiss. Supported by stilts on one side, this unusual home crafted from rough-cut spruce and fir juts out over the western slope of a steep, forested hillside. A wraparound deck surveys compelling views of the Oregon coastline; salty breezes rustle the branches of the towering evergreens and gently caress the untamed ferns and foliage that enfold the property. The interior is equally stunning, with cathedral-style pine ceilings and expansive floor-to-ceiling windows. Bright blue tiles accent the spacious sunken kitchen, where a basket of breakfast goodies (chilled champagne, baked goods, and fresh fruit) awaits guests upon arrival. A wood-burning stove sheds more than enough warmth to heat the entire home, and interesting knickknacks add charm to the modest decor. You won't want for space in the spacious two-level master bedroom, which has an open rock-lined shower and an oversize spa tub set overlooking the trees. You can also cozy up under a patchwork quilt on the king-size bed and watch a fire crackling in the stone hearth. In the open loft above the sitting room, a second bedroom with several additional beds is designed more for kids, but can also accommodate another romance-minded couple if they don't mind the limited privacy.

If you are looking for something more affordable, ask about the unassuming cottage or studio next door, both of which enjoy quiet views of the trees and distant ocean. Mismatched furnishings and dated linens make these choices homey rather than romantic (worthy of only one lip), but amenities such as skylights, TV/VCRs, and kitchenettes help to compensate. The ground-floor studio offers a cedar-paneled double shower, and the spacious cottage upstairs has a whirlpool bathtub. **50 Highway 101; (503) 436-1809; www.clatsop. com/turkslodging; moderate to unbelievably expensive; minimum-stay requirement on weekends and holidays seasonally.**

❦❦❦ **THE WAVES OCEANFRONT MOTEL, Cannon Beach** It doesn't get more eclectic than the sprawling Waves Motel. The enormous property meanders for several blocks along the water's edge, offering a hodgepodge of accommodations. Some units have scintillating views of the ocean and are perfectly designed for cozy twosomes; others overlook the cement parking lot and are geared more for a family of five. For guaranteed inspiration, we recommend a unit in La Colina or the Flagship Building. Rooms in both have unobstructed ocean views, and the resonant sound of the surf striking the steadfast shore is a welcome reminder of just how far behind you've left city life. La Colina is cozy and somewhat rustic; rooms in this building feature open beams, river-rock fireplaces, and nondescript furnishings. Rooms in the Flagship Building are slightly more spartan but still enticing, with pine furnishings, fireplaces, vaulted ceilings, and tiny decks. In the Southwind units, ocean views, down comforters, and gas fireplaces ensure romantic possibilities; modern amenities such as Jacuzzi tubs and upscale kitchens are alluring as well. Steer clear of the rooms in the Garden Court, which lack ocean views and suggest a typical economy motel. Guests in each of the buildings are welcome to use the glass-enclosed Jacuzzi tub overlooking the beach. **188 West Second Street; (503) 436-2205, (800) 822-2468; inexpensive to unbelievably expensive; minimum-stay requirement on weekends seasonally.**

❦❦ **WHITE HERON LODGE, Cannon Beach** In spite of its proximity to downtown Cannon Beach, the quiet residential area surrounding the White Heron Lodge remains peaceful and enticing. Sea grass sways at the edge of the front lawn, eventually giving way to a vast expanse of sand, while seagulls soar above the foamy waves that roll onto the beach. A Victorian-style fourplex and a contemporary duplex stand side by side on this secluded property. For romantic purposes, we recommend the relatively new studios in the fourplex, which are modestly appointed and fully equipped. Tiny private decks look out to the shore, and gas fireplaces glow with inviting warmth. Lace curtains lend privacy to the cozy bedrooms, and the beds are adorned with thick floral comforters. In addition, all of the rooms have private baths and small kitchens, and the upper units boast vaulted ceilings. The units in the contemporary duplex are larger, but they share a common entryway and have mismatched decor. Whether you opt for a unit in the duplex, which can accommodate up to five people, or choose one of the studios, with just enough room for two, you'll have all the space you need to spoil yourselves with utter relaxation and quiet. **356 North Spruce; (503) 436-2205, (800) 822-2468; expensive; minimum-stay requirement on weekends seasonally.**

Restaurant Kissing

❦❦❦ **BISTRO, Cannon Beach** Nestled within a cluster of small shops, this Tudor-style cottage fronts a charming little courtyard a comfortable distance away from the main thoroughfare. Past the bustling bar area, you'll find a snug dining room handsomely appointed with dark wood trim, blue tablecloths, and glowing candles. A plethora of rural knickknacks, everything from dried flowers to plates, baskets, plants, and birdcages, ornaments the white stucco walls, and soft track lighting creates a cozy atmosphere in which to enjoy some of the best food in town.

You might begin your feast with mouthwatering Manila clams dipped in herbed broth and drawn butter, then move on to spicy spaghetti marinara with fresh vegetables or baked salmon served with leeks, asparagus, and an intriguing black bean sauce. All entrées may be ordered à la carte or as part of a full dinner that includes antipasto, soup, salad, and fresh bread.

Although Bistro is slightly noisier than most places we recommend for amorous encounters, the constant hum can work to your advantage by drowning out neighboring conversations and possible kitchen clamor. The tables are far enough apart to ensure all the privacy you need for a kiss or two. **263 North Hemlock Street; (503) 436-2661; expensive; call for seasonal hours.**

❦❦❦ **CAFE DE LA MER, Cannon Beach** After a late-afternoon or early-evening stroll along the beach, head inland to Cafe de la Mer. This tiny blue house is fronted by window boxes overflowing with tulips and greenery, and the rustic interior is just as inviting. Well-spaced tables are draped with lavender linens and topped with glowing candles and fresh flowers. The first dining room holds only a handful of tables and is within earshot of the open kitchen. Opt instead for a table in the second, more spacious dining room with its row of windows lining an entire wall. Knotty pine wainscoting and framed prints adorn the walls, while sconces shed soft light throughout.

Choose from a tempting selection of appetizers, salads, and soups before delving into the main course. We found the roasted sweet potato bisque with maple crème fraîche to be a smooth taste of heaven. The attentive staff delivers enticing dinners, such as hazelnut-crusted halibut served with a saffron–black currant beurre blanc, or lamb stew with vegetables. **1287 South Hemlock Street; (503) 436-1179; moderate to expensive; call for seasonal hours.**

❧❧ **IRA'S, Cannon Beach** Ira's tries hard to create an intimate ambience, and to some extent it succeeds. All the romantic elements are in place: glowing candlelight, soothing jazz, attentive service, and white linen–draped tables for two. Unfortunately, the confines of the building work to its disadvantage. The nondescript exterior is less than inviting, and once inside, conversations carry easily across the open dining room. Purple vinyl booths line the perimeter of the restaurant—possibly a relic left over from the Mexican restaurant that previously occupied this space—and cheap-looking blinds shield diners from the main road. The end result is a hybrid of fine dining and your local Denny's. Still, the quality of the food makes it worth your while to overlook these distractions.

We went head over heels for the ravioli appetizer stuffed with duck and walnuts. Entrées include trout stuffed with apple, fennel, and leeks, or grilled duck breast topped with an apricot-jalapeño glaze and macadamia nuts. The salmon with pear chutney baked in parchment paper isn't anything to write home about, but it's satisfactory nonetheless. And when it comes to desserts, you won't want to leave town without trying Ira's famous peanut butter pie. **3401 South Hemlock; (503) 436-1588; expensive; lunch Wednesday–Sunday, dinner daily.**

❧❧❧ **KALYPSO, Cannon Beach** Kalypso, the newest addition to the Cannon Beach dining scene, describes itself as an "odyssey of alluring flavors"; we think it could just as easily be called an "odyssey of alluring colors." Its pale blue exterior, fronted by potted plants and large picture windows, is only the beginning. Inside, the dining room is a delightful blend of contemporary and whimsical decor, from the lavender sponge-painted walls to the Chinese paper lanterns hanging from the ceiling. Green chairs encircle intimate tables topped with fresh flowers and glowing candles, and purple cloth napkins add splashes of color to the white and beige linens.

For a sophisticated prelude to dinner, try the Italian salsa verde drizzled over grilled squid stuffed with prosciutto, shallots, and mushrooms. Dinner choices include Pacific snapper served over prosciutto hash and accompanied by a Creole crayfish sauce. Seafood dishes here show promise, but other selections could use some fine-tuning. (Our rack of lamb was presented in a manner more appropriate for spareribs, and the marinara sauce on the polenta lasagne was almost like tomato paste.) Still, given the newness of this restaurant and the obvious dedication of the chef and staff, there is every indication the kitchen will correct these minor shortcomings. Thankfully, our caramel-walnut tart edged with a cinnamon crust was a sheer delight, making Kalypso a worthwhile stop on your odyssey together. **140 North Hemlock Street; (503) 436-1585; moderate to expensive; call for seasonal hours.**

❤❤ **LOCAL SCOOP, Cannon Beach** There was a time when a boy would take a girl to the local ice cream shoppe and they would share whatever gooey offering they could handle with two spoons or two straws. Well, times have changed, and the Local Scoop has updated that innocent scene with striking Northwest flair. Towering pine ceilings, floor-to-ceiling windows, wrought-iron tables with cushioned chairs, and an authentic soda-fountain counter set an appropriately sweet mood. Yes, during the summer and on weekends parents may be treating their children to a sugar rush. But during off-hours, after a long stroll along the beach on a sunny afternoon, order a soda with two straws and gaze into each other's eyes until the last slurp is gone. Enjoy your refreshments in the glass-enclosed garden room or outside on the brick wrap-around patio if the day is sunny and warm. **156 North Hemlock Street; (503) 436-9551; inexpensive; call for seasonal hours.**

Outdoor Kissing

❤❤❤ **ECOLA STATE PARK, Cannon Beach** State parks are not usually considered good places for conducting affectionate business. They may be well kept, they may offer supreme scenery, but they also tend to be crowded and inundated with RVs and kids. Ecola State Park is an exception. The character of this area is so exceptional, the potency of the sights so remarkable, you won't notice anyone but yourselves and the splendor of nature.

Ecola State Park begins just outside Cannon Beach and extends nine miles north toward Seaside. From the park's entrance, a narrow road winds through a dense forest, where emerald green moss clings to tree branches above a fern-laden carpet of undergrowth. Even on the foggiest days, Ecola Point is a good place to catch a sunset; fog simply means fewer crowds and more mystical scenery. The point offers expansive views of Haystack Rock, and you can also watch the tumultuous surf crashing against the basalt headlands; past erosion and landslides have sculpted these headlands into the rugged panorama that exists today.

From Ecola Point, continue northward either by foot, following a two-mile trail with views of the coastline, or by car, winding farther into the forest until you reach the wind-sculpted trees of **INDIAN BEACH**. Hold hands as you take in views of Tillamook Rock, a 100-foot-high sea stack of basalt that broke away from the mainland years ago and now stands roughly a mile off-shore. Tillamook Head, the cape separating Seaside from Cannon Beach, was traversed by the Lewis and Clark expedition in 1806; nowadays it is explored by scenery-seeking hikers. (Watch for the sign at Indian Beach marking the six-mile Tillamook Head National Recreation Trail.) Both Ecola Point and Indian Beach offer grassy picnic areas overlooking sandy beaches. What better place to inspire romance than in the heart of nature? **(503) 436-2844, (800) 452-5687 (for campground reservations only); $3 entrance fee per vehicle.** *Two miles north of Cannon Beach, off Highway 101.*

Tolovana Park

Outdoor Kissing

❤❤❤❤ **HUG POINT, Tolovana Park** Even when the parking lot is full, there is still plenty of room at this windswept beach to make you feel like you're all by yourselves. If you find yourselves at Hug Point during low tide, give in to your curiosity and permit those kids inside you to play for the duration of your stay. The soaring cliffs along the beach are gouged with caves and crevasses of varying shapes and proportions. For the timid there are gentle tide pools and rocky fissures where you can easily observe marine life; for the more daring there are dark, ominous sea caves in which to hide. When your exploring is done and the tide reclaims your playground, the grown-ups in you can end the day by watching the dazzling sunset over the Pacific while you hug. **Free admission.** *Four miles south of Cannon Beach, off Highway 101.*

Arch Cape

❤❤❤ **ST. BERNARDS—A BED AND BREAKFAST, Arch Cape** Ensconced on one and a half acres of lovingly landscaped grounds, St. Bernards surveys views of the ocean across the street. Reminiscent of an old-world castle, the expansive wood-shingled chateau is like a treasure box waiting to be explored, with its collection of unusual European antiques, unexpected staircases, and dramatic guest rooms. Plush white carpets extend throughout the home, which is accented with French doors, beautiful tile work, and pieces from the owners' private art collection. A carousel horse is the highlight of the spacious living room, where the sometimes-boisterous innkeeper hosts an afternoon social hour next to the warmth of a blazing fire.

The inn's seven guest rooms are bona fide masterpieces, and all of them enjoy distant ocean views. White lace and pale peach walls decorate the Tower Room, which hosts a Louis XIV carved bed and a raised sitting area with a handsome settee situated beneath a pointed turret. Everything about the Tapestry Room is spacious, including its king-size bed and large bathroom with a two-person soaking tub. When the gas fireplace is lit, this room becomes especially cozy. For a taste of the French countryside, request the Provence Room, with its cathedral ceilings, authentic French linens, terra-cotta floors, and French doors that lead to a private terrace. A wood-accented tiled Jacuzzi is an added luxury here. The appropriately named Gauguin Room, decorated in muted shades of purple, pink, and peach characteristic of Gauguin's artwork, showcases a unique headboard made from an antique Polynesian porch railing.

Breakfast at St. Bernards is an all-out affair. French country pine tables clustered beneath a peaked turret in the conservatory allow lovely views of the patio garden area. One of the innkeepers is a former chef, and she spoils her guests with gourmet goodies like broiled grapefruit, cranberry upside-down coffee cake, and a corn bread and Dungeness crab quiche. A morning meal like this might keep you going until the baked goodies are set out in the early afternoon. **3 East Ocean Road; (503) 436-2800, (800) 436-2848; expensive to very expensive; minimum-stay requirement on weekends.**

Manzanita

The town of Manzanita is nestled between the endless Pacific Ocean and the base of Neahkahnie Mountain. Although this small, nondescript village has grown a bit over the past few years, it remains relatively undiscovered by tourists, particularly in comparison with Cannon Beach and Seaside. For beach roaming, kite flying, or an exhilarating day by the sea, this area is sheer perfection. Manzanita is close enough to Cannon Beach for you to take advantage of the nightlife and many dining spots, yet far enough from the crowds to give you a comforting sense of calm.

Hotel/Bed and Breakfast Kissing

THE ARBORS BED AND BREAKFAST, Manzanita Cozy up here after a windblown day spent exploring sandy beaches and flourishing tide pools. Set just a block from the beach on a quiet corner of Manzanita, this English-style cottage is embraced by gardens and a white picket fence. Choose between two small but comfortable guest rooms with hardwood floors, well-maintained private baths, and glimpses of the ocean. Dressed in white with country accents, these airy rooms make lovely retreats. Thick down comforters and patchwork quilts drape the queen-size beds in both of the modestly decorated rooms. Guests and innkeepers share a generous breakfast of muffins, scones, a baked entrée, and fruit, served family-style in the homey downstairs dining room. At these reasonable rates, you couldn't ask for more—you'll feel rejuvenated and ready for another day at the beach. **78 Idaho Avenue; (503) 368-7566; www.doormat.com/lodging/arbors.htm; moderate; minimum-stay requirement on holiday weekends; call for seasonal closures.**

❤❤❤❤ **THE INN AT MANZANITA, Manzanita** Set amid coastal pines and spruce trees, this contemporary Northwest inn sits a mere 200 feet from Manzanita's seven-mile stretch of beach. Guest rooms in the main building are a hybrid of sunny log cabin and comfortable hotel room, with pine and cedar walls that rise dramatically to form vaulted ceilings, and private decks that allow partial views of the ocean through the treetops. The rooms are further enhanced by all the amenities a couple could ever need to ensure romance: two-person Jacuzzi tubs, gas fireplaces, stocked wet bars, and firm, cozy beds with down comforters. All that's missing are a few personal touches to warm up the somewhat barren interiors.

Adjacent to the main building is a stunning two-level cottage known as the North Building. The four units here are decorated in subtle shades of nautical blue with wood paneling, Jacuzzi tubs, and small decks. Captain's beds with down comforters are tucked into cozy sunlit nooks separated from the living area by curtains. The downstairs units offer full kitchens; however, advantages in the upstairs units include vaulted ceilings, superior views, and a skylight over the bed for stargazing.

Three new units have recently been added in a second cottage, giving guests a total of 13 rooms from which to choose. The downstairs unit in this cottage has a kitchenette and a king-size bed, but the two units on the second floor offer better views of the nearby ocean. Other amenities include Jacuzzi tubs, contemporary interiors, and double-sided fireplaces that warm both the bedroom and living area. Considering the prices and the luxurious Northwest-style comfort, the Inn at Manzanita could easily become one of your favorite getaways along the coast. **67 Laneda Avenue; (503) 368-6754; moderate to expensive; minimum-stay requirement on weekends and seasonally.**

Romantic Suggestion: Head to the nearby town of Nehalem for hearty breakfast fixings at the **HILL HOUSE DELI & CAFE** (12870 Highway 101; 503-368-7933; inexpensive; breakfast and lunch daily). A cup of espresso with a side of hometown hospitality ought to get your day off to a wonderful start.

❤❤❤ **MANZANITA RENTAL COMPANY, Manzanita** If you've ever fantasized about living on the rugged Oregon coast with the pounding surf as the backdrop for your comings and goings, you're in luck. Manzanita Rental Company has a remarkable assortment of homes that you can call your own (for a little while, anyway). The 60 or so rental properties range from loft studios to spacious five-bedroom homes. Some have breathtaking ocean views; others are set back in wooded glens secluded from the rest of the world by old-growth trees. Many of the older properties have outdated furnishings and mismatched decor, so choose carefully. Interiors range from beach-frolic residences best for families to unique designer abodes that will delight the most finicky of travelers. Kick off your shoes, cuddle on the deck as you drink in the view, and revel in your home away from home on the Oregon coast. **32 Laneda Avenue; (503)**

368-6797, (800) 579-9801; www.doormat.com/mr/mr-cov. htm; inexpensive to expensive; minimum-stay requirement.

❀❀❀ **OCEAN INN, Manzanita** Situated at the very end of Manzanita's main thoroughfare, the Ocean Inn offers superior location and comfortable accommodations. Four mini-apartments are literally perched on a white sandy beach that reaches to the ocean's edge, while six newer units sit slightly back from the beach on the adjoining property. As advantageous as this sounds, the time-worn motel across the street detracts from the otherwise ideal location. Still, the four mini-apartments are endearing places to spend a cozy weekend together. Wood-burning stoves in three units warm the knotty pine interiors, which are accented with floral wallpapers, country antiques, and plenty of sunshine. Contemporary full kitchens (breakfast provisions are your responsibility), TV/VCRs, full bathrooms, and even private garages ensure that you will have all the comforts and conveniences of home. Two of the suites are equipped with glass doors that slide open to private outdoor decks where you can sit and watch the waves roll onto the shore for hours on end. Who could ever tire of these views?

Less endearing are the spacious one-bedroom units in the newer building. While they do allow couples plenty of space to spread out, the interiors are just too sparse to be cozy. Old-fashioned stoves and quilt comforters seem out of place amid the vaulted ceilings, modern bathrooms, and contemporary pine furnishings. Most of the units have full kitchens as well as private patios with views of the ocean over nearby rooftops. **32 Laneda Avenue; (503) 368-6797, (800) 579-9801; www.doormat.com/mr/mr-cov.htm; inexpensive to expensive; minimum-stay requirement.**

Restaurant Kissing

❀❀ **BLUE SKY CAFE, Manzanita** Casual is the word at the Blue Sky Cafe (the wait staff seem quite comfortable in their jeans and T-shirts), but the food is anything but ordinary. Simple wooden tables are topped with candles, and an eclectic mix of local artwork adorns the inviting dining rooms. Even though there is no special view, tables along the windows are preferred—this is a very popular restaurant, but it feels most calm around the perimeter. Organic ingredients are used in such remarkable appetizers as grilled polenta crostini and build-them-yourself rock shrimp rolls. Scrumptious entrées include filet mignon, crab and shrimp wontons, and Thai peanut chicken. Leave room for dessert, because anything prepared here is worth the effort. **154 Laneda Avenue; (503) 368-5712; moderate to expensive; no credit cards; dinner Wednesday–Sunday.**

❀❀❀ **JARBOE'S IN MANZANITA, Manzanita** Jarboe's is a must for an intimate, truly gourmet dinner. This charming, exceedingly small restaurant is situated in a wood-shingled cottage not far from Manzanita's beach. The two cozy dining rooms are decorated with crisp white walls, simple artwork, and innovative flower-pot lamps that hang from the vaulted ceiling. Both the crayfish bisque and the gravlax-and-potato terrine are superb. For your main course, try duck with lamb sausage or sturgeon displayed on a bed of fennel, asparagus, and roasted garlic. If you have difficulty deciding between the many enticing entrées, why not simplify the matter by choosing the three-course prix fixe dinner? Garden-fresh garnishes are sure to accompany whatever you choose. The service here is efficient enough, but lacks the warmth of genuine small-town hospitality. **137 Laneda Avenue; (503) 368-5113; expensive; call for seasonal hours.**

Outdoor Kissing

❦❦❦ **OSWALD WEST STATE PARK** Oswald West State Park is one of the most inspiring campgrounds in these parts—just ask any Northwest camping enthusiast. Its superior desirability has to do with its mode of access. In order to set up camp, you must walk a third of a mile down a rain-forest path, wheeling a cart (provided) with your things piled on top. This jaunt tends to eliminate featherweights and RVs, giving you and your loved one much-needed privacy. The forested setting is within arm's reach of the water, with footpaths that take you briskly down to a 13-mile stretch of surging surf. The scenery to the south is a succession of overlapping mountains jutting out of the ocean; their dark, jagged profiles are silhouetted against the distant horizon. White sand, effervescent surf, and a rock-clad shore make exploring here a treasure hunt. **$10 per campsite, $7 per extra car.** *Ten miles south of Cannon Beach, on the west side of Highway 101. Look for signs pointing the way.*

Wheeler

Outdoor Kissing

❦❦ **NEHALEM BAY KAYAK COMPANY, Wheeler** When the summer sun beats down and the gentle waters of the Nehalem River gleam invitingly, outdoor enthusiasts head to the tiny town of Wheeler with only one thought on their minds: kayaking. What could be more relaxing than cutting through the water at waist level, with a soft breeze on your face and your loved one in tow? Follow the curve of the river southward past country meadows and groves of trees to Nehalem Bay, or simply spend the afternoon exploring the river's edge. Whether you're a pro or a beginner, there's something here for everyone. Beginners receive a 20-minute orientation and an hour-long lesson by a skilled instructor before setting off on their own private adventure. Several days a week during the summer months, you can opt to join others for a three-hour tour down the river ($40 per person, includes gear, guide, and lunch); while this is a less romantic option, nature lovers will enjoy learning about the area's wildlife and ecology from the tour guide. Whether you decide to kayak alone or with others, a day on the river is a day you will never forget. **395 Highway 101; (503) 368-6055; $18 per hour, $26 per half-day, $36 per day for double kayaks; call for seasonal hours.**

Oceanside

Located about eight miles west of the main road on the small peninsula that forms Tillamook Bay, Oceanside offers sweet reprieve from the crowds that haunt the coast in the summertime. Harbored right on the coast, Oceanside is small and unassuming, which is part of its charm. There are only a few dining and lodging establishments worth recommending here, but the magnificent Oregon coastline is invitation enough. As the mist mingles with the cries of seabirds along this stretch of inviting but rugged beachfront, you'll find the stresses and cares of your busy life simply fading away.

Romantic Suggestion: For magnificent views of the surrounding area, head east to nearby Tillamook and hop on a 1942 "gull-wing" Stinson aircraft at **TILLAMOOK AIR TOURS** (503-842-1942). Private charters, scenic tours, and whale-watching expeditions are available daily. Twenty-minute tours are $30 per person; 30-minute tours are $40.

Hotel/Bed and Breakfast Kissing

❦ **HOUSE ON THE HILL MOTEL, Oceanside** You know what they say: Location is everything. Romantics know there's more to heart-stirring accommodations than a spectacular view, but we have to admit it helps. This very standard motel is an anomaly in a book such as ours; but what it lacks in romantic ambience, it makes up for in surrounding splendor. Balanced atop one of the highest points along the entire Oregon coast, these pale blue, contemporary buildings boast absolutely spectacular ocean views. One look through the telescope in the lobby's viewing room, and you'll be hooked. (You'll be so enthralled, you probably won't even mind the tacky sea paraphernalia cluttering the room.) Witness migrating whales that occasionally breach on the horizon or the hundreds of resident sea lions basking in the sun on rocky outcroppings. The telescope also provides excellent viewing of the Three Arch Rocks National Wildlife Refuge, the largest seabird sanctuary in North America.

It's a shame the owners haven't done more with the guest rooms, which don't begin to live up to the property's views. The accommodations are clean and well maintained, but the cheap linens, artwork, and furnishings are more functional than attractive. Even the Anniversary Suite, with its floral linens and private deck, is disappointing. All 16 units offer amazing ocean views, but the paper-thin walls make it possible to overhear entire conversations from adjacent rooms. Nevertheless, with views of this caliber at your fingertips, a stay here can make you feel a little closer to heaven, and a lot closer to the mesmerizing sea. **1816 Maxwell Mountain Road; (503) 842-6030; www. choicemall.com/houseonthehill; inexpensive to moderate; minimum-stay requirement on holidays.**

Restaurant Kissing

❤❤ **ROSEANNA'S RESTAURANT, Oceanside** Roseanna's is Oceanside's only oceanfront restaurant. In fact, except for the little coffee shop down the road, it's literally the *only* restaurant in town. But even if there were a number of dining establishments to choose from, we would still recommend eating here. Views of the ever-changing ocean surround this vintage Northwest dining establishment. An assortment of shells and other eccentric seaside trinkets ornament the dining room's wooden walls. Pink floral tablecloths and green plastic chairs create a casual mood, augmented by swivel stools that flank a counter at the front of the restaurant. While Roseanna's atmosphere is easygoing, the kitchen takes its job seriously, producing healthy breakfasts, lunches, and dinners. The menu highlights regional cuisine and fresh seafood; expect salads chock-full of crisp, fresh vegetables and a variety of creative pasta dishes that are sure to satisfy. In the evening, nature prepares another treat to enhance your meal: an ambrosial sunset for two. **1490 Pacific Street; (503) 842-7351; moderate; lunch and dinner daily.**

Romantic Warning: Roseanna's doesn't accept reservations, and due to Oceanside's limited dining options, the wait for a table here can be *ridiculously* long. But look on the bright side. You'll have time for a stroll on the beach, and the longer you wait, the more likely you are to enjoy a late summer sunset while you dine.

Outdoor Kissing

❤❤❤❤ **THREE CAPES SCENIC LOOP** Near Tillamook, Highway 101 abandons the seashore and veers through a long stretch of overdeveloped and unsightly shopping areas. To avoid these distractions, we recommend taking a detour along the Three Capes Scenic Loop. Even at the height of summer the tourists seem to be elsewhere, and you can explore this exquisite passage at a slow, cruising pace. You'll begin near Tillamook Bay, where wispy trees outline marshy mudflats and fishing boats dot the horizon. Follow the winding road toward **CAPE MEARES STATE PARK**, where you can survey the ocean from forested hilltops or from inside a small lighthouse. Migrating seabirds and resident orcas, sea lions, and porpoises are easily seen from this exquisite vantage point, while waterfalls trickle down rocky cliffs into the crashing waves below. Though Cape Meares does draw crowds on hot summer days, if you follow signs to the park's wind-sculpted Sitka spruce (better known as the Octopus Tree) and the private lookout beyond, you'll find a bit more privacy and breathtaking views of the coastline.

Continue south (by car) toward Oceanside and Netarts, where the road drops back to sea level. Both hikers and romantics will appreciate **CAPE LOOK-OUT STATE PARK**, which has gorgeous walking paths that lead down to the beach and nature trails that climb to the tip of rocky lookout points. Unfortunately, easy-access camping facilities here also mean more crowds.

Follow the loop farther south to **ANDERSON VIEWPOINT**, a precipitous mountain bluff that overlooks everything north, south, and west. Just a little farther south, you'll find vast expanses of sand dunes along the placid shores of Sand Lake before reaching the third and final cape: **CAPE KIWANDA**. This sandy stretch of beach is home to a magnificent offshore haystack rock, not far from the heart of Pacific City. *North of Tillamook you will see signs for the Three Capes Scenic Loop. Turn west off Highway 101 and follow the signs along this loop to Cape Meares, around and south to Oceanside, and down to Pacific City, where the 38-mile loop rejoins Highway 101.*

Netarts

Restaurant Kissing

❀❀ **MARINA'S RESTAURANT, Netarts** Granted, this roadside restaurant doesn't look like much from the outside, but it would be a shame to pass up such an enticing Italian dining experience. Inside, knotty pine walls lend a rustic flavor to the restaurant's two small dining rooms, which are adorned with eclectic local artwork and fluffy floral curtains. Closely spaced tables are draped with burgundy-and-green floral linens and topped with fresh flowers. The adept kitchen staff more than makes up for what the restaurant lacks in exterior charm. Though at first glance the menu seems to offer little more than steak and seafood, this restaurant has won local acclaim for its delicious Italian fare. The sautéed scallops, manicotti, and antipasto are all sheer perfection. After one bite, Marina's will have your vote of approval too. **4785 Netarts Highway West; (503) 842-8525; moderate to expensive; call for seasonal hours.**

Sandlake

Hotel/Bed and Breakfast Kissing

❀❀❀❀ **SANDLAKE COUNTRY INN, Sandlake** When planning a romantic getaway to the Oregon coast, most couples look for oceanfront accommodations, or at least an ocean view. Although this attitude is perfectly understandable, it deprives amorous-minded travelers of the wonderful Sandlake Country Inn, which is definitely a very good place to kiss. Bountiful flower gardens fill the front yard of this 100-year-old farmhouse hidden on a quiet country road off the **THREE CAPES SCENIC LOOP** (reviewed on page 482). Rasping frogs and chirping crickets provide the only sounds to pierce the country quiet. Guests can wander through the property's tranquil acreage and watch three resident beavers busy at work on a dam in the nearby creek.

The inn's countrified, farm-like surroundings give no hint of the elegance and luxury that await you in the four very private suites. Gracious innkeepers tend to all the affectionate details to ensure that your stay is comfortable. The smell of freshly baked cookies and sweet apple cider permeates the house, enticing guests to stop for refreshments in the downstairs parlor before checking in to their rooms. Creaking hardwood floors give historic flavor to the unusually elegant rooms, while dramatic floral fabrics and wallpapers add personality. The spacious Starlight Suite is situated behind a curtain at the top of the stairs in the original farmhouse. (The four connecting rooms in this spacious suite have doors that can be closed for privacy.) A double-sided fireplace warms the suite's master bedroom and extra sitting room; you'll also find a TV/VCR, French doors that open onto a private deck, and a wood-paneled bathroom with a whirlpool tub for two.

Downstairs in the Timber Room, sumptuous linens drape a four-poster king-size bed, French doors open onto a private deck and gardens, Oriental rugs cover hardwood floors, and a large bathroom boasts a sunken whirlpool tub set behind lace draperies. The Rose Garden Room is smaller but equally charming, with a netted, canopied king-size bed and a sitting area that faces an abundant flower garden. For total privacy we recommend the neighboring self-contained Cottage, with its atrium doors that open onto a deck beside a burbling creek. In the inviting bedroom, a gleaming black whirlpool tub also offers creek-side views. A full kitchen, cozy breakfast nook, and TV/VCR are additional luxuries.

Because the owners value your privacy almost as much as you do, an overwhelmingly generous three-course breakfast is delivered for you to enjoy undisturbed in your room. Imagine waking to fresh-squeezed orange juice, Oregon hazelnut toast, grapefruit with raspberry sauce, pumpkin–chocolate chip muffins, baked apple oatmeal, and zucchini frittata. The menu changes daily, making every morning a special event.

Romantic Suggestion: Your hospitable hostess can also provide a "Togetherness Basket" ($34) for you to take along on a tour of nature's glory. Enjoy local goodies such as smoked salmon and Tillamook cheese, sourdough baguettes, hot clam chowder, fresh fruit, sparkling cider, and chocolate truffles. Consider a picnic at **SAND LAKE** (see Outdoor Kissing), just a mile down the road, for an exemplary Northwest experience. **8505 Galloway Road; (503) 965-6745; inexpensive to expensive; minimum-stay requirement on weekends seasonally.**

Outdoor Kissing

❧❧❧❧ **SAND LAKE** Seabirds seek refuge at this quiet lake and estuary surrounded by sand flats and grass-covered dunes. When the tide is out, you can walk around the perimeter of the lake and explore the tide pools that eventually merge with the raging Pacific. Astonishingly, this exquisite beach area is not popular with locals or tourists (we don't know why), and the odds of having the beach to yourselves are in your favor. We can't think of a better place for an inspirational romantic interlude. *From southbound Highway 101, take the Sandlake turnoff, go 5.5 miles to the fire station, and turn right onto Galloway Road. Follow Galloway Road until it dead-ends at a campground. Turn left just before the campground entrance at a sign that reads "FISHERMAN'S DAY USE AREA," and follow this road into the parking lot. The lake and estuary are on the other side of the sand dunes.*

Pacific City

Hotel/Bed and Breakfast Kissing

❧❧❧ **EAGLE'S VIEW BED AND BREAKFAST, Pacific City** Eagle's View wins hands down as the best kissing bargain along the Oregon coast. Set inland and surrounded by gently rolling countryside, this newly constructed home commands sweeping views of Nestucca Bay from its perch atop a quiet hill. Four acres of nature and all its glories can be yours for a weekend at prices that will make your hearts sing. Here eagles soar overhead, a series of decks call for quiet reflection, and walking paths lead to private sitting spots. And how can we ignore a place that has a heart-shaped pond in the backyard?

Country quilts adorn the crisp white walls throughout this two-story home. All five guest rooms have been tastefully appointed with plush comforters, European armoires, and plenty of sunshine. Colorful stenciling in each of the private bathrooms is an endearing touch as well. The Yellow Room downstairs offers a private entrance and a whirlpool tub; however, we prefer the four rooms upstairs with their tall, knotty pine ceilings and serene vistas. Honeymoon and Deerfield boast whirlpool tubs and incredible views of Nestucca Bay, while the remaining two rooms overlook the landscaped backyard.

In the morning, you'll be tempted out of bed by the aroma of a full country breakfast. Eat in the privacy of your own room, or join other guests downstairs in the Great Room for fresh fruit, granola, homemade pastries, and the innkeepers' famous Nestucca Eggs: scrambled eggs combined with smoked salmon, cream cheese, and green onions, served over a warm croissant. Sound enticing? It is. All this, and you're only minutes from the sandy beaches of Pacific City. **37975 Brooten Road; (503) 965-7600, (888) 846-3292; inexpensive.**

Unrated INN AT CAPE KIWANDA, Pacific City Although construction was still in progress at the time this book went to press, we have high hopes for the Inn at Cape Kiwanda. From the shingled exterior to the exposed wooden beams to the rustic pine furnishings, this ocean-view hotel exudes a distinctive Northwest ambience. The inviting lobby wraps around a central fireplace, with a wall of windows showcasing Cape Kiwanda's haystack rock. All 35 guest rooms feature gas fireplaces, down comforters, mini-bars, and ocean views from private decks; a few rooms have the added luxury of Jacuzzi tubs. If all goes as planned, the Bridal Suite promises to be extra-special. Its king-size bed, small kitchenette, two fireplaces, tiled bathroom, and Jacuzzi tub with ocean views distinguish this room from all the others. In the morning, guests at the inn can head downstairs to the coffee shop for breakfast. **33105 Cape Kiwanda Drive; (888) 965-7001; www.capekiwanda.com; expensive to very expensive.**

Lincoln City

Lincoln City isn't a destination around which to plan a romantic itinerary. Instead, bring along your shopping list and take advantage of Oregon's tax-free outlet stores. To its credit, Lincoln City does offer one kiss-worthy spot for dining after a long day of shopping; however, you would do better looking elsewhere for romantic accommodations. This section of the Oregon coast is too commercialized to feel like the Northwest getaway most of us are seeking.

Romantic Warning: With the opening of the Chinook Winds Casino at the north end of town, traffic on weekends and holidays can be maddening (even if you are just passing through on your way to a more endearing destination).

Restaurant Kissing

❀❀❀❀ **BAY HOUSE, Lincoln City** This weathered building, all by itself on a steep bank off the main highway, is hardly what you'd call a showcase. But pull over! Bay House enjoys a flawless view of tidal Siletz Bay, the driftwood-strewn shoreline, and the flow of the calm, clear blue water. Just about every table is blessed with its share of the lovely scenery. The newly renovated interior is elegant and modern, with large picture windows, upholstered chairs, and private booths edged in cherry wood. Colorful tulips and glowing votive candles top each of the white-cloaked tables. Service can be leisurely at times, but you won't mind lingering over these views.

The menu lists an enterprising assortment of Northwest creations made from local fish and meats. Meals here are consistently outstanding. Creamy onion soup or portobello mushrooms with grilled polenta make excellent appetizers. When choosing an entrée, don't miss the shellfish pan roast linguine: prawns, clams, scallops, and mussels are pan roasted with capers, tomatoes, roasted garlic, and kalamata olives in an herb broth. Simply splendid! Equally wonderful are the desserts; if you forget to save room, at least order one and sample it together. **5911 Southwest Highway 101; (541) 996-3222; expensive; call for seasonal hours.**

Kernville

Restaurant Kissing

❧ **KERNVILLE STEAK AND SEAFOOD HOUSE, Kernville** From its weathered wood exterior to its knotty pine interior, this is a casual, down-home eatery where portions are more than generous. The emphasis is strictly on meat and seafood dishes. Although appetizers often include deep-fried Kernville potatoes or mushrooms sautéed in a garlic-wine sauce, that's where the vegetables start and stop. We loved the fresh halibut encrusted in Parmesan, but the teriyaki steak was drenched in an overly sweet sauce. Those with large appetites can tackle a king cut of prime rib, the steak and prawns dinner, or a bucket full of sweet butter clams. You might not experience elegant intimacy here, but you are right on the Siletz River, where great blue herons often feed at the water's edge. So sit back, admire the view, and enjoy the hearty fixings. **186 Siletz Highway; (541) 994-6200; moderate to expensive; dinner daily.**

Gleneden Beach

Restaurant Kissing

❧❧❧❧ **CHEZ JEANNETTE, Gleneden Beach** Thick branches curl around the roof and walls of this stone-fronted house resting snugly upon a vine-covered hill. The interior is divinely elegant, yet remarkably cozy and welcoming, with two blazing fireplaces warming the softly lit dining rooms. Soothing piano music envelops you as you gaze out the windows at lush foliage and colorful flower boxes. Velvety green draperies, lush carpet, regal high-backed chairs, and tables set with bone china and crystal create a thoroughly intimate and romantic atmosphere in which to enjoy delectable French dishes.

Just about everything is made from scratch at Chez Jeannette, from the oven-fresh herb baguettes to the enticing homemade desserts. We suggest you begin your meal with escargots à la bourguignonne or ragout of wild and button mushrooms served on toasted bread. As for the main course, you can't go wrong with any of the chef's nightly seafood, game, or pasta selections. (Our spinach pasta with scallops was superb!) One look at the dessert tray and we guarantee you won't escape without a little taste of heaven. **7150 Old Highway 101; (541) 764-3434; expensive; dinner daily.**

Depoe Bay

Depoe Bay is the Oregon coast's prime spot for whale watching, especially from December through April, when cetacean migration is in full swing. Regardless of whether you come here to whale watch or not, this small strip of a town is an entertaining place to spend a day. Massive waves crash endlessly against its rocky shores. There is no beach separating the town from the sea, just formidable black rocks rising up out of the water. Sun-starved Northwesterners usually hope for clear days, but witnessing a turbulent storm here is a moving experience, not soon forgotten.

Hotel/Bed and Breakfast Kissing

❤❤❤ **CHANNEL HOUSE INN, Depoe Bay** If you're looking for a cozy getaway with fantastic ocean views, Channel House Inn is definitely worth a visit. Don't let its rather ordinary appearance disappoint you: A world of closeness with each other and the sea awaits inside. Appropriately named, this towering blue building sits high upon the rocky cliffs of Depoe Bay and overlooks one of the world's smallest channels (only 50 feet wide). The interior displays a nautical theme, from the whales etched into the glass doors at the entrance to guest rooms with names like Channel Watch, The Bridge, and Crow's Nest. Scattered throughout the hallways are maritime antiques such as brass ship fittings, a polished captain's wheel, and part of an archaic diving suit.

Almost all of the 12 contemporary units feature views of waves crashing against the venerable coastline. The larger, more desirable oceanfront rooms and suites have their own private decks, where you can lie back in a steaming hot tub for two and watch the evening sun disappear beneath the sea. After a relaxing soak, let the gas fireplace warm and dry you while the stresses of life ebb away. In rooms like Whale Watch, the bedroom seems to jut out over the water like the cliffs themselves; here you can lie in bed, surrounded by two walls of windows, and bask in the sights, sounds, and smells of the ocean in total privacy. (Boat traffic during the day may be your only distraction.) Each room is decorated in subtle shades of blue, with pine furnishings, plush new comforters, and a pair of binoculars for whale watching. Several units offer the additional convenience of small kitchenettes. In the morning, head downstairs to the cheery breakfast nook for a buffet of fresh fruit and pastries. **35 Ellingson Street; (541) 765-2140, (800) 447-2140; www.channelhouse.com; inexpensive to very expensive.**

Outdoor Kissing

❤❤ **FOGARTY CREEK STATE PARK, Depoe Bay** Fogarty Creek State Park may not look like much at first; the signs from the highway lead you east to a rather unattractive parking area with a few picnic tables scattered about. But once you leave your car behind and take the pedestrian underpass to the other side of the highway, you're in for a treat. This small stretch of sandy beach is an ideal setting for picnics and whale watching. Take in the dramatic display of waves and mist as the turbulent surf breaks against the rugged rock formations or, if the sea is in a more tranquil mood, explore sea life in the peaceful tide pools. Such a striking seascape is bound to inspire a kiss or two. **$6 day-use fee for parking.** *One mile north of Depoe Bay, on Highway 101.*

Otter Rock

Hotel/Bed and Breakfast Kissing

❧ **INN AT OTTER CREST, Otter Rock** If it's natural splendor you're seeking, the Inn at Otter Crest offers more than its share. From the moment you turn off the highway and embark upon the curvy descent to the inn, the magic of the area is clearly evident. One moment the road hugs a perilous cliff; the next it disappears beneath dense canopies of foliage. Disappointingly, once you reach the inn's entrance, it is also clearly evident that the accommodations do not come close to matching the quality of the surroundings.

The half-dozen or so gray wooden buildings scattered over the property's 35 acres are overdue for refurbishing. All 286 units are individually owned and decorated by private owners; the inn simply rents out vacant rooms to guests when the owners have not reserved them. Rates vary, depending on the decor and amenities of each room. Most are modestly appointed with outdated furnishings, full kitchens, standard baths, and private entrances. Some come equipped with TVs and VCRs as well, and all suites and studios have fireplaces. On the positive side, each room has a private deck that allows incredible views of the craggy coastline and the churning ocean beyond. (This is the perfect place to catch glimpses of the gray whales and seals that occasionally visit the coves.) It's doubtful that these extremely average rooms will spark romance, but the quiet tranquillity of the property is bound to turn your thoughts inward toward matters of the heart.

At the foot of the hillside, **THE FLYING DUTCHMAN RESTAURANT** (expensive; breakfast, lunch, and dinner daily) features wonderful views of the ocean, although the food will leave your palate wanting. Nearby you'll also find the inn's community saunas, heated outdoor pool, hot tubs, and outdoor sports area. **301 Otter Crest Loop; (541) 765-2111, (800) 452-2101; moderate to very expensive; minimum-stay requirement on holidays.**

Newport

Tourists flock to Newport during the summer to eat fish 'n' chips at the tired bayfront, frequent the **OREGON COAST AQUARIUM,** and take in the sights at **YAQUINA HEAD OUTSTANDING NATURAL AREA.** Don't be dismayed by your first impression of this small, nondescript seaside town. Once you step beyond the commercialized strip of Highway 101, the dramatic ocean surf and wide stretches of sandy beach are a lover's paradise.

Hotel/Bed and Breakfast Kissing

❤❤ **NYE BEACH HOTEL, Newport** Gleaming brightly amid its rundown neighbors, this cosmopolitan hotel is a diamond in the rough, so to speak. The hotel's striking shingle-sheathed facade has been painted chile-pepper red. Inside, the color scheme is equally eye-catching, with a hunter green lobby and banisters accented with splashes of taupe and cranberry. The lobby is also home to several lovebirds and canaries that twitter at guests from the safety of their cages.

Overall, this hotel is more eclectic than romantic. All 18 guest rooms are identical, with fireplaces, bent-willow love seats, small private baths, thick down comforters, and black-lacquered bed frames imported from Holland. For the purposes of our book, we recommend the six rooms with Jacuzzi soaking tubs and unobstructed ocean views. In a half-hearted attempt to decorate the maize-colored walls, a few theater posters have been tacked haphazardly around the rooms; unfortunately, they do little to liven up the unusually spartan, hostel-like atmosphere. Still, if you open the sliding glass door to your tiny balcony, you can doze off to the continuous melody of the nearby ocean surf. **219 Northwest Cliff Street; (541) 265-3334; www.teleport.com/~nyebeach; inexpensive to moderate.**

Romantic Note: For a casual lunch or dinner, simply head downstairs to the brightly decorated oceanfront **NYE BEACH CAFE** (inexpensive; all-day bistro menu). Your senses will be overstimulated by the red-and-yellow-tiled floor, the colorful posters peppering the walls, and the eclectic mix of Mediterranean, Caribbean, and Mexican food on the menu. Hanging from the ceiling are pots of cacti with branches reaching downward like long tresses of hair. To top it all off, a small aviary is located outside on the main deck. This place is anything but boring!

❤❤❤ **OCEAN HOUSE BED AND BREAKFAST, Newport** For over a decade Ocean House has maintained its reputation as a treasured place to stay. Rain or shine, you will find many reasons to prolong your visit. A sweeping lawn and meticulously maintained gardens envelop this 1941 Cape Cod home. A private staircase winds down to Agate Beach, where four miles of firm sand summon those who want to shed their shoes and comb the beach for seashells and agates. A series of cedar decks strategically placed along the bluff take full advantage of sunset's magic, and the homey common rooms, including a glass-enclosed sitting room, share this same enchanting perspective.

Recent renovations have turned the Ocean House's five guest rooms into ultra-romantic retreats; unfortunately, dated touches and unattractive artwork still show up occasionally. Michelle's Room has been done up in an airy white and green color scheme. It offers a four-poster canopied bed and an adjacent glass-enclosed sunroom featuring magnificent ocean views. In the Rainbow Room, cathedral ceilings soar above a four-poster bed covered with plush linens and colorful pillows. French doors open onto a private porch serenaded by the sound of the surf. A corner Jacuzzi tub is situated in the wonderfully spacious white-tiled bathroom. The Overlook Room has its own fireplace and a wraparound porch that surveys the gardens and the ocean. An inviting king-size bed is framed by picturesque bookcases adorned with baskets, books, and seashells. Unusual wallpapers accent the bathroom, which also boasts a corner Jacuzzi tub. Even the smallest room, Melody's Room, has been lovingly redecorated with light blue walls, a four-poster bed, and a bathroom with a Jacuzzi tub. The remaining room offers a king-bed and a tiny sitting area.

Enjoy a satisfying breakfast of Belgian waffles or quiche, served downstairs in the dining room each morning. Views of the garden and water beyond can be enjoyed from the solarium, located just off the breakfast nook. **4920 Northwest Woody Way; (541) 265-6158, (800) 562-2632; www.ocean house.com; inexpensive to expensive.**

❤❤ **STARFISH POINT, Newport** The freshly painted buildings at Starfish Point are a welcome change of pace after the industrial scenes along Highway 101. Set atop an oceanfront bluff, the six condominium-style units have bay windows that emphasize stunning views of the ocean. Each spacious two-bedroom, two-story townhouse provides everything you could possibly think of to ensure a totally luxurious getaway: a sunken dining and living room, private decks, a stereo, TV/VCR, fireplace, full kitchen with modern appliances, and two bathrooms. The romantic highlight of every unit is an enormous tiled Jacuzzi tub set beneath skylights and overlooking the ocean. Despite the luxurious amenities and architecture, we must warn you that the decor could use some sprucing up—particularly the dated carpeting, drab linens, and unattractive artwork.

Outside, a landscaped deck area extends toward the water, providing lovely views of the water through stands of trees. For an even closer look at the water, guests can follow the well-groomed but steep trail leading down to a relatively secluded four-mile stretch of shoreline. **140 Northwest 48th Street; (541) 265-3751; www.ohwy.com/or/s/starfish.htm; expensive.**

❤❤❤ **TYEE LODGE OCEANFRONT BED AND BREAKFAST, Newport** Named for the Chinook word for salmon, this newly renovated contemporary home embraces the Native American heritage of the Pacific Northwest. Situated on a cliff overlooking the ocean, Tyee Lodge offers breathtaking views of Agate Beach and Yaquina Head from almost every part of the house. Each guest room honors a different local tribe, with names like Tillamook, Siletz, and Alsea. All five are sparsely appointed, with sage and burgundy color schemes, down comforters, queen-size beds, private baths with skylights, pine furnishings, and wrought-iron mirrors. Distinctive theme-inspired artwork adorns the cream walls in each room. In the Yaquina Room, an inviting bay window is a perfect spot for watching the waves roll in on the beach below. The Chinook Room outshines the others, with its gas fireplace and extraordinary view to the southwest.

Follow the switchback trail down to the sandy beach, where you can explore tide pools to your hearts' content. Or catch a brilliant sunset from the outdoor fire pit. More serene souls will find contentment in the sunlit grand room, which has been tastefully decorated in subtle greens and beiges, with large windows facing the sparkling ocean. Snuggle up in the plaid overstuffed chairs near the slate fireplace as you sip complimentary coffee or tea. In the adjacent dining room, you'll discover a glass etching of the lodge's logo: a salmon done in traditional totem style. Mornings here begin with a full breakfast of fresh cinnamon rolls and smoked-salmon quiche. Honeymoons, anniversaries, and other special occasions often merit breakfast in bed, so be sure to make arrangements with the innkeepers beforehand. **4925 Northwest Woody Way; (541) 265-8953, (888) 553-8933; www.newportnet.com/ tyee/home.htm; moderate.**

Waldport

Hotel/Bed and Breakfast Kissing

☙☙❣ **CLIFF HOUSE, Waldport** Perched on a cliff overlooking the clamorous surf, this bed and breakfast is full of personality, from its bright blue exterior to its eclectic decor to its flamboyant innkeeper. The interior is filled (and we mean *filled*) with intriguing antiques, heirlooms, and knickknacks. The common area feels a bit cramped, but the vaulted ceiling, knotty pine walls, hardwood floors, hanging ferns, and beach-stone fireplace make it an inviting spot from which to admire the ocean view.

All four guest rooms are plushly decorated with chandeliers and exquisite European antiques. Like the common area, some guest rooms feel a bit too cluttered for comfort, but guests with a taste for the eclectic will undoubtedly find them charming. Done up in deep shades of maroon and green, the Library offers views of the glorious sea from its queen-size cherry-wood bed with lace canopy. Its detached private bath is only two steps away. In the Morning Star Room, inhale the fresh ocean air on the private balcony or stargaze through skylights above the king-size bed. A panoramic view and a private entrance make the Alsea Room a pleasing choice; however, the best room in the house is the Bridal Suite. This suite features supreme privacy, in addition to ocean views, a wood-burning stove, and its own balcony. Taking up center stage is a queen-size 15th-century sleigh bed, adorned with a canopy and powder blue tufted velvet. Soak your cares away in the large Jacuzzi tub in the suite's fully mirrored bathroom, or try out the two-headed shower for some good, clean fun. Breakfast is served to the Bridal Suite each morning at a small table overlooking the thunderous waves.

Breakfast entrées such as Dutch babies, crab quiche, or French toast are accompanied by a fruit compote and coffee, tea, or juice. Guests in rooms other than the Bridal Suite partake at one large table in the oceanfront breakfast area. After your morning meal, be sure to take advantage of the large, adjacent common deck, which has a panoramic view of the ocean to the north, west, and east. In the center of the glassed-in deck you'll find a massive hot tub with massaging jets that move up and down your spine—a wonderful way to begin your day on the Oregon coast. **1450 Adahi Road, on Yaquina John Point; (541) 563-2506; www.virtualcities.com/ons/or/z/orb5z01.htm; moderate to very expensive; minimum-stay requirement on weekends and holidays; closed mid-November–February.**

Yachats

In spite of its popularity as a tourist destination, the tiny oceanfront town of Yachats retains a spirit of obscurity, lacking the urban sprawl that proliferates in many of the other coastal towns along Highway 101. Luckily, Yachats is unlikely to change since it is protected from developers by several surrounding state and federal parks. Harbored in the Siuslaw National Forest, Yachats is one of the few places where the coastal mountain range actually merges with the shoreline. The hiking terrain ranks with the best on the coast, and the beaches are relatively remote and empty. Better yet, Yachats has some of the most impressive and romantic bed and breakfasts in the area.

Hotel/Bed and Breakfast Kissing

❤❤❸ **KITTIWAKE, Yachats** The ocean views from this gray contemporary home are so sensational, you'll wonder if the innkeepers ever experience high tide in their living room—the careening ocean surf seems *that* close. The two light and airy oceanfront rooms are appointed with brightly colored linens (handmade by the innkeeper herself), lovely wood furnishings, and French doors that open out to the crashing surf. Guests in Room 2 can appreciate the inn's gorgeous location from the vantage point of a large, private whirlpool tub.

Whether your experience here falls into the moderate or expensive price range depends entirely on which breakfast option you chose. A continental breakfast is included in the price of your stay and served in the privacy of your room at a specified time. On weekends only, you can choose to pay a bit more for a full breakfast presented upstairs in the dining room or outside on the deck when weather permits. Although we found it a bit awkward to wander through the innkeepers' quarters to the upstairs dining room, the views from the second story are magnificent. Your six-course, full breakfast may begin with fresh juices, home-baked coffee cake, and lox and bagels, followed by a European entrée such as stuffed crêpes, egg blossoms, or Austrian pancakes. This feast is served to guests at one shared table, which isn't great for kissing, but with this array of goodies your appetites will keep you too busy to remember your lips anyway.

You can walk along the beach at any time of day or night in any season, thanks to the innkeepers' thoughtful supply of beach amenities, which includes boots, hats, scarves, rain ponchos, warm jackets, and flashlights. If you've decided on the full breakfast option, we highly recommend taking an extended walk before breakfast to whet your appetites for the extravaganza to come. **95368 Highway 101; (541) 547-4470; www.ohwy.com/or/k/kittiwbb. htm; moderate to expensive; minimum-stay requirement on weekends and holidays; call for seasonal closures.**

❤❤ **MORNING STAR BED AND BREAKFAST, Yachats** At first glance, you might not expect too much from this gray-shingled bed and breakfast set directly on busy Highway 101. But we strongly urge you to take a second look, as we did: Morning Star is full of small surprises. Although the common areas and breakfast nook are somewhat cluttered and a bit on the homey side, French doors at the back of the house open up to reveal an outdoor hot tub sporting some of the best views around.

The three guest rooms, located on the upstairs level, are named for well-known artists. Each one is appointed with plush linens, a private bathroom, and art in keeping with the room's namesake. Icart is the most impressive, thanks to its intricate queen-size steel canopy bed, rich window treatments, shoji screens, gas fireplace, and original Icart etchings. Its brightly tiled private bathroom doesn't quite go with the room's decor, but is still spacious and pretty. Matisse has been done up in shades of purple and pink, and offers a king-size bed and a peekaboo view of the water; unfortunately, traffic noise is quite audible from this room. O'Keeffe features great ocean views, a black Jacuzzi tub in the bathroom, and pastel linens.

After you have enjoyed your full country breakfast, wander over to the adjacent Morning Star Gallery, which is run by the innkeeper and filled with wonderful local art and crafts. **95668 Highway 101; (541) 547-4412; www.teleport.com/~artgal; inexpensive to expensive; minimum-stay requirement on weekends.**

❤❤❤❤ **SEA QUEST BED AND BREAKFAST, Yachats** If we could award a five-kiss rating to this bed and breakfast, we would. Everything you could possibly want in a romantic getaway is here, and much, much more. Residing a mere 50 feet from the ocean's edge, this contemporary 7,000-square-foot wood home exemplifies Oregon coast architecture at its best. The five beautifully designed guest rooms feature bright linens and wallpapers, thick down comforters, queen-size beds, private entrances, and tantalizing views. Shutters open from the bedrooms onto spacious Jacuzzi soaking tubs in the tiled bathrooms.

Eclectic is the only word that accurately describes the ever-changing decor throughout the home. Framed artwork covers just about every inch of wall space, while corners and sitting areas overflow with knickknacks and trinkets. You'll find a little bit of everything here, from the whimsical to the mundane. A room off the common area called "General Mess" is filled with beach toys, boots, and jackets for guests to use.

Upstairs, a crackling fire warms the dining/living room, where three walls of windows showcase the fantastic ocean view. An enormous brick fireplace boasts a different, imaginative mantelpiece each season; when we visited, large sunflowers adorned an old-fashioned bicycle hung from the ceiling. This comfortable room is filled with games, books, and clusters of tables and overstuffed chairs; it's also a perfect spot to enjoy the full buffet-style breakfast. Morning repasts may include homemade granola and jams, fresh fruit, a variety of baked breads, coffee cake, and delicious croissants stuffed with eggs, cheese, and mushrooms. The enthusiastic innkeepers are a delight, but if you want privacy clearly specify this—or during breakfast you may encounter unwanted social introductions. **95354 Highway 101; (541) 547-3782, (800) 341-4878; www.seaq.com; expensive; minimum-stay requirement seasonally and on holidays.**

♥♥♥♦ SERENITY BED AND BREAKFAST, Yachats Don't make the mistake of bypassing this outstanding romantic destination simply because it's not on the ocean. A six-mile drive inland from Highway 101 brings you to this large, white home and accompanying guest house, spread out on a ten-acre sweep of lawn lined with red alders and kissed by distant ocean breezes. Inside, you'll find a haven filled with unexpected luxury and opulence.

We had difficulty choosing between the four ornate guest suites because each one has been lavished with sensuous details and appointed in a unique theme. Alt Heidelberg, the smallest suite, features a double bed and antiques from Heidelberg, Germany, while Bavaria is brimming with Bavarian knickknacks and accented with beautiful blond wood. Europa holds an enticing assortment of fine European antiques, including an iron bed draped in blue-and-white linens. The most opulent room is La Italia, also called the Honeymoon Suite, with its white-veiled wrought-iron canopy bed, tall ceilings, and large, tiled Jacuzzi tub. Skylights overhead and a wall of windows enhance its sunny disposition. Each suite boasts a two-person Jacuzzi tub and French doors that open to private decks or patios overlooking the nearby gardens and distant mountains.

If you can tear yourselves away from your romantic oasis for breakfast, you certainly won't be disappointed. The innkeeper is known for her authentic German-style breakfasts, served at one shared table in the main house, amid European antiques and lace curtains. **5985 Yachats River Road; (541) 547-3813; www.ohwy.com/or/s/serenibb.htm; inexpensive to expensive; minimum-stay requirement in the Honeymoon Suite.**

❦❦❦ **ZIGGURAT BED AND BREAKFAST, Yachats** Believe us when we tell you that Ziggurat is truly unique, an architecturally striking specimen of coastal escapism. True to its name, the building is a towering four-story shingled pyramid that sits on a grassy bluff overlooking the untamed ocean. The inn's interior, equally unusual, is schizophrenically appointed with a strange combination of black carpeting, slick gray tile and laminate, homey accents, abstract artwork, and handsome locally crafted furniture.

Two spacious guest rooms take up the lower level of the home. Both sport wraparound windows, scintillating views, comfy linens, and a slick ambience. The West Suite is the more alluring by far, with its immense round glass-block shower, mirrored ceiling, handmade maple bed, and private deck accessible via French doors. The Southeast Suite has a canopy bed, rather spartan decor, and a private sauna. A third, smaller guest room fills the top level of the pyramid, offering incredible views of the windswept bluff and ocean surf. This room contains a sink and toilet, but guests must make their way to the second floor for shower facilities.

A full, carefully prepared breakfast is served in the ultramodern (almost space-age) dining room, accompanied by extraordinary views of the ocean. Although there are only three guest rooms, until you get used to the multilevel, maze-like floor plan, you can actually get lost here. **95330 Highway 101; (541) 547-3925; www.newportnet.com/ziggurat; moderate to expensive; no credit cards; minimum-stay requirement on holidays; call for seasonal closures.**

Restaurant Kissing

❦❦ **LA SERRE RESTAURANT, Yachats** Although the ambience isn't exactly heart-stirring, La Serre is your best bet for a pleasant evening out in Yachats. Set just off Highway 101, the casual restaurant is filled with large, leafy potted plants and thriving greenery that hangs from the atrium-like ceiling. The oak tables are topped with oil lamps, and frilly white curtains partly shield diners from the outside world. An open kitchen and the popularity of this place mean the atmosphere in the two dining rooms can get noisy. Service is friendly, but may be a slow on busy nights.

Fresh, local seafood is the kitchen's specialty. We recommend starting your meal with steamed clams with drawn butter and lemon, then moving on to either Dungeness crab cakes with Cajun tartar sauce and mild red peppercorns, or filet mignon wrapped with bacon and topped with sautéed mushrooms in a light cream sauce. A meal at La Serre will satisfy both your palate and your need to be close to your special someone. **160 West Second Street; (541) 547-**

3420; moderate to expensive; dinner Wednesday–Monday; closed January.

Outdoor Kissing

❀❀❀❀ **DEVIL'S CHURN AND CAPE PERPETUA, Yachats** If you thought the drive from Cannon Beach to Yachats was incredible, you haven't seen anything yet. Every mile between Yachats and Gold Beach is stupendous. The coast is even more rugged and mountainous, and bordered on the east by the Siuslaw National Forest. The vista turnoffs along this stretch of highway are located on soaring cliffs that offer arresting panoramas of the coastline due south and north. Take your time during this drive, and take advantage of every wayside opportunity for kissing and viewing.

Two of the best places to observe the astounding mixture of rock, sand, and surf are the **DEVIL'S CHURN** and the 2,700-acre **CAPE PERPETUA SCENIC AREA**. The Devil's Churn is accessible via an exciting descent down a steep flight of wooden stairs that leads to a rocky, narrow channel. At the exchange of tides, the movement of water through this natural cut into the land is electrifying. If you feel like stretching your legs, stop at the Cape Perpetua Interpretive Center, which offers hiking maps for a diverse range of trails. An auto tour map is also available for those who want to see the area by car; the drive is fantastic. **$3 day-use fee per vehicle for each location.** *Two miles south of Yachats, just off Highway 101, on the west side of the road. Look for the signs to the turnoff.*

Florence

There is nothing remotely romantic about *new* Florence; it straddles Highway 101 and offers an overabundance of gas stations and mini-marts. For romantic moments, we recommend visiting the nearby seaside and sand dunes and historic **OLD TOWN FLORENCE**, harbored on the Siuslaw River. In the relatively quaint surroundings of Old Town Florence you can park your car and browse through the gift, coffee, and sweet shops along the placid riverfront.

Hotel/Bed and Breakfast Kissing

❀❀❀❀ **COAST HOUSE, Florence** A short lantern-lit pathway meanders through a grove of evergreens to this round, cedar-shake rental home set high on a towering cliff overlooking the blue waters of the Pacific. An expansive deck complete with outdoor shower and wooden chairs offers a stunning view of the mesmerizing terrain. (Please note that the deck is somewhat perilous due to its height and lack of fencing.) Inside, throw rugs cover hardwood floors and an antique woodstove supplies cozy warmth. Floor-to-ceiling windows in the comfortable living room allow a view of the ocean through lofty pines. Ladders lead to two sleeping lofts, where you can stargaze through windows and skylights. In the bathroom, a claw-foot tub sits next to windows with more views of the ocean.

Stock up on provisions in Florence before you arrive, because the only staples you'll find here are coffee, tea, and a complimentary bottle of wine (a wonderful romantic touch). The house is equipped with a full kitchen, a microwave oven, and a stereo along with a collection of tapes and CDs; but thankfully there is no TV or telephone to distract you from each other. **Ten miles north of Florence; (541) 997-7888; very expensive; no credit cards; minimum-stay requirement.**

☙☙❦ **THE EDWIN K BED AND BREAKFAST, Florence** Beautifully tended flower gardens trim this white Craftsman-style home, located at the edge of Old Town Florence and across the street from the Siuslaw River. (Unfortunately, the inn's river views are obstructed by a building and a large parking lot.) Built in 1914, the home has been lovingly refurbished to provide thoroughly comfortable accommodations.

The six guest rooms are named after seasons and times of the year. We prefer the four very spacious upstairs rooms, appointed with stained and leaded glass windows, period antiques, and contemporary pastel fabrics and linens. Some even have patios that overlook a rock waterfall at the back of the house. Winter is the most elegant room of all, with its apricot and cream color scheme, a claw-foot tub displayed in its step-up bathroom, and a queen-size four-poster bed crowned by a lovely wall canopy. Each room upstairs has a tiled bathroom, containing a large shower or tub, that opens to the bedroom. (The toilet is just as visible, which might make you as uncomfortable as it made us.) Two additional country-style guest rooms are located on the main floor, just off the antique-filled common area, but they are not as lavish as the upstairs rooms.

When you awake, follow your nose to the wood-paneled Victorian dining room for a formal breakfast served on fine china at one large table. Quiches, soufflés, freshly baked breads, and puff pastries with fruit are just a few of the culinary creations presented each morning. Complimentary sherry and tea are offered each afternoon. **1155 Bay Street; (541) 997-8360, (800) 8-EDWIN-K; www.edwink.com; inexpensive to moderate.**

Romantic Note: A rental apartment for families (moderate) is located in a recent add-on to the home. Unfortunately, this unit is even less enticing than the two main-floor rooms, with drab, motel-like furnishings, a visually intrusive TV, and thin linens. It does have a full kitchen, however, as well as a washer and dryer.

☙☙☙ **THE JOHNSON HOUSE BED AND BREAKFAST INN, Florence** Built in 1892, the Johnson House is one of Old Town Florence's original fixtures. The property comprises a pair of white Victorian farmhouses and a small adjacent cottage, all surrounded by a lush green lawn and brilliantly colored flowers. The five quaint guest rooms located in one of the farmhouses (the owners live in the other) are as authentic as they come, showcasing period antiques, feather beds, and hand-embroidered curtains and linens. Unfortunately, only two of these rooms have private bathrooms, leaving guests in the other three rooms to share a detached bath off the upstairs hallway. The absolutely adorable Rose Cottage is snug, even for two, and set amid an overflowing wildflower garden. A sunny porch, fresh flowers, hardwood floors, a queen-size feather bed, a tiny bathroom, and an antique claw-foot tub make this a delightfully romantic option.

In the morning, you can look forward to the innkeepers' pleasant conversation as you enjoy sweet French toast, fresh fruit, homemade muffins and breads, and a hot egg dish. Breakfast is served at one large table in the main house, adjacent to a lovely parlor area filled with antiques and adorned with old-fashioned portraits. **216 Maple Street; (541) 997-8000, (800) 768-9488; www.touroregon.com/thejohnsonhouse; inexpensive to moderate.**

❤❤❤❤ **MOONSET, Florence** Specifically designed as a romantic oceanfront getaway, this phenomenal property is owned and operated by the people who run **THE JOHNSON HOUSE** (see above). Octagonal in shape, Moonset is a one-of-a-kind contemporary home set on an acre of meadow and trees eight miles north of Florence. The interior of this architectural masterpiece features wood-paneled walls and wraparound floor-to-ceiling windows that showcase views of the nearby woods, the sprawling ocean dunes, and the blue waters of the Pacific Ocean in the distance. A loft bedroom holds a king-size bed covered with colorful goosedown pillows and a down comforter. The full sunken kitchen (breakfast provisions are up to you) and tiled bath are modern and luxurious. Romantic amenities include a sauna, an outdoor Jacuzzi tub and shower, a video library, and a wood-stocked fireplace. When you tire of being indoors, retreat to the circular decks outside and get closer to nature and each other. **90675 Highway 101; (541) 997-8000, (800) 768-9488; www.touroregon.com/moonset; very expensive; minimum-stay requirement; call for seasonal closures.**

Outdoor Kissing

❤ **SANDLAND ADVENTURE FAMILY FUN CENTER, Florence** The Oregon Dunes National Recreation Area is one of the most beautiful sections of this coast, and much of it is accessible only by dune buggy. Renting these nifty little vehicles opens up the phenomenal ecosystem of the dunes to your personal perusal. Imagine 600-foot sand dunes dotted with wisps of sea grass, secret lakes, and islands of trees. The area is immense. During the summer you are likely to run into reckless kids (hopefully not literally), but depending on how you navigate your excursion, you can cleverly avoid them. **85366 Highway 101; (541) 997-8087; www.ohwy.com/or/s/sandland.htm; $30 or $35 per hour per person, plus a $50 or $100 deposit depending on vehicle; open daily.**

Winchester Bay

Hotel Bed and Breakfast Kissing

💋💋 SALMON HARBOR BELLE BED AND BREAKFAST, Winchester Bay

Those in search of a unique bed-and-breakfast experience need only step aboard the *Salmon Harbor Belle*. This three-story, stern-wheeler riverboat is firmly docked at the Salmon Harbor Marina, its white and cherry red exterior gleaming invitingly on Winchester Bay's quiet waters. The massive paddle wheel at its stern lies dormant, except when the owner starts up the boat to give the paddles their weekly workout. Even though you won't be braving the high seas during your stay, a night here is guaranteed to rock the boat when it comes to romance.

Built in 1991, the 97-foot-long riverboat offers a surprising amount of space, with six guest rooms, three decks, and a main salon. All six staterooms are on the snug side (which encourages snuggling), with private full baths, maroon and green color schemes, down comforters, and views of the harbor. Most feature either a king- or queen-size bed, although one room is equipped with a double and a twin day bed. Room 6 is the most romantic; its corner top-floor location affords the best views through an extra set of windows. Although the staterooms sport similar decor, each has a subtle motif that sets it apart, from cowboy hats and a rocking horse in the Montana-inspired room to sheepskin and a stuffed koala bear in the Australian-theme room. Whichever room you choose, don't be alarmed by the orange life jackets stowed above your open closet; the law requires one per person, even though the boat remains stationary.

Awake early to catch views of the sunrise from the *Belle*'s bow, then steal away to the stern around dusk for a brilliant sunset. In between, you can set crab pots near the dock or simply cozy up in the main salon. Polished hardwood floors and ceilings give the salon its warm glow, and generous windows let in plenty of natural light. Curl up on the comfy couches next to a pellet stove and listen to a melody on the old-fashioned gramophone. The amiable hostess serves a buffet-style gourmet breakfast here each morning, which may include omelets, waffles, French toast, or quiche, along with fresh fruit and homemade granola. Take your plateful of goodies to one of the tables that hug the windows, or head outside to catch some rays on one of the decks. **F Charter Dock, at the Salmon Harbor Marina; (541) 271-1137, (800) 348-1922; moderate to expensive.**

Charleston

Outdoor Kissing

💋💋💋💋 CHARLESTON STATE PARKS, Charleston This trio of state parks
south of town are well marked and well worth the detour from the main road.

Despite the fact that they are separated from one another by only a few miles, each one has its own distinctive personality. The northernmost park is **SUN-SET BAY**, where majestic cliffs and thick forest flank a small, calm ocean inlet. A bit farther south, **SHORE ACRES** ($3 day-use fee) is where the remains of an estate sprawl on a cliff soaring high above the coast. Intriguing paths ramble over rock-strewn beaches gouged with caves and granite fissures where the water releases its energy in spraying foam and crashing waves. This park is renowned for its extensive botanical gardens, which are maintained to resemble their former glory. Don't miss the numerous lookouts. The most informal park is **CAPE ARAGO**, an outstanding picnic spot high above the shoreline with a northern view of the coast. It is best known for the sea lions and harbor seals that can be seen romping in the surf or sleeping languidly on the rocks below. Bring along your binoculars for optimum viewing of these friendly creatures. *The town of Charleston is south of Coos Bay, on a small peninsula 30 miles due west of Highway 101. Watch for signs to the parks.*

Bandon

Bandon is one of the few relatively undiscovered seaside towns along the Oregon coast, although that probably won't last much longer. Real estate signs abound, which isn't surprising. The beach here is just as spectacular and interesting as the more popular sites farther north, with a multitude of haystack rocks that rise in tiers from the ocean. There are only a few noteworthy restaurants in this small community, and even fewer bed and breakfasts. If you yearn for a quiet retreat from the busy coastal towns, this small beachside community is definitely your answer.

Hotel/Bed and Breakfast Kissing

❦❦❦ **BANDON BEACH HOUSE BED AND BREAKFAST, Bandon** This sprawling wood-shingled home sits comfortably on a 40-foot bluff overlooking Bandon's spectacular sandy beach. Due to its location in a residential neighborhood, you could easily drive right by this property without realizing it's a bed and breakfast. That would be a shame, because this lovely home is your best bet for romantic, oceanfront accommodations in Bandon.

A landscaped yard and expansive porch welcome you even before the hospitable hosts greet you at the door. Inside, the home's common area features blue and cream couches, hardwood floors covered with Oriental rugs, a large stone hearth, and a subtle nautical theme. This room would be perfectly inviting if it weren't for a few slightly homey touches and some unattractive artwork. You probably won't mind, however, once you catch a glimpse of the ocean showcased through large picture windows; the view is simply sublime.

The two guest rooms here rate high in privacy and comfort. One end of the house has been dedicated exclusively to guests, with a separate entrance that allows you to come and go privately. Both rooms are incredibly spacious, with large, private bathrooms, hardwood floors, wood furnishings, and generous windows facing the crashing surf. Although the accommodations are not luxurious, you'll definitely have plenty of room to spread out and make yourselves at home; the king-size beds don't even begin to fill the abundance of space. A blue and white sailboat theme prevails in the downstairs room, while the room upstairs boasts vaulted ceilings and a burgundy and cream color scheme. In each room, comfy chairs are arranged invitingly in front of a river-rock fireplace; simply throw on a log, snuggle up, and relax as the night heats up.

In the morning, breakfast is served family-style at one long, wooden table in the common room. Fill up on a soufflé, quiche, or other egg dish before heading outdoors. A wooden stairwell at the bluff's edge descends to a 105-foot expanse of sandy beach that's just waiting to be explored. **2866 Beach Loop Drive; (541) 347-1196; www.bandonbeach.com; expensive; no credit cards.**

Restaurant Kissing

❧❧❧ **HARP'S-ON-THE-BAY, Bandon** Harp's is acclaimed up and down the coast for its superlative cuisine and gracious service. The new location, in a pastel blue shingled building just outside of Old Town Bandon, offers diners an enhanced romantic ambience. White tablecloths drape each table, while wood wainscoting, taupe walls, and wallpaper adorned with grapevines add a touch of elegance. Large windows afford fabulous views of the bay and Bandon's historic lighthouse. While the restaurant's location may have changed, the food remains superb: The poached salmon with capers marinated in vermouth is impeccable, and the halibut in a hot pistachio sauce is even better. Another tasty treat is the rack of lamb charbroiled with garlic and thyme. Save room for a slice of New York–style cheesecake, or top off your meal with a glass of port served with walnuts and cheese. **480 First Street Southwest; (541) 347-9057; moderate to expensive; call for seasonal hours.**

❧ **LORD BENNETT'S RESTAURANT AND LOUNGE, Bandon** Named after Bandon's founder, this contemporary restaurant sits across the street from the beach. Floral watercolors and hanging greenery enliven the modern dining room's temperate mood, and a long wall of windows showcases views of the surf. We've heard locals rave about Lord Bennett's traditional fare, but after eating there we can't figure out why. Year after year, the food remains mediocre, and the service can be slow. The real attraction is the stellar location. The panorama of jagged coastline, sparkling water, and haystack rocks is spellbinding. **1695 Beach Loop Road; (541) 347-3663; moderate to expensive; lunch and dinner daily, brunch Sunday.**

Outdoor Kissing

☙☙☙ **FACE ROCK WAYSIDE, Bandon** Many sections of beach and shoreline along the Oregon coast possess unparalleled views and stupendous scenery, and the beachfront at the Face Rock Wayside is no exception. A few picnic benches are scattered on the grassy bluff, allowing the few tourists who have discovered this area a place to congregate around lunchtime. Follow the short path from the picnic area to the edge of the wayside, which juts out over the water and provides a 180-degree view of the crashing surf. Dramatic rock formations rise out of the sand and water directly in front of you. The rock-studded water and damp, firm expanse of sandy beach below are truly magical. *Turn off Highway 101 at the signs indicating Beach Loop Drive. Follow Beach Loop Drive until you reach the wayside.*

Langlois

Hotel/Bed and Breakfast Kissing

☙☙❧ **FLORAS LAKE HOUSE BED AND BREAKFAST, Langlois** If you windsurf (or want to learn), this place has a definite kissing bonus. Floras Lake's steady Northwest winds and proximity to the ocean make it ideal for windsurfing. The owners of this bed and breakfast rent sailboards and wet suits, and even give lessons for those of all skill levels. But you don't have to windsurf to appreciate this lovely wood-and-brick contemporary home.

The four attractive guest rooms are very spacious, with cathedral ceilings and abundant windows, and decorated with antique beds, patchwork quilts, wicker furnishings, and pastel accents. We prefer the South Room, thanks to its king-size four-poster bed and country-Victorian touches, and the Nautical Room, which boasts a navy and red color scheme. Two rooms have fireplaces, and all have private entrances that open onto a weathered wraparound deck facing the beautiful gardens, Floras Lake, and the ocean in the distance.

This same view can be enjoyed from the airy common room, crowned by a 20-foot-high, open-beamed ceiling and furnished with several comfy couches and a woodstove. A continental breakfast buffet is served here each morning. Before or after your morning meal, take a long walk on the beach or follow one of the hiking trails that wind along the bluffs to secluded coves and a waterfall. These areas remain empty most of the year, so you can privately kiss to your hearts' content. **92870 Boice Cope Road; (541) 348-2573; www. floraslake.com; moderate; closed mid-November–mid-February.**

Romantic Alternative: A small campground called **BOICE COPE CAMP-GROUND** sits directly on the shore of Floras Lake, hidden by trees from the bed and breakfast. If camping is more your style, try this wonderfully secluded spot. And you can still rent sailboards and wet suits from Floras Lake House.

Gold Beach

Hotel/Bed and Breakfast Kissing

❤❤❥ **INN AT NESIKA BEACH, Gold Beach** One of the last stops for romance before the California border is this pale blue, Victorian-style home located in a residential neighborhood, on a steep bluff overlooking the dramatic Pacific Ocean. Each of the four spacious and tastefully decorated guest rooms has a ringside view of the crashing surf and brilliant sunsets. Three of the rooms have black marble fireplaces, and all boast cozy sitting areas, whirlpool tubs in private bathrooms, a few homey touches, down comforters, and lace curtains that billow in the breeze. We prefer the sunny third-floor room called Starkissed, thanks to its supreme ocean views, king-size bed, and skylight over the Jacuzzi tub in the bathroom.

Breakfast is served at a common table in the formal dining room, along with more ocean views. You can take your coffee out on the enclosed sundeck after you feast on warm scones, apple crêpes, and pancakes stuffed with peaches. Morning delights like these will keep you going all day long. **33026 Nesika Road; (541) 247-6434; moderate; no credit cards.**

❤❤❤ **TU TU' TUN LODGE, Gold Beach** Prepare to be enchanted. Located seven miles from Gold Beach, Tu Tu' Tun (meaning "People by the River") is nestled in the heart of a quiet forested valley, next to the winding Rogue River. Ivy cloaks the wood pillars that flank the cedar lodge, colorful flower boxes line the stairs, and the manicured grounds envelop a heated outdoor lap pool and stone terrace.

The lodge's 16 attractive rooms, two suites, and two private homes have a distinctive Northwest flavor; all are decorated with unique art pieces, sumptuous linens and fabrics, and open-beamed ceilings. Tile entryways, wool carpeting, and small refrigerators are additional features. Some units offer slate fireplaces; others are blessed with sliding doors that open onto private balconies or patios where guests can relish river views from a "moon soaker" tub. (Be sure to specify the amenities you desire, since only five rooms have a hot tub and only six have a fireplace.) Bouquets of fresh flowers adorn each room, and turndown service and fresh cookies are provided nightly. The only accommodation here that does not have a river view is a private three-bedroom home sheltered in a nearby apple orchard.

For an extra charge, breakfast, hors d'oeuvres, and dinner are served in a comfortable common lodge, warmed in winter by a crackling fire in an immense river-rock fireplace. Unfortunately, all of the meals are served family-style at several round eight-person tables, which precludes the possibility of a romantic encounter. However, guests who desire more privacy can request a candlelit dinner for two served in the comfort of their own room. **96550 North Bank**

Rogue; (541) 247-6664, (800) 864-6357; www.tututun.com; expensive to very expensive; minimum-stay requirement seasonally; call for seasonal closures.

"I have found men who

didn't know how to

kiss. I've always found

time to teach them."

Mae West

Oregon Cascades

Where can you slice up the slopes on an extinct 11,234-foot volcano one day and the next day run the rapids or chase a golf ball from hole to hole? The answer is the Oregon Cascades region, an outdoor playground that's easily accessible from metropolitan areas, but far enough away for peace and solitude. From the windsurfing capital of the world (Hood River) to the high-desert town of Bend, this region's wealth of opportunities will keep you hopping from sunup until sundown.

Troutdale

Set at the west entrance of the Columbia River Gorge, Troutdale is located 25 miles west of Hood River and 20 miles east of Portland. New development and residential areas cover most of the town, but we discovered one noteworthy stop you can check out on your way into or out of the Gorge.

Restaurant Kissing

❧❧ **THE BLACK RABBIT RESTAURANT, Troutdale** As most Portlanders know, the McMenamins have cornered the Northwest microbrew market. They currently own almost three dozen pubs and brewpubs in Oregon and Washington, and the chain's popularity is continually growing. With this site, however, they have crossed over into another segment of the hospitality industry: fine dining and accommodations. The modestly elegant Black Rabbit Restaurant is a great place to nibble on Northwest specialties and gourmet delights. Wall sconces cast subdued light upon the dining room, with its hardwood floors and high-backed wooden booths. (Be sure to request one of these booths; the tables are packed in tightly.) Overall, the wait staff is friendly and the food above average, with generous portions being the norm. **2126 Southwest Halsey, at McMenamins Edgefield; (503) 669-8610, (800) 669-8610; www.mcmenamins.com; moderate to expensive; breakfast, lunch, and dinner daily.**

Romantic Warning: Overnight lodging at MCMENAMINS EDGEFIELD (inexpensive to expensive) is not for everyone. Built in the early 1900s as the county's poor farm, this complex of buildings eventually became a nursing home. It was almost demolished in the late 1980s, but the McMenamins stepped in with big plans. We applaud the rescue and restoration of this historic property; unfortunately, however, the guest rooms have retained the sterile feeling of an institution. Thin bedspreads, sparse furnishings, exposed pipes, and detached baths down each hall add to this cold ambience. The extravagant murals along the walls and doors are interesting, but the surreal theme throughout the building is somewhat eerie. If you are a big fan of the McMenamins brewpubs, you might appreciate the charms of this property and enjoy the several on-site pubs and movie theater. Otherwise, the drafty halls and funky artwork will probably not tug at your heartstrings.

Columbia River Gorge

In Oregon, Interstate 84 borders the south side of the Columbia River; Highway 14 runs parallel to it on the north side of the river in Washington state. Several bridges span the river between Oregon and Washington. Reviews of kiss-worthy places on the Washington side of the Columbia River Gorge are included in the Washington Cascades chapter of this book.

The Columbia River Gorge is a most fitting region to include in this kissing travelogue. The 60 miles or so of scenery formed by the river carving its way through the Cascade Mountains contain a kaleidoscope of heart-stirring images. To travel this passage is to sense the magic afoot in the emerald mountains to the west and emblazoned across the sunburnt mountains and grasslands to the east.

The Gorge is a vast collage of all the intensely beautiful features the Northwest has to offer. There are scores of ponds, mountain lakes, and trails, but the waterfalls are undoubtedly the most remarkable natural feature. Depending on the season, they rush to earth in a variety of contours and intensities. **ONEONTA FALLS** drops abruptly off a sheer ledge for several hundred feet. **ELOWAH FALLS** sprays a fine, showery mist over deciduous forest, while **PUNCH BOWL FALLS** pours into crystal-clear Eagle Creek. **UPPER HORSE-TAIL FALLS** is forced out in a jet stream through a portal centered in a wall of rock, and **WAHKEENAH FALLS** rushes over rocky steps and beds of stone. Wherever you happen to be in the Columbia River Gorge, its stunning natural pageantry will make you feel that you've found paradise.

Outdoor Kissing

❤❤❤ **COLUMBIA RIVER GORGE NATIONAL SCENIC AREA, Columbia River Gorge** This highway, the first paved road to cross the Cascades, was constructed in 1915 and is considered an engineering marvel. Once you drive this sinuous, moss-covered work of art, you will swear it was really built by wizards. It lacks any hint of the commercialism associated with road travel; you won't be bothered by neon, billboards, traffic signs, or speeding cars. This is one scenic route that really accentuates the scenery. It reflects an earlier time, when driving was called touring and cars moseyed along at 30 miles an hour. You can go a tad faster through here now, but not much, and why bother? You won't want to miss the falls, hikes, and roadside vistas that suddenly appear along the way. **Columbia River Gorge National Scenic Area, U.S. Forest Service; (541) 386-2333.** *The Columbia River Historic Highway (Route 30) begins at the Troutdale exit on Interstate 84 (east of Portland) and extends 30 miles east.*

Romantic Warning: In summertime, when family vacations are under way, this can be a very crowded strip of road. The best time for romance here is when school is in session.

Romantic Option: We don't generally recommend tourist attractions; the crowds associated with them usually prevent intimate moments and privacy. The restaurant in **MULTNOMAH FALLS LODGE** (Highway 30 East, Troutdale; 503- 695-2376; moderate) is indeed a tourist attraction, and were it not for one unbelievable feature this would be just another Northwest wood-and-stone dining room serving three decent meals a day. That attraction, of course, is the lodge's namesake, a plummeting waterfall that spills a dramatic 620 feet, almost in the lodge's backyard. This spectacle makes any snack or meal here a momentous occasion.

Hood River

Though the Columbia River Gorge is visually stunning, and the trails, natural wonders, and fruit-laden orchards are totally splendid, this area has yet another attraction: windsurfing. Hood River is at the heart of this activity, and this is where you'll find the reliably exciting air currents that windsurfers relish. Sit and watch these enthusiasts and their multicolored sails whip across the Gorge, or get out there and try it yourselves—several places in town offer classes.

Hotel/Bed and Breakfast Kissing

✿✿✦ **COLUMBIA GORGE HOTEL, Hood River** Vast, meticulously maintained grounds surround the Columbia Gorge Hotel, a prestigious Spanish-style villa set on a high, forested bank above the Columbia River. Wah Gwin Gwin Falls tumbles down the bluff in front of the hotel; below, windsurfers take on the windswept waters. The impressive lobby embodies the grandeur of this landmark hotel, built in the 1920s by a Portland lumber baron, and the elegance continues in the hotel's restaurant, **COLUMBIA RIVER COURT DINING ROOM** (see Restaurant Kissing). Sometime during your stay, stroll around the manicured grounds, complete with a stream and plenty of kissing spots near the cliff and out on the velvety lawns.

The 40 individually decorated guest rooms are attractive, but a bit of a letdown after seeing the lavish lobby, restaurant, and grounds. Each room is appointed with antique reproduction furniture, a king- or queen-size bed, TV, and telephone. One of the most romantic is Room 329, a corner hideaway with a beautiful canopied king-size bed, gas fireplace, and sitting area. Pull back the lace curtains to reveal river views below. The waterfall rooms are another nice option, albeit a very expensive one. These small corner rooms offer a partial view of the falls as well as great cross ventilation. Speaking of ventilation, air conditioners in each room provide comfort, but at a cost. They are noisy and a bit of an eyesore.

More than anything, the price tag on these accommodations is what makes you expect more than you get. One saving grace is the phenomenal five-course breakfast included with your stay (nonguests pay $46 for two). Take seriously the menu's declaration—"It's not a choice, you get it all"—and plan on spending an hour and a half slowly consuming the delicious, seemingly never-ending courses. The meal starts with fresh fruit, then continues with hot apple fritters, oatmeal, three eggs, breakfast meats or grilled Idaho trout, golden hash browns, biscuits with honey, and, finally, a stack of buttermilk pancakes. Even if you were not completely thrilled with your room, you will surely leave the hotel feeling you got your money's worth at breakfast. **4000 Westcliff Drive; (541) 386-5566, (800) 345-1921; www.gorge.net/lodging/cghotel; very expensive to unbelievably expensive; recommended wedding site.**

❤❤❤ **HOOD RIVER HOTEL, Hood River** Visit days gone by with a night at Hood River's oldest hotel. This venerable 1913 red brick building is located in the core of downtown Hood River. The handsome lobby beckons through stylish French doors, promising to embrace you with posh sofas, large potted plants, high ceilings, and abundant morning sunlight.

Upstairs, hallways with high ceilings and Oriental carpets set a welcoming tone. None of the 41 guest rooms escapes the perpetual hum of traffic (after all, you are downtown), but if you can get used to this you're likely to appreciate these accommodations. The two-bedroom suites, with full kitchens, hardwood floors, Oriental carpets, antique mirrors, and plenty of windows, feel more like apartments than hotel rooms. The less expensive rooms are smaller but also cozier, with personal touches like dried floral wreaths and canopied beds. From some, you can even catch a glimpse of the Columbia Gorge beyond the nearby buildings, roads, and railroad tracks. Unfortunately, many bathrooms are just slightly larger than a closet, and some suites, especially those with kitchens, are beginning to look timeworn. (The smaller rooms seem a bit less faded.) If you're visiting in summer, be sure to ask for a cool third-floor river-view room (avoid the courtyard rooms, which are dark). Due to historical preservation codes, air conditioners couldn't be installed in the lower-level rooms.

Exercise buffs can work out in the basement workout room or, better yet, enjoy a soak in the glass-enclosed hot tub or sit in the cedar sauna. A continental breakfast, served in Pasquale's (see below), is included in your stay at the hotel. **102 Oak Avenue; (541) 386-1900, (800) 386-1859; www.hoodriver hotel.com; inexpensive to expensive.**

Romantic Note: A restaurant called **PASQUALE'S** (moderate; breakfast, lunch, and dinner daily) is adjacent to the downstairs lobby, and you might consider having lunch here. The atmosphere is casual, and the fare ranges from creamy pasta dishes to homemade minestrone soup served with a baguette to broiled salmon with dill-garlic butter.

Romantic Suggestion: If a day trip to Mount Hood or a breezy picnic by the river sounds intriguing, pick up provisions at **THE WINE SELLERS** (514 State Street; 541-386-4647; inexpensive). The back of this charming gift boutique houses a small coffee bar, an assortment of gourmet foods perfect for picnics, and a large selection of local wines.

❤❤❤ **LAKECLIFF ESTATE BED AND BREAKFAST, Hood River** Rather than staying in the costly accommodations at the **COLUMBIA GORGE HOTEL** (see above), consider a sojourn at Lakecliff Estate Bed and Breakfast, only a half mile down the road from the hotel. This large, beautiful, historic summer home is tucked away on three magnificent acres of prime Columbia River property, and almost every room in the house has a commanding view of the river. An outside deck at the back of the house is an ideal location for lounging and gazing, as is the pleasant sunroom with wicker furniture and a ceiling fan.

All four guest rooms are spacious and appealing. The Garden Room is an especially cozy hideaway, with dark green linens, views of the surrounding garden and woods, thick quilts, a native stone fireplace, and a private bath. Emily's Room, decorated in light florals, has a river view and is the only other room with a private bath. (Just be sure to ask the owners to convert this room's two twin beds into a king-size bed). The other two rooms share a separate shower and bathroom; each has a stone fireplace, a washbasin, plush carpets, and attractive decor. If it weren't for the shared bath, we'd highly recommend light and airy Lynn's Room, decorated in blues and yellows, with big windows that offer river and wooded views.

A hearty breakfast awaits you in the morning, making this bed and breakfast an easy place to call home. As the wind begins to whip up outside, sit in the tranquil dining room enjoying puff pancakes, oatmeal with sautéed nectarines, heart-shaped waffles, and the house specialty—caramelized Lakecliff bacon. Breakfast is served family-style at one large table, and the milk-bottle collection that lines the wall mantle makes for interesting morning conversation. **3820 Westcliff Drive; (541) 386-7000; inexpensive to moderate; no credit cards; call for seasonal closures.**

Restaurant Kissing

❤❤❤ **COLUMBIA RIVER COURT DINING ROOM, Hood River** Fine crystal, silver, and white linens adorn the tables in the elegant dining room of the **COLUMBIA GORGE HOTEL** (see Hotel/Bed and Breakfast Kissing). Yet the main attractions are the arched bay windows that overlook the mighty Columbia River. If you crave a big breakfast, you may want to consider a morning stop here. The trademarked World Famous Farm Breakfast is pricey if you aren't a guest, but you may end up saving money because you surely won't need lunch after this multicourse extravaganza. Dinner is an equally sumptuous affair, and the menu offers gourmet Northwest fare such as roast pork tenderloin stuffed with Hood River apples, and baked salmon fillet crusted with sesame seeds and orange zest. Try the chef's signature salad, with wilted spinach, smoked duck, and bacon, prepared and flambéed tableside. Keep your hearts ablaze with the signature flambé dessert, an apple tart topped with French vanilla ice cream. **4000 Westcliff Drive, at the Columbia Gorge Hotel; (541) 386-5566, (800) 345-1921; expensive to very expensive; breakfast, lunch, and dinner daily.**

❤❤❤ **STONEHEDGE INN, Hood River** Considered one of the state's best-kept romantic secrets (according to an Oregon newspaper poll), Stonehedge consistently lives up to its well-deserved reputation. The restaurant is quietly tucked away from town up a potholed gravel road, concealed by dense shrubbery, and identified only by a small sign that gives no indication as to what lies beyond.

This century-old, stone-clad home is an intriguing find. The former dining and living rooms have been beautifully transformed to accommodate intimate seating in a comfortable setting, the windows face the woods and gardens outside, and the food is classic continental with a Northwest accent. Entrées are incredibly fresh and generously accompanied by soup, salad, and fresh warm bread. **3405 Cascade Drive; (541) 386-3940; moderate to expensive; call for seasonal hours.**

Mount Hood

At 11,235 feet, Mount Hood is Oregon's highest mountain. It is also one of the most popular winter destinations in the state. The skiing is outstanding, and there are many trails for hiking in the summer. For the most part, accommodations in this region (including the towns of Government Camp and Welches) cater to outdoor enthusiasts; guest rooms tend to be plain, because most of the people who come here spend the majority of their time outside, not in their room. The rugged beauty of the area is likely to make up for any shortcomings in romantic accommodations, though, and your time here is sure to be relaxed and casual—something all Northwesterners can appreciate.

Hotel/Bed and Breakfast Kissing

❤❤ **INN AT COOPER SPUR, Mount Hood** Best described as a romantic anomaly, this lodge definitely has all the outward signs of a provincial mountain snuggery. At the foot of a gentle, less-traveled slope, about a half hour from the Timberline ski area, a stone path leads to a charming wood-sided cottage that houses the lodge's restaurant. Inside, you will be greeted by the aroma of either just-baked pies or freshly grilled thick steaks. The 14 rooms and cabins have the same type of rustic exterior, and the wood-paneled interiors are all equipped with stone fireplaces. Almost a dozen hot tubs wait outdoors to assuage tired, overused muscles. (They all occupy the same cement slab, so there is no privacy, but they are soothing just the same.)

Who could deny how quaint and cozy all this sounds? And it is, but only up to a point. The homey, ultra-basic decor and furnishings and laid-back atmosphere make this place more suitable for hiking or skiing chums than for starry-eyed lovers. Though this may not be exactly the kind of intimate destination you are looking for, the Inn at Cooper Spur has mountain hospitality aplenty and all the warmth and social activity you could want. **10755 Cooper Spur Road; (541) 352-6692, (888) 541-6894; inexpensive to expensive; minimum-stay requirement on holidays.**

❤❤❤ **TIMBERLINE LODGE, Mount Hood** Mount Hood stands as an overwhelming example of nature's potency and formidable genius. At the 6,000-foot-level rests an example of human tenacity and creativity: Timberline Lodge. This grand structure was built in 1937, during the Depression, as part of President Roosevelt's WPA (Works Progress Administration) program to create jobs. Every aspect of the building is endowed with character and masterful craftsmanship, evidenced in the metal filigree, stone chimneys, archways, and massive hand-hewn beams. Great attention has gone into keeping the lodge as authentic as possible, from the handmade tapestries and fabrics in the main lodge to the glass mosaics in the Blue Ox Bar.

The lodge holds 70 guest rooms, including ten Chalet units that are beyond rustic, with bunk beds and a shared bath. The eight Fireplace Rooms have the most romantic potential, with pine-planked walls, wood-burning fireplaces, king-size beds, and watercolors of native wildflowers. But we must mention that the authenticity of the units makes for less than plush surroundings, and the bathrooms tend to be drab. Still, if you are here primarily to enjoy the great outdoors, this handsome, historic lodge and the riveting countenance of Mount Hood together will create a scene of rugged romance perfect for two. **South side of Mount Hood off Highway 26; reservations, (503) 231-5400, (800) 547-1406; general information, (503) 272-3311; www.timberlinelodge.com; inexpensive to very expensive; minimum-stay requirement on holidays.**

Romantic Note: As you might expect, the peak season here is winter, when skiing is in full force. However, this mountaintop destination is one of Oregon's top tourist attractions and can be booked year-round, so plan ahead.

Romantic Suggestion: Timberline's **CASCADE DINING ROOM** (moderate to expensive; breakfast, lunch, and dinner daily) is definitely worth trying after a day of skiing or hiking. You'll find the excellent Northwest-style cuisine is served up in Paul Bunyan–size portions, and the kitchen specializes in luscious desserts such as Swedish cream with strawberries.

Brightwood

Hotel/Bed and Breakfast Kissing

❧❧ **THE BRIGHTWOOD GUEST HOUSE, Brightwood** Cross the koi pond bordered by rustling wild grass and pass through the red door into your own little Japanese-style guesthouse. Situated on two acres of land and separate from the main house, this one-room hideaway bestows peace and privacy on romantic-minded couples. Japanese fans and lanterns, a futon, and Asian artwork adorn the cedar-planked house. In the modest kitchen, Japanese tea sets are complemented by the largest selection of teas we've ever seen. Comfortable kimonos and slippers are also provided. For entertainment, watch a video, play a board game, or ride the bicycles. Better yet, succumb to the Zen-like feel of this place and enjoy such simple pleasures as feeding the fish and birds (food is provided). Upstairs in the loft, a feather bed rests on the floor, flanked by delicate paper lanterns. We half expected to find a deep Japanese-style soaking tub in the bathroom, but, alas, we were met with a standard tub. Oh well.

Sit on the covered patio if the weather is nice and enjoy a breakfast that may include waffles with berries and cream, muesli with homemade preserves, or a frittata. **64725 East Barlow Trail Road; (503) 622-5783, (888) 503-5783; moderate; minimum-stay requirement on weekends.**

❧❧❧ **MAPLE RIVER INN, Brightwood** On every trip, we usually come across at least one wonderful find. The Maple River Inn is our special discovery in the Mount Hood area. This beautifully appointed home actually overlooks the Salmon River; the inn's name refers to an outstanding collection of Japanese maples in the front yard. Name plates identify each variety surrounding the lovely yard, pond, and miniature red barn out front. The home, a contemporary that has been beautifully refurbished by the owners, combines Craftsman-style detailing and wood accents with a subtle lodge look, including a river-rock fireplace embellished with a Mount Hood wood carving above.

The two charmingly decorated guest rooms reside on the lower level. The Northwoods Room, with a queen-size bed and big private bath, features a Northwest nature twist, from the moose-print wallpaper border to the wooden canoe sculpture on the fireplace mantel. Windows face the river below, and a private entrance leads to the shaded backyard patio. Walk a short way up the bluff to find the inn's hot tub, which overlooks the river. Equally nice, but larger, the St. Andrews Suite sports a golf and duck theme. It has the same features (and view) as the Northwoods Room, with the added elegance of a queen-size sleigh bed and matching armoire. When we visited, the innkeepers were transforming the charming mini-barn into a honeymoon suite. By the looks of things, future couples will have a heyday at this private retreat.

On special occasions, breakfast can be delivered to your room. Otherwise, wander upstairs to the elegant dining room, where pear soufflés, Swedish pancakes, or marionberry biscuits are served in style. If you can, visit the inn during a holiday. The innkeeper takes special pride in customizing the home for those special days. **20525 East Mountain Country Lane; (503) 622-6273; inexpensive to expensive; minimum-stay requirement on weekends.**

Welches

Hotel/Bed and Breakfast Kissing

❀❀ **THE RESORT AT THE MOUNTAIN, Welches** Rushing waterfalls, dense forest, and diverse wildlife fill this area with raw natural beauty. Finding a place to stay amid all the gorgeous scenery is not always easy: You should call far in advance to make a reservation when visiting this area, especially during the height of ski season—and even then you might be out in the cold. However, your chances are better at this resort, which offers 160 guest rooms.

We would not usually recommend a resort of this magnitude, not only because its size reduces your sense of privacy, but also because the grounds resemble an apartment complex and the rooms are reminiscent of a standard hotel. Nevertheless, the setting is sublime; the resort is nestled in 300 acres of evergreen woodland in the foothills of the Huckleberry Wilderness Area of the Mount Hood National Forest. It's truly a special place to be in any season, but it's particularly spectacular when the grounds are covered in snow.

Catering to sports enthusiasts, the resort has a golf course, tennis courts, an outdoor heated pool, a Jacuzzi tub, a fitness center, hiking trails, volleyball courts, and more. It is a perfect place for athletes, but for those of you who have come looking for some peace and quiet, we suggest walking in the still woods and taking in the enthralling mountain views. As you fill your lungs with the sweet, fresh air, you will be thankful for this mountain vacation spot, even if it was your only option. **68010 East Fairway Avenue; (503) 622-3101, (800) 669-7666; www.theresort.com; moderate to very expensive.**

Romantic Note: Dinner at **THE HIGHLANDS** (503-622-2214; expensive; breakfast and lunch Monday–Saturday, dinner daily, brunch Sunday) brings you into a realm of formal (and pricey) dining not common in these parts. Conveniently located in the resort's complex, the restaurant offers serene intimacy in an elegant green and peach room with a view of the evergreens and grounds beyond. Lobster bisque, salmon piccata, and hazelnut-chicken linguine are just a few of the dishes you can relish by candlelight.

❀❀ **SUITE RIVER BED AND BREAKFAST, Welches** For the couple looking for a true bed-and-breakfast experience with plenty of privacy, Suite River is a noteworthy kissing option. With the exception of the innkeepers and their two dogs, you'll have the entire home to yourselves since there is only one guest suite. Located along a quiet gravel road, the average-looking 1970 contemporary home is enhanced by a beautiful backyard garden full of flowers and bird feeders. Below the home, lush foliage hides the Sandy River from view, but does not obscure the mountains above. The only jarring touches inside the home are some 1970 leftovers—e.g., lime-green stained glass windows—but thankfully the owners have tried hard to update.

The green and rose Marie Frances Suite off the dining room area has a sitting area, queen-size brass bed, and a tiled bathroom with a two-person Jacuzzi tub. Only the birds and bees will keep you company as you steal a kiss on the secluded back porch overlooking the garden.

Ordering breakfast (the night before) is much like being in a restaurant: The menu is full of delicious options. Choose from among four types of juice, a dozen pastry and pancake selections, four types of egg dishes, breakfast meats, and, last, but not least, a fruit salad. With all the food, combined with the privacy and serenity, you might get a little spoiled staying at Suite River. **(503) 622-3547; moderate.**

Restaurant Kissing

☙☙ **THE RENDEZVOUS GRILL AND THE TAP ROOM, Welches** Don't let the truck-stop sounding name detour you from considering this restaurant; it's definitely worth a visit. In fact, the restaurant is packed on weekends with Portlanders who drive out to the mountains for a breath of fresh air and a bite of the Rendezvous' outstanding desserts. The comfortable main room, complete with tall ceilings, an assortment of tables and booths, and vines wrapped around the windows, isn't outright romantic, but can be at night when it is enhanced by candlelight and soft classical music. (The adjacent Tap Room is more suited for couples who want to hoist a pint rather than pucker up.)

What really stands out here is the food: Everything is made from scratch, right down to the mayonnaise. Rigatoni and alder-smoked chicken is the house specialty, but don't miss out on other delectables, such as Asian grilled pork loin sparked with mango salsa, or pan-fried Alaskan razor clams served with a sesame-ginger dipping sauce. Desserts are a must. (Take one for the road if you don't have enough stomach space—you'll be glad you did!) The pear-hazelnut bread pudding and white chocolate–mocha cheesecake are culinary creations worth driving a million miles for. **67149 East Highway 26; (503) 622-6837; moderate to expensive; reservations recommended on weekends.**

Government Camp

Hotel/Bed and Breakfast Kissing

☙☙☙ **FALCON'S CREST INN, Government Camp** The gracious hosts here are eager to make you feel right at home. The contemporary chalet-style mountain house holds five guest rooms, and each has a private bath, in-room telephone, and a forest or mountain view. The Mexicali Suite is the only ground-level unit, making it a particularly private option (and our favorite). The color scheme mixes subtle desert hues with vibrant Southwest patterns; a queen-size bed and a two-person Jacuzzi tub with dimming lights make the suite even more sumptuous. Up a flight of stairs and adjacent to the dining room, the Master Suite has a four-poster queen-size bed, knotty pine walls, and a luxurious soaking tub on the back deck—another excellent room for romantics. The Safari and Cat Ballou Rooms may be a bit overdone for some tastes, with stuffed animals and wild prints in one and rich red velvet, satin, and lace accents in the other, but the Cat Ballou Room is the only room with a king-size bed. Sophia's Room has two twin beds, which means it is not a romantic option. A comfortable sitting loft on the third floor with a TV/VCR and a CD player is available for guests' use. Common areas throughout the house are comfortable and furnished with various collections from the innkeepers' family and travels.

In the morning, fresh muffins complete with two fruit butters are delivered to your room along with a carafe of coffee or tea. Following this, a full gourmet breakfast is served in the dining room and may include such tasty treats as orange French toast, hash brown potato pie, or sausage patties with spicy mustard. The lavish morning meal should keep you satisfied as you spend the day skiing, sightseeing, hiking, or golfing. **87287 Government Camp Loop Highway; (503) 272-3403, (800) 624-7384; moderate to very expensive; minimum-stay requirement on holidays and for the Mexicali Suite.**

Romantic Note: If you visit Falcon's Crest in the winter, you should know that from the day after Thanksgiving through the month of March, the inn celebrates an extended Christmas. Each room has its own custom-designed tree and is dressed with garlands and lights.

Romantic Suggestion: Elegant dinners are served in the inn's dining room, and we highly recommend an evening here. Six-course Euro-American extravaganzas are the specialty, and you will surely be satisfied by a main course such as Cornish game hens with apricot stuffing or prime rib with horseradish sauce. Reservations for dinner are required at least 24 hours in advance, and the price starts at $76 per couple.

❀❀ **MT. HOOD INN, Government Camp** Although the Mt. Hood Inn is obviously a chain hotel that borders the highway, some of the King Spa Rooms are more romantic than those rooms at **THE RESORT AT THE MOUNTAIN** and the **INN AT COOPER SPUR** (reviewed on pages 515 and 512, respectively). All 56 guest rooms are tastefully decorated with plush carpeting; contemporary natural-wood furniture; and matching linens, comforters, and curtains. While the pastel decor and nondescript hotel interiors may not be incredibly stylish or impressive, the above-mentioned King Spa Rooms offer private, beautifully tiled, two-person Jacuzzi tubs—perfect for ski-weary bodies. Given the fact that the mountain setting is just moments away, this is a good option for those seriously into snow sports or hiking. **87450 East Govern-**

ment Camp Loop; (503) 272-3205, (800) 443-7777; expensive to very expensive; minimum-stay requirement on holidays.

Sisters

Hotel/Bed and Breakfast Kissing

❤❤ **BLACK BUTTE RANCH, Sisters** For some, a romantic retreat consists of shutting out the world for hours or even days and focusing solely on each other. For others, romance means actively exploring the world together, side by side or hand in hand. You can have the best of both worlds at Black Butte Ranch, although it caters more to those who want to see and do it all.

Encircled by seven impressive mountains, the ranch is set on a flat, grassy plain sparsely covered with ponderosa pines, meandering streams, and fertile meadows. Your interlude begins in the three-story registration lodge; the ranch-style interior boasts open wood beams, high ceilings, terraced landings and stairways, cozy nooks and crannies, and a live tree growing through its center. Encircling glass windows showcase calming views of the far-reaching plain, the glorious mountains, and a nearby lake that is dotted with geese in the summer.

You can rent one-, two-, or three-bedroom condominiums, all set in contemporary gray wood complexes with wood walkways and views of the grounds. Inside, the condos feature high ceilings, fireplaces, full kitchens, and ranch-style decor that can look somewhat dull and outdated, depending on the condo. One- and four-bedroom homes scattered around the ranch are also available for rent. Because each home is privately owned, furniture, amenities, and decor vary significantly from one to another. Neither luxurious nor elegant, Black Butte is nevertheless a pleasant place to enjoy some country privacy together.

Black Butte's stables are only moments away. For a real Western experience, befriend a horse and take a guided tour on horseback through the silent, lush backwoods. Choose from various trail rides (some include a barbecue dinner in the barn afterward), design your own ride, or get lessons if you're a tenderfoot. As if this were not enough, Black Butte Ranch also offers the standard resort amenities: tennis courts, four outdoor swimming pools, bike rentals, jogging trails, golf courses, and acceptable restaurants. **13653 Hawks Beard Road (Highway 20); (541) 595-6211, (800) 452-7455; www.black butteranch.com; moderate to unbelievably expensive; minimum-stay requirement for the homes.**

❤❤❤ **CONKLIN'S GUEST HOUSE, Sisters** Set amid sprawling farm fields on the outskirts of Sisters, this sparkling white turn-of-the-century farmhouse is surrounded by five acres of land, two ponds, and a large grassy yard complete with a swimming pool.

Outside, the front porch is festooned with an international array of flags. Inside, the main living area's eclectic Victorian/country decor is accented by an even more eclectic collection of furnishings, including a piano, a water fountain, an old-fashioned telephone booth in the entryway, and a birdcage that holds African bluecaps that love to sing and dance for guests. The rich burgundy color scheme lends a cozy darkness to the room, which is perfect for hot summer days.

The five guest rooms do not share the living room's mix-and-match decor. Our favorite is the downstairs Forget-me-not Room, decorated in dark green and white. A black iron canopied queen-size bed stands as the room's centerpiece, complemented by white wicker furniture, a gas fireplace, private entrance, and a day bed. A claw-foot tub and shower grace the sun-filled bathroom. Upstairs, the refined Morning Glory Suite inspires romance with classical artwork, terra-cotta-colored walls, and a black iron canopied queen-size bed. A private patio overlooking the pool below and the Three Sisters beyond is a wonderful morning spot. That same view can be enjoyed from the claw-foot tub in the bathroom.

Romance-minded couples gravitate to the gazebo that juts out over the pond or to one of several benches along the pond's banks. A lovely terra-cotta-tiled solarium next to the pool makes the perfect place for a breakfast that may bring forth corned beef hash with baked eggs, eggs Benedict with grated kielbasa, or an assortment of muffins. Fresh flowers and herbs from the garden adorn each dish. **69013 Camp Polk Road; (541) 549-0123, (800) 549-4262; www.informat.com/bz/conklins; inexpensive to expensive.**

Bend

Parched in the summer and frozen in the winter, Bend is a lively resort community snuggled in the heart of the Oregon Cascades. (Unfortunately, parts of town resemble Marlboro Country rather than a captivating Northwest enclave.) Mount Bachelor and the Deschutes River are a short drive away, and more than a dozen parks and national forests offer unlimited adventure. Summertime brings white-water rafters, hikers, bikers, rock climbers, and families; in the winter, skiers and boarders hit the slopes. While Bend's primary romantic draw is the great outdoors, in the summer the **CASCADE FESTIVAL OF MUSIC** (541-382-8381) presents live performances of jazz, pop, blues, and classical music next to the Deschutes River at Drake Park. Whatever the season, activities abound, and lovers of the outdoors fall in love with Bend.

Hotel/Bed and Breakfast Kissing

❧ **INN OF THE SEVENTH MOUNTAIN, Bend** For those dynamic couples who just can't sit still, the Inn of the Seventh Mountain is ideal. White-water river rafting, roller skating, and horseback riding, plus challenging mountain trails, sturdy mountain bikes, a large pool where roughhousing is acceptable, lots of hot tubs, and a world-class golf course are right outside your door, and that's just in the summer! Winter brings a whole new set of activities, such as ice skating, snowmobile touring, sleigh rides, and, of course, skiing at nearby Mount Bachelor. Outdoor activities are the specialty here, and the inn's knowledgeable staff will be happy to set you up with the activities that interest you most.

We recommend this inn only for active, outdoor-oriented people, because you won't want to spend too much time in your room. The 400 condo-like accommodations are privately owned and reflect each proprietor's individual tastes, ranging from tacky '70s decor and "resort simplicity" to contemporary accoutrements. Although most rooms have views of the forest and snowcapped Mount Bachelor, the furnishings tend to be dismal, outdated, and plain. A fireside studio or loft room is your best bet, because the layout of these rooms offers ample space. **18575 Southwest Century Drive; (541) 382-8711, (800) 452-6810; www.7thmtn.com; inexpensive to unbelievably expensive.**

Romantic Note: The pace here is almost always vigorous and busy. In summer the inn becomes the setting for family vacations, and the winter months bring the ski crowds. Off-season, when kids are in school and the first snows are still a few weeks away, is the best time to enjoy each other while participating in as many activities as you desire.

❀❀ LARA HOUSE BED AND BREAKFAST, Bend

One of the oldest homes in Bend, Lara House was built in 1910, and its location on a residential corner offers views of tranquil Drake Park and Mirror Pond from the bay windows and large front porch. The common rooms are dignified, with well-polished hardwood floors, a brick fireplace with nearby comfy armchairs, and antique sofas. A cheery, glass-enclosed sunroom serves as a breakfast room. Guests also have access to an outdoor hot tub, perfect for soaking weary muscles at the end of a busy day spent skiing, biking, or hiking.

The five guest rooms and one two-bedroom suite upstairs are all comfortable and equipped with private baths. The hand-sewn quilts give the queen-size beds an old-fashioned aspect; the somewhat tired antiques, fabrics, and color schemes could use some updating. However, the prices here are extremely reasonable, and the innkeeper goes out of her way to ensure that your stay is enjoyable. A genuine smile and a cup of steaming, delicious spiced cider greet your arrival. In the morning, an ample full breakfast of stuffed French toast, fresh fruit, and almond-flavored coffee is served at your private table in the solarium. Although Lara House is not exceedingly elegant, it's still a wonderful place to let your hair down, loosen your tie, and liberate your hearts. **640 Northwest Congress; (541) 388-4064, (800) 766-4064; inexpensive, minimum-stay requirement on holidays.**

❀❀❀❀ PINE RIDGE INN, Bend

In an area dominated by sprawling resorts, this small luxury inn perched on a bluff above the Deschutes River is a wonderful find. Pine Ridge caters to the romantically inclined, offering the ultimate in personal attention and seclusion. Amenities in most of the inn's 20 guest rooms include private baths, TV/VCRs, kitchenettes, Jacuzzi tubs, and evening turn-down service. Despite their hotel ambience, even the least expensive courtyard rooms are wonderful. Each room is decorated in one of three themes: fly-fishing, Western, or floral. Classy, and not overcrowded with detailing, the rooms are simply delightful. Other appointments include light wood furniture, four-poster or library-style beds, private balconies or patios, and gas fireplaces to warm the cozy sunken living rooms. Aveda products grace each tiled bathroom, many of which have a double Jacuzzi tub and glass-enclosed shower. Fourteen guest rooms have lovely views of the river and the ponderosa pines beyond. The other six face the front yard and parking lot.

If you can stretch your budget a bit, spend a night in Pine Ridge's designer Hyde Suite: 900 square feet of sheer Northwest luxury. Watch the sunrise from the king-size library bed fitted with luxurious Ralph Lauren linens and adorned with large pillows. In the living room, a fire blazes in the stone fireplace during colder months. French country–style furnishings, warm earth tones, and double closets make this room extra-special. A two-person Jacuzzi tub is the centerpiece of the large, airy bathroom, which also boasts a glass-enclosed shower. Best of all, two private decks and expansive windows offer glorious views of the river below.

Wine and cheese are served every evening in a communal fireside parlor. In the morning, a delicious complimentary breakfast is served in the same room, complete with a hot entrée, fruit, breads, and cereals. Later in the day, be sure to take advantage of the inn's affiliation with the Athletic Club of Bend (within walking distance of the inn), which has wonderful exercise facilities, including a huge outdoor pool. **1200 Southwest Century Drive; (541) 389-6137, (800) 600-4095; www.pineridgeinn.com; moderate to very expensive; minimum-stay requirement on holidays; recommended wedding site.**

❀❀❀❀ RIVER RIDGE AT MOUNT BACHELOR VILLAGE RESORT, Bend

Nestled in the heart of Mount Bachelor Village Resort, this series of sprawling, two-story contemporary buildings is privately owned, but available for rent through the Village's registration office. You can choose to rent one-, two-, or three-bedroom suites or an executive suite. No matter which you choose, all are seductively sensuous, with the same sumptuous decor. The executive units, similar to upscale hotel rooms, are the smallest and least expensive—a real bargain, although they lack forest or river views. The one-bedroom suites have plentiful space for two, a full kitchen, and enough opulence and natural beauty to last a lifetime. The two- and three-bedroom suites are the crème de la crème, each sporting a complete kitchen, a hot tub on the deck, a Jacuzzi tub in the master suite, a gas fireplace, and an unbelievably expensive price tag. Go ahead and splurge if you can. Each exquisitely detailed unit is replete with walls of windows, a private deck with an outdoor hot tub, and upscale, stylish furnishings. A plethora of plump pillows makes the expansive couch an ideal spot to cuddle together by the gas fireplace and relish views of the rapids below. Blond wood and plentiful sunlight highlight the modern, fully stocked kitchen; in the spacious bedroom, sumptuous linens adorn a comfy king-size bed. A second, indoor spa resides in the contemporary white-tiled bathroom, along with a step-up, glass-enclosed shower.

Fortunately or unfortunately, depending on how you look at it, the River Ridge is part of a bigger resort. This means more people in the surrounding area, but it also means that you have access to all of the resort's amenities. You can bring your fishing pole and cast in the Deschutes River, take a romantic walk on the 2.2-mile nature trail that runs through the Village and next to the Deschutes, or tone your muscles at the outstanding athletic club. In the warmer months you can splash in the outdoor pool (open year-round); in snowy seasons, you can ski Mount Bachelor, just 20 minutes away.

One- and two-bedroom Ski Houses in various other buildings at the Village are also available (moderate to very expensive). Decorated individually by their private owners, many of these condo-style rooms are adequate and comfortable. There's a wide variety to choose from, so you're sure to find one that's right for the two of you. Just keep in mind that they don't come remotely close to the River Ridge units when it comes to romance. **19717 Mount Bachelor Drive; (541) 389-5900, (800) 452-9846; www.empnet.com/mbvr; inexpensive to unbelievably expensive; minimum-stay requirement.**

☙☙ **ROCK SPRINGS GUEST RANCH, Bend** Step off the dusty trail and unpack your saddlebags, pardners; you've reached the Rock Springs Guest Ranch. To adequately portray this diamond in the rough, we should probably rhapsodize about the 12,000 acres of arresting mountain scenery and rambling streams, or elaborate on the rustic cabins and the boot-shaped hot tub and duck-shaped swimming pool. But the essence of Rock Springs Guest Ranch is not revealed by such particulars; rather, it is displayed when you traverse this land on horseback with the one you love, the breeze cooling your brow and the balmy summer sun warming your face.

Vacations at the ranch are a family affair and a social affair as well; some groups return year after year to see old friends and have fun with their whole family. Stays last one week, and lodging, three hearty meals a day, horseback riding, and all activities are included in one fee. All of the 26 dated but cozy cabins have knotty pine walls, many have wood-burning fireplaces, and some have loft bedrooms. The hospitable, qualified staff plans separate daily activities for youngsters and grown-ups, something both parents and kids appreciate. Meals are served family-style at large wooden tables in the casual main lodge, and horseback rides are taken in groups every morning.

If you are looking for total privacy and luxurious seclusion, go somewhere else. But if a playful, casual escape is more your style (and you want to bring the kids along), we suggest giving Rock Springs Guest Ranch a call. **64201 Tyler Road; (541) 382-1957, (800) 225-DUDE (in the U.S.); www.**

rocksprings.com; expensive; minimum-stay requirement on holidays and seasonally.

Restaurant Kissing

❧❧❧ **BROKEN TOP CLUB RESTAURANT, Bend** We usually recommend steering clear of exclusive country clubs for romantic encounters, but Broken Top Club is an extraordinary exception to our rule. Set at the edge of a sloping, emerald green golf course, Broken Top's dining room (open to the public) overlooks tall stands of evergreens, a shimmering pond, and views of Broken Top Mountain in the distance. Floor-to-ceiling windows wrap around the expansive series of dining rooms, which are accented with natural wood, crisp white linens, and candlelight. For the most intimacy and comfort, request that your meal be served in the front lounge. Here, immense windows showcase the spectacular setting, and a fire roars in a floor-to-ceiling hearth. Cathedral ceilings and Northwest artwork create a stylish atmosphere. Cozy up together on a plush, oversize couch and enjoy savory crab cakes served with mascarpone cheese and caviar, grilled salmon with papaya-mango confetti, or sea scallops and mussels in saffron. In the dining room you can enjoy heartier entrées such as roasted rack of lamb with a huckleberry demi-glace, poached halibut wrapped in a pear-port crêpe, or grilled salmon topped with red gooseberry beurre blanc. Desserts are little slices of heaven—just try the Bailey's ice cream pie and you'll see what we mean. **61999 Broken Top Drive; (541) 383-7600, (800) 382-7690; expensive; lunch and dinner Tuesday–Saturday; recommended wedding site.**

❧❧ **ROSETTE, Bend** Bend is better known for its outdoor recreation than for romantic, indoor kissing spots. Don't expect to find dark, cozy restaurants with little tables lit by candlelight. However, this downtown spot manages to fit the definition of romantic dining better than most local restaurants. Soft yellow walls, white linen tablecloths, and nature photographs adorn the elongated room. Five high-backed booths against the wall are the most kiss-worthy spots, along with the front window table for two (although you'll be in full view of the outside world).

The menu features standard chicken, beef, lamb, and pasta dishes, with lots of soy-Dijon accents and some interesting spice twists. Just steer clear of any exotic fish item. Our shark kabob was older than a *Jaws* rerun, although the local salmon proved much fresher. The grilled portobello mushroom is excellent and served with real garlic mashed potatoes. (Keep a few breath mints handy for later on.) Entrées are accompanied by house salads topped with an excellent miso dressing. **150 Northwest Oregon Avenue; (541) 383-2780; expensive; dinner Monday–Saturday.**

❧ **TOOMIE'S THAI CUISINE, Bend** Set in the heart of downtown Bend, this expansive dining room has oversize windows with views of the storefronts across the street. Curtains blocking this less-than-inspiring view would be a welcome addition. The space once housed a popular Italian eatery, but the only remnants of its Mediterranean past are the columns and archways commonly found in Italian restaurants. Bright and airy by day and dimly lit at night, Toomie's dining room is now appointed with Eastern artifacts, sculptures, and wall murals. Red tablecloths with Thai prints drape snugly arranged tables illuminated by candle lanterns. A gracious wait staff serves up tantalizing Thai food. You can't go wrong with anything on the menu, but we were particularly impressed with the sweet-and-sour lemongrass-and-coconut soup and the just-right spicy vegetarian phad Thai. **119 Northwest Minnesota Avenue; (541) 388-5590; moderate; lunch Monday–Friday, dinner daily.**

Outdoor Kissing

❤❤❤❤ **CASCADE LAKES HIGHWAY, Bend** Depending on the season, adventurous souls (with good snow tires) can journey together on this 89-mile paved loop with stirring views. Mount Bachelor, the Three Sisters, and Broken Top Mountain tower overhead in astonishing panoramas. Celebrate the area's beauty, stopping frequently for closer looks at the numerous lakes, streams, and unique environments, all teeming with wildlife. Take a moment to bird-watch at the osprey observation area, or investigate lava caves with the aid of provided flashlights and hard hats. Keep your eyes open for the deer, rabbits, hawks, and other wild creatures that inhabit this heavenly domain. We can't think of a more opportune spot for kissing, as long as you don't cause traffic to back up (maybe you should pull over). *From Highway 97 just south of Bend, turn west onto Cascade Lakes Highway and follow the signs.*

Sunriver

Hotel/Bed and Breakfast Kissing

❤❤ **SUNRIVER RESORT, Sunriver** Although not officially a town, Sunriver has all the makings of one. Set on 3,200 riverside acres, this self-sufficient community is complete with its own post office, grocery store, three golf courses, a paved runway for private planes, and several realty offices. Various companies manage vacation rentals, but contacting the Sunriver Resort is the most efficient way to plan a vacation here. Rooms, condominiums, and homes (some owned by the resort, others privately owned) are available for rent through the resort's main office. Because of Sunriver's vast size, we won't even attempt to describe in detail all of the options you have here. We can tell you, however, that the professional staff should be able to help you decide which accommodations will best suit your needs.

Sunriver Resort's main attraction will vary depending on what you like.

Much of its reputation is built around the three 18-hole championship golf courses. Yet the surrounding mountains and Deschutes River offer recreational opportunities of all kinds, from biking to hiking. Top that off with 28 tennis courts, 35 miles of paved bike paths, swimming pools, horseback riding, cross-country skiing, and white-water rafting, and you have the makings of an all-around vacation destination. Unlike many resorts, Sunriver is sufficiently spread out, so you aren't forced to have a family experience even if you are traveling without children.

No matter where you stay, be sure to stop by the recently renovated Sunriver Lodge, a spectacular study in Northwest design. There are several restaurants here, but for a romantic meal, we recommend you travel up the road to **THE GRILLE AT CROSSWATER** (expensive; call for seasonal hours), a golf-course restaurant that's above par and open to Sunriver guests only. **1 Center Drive; (541) 593-1000, (800) 547-3922; www.sunriver-resort.com; moderate to unbelievably expensive; minimum-stay requirement on holidays and seasonally.**

"There are swords

about to keep me safe:

They are the kisses

of your lips."

Mary Carolyn Davies

Southern Oregon

From magnificent national parks and forests to a world-renowned Shakespeare festival, Southern Oregon offers something for everyone. Outdoor enthusiasts will appreciate river rafting on the Rogue or touring Crater Lake, while even the most discriminating traveler will enjoy Ashland's highly acclaimed theater and gourmet restaurants. Whatever your preference, or if you like to combine outdoor and cultural activities, as many Northwesterners do, Southern Oregon is a unique, worthwhile destination.

Steamboat

The riverside community of Steamboat is located on Highway 138, approximately 38 miles east of Interstate 5 and the town of Roseburg. Cradled by the deep green hillsides of the Umpqua National Forest and the rushing waters of the Umpqua River, Steamboat is home to one of the most popular fishing resorts in the state (see Hotel/Bed and Breakfast Kissing).

Hotel/Bed and Breakfast Kissing

❁❁❁ **STEAMBOAT INN, Steamboat** It may feel like the middle of nowhere, but the Steamboat Inn is approximately halfway between Interstate 5 and Crater Lake, in the heart of the Umpqua National Forest. Its remote location along the rushing North Umpqua River is the best reason to visit this rustic lodge. Hiking to a dozen different waterfalls, wading in the river, and fly-fishing top the list of possible activities. If the great outdoors is not calling you, other options include perusing the inn's fabulous library, which is warmed by a gas fireplace, or relaxing in your own deep soaking tub (almost half of the rooms offer this amenity).

Accommodations come in a variety of shapes and sizes. The five Hideaway Cottages set in forested surroundings are spacious and particularly private. Each one features comfortable furnishings, knotty pine walls, a white-tiled soaking tub, a wood-burning fireplace, a small kitchenette, and a spacious bedroom and living room area. The only thing lacking is a river view. That feature is available in the two higher-priced River Suites, which feature king-size beds, soaking tubs, fireplaces, and private decks that overlook the river. Three ranch-style homes, located about a mile upstream, are geared for families. Finally, at the inexpensive end of the price spectrum, there are eight small cedar-paneled Streamside Cabins without any extras except a pleasant common veranda that overlooks the river. These spartan but clean cabins serve as a reminder that many guests come here to fish, not to kiss. The rusticity is part of the fun of this lodging, and the secluded setting really does allow you to get away from it all. **42705 North Umpqua Highway (Highway 138); (800) 840-8825; www.europa.com/~timp/steamboat/index.html; expensive to very expensive; call for seasonal closures.**

Romantic Note: The inn is known for its Fisherman's Dinner (expensive), served in the dining room around a long wood-slab table. Meals include aperitifs, hors d'oeuvres, a hearty main course and savory side dish, Oregon wines, and a grand dessert. The set menu changes nightly and may not include fish (despite the name), but the food is always plentiful and good. Family-style seating encourages a warm, conversational atmosphere around the table. Although it might not be a romantic encounter, the Fisherman's Dinner is a great value, considering all of the food and beverages included, and you should give it a try at least one night during your stay. Reservations are required; try to reserve at least two days in advance if you have any special requests or dietary restrictions.

Crater Lake

Hotel/Bed and Breakfast Kissing

❧❧ **CRATER LAKE LODGE, Crater Lake** This 1915 lodge—renovated in the mid-1990s—sits on the southern rim of the Crater Lake caldera near Rim Village, where it proudly displays its stone-and-wood exterior accentuated with chalet-style shutters. Inside, an extensive collection of black-and-white photographs and a detailed display area recount the history of the original building and its recent (and extraordinary) transformation. One of the original stone fireplaces still stands in the main lobby, where Douglas fir floors, columns made from tree trunks, and walls of stone and wood create a rustic Northwest ambience not soon forgotten. Next to the lobby is the Great Hall, which was part of the original 1915 lodge. Here you'll find a gigantic stone fireplace and an assortment of Craftsman-style chairs and sofas. After a day of outdoor adventures, take in the breathtaking views of Crater Lake from the lodge's large patio area.

You won't find any phones or TVs in the lodge's 71 guest rooms. Luckily, there's plenty to see right outside your window. Half the rooms offer incredible views of Crater Lake, and the other half face the Klamath Lake basin. Nicely decorated, the rooms are a small step up from standard hotel rooms, with contemporary oak furnishings, rather ordinary linens, and small private bathrooms; some have cushioned window seats. Rooms on the third and fourth floors have sloped ceilings. Four spacious loft rooms are also available, but unfortunately these rooms are better suited for families than for couples looking for a romantic getaway. Few activities or recreational amenities are available inside the lodge, aside from a selection of board games and cards. This can translate into boredom when bad weather ruins outdoor plans. If the rooms were more romantic, we wouldn't mind so much. Bring a good book just in case.

The lodge's dining room, although spectacular in appearance, is a perfect example of what happens when no other culinary competition exists for miles. Substandard food, boring presentations, and tables so close you could kiss your neighbor put a damper on dining here. **On the southern rim of the Crater Lake caldera at Rim Village; (541) 830-8700; www.crater-lake.com; moderate to expensive; call for seasonal closures.**

Romantic Suggestion: June through August is the busiest time at Crater Lake Lodge. Consider making reservations as early as January if you plan to visit during the summer months.

Outdoor Kissing

❀❀❀❀ **CRATER LAKE NATIONAL PARK, Crater Lake** It's hard to fathom the dimensions of this volcanic formation, cut into the earth thousands of years ago by forces that make the Mount St. Helens eruption look like a firecracker on the Fourth of July. At 1,932 feet deep, Crater Lake is the deepest lake in the United States, and the seventh-deepest in the world. A towering border of golden, rocky earth encompasses this inconceivably blue body of water. It is an astounding spectacle to behold. You can revel in the views as you drive around the entire perimeter (except in the winter and early spring), take a two-hour boat ride from Cleetwood Cove to Wizard Island, or hike down to the lake and embrace amid scenery that will take your breath away. Alas, the caravans of tourists during the summer can also take your breath away, and mar some otherwise pretty good kissing opportunities. Snow lasts nine months of the year here, which is good news for cross-country skiers; trails ranging in length from one to ten miles will delight skiers of all abilities. **(541) 594-2211, (541) 830-8700; $10 per car per week.** *Crater Lake is off Highway 62, 80 miles northeast of Medford, and 60 miles northwest of Klamath Falls. It is about a two-hour drive from Ashland.*

Romantic Note: For overnight accommodations, we recommend the renovated **CRATER LAKE LODGE** at Rim Village (see Hotel/Bed and Breakfast Kissing). Camping at the **MAZAMA CAMPGROUND** (541) 830-8700) is also an option for those who can't get enough of the crisp mountain air.

Merlin

Near Grants Pass, Merlin is a small, mostly residential community approximately one hour north of Ashland.

Hotel/Bed and Breakfast Kissing

❀❀❀ **PINE MEADOW INN BED AND BREAKFAST, Merlin** Set in a quiet rural area, crowning a grassy, wooded knoll, this large country home is reminiscent of a Midwestern farmhouse. The owners helped design and build the house and its surrounding gardens. From the diligently cultivated vegetable garden, fruit trees, and pretty flowers to the serene koi pond and the house itself, the tender loving care they have invested is evident. These efforts include the creation of wonderful kissing spots for guests. You can kiss near the koi pond, in the hot tub, or on the front yard hammock, but we think the best spots are the private benches tucked away in the woods.

The comfortable furnishings in the main-floor living room are indicative of the comforts that await in the four upstairs guest rooms. Each room has its own private bath. The Willow Room is the largest, with English antiques, a sitting area, and a window seat that views Mount Walker in the distance. The bath is standard, but has a double vanity so both of you have space. Both the Heather Room and the Garden Room look out to the gardens and woods, but the Garden Room also has a bay window overlooking the koi pond. Finally, the Laurel Room is furnished with oak antiques, a handmade quilt, and lace curtains. A long window seat is perfect for stargazing or watching the sun rise through the woods.

Heavy breakfasts can put passion on the back burner, so the focus here is on low-fat, vegetarian-oriented meals. The delightful innkeepers keep everyone entertained between courses with stories about their comical resident squirrels, details of the house-building project, and information about the beautiful surroundings. As you listen, fill up on just-picked berries from the garden, yogurt dishes, or baked orange-pecan French toast. With such a healthy start, your heart will be all the more ready for romance. **1000 Crow Road; (541) 471-6277, (800) 554-0806; www.pinemeadowinn.com; inexpensive to moderate.**

Restaurant Kissing

❦❦ MORRISON'S ROGUE RIVER LODGE, Merlin If you find that food always tastes better when you eat outside, travel the long, winding road along the Rogue River to this fishing lodge. Each summer evening the large deck surrounding the rustic, 50-year-old lodge is transformed into a dining room complete with linen-covered tables, fine silverware, and candles. Enjoy a four-course, prix fixe dinner as you watch the sun disappear behind the hills. Before you, manicured lawns stretch out to the banks of the mighty and majestic Rogue River.

The lodge's kitchen does a fine job of complementing the outstanding scenery with good yet simple food. Some dishes border on mediocre, such as our appetizer of tortellini with creamy pesto. Others, like the golden baked halibut with lemon sour-cream sauce, are above average. Be sure to linger over the Oreo cheesecake until you see the stars. **8500 Galice Road; (541) 476-3825, (800) 826-1963; www.morrisonslodge.com; moderate to expensive; reservations required; dinner daily May–late August.**

Romantic Suggestion: If your sweetie is into fly-fishing, he or she might spend too much time eyeing the river instead of you. To turn his or her attention away (for a while), promise to return in autumn to fish together. That's when the lodge offers fishing packages for couples. You'll stay in the accompanying cabins or lodge, which are clean and rustic, but not very romantic. However, being outdoors in this spectacular setting with your beloved certainly is.

Grants Pass

Hotel/Bed and Breakfast Kissing

❦❦❦ **FLERY MANOR, Grants Pass** Those seeking opulence combined with the quietness of the country will adore this large blue house a few miles north of Grants Pass. The lavish window treatments, plush carpeting, and ornate decorations inside come as quite a surprise considering the rural mountainside location.

Each of the four guest rooms is richly appointed with lace and satin accents, fluffy pillows, classical art, faux-textured walls, and plenty of antiques. Double doors lead into the Moonlight Suite, which takes the prize when it comes to romance. Red satin sheets await on the king-size bed (reserved for special occasions), and a love-note pillow by the bed lets you write sweet nothings in addition to whispering them. The room—larger than most apartments—has a private balcony for great sunset viewing, along with a marble fireplace for cooler nights. Perhaps most spectacular is the suite's spa room, where the two of you can soak in the pink double Jacuzzi tub, surrounded by glowing candles and fluffy clouds, which are painted on the ceiling.

A bubbling little waterfall fountain provides background music as you savor a three-course breakfast in the formal dining room. Scottish shortbread, baked apples stuffed with wild blackberries, eggs on a cloud, and other savories arrive on fine china. Later in the day, sip the innkeeper's wild blackberry and mint iced tea, one of the best combinations we've tasted. Outside, in the seven acres of yard, little pathways weave around the garden and ponds. Plenty of lawn ornaments and a gazebo add interest to the grassy landscape, and, when we visited, a koi pond and waterfall were in the works. **2000 Jumpoff Joe Creek Road; (541) 476-3591, (541) 471-2303; www.flerymanor.com; inexpensive to expensive.**

Restaurant Kissing

❦❦ **THE COUNTRY COTTAGE CAFE AND TEA ROOM, Grants Pass** High tea is such a refined afternoon activity, and in a charming setting like this one, you really can't go wrong. Since this casual tearoom is located at Meadow View Country Gardens, you can find a lot more to do here than just sip tea. Three different gardens—one for organic vegetables, one for herbs, and a classic English flower garden—can be toured before or after your meal, as well as the Harvest Room, which sells just-picked produce, fresh vegetables, and herbs you can take home with you.

Everything in the restaurant is homemade, using Oregon-made products, organic produce, and herbs from the gardens whenever possible. Lunch options include a variety of sandwiches and fresh soups. High tea includes the traditional scones with hand-whipped cream and jam, lemon tarts, dainty finger sandwiches, home-baked shortbread, and, of course, a pot of tea. The open-air covered patio with skylights is a quiet, lovely setting where romance is free to bloom along with all the flowers around you. **2315 Upper River Road Loop, at Meadow View Country Gardens; (541) 476-6882; www. country-cottage.org; inexpensive; reservations recommended; lunch and high tea Tuesday–Saturday.**

Jacksonville

Jacksonville is remembered as the first place gold was discovered in Oregon during the 1850s gold rush. Today it remains a truly charming, revitalized Old West town that gives only the subtlest hint that it is a tourist attraction. You will be pleased to discover this lovely escape.

Four distinct seasons sweep across the area's rolling hills, distant mountains, and pristine farm country, filling them in turn with sultry warmth, stunning colors, and mild frosts. During the summer, don't miss the exhilarating **BRITT FESTIVALS** (see Theater Kissing), the town's outdoor music and performing arts series. In addition, Jacksonville is conveniently located for **RIVER RAFTING ON THE ROGUE** (see Outdoor Kissing), and only 15 miles from Ashland and the **OREGON SHAKESPEARE FESTIVAL** (reviewed on page 554). Trolleys and horse-drawn carriages tour downtown on most summer days, quaint shops and historic museums abound, and some of the first-class bed and breakfasts and restaurants are thoroughly romantic.

Hotel/Bed and Breakfast Kissing

❧❧❧ **JACKSONVILLE INN, Jacksonville** This landmark brick hotel is set in the heart of Jacksonville. Built in 1861 and lovingly restored over the years, the Jacksonville Inn blends old and new to create comfortably elegant lodgings. All of the eight second-floor rooms have exposed brick walls, private baths, handsome antique armoires, oak furnishings, comfortable beds, and a great deal of polish. The blue-toned Peter Britt Room even has a wonderful whirlpool tub—not exactly authentic, but very luxurious. A full breakfast of your choice is served in the inn's famous Victorian dining room (see Restaurant Kissing).

The inn also rents out three charming, private guest cottages, approximately a block away. A white picket fence borders these side-by-side cottages, and gardens line the walkways. Two are newly built, with vaulted ceilings, large Jacuzzi tubs with steam showers, and double-sided gas-log fireplaces. The oldest cottage is also a wonderful little hideaway, with country Victorian furnishings, a lace-canopied bed, gas fireplace, kitchenette, and a steam shower with Jacuzzi tub. A fruit-and-champagne breakfast can be delivered to these cottages, but you may want to walk over to the inn for a fine breakfast that will tide you over until dinnertime. **175 East California Street; (541) 899-1900, (800) 321-9344; www.jacksonvilleinn.com; moderate to very expensive.**

❀❀❀ **TOUVELLE HOUSE, Jacksonville** This lovely Craftsman-style home sits a stone's throw away from the charming town of Jacksonville. Inside the well-preserved 1916 home, you'll find many of the original features, including built-in hutches, push-button light switches, and a wonderful wraparound porch that provides much-needed shade on hot summer days.

After you've been greeted by the personable innkeepers, saunter through the inn and soak in the grandeur of the common areas, including the Great Room, where an eclectic assortment of plush couches and chairs sit beside a grand stone fireplace. Ornate window treatments and period wallpaper add richness to the room. The loving work that went into this place is unmistakable, and extraordinary attention to detail is apparent throughout.

Each of the six rooms has an individual style, most have queen-size beds, and all have private baths. We liked the Garden Suite for its abundance of natural light and the third-floor Granny's Attic for its coziness. Thanks to two gigantic oak trees that shade the entire home, some of the rooms are a bit on the dark side (which can prove soothing in the summertime). Yet all the rooms are brightened by subtle motifs. Prairie West is loaded with early Jacksonville charm, accented by bent willow furnishings and a handmade quilt; and Americana, patriotically furnished in burgundy, white, and navy blue, has a lovely outdoor patio.

A dip in the outdoor pool and spa provides welcome refreshment at the end of a hot summer day. (Summer days here can be unbearably hot, so the pool really is a treat.) Generous three-course breakfasts are served on fine china with antique crystal each morning, and the cooking is just as wonderful as you would expect from everything else here. Breakfast starts with a yogurt-granola-fruit bowl, followed by an herb egg soufflé, ham, and a dessert of baked pear with caramel-pecan sauce. Yes, breakfast comes with dessert. Now that's a sweet way to start the day. **455 North Oregon Street; (541) 899-8938, (800) 846-8422; www.wave.net/upg/touvelle; moderate to expensive.**

Restaurant Kissing

❀❀ **GOGI'S, Jacksonville** At the edge of town, Jacksonville's newest restaurant is housed in a turn-of-the-century replica building that delights the eye with its authenticity. The interior is rather nondescript, but the butter-colored walls, classical artwork, and dim lighting make this a pleasant place for an evening out. Gogi's holds only a dozen or so tables and a few booths, plus a hand-built pine bar that truly can be called the room's centerpiece. While the booths provide some privacy, try the two-person outdoor tables if the weather is nice. Unfortunately, you'll get a view of the parking lot.

The kitchen serves mostly straightforward dishes, with a few interesting entrées thrown in here and there. Smoked salmon and linguine, grilled chicken breast, rack of lamb, and a variety of steaks make up the main dinner menu. Salads, such as the grilled mushroom or Cuban rice salad, are specialties, and big enough to have as entrées. We went tropical and tried the Hawaiian wild rice salad, like fried rice (sans grease) with lots of tropical flavors. If you are heading to the **BRITT FESTIVALS** (see Theater Kissing), inquire about their take-along Britt baskets. **235 West Main Street; (541) 899-8699; moderate to expensive; lunch Monday–Saturday, dinner daily, brunch Sunday.**

❦❦ JACKSONVILLE INN RESTAURANT, Jacksonville
One of the better-known restaurants in the area, this plush, demurely lit dining room is constantly busy. We are not sure what all the commotion is about; the service is not worth raving about, and parts of the extensive menu leave much to be desired. The salmon crêpes with cream sauce were mushy and the sauce too thick, and the spanakopita was greasy and tough. You are better off ordering the simpler entrées, because they can be delicious. Meat dishes, particularly the filet mignon and the fresh fish, are just fine and quite tender.

The dining rooms themselves are definitely romantic settings for any meal. Sketches of old buildings, exposed brick, and old-fashioned lamps create a quaint atmosphere in the main-floor dining room, although the overall redness of the room can be relentless. The lower-level dining room is more intimate feeling, but the stone walls can make for poor acoustics and the smoky mirrors are too outdated for our taste. Consider coming to the Jacksonville Inn for Sunday brunch—champagne from local wineries is served with the meal. If you choose carefully, this can be a four-lip dining rhapsody. If not, well, you can still kiss. **175 East California Street, at the Jacksonville Inn; (541) 899-1900, (800) 321-9344; moderate to expensive; breakfast and dinner daily, lunch Tuesday–Saturday, brunch Sunday.**

Romantic Note: Lovely accommodations await upstairs (see Hotel/Bed and Breakfast Kissing).

❦❦❦ MCCULLY HOUSE INN, Jacksonville
You might not expect to find world-class cuisine in a small town like Jacksonville, but that's exactly what you will encounter at the McCully House Inn. This historic Gothic Revival mansion sits proudly at the edge of Jacksonville's downtown area. Remarkable gourmet cuisine is served in two separate indoor dining rooms, in the garden, or out on the rose-bordered front lawn. The first dining room, near the entrance, feels like part of an elegant home, with its glowing fireplace and warm peach-toned walls. Our favorite place (if you can't venture outside) is the sunny indoor garden patio with French doors and floor-to-ceiling windows looking out to the English country garden. Patio chairs with green cushions and white tables, along with striking sunflowers painted on the walls, make this room inviting, casual, and light. On warm days or for special events,

outdoor seating at umbrella-shaded tables may be arranged either on the front lawn (which can be noisy due to traffic) or on the more secluded back garden patio, where a bubbling waterfall awaits.

Not only are the dining rooms and outdoor patios lovely, but dinner itself is a culinary treat. The internationally inspired cuisine combines flavors that work wonderfully. The tuna and shrimp–filled wontons surrounded by a blackberry beurre blanc are absolutely succulent, and so is the aromatic cedar-planked halibut topped with mushrooms and bacon. Be sure to give the dessert menu a once-over. What chocolate lover could resist the chocolate soufflé? **240 East California Street; (541) 899-1942, (800) 367-1942; www.mccullyhouseinn.com; expensive; lunch Thursday–Monday, dinner daily.**

Romantic Note: Three second-story guest rooms at the McCully House Inn (inexpensive to moderate), while not overflowing with romantic amenities, have been nicely renovated and are decorated with antiques.

Outdoor Kissing

❦❦❦ **RIVER RAFTING ON THE ROGUE, Jacksonville** The area between Grants Pass and the coast (where the Rogue River empties into the Pacific) has attracted more than 45 different rafting and boat companies that offer all kinds of excursions down the Rogue River and the Upper Klamath River. Some of these jaunts are totally tame, allowing you to float freely in the midst of towering pines and mountains, while others are radically exhilarating, with rapids to shoot and rocky channels to navigate. Boats built for one, two, eight, or even larger groups are all part of the Rogue adventure; what you choose depends on your skill and your level of confidence. A trip down the Rogue might seem touristy, but once you challenge the rapids and feel the adrenaline rush of riding a waterborne roller coaster, everyone else disappears and it is only the two of you and the river. **Adventure Center: (541) 488-2819, (800) 444-2819; www.raftingtours.com. Noah's World of Water: (541) 488-2811, (800) 858-2811; www.noahsrafting.com. Orange Torpedo Trips: (541) 479-5061, (800) 635-2925. Rogue/Klamath River Adventures: (541) 779-3708, (800) 231-0769; www.rogueklamath.com. Prices start at $50 per person.** *Many of the rafting companies offer pickups in Jacksonville and Ashland.*

Theater Kissing

❦❦❦ **BRITT FESTIVALS, Jacksonville** From June through early September, Jacksonville is filled with crowds attending the annual Britt Festivals. This summer-long series hosts internationally recognized musicians, bands, and dance ensembles, as well as a handful of comedians and musical-theater troupes. All perform under the stars in an outdoor amphitheater, surrounded by ponderosa pines and madronas, on land that was once the estate of pioneer photographer Peter Britt. Bring a blanket and a picnic dinner, and find your own stretch of musical heaven on the grassy hillside facing the stage. Just about every type of music is represented: classical, jazz, rhythm and blues, folk, country, and rock. The lineup changes seasonally, so call ahead for details and tickets. **(541) 773-6077, (800) 882-7488; www.mind.net/britt; ticket prices range from $16–$46.** *Two blocks from downtown Jacksonville.*

Talent

Just north of Ashland is Talent, a small village that is little more than a stretch of two-lane highway dotted with businesses. Chances are you will pass through Talent on your way to or from Ashland without even noticing the intriguing little restaurant that is a desirable kissing destination.

Restaurant Kissing

🐛🐛 **NEW SAMMY'S COWBOY BISTRO, Talent** All right, all right, we know what you are thinking: How can romance and Sammy the Cowboy go together? Well, we weren't so sure at first either. From the outside, this bistro looks like a rundown roadside shack; the exterior is painted in bright, vivid shades, and a flashing arrow (with lots of bulbs missing) is the only sign indicating the restaurant. As you enter the first set of doors, you may wonder if you are in the right place. Venture on: Half of the romantic fun is what awaits inside.

Attractive country wallpaper, pastel accents, Fiestaware, and candles on the tables allow you to forget the outside and appreciate what you've found—a dining room reminiscent of a quaint little dollhouse. The kitchen emphasizes fresh, organic, regional ingredients, and the food ranks among the best in the Northwest. The extremely tiny dining room holds only six tables, so you'll have to make reservations up to three months in advance to get a taste of this place. We recommend the baby vegetable stew with new potatoes, snow peas, asparagus, onions, and carrots combined with cheese, pesto ravioli, and morel mushrooms. The grilled quail Provençal with rice pilaf is another possibility. If you are looking for a unique experience, have a sense of adventure, and want to plan far in advance, New Sammy's Cowboy Bistro will not let you down. **2210 South Pacific Highway; (541) 535-2779; expensive; no credit cards; reservations required; call for seasonal hours.**

Ashland

Tranquil neighborhoods, a dynamic downtown teeming with shops and restaurants, a world-class cultural center, pristine countryside, and mountainous terrain bordering fertile river valleys make up the utopian world of Ashland, the southernmost point covered in this book. Not only is the town attractive, with many delightful accommodations, but the Ashland theater season, which begins in February and runs through October, almost makes Broadway pale by comparison. It will take only one visit to make both of you sustaining members of Ashland's annual **OREGON SHAKESPEARE FESTIVAL** (see Theater Kissing).

Ashland offers more to do than almost any other small town in the Northwest. Besides the in-town activities, you can try white-water rafting down the nearby Rogue and Klamath Rivers (reviewed on page 535), horseback riding, hiking with llamas, mountain climbing, and, during the winter, downhill and cross-country skiing, available minutes away on **MOUNT ASHLAND** (see Outdoor Kissing). The town is chock-full of wonderful bed and breakfasts, and many offer very enticing winter rates. Summer lodging reservations should be made months in advance because rooms fill quickly when the weather is hot and the theater is in full swing. If you are having a hard time finding a place to stay, two very helpful services are **ASHLAND'S B&B NETWORK** (800-944-0329; www.abbnet.com) and the **OREGON BED AND BREAKFAST GUILD** (800-983-4667; www.opendoor.com/aaa-obbg).

Hotel/Bed and Breakfast Kissing

❧❧❧ **ANTIQUE ROSE INN, Ashland** As you ascend the steep stairs leading to this beautifully renovated 1888 Queen Anne Victorian home, you'll know right away that something special is in store. Romance inhabits every corner of the house, which is decorated with authentic Victorian furnishings, lace curtains and table coverings, Oriental rugs, and enough antiques to make you think you've traveled back in time.

An abundance of love and attention has gone into all three guest rooms. The Rose Room is nicely tucked away upstairs and features a king-size four-poster bed with down comforter, a uniquely carved wood fireplace, a private balcony, and a separate sitting area with an antique fainting couch. The Lace Room, also located upstairs, has a canopied oak Victorian bed and a delightful private bath with a claw-foot tub. The smaller Mahogany Room is set directly off the downstairs entry hall, which means that other guests can be heard coming and going. Still, this room is just as lovely as the others, with rich mahogany walls, antique wedding photos, antique baby christening gowns, a queen-size four-poster bed, lace curtains, and a private bathroom with an antique claw-foot tub.

The Rose Cottage, adjacent to the inn, is a private two-bedroom retreat with a gas fireplace, Jacuzzi tub, skylights, lace-canopied four-poster beds, and many elegant antiques. It also boasts a dry sauna and a tiny deck out back. Gourmet breakfasts are delivered to this unit to allow for a thoroughly intimate breakfast just for two.

Guests staying in the main house eat in the formal dining room downstairs, at a long table topped with lace and crystal. The satisfying meal features fresh fruit, homemade breads and pastries, gingerbread pancakes or tortilla-rolled brunch eggs, and plenty of hot coffee and tea. **91 Gresham Street; (541) 482-**

6285, (888) 282-6285; www.wvi.com/~dhull/antiquebnb; moderate to expensive; minimum-stay requirement on holiday weekends and seasonally; main house closed November–February.

❤❤ **COOLIDGE HOUSE, Ashland** We have said it before and we will say it again: Ashland's Main Street is not the most tranquil location for a bed and breakfast. On the other hand, it *is* one of the most convenient places to stay if you do not want to bother with hopping in and out of your car and finding a parking spot whenever you go to town.

Coolidge House is a finely restored Victorian just two blocks from downtown. Manicured shrubs and gardens adorn the front yard, and flower baskets line the porch. Of the six guest rooms here, four are in the main house and two are in the Carriage House behind it. Rooms in the main house vary in size, but all have private baths and are furnished with gorgeous antiques. The Baker Suite, dressed all in blue, features a lovely 1880s hand-painted French bed set, and the bathroom holds a claw-foot tub and pedestal sink. Romantics will especially love the regal Parlor Room, with its hardwood floors, fabulous window seat, luxurious furnishings, and spacious bathroom with Jacuzzi tub for two. The Rose Room and the Garden Room are smaller; an antique iron bed and claw-foot tub make the Rose Room a cozy choice, while the sunny Garden Room features white wicker furniture, a handmade quilt, and views of the garden.

The Carriage House rooms have the advantage of being larger, but mostly lack the lovely antiques found in the main house. The contemporary style of these rooms is a bit of a letdown if you've had the opportunity to admire the furnishings in the main house. However, these two units are still desirable, both for the extra space they offer and for the fact that they are tucked behind the main house, which means noise from Main Street is hardly evident. The Cottage is a two-room suite with a gas fireplace, TV, and huge round Jacuzzi tub. The Sun Suite (available in summer only) is appropriately named given its bright and airy feel. Vaulted ceilings and white wicker furniture contribute to this effect, and a gas fireplace and a whirlpool tub are additional romantic amenities.

Full gourmet breakfasts are presented each morning. Depending on the season, you may enjoy your morning meal in the dining room, on the flower-trimmed brick patio behind the house, or on the second-story balcony at charming white iron tables for two. **137 North Main Street; (541) 482-4721, (800) 655-5522; expensive to very expensive; minimum-stay requirement on weekends seasonally.**

❤❤❤❤ **COUNTRY WILLOWS BED AND BREAKFAST, Ashland** This ranch estate two and a half miles from downtown Ashland has been a wonderful kissing destination for years, and the enthusiastic and detail-oriented innkeepers keep improving things. Who knows? If they keep up the good work, we may have to create a five-lip category!

A bright yellow sign, reminding you to drive slowly because of the "Geese and Quackers," greets you as you drive up the gravel road. However, Portia and Juliet, the two resident goats, or the horses that graze in the pasture will most likely be the first residents you'll see. Huge willows, a manicured lawn bordered by lovely gardens, and a duck pond decorate the property, which lies at the foot of wooded hills. But don't get the idea you're visiting Old McDonald's Farm. While there are plenty of animals to complement the lovingly restored ranchhouse and barn, a stay here is many steps up from life on the farm.

The bucolic landscape can be enjoyed from almost every part of the house. Four rooms are located on the second floor of the farmhouse, where an expansive deck with willow furniture provides a place to sit and appreciate the country landscape. Across the yard and right beside the pond is an individual unit called the Cottage, which has a kitchenette, a little patio overlooking the duck pond, and a standard but bright bathroom. If you don't mind a quack-quack here and a quack-quack there outside your door, it's a nice private option.

For the ultimate in privacy and comfort, the Barn Suites have to be the absolute best places to kiss on the property. Our first favorite is the luxurious Pine Ridge Suite, a stunning, spacious room with a fireplace, high open-beam ceilings, skylights, and a dazzling slate bathroom with a two-person open shower and a Jacuzzi tub for two. The fresh Northwest-style decor—a peeled-log bedframe cradling the king-size bed, pine furnishings, and coordinating pine-tree wallpaper and linens—creates an overall effect that is simply glorious, yet entirely tasteful. Our other favorite is the Sunrise Suite, a masterpiece of white-washed pine walls set off by rich eggplant-colored carpet. A secluded deck overlooks the river, a gas-log fireplace provides a warm glow, and a wonderfully enormous bathtub is nestled in an alcove and surrounded by bay windows that overlook the trees. A smaller, less fancy version of this suite (minus the bathtub) is the adjacent Bunk Room, with similar stylish furnishings, leaf-print wallpaper, birch paper on the ceiling next to the skylights, and a small private deck. The Hayloft Suite, with a kitchenette and sitting area on the entry floor and a skylighted bedroom on the upper level, is handsomely appointed in hunter green and rich burgundy.

Sunrise is accompanied by fresh coffee, homemade breads, and whatever gourmet creation the inspired innkeepers can think of. The pleasant sunroom is a lovely breakfast area, with a soft fabric ceiling and several glass tables for two, topped with fresh flowers. After breakfast retreat into the cozy library, which is filled with plenty of Shakespearean literature, including a book filled with theater reviews. If exercise is more your style, grab a mountain bike and pedal downtown. Last, but certainly not least, we must also mention the huge heated pool out back (complete with a complimentary selection of sunscreens) and the hot tub where you can steam away aches and pains. Impressed yet? We were. Places like Country Willows inspire us to keep kissing and telling. **1313 Clay Street; (541) 488-1590, (800) WILLOWS; www.willowsinn.com; moderate to very expensive.**

❧❧❧ **COWSLIP'S BELLE, Ashland** Once upon a time people sought out bed and breakfasts just for a clean and simple place to stay overnight. Today, ask couples why they choose to stay at an intimate inn rather than a hotel, and the answer is often "For the breakfast, of course." In honor of this tradition, the morning meal at Cowslip's Belle is an event in itself. (The innkeepers also operate a popular cookie company, so you know things have to be good!) Served on the main floor of this 1913 Craftsman bungalow, breakfast is an extravagant affair that may include fresh fruit, homemade coffee cake, and sour cream Belgian waffles with pecan-maple syrup or cornmeal crêpes with shrimp-vegetable stuffing. Needless to say, you will not be left hungry.

The four guest rooms are renovated on a revolving basis, so they are all beautifully kept up. Every room is named for a flower cited in a Shakespearean play. Our favorite rooms are the two in the adjacent carriage house and the Rosebud Suite in the main house. Each has a private entrance, a down comforter, and the softest linens you've ever snuggled in. The two rooms in the carriage house feel especially private, tucked away in a lovely backyard with a colorful flower garden, stream, and koi pond (which was a work in progress when we visited and looks promising). Cuckoo-Bud has a daybed and a magnificent four-poster bent-willow canopied bed entwined with roses. It also features an antique stained glass window, a beamed ceiling, upholstered floral chintz walls, and a star-quilt wall hanging. Love-in-Idleness has a beautiful antique brass bed and a damask love seat. Although the cottage is newer than the home, the owners have done an outstanding job of re-creating Craftsman-style touches throughout. Air-conditioning in all four rooms provides comfort during the sweltering heat of Ashland's summers.

At night, when you return from the theater, you will find a tucked-in teddy bear and homemade, hand-dipped chocolate truffles placed lovingly on your pillows. Now this is the kind of pampering you could get accustomed to. **159 North Main Street; (541) 488-2901, (800) 888-6819; www.cowslip.com/cowslip; moderate to expensive; no credit cards.**

❧❧❧ **GRAPEVINE INN, Ashland** Given the abundance of high-quality establishments in Ashland, innkeepers face some stiff competition. Fortunately, the GrapeVine Inn has just the right blend of style, elegance, and comfort to set it apart it from the rest. The outside of this Dutch Colonial home is distinguished by a lovely wraparound porch and a colorful garden with a trellised patio and charming gazebo. Inside, a comfortable common area on the main floor features plush tan furnishings, hardwood floors, and a contemporary motif.

Upstairs are two of the guest rooms, both named after wines. Chardonnay, decorated in beige tones, has a sitting area with a fireplace, along with a stunning queen-size French iron bed draped with muslin. Cabernet features a deep burgundy comforter on a queen-size iron bed. Both rooms are elegant and cozy, and each has a spacious tiled bathroom. Guests enter the third room, the

Grape Ivy Suite, through its trellised garden entrance near the back of the house. Its bright and airy atmosphere is enhanced by soft green carpet, ivy-patterned linens, a sitting area with fireplace, a private bath, and a full kitchen. All three rooms are graced with down comforters and cooled by air-conditioning.

A full breakfast, served at an antique pine table in the dining room, features fresh fruit, creative egg dishes, blintzes, freshly baked breads and sticky buns, and fresh coffee and tea. In hot weather, guests can choose to eat outdoors in the garden gazebo. During their stay at the GrapeVine Inn, guests are presented with a complimentary bottle of wine from a local Oregon winery. Enophiles and even casual wine appreciators will find it extremely romantic to be surrounded by grapes and the precious elixir they yield. **486 Siskiyou Boulevard; (541) 482-7944, (800) 500-VINE; www.mind.net/grapevineinn; moderate to expensive; no credit cards; minimum-stay requirement on weekends; closed October–April.**

❀❀❀❀ **MORICAL HOUSE GARDEN INN, Ashland** When a bed and breakfast calls itself a garden inn, you know things are going to be green. This enchanting bed and breakfast has one of the most romantic and lovely gardens in Ashland, with a large lawn, several duck ponds, a variety of special gardens, and plenty of secret alcoves for kissing. Sit on the sundeck, which wraps around boulders, or watch the activity in the butterfly gardens. The greenery here acts as a centerpiece, while distracting and buffering you from the nearby street noise. Growing hedges shelter the home from the street, and the gardens draw you away from the road to the back of the property, which borders undeveloped grasslands.

This flawlessly renovated Eastlake-style Victorian farmhouse offers five guest rooms on the upper floors of the main house and two lovely garden suites in the backyard. Color schemes and styles vary in each guest room, but the ones in the main house are embellished with antiques and have private baths. Foxglove, an elegant top-floor unit with a creamy color scheme, lace curtains, and a claw-foot tub, has views of the neighboring valley that stretch for miles. Garden Party is tastefully done in pastels, and the Berries, with a portion of exposed brick from the old chimney, is handsomely appointed with dark burgundy wallpaper. The other two main-house rooms are just as attractive, but they face Main Street, so road noise is noticeable.

The best rooms are those you'll come to last; these magnificent rooms are worth waiting for—and worth planning your vacation around. Set off to one side of the gardens is a modest building that resembles a carriage house. The two lovingly crafted units inside epitomize a romantic traveler's dream come true. Though the styles are different, both have exquisite furnishings, corner gas-log fireplaces, small private patios, two-person Jacuzzi tubs, walk-in showers, and king-size beds with piles of pillows and top-quality linens. Personal touches in each of the garden rooms include locally crafted stained glass and etched windows, hand-carved mantels, and stunning watercolors. As for added conveniences, both garden rooms have their own temperature controls, air-conditioning, wet bar with fridge, and coffeemaker. The front doors are soundproof, so outside noise isn't a problem.

An integral part of your stay at Morical House is the hearty country breakfast, beautifully presented on fine china or colorful glass dishes. The sunroom, overlooking the lawn and garden, serves as the breakfast room, with several two-person tables. Start with a fruit smoothie, then continue with cranberry scones, smoked salmon in a phyllo pocket, or Italian eggs with fresh asparagus. In the afternoon, enjoy wine and hors d'oeuvres while discussing the plays of the season with your friendly hosts and other theatergoing guests. Or, just relax in the garden, because that's what this inn is all about. **668 North Main Street; (541) 482-2254, (800) 208-0960; www.garden-inn.com; moderate to very expensive; minimum-stay requirement seasonally.**

❤❤❤ **MOUNT ASHLAND INN, Ashland** Enjoy breathtaking views as a winding road leads you high into the Siskiyou Mountains. Sheltered by pine trees near the summit of Mount Ashland, this handcrafted cedar cabin will make you feel like lacing up your hiking boots and shrugging on your Northwest flannel. Mount Ashland Inn is a nature lover's retreat. In wintertime, the inn provides lightweight high-tech snowshoes for adventurous, snow-clomping types. Downhill and cross-country skiers will find ecstasy only three miles away at the **MOUNT ASHLAND SKI AREA** (see Outdoor Kissing). Spring and summer bring beautiful weather, budding wildflowers, and the opportunity to explore the Pacific Crest Trail, which cuts through the inn's 40 acres. (The owners' two energetic golden retrievers will gladly accompany you on hikes.)

A cedar-log interior adds charm to the Mount Ashland Inn. The main living room resembles a cozy mountain lodge, with peeled log columns and a 17th-century fireplace in a massive stone wall. Some of the guest rooms are on the snug side, but all five are appointed with handmade quilts, Early American furnishings, and private bathrooms (although one is a detached bath across the hall). Especially romantic are the McLoughlin Suite and the Sky Lakes Suite. Second-story McLoughlin is reminiscent of a cabin, with its exposed log walls and a rose marble gas fireplace near the foot of the bed. A lovely rectangular window above the king-size bed perfectly frames Mount McLoughlin, while Mount Shasta rises off to the south. However, for the ultimate in romantic hideaways, journey upward to the third-floor Sky Lakes Suite. The stunning bathroom's centerpiece is a small river-rock waterfall that sends water cascading into a two-person Jacuzzi tub. A skylight, a walk-in double-headed shower, and forest views from the window above the tub complete the picture. Just be aware that the exquisite log-arch doorway to this wonderful bathroom doesn't have a door. The suite offers plenty of extras, including a wet bar with microwave and refrigerator, a river-rock fireplace, a king-size bed, and picture-perfect views of Mount Shasta.

Days at the Mount Ashland Inn start in the main-floor dining room with a full breakfast that may include chilled mango and kiwi soup or poached pear in a blackberry–sweet vermouth sauce, followed by an entrée such as eggs picante with cornbread. Afterward, venture outside to the inviting wrap-around deck, where you'll find clear, crisp views of Mount McLoughlin and Mount Shasta.

A long day of hiking, skiing, or just playing with the two dogs can tire even the most energetic outdoor enthusiasts. Refresh yourselves with a dip in the outdoor jetted tub or heat up in the Finnish cedar sauna. With such relaxing surroundings, you might not want to descend to Ashland for dinner (about a 20-minute trip). So, if you feel the nesting urge coming on, be sure to pack extra snacks for suppertime. **550 Mount Ashland Road; (541) 482-8707, (800) 830-8707; www.mtashlandinn.com; moderate to very expensive; minimum-stay requirement seasonally.**

Romantic Note: Due to the sometimes snowcapped location, traction tires and/or chains may be required during the winter. Also, be careful of deer darting into the road at night.

❀❀ **THE PEDIGRIFT HOUSE, Ashland** A white picket fence frames this cheerful grayish blue and white 1888 Queen Anne Victorian set in a quiet Ashland neighborhood. Judging from the historic exterior, one would expect to find a clutter of antiques and an elegant array of furnishings inside the home, but instead it is freshly appointed in a combination of contemporary and classic styles. The original maple hardwood floors are polished to a high sheen in the parlor, where green leather couches sit beside an Italian granite gas fireplace. Adjacent to the parlor is the open, airy breakfast room, where full breakfasts are presented in the morning and beverages, cheese, and crackers are offered each afternoon. Later on, after the evening performances are concluded, a warm dessert à la mode is set out here for all guests to enjoy.

There is only one guest room on the main floor, the light and bright East Room. High ceilings, pale hardwood floors, antique furnishings, and a window seat make this our favorite room. The remaining three guest rooms are upstairs. Two are best suited for groups of three, since they are furnished with both a queen-size and a twin bed, but the last room, Cypress, is a cozy choice. It is considerably darker than the rest of the rooms, but antiques and a clawfoot tub hand-painted with vines lend authentic charm. **407 Scenic Drive; (541) 482-1888, (800) 262-4073; www.opendoor.com/pedigrift; expensive; minimum-stay requirement seasonally; call for seasonal closures.**

❀❀❀ **PEERLESS HOTEL, Ashland** A bold name like "Peerless" sets up lofty expectations in a traveler's mind. Luckily, this inn lives up to its name by offering a memorable and unique-to-Ashland experience. With colorful flower boxes adorning the windows and an old Coca-Cola sign painted on one outer wall, the exterior of this turn-of-the-century brick building gives no indication of the magnificent polish found inside. Upon entering the elegant, small lobby, however, you'll begin to see the romantic potential. Finally, your room will take your breath away.

All six of the grand rooms are decorated with large murals or intricate stencilwork, towering 12-foot ceilings, original woodwork, rich colors and fabrics, and glistening hardwood floors with Oriental rugs. Although each room is different, a flamboyant and stylish Victorian theme prevails throughout, with antiques, queen-size beds, and sumptuous furnishings and linens. Suite 3 has side-by-side claw-foot tubs and a spacious sitting area adjacent to the bedroom; French-influenced Room 5 has a two-person Jacuzzi tub set beneath a skylight; and Suite 7 (our favorite) features a four-poster mahogany bed, two-person shower, and a jetted tub for two framed by lace curtains. An amateurish tropical-theme wall mural, complete with creeping vines, covers Suite 7's sitting-room walls. The remainder of the suite is much more elegant, painted a calming green that's complemented by hardwood floors and white shutters. Ceiling fans help cool the sunlight-filled room, and a private patio adds an extra-special touch. Turndown service is provided in the evening, but you are otherwise left alone once you check in.

After an early-morning bicycle tour around town (bikes are supplied by the inn), return for breakfast at the inn's new bistro and restaurant (See **THE CONNOISSEUR** under Restaurant Kissing). **243 Fourth Street; (541) 488-1082, (800) 460-8758; www.mind.net/peerless; moderate to very expensive.**

❤❤❄ **PINEHURST INN AT JENNY CREEK, Ashland** Nestled in the Cascade Mountains a good distance from the nearest city or village, this unassuming country inn is just about the most enchanting place for miles around. Once a stage stop along the Applegate Wagon Trail, the original inn was restored as a roadhouse in the 1920s. Today, as in days gone by, the Pinehurst Inn offers travelers a secluded spot to rest. But, in keeping with modern times, the inn also offers a wonderful base for day hikes, mountain biking, or fishing in Jenny Creek.

The inn's entry room is all cedar and pine, with a huge stone fireplace for welcoming warmth. Just beyond the parlor is the restaurant, with its rich scarlet wool carpet, cream walls, and lace curtains. At the back of the restaurant stands an antique wood-burning stove that heats the dining room in wintertime. These touches, along with the antique chairs, wood tables, and peeled-log columns, create a rustic setting in which to enjoy innovative Northwest cuisine. You certainly won't want to miss the delicious English muffins or the homemade desserts.

Upstairs the simple guest rooms offer views of the surrounding woods and Jenny Creek. One of the suites has burgundy walls and an old-fashioned stained glass window above its entryway. Room 5 has a wedding-ring quilt, a bent-willow headboard, and an extra-long tub. All six rooms feature down comforters, antique furnishings, and private baths with claw-foot tubs and showers. These rooms aren't exactly suitable for high romance, but the entire experience is pleasant and serene.

Enjoy views of the property's 23 acres from the inn's wraparound porch, or relax in the screened patio overlooking ponderosa pines and a terraced garden. An upstairs sunroom, filled with wicker furniture and hanging plants, provides an amazing panorama of the forested mountainside. The breakfast is superb, and the hospitality is unparalleled. If getting away from civilization is what you want, you'll be happy at this out-of-the-way location. **17250 Highway 66; (541) 488-1002; inexpensive to expensive; breakfast, lunch, and dinner Wednesday–Sunday, brunch Sunday; call for seasonal closures.**

Romantic Note: When making reservations, ask about the Pinehurst Inn's year-round package that includes both breakfast and dinner with your lodging. This package is quite economical when you consider the restaurant's convenient location and the quantity of food you receive (you can order whatever you'd like, and you can eat as much as you want). Dinner usually begins as early as 4 P.M. to accommodate theatergoers (see Romantic Warning).

Romantic Warning: For those wishing to attend Ashland's Shakespeare Festival, the Pinehurst Inn's distance (26 miles) from the town center may be a disadvantage. Evening theater performances in Ashland can get out as late as midnight, and the slow, winding, uphill drive to the inn isn't enjoyable when you're tired or when it's dark outside. Our suggestion: Take in a matinee and enjoy your evening in the mountains.

❄️❄️❄️ **THE QUEEN ANNE, Ashland** The Queen Anne is one of the more appealing Victorian bed and breakfasts in Ashland. Lovingly renovated, the stately 1880 home is graced by well-tended English gardens, abundant rosebushes, a handcrafted stone waterfall, a white gazebo, and an outdoor deck with mountain views. Unfortunately, it overlooks busy Main Street, and traffic noise can be a problem (although the owner has attempted to curb the noise by installing soundproofing blinds in the guest rooms).

Inside, the four ample guest rooms have lace curtains, cozy sitting areas, and private baths with antique claw-foot tubs. All are extremely sunny and comfortable, with queen-size beds and old-fashioned patchwork quilts, and three of the four are equipped with a TV, hidden inside an amoire. Lady Lora is appointed with pine furnishings and decorated in pretty pastel blues. It is the only room located on the main floor and has a detached private bath across the hall. In the evening, its French doors open onto the parlor, providing exclusive use of the sitting area (the parlor is closed to other guests during this time). Upstairs, the clean and crisp Queen Victoria Room features a lovely antique vanity and an old-fashioned, hand-painted pedestal sink, as well as a cozy queen-size bed tucked away in a small bay window. The Prince Hal Room has some of the best views in the house, primarily from the bathroom's large window. The most spacious room in the house is the King George: Its bedroom is connected to a sitting area by an arched doorway, and a six-foot-long claw-foot tub and double vanity adorn its bathroom.

Fresh breads and hot coffee and tea accompany a full breakfast that is served in the dining room, complete with bone china, sterling silver flatware, and antique crystal glasses. Most guests eat at the large table, although those seeking more intimacy can dine at the small windowside table. Spinach enchiladas, cranberry popovers, fruit smoothies, and custard-baked French toast are just a few of the savory dishes prepared by the innkeeper. **125 North Main Street; (541) 482-0220, (800) 460-6818; moderate to expensive; no credit cards; minimum-stay requirement on weekends.**

❀❀ **ROMEO INN, Ashland** Two years ago when we visited, the Romeo Inn was caught in a '70s time warp, complete with shag carpet and outdated furnishings. Luckily, new owners have taken over since then, and they are refurbishing the interior with refreshing, contemporary decor. So far, three rooms in the charming, Cape Cod–style main house have been redecorated, while the two largest suites with private entrances are still awaiting an uplift. Although all are nice, the spacious Stratford Suite, above the detached garage, is your best bet for romance. A two-person whirlpool tub beneath a skylight, vaulted ceilings, a complete kitchen, and marble fireplace provide you and your Romeo (or Juliet) with all you need.

In the dining area, overlooking the backyard, enjoy a breakfast that may include ham soufflé with chili potatoes, apricot scones, or eggs Creole on polenta. Lovely terraced gardens surround a backyard hot tub, pool, and patio. You can dine on the patio in summertime and visit with Cleo, the outdoor kitty. **295 Idaho Street; (541) 488-0884, (800) 915-8899; expensive to very expensive; minimum-stay requirement seasonally.**

❀❀ **WATERSIDE INN, Ashland** You could call these apartment-style suites a home away from home, but only if you live in a super-stylish, antique-filled designer home. Even if you do happen to be so blessed, you will still envy the élan with which each room here has been outfitted. The innkeeper was once a cinematic set designer, and she has used her appreciation of sumptuous, intriguing, and sometimes flamboyant details to distinguish each suite. The Normandy, Kafuzo, and Taos Suites are the loveliest options; the other two could use some freshening. Each of the suites we recommend offers a dining and living room with plush furnishings and 20-foot ceilings; a TV/VCR and stereo; an incredible full kitchen; a sensuous bedroom with down comforters, overstuffed pillows, and floral fabrics; a full loft; and wraparound windows facing a babbling stone-scattered creek. The only hesitation we have about this unique place is that some parts look worn and the main entrance smells musty. Granted, a recent flood destroyed the backyard patio, but that's not the area we are talking about. For the price you pay here, things should look better.

A full hot breakfast is served on the lower creekside patio every morning. Long hours can be spent at the Waterside Inn, listening to the flow of rushing water and enjoying each other's company. At the time of our visit, a new restaurant was under construction. **70 Water Street; (541) 482-3315; www.thewatersideinn.com; very expensive to unbelievably expensive; no credit cards; call for seasonal closures.**

❦❦❦ **WEISINGER'S VINEYARD COTTAGE, Ashland** If a private cottage set on ten acres of luscious vineyards and quaint farmland is your idea of romance, then you and your love will have a time to remember. This petite modern home has everything you could want for an affectionate interlude: a comfy floral love seat positioned directly across from a gas fireplace, a private hot tub on the outside deck, a TV/VCR and stereo hidden away in an attractive armoire, air-conditioning, and a basket of wine, cheese, crackers, and light breakfast items awaiting your arrival. The full kitchen is stocked with utensils, a toaster oven, and a microwave, but you're on your own if you would like a breakfast of more than just pastries and coffee.

In the spacious bedroom, where green-and-white decor sets the mood for rest and relaxation, you'll find a queen-size bed, ivy-patterned linens and wallpaper, and a skylight ideal for midnight stargazing. Yet this is not a perfect paradise: The cottage is within earshot of a nearby home, and, when we visited, two huge antennas and an unsightly shack cluttered the landscape. Luckily, you can't see these eyesores while soaking in the bubbling hot tub. From this vantage point, all that is before you is vineyard. **3150 Siskiyou Boulevard; (541) 488-5989, (800) 551-9463; www.weisingers.com; expensive; minimum-stay requirement seasonally; call for seasonal closures.**

Romantic Suggestion: Check out Weisinger's tasting room and gift shop, just across the driveway and parking lot. If you discover some vintages that you are especially fond of, or if you need wine for a picnic or other outing, take advantage of the wine discounts offered to overnight guests.

❦❦❦ **WINCHESTER COUNTRY INN, Ashland** Located on a side street in downtown Ashland, the Winchester Country Inn is actually three buildings: a stately Queen Anne Victorian, a two-suite cottage, and a neighboring heritage house. Bountiful flowering gardens line the walkways, a charming gazebo sits on the front lawn, and magnificent trees shade the entire property. Here is a place where the elegance of the Victorian era radiates in grand style, but the comforts and conveniences of the 20th century abound.

While charming at first glance, closer inspection reveals that parts of the inn are looking run-down. Chipping paint blemishes the main house, carpets throughout are spotted, luggage scuffs mar many walls and doors, and boxes of junk crammed under stairways are visible to guests. Is all this serious enough to ruin your romantic getaway? Not quite, but it does diminish the romance and charm of this inn.

Eighteen guest rooms are available, and some are better than others. At the lowest end of the price range are the 12 Victorian rooms, some of which have claw-foot tubs and sparse antique furnishings. The helpful, professional staff will gladly assist you in choosing a room, but we found the more contemporary suites and heritage house units to be especially endearing, with two-person Jacuzzi tubs, gas fireplaces, two-person showers, and space to spare. Both the Belvedere Suite and the Barbara Howard Suite also have bay windows overlooking the tiered gardens and lovely grounds. Pack light if you stay in one of these two secluded suites—the three-story climb is quite a challenge with luggage.

A complimentary breakfast with a choice of three different entrées is served in the main-floor restaurant, which we also recommend as a dinner destination (see Restaurant Kissing). You should also inquire about the inn's off-season getaway packages, which include overnight lodging and breakfast along with dinner for two. Prices for the packages do not exceed the very expensive range, which is a great bargain in this part of the world. **35 South Second Street; (541) 488-1113, (800) 972-4991; www.mind.net/winchesterinn; moderate to very expensive; call for seasonal closures.**

Romantic Warning: The popular restaurant downstairs (see Restaurant Kissing creates a potential for noise disturbance in the second-story rooms of the main house.

❧❧ **WOLFE MANOR INN, Ashland** The lavender-colored Wolfe Manor Inn, a large two-story Craftsman bungalow, is poised on a corner in a residential area that is conveniently close to Ashland's shops and theaters. Victorian-era antiques, lace curtains, and plenty of silk flower arrangements beautify (or clutter, depending on your perspective) the main-floor parlor and formal dining room of this bed and breakfast. Upstairs, five modest guest rooms await, each with a down comforter, private bath, and air-conditioning. Mementos of the innkeepers' family and travels adorn each of the rooms. Of the five, we had three favorites. Madeleine's Memories, done in a turn-of-the-century theme with an antique iron bed, is dedicated to the owner's accomplished mother and filled with family keepsakes. Lighthearted and bright, Norman's Nook is furnished with Norman Rockwell memorabilia and has plenty of windows, a 180-degree view, and a large bathroom. The Swazi Safari Room, done up in an African theme that is a refreshing change from the fluffy decor found elsewhere, holds two full-size beds, which can be made into a huge king-size bed. The carvings, batiks, and masks that line the walls are from the innkeepers' exotic journeys abroad.

Breakfasts, such as broiled grapefruit with apricot brandy, vegetarian quiche and fried potatoes, or French toast with banana-blueberry sauce, are served at one long table in the dining room. After you have enjoyed your morning meal, cuddle up on the chaise lounge in the sunny, lace-filled reading room. **586 B Street; (541) 488-3676, (800) 801-3676; www.wolfemanor.com; moderate to expensive; minimum-stay requirement seasonally.**

Restaurant Kissing

During the summer, when a cast of thousands comes for the Shakespeare Festival, quiet, romantic dining spots can be difficult to find. Everyone wants to eat before the show, so restaurants are packed and rushed between 5 and 7:30 P.M. If you don't have evening tickets, and if your stomachs can hold out, book a reservation for later in the evening.

❧❧❧❧ **CHATEAULIN RESTAURANT, Ashland** Conveniently located in the heart of Ashland's theater district, this ivy-covered French country restaurant will win a place in your hearts. Inside, the subtle lighting is augmented by flickering candlelight. Exposed brick walls are decorated with champagne bottles and copper kettles, and rosy stained glass windows frame the restaurant's bar area. Lace window treatments, scarlet carpeting, and dark woodwork create a romantic milieu. The seating is intimate—perhaps too intimate (meaning too close to other diners), particularly just before show time. Try booking one of the window tables for more personal space. Still, the food produced by the serious kitchen is excellent, and the menu changes seasonally. Creatively prepared pâtés and free-range veal dishes with subtle sauces are the specialties here, and the seafood is always fresh and delicious. Desserts at Chateaulin border on euphoric, so save room for one of our favorites: the Chambord pot de crème with raspberry coulis. This is one of the most romantic restaurants in Ashland. **50 East Main Street; (541) 482-2264; www.chateaulin.com; expensive; dinner daily.**

Romantic Suggestion: If dinner at Chateaulin isn't feasible, the next best thing is a visit after the final curtain call for drinks and dessert. The bar is open until midnight, and they can whip up, among other things, some interesting steamed milk specialty drinks.

❧❧❧ **THE CONNOISSEUR, Ashland** British colonialism meets the Northwest at this unique restaurant next to the **PEERLESS HOTEL** (see Hotel/Bed and Breakfast Kissing). Taupe walls, chocolate brown carpets, leopard-print chairs, lush plants, and ceiling fans contribute to the colonial impression, while the sandstone fireplace and planked wood ceiling serve as reminders that you are still in Oregon. It's certainly one of the classiest restaurants in this casual town, and men are requested to wear jackets. The eight-table room can be intimate if it's shared by just a few couples, but very noisy when parties with four or more fill the space.

When we visited, the restaurant had been open for only a few weeks, and it was evident from the slow service, limited menu, and lack of certain items that some bumps hadn't been ironed out yet. Hopefully that will change—along with the food. The menu mainly consists of French and Northwest fare with some tropical and Asian twists, and could prove exciting once all smooths out in the kitchen. While not disappointing, some dishes lacked flavor, such as the skillfully prepared but bland shiitake mushroom soup topped with a spinach soufflé. The deep-fried ahi tuna with lemon pepper aioli was delicious; however, the osso bucco braised coq au vin–style proved only satisfactory. **265 Fourth Street; (541) 488-6067; reservations recommended; dinner Wednesday–Sunday.**

Romantic Suggestion: For a more casual (and less expensive) meal, visit the adjoining **PEERLESS RESTAURANT AND BISTRO** (same phone and address), which features salads, pizzas and pastas, grilled items, and some inventive specialties. The decor is similar to that at the Connoisseur, but much more easygoing and hip, with murals, a giraffe statue, and papier-mâché parrots hanging from the ceiling.

CUCINA BIAZZI, Ashland A few blocks from the town center, you'll find a touch of Tuscany in this pleasant home turned restaurant. If the weather permits, walk beneath the vine-covered arbor and sit outside on the sunken backyard patio, enclosed by stucco walls and lined with terra-cotta tile. Green iron furniture, potted plants, and linen-covered tables accent this delightful retreat. On the downside, the parking-lot view is dull, traffic noise can be distracting, and, like every other place in town, it gets crowded before show time. Inside may be quieter (if everyone else is outside). Here, textured dark yellow walls, lace curtains, wine bottles, and reproductions of Leonardo da Vinci paintings adorn the small, narrow room that packs the tables in tight.

A three-course menu changes daily. The antipasto appetizer plate on our visit was ordinary, while our second course—ravioli in browned butter and fresh sage—proved more inventive. Its richness was further enhanced by the addition of crumbled Italian amaretto cookies. Unfortunately, the dish tasted too dessert-like, but you do have to admire the kitchen's creativity. Our entrée of grilled chicken in a spicy cayenne-mustard vinaigrette wasn't as wild as the server said, and proved just right for our taste buds. Cool off with the homemade espresso ice cream, a dessert guaranteed to keep you wide awake for whatever plans you have for the night. **568 East Main; (541) 488-3739; moderate to expensive; dinner daily.**

THE FIREFLY, Ashland Pardon the pun, but this wonderfully creative restaurant really brightens up Ashland's dining scene. Not that it's a dark, dull scene, but the creations that come out of this kitchen are outstanding, original, and very international.

The interior is quite subdued, as it should be when food is the main feature. Fresh flowers, brass sconces, and blue glass accents help warm the modest dining room. Two tables in particular are ideally suited for romantic dining: the little table tucked away near the front window and the larger back corner table, slightly hidden behind half walls. No matter where you sit, everyone wants to see what everyone else has ordered. Why? The three-dimensional, slightly whimsical presentations are all head-turners. And, luckily, the artistic dishes are equally engaging to the palate. Ignite your taste buds with fiery sambal grilled prawns with lime-peanut couscous, crispy-skinned grilled teriyaki salmon, blue corn glazed mahimahi, or cinnamon-seared rock hen. Deciding on dessert is delightfully difficult. It's impossible to choose between the caramel custard in a pastry shell and the frozen cappuccino. We suggest you try both. **15 North First Street; (541) 488-3212; expensive; call for seasonal hours.**

✿✿✿ IL GIARDINO CUCINA ITALIANA, Ashland You'll surely succeed in wooing your beloved at Il Giardino. This family-run restaurant is both casual and personal, with family photographs and colorful art deco advertisements covering the bright blue walls. Italian-speaking waiters deliver steaming pasta to linen-draped tables while opera plays in the background. Just off the dining room, a garden patio allows alfresco dining beneath wisteria vines and hanging baskets of flowers. No matter where you sit, be aware that the restaurant is usually too noisy and bustling for intimate conversation; instead, you may just want to gaze into each other's eyes and let the food speak for itself.

Authentic Italian cuisine is prepared with the utmost care and expertise here. We highly recommend the linguine with clams in a light tomato sauce, or the capellini with tomato and basil. You'll want to linger over the black ravioli stuffed with shrimp-and-salmon mousse and topped with a light cream sauce. Even the classic spaghetti Bolognese is a masterpiece. *Bravo!* **5 Granite Street; (541) 488-0816; moderate; dinner daily.**

✿✿✿ MONET RESTAURANT, Ashland Contemplate an exquisite French meal, with every dish more delectable than the last, and you'll have only a hint of what awaits you at Monet. Culinary masterpieces include smoked salmon wrapped around a heavenly avocado mousse, creamy broccoli soup drizzled with sour cream, and the robust *poulet alsacienne*, paprika-spiced chicken on a bed of linguine. Most meals come with fresh whole-grain French bread. From appetizers to entrées, all portions are unexpectedly generous, so be sure to save room for dessert.

Named after the famous French Impressionist, this restaurant is as pretty as a picture. A delightful garden area outside, filled with plants similar to those in Monet's garden, is a perfect spot for dining in the summer. Emulating the colors of the artist's palette, the interior has been decorated in pale pinks and greens, with peach curtains framing the front windows. The walls are appropriately adorned with replicas of Monet's oil paintings. Fresh flowers, floral tablecloths, and elegantly comfortable chairs complement each table. Our only complaint is that the tables are a little too close together, but all is forgiven once the formal procession of delicacies begins. **36 South Second Street; (541) 482-1339; www.mind.net/monet; expensive; call for seasonal hours.**

❤❤❤ **PRIMAVERA RESTAURANT, Ashland** Located on the lower level of the OREGON CABARET THEATRE (see Theater Kissing), Primavera earns a full four lips for romantic ambience, but only one lip for its inconsistent food. This averages out to a two-and-a-half-lip rating on our kissometer. It's too bad, really; a restaurant this elegant ought to serve equally wonderful cuisine. The dinner menu is full of delicious-sounding dishes such as mustard-fennel halibut with tomato-mint compote and saffron couscous, and eggplant-and-rice-stuffed roasted pepper with crisp polenta and green sauce. Such creativity, however, appears to be difficult for this kitchen to achieve on a regular basis.

To add to our disappointment, we found the menu setup rather odd. Like many restaurants, Primavera offers its guests a choice between full dinners or lighter bistro fare. However, Primavera's wait staff asks for your preference as soon as you arrive (before you've seen either menu), so they can seat you in the appropriate part of the restaurant. And once you've made your decision, you can't order items off the other menu. That's a lot to decide before you even sit down.

Food and service aside, though, this restaurant is truly striking. The dining room has all the makings of a 1920s-style speakeasy, with its etched bronze-and-black pillars, subdued lighting, handsome floor-length curtains, and baby grand piano at center stage. Walls of dark blue and fiery orange are adorned with colorful exotic canvases of dancing gypsies. Crystal sparkles on snowy white tablecloths, small lamps at each table give the room a subtle glow, and black-lacquered chairs add to the overall drama. Weather permitting, the terraced garden patio at the rear of the restaurant is laced with tables for dining beneath the stars. **241 Hargadine Street; (541) 488-1994; expensive; reservations recommended; call for seasonal hours.**

❤❤ **THAI PEPPER, Ashland** Authentic Thai cuisine—heavy on the curry and impeccably fresh—is a spicy change of pace from the European-oriented cuisine offered by most of the restaurants here. In the summer, sip Thai iced tea and dine outside on the patio, where birch trees border flowing Ashland Creek. You'll have to speak up to overcome the sound of rushing water, but the stream's music is soothing and helps to muffle the noise from Main Street, which parallels the restaurant. Inside, the setting is contemporary, with glass-brick walls that allow light to reflect throughout the all-white interior. The single dining room has a casual and airy atmosphere, but it doesn't really compare with the charm of the patio.

Spend a midsummer night's eve here eating tiger rolls with cream cheese, crab, and shrimp, dipped in a sweet hot-and-sour sauce; green coconut chicken curry with lemongrass and fresh spearmint; and juicy shrimp with coconut-peanut sauce and fresh spinach. Thai food is always great for sharing, especially with the one you love. **84 North Main Street; (541) 482-8058; moderate; lunch Tuesday–Saturday, dinner daily.**

Romantic Warning: Despite our rave review, we have to report that Thai Pepper cannot be counted on for swift service. In fact, service can be terribly slow, and if you are in a hurry to make a show, this is a huge problem.

❤❤❤ **WINCHESTER COUNTRY INN, Ashland** The main floor of a renovated Queen Anne Victorian houses this romantically winning restaurant; tables are placed casually throughout the two front rooms, with plenty of privacy and space in between. Windows look out onto tiered gardens where you can also dine, and the mood is always cordial and relaxed. The kitchen specializes in international cuisine, prepared with finesse and skill. The Teng Dah beef (filet mignon marinated in soy, garlic, nutmeg, anise seed, and lemon zest) orchestrates an incredible harmony of flavors; the boneless chicken breast stuffed with pear, currants, and ricotta and served with a brandy cream sauce is rich yet subtle. Bread and soup or salad accompany the entrées, and a different prix fixe meal is offered each night—an affordable option if you have a large appetite. Service is prompt and eager to help you make it to your performance. Just make sure you leave time for dessert. Our pear strudel with caramel sauce, which was actually more like a crumble, was outstanding. **35 South Second Street; (541) 488-1115, (800) 972-4991; www.mind.net/winchesterinn; moderate to expensive; dinner daily.**

Romantic Warning: During our visit, a busload of visitors arrived and took over the more formal (and nicer) of the two separated dining rooms. Such mass arrivals occur occasionally, but didn't greatly disrupt our side of the dining room or the speed of the service.

Romantic Note: The Winchester Country Inn is also a lovely place to spend the night (see Hotel/Bed and Breakfast Kissing).

Outdoor Kissing

❤❤❤❤ **LITHIA PARK, Ashland** Lithia Park is a national historic landmark that begins in the heart of Ashland's theater district and extends southward for roughly a mile. With more than 100 acres of forest, lawns, ponds, and flower gardens, this lovely playground has plenty of space for intimate moments. Stroll arm in arm beneath the ponderosa pines, or share a kiss on one of the small bridges spanning a burbling creek. Rhododendrons, dogwood trees, azaleas, and forget-me-nots grace the park with brilliant displays of color each spring. Picnic tables are liberally sprinkled throughout the park, surrounded by 100 different kinds of trees and shrubs. Immaculate paved walkways eventually turn into trails as you wind your way upward to a panoramic view of Ashland and the valley beyond. Lithia Park also features tennis courts, a volleyball court, a children's playground, and a small open-air amphitheater used for performances by local entertainers. **Free admission.** *Located in Ashland's theater district.*

❀❀❀❀ **MOUNT ASHLAND, Ashland** The town of Ashland is crowned by the 7,500-foot summit of Mount Ashland. In winter, outdoor buffs hit the more than 100 miles of cross-country ski trails that snake their way through forests, across open fields, past crystal-clear mountain lakes and flowing rivers, and over rolling hillsides. The views are spectacular. As you glide over endless stretches of white powder, you can see the peaks of the Cascade Range to the north and Mount Shasta to the south. Mount Ashland is also considered one of the most challenging downhill ski areas around, with more than 23 runs (along with open bowl skiing) catering to intermediate and advanced skiers. For information on skiing, call the **MOUNT ASHLAND SKI AREA** (541-482-2897). In spring and summer the steep trails are equally challenging and beautiful, and perfect for hiking. *At the heart of the Siskiyou Mountain Range, 18 miles southwest of downtown Ashland. Take Interstate 5 south until you see signs for the ski area, then drive several miles up Mount Ashland Road.*

Theater Kissing

❀❀❀ **OREGON CABARET THEATRE, Ashland** After you've had your fill of Shakespeare and contemporary drama at the festival, try a taste of musical comedy at the Oregon Cabaret Theatre. Don't let the name deter you; this is not a small, crowded, noise-filled room, but a handsomely decorated theater housed in Ashland's historic First Baptist Church. Stained glass windows throw muted light onto the dark green walls. Suspended overhead is an enormous crystal chandelier that has been transplanted from a vintage movie palace. Tables draped in burgundy linens and adorned with glowing candles line the tiered first floor and the second-floor balcony area. Just about every seat in the house has an excellent view of the stage.

The Oregon Cabaret Theatre is a professional (non-Equity) company that performs some of the most innovative musical theater around. Many of the productions are original and some are well-known off-Broadway hits, but all are delightfully entertaining. Shows change every two to three months, so call ahead to find out what is currently playing.

Dinner or brunch is served an hour and a half before show time, and appetizers, soups, salads, and desserts can also be ordered at intermission if you so choose. On our previous visit, the food was catered by a local restaurant that we didn't rate highly. However, things have changed for the better with a new chef who prepares dinners on-site. **First and Hargadine Streets; (541) 488-2902; www.oregoncabaret.com; ticket prices range from $12–$20 (meals separate); call for seasonal closures.**

❀❀❀❀ **OREGON SHAKESPEARE FESTIVAL, Ashland** For those who have a passion for Shakespeare, what could be more romantic than snuggling close together at dusk in an outdoor Elizabethan theater, listening to romantic love poetry written by England's leading authority on the subject? At the Oregon Shakespeare Festival, you can see a variety of the master's works in several different theaters (both indoor and out) in downtown Ashland. Who would have imagined that such a small town would be home to the oldest existing full-scale Elizabethan stage in the Western Hemisphere? Season after season, the costumes are spectacular, the sets are imaginative, and the acting is superb. Be sure to arrive early to catch "The Green Show," a musical and dance presentation that precedes every outdoor performance. This 30- to 45-minute production can be as engaging and enjoyable as the main features.

If you are not a Shakespeare fan, don't let that stop you from attending; Shakespearean drama is only one component of each season's theatrical offerings. Established in 1935, the Festival boasts one of the largest regional theater companies in the United States, and it performs plenty of contemporary plays that will surely spark your interest. You can call the festival directly for tickets, or phone the **SOUTHERN OREGON RESERVATION CENTER** (541-488-1011, 800-547-8052; www.sorc.com), a professionally run ticket agency that can help you with both tickets and lodging. **(541) 482-4331; www.orshakes.org; ticket prices start at $21 in summer, prices are slightly lower in spring and fall.** *Located in downtown Ashland.*

"Her lips on his

could tell him

better than all her

stumbling words."

Margaret Mitchell

Index

A

A Bungalow on the Bluff, 342
A Coach House on Oyster
    Bay, 142
A Haterleigh Heritage Inn, 64
A Little Green House
    on the Park, 15
A Perfect Perch Bed and
    Breakfast, 138
A Quail's Roost Inn, 387
A Snug Harbour Inn, 122
A Touch of Europe Bed and
    Breakfast, 414, 416
ABC Yacht Charters, 247
Abendblume Pension, 374
Abigail's Hotel, 58
Adam's Place, 453
Adriatica, 202
Adventure Ranch, The, 190
Aerie Resort, The, 96
Aerie Resort, The, 97
Ajax Cafe, 336
Al Boccalino, 202
Alexander's, 429
Alexander's Country Inn, 401
Alexis Hotel, 193
Alki Beach, 223
All Seasons River Inn, 375
Alpine Lakes
    Wilderness, 374, 385
Ambleside, 41
American Camp, 305
Amy's Manor, 391
Anacortes, 247
Anchorage Cove Bed and
    Breakfast, 132
Anchorage Inn, 273
Anchorage Inn, The, 307
Andaluca, 200, 203
Andersen House, 59
Anderson Viewpoint, 483
Andiamo, 253
Ann Starrett Mansion Bed and
    Breakfast, 338
Anne's Oceanfront
    Hideaway, 132
Anthony's Pier 66, 203
Antique Rose Inn, 537

Aquabus, 9
Arbors Bed and Breakfast,
    The, 477
Arbutus House, 10
Arbutus Lodge, 294
Arch Cape, 476
Argonauta Inn, 467
Argyle House Bed and
    Breakfast, 294
Ark Restaurant, The, 371
Arthur's, 179, 181
Artisan Sundays, 141
Artist's Studio Loft Bed and
    Breakfast, 277
Ashford, 401
Ashland, 536
Ashland's B&B Network, 537
Assaggio Ristorante, 204
Astoria, 460
Astoria Inn Bed and
    Breakfast, 460
Atwater's Restaurant and
    Bar, 430
Avenue One, 204
Azaleas Fountain Court, 228

B

B.C. Transit, 56
Bacchus, 21, 22
Backeddy Marine Pub, 167
Bacon Mansion, The, 194
Bainbridge Island, 274
Balloon Depot, 225
Bandon, 501
Bandon Beach House Bed and
    Breakfast, 501
Bay Cafe, 326
Bay Cottages, 339
Bay House, 486
Bayside Cottages, 307
Beach Cafe, The, 232
Beach Cottage, 60
Beach Cottage, The, 274
Beach House at Dundarave
    Pier, 37
Beach House on Sunset, 133
Beach Side Cafe, 37
Beachside Bed and Breakfast, 34
Beachwood, 115

Beaconsfield Inn, 61
Bearfoot Bistro, 181
Beddis House Bed and
    Breakfast, 134
Bedford Regency Hotel, The, 62
Beggar's Purse, 155, 156
Belfair, 330
Bell Street Diner, 203
Bella Italia, 350
Bellevue, 227
Bellevue Botanical Garden, 229
Bellevue Club Hotel, 227
Bellevue Downtown Park, 229
Bellhouse Inn, The, 146
Bellingham, 237
Belmont, The, 345
Bend, 519
Bengal Lounge and Patio, 63
Benson Beach, 362
Benson Hotel, The, 423
Bentley's on the Bay, 69
Betty Macdonald Farm Guest
    Cottage, 277
"Bhy" Kracke Park, 223
Big Trees Bed and
    Breakfast, 237
Bilbo's Festivo, 317
Bingen, 405
Birchfield Manor, 412, 415
Bird Song Cottage Bed and
    Breakfast, 104
Bishop's, 22
Bistro, 473
Bistro Provençal, 231
Black Ball Ferry Transport, 57
Black Butte Ranch, 518
Black Rabbit Restaurant,
    The, 507
Blackberries Restaurant, 346
Blackcomb Helicopters, 186
Blackwood Beach Cottages, 367
Blethering Place, 77
Bloedel Floral
    Conservatory, 32
Bloedel Reserve, The, 276
Blue Fjord Cabins, 323
Blue Gull Inn, 339
Blue Heron Inn, 164, 165

Blue Poppy Restaurant, The, 80
Blue Sky Cafe, 479
Boathouse Bed and Breakfast,
    The, 83
Boatyard Inn, 259
Boice Cope Campground, 503
Bold Bluff Retreat, 134
Bombay House Bed and
    Breakfast, 275
Bonair Winery, 410
Bonniebrook Lodge, 157, 159
Booth Bros. Apartments, 464
Boreas Bed and Breakfast
    Inn, 365
Botanical Beach, 96
Botanical gardens, 32
Bothell, 234
Boulevard Park, 237, 241, 243
Bouzouki Greek Cafe, 140
Bow, 245
Bowen Island, 154
Bowen Island Sea
    Kayaking, 154
Boyle Point Park, 150
Brandywine Falls, 187
Bread Garden, 22
Bremerton, 329
Brentwood Bay, 83
Brew Creek Lodge, 172
Brighton House, 10
Brightwood, 514
Brightwood Guest House,
    The, 514
British Columbia Ferries, 58, 167
Britt Festivals, 532, 534, 535
Broken Top Club
    Restaurant, 523
Budd Bay Bungalow, 291
Burton Acres Park, 279
Butchart Gardens, The, 78, 80
Butchart Gardens Dining
    Room, 78, 80

C

C'est Si Bon, 351
Cabin, The, 340
Cabins-on-the-Point, 308
Cable Cove Inn, 115
Cafe Brio, 72
Cafe Campagne, 206
Cafe de la Mer, 473

Cafe Deli, 76
Café des Amis, 430
Cafe Dilettante, 205
Cafe Flora, 205
Café Il Nido, 23
Cafe Juanita, 233
Cafe Langley, 269
Cafe Laurel, 67
Cafe Mozart, 382
Cafe Olga, 317
Caffe de Medici, 23
Camano Island, 256
Camille's, 72
Campagne, 205
Campbell House, The, 451
Campbell River, 127
Canlis Restaurant, 206
Cannon Beach, 466
Cannon Beach Hotel and
    Restaurant, 468
Cannon Beach Vacation Rental
    Homes, 468
Cape Arago, 501
Cape Disappointment
    Lighthouse, 362, 372
Cape Flattery, 354
Cape Kiwanda, 483
Cape Lookout State Park, 483
Cape Meares State Park, 482
Cape Perpetua Scenic Area, 497
Cape Scott Provincial Park and
    San Josef Bay, 129
Capers Cafe, 37
Capitol Lake, 290
Carberry Gardens, 62
Carmelo's Pastry Shop, 23
Carter Beach, 301
Cascade Bay Cafe, 319
Cascade Dining Room, 513
Cascade Falls, 321
Cascade Festival of Music, 519
Cascade Lakes Highway, 524
Cascades Lounge, 18, 29
Cashmere, 386
Cassis, 207
Cassis Bistro, 73
Caswell's on the Bay Bed and
    Breakfast Inn, 368
Cates Park, 40
Cedar Creek, 172

Centrum, 337
Chalet Luise, 173
Channel House, 247
Channel House Inn, 488
Chanterelle Restaurant and
    Lounge, 454
Chanticleer Inn Bed and
    Breakfast, 340
Charleston, 501
Charleston State Parks, 501
Chartwell, 12, 24
Chateau Benoit, 442
Chateau Ste. Michelle
    Winery, 233
Chateau Whistler Resort, 186
Chateaulin Restaurant, 549
Chauntecleer House, 259, 262
Chelan, 387
Chelan Airways, 388
Chelsea Station on the
    Park, 195
Chemainus, 104
Chemainus Theatre, 104
Cheri Walker's 42nd St.
    Cafe, 364
Chesa Restaurant, 38
Chestnut Cottage, 351
Chestnut Hill Inn, 309
Chetzemoka Park, 348
Chez Daniel, 73
Chez Jeannette, 487
Chez Nous, 207
Chez Philippe
    Restaurant, 157, 159
Chez Shea, 208
China Beach and French
    Beach, 95
Chinaberry Hill, 283
Chinook, 361
Chinook Pass, 399
Chinook Wines, 410
Christine's on Blackcomb, 181
Christy's Country Cottage, 260
Chuckanut Drive,
    237, 243, 246
Cincin, 24
Clatsop Spit, 462
Cliff Gilker Park, 163
Cliff House, Bellingham, 241
Cliff House, Freeland, 271

Index

Cliff House, Tacoma, 288
Cliff House, Waldport, 492
Clinton, 257
Coast House, 497
Coffee Cottage, The, 444
Collins' Sanctuary, 438
Colonel Crockett Farm Bed and
    Breakfast, 274
Columbia Cottage Guest
    House, 11
Columbia Gorge
    Hotel, 509
Columbia River Court Dining
    Room, 509, 511
Columbia River Gorge, 508
Columbia River Gorge National
    Scenic Area, 508
Columbia Winery, 234
Commander's Guesthouse, 341
Commencement Bay Bed and
    Breakfast, 284
Comox, 127
Company Town Cottages, 305
Compass Room, 318
Conklin's Guest House, 518
Connoisseur, The, 544
Cook's Landing Lounge, 67
Coolidge House, 538
Copalis Beach, 360
Cottage by the Sea, 244
Cottage on Driftwood Beach,
    The, 160
Country Cottage Bed and
    Breakfast, 160
Country Cottage Cafe and Tea
    Room, The, 531
Country Cottage of
    Langley, 261
Country Willows Bed and
    Breakfast, 538
Coupeville, 273
Courtenay, 125
Courtyard, The, 469
Couvron, 431
Covey Run Winery, 410
Cowichan Bay, 99
Cowslip's Belle, 540
Cozy Rose Bed and
    Breakfast, 418
Cranberry Ridge Bed and
    Breakfast, 135

Crater Lake, 528
Crater Lake Lodge, 528, 529
Crater Lake National Park, 529
Creekhouse Restaurant, 162
Crêpe Montagne, 182
Crow and Gate Neighborhood
    Pub, The, 108
Crystal Springs Rhododendron
    Garden, 436
Cucina Biazzi, 550
Cypress Provincial Park, 40, 41

D
Da Tandoor, 74
Dahlia Lounge, 208
Daisy Cabin, 309
Dashpoint Lobster Shop,
    The, 282
Dashwood Manor, 63
Dayton, 445
Deep Cove Chalet, 81
Deer Park, 353
Deli de Pasta, 415
Delilah's, 24
Delta Whistler Village
    Suites, 174
Denman Island, 150
Depoe Bay, 488
Devil's Churn, 497
Devoe Mansion, 285
Dining Room, The, 403
Discovery Park, 224
Diva at the Met, 16, 25
Domaine Madeleine, 349
Dorrington Bed and
    Breakfast, 45
Dove House, 260, 261
Doveshire Bed and Breakfast,
    The, 369
Dr. Sun Yat-Sen Classical
    Chinese Garden, 32
Dream Log Home With Private
    Hot Tub, 171
Dubh Linn Gate, The, 179
Duck Inn, The, 42
Duck Soup Inn, 303
Duffy House Bed and
    Breakfast, 295
Dulces Latin Bistro, 209
Duncan, 100
Dundee, 444

Dunsmuir Lodge and
    Restaurant, 82
Durlacher Hof, 175
Dykstra House, 419

E
Eagle Creek Ranch, 386
Eagle Pine Chalets, 393
Eagle watching, 397
Eagles Nest Honeymoon
    Cottage, 262, 263
Eagles Nest Inn, 262, 263
Eagle's Reach, 47
Eagle's View Bed and
    Breakfast, 485
Earl's Cove, 164, 166
East Point, 144
East Sooke Regional Park, 95
Ecola State Park, 475
Edenwild Inn, 323
Edgewater Beach Bed and
    Breakfast, 332
Edgewater Lodge, 175
Edgewater Lodge
    Restaurant, 176, 183
Edwin K Bed and
    Breakfast, The, 498
Egmont, 167
El Gaucho, 209
Elk Rock Garden, 437
Elowah Falls, 508
Empress Dining Room,
    The, 63, 74
Empress Hotel, The, 63
Empress Tea Lobby, The, 63, 78
English Bay Inn, 11
English Camp, 306
Esplanade, The, 438
Esplanade Restaurant,
    The, 429, 431
Estuary Estate Bed and
    Breakfast, 107
**EUGENE AND
    ENVIRONS, 451**
Eugene, 451
Excelsior Inn Restaurant and
    Lounge, 454
Express Cuisine, 281

F
Face Rock Wayside, 503
Falcon's Crest Inn, 516

Fanny Bay, 124

Featherwind's Bed and
Breakfast, 376

Federal Way, 281

Fernhill Lodge, 85, 86, 100,
137, 144

Fifth Street Public Market, 451

Fillongley Provincial Park, 150

Firefly, The, 551

Fireside Room, 201

First Street Haven, 351, 352

Fish Bar, 203

Fisherman Bay Guest
House, 324

Five Sails, 18

Flery Manor, 531

Fleuri Restaurant, 19, 25

Flick Creek House, 389

Floras Lake House Bed and
Breakfast, 503

Florence, 497

Flying Dutchman Restaurant,
The, 489

Fogarty Creek State Park, 489

Fort Canby State Park, 362

Fort Langley, 47

Fort Stevens State Park, 462

Fort Worden State Park, 346

Foskett House Bed and
Breakfast, 127

Fountain Cafe, The, 346

Four Seasons Hotel, 12, 24

Four Seasons Olympic
Hotel, 195

Four Swallows Restaurant,
The, 276

Four Winds Motel, 464

Fowl & Fish Cafe, 72

Foxglove Cottage, 310

Franklin Street Station Bed and
Breakfast Inn, 461

Freeland, 270

Freestone Inn and Cabins, 395

French Beach Retreats, 86

French Road Farm Cottage, 257

Friday Harbor House, 295

Friday Harbor House
Restaurant, 303

Friday Harbor Seafood, 303

Friday's Historical Inn, 296

From the Bayou, 289

Fullers, 210

G

Gables, The, 176

Gabriola Island, 148

Gahr Farm Bed and
Breakfast, 446

Galiano Island, 146

Galittoire—A Contemporary
Guest House, 263

Garden Court Lounge, 196

Garden Path Inn, 264

Garden Terrace, 12

Gaslight Inn, The, 196

Gasperetti's Restaurant, 416

Gate Lodge Restaurant, 438

Gearhart, 462

Genoa, 432

Georgian Court Hotel, 12

Georgian Room, The, 196, 210

Gerard Lounge, 19

Gianni Restaurant, 26

Gibsons, 157

Gig Harbor, 283

Gilbert Inn, 464

Giraffe Restaurant, 46

Glen Eagles, 171

Gleneden Beach, 487

Gogi's, 533

Gold Beach, 504

Goldendale, 406

Goldendale Observatory,
406, 407

Good Life Bookstore
Cafe, The, 94

Government Camp, 516

Governor Hotel, The, 424

Grandview, 418

Grants Pass, 531

Grape Escape Winery
Tours, 441

Grapevine Inn, 540

Green Cape Cod Bed and
Breakfast, The, 285

Green Lake, 195

Green Rose Bed and
Breakfast, 135

Greenbank, 272

Griffins Restaurant, 14

Grille at Crosswater, The, 525

Grouse Mountain, 33, 36,
40, 41

Grove Hall Estate, 100

Guest House Log Cottage, 272

GULF ISLANDS, 131

Gull Cottage, 116

H

Halfmoon Bay, 165

Halfmoon Bay Cabin, 165

Hallmark Resort, 469

Hamilton Viewpoint, 223

Harbinger Inn Bed and
Breakfast, 290

Harbor Inn Bed and
Breakfast, 278

Harbour View Bistro, 125

Harp's-on-the-Bay, 502

Harrison Hot Springs, 50

Harrison Hot Springs
Hotel, 50, 51

Harrison House Suites, 296

Harrison Mills, 48

Harrison Mills Country
House, 48

Hartmann House Bed and
Breakfast, 87

Hart's Pass, 392

Hastings House, 136, 140

Hastings House
Restaurant, 136, 140

Haus Lorelei on the River, 376

Haus Rohrbach Pension, 377

Haystack Gardens, 471

Hearthstone Inn, 469

Heathman Hotel, The, 424

Heathman Restaurant, 432

Heaven's Edge Bed and
Breakfast, 331

Helijet Airways, 57

Hendricks Park, 455

Herald Street Caffe, 74

Heritage Harbour Bed and
Breakfast, 13

Hermitage, 26

Heron, The, 249, 253

Heron Beach Inn on Ludlow
Bay, 334

Heron Haus, 425

Higgins Restaurant
and Bar, 433

Index

Highland Drive/Kerry Park, 224
Highlands, The, 515
Highlands House, 308
Highway 99, 187
Hill House Bed and
  Breakfast, 197
Hill House Deli & Cafe, 478
Hillside House Bed and
  Breakfast, 297
Hobuck Beach Park, 355
Hoh Rain Forest, 353, 356
Holland House Inn, The, 64
Holly Hill House, 341
Home by the Sea Cottages, 258
Home Fires Bakery, 383
Honey Moon Cabin on
  Marrowstone Island, 337
Hood River, 509
Hood River Hotel, 510
Hoquiam, 359
Hornby Island, 150
Horse-Drawn Carriage Services
  of Leavenworth, 385
Horstman Estates Home, 171
Hot-air ballooning, 224
Hotel de Haro, 305
Hotel Edgewater, 197
Hotel Monaco, 198, 220
Hotel Pension Anna, 377
Hotel Planter, 250
Hotel Vancouver, 13
Hotel Vintage Park, 199
Hotel Vintage Plaza, 426
House on the Hill Motel, 481
House Piccolo, 140
Huckleberry House Bed and
  Breakfast, 161
Hug Point, 476
Humboldt House, 65
Hummingbird Tea
  House, 106
Hunt Club Restaurant,
  202, 210
Hurricane Ridge, 353
Husum, 403
Hy's Steakhouse, 175, 183
Hyak Wilderness Adventures
  Ltd., 32

I

Icicle Outfitters and Guides, 386

Il Fiasco, 241
Il Fornaio, 433
Il Giardino, 26
Il Giardino Cucina Italiana, 551
Il Terrazzo Carmine, 211
Il Terrazzo Ristorante, 75
Illahee Manor, 329
Ilwaco, 362
Ilwaco Heritage Museum, 362
Indian Beach, 476
Inglenook Restaurant, 102
Inn at Cape Kiwanda, 486
Inn at Clifftop Lane, The, 176
Inn at Cooper Spur, 512
Inn at Langley, The, 265, 335
Inn at Manzanita, The, 478
Inn at Nesika Beach, 504
Inn at Otter Crest, 489
Inn at Swifts Bay, 324
Inn at the Market, 199
Inn of the Seventh
  Mountain, 519
Inn of the White Salmon, 405
International Rose Test
  Gardens, 437
Ira's, 474
Isabella Ristorante, 211
Island Tyme Bed and
  Breakfast, 265
Italian Gardens at Royal Roads
  University, The, 84

J

Jack's Hut at Freestone Inn, 396
Jacksonville, 532
Jacksonville Inn, 532
Jacksonville Inn
  Restaurant, 534
Jake's Grill, 424
James Bay Tea Room and
  Restaurant, 79
James House Bed and
  Breakfast, 342
Japanese Gardens, The, 437
Jarboe's in Manzanita, 480
Jasmer's at Mt. Rainier, 401
Joan Brown's Bed and
  Breakfast, 66
Joel Palmer House, The, 446
Joel's Restaurant and Fireplace
  Lounge at Nicklaus, 184

Johnson Heritage House Bed
  and Breakfast, The, 14
Johnson House Bed and
  Breakfast Inn, The, 498
JP's at Cannon Beach, 468
Juanita, 233
Judith's Tea Room, 333

K

Kalaloch, 356
Kalaloch Lodge, 356
Kalypso, 474
Kaspar's, 212
Katy's Inn, 250
Kenmore Air, 57, 293
Kernville, 487
Kernville Steak and Seafood
  House, 487
Kilby Store and Farm, 49
Kiona Vineyards Winery, 411
Kipling's, 63
Kirkland, 230
Kittleson Cove, 258

L

La Berengerie, 147
La Conner, 249
La Conner Chamber of
  Commerce, 249
La Conner Channel Lodge, 251
La Conner Country Inn, 251
La Côte d'Azur, 52
La Crémaillère, 125
La Fontana Siciliana, 212
La Push, 355
La Rua, 177, 184
La Serre Restaurant, 496
La Toque Blanche, 38
Laburnum Cottage, 34
Ladner, 42
Ladysmith, 107
Lake Chelan, 374
Lake Chelan Boat
  Company, 388
Lake Chelan Chamber of
  Commerce, 388
Lake Chelan Tours, Inc., 388
Lake Crescent, 353
Lake Crescent Lodge, 353
Lake Quinault Lodge, 357
Lake Wenatchee, 374

Lakefront Home, 171
Lakewood, 289
Lampreia, 212
Langley, British Columbia, 46
Langley, Washington, 259
Langley Tea Room, 269
Langley Village Bakery, 270
Langlois, 503
Lanza's Ristorante, 346
Lara House Bed and
  Breakfast, 520
Larrabee State Park, 243
Latch Country Inn, The, 82
Latitudes at Silva Bay, 149
Laurel Point Inn, 66
Le Chamois, 177
Le Crocodile, 27
Le Gavroche, 27
Le Gourmand, 213
Leavenworth, 373
Leavenworth Village Inn, 378
Leo Melina, 213
Lewis and Clark Interpretive
  Center, 362
Liberty Marina Park, 332
Light House Retreat, 88
Lighthouse Park, 40
Lightship Restaurant, The, 365
Lincoln City, 486
Lincoln Park, 223
Lion and the Rose, The, 427
Lithia Park, 553
Little House on the Lake Bed
  and Breakfast, 51
Little Inn on Willow
  Street, 105, 106
Little Italy, 23
Lizzie's Bed and Breakfast, 343
Local Scoop, 475
Log Castle, 266
Log House Bed and Breakfast
  Inn, The, 189
Lomas' Murphy House Bed and
  Breakfast, 333
London Grill, 424, 434
Lonesome Cove Resort, 298
Long Beach, British
  Columbia, 121
Long Beach, Washington, 365

Long Beach Peninsula, 361
Lonny's, 347
Lopez Farm Cottages, 325
Lopez Island, 322
Lord Bennett's Restaurant and
  Lounge, 502
Lorimer Ridge Pension, 177
Lorraine's Edel Haus, 383
Luciano's, 288
Lumiere, 27
Lummi Island, 243
Lynn Canyon Suspension
  Bridge, 41
Lytle House, 359

M

MacKaye Harbor Inn, 326
Macleay Park, 437
Maclure House Inn
  Restaurant, 113
Macmaster House, 427
MacMillan Provincial Park, 114
Magnolia Boulevard, 224
Mahle House Restaurant, 110
Majestic Hotel, 248, 249
Malahat, 96
Malaspina Galleries, 150
Mallard Bar, 174
Mallard's Mill Bed and
  Breakfast, 137
Mamita, The, 67
Mangiamo, 28
Manresa Castle Restaurant and
  Lounge, 347
Manzanita, 477
Manzanita House, 279
Manzanita Rental
  Company, 478
Maple Meadow, 44
Maple River Inn, 514
Margison Guest House, 88
Marina House, 158
Marina Restaurant, The, 75
Marina's Hideaway, 148
Marina's Restaurant, 483
Marine Drive, 41
Markham House Bed and
  Breakfast, 89
Marrakesh Moroccan
  Restaurant, 434

Marrowstone Island, 336
Maryhill Museum
  of Art, 406
Masthead Restaurant, The, 99
Matterson House Restaurant,
  The, 123
Mattey House, 447
Maximilien, 214
Mayflower Park
  Hotel, 199, 203
Mayne Island, 142
Mazama, 395
Mazama Campground, 529
Mazama Country Inn, 396, 397
Mazama Country Inn Dining
  Room, 397
McCully House Inn, 534
McKenzie View, 456
McMenamins Edgefield, 507
McMinnville, 446
Meerkerk Rhododendron
  Gardens, 272
Merlin, 529
Metchosin, 83
Metropolitan Hotel, The, 15
Middle Beach Lodge, 116
Mimi's Cottage, 279
Mission Ridge, 374
Moclips, 361
Molly Ward Gardens, 334
Monet Restaurant, 551
Montinore Vineyards, 442
Moon and Sixpence, 298
Moonset, 499
Moran State Park, 320
Morical House Garden Inn, 541
Morning Star Bed and
  Breakfast, 494
Morrison's Rogue River
  Lodge, 530
Mount Ashland, 537, 554
Mount Ashland Inn, 542
Mount Ashland
  Ski Area, 542, 554
Mount Constitution, 306, 320
Mount Douglas Park, 80
Mount Hood, 512
Mount Maxwell Park, 141
Mount Pisgah, 456
Mount Rainier, 398

Index

Mount Rainier National Park, 399
Mount Seymour Provincial Park, 40
Mount Vernon, 254
Mount Washington, 125, 126
Mountain Home Lodge, 379, 384
Mountain Meadows Inn Bed and Breakfast, 402
Mountain Springs Lodge, 379
Mountain Star, 177, 178
Mt. Hood Inn, 517
Mulberry Manor, 68
Multnomah Falls Lodge, 509
My Mom's Pie Kitchen, 364

N

Nahcotta, 370
Nanaimo, 109
Nanoose Bay, 111
Nantucket Manor, The, 335
Natapoc Lodging, 380
National Park Inn at Longmire, 398
Neah Bay, 354
Nehalem Bay Kayak Company, 480
Netarts, 483
New Deluxe Log Home With Den, 171
New Sammy's Cowboy Bistro, 536
Newberg, 443
Newport, 490
Nick's Italian Cafe, 449
900 West, 14
Nordland General Store, 337
North Cascade Heli-Skiing, 392
North Cascades National Park, 373, 388
North Cascades Stehekin Lodge Dining Room, 389
North Head Lighthouse, 362, 372
Northern Lights, 178
Nye Beach Cafe, 490
Nye Beach Hotel, 490

O

"O Canada" House, 16
Oak Bay Beach Hotel, 68

Ocean House Bed and Breakfast, 490
Ocean Inn, 479
Ocean Park, 367
Ocean Pointe Resort Hotel and Spa, 69, 76, 81
Ocean Wilderness Inn and Spa Retreat, 90
Oceanside, 481
Oceanside Restaurant, 463
Oceanwood Country Inn, 142, 144
Ogden Point Bed and Breakfast, 17
Ohme Gardens County Park, 387
Okanogan, 392
Okanogan National Forest, 392
Old Consulate Inn, 343
Old House Cafe, The, 289
Old House Restaurant, The, 126
Old Mill Cottage, 280
Old Town Florence, 497
Old Trout Inn, The, 310
Olde England Inn, 69
Oliver's, 200
Olympia, 290
Olympia Brewery, 290
Olympic Lights Bed and Breakfast, 298
Olympic Music Festival, 336, 338
Olympic National Park, 353
OLYMPIC PENINSULA, 329
On the Sea Bed and Breakfast, 154
Once upon a Time Inn, 105
Oneonta Falls, 508
Orca Lodge, 119
Orca Lodge Restaurant, 119
Orcas Dining Room, 318
Orcas Hotel, 311
Orcas Island, 306
Orcas Wine Company and Oyster Bar, 318
Orchard Bed and Breakfast, 155
Orchard Inn Bed and Breakfast, 413
Orchard Street Brewery, 241
Oregon Bach Festival, 451

Oregon Bed and Breakfast Guild, 537
Oregon Cabaret Theatre, 552, 554
OREGON CASCADES, 507
OREGON COAST, 459
Oregon Coast Aquarium, 490
Oregon Lodging Association, 460
Oregon Parks and Recreation Areas, 459
Oregon Shakespeare Festival, 532, 537, 555
Oregon Wine Advisory Board, 441
Osprey River Adventures, 392
Oswald West State Park, 480
Otter Magic, 301
Otter Rock, 489
Otters Pond Bed and Breakfast, 312
Our House in Nahcotta, 370
Outlook Inn, The, 312
Over the Rainbow, 225
Owen Memorial Rose Gardens, 456
Oyster Bar, 246
Oyster Creek Inn, 246

P

Pacific Cafe, 242
Pacific City, 485
Pacific Crest National Scenic Trail, 392
Pacific Palisades Hotel, 17
Pacific Sands Beach Resort, 117
Pacific Shores, 163
Pacific Shores Inn, 106
Pacific Shores Nature Resort, 111
Pacific Way Bakery and Cafe, 463
Painted Cliffs, 178
Painted Table, The, 193, 194
Painter's Lodge, 127
Painter's Lodge Restaurant, 128, 129
Paley's Place, 434
Palisade, 214
Palisades Bed and Breakfast, 282

Palm Court, 63, 78
Palmer's Restaurant and Pub, 253, 254
Palms Guest House, The, 35
Pan Pacific Hotel, The, 17, 20, 29
Panacea, 299
Pantages Theater, 283
Paradise, 399, 400
Paradise Inn, 398
Parkland, 289
Parksville, 112
Pasayten Wilderness, 392
Pasquale's, 510
Pastázza, 242
Pateros, 390
Pazzo Ristorante, 426
Pedigrift House, The, 543
Peerless Hotel, 543, 549
Pemberton and Mount Currie, 188
Pemberton Helicopters, Inc., 187
Pemberton Valley Golf and Country Club, 189
Penny Farthing Inn, 18
Penthouse, The, 266
Pepper Muffin Country Inn, The, 109
Perche' No, 215
Pewter Pot, The, 386
Phoenecia at Alki, 216
Piccolo Mondo Restaurant, 28
Pike Place Market, 198, 199, 200, 205, 214
Pine Meadow Inn Bed and Breakfast, 529
Pine Ridge Inn, 520
Pine River Ranch, 381
Pinehurst Inn at Jenny Creek, 544
Pinnacle International Hotel, The, 179, 185
Pittock Mansion, 438
Place Next to the San Juan Ferry, The, 304
Plainfields' Mayur Cuisine of India, 435
Plaza Park Suites, 200
Point Defiance Zoo and Aquarium, 283

Point Ellice House, 79
Point-No-Point Resort, 90
Point Roberts, Washington, 44
Pointe Restaurant, The, 119, 120
Polaris Restaurant, The, 228
Pontevecchio, 216
Ponti Seafood Grill, 216
Port Angeles, 349
Port Hardy, 129
Port Ludlow, 334
Port Renfrew, 96
Port Townsend, 337
Port Townsend Chamber of Commerce Visitor Information, 338
PORTLAND, 423
Portland Saturday Market, 423
Portland's White House, 428
Potting Shed, 260, 262
Poulsbo, 332
Prefontaine Trail, 451
Priest Point Park, 291
Primavera Restaurant, 552
Princess Marguerite, 57
Printingdun Beanery, The, 108
Prosser, 419
Prow, The, 29
PUGET SOUND AREA, 237
Punch Bowl Falls, 508

Q

Quadra Island, 151
Quamichan Inn, 102
Quarter Moon Cruises, 321
Quattro, 180, 185
Queen City Grill, 217
Queen Elizabeth Park, 11, 30, 32
Queen Mary, 217
Quimper Inn, 344
Quinault, 357

R

Rain Coast Cafe, 120
Rainbow Inn, 252
Raincity Grill, 29
Ravenscroft Inn, 344
Red Currant Cafe, 62
Red Hills Provincial Dining, 444

Redmond, 229
Reiner's, 218
Relais, 234
Rendezvous Grill and The Tap Room, The, 516
Renee's on Camano, 256
Reservations Northwest, 459
Resort at Deer Harbor, The, 310, 313, 319
Resort at the Mountain, The, 515
Restaurant Araxi, 185
Restaurant at Hotel Edgewater, 198
Restaurant Österreich, 384
Rex Hill Vineyards, 442, 443
Rhododendron Cafe, 246
Richview House, 91
Rim Rock Cafe, The, 185
Ristorante Salute, 218
River rafting, 391
River rafting on the Rogue, 532, 535
River Ridge at Mount Bachelor Village Resort, 521
River Rock Lounge, 403
River Run Cottages, 42
RiverPlace, 438
RiverPlace Hotel, 429, 431, 438
River's Edge Resort, 393
Riverside Inn, 465
Roberts Creek, 160, 162
Roberts Creek Beach Park, 163
Roche Harbor Rabbit Farm, 300
Roche Harbor Resort Restaurant, 304
Rock Springs Guest Ranch, 522
Rockaway Beach Guest House, 275
Rockport, 397
Rockwood Adventures, 33
Rogers' Chocolates, 76
Romeo Inn, 546
Rosario Resort, 313
Rosario Restaurants, 318
Roseanna's Restaurant, 482
Rosebriar Hotel, 461
Roses Bread and Specialties, 321

Rosette, 523
Rover's, 218
Rowena's Inn on the River, 49
Ruby Beach, 357
Run of the River Bed and
Breakfast, 382

S

Sahtlam Lodge and
Cabins, 101, 103
Sahtlam Lodge
Restaurant, 101, 103
Sail the San Juans, 237
Saleh Al Lago, 219
Salisbury House, 201
Salish Lodge and Spa, 235
Salish Lodge Dining Room, 235
Salmon Harbor Belle Bed and
Breakfast, 500
Salmon House on the Hill, 39
Salmon Run, The, 248, 249
Salt Spring Island, 131
Saltery Bay, 166
Salty Springs Spa and Seaside
Retreat, 138
Salute, 39
Salvatore, 219
Samish Point by the Bay, 245
San Juan Boat Tours, 306
San Juan Island, 294
SAN JUAN ISLANDS, 293
San Juan Real Estate
Company, 300
Sanctuary Restaurant, 361
Sand Lake, 485
Sandlake, 483
Sandlake Country Inn, 483
Sandland Adventure Family Fun
Center, 499
Saratoga Inn, 267
Saturday Market, 451
Saturna Island, 144
Saturna Lodge, 144, 145
Saturna Restaurant, 145
Sauvie Island, 439
Savoury Restaurant, The, 39
Sawatdy Thai Cuisine, 276
Sazerac, 198, 220
Scandinavian Gardens Inn Bed
and Breakfast, 366

Scenic Ilwaco Loop, 362
Scenic Ilwaco Loop, 372
Schnauzer Crossing Bed and
Breakfast Inn, 238
Scholefield House, 70
Sea Bus, 9
Sea kayaking, 321
Sea Lotus Day Spa Bed and
Breakfast, 280
Sea Quest Bed and
Breakfast, 494
Sea Side Inn, 465
Sea Suns, The, 350
Seabeck, 330
Seacliff Cottage, 271
Sean Paul's at Deer Harbor, 313
Seaside, 463
Seaside Bed and Breakfast, 83
Seasons in the Park
Restaurant, 30, 33
**SEATTLE AND
ENVIRONS, 193**
Seaview, 363
Seawall Promenade, 33
Sechelt, 163
Secret Garden, The, 452
Selah, 411
Selah Inn, 330
Serafina, 220
Serenity Bed and Breakfast, 495
Serenity's, 404
Seven Gables Restaurant, 291
Shannon Falls, 187
Shaw Island, 326
Shawnigan Lake, 98
Shelburne Inn, The, 363
Ship Bay Oyster House, 320
Ships Point Beach House, 124
Shoalwater Restaurant,
The, 364, 365
Shore Acres, 501
Shumway Mansion, 230
Sidney, 81
Silver Bay Inn, 390
Silverdale, 331
Silverwater Cafe, 348
Sisters, 518
Skamania Lodge, 402
Skinner's Butte Park, 451
Skookumchuck Narrows, 167

Sky Train, 9
Slate Peak, 392
Sluys Bakery, 332
Smuggler Cove, 166
Snoqualmie, 235
Snug, 136, 140
Solimar, 139
Sooke, 85
Sooke Harbour House, 92, 94
Sooke River Estuary Bed and
Breakfast, 92
Soríah Café and Bar, 455
Sorrento Hotel, 201
Sostanza Trattoria, 221
Sound Food Restaurant and
Bakery, 281
South Bay Bed and
Breakfast, 239
South Jetty, 462
SOUTHERN OREGON, 527
Southern Oregon Reservation
Center, 555
**SOUTHERN WASHINGTON
COAST, 359**
Southlands House by
the Sea, 43
Spa, The, 174
Space Needle Restaurant, 221
Spindrift, 118
Spirit Circle, The, 189
Spring Bay Inn, 314
Springfield, 456
Springtree Grill, 305
St. Bernards—a Bed and
Breakfast, 476
Stanley Park, 12, 21, 33, 37, 42
Starfish Point, 491
Staton Hills, 411
Steamboat, 527
Steamboat Inn, 527
Stehekin, 388
Stehekin Pastry Company, 389
Stehekin Valley Ranch, 389
Steiger Haus, 448
Stephanie Inn, 470
Stevens Pass, 374
Stevenson, 402
Stone House Farm Resort, 145
Stonehedge Inn, 512
Stoneridge, 180

Storyville Bed and Breakfast, 254
Stratford Manor, 240
Strathcona Park Lodge, 128
Strathcona Provincial Park, 127, 129
Suite River Bed and Breakfast, 515
Summerside Text Centre, 56
Sun Mountain Lodge, 394, 395
Sun Mountain Lodge Dining Room, 394, 395
Sundance, 180
Sunflower Cafe, 99
Sunrise, 400
Sunriver, 524
Sunriver Resort, 524
Sunset Bay, 501
Sunset Bed and Breakfast, 149
SUNSHINE COAST, 153
Surfsand Resort, 471
Sutton Place Hotel, 19, 25
Swans, 71
Szmania's, 222

T
Table for Two, 435
Tacoma, 283
Tacoma Actors Guild, 283
Tacoma Art Museum, 283
Talent, 536
Tea Court, 425
Teahouse Restaurant, The, 30–31, 34
Terra Blanca Vintners, 411
Terra Breads, 23
Terrace Room, 67
Thai Pepper, 552
Third Beach, 355
Third Floor Fish Café, 231
Third Street Grill, 449
Thistle Down House, 36
Thornewood Castle, 286
Three Capes Scenic Loop, 482, 484
Tigh-Na-Mara Resort Hotel, 112
Tigh-Na-Mara Restaurant, 113
Tillamook Air Tours, 481
Timberframe Country Inn, 406

Timberline Lodge, 513
Timbers, The, 403
Tina's, 445
Tofino, 114
Toga's, 352
Tolovana Park, 476
Toomie's Thai Cuisine, 523
Touvelle House, 533
Tranquility Bay, 164
Trattoria Giuseppe Italian Restaurant Bar and Gril, 270
Trattoria Russo, 417
Treehouse Bed and Breakfast, 19
Tribune Bay, 151
Tropea Ristorante Italiano, 229
Trout Lake, 404
Troutdale, 507
Trumpeter Inn Bed and Breakfast, 301
Tryon Creek State Park, 439
Tsa-Kwa-Luten Lodge, 151
Tsawwassen, 43
Tu Tu' Tun Lodge, 504
Tualatin Vineyards, 442, 443
Tudor Inn, 350
Tulio Ristorante, 199
Tulip Festival, 249
Tumwater Falls, 290
Turk's Lodgings, 471
Turtleback Farm Inn, 315
Tuscan Farm Gardens, 46
Tyax Heli-Skiing, 187
Tyee Lodge Oceanfront Bed and Breakfast, 491

U
Ucluelet, 122
Union Bay, 125
Union Bay Cafe, 222
University of British Columbia Botanical Garden, 32
Upper Horsetail Falls, 508

V
Val d'Isère, 186
Vancouver, 10
VANCOUVER AND ENVIRONS, 9
Vancouver Art Gallery, 9

VANCOUVER ISLAND, 55
Vancouver Opera, 9
Vancouver Symphony Orchestra, 9
Vancouver Tourist Information Centre, 10
Vandusen Botanical Gardens, 32
Vashon Island, 277
Victoria, 56
Victoria Clipper, 57
Victoria Express, 58
Victoria Harbour Ferry Company, 79
Victorian Garden Tours, 80
Victorian Restaurant, The, 69, 76
Villa, The, 287
Villa del Lupo, 31
Villa Isola, 268
Vineyard at Bowen Island, The, 155
Vista Balloon Adventures, Inc., 441
Vista Sea Cafe, 466
Vito's Pastry Shop, 23

W
Wahkeenah Falls, 508
Waldport, 492
Warrenton, 462
WASHINGTON CASCADES, 373
Washington Park Arboretum, 225
Washington State Ferries, 58, 226, 273, 293
Washington State History Museum, 283
Washington Wine Commission, 410
Waterfall Garden, 226
Waterford Restaurant, The, 106
Waterfront Bungalow, 301
Waterfront Centre Hotel, 20
Water's Edge Cottage and Bed and Breakfast, 93
Waters Lakeside Bistro, 231
Waterside Inn, 546
Waves Oceanfront Motel, The, 472

Index

Wedgewood Hotel, 21, 22
Weisinger's Vineyard
    Cottage, 547
Welches, 515
Welcome Aboard Sailing
    Charters, 142
Wenatchee, 387
Wenatchee National
    Forest, 374, 381
Wesley Street Restaurant,
    The, 111
West Coast Crab Bar, 120
West Vancouver and North
    Vancouver, 34
Weston Lake Inn, 139
Westwinds Harmony
    Cottage, 302
Whale Watch Cottage, 300
Whale Watch Park, 306
Whale-watching, 81,
    94–95, 121
Whale watching cruises, 322
Wharfside Bed and
    Breakfast, 302
Wheeler, 480
Whidbey Inn, The, 269
Whidbey Island, 257
Whiffin Spit, 91
Whistler, 170
Whistler Activity and
    Information Centre, 188
Whistler Air, 184
WHISTLER AND
    ENVIRONS, 169
Whistler Cay Heights Log
    Home, 171
Whistler Chamber of
    Commerce, 170
Whistler Reservation
    Companies, 170
Whistler Resort
    Association, 170
Whistler River Adventures, 188
Whistlestop Shawnigan
    Lakeside Bed and
    Breakfast, 98
White Heron Lodge, 473
White Rock, 45
White Salmon, 405
White Swan Guest House, 255

White-water rafting, 457
Wickaninnish Inn, The, 118
Wickaninnish Restaurant, 123
Wild Garlic, 243
Wild Iris, The, 249, 252
Wild Mushroom, The, 406
Wildflower, The, 174, 186
Wildflowers Restaurant and
    Wine Merchants, 256
WILLAMETTE VALLEY, 441
Willcox House Country
    Inn, 331
William Tell Restaurant, 13, 31
Willie's on 7th Street, 455
Willows Inn, 162
Willows Inn, The, 244
Winchester Bay, 500
Winchester Country
    Inn, 547, 553
Wind River Cellars Winery, 403
Windridge Cottage, 345
Windsong Bed and
    Breakfast, 316
Wine Country Farm, 445
Wine Country Inn, 419
Wine Sellers, The, 511
Winthrop, 393
Wolfe Manor Inn, 548
Wolfridge Resort, 394
Woodinville, 233
Woodland Park Zoo, 195
Woodmark Hotel, The, 230
Woodrun, 180
Woodstone Country
    Inn, 143

Y

Yachats, 493
Yacht Haven, 300
Yakima, 412
YAKIMA VALLEY, 409
Yakima Valley Winegrowers
    Association, 410
Yaquina Head Outstanding
    Natural Area, 490
Yarrow Bay Grill, 232
Yashiro Japanese Garden, 290
Yellow Point Lodge, 107
Yesteryear Farm and Guest
    House, 110

Youngberg Hill Vineyard Bed
    and Breakfast, 448

Z

Zefiro, 436
Ziggurat Bed and Breakfast, 496

From the creators of **The Best Places to Kiss** series:
a unique catalog specializing in tasteful, thoughtful gifts
for all the ones you love.

Affectionate Gifts for Every Occasion

For all those moments when a special gift can say more than words, **Sealed with a Kiss** will help you send your message with ease and distinction. Whether you are looking for a birthday or anniversary gift or celebrating a particular holiday or event, **Sealed with a Kiss** offers a selection of premium gifts to fit every and any occasion. From English picnic baskets to semiprecious jewelry, unique picture frames to stylish candles, **Sealed with a Kiss** will help you make a lasting, meaningful impression.

Call (888) 345-7925
or (206) 444-1611 for a free catalog

or send your requests to:
Sealed with a Kiss
13075 Gateway Drive, Suite 300
Tukwila, WA 98168

✂ -

Please send a catalog to:
Name:_____
Address:_____
City:_____State:_____Zip:_____

Please send a catalog to:
Name:_____
Address:_____
City:_____State:_____Zip:_____

13075 Gateway Drive, Suite 300, Tukwila, WA 98168
(888) 345-7925/fax (206) 444-1625